Pg

Learning Theory and Behavior

Learning Theory

and

Behavior

O. HOBART MOWRER

Research Professor of Psychology
University of Illinois

ROBERT E. KRIEGER PUBLISHING COMPANY
HUNTINGTON, NEW YORK
1973

ORIGINAL EDITION 1960
Reprint with supplemental material 1973

Printed and Published by
ROBERT E. KRIEGER PUBLISHING CO., INC.
BOX 542, HUNTINGTON, NEW YORK, 11973

©Copyright 1960 by
JOHN WILEY & SONS, INC.
Reprinted by arrangement

Library of Congress Card Number 59-15671
ISBN 0-88275-127-1

Printed in the United States of America

To

MAX F. MEYER

and the memory of

KNIGHT DUNLAP

and

RAYMOND DODGE

I propose . . to argue that up to now we have had no explicitly stated *complete* psychological theory, but rather. that we seem to have contented ourselves with a collection of discontinuous, unrelated "theorettes." It is my opinion that psychology has now reached the stage where it has accumulated sufficient data and understanding to reformulate, explicitly, its entire theoretical framework (p. 66).

David Krech (1949)

Pure empiricism is a delusion. A theorylike process is inevitably involved in drawing boundaries around certain parts of the flux of experience to define observable events and in the selection of the events that are observed. Since multitudinous events could be observed and an enormous number of relationships could be determined among all of these events, gathering all the facts with no bias from theory is utterly impossible. Scientists are forced to make a drastic selection, either unconsciously on the basis of perceptual habits and the folklore and linguistic categories of the culture, or consciously on the basis of explicitly formulated theory (p. 200).

Neal E. Miller (1959)

If any large trends are detectable, they would be the finer and finer differentiating of the subject matter falling under the rubric of learning and a gradual merger of "learning theories" with theories of perception, neuro-physiology, motivation, and personality into "behavior theories." One might predict that rather than a third edition of *Theories of learning*, Hilgard might well write a book 10 years hence titled *Theories of behavior*. We shall see (p. 134).

Edward L. Walker (1957)

PREFACE

to 1973 Reprint

The announcement from Mr. Krieger that he was planning to re-issue this book was certainly a welcome one, but his request that I write a special preface for this new edition posed certain difficulties. Since this volume, along with its companion, *Learning Theory and the Symbolic Processes*, was originally published (in 1960), I have not followed the literature on the psychology of learning at all systematically; and I immediately saw that I would need assistance in updating my knowledge of this field in order to give an accurate appraisal of this book's current status and value.

While on another university campus recently, it happened that my host's field of specialization is learning, so I asked him for references he thought might be helpful in this connection. He gave me some particularly pertinent ones and then added, to my considerable surprise and satisfaction: "You know, I have just finished rereading *Learning Theory and Behavior,* and in my opinion it is still as good a book as there is in this field." And a few days later, I sought the counsel of a colleague in my own department, and, after he had given me some additional references, he said: "Your book has had a fundamental and continuing impact, and I have more requests to borrow it than any other book on my shelves."

Not everyone, of course, would be so positive in their evaluation of this volume—in fact, one reader of the original manuscript said it was intrinsically fallacious and advised against its publication. As I now re-examine this book and survey the contemporary literature, it strikes me that the book performs a basic function which has not been duplicated, and it has also stimulated intensive research on a number of special problems that are not without interest and significance.

The advent of Radical Behaviorism in the second decade of this century, under the leadership of John B. Watson, collided head-on with the more traditional Psychology of Introspection, resulting in a major cleavage in this field. During the early years of my professional career, I was strongly influenced by and identified with Behaviorism, but I also became interested in Freudian psychoanalysis, which was highly introspective in its approach; and in the 1930's I found myself moving away from "pure" Behaviorism toward a much more eclectic, or what Neal Miller has termed "liberal," position. This change came about not only because of the increasing popularity and influence of psychoanalysis but also because Radical Behaviorism was at variance with common sense and—what was, in some respects, even more important—because the findings of many experiments performed with laboratory animals by behaviorists (including myself) could be accounted for only if one introduced what Edward Tolman termed "intervening variables."

As it happened, I became involved in a series of experiments which yielded findings that could be explained only if one was willing to recognize the subjective phenomenon of *fear*. Several of these experiments have been reported in detail in my *Learning Theory and Personality Dynamics* (1950), and they have stimulated many other related studies which now constitute an extensive literature on which is commonly called "avoidance learning," well reviewed in Chapter 8 of M. R. D'Amato's *Experimental Psychology* (1970). But useful as it was, this line of development involved a certain theoretical onesidedness; and, for reasons given in the present volume, it became necessary to introduce the concept of *hope*, which is now also widely accepted. Many writers, for example, Jeffrey Gray in *The Psychology of Fear and Stress* (1971), today speak of safety signals (as opposed to danger signals) and the hope (relief, appetite) they produce; and Ezra Stotland has devoted an entire book to what he terms *The Psychology of Hope* (1969). In thus incorporating the concept of hope as well as fear, neo-behavioristic learning theory gained a new and powerful type of symmetry, but certain problems remained which demanded the introduction of the concept of *images*. Some of the circumstances which necessitated this move are described in this book and others are discussed at greater length in *Learning Theory and the Symbolic*

Processes. Carol McMahon has published a particularly pertinent article, "Images as motives and motivators: An historical perspective" (*American Journal of Psychology,* 1973); and Peter W. Sheehan has edited a book, *The Function and Nature of Imagery* (1972).

It would thus seem that, in 1960, this book and its companion volume laid a sound basis for the development of a comprehensive science of learning and behavior which reconciled and unified both the objective and subjective approaches. But there was again to be a sharp bifurcation in this field. Under the leadership of B. F. Skinner, there has been a revival of Radical Behaviorism with practical applications far exceeding those of Watsonian Behaviorism. There is a special division of the American Psychological Association for Skinnerian Behaviorism, and there are several journals devoted both to pertinent laboratory and clinical studies. Moreover, the presuppositions of this approach are so simple that it is essentially atheoretical. In the volume already mentioned, D'Amato says: "The strategy is always clear. Behavior is [developed and] maintained by reinforcement; to eliminate the behavior, find and eliminate the reinforcement" (p. 394). And later this author refers to "the ever-increasing acceptance of [this] operant methodology" (p. 416).

But there has also been a powerful counter movement on the part of many students of both animal and human learning. This is perhaps best epitomized by Francis W. Irwin's 1971 book, *Intentional Behavior and Motivation.* It is replete with such terms as cognition, desire, volution, consciousness, choice, expectancy, frustration, responsibility, and preference. And F. J. McGuigan and D. Barry Lumsden have edited a book, *Contemporary Approaches to Conditioning and Learning* (1973), in which many of the chapters are concerned with "higher mental processes," such as volition, cognition, teleology, covert behavior, and memory. There are relatively few references to the work of Skinner and the purely objective stance of Behaviorism is hardly represented at all. So, once more, the psychology of learning is a house divided, and *Learning Theory and Behavior* represents today, as it did in 1960, an intermediate, eclectic, conciliatory position. Here I am reminded of a comment attributed to the late Robert S. Woodworth. When once chided for having "sat on the fence" with respect to many of the great issues and debates in psychology, he is supposed to have said: "Yes, I suppose I have, as you say, sat on the fence a good deal. But you get a good view from up there. And, besides, it's cooler!" *Learning Theory and*

Behavior does not avoid crucial issues but takes the position that adequate psychological theory must deal with what goes on within as well as outside living organisms as parsimoniously possible.

If one explores the effects of positive reinforcement (reward) and negative reinforcement (punishment, extinction) in association with stimuli produced both by an organism's own behavior and by the external environment, one has theoretical command of both habit formation and inhibition, on the one hand, and so-called "field behavior," on the other. But then it is obvious that behavior may be followed by both reward and punishment, and this introduces the problem of conflict and integrative learning. Since the publication of *Learning Theory and Behavior,* this problem has been most systematically pursued by K. E. Renner, with findings which have been summarized in an article appearing in *Psychological Reports* (1964) and in an unpublished paper entitled "Coherent Self-Direction and Values."

A special case of failure of integrative learning involves the so-called vicious circle. This phenomenon is discussed in considerable detail and an explanation proposed in the present volume. Subsequent research and theorizing has been reviewed by Judson S. Brown in a chapter in *Punishment and Aversive Learning* (B. A. Campbell and R. M. Church, eds., 1969).

In 1948, Peter Viek and I published a paper entitled "An experimental analogue of fear from a sense of helplessness" which was reproduced in the 1950 volume and is discussed in the present one. This phenomenon has been further investigated and its implications pursued by M. E. P. Seligman in a number of papers, and H. D. Kimmel has written a paper entitled "Conditioned Fear and Anxiety." In the latter the author makes the probably valid distinction between anxiety as a state in which an organism is helpless, overwhelmed, unable to cope, and a situation of danger (fear) for which there is a possible solution. As early as 1953 Rollo May suggested that anxiety threatens the organization, indeed the very existence, of what is known in human beings as the ego, whereas the ego is able to cope with fear with a certain sense of competence.

The implications of failures in integrative learning, the vicious circle phenomenon, and the anxiety-provoking (ego-threatening) nature of states of helplessness all have manifest implications in the domain of psychopathology and have been utilized by various writers.

In the present volume considerable emphasis is placed on the importance of response-produced sensory feedback in the acquisition and refinement of instrumental learning or habit formation. Recent researches have demonstrated that gross responses can be executed without sensory feedback, but even in this book it is shown that some central process is necessary to get responses *started,* before they can produce and be guided, facilitated or inhibited by response-produced stimuli. So the new research does not pose a new problem and seems to be adequately handled within the existing theoretical frame of reference.

Within the past decade there have been a number of studies suggesting that responses mediated by the autonomic nervous system, which have long been regarded as subject to learning only through the process of conditioning, can also be modified by reward and punishment, and the latter have been regarded as effective only with behavior mediated by the central nervous system and the implicated skeletal muscles. It has also been shown that responses long regarded as involuntary can be brought under voluntary control if the subject is provided with information about these responses ("biofeedback") not ordinarily available as they occur. This area of inquiry is still controversial, but even if the positive findings which have been reported should all be unequivocally confirmed, they would not necessarily controvert traditional suppositions. It has long been known that the fakirs of India could modify heart rate and certain other physiological processes "at will." It seems likely that these and the changes reported in recent experimental studies involve a "trick" of some sort. For example, change in the size of the eye's pupillary aperture are not subject to direct voluntary control; but anyone can easily produce such changes by fixating on a near object (pupillary contraction) and then on a remote object (pupillary dilation). It is less clear how certain other normally involuntary responses (such as heart rate or blood pressure) can be altered voluntarily or—what amounts to much the same thing—by instrumental learning. But it seems likely that in all such cases some type of *mediating* process, behavioral or symbolic, is involved.

In contrast to the type of research just described, there is considerable interest in learning problems imposed by "species-specific" behavioral limitations, i.e., limitations in the readiness with which certain responses can be made by different animal species. These variations in behavior plasticity, or specific learning capacities, probably account for a good many paradoxical results previously obtained in experiments with animal subjects. Although new details are thus being brought to light, the basic phenomenon is an old and familiar one. For example, it has long been known that chimpanzees have the physical apparatus needed to produce human speech and that their failure to do so represents a lack of the necessary connections between certain muscles and the cerebral cortex. These muscles are controlled thalamically and can be activated, in stereotyped ways, only when the animal is experiencing certain emotional states.

George Albee has recently pointed out that half of the psychologists today holding the Ph.D. degree received that degree within the last decade. There has, of course, been a corresponding increase in psychological literature, but none of it seems to have invalidated the systematic position represented by *Learning Theory and Behavior,* and much of it has provided strong collateral support. If I were rewriting this book today, the research literature could be usefully updated, but the book's basic structure and thesis would not, it seems, require any fundamental modification. .

Preface

If the proverbial Man from Mars or, what would amount to much the same thing, an intelligent layman were to examine a cross-sectional "slice" of the technical literature on the psychology of learning, he would find it very confusing. If, for example, he confined himself to the contents of our specialized journals and monographs for a given year, he could hardly escape the impression that, while extremely vigorous, the field is fragmented and disorderly. A colleague has estimated that each month approximately 80 new titles appear in this field; and if our hypothetical analyst worked a five-day week, there would be an average of four articles or monographs a day for him to master. But after thus immersing himself in this relatively immense literature, he might still emerge with the feeling of having learned very little about learning. Even some professional psychologists would agree with an opinion recently expressed to the effect that "all this work on learning is a maze of 'crucial experiments,' none of which is ever quite confirmed and any one of which almost certainly has been contradicted!"

If, however, one takes a sufficiently long view of the situation, movement of an unmistakable and meaningful kind is apparent. It is the purpose of this book to trace and interpret this movement.

There are, of course, a number of excellent summarizing volumes in the area of learning which are organized along other lines. Some of these attempt to order the field *topically*, with only incidental attention to the historical dimension; others synopsize major *theories*, with varying interest in the possibility of unifying them. Here we shall be concerned both with conventional topics and with salient theoretical positions; but our approach will be predominantly developmental, in

the historical sense of the term. In this way, it is believed, both empirical facts and divergent theories become maximally meaningful and
most significantly related.

Our aim then, in short, is to achieve a high-level *synthesis* of the field.
This, of course, is what every theory of learning has attempted to do.
That such efforts have not been entirely successful is, of course, attested by their very diversity. So why should we expect yet another
attempt to be more successful? Two considerations, already alluded
to, are relevant: (1) the fact that we shall examine both research and
conjecture in a broadly historical context and (2) the fact that today
we have access to many new experimental findings not available to
earlier system makers.

From all this it should not be inferred, however, that we shall here
discard or disregard earlier theories of learning. Quite the contrary!
We shall, indeed, use them as the very cornerstones and building blocks
for our present edifice, but with the privilege of reshaping and rein-
terpreting them, so as to make them fit more smoothly into a new, over-
all system which, hopefully, will have both greater scope and power
than any of the earlier conceptual schemes, taken separately. Here we
shall assume, more specifically, that almost all the great traditional and
contemporary theories of learning have an element, perhaps a very
large element, of validity; and our quest will be for that scheme which
most fully utilizes these theories but, at the same time, permits us to see
the errors and inadequacies of each.

Recently a wag observed that a *psychologist* is "an individual who
thinks that the human race is directly descended from the white rat."
From the extent to which rat experiments are cited in this book, the
reader may conclude that this definition is more true than humorous.
These experiments are cited so extensively, not because our interest is
primarily in the white rat (or any other infrahuman organism) as
such, but because, over the course of half a century, the great, systematic thinkers in the field have gravitated toward animal research; and
the persevering reader will see why this should have been the case.
However, this is not to say that even those who most assiduously culti-
vate this approach to knowledge necessarily believe that it will unlock
all the mysteries of human experience and existence. It is simply *one*
approach—the approach, so to say, from *below;* and most of its de-
votees are modest, though sincere, in the claims they make for it. With
Hamlet they would agree, when he says, "There are more things in
heaven and earth, Horatio, than are dreamt of in your philosophy."

Some readers may deplore the absence, at the end of this volume, of a summary chapter. Such a chapter is omitted for a variety of reasons, one being that the basic argument is epitomized in Chapter 7. Earlier chapters provide the logical and factual background from which this argument evolves; and the five subsequent chapters amplify and apply the argument in more specific ways. Thus, the reader who wishes a quick "look" at this volume as a whole may first read the chapter indicated; but the argument will unfold most naturally and persuasively if the chapters are read in the order in which they appear.

A second reason why there is no summary chapter at the end of this book is that such a chapter appears as the Introduction to a companion volume entitled *Learning Theory and the Symbolic Processes* (John Wiley & Sons, Inc., 1960). Experience has shown that the contents of the present book, when properly supplemented by collateral reading and classroom discussion, makes a full semester's work for advanced undergraduate or graduate students. Yet this material does not by any means exhaust available knowledge in the field. Instead it provides a broad and apparently secure foundation for study of the more intricate topics considered in the second book. Because of the close continuity between these books, there would have been an advantage, for some readers, in having their combined contents appear as a single volume. But the greater convenience for students of the two-volume format has seemed to be a weightier consideration. The device of summarizing the present volume at the outset of the ensuing one increases the feasibility of this arrangement.

This word, now, of forewarning—and encouragement—to students and their teachers. When I have used this book (in mimeographed form) as a classroom text, it has been my unvarying experience that for the first third or half of the course, students are not a little bewildered. In their own words, they don't see "what it's all about." And for examinations they say they just have to *memorize* certain phrases and facts. But then something exciting happens! They discover, often quite suddenly, that they have command of a conceptual scheme which gives order and meaning to all they have routinely learned and which also opens up for them new vistas of insight and inquiry. Once this point is reached, the battle is, of course, won. And to the end of keeping them in the frey up to this point and preventing premature desertions, I have introduced what may be termed recurrent progressive summaries (see "Summaries" in Subject Index). As already indicated, the argument as a whole is nowhere fully reviewed in this volume. But repeatedly we stop and, in effect, ask: Now where are we and where do we go from here? At some point—usually in Chapter 5 or Chapter 6

—the student begins to grasp the logic of the argument in its totality and from that point on needs no such aids. Details click into place, and he sees the picture whole. Other instructors who employ this book may find ways of speeding up this comprehension of the system, but it seems that a certain minimum period of "maturation" is essential as a preliminary and cannot be altogether eliminated.

Persons in other professional disciplines are invited to examine this and the ensuing volume in the context of their particular interests. In a number of related fields the psychology of learning is admittedly basic, and it is believed that the approach here followed provides a maximally satisfactory introduction and guide to the understanding thereof. Criticisms and suggestions from readers will be gratefully received by the author and incorporated in later editions, if there is continuing demand for this work. Also, readers are invited to write to the author and obtain, without charge, one of the phonograph recordings alluded to in Chapter 7.

To Mrs. Herbert Goldstein, Miss Anita Jeanne Elder, and Miss Leona D. Pedigo, consecutively my secretaries during the five years that this book and its sequel have been in preparation and in press, go my sincere thanks for their sustained interest and efficiency. It is likewise a pleasure to acknowledge my indebtedness to several "generations" of graduate students for much help and stimulation in the preparation of these two volumes; and to Dr. Donald W. Zimmerman and Dr. Janusz Reykowski, who thoughtfully read all of the final typescript copy, go my special thanks. But I am most deeply indebted to those three seasoned experts on behavior theory—John P. Seward, Richard L. Solomon, and M. E. Bitterman—who read and mercilessly criticized the early, mimeographed version of these two volumes. Whatever their remaining defects, these books have been substantially improved by the trenchant commentary of these men; and here I record not only my appreciation of their assistance, but also my delight in working with them in this venture.

O. Hobart Mowrer

Urbana, Illinois
December, 1959

Contents

1

Introduction: Historical Review and Perspective

Sometimes the best way to understand and evaluate contemporary events is to examine them in historical perspective. Such is the method employed in this introductory chapter, as a means of providing context for the more specific and technical discussion of the psychology of learning which follows.

I. Biological Concepts and the Birth of Scientific Psychology

In his book, *Limitations of Science*, J. W. N. Sullivan (1949) quotes Lord Kelvin to the effect that "he could understand nothing of which he could not make a working model" (p. 39). As will become evident in later chapters, psychologists have often been greatly influenced by models and modes of thought taken—sometimes, it seems, quite unconsciously—from physics and practical mechanics (see Wiener, 1948, pp. 49–50; English, 1954, pp. 1–4; also Mowrer, 1960, Chapter 7). But psychology has also drawn heavily from and been much influenced by developments in the more immediately adjacent field of biology.

At the beginning of the present century, the prevailing conception, or "school," of psychology in this country was what has since come to be known as *Structuralism*. Here the emphasis—as Ladd, writing in 1902, phrased it—was upon "the systematic description and explanation of the phenomenon of consciousness, as such" (p. 1). The mind, or psyche, was seen as an entity or structure, and the task of psychologists was to identify its limits and to relate and classify its various sections and subdivisions, sometimes called "faculties." Like Gaul, the mind, as conceived by most Structuralists, was divided into three parts: cognition (knowing), conation (willing), and affection (feeling). And textbook writers spent much space arranging and rearranging various mental activities and capacities under these three salient categories. Labels and definitions were highly important; and the whole approach was essentially descriptive, taxonomic, static. In fact, the main objective of the enterprise seemed focused on an effort to do for psychology what Karl von Linne, in 1735, had done for biology in announcing his great classificatory system, beginning with *phyla* and proceeding down through *classes, orders,* etc., to the *species.*

But then, in 1859, Charles Darwin published his book, *Origin of the Species,* and a revolution shocked and shook biology and related sciences. Like von Linne, Darwin too was interested in *species,* i.e., in the problem of ordering and classifying living organisms; but he took the further, momentous step of also asking how they "got that way." In other words, he was concerned, as Linnaeus had not been, with the problem of *origin,* or development; and this interest, combined with exhaustive, painstaking observation and analysis, led to a dynamic, *functional* conception known as Organic Evolution. Slight variations in structure, reasoned Darwin, would give to certain individual organisms, in a particular environment, slight or perhaps crucial advantages in the "struggle for existence," with the result that the "fittest" would survive best and would leave more offspring than those individuals not showing the same "natural," or "spontaneous," variation. By this process, or "mechanism," organic evolution, whereby all present life had developed from simpler forms, was thought to have come about.[1]

For biology, this conception of evolution of form, on the basis of function, ushered in a new era. Definition, description, classification were no longer all-important. Consuming interest now centered upon a dynamic phenomenon known as *adaptation.* Behavior and process suddenly took on special significance, and the whole of life

---

[1] Present thinking about the "origin of species" seems to differ from that of Darwin chiefly in that new knowledge from the field of genetics has introduced the concept of *mutation,* which has importantly supplemented and, in some degree, replaced the notion of "spontaneous" variations. Otherwise, a century later, the theory stands intact.

became progressive, developmental, forward-looking. "Ontogeny repeats phylogeny" became a new and majestic phrase; and if Man lost something of the status he had enjoyed in the earlier conception of a Special Creation, *all* life now gained new importance, direction, and meaning in the evolutionary scheme of things.

This revolution in the field of biology gradually made itself felt in psychology; and by the turn of the century a new school of thought, known as *Functionalism*, was coming rapidly to the fore. In fact, by 1906, it was so well established and so respectable that one of its great leaders, Dr. James Roland Angell, was in that year elected president of the American Psychological Association. And in his presidential address (1907), entitled "The Province of Functional Psychology," he gave a masterful summary and appraisal of the nature and significance of this new movement.

At the outset, Angell acknowledged the relationship between Functionalism and Darwinian evolution. He said:

Whatever else it may be, functional psychology is nothing wholly new. In certain of its phases it is plainly discernible in the psychology of Aristotle and in its more modern garb it has been increasingly in evidence since Spencer wrote his *Psychology* and Darwin his *Origin of species* (p. 62).
This involves the identification of functional psychology with the effort to discern and portray the typical *operations* of consciousness under actual life conditions, as over against the attempt to analyze and describe its elementary and complex contents (pp. 62–63).

After referring to the "much-abused faculty psychology," or Structuralism, Angell continued:

The mention of this classic target for psychological vituperation recalls the fact that when the critics of functionalism wish to be particularly unpleasant, they refer to it as the bastard offspring of the faculty psychology masquerading in biological plumage (pp. 63–64).

But what, more specifically, were the functionalist's position and program? Said Angell:

The psychologist of this stripe is wont to take his cue from the basal conception of the evolutionary movement, i.e., that for the most part organic structures and functions possess their present characteristics by virtue of the efficiency with which they fit into the extant conditions of life broadly designated by the environment. With this conception of mind he proceeds to attempt some understanding of the manner in which the psychical contributes to the furtherance of the sum total of organic activities, not alone the psychical in its entirety, but especially the psychical in its particularities —mind as judging, mind as feeling, etc. (pp. 68–69).
This is the point of view which instantly brings the psychologist cheek by jowl with the general biologist (p. 69).

In other words, in this new frame of reference, mind was to be viewed as an organ of adaptation and the focus of interest was to be upon its activities, rather than upon its structure or contents.

Such an effort if successful [said Angell] would not only broaden the foundations for biological appreciation of the intimate nature of accommodatory process, it would also immensely enhance the psychologist's interest in the exact portrayal of conscious life. It is of course the latter consideration which lends importance to the matter from our point of view. Moreover, not a few practical consequences of value may be expected to flow from this attempt, if it achieves even a measurable degree of success. Pedagogy and mental hygiene both await the quickening and guiding counsel which can only come from a psychology of this stripe. For their purpose a strictly structural psychology is as sterile in theory as teachers and psychiatrists have found it in practice (p. 69).[2]

In a later chapter, we shall have occasion to refer again to this important paper by Angell; but if we are to be faithful to history, we must now consider another development which was to intervene before the objectives of Functionalism were to see anything like fulfillment. If Angell, at the time he delivered his presidential address, could have glimpsed the future a decade hence, he would have seen the same function being performed, not by a member of his own school, but by the leader of this other movement (Watson, 1916b).

II. Behaviorism: Revolt and Reformation

Frequently Behaviorism is dated from the appearance of two books by John B. Watson (1914, 1919) during the second decade of the century. But behaviorism (with a little "b") certainly had its inception well before 1900. During the first decade of the century, Structuralists and Functionalists alike continued to stress the phenomenon of consciousness. But as early as 1896, John Dewey had already voiced a growing dissatisfaction with this emphasis and had indicated the mode of thought that was to go far toward replacing it. Said Dewey:

That the greater demand for a unifying principle and controlling working hypothesis in psychology should come at just the time when all generalizations and classifications are most questioned and questionable is natural enough. It is the very culmination of discrete facts creating the demand for unification that also breaks down previous lines of classification. . . . The idea of the *reflex arc* has upon the whole come nearer to

[2] For another, more recent review and appraisal of the impact of the theory of evolution upon American psychology, see Boring (1950); also Roe & Simpson (1958).

meeting this demand for a general working hypothesis than any other single concept. It being admitted that the sensori-motor apparatus represents both the unit of nerve structure and the type of nerve function, the image of this relationship passed over into psychology, and became an organizing principle to hold together the multiplicity of fact (p. 375, italics added).

Even earlier, in his *Principles of Psychology* (1890), William James had adopted a method of approach to certain psychological topics which was clearly behavioristic, as the concept was later to develop. Formally trained in physiology and medicine, this writer freely imported from these disciplines observations and theories which departed radically from what was then considered psychology. For example, in his chapters on "The Functions of the Brain," "Some General Conditions of Brain Activity," and "Association," James showed a good grasp of (though he did not have the term for) reflex conditioning. In fact, he even went so far as to reproduce Meynert's earlier (1874) "brain-scheme" (really a constellation of reflex arcs) purporting to show how a child, once burnt, will thereafter avoid touching a candle.

Writing retrospectively of this same decade (1890–1900), Pavlov (1927) was later to remark:

Under the influence of these new tendencies in biology, which appealed to the practical bent of the American mind, the American School of Psychologists—already interested in the comparative study of psychology—evinced a disposition to subject the highest nervous activities of animals to experimental analysis under various specially devised conditions. We may fairly regard the treatise by Thorndike, *Animal Intelligence* [1898], as the starting point for systematic investigations of this kind. . . .

At about the same time as Thorndike was engaged in this work, I myself (being then quite ignorant of his researches) was also led to the objective study of the hemispheres. . . . As a result of this investigation an unqualified conviction of the futility of subjective methods of inquiry was firmly stamped upon my mind (pp. 5–6).

While Behaviorism was not to find its most explicit spokesman for another decade, it was clear by the turn of the century that the "study of consciousness," whether by the approach of the Structuralists or that of the Functionalists, was rapidly giving way to a lively interest in something called *behavior*. Thus, as early as 1904, Cattell, in speaking of psychological research done at Columbia University, was able to say:

It seems to me that most of the research work that has been done by me or in my laboratory is nearly as independent of introspection as work in physics or in zoology. The time of mental processes, the accuracy of perception and movement, the range of consciousness, fatigue and practice, the motor accompaniments of thought, memory, the association of ideas, the perception of space, color-vision, preferences, judgments, individual differences, *the behavior of animals and of children*, these and other topics I have investigated without requiring the slightest introspection on the part of the subject or undertaking such on my own part during the course of the experiments. It is usually no more necessary for the subject to be a psychologist than it is for the vivisected frog to be a physiologist (p. 180, italics added).

Hence, the formal enunciation of the tenets of Behaviorism by Watson, between 1910 and 1920, came as something of an anticlimax, since both the ideology and many of the experimental techniques of this type of psychology were already well established. Yet Watson marshaled forces and led the revolt against the older order in a way not equaled by any other figure during the period under review.[3]

As later chapters of this book will show, Behaviorism is today notable, not so much for its own inherent durability, as for the role it has played in a highly creative dialectical process. If Subjectivism (or Introspectionism) was the original theme, or *thesis*, in American psychology (as it became an independent discipline, distinct from philosophy and theology), Behaviorism was the strident *antithesis*. And something which, for want of a better term, may be called neo-behaviorism is the present-day outcome, or *synthesis*. The present

[3] Recently Dr. Max F. Meyer (who, in 1911, published the first book on psychology with "behavior" in the title) wrote a letter to the author which reads, in part, as follows:

"Skinner says in the last [January, 1959] issue of *Science* that Watson—who is compared with Darwin, strangely—'cleared the way for a scientific analysis.'

"That way was already pretty clear in 1896. In that earlier year, still in the Nineteenth century, I attended the International Congress of Psychology in Munich. There was a vigorous debate on that same 'way' between Lipps of Munich and a Russian psychologist of the name of Bekhterev. The question was simply which way should be preferred by university professors. But it was certainly not 'unclear' in the Nineteenth century. That is, on the continent of Europe.

"What one can truly say of Watson is: He knew how to advertise that 'way' among English-speaking psychologists."

And Woodworth (1958) makes the same point when he says: "Even before the advent of behaviorism about 1912, psychologists were beginning to regard the word *behavior* as a good term for the subject matter of their science, a better term for the purpose than *consciousness* or *mind* or even *mental processes*" (p. 20). For example, "William McDougall in 1905 had offered a new definition of psychology: 'Psychology may be best and most comprehensively defined as the positive science . . . of the activities by which any creature maintains its relations with other creatures and with the world of physical things.' Other psychologists offered similar comprehensive definitions" (p. 21).

volume is "behavioristic" in the sense of approaching the topic of learning in the tradition of Pavlov, Thorndike, Hull, and other objectivists. But it deviates from or transcends this tradition in that it re-admits to consideration various problems which the behaviorists had renounced: hence its qualification as *neo*behavioristic.

Yet the position here adopted is not one of mere conciliatory eclecticism. If, for example, we sometimes speak of "consciousness" (a tabued word for the Behaviorists), this is not just a friendly gesture to the past or concession to common sense; it represents instead the growing conviction that the objective study of behavior has now reached the point where some such concept is essential if systematic progress in theory construction is to go forward. Indeed, it is perhaps not too much to say that we have now reached a point at which, if consciousness were not itself experienced, we would have to invent some such equivalent construct to take its place. Behaviorism was thus no idle "detour" or meaningless aberration. It was instead a new foundation which had to be laid before a sounder total psychology could be constructed (see also Mowrer, 1960).

III. Learning Theory: Limitations and Possibilities

Perhaps we can say that only now, half a century later, after the rise and decline of Behaviorism, are we in a position to embark upon some such approach to the problems of psychology as that envisioned by Angell and the other early Functionalists. But if the body of objective observation and theory accumulated during the era of Behaviorism has provided a new and sounder basis for attacking certain problems, it also warrants a word of caution and circumspection. Probably the greatest single accomplishment of this movement has been the gradual development of learning theory, as we know it today. And although it is still in its formative stage, many hopeful aspirations have been expressed for it, as a basis upon which many other types of problems may find new and better solutions. There is, however, a sense in which learning theory is severely limited. At best, it gives us a picture of the basic, biologically determined principles, or *laws*, of learning. It has little or nothing to say about what living organisms, and human beings in particular, *ought* to learn or what they in fact *do* learn: yet this is a question with which parents, teachers, ministers, jurists, and many others are deeply concerned. Learning theory may help such persons, once they have decided upon their objectives, to attain them; but it never, or at least only rarely, dictates what these objectives should be (cf. Skinner, 1953a, and Jourard, 1958).

In a paper entitled, "Ethics and Theories of Motivation and Learning," Professor B. J. Diggs (1957) has put the matter well in these words:

In regarding human action from the standpoint of learning theory, we have been looking at moral problems primarily from the standpoint of the individual. The means most essential to the promotion of individual goals, however, as well as a primary determinant of those goals, is the set of interpersonal structures collectively designated as society or culture. The family or some substitute therefor is essential to the maturation of the infant and the elementary education of the child in the ways of the group; it supplies the "learning" originally lacking. In various ways, other [groups] continue the education begun by the family circle, until finally the matured individual is given the opportunity of selecting, or is assigned to, some position from a set [of "positions" or "roles"] which his culture makes available. The ultimate acquisition of such social status is even from the standpoint of the individual the most essential condition in his having the means at hand for the gaining of his goals, however narrowly these goals are conceived. Thus society or culture provides the individual with sustenance, protection, and education, all of which culminate in social status; and in the process it gives the individual (beyond his primary drives) his characteristic wants, a knowledge of how these wants can be satisfied, and actual means-at-hand. At the same time and, if you like, in return therefor, it imposes rules to be obeyed. Just as individual learning must follow rules, so society must embody rules—if either of them is to be goal-attaining. All of this is common-place.

The so-called distinctively human values are no doubt products of this social learning; or if we regard societies themselves as the products, these values are the products and by-products. Such values thus arise from man's ability to learn, but this ability itself is strongly conditioned and is brought to fruition by the kind of society into which the individual is born. Among these values are classes of valued objects, sets of valued courses of action, and sets of norms—all of these expressing the "habits" or the "learning" of the group. Justice, conceived as a general virtue, consists simply in obedience to the rules. This might lead one to interpret statements of obligation "You ought to do X" (at least a large class of them) as commands expressing the rules of the group. The most important of such statements command categorically. They don't prescribe action contingently, depending on what the individual wants; they don't even say "If you wish to remain in our society, you ought. . . ." Since the actions prescribed by the rules are essential (or are assumed to be essential) to the society, the rules simply command. Behind the commands, and expressing them, are the institutions of the society and the combined force of all individual pursuits of goals, for which society is necessary. Society says to the individual, "We have given you your ability to see; do not lose sight of us." If it be asked "Why are men subject to these commands," this in one sense, as Dewey puts it, is equivalent to asking "Why live?" The only way of escaping such categorical commands is not to be born (pp. 106–107).

It has often been pointed out that man has, and is a product of, two great heritages: the one *biological*, the other *social*. His biological heritage is carried by and transmitted through the *chromosomes* he receives from his progenitors; whereas his social heritage, as Professor Diggs indicates, is the *culture* of his group, and this is acquired, extra-organically, through learning. But the *capacity* to learn is biologically given; and it is with this set of innate processes and principles that learning theory is most directly and importantly concerned. In this frame of reference, it is of no particular consequence *what* an organism learns: the basic question is *how?*

"Personality," or what a particular human (or infra-human) organism, as a result of his particular social and other experiences, eventually *becomes*, is thus beyond the scope of learning theory, strictly speaking. Much laboratory research on learning is still at the stage of using "naive" subjects: rats and other small mammals or birds which have been permitted to learn as little as possible before coming into the experimental situation. Only in this way, it is reasoned, can we get at the basic, biologically given laws of learning. If we study the learning, or problem-solving, abilities of a highly "acculturated" organism (such as man or, to a lesser extent, a trained or "pet" animal), our results may easily be confounded: we cannot tell what the organism is able to do "on his own," as opposed to what he can do *through* culture. Culture is an accumulation of "answers" or problem solutions; and if we wish to study the problem-solving process in the raw, we do not want a subject who has learned a lot of problem solutions vicariously, i.e., through instruction from or the example of others.

Great hopes have often been expressed in recent years for learning theory as the master science of psychology. A knowledge of the congenital mechanisms whereby we learn is undoubtedly necessary for a complete understanding of human personality; yet one wonders if, on the basis of such knowledge alone, one could ever deduce or predict either the development of personality in a particular individual or the development of culture, historically speaking. With Professor Diggs, we may rightly wonder if many of man's distinctive institutions, practices, and values are not *emergent* phenomena, i.e., compatible with but not rigorously determined by antecedent conditions (cf. Kroeber, 1952; White, 1949; and Childe, 1951,

1955). It is generally agreed by anthropologists that human beings are today probably not very different, organically, from what they were when they first started using language and accumulating and transmitting "culture," fifty or a hundred thousand years ago. Query: If all we now know about the learning process, or can reasonably hope to know in the next several decades, had at that point been put into a "giant computer" or "logical-consequences machine," could the machine have deduced or predicted anything very close to what has been the actual course of human development during this period of time? Answer: Perhaps—but very probably not!

Learning itself makes for a sort of indeterminacy in the behavior of living organisms, i.e., it makes them, fortunately, *changeable*. We assume, of course, that there is a certain lawfulness about this changeability, this capacity for being modified by experience. But no matter how completely we know *how* learning takes place, it does not enable us at all accurately to predict *what* will be learned—much less *what ought* to be learned. Miller & Dollard (1941) have put the matter picturesquely by saying that in order to understand or predict what a rat will learn to do in a maze, one has to "know both the rat *and the maze*." [4] In other words, on the basis of learning principles alone, one cannot at all accurately foretell what an organism will or will not do; one must also know what both his internal environment (tissue needs) and his external environment (physical and social) are going to be. A psychology of the total person must, therefore, be anchored no less in sociology, history, culture theory, and even geography than it is in biology. While learning capacity has made both society and culture possible, learning, as this term is usually understood, refers to biologically determined processes and, in and of itself, is not at all adequate to "explain" personality, culture, society, or any similarly complex derivative of human experience.

At the same time, these disclaimers are not meant to be taken too categorically. For example, the distinction between learning as a process, as opposed to content, is not always easy to maintain.[5]

[4] Sears (1951) has put the matter this way: "Changes in behavior are of two kinds. For a theory to be dynamic, both must be systematized, separately but congruently. One is ongoing action, or performance, and the other is learning, or *acquisition*. . . . The combining of these two approaches to behavior has not yet been fully accomplished" (p. 478). See also Sears, Maccoby, & Levin (1957).

[5] For an illuminating and historically sophisticated discussion of the relationship between the study of process and content in psychology, see McClelland (1955). He notes that, under the sway of Titchener and the Introspectionists, psychology was much concerned with content but that, later, it became almost exclusively pre-

Harlow (1949) and others have recently reported convincing work on the acquisition of what they call "learning sets," or "learning to learn," in monkeys and other mammals. And, as indicated elsewhere (Mowrer, 1960), the learning of language by a human infant opens up for him further learning capacities or at least opportunities. Moreover, in insisting that the learning theorist, as such, is not properly concerned with *values*, i.e., with questions of what any given person ought to learn or teach, we are not, of course, holding that these are not entirely legitimate concerns for other psychologists, or even for the erstwhile learning theorist, at other times. *Behavior theory* is a somewhat more inclusive term than is learning theory; and *personality theory* is, of course, more inclusive still. The point is that the psychologist when functioning as a learning theorist must be allowed to define for himself an appropriately modest and scientifically manageable task.[6]

---

occupied with process. Now, he suggests, there is a revival of interest in content and that it is only by studying *both* that we can have anything like a psychology of the total person. The issue, McClelland holds, devolves upon the selection of the proper contentual *categories*. Titchener's "content categories" failed to work because they were "not related to experimental operations on the one hand or to other types of behavior on the other. For these or other reasons, they simply did not lead to theoretical development" (p. 301). "If psychologists are to re-enter the field of mental content and start classifying it according to categories of genuine theoretical fruitfulness, I fear they will have to return to disciplines they have long neglected . . . religion, art, history, economics, politics" (p. 302). "If my analysis is correct, we are on the brink of an important new development in psychology. Because of methodological improvements, we are about to take up again some of the problems in mental content that formerly were considered to be an essential part of psychology" (p. 302). It is believed that the type of learning theory whose development we shall follow in this volume, while not itself directly concerned with the content issue, is nevertheless logically hospitable to the concept of content, as opposed to an exclusive emphasis upon process.

[6] Passing reference to the relationship between the sciences of genetics and embryology may be helpful here. Genetics is ordinarily thought of as concerned with the *heredity* of organisms, as opposed to their *environments*. Yet it is well known that individual development, especially during the embryological period, is dependent upon the organism's *medium* or milieu, quite as much as upon its chromosomes. The latter do not determine development irrespective of environment; rather they determine how the individual will react, developmentally, *given* more or less favorable conditions. Yet genetics has justified itself as an independent and distinct science. The analogy with learning theory, in contrast to the more "substantive" areas of psychology, will be apparent. A thoughtful graduate student has made the following comment in this connection: "This is another way of saying that instead of regarding the organism's behavior 'as a function of variables' (the Hull-Spence model), one should regard the organism *together*

As briefly indicated in the Preface, it is believed by some, including the writer, that the continued pursuit of knowledge concerning the psychology of learning is scientifically and socially worth while. Already it has been of value, practically, in various minor ways, and eventually it may yield more impressive dividends. However, the student as well as the specialist in this field does well to keep in mind the strictures set forth, a decade ago, in a paper entitled "Scientific Models and Human Morals" (Allport, 1947). Here the author argues that we have been

. . . so stupidified by admiration of physical science that we believe psychology in order to succeed need only imitate the models, postulates, methods and language of physical science (p. 182).

The machine model in psychology had its origin not in clinical or social experience, but rather in adulation of the technological success of the physical sciences. Since psychologists, like everyone else, are enmeshed in the prevailing ethos, they too, unless especially on guard, are likely to allow their subservience to technology to outrun their moral sense (p. 183).

The foregoing was written before the principles of mechanical automation ("cybernetics") were widely known and is more strictly applicable to those less "intelligent" types of machines which were developed during the 19th Century and which were indeed "mechanical" and lacking in the capacity for self-regulation and self-direction which living organisms manifest in such remarkable ways. In later chapters we shall see that contemporary learning theory posits principles more like those involved in modern servomechanisms than those of the mere "power-transmitting" machines of the last century (see also Mowrer, 1960, especially Chapter 7).

However, Allport warns not only against mechanical models in general, but also against the "phylogenetic" (animal) and the "infant" models. In concluding his paper, he says:

The designs we have been using in our studies of motivation, of symbol, and hence of the foundations of moral behavior, are not—to borrow Morris's crisp term—sufficiently iconic with our subject-matter. Addiction to machines, rats, or infants leads us to overplay those features of human behavior that are peripheral, signal-oriented, or genetic. Correspondingly it causes us to underplay those features that are central, future-oriented, and symbolic (p. 190).

with its surrounding environment, physical and social, as a single system undergoing various states through time (thermodynamic model). Comparative psychologists have urged a similar position for some time." However, for present purposes we shall adhere to the more conventional mode of analysis, which assumes the distinctness of organism and environment, the principles and the results (content) of learning, the *how* and the *what*.

Here, in the present volume, we are by no means assuming that man is "just a machine," or "just an animal," or "just a big baby." A normal, adult human being is manifestly "something more," a truly transcendant creature, so that, admittedly, none of these models is at all fully "iconic." However, there are certain processes which adult man indubitably shares with the infant, the animal, and, quite possibly, with certain types of machines. And since, as indicated in the Preface, we are here avowedly using the Approach-from-Below, it is proper that we should operate at these lower levels. We must simply make a point of avoiding the reductionist's fallacy and of remembering that we are trying, not to pull human nature down to a lower and inappropriate level of conceptualization, but rather to build our conceptual scheme up to the point that it will connect, naturally and meaningfully, with human personality in all its complexity and wonder.

IV. But Why Learning "Theory"?

Theory, to be sure, is a feature of all science. But the area of psychology which deals with the learning process—or processes—seems to be especially characterized by theory and theorizing. Why should this be so?

In the psychology of *sensation*, theories are, of course, not entirely lacking; but it is notable that the expression, "sensation theory," has no great currency; whereas one is today more likely to speak of "learning theory" than simply of "learning." Perhaps this is an oblique way of saying that we are really more interested here in what learning theorists are themselves thinking and saying than in the "thing itself." At first brush, this strikes one as a rather singular situation. But a moment's reflection will make it more intelligible. Everyone has sensations; everyone, on the basis of immediate experience, knows what tastes, odors, colors, and sounds are like. But it seems that no one ever has a "sensation" of learning.[7] Therefore this phenomenon has the status of a *construct* and is knowable only inferentially. It is capable of being scientifically studied and even

---

[7] Two or three decades ago a movement, known as *Gestalttheorie*, tried to develop a psychology of learning based on the premise that learning is directly knowable, as "insight" or the "ah-ha" experience. Although sound and scientifically productive in some of its tenets, *Gestalttheorie* has not been fruitful in the learning area. We are today much nearer to explaining insight (or so-called "discontinuity") in terms of learning principles than we are to being able to explain learning ("continuity") in terms of Gestalt principles. (See Mowrer, 1960, especially Chapter 6).

casually observed in terms of its conditions and consequences; but the operation itself is completely "silent." Everyone knows a good deal about what he has to do to learn this or that, and we all have rough ways of testing ourselves for learning. But never, apparently, do we have any awareness of the "wheels going 'round' " *as we learn.*

In the evolution of living organisms, there was presumably no premium on their being directly conscious of the learning process. Just as there is ordinarily no gain in brain tissue being "sensitive" to pressures or lesions (since the skull usually protects the brain so adequately), so likewise was there no reason for living organisms to have a sensation whenever the learning process takes place. But this fact constitutes a problem for psychology and was certainly one of the shoals on which Structuralism foundered. If learning is accompanied by no distinctive sensation or state of consciousness, then it is not open to investigation by means of introspection. Accordingly, Structrualism gave us no psychology of learning, no "learning theory," and as a total psychology was not viable.[8]

As we have seen, Functionalism accented *behavior* in a way which Structuralism had not. But, at the turn of the century, hypotheses and methods for the study of behavior were still primitive and vague; so it is understandable that the Functionalists and early Behaviorists should have seized upon the concept of the *reflex.* Various methods for its study had been developed by the physiologists. But, by traditional definition, one of the salient and identifying features of a reflex is its invariability, its mechanical regularity and dependability. Yet the characteristic and distinguishing thing about most behavior, and especially those forms of behavior in which psychologists are especially interested, is its flexibility, fluidity, "freedom," non-fixity.

In an attempt to remedy this situation, psychologists were obliged to turn their attention, more seriously than ever before, to the phenomenon of learning. Behavior is clearly and manifestly subject to *modification, change.* How, precisely, does this come about? *That* was the question.

Two answers were soon forthcoming. The work of I. P. Pavlov (1927)—a Russian physiologist who, in studying certain "digestive reflexes," became impressed with their modifiability—showed one way (for Pavlov the *only* way) in which behavior can be modified,

---

[8] By the same token, learning lent itself particularly well to the type of inquiry which Behaviorism, or S—R psychology, fostered. This approach presupposed no observation or knowledge of any mental state but rather a change in the relationship between stimulus and response, between conditions and consequences.

i.e., by so-called *conditioning*. If a formerly neutral stimulus is paired a few times with a stimulus that dependably ("reflexly") produces a given response, soon the erstwhile neutral (ineffective) stimulus will be capable, alone, of eliciting this response. The response, in other words, will have been "associatively shifted," to borrow an apt expression from Thorndike, to a *new* stimulus (see Fig. 1–1). This and this alone, Pavlov averred, was the basis of behavior flexibility and adaptability. But, it will be noted, responses which had been thus conditioned were *still* reflexes, "conditioned reflexes."

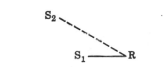

Fig. 1–1. Learning, or "conditioning," as it was conceived by Pavlov. The three little diagrams are to be read from left to right. Initially, some response R can be elicited only by its "physiologically adequate," or "unconditioned," stimulus S_1. But it may happen that S_1 is regularly and closely associated with (preceded by) some other stimulus S_2. As a result of this association, conjunction, or "temporal contiguity," response R gets "associatively shifted" from S_1 to S_2.

The biological utility, i.e., the advantage to living organisms in their struggle for existence, of the conditioning process is clear: it enables them to *anticipate* forthcoming events and to make more intelligent, more adaptive reactions thereto (cf. Chapter 10, Section I).

Pavlov and his numerous co-workers and students, both in Russia and in many other countries, obviously "had something," but did they "have anything"? Pretty clearly they did not.[9] One of the most palpable difficulties was the fact that so-called conditioned reflexes, instead of being exact replicas of their unconditioned prototypes, are often perceptibly and, sometimes, radically different. Specific instances of this sort will be cited in connection with the discussion of avoidance learning in animals in Chapter 3; and the phenomenon is likely to be even more conspicuous at the human level. For example, several years ago Wickens (1938) showed that if human subjects are trained ("conditioned") under threat of electric shock to lift a finger, by *extension*, from a grill on which the finger has been lying *palm down*, they will, with no further training, also lift the finger, by *flexion*, at the appropriate signal, when the finger has been placed on the

[9] For a detailed account of the status of Pavlovian reflexology, both as science and as ideology, in Russia today, see Razran (1957).

grill *palm up!* Here, in the latter situation, the response of lifting the finger off the grill involves an entirely different set of muscles and motor nerves from those involved in the original training, so one can hardly characterize such a response as a "conditioned reflex." Indeed, common sense would suggest, and laboratory observation would probably confirm, that if, after such training, the subject's *foot* were placed on the grill, it might well be lifted when the danger signal occurred. Or, a subject so trained might even shout a warning to another person who happened to be near the grill when the signal came on. Clearly the paradigm of learning offered by Pavlov, while intuitively recognized by everyone as having some validity, has serious limitations and does not provide a master formula for the interpretation and prediction of all behavior.

The other early attempt to account for behavior modifiability was, of course, that made by E. L. Thorndike (1898; see also Jennings, 1906), with the concept of "habit." This concept was strong precisely where the conditioned reflex idea was weak, in that it accounts, at least within limits, for response variability. The basic notion here is that living organisms have drives, such as hunger, thirst, and cold, and that the response first made to a given drive in a given situation may not achieve the desired ends. Therefore, living organisms must have provision for *response substitution*, i.e., some means whereby

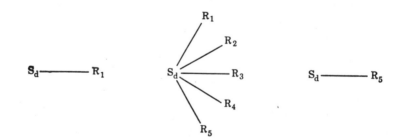

Fig. 1–2. Thorndikian habit formulation or trial-and-error learning. Some drive stimulus S_d characteristically produces some response R_1, because in the past R_1 has served to reduce and gratify the drive. But conditions change and R_1 no longer "works." The organism is thrown into variable, trial-and-error behavior (middle diagram) and "tries," in succession, responses R_1, R_2, . . . R_5, the last of which produces the desired effect. On successive repetitions or trials, R_5 gradually rises in the "response hierarchy" (Miller & Dollard, 1941) until, as shown at the right, whenever S_d occurs R_5 promptly and specifically follows. This type of behavior modification has often been called response substitution or selective learning.

a reaction made originally, but inappropriately, to a given source of stimulation can be replaced by a more effective one. This, for Thorndike, was the gist of *habit formation* (Fig. 1–2).

We have already seen how Pavlov's theory of conditioning articulated with evolutionary thought: in being able to learn to react to *signals*, as well as to the things signalized, living organisms have a better chance in the struggle for existence. But, as Campbell (1956) has pointed out, Thorndike's theory also shows the imprint of Darwinian influence. It was, in fact, a theory of the evolution of *acts*, as opposed to individuals. In so-called organic evolution, the "trials" and the "errors" are individuals possessing more or less advantageous structural characteristics, and the competition is between these individuals; whereas, in learning, according to Thorndike's view, the competition is between different response tendencies within the *same* individual, and learning is the process that ensures "survival" of the effective and elimination of the ineffective ones. As Campbell observes:

Selective survival among random variations is taken as a general paradigm for instances of organismic fit to environment. Darwinian theory of natural selection applies the model to the fit between the inherited characteristics of organisms and the opportunities provided by their habitats. Trial-and-error doctrines apply the model to learned fit between organismic response and environment (p. 341).[10]

Naturally enough, Thorndike made much use of this latter means of behavior modification. Although he did not deny the reality of conditioning, he attached, as we shall later see, little significance to it. But "habit" had its troubles, too. Whereas conditioned-reflex theory spoke of attaching *new stimuli* to established (unconditioned, or unconditional) responses, habit theory spoke of attaching, or connecting, established stimuli (drives, needs) to new responses. In other words, in conditioning the response remains constant (in theory) and stimulus potency changes; whereas, in habit formation, the stimulus remains constant and the response changes. As between these two mechanisms, it might seem that nothing was left to be desired. But both suffered from the common weakness of being modeled on the concept of the reflex.[11] As already noted, a reflex modified by con-

---

[10] Cf. also Darwin's terms "natural variation" and "natural selection" and expressions employed by contemporary learning theorists (e.g., Miller & Dollard, 1941) such as "response variation" and "response selection."

[11] Pavlov was quite open and direct in characterizing his theory of learning as *reflexological;* whereas Thorndike spoke of his theory as being *connectionistic.*

ditioning is still, at least by definition, a reflex; and a "reflex" modified by the kind of learning called habit formation is, also, still essentially reflexive. The latter point can be simply illustrated.

Critics of habit theory have often pointed out that it makes all behavior, whether learned or unlearned, "mechanical," "blind," and, of necessity, more or less blundering; whereas the truth seems to be that, at least on occasion, living organisms can be exceedingly clever—foresightful, intelligent, resourceful. Put a little differently, the objection is this. Thorndike, on the basis of his theory, popularized the notion that we "learn only by *doing*." This follows, directly enough, from his theory, which says, in effect, that before an existing "habit" (or "reflex") can be modified, i.e., before its chances of recurrence can be either increased or decreased, it must *occur* and be either rewarded or punished. There is, in other words, no possibility for the organism to be "smart," and do the "right thing" in the first place. If a given response is wrong and will be punished if performed in a given situation, there must be at least one *error* (perhaps several), says the theory, before the organism can "mend its ways." And if a response is the correct one for a given situation, it must likewise occur one or more times before the organism can have increased confidence in it. Hence the familiar characterization of habit formation as *trial-and-error* learning.

Now it is only too evident, alas, that those creatures with even the best brains do far more foolish things than we (or they) might wish; but it is also true—habit theory notwithstanding—that *some* of the time living organisms are able to by-pass even that *one* trial, or "error," and behave quite adaptively (i.e., change, learn) *without* "doing." Here, then, is habit theory's Achilles' heel, into which a number of arrows have, in the past few decades, been deeply driven.[12]

Clearly the distinction is more terminological than real. Woodworth (1918), writing at a time when he was much under the sway of Thorndike's views, said: "A man carries around with him a vast assortment of possibilities of action. The best conception of a 'possibility of action' is undoubtedly that of a neural mechanism so connected with other neural mechanisms and with the sense organs and muscles as to give the action when aroused" (p. 106). One could hardly formulate a better description of reflexology. However, granting that Thorndike's theory of learning was no less "reflexological" than was that of Pavlov, the fact remains that the one stressed *response* substitution while the other stressed *stimulus* substitution.

[12] It is probably fair to say that much of the vogue which Gestalt psychology, with its emphasis on *insight*, enjoyed in this country during the 1930's and 1940's arose from the manifest inadequacy of the notion that we learn only by doing. But *Gestalttheorie* was itself critically weak in certain important respects; and

V. Methods and Objective

As the preceding section indicates, neither of the two conceptions
of learning which were most influential during the first half of
this century provided a wholly satisfactory explanation of all learning.
Like the corpuscular and the wave theories of light (in physics),
these two conceptions of learning were apparently *both* necessary
to account for different types of experimental and commonplace
data; so it was natural that many investigators should have concluded
that learning involved two distinctively different processes, a view
which was eventually dubbed *two-factor* learning theory (Mowrer,
1947). In the next two chapters we shall see how, between 1935
and 1950, this view was elaborated and systematized. But then, in Chapters 4 to 6, we shall see that, while an advance over the classical views
of Pavlov and Thorndike, considered separately, two-factor theory was
likewise unsatisfactory in certain important ways, including its inability to account for a form of so-called secondary reinforcement
which was being increasingly studied from about 1945 on.

This work on secondary reinforcement led to a major revision
of two-factor theory, which was enunciated in 1956 (Mowrer). Here
an attempt was made to show that, in the final analysis, all learning
can be reduced to conditioning, if that process is properly defined.
However, according to this view, learning is still "two-factored"
in the sense that it occurs under two different conditions of reinforcement: drive reduction (reward) and drive induction (punishment). Thus, instead of invoking Pavlovian theory to explain certain
instances of learning (so-called conditioning) and Thorndikian theory
to explain other instances (so-called trial-and-error learning, or habit
formation), the attempt is made to integrate these two conceptions
into a more powerful and truly united conceptual scheme.

This new conceptualization carries us far, as will be apparent in
Chapters 7 through 12. But, in the sequel to this volume (Mowrer,
1960), which deals with the *vicarious* learning which language makes
possible, it is necessary to come to grips with the problem of *semantics*.
Here it is found that the meanings of words have both a connotative
(evaluative, good-bad) and a denotative (or "cognitive") dimension;
and while the revised version of two-factor learning theory can

---

as S—R psychology has become more sophisticated and more adequate, there has
been a steady falling-off of interest in this alternative approach (see Chapter 9; and
Mowrer, 1960, Chapters 2 and 6).

readily account for the evaluative aspect of meaning (through the association of words with the experience of reward or punishment), it cannot explain, without further development, the purely denotative aspect of meaning—or certain familiar aspects of *memory*. In Chapters 5 and 6 of this book and in Chapters 5–7 of *Learning theory and the symbolic processes* (Mowrer, 1960), an attempt is made to work through this complication; and, as a result, it is discovered that psychology is today again concerned, although under a new terminology, with those banished "faculties," or "mental functions," once known as cognition (knowing), conation (willing), and affection (feeling). However now, instead of having either a psychology without learning (as we may characterize Structuralism) or learning without psychology (radical Behaviorism), we have a conceptual scheme in which learning and the more distinctive "mental" functions are integrally and inseparably related.

As is thus apparent, the approach to be followed in this volume is heavily historical; but it is one which catches in its sweep most of the great issues and problems that have occupied the creative thinkers and investigators in the field. It is hoped that the reader will find in the ensuing account of these developments some of the challenge and fascination which the field has held for those who have been personally immersed in it.

2

The Law of Effect, Conditioning, and the Problem of Punishment

The preceding chapter has indicated something of the influence which E. L. Thorndike and I. P. Pavlov were to exercise on the development of learning theory during the first half of this century. In the present chapter we shall be concerned, more specifically, with the problem of *punishment* and with the contribution which the views of each of these investigators and the research they have stimulated have made to the better understanding of the problem and, in this way, to the development of a more comprehensive, more self-consistent, and more unified theory of learning in general. This may seem an awkward and perverse way of approaching the psychology of learning, to begin with its more "negative" aspect; but this is how the matter has moved historically. Moreover, such a course leads quite naturally and with certain logical advantages to a consideration, in later chapters, of the psychology of learning in its totality (see also Mowrer, 1960).

I. Thorndike's Early Position Re-evaluated and Revised

A possible source of misunderstanding should be dispelled at the outset. Here we are to take, as basic, a conception of punishment which Thorndike himself later repudiated—or at least seriously questioned. Such a strategy, without explanation, might suggest that a "straw man" was being set up only to be knocked over. Such is not at all the case.

Thorndike's original position was to the effect that learning is a reversible process, reward strengthening and punishment weakening it. However, as a result of a long series of experiments on verbal learning in human subjects carried out later in his professional life, Thorndike (1931, 1932b) came to the conclusion that his original position had been in error and that, while reward does indeed facilitate learning, punishment does not weaken it. The details of this remarkable interlude in Thorndike's thought have been carefully reviewed by Postman (1947) and need not be repeated here, but it is relevant to note some of Postman's own comments on this score.

Thorndike's revised view of punishment startled the psychological public. Not only did it contradict the belief in the practical value of punishment which had become almost an axiom of our social life, it was also clearly at variance with a considerable body of other experimental data (p. 502).

When we turn to punishments other than an announcement of *wrong* or slight monetary losses, the uncertainty of Thorndike's generalization becomes even more apparent. . . . As against the blanket assertion that punishment is not instrumental in the elimination of the wrong responses it is possible to cite a long list of papers covering more than half a century of experimental work [cf. also Thorndike, 1932a] which report that punishment is an effective condition of learning (pp. 505–506).

When Thorndike moved from his earlier, "classical" theory to the new position (which was to be espoused and elaborated by Hull and his followers; see Chapters 3 and 8), he was clearly on less firm ground than he had initially been; so we shall here deliberately take as our point of departure his *earlier* formulations which, while admittedly incomplete and inadequate, at least give us a good first approximation to the truth.

As Deese (1952) has remarked, "Thorndike, for many years, dominated the theory of punishment. Because his influence is still felt to a very considerable degree today, it is best to begin with his notions concerning the effects of punishment" (p. 112). In the end, these notions broke down (or were abandoned), it seems, not because they were wrong in any global sense, but because Thorndike refused to *develop* them in keeping with certain ideas which have been put forward, with much empirical support, by Pavlov and other students of conditioned-response learning. By taking Thorndike's *original* rather than his revised theory as a starting point and by incorporating rather than ignoring the work of Pavlov, we find ourselves on a road which promises to carry us far toward the development of a more nearly "whole" conception of the topic under consideration.

Perhaps, therefore, the quickest way to come to the heart of the issues with which we are here concerned will be to re-examine Thorndike's early statement of both "sides" of the Law of Effect. Writing in 1913, Thorndike said:

> When a modifiable connection between a situation and a response is made and is accompanied or followed by a satisfying state of affairs, that connection's strength is increased: When made and accompanied or followed by an annoying state of affairs, its strength is decreased (p. 4).

And by way of amplification, Thorndike added:

> By the strength of a connection is meant roughly the probability that the connection will be made when the situation recurs (p. 3).
>
> The strengthening effect of satisfyingness (or the weakening effect of annoyingness) upon a bond varies with the closeness between it and the bond (p. 4).

In a grossly empirical, descriptive sense, the Law of Effect is almost certainly valid: other things being equal, an act is more likely to recur if its prior occurrence has led to reward, and it is *less* likely to recur if its prior occurrence has led to punishment. Such a bifurcated principle is, to say the least, congruent with common sense; and it seems well calculated to make behavior adaptive, in the biological scheme of things.

However, at another level of interpretation, the Law of Effect has come under increasingly critical scrutiny. For at least two decades now, it has been clear that the "negative" half of the law, in its more molecular aspects, was miscast. Just as reward was said to "stamp in" bonds, associations, or connections, punishment was thought to weaken, or "stamp out," such connections. Learning, or S—R "bonding," was thus, as already noted, a reversible process. Just as reward caused it to proceed in a forward direction, punishment caused it to recede. If rewards, so to say, opened neural pathways, punishment closed them. And the one action was assumed to be just as immediate and direct as the other.

Whatever learning may be in its "forward," positive phase, it became increasingly clear that unlearning, or "punishment," is not a simple matter of obliterating, stamping out stimulus-response "bonds." But a more declarative approach to the negative side of learning could not occur until at least certain forms of that type of learning known as *conditioning* were taken into account. And here our story starts with the phenomenon of *fear* conditioning.

It has long been known, of course, that fear can be attached to a formerly neutral, or "indifferent," stimulus by associating that stimulus with some painful experience. W. A. Bousfield, writing in the *American Psychologist* for 1955, documents this statement in an unusual way when he says:

Professor J. H. Arjona of the University of Connecticut, the leading authority on the Spanish playwright Lope de Vega, recently sent me a copy of his admittedly free translation of a story in Lope's play *El Capellán de la Virgen* (The Chaplain of the Virgin). This play was probably written in 1615. Accompanying the translation was the pointed observation, "This antedates your scientific experiments by about three centuries."

With Professor Arjona's permission, I am submitting his translation for the possible edification of the profession. . . . It would appear that the highly prolific Lope was somewhat of an authority on classical conditioning.

"Saint Ildefonso used to scold me and punish me lots of times. He would sit me on the bare floor and make me eat with the cats of the monastery. These cats were such rascals that they took advantage of my penitence. They drove me mad stealing my choicest morsels. It did no good to chase them away. But I found a way of coping with the beasts in order to enjoy my meals when I was being punished. I put them all in a sack, and on a pitch black night took them out under an arch. First I would cough and then immediately whale the daylights out of the cats. They whined and shrieked like an infernal pipe organ. I would pause for awhile and repeat the operation—first a cough, and then a thrashing. I finally noticed that even without beating them, the beasts moaned and yelped like the very devil whenever I coughed. I then let them loose. Thereafter, whenever I had to eat off the floor, I would cast a look around. If an animal approached my food, all I had to do was to cough, and how that cat did scat!"

Here was a situation in which the character who is telling the story was not able to punish the voracious cats directly, lest Saint Ildefonso see him do it. Yet he manages *to inhibit* their behavior, in a simple yet ingenious way. He conditioned the cats so that they would be afraid whenever he *coughed*, a sound which he could make innocently enough in Ildefonso's presence; and later, when the cats were about to advance and devour his food, this stimulus alone was enough to keep them at a distance. Here one cannot legitimately speak of the "stamping out," by means of direct punishment of the cats, of the habitual bonds that caused the cats to eat the boy's food; but such behavior was none the less effectively controlled. And this observation suggests that even in the more direct and simpler instances of punishment, inhibition is achieved in another way.

First of all it is to be observed that the procedure described in Lope's play made coughing one of the stimuli which the cats, in effect, "produced" when they started to advance upon the boy's food. Now suppose that, instead of this artificially introduced stimulus, we make use of those stimuli which are *naturally* correlated with the behavior in question. To do this we let the behavior itself start to occur and then, on the spot, punish the cats. Now, by the principle of associative learning, or conditioning, already described, we would expect fear to become attached to *these* stimuli, so that the special procedure described by Lope would not be necessary: as soon as the cats started to perform the punished act they would, so to say, *automatically* (i.e., without anyone's intervention) become afraid and remain at a safe distance. This notion of punishment is obviously and importantly different from Thorndike's conception of bond erasure; and it is now generally conceded that punishment achieves its inhibitory effect, not by the direct stamping out of S—R bonds, but by the intermediation of fear. An action, previously strengthened by reward, which is followed by punishment, produces certain stimuli, both internal and external to the organism, which, by virtue of their contiguity with the punishment, take on the capacity to arouse fear; and when the organism subsequently starts to repeat such an action, the resulting fear produces a *conflict* with the drive or motive underlying the original act. If the fear is sufficiently strong, the act will, in consequence, be inhibited, or at least in some fashion modified.

This revised conception of the way in which ordinary punishment operates has had two rather momentous consequences. First of all, it "integrates" the views of Thorndike and Pavlov in a way which neither of these men alone was able to do. Pavlov, for reasons which will gradually emerge as our discussion continues, never really interested himself in the problem of punishment; and Thorndike, although fully aware of and concerned about the problem, refused to take seriously the principle of conditioning. But if we combine the *principle* of (fear) conditioning with the *problem* of punishment, a new and powerful hypothesis emerges—a hypothesis which not only provides a superior explanation of punishment (in both its passive and active aspects, see below) but which leads ultimately, as we shall see, to a revised and sounder conception of habit formation itself.

Moreover, the developments just sketched opened the way for the integration of learning theory and clinical psychology, in general, and psychoanalysis in particular. Thorndike's original theory of punishment, while sound as a first approximation, made no provision for the manifest phenomenon of conflict, and conflict is the very essence of the clinical problem. Although in this book we shall be only incidentally concerned with the latter (see Chapter 11; see also Mowrer, 1960), yet it is reassuring to know that we are pursuing a conception of learning which leads naturally to such matters, rather than automatically excluding them or denying their very existence.

II. Punishment and Fear Conditioning

Punishment thus emerges, not as one of two aspects of a single (reversible) learning process, but rather as a subprinciple, or "application," of another seemingly separate type of learning. This other type of learning is fear conditioning and, in its most general form, can be conveniently depicted as shown in Fig. 2–1. If fear, with its powerful motivational properties, is conditioned to stimuli which are response-produced, occurrence of that response will tend, as already indicated, to be blocked: the occurrence or continuation of the response arouses fear and its discontinuation causes the fear to abate. If, on the other hand, fear is conditioned to stimuli not specifically associated with behavior, resolution of the fear will very likely be best achieved, not by inaction, but by *action*—action which will eliminate the fear-producing stimulus or situation either by removing the affected organism therefrom or by changing the situation. In the one case, i.e., where the stimuli are response-produced, we are likely to speak of "punishment"

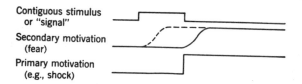

Fig. 2–1. Diagrammatic representation of fear conditioning. This emotion is originally elicited by some primary drive, such as electric shock; but if some other, formerly neutral stimulus immediately precedes the primary drive, the fear response, after a few pairings of signal and drive, will become attached to the signal and "move forward," as shown by the dotted line. When this occurs, the fear response is said to have become "anticipatory." The above diagram is schematic, but very similar actual records can be obtained by using the GSR (galvanic skin reaction) as an indicator of fear (Mowrer, 1938; Woodworth & Schlosberg, 1954, Ch. 6).

and, in the other case, of "avoidance learning," although it is now evident that "avoidance," in the sense of averting painful, noxious stimulation, is achieved in *both* instances through the arousal of fear and appropriate (though different) reactions thereto.

The term, "punishment," is usually applied to the procedure employed when an organism, prompted by some drive such as hunger, exhibits a mode of behavior which has previously satisfied this drive and an effort is then made (usually by another organism) to disrupt or eliminate this "habit" by the introduction of a competing drive or drives. Suppose, for example, that a hungry laboratory rat has learned to run to a small iron rod (or "spatula") with a bit of mash pressed on its flattened end whenever this rod is inserted up through the grill-like floor of the apparatus in which the rat is located. The rat will have received considerable training in getting food in this way, over a period of two or three days, so that, at the time of the demonstration, its response to the insertion of the food-bearing rod will be prompt and specific ("habitual"). Now suppose that we have decided to "break" the rat of the "habit" of running to and taking the food from this rod by means of punishment in the form of an electric shock of, say, two seconds duration—administered to the rat's feet from the grill floor of the apparatus. (A 125-volt alternating current will be used, with a limiting resistance of 175,000 ohms. The charge thus imposed upon the grill is so slight that it is hardly perceptible to a human hand, but it is mildly painful to the rat.)

One can easily surmise what would happen to the rat's behavior as a result of the introduction of this sort of punishment; but let us reproduce here notes made in connection with an actual demonstration of the kind described.

1st trial: On insertion of food rod, rat dashed, quite as usual, to the rod and, taking it in his forepaws, started eating. Shock was applied. Rat dropped rod and "danced" around on the grill until shock went off.

2nd trial: After an interval of 2 minutes, food rod was again presented. Rat immediately ran to the rod, took it in forepaws, and started eating. When shock was applied, rat dropped rod, danced much as before, and squealed slightly.

3rd trial: This time rat ran toward rod and tried to grab the food off it, with teeth, without taking rod in forepaws. Probably got some food, but also got shocked. Danced and squealed.

4th trial: Very much like preceding trial.

5th trial: Rat would run toward food rod, then suddenly withdraw, pause a moment, and then repeat this performance. The "conflict," between hunger and fear of being shocked, was thus very evident [see Chapter 11].

After four or five successive advances toward and retreats from the food bar (without actually touching it), the rat came briefly to rest at some distance, and the experiment was discontinued.

While instructive, such a demonstration leaves some unanswered questions. What would the rat, in this particular demonstration, have done on the next few trials? Would it soon have been so thoroughly "beaten" that, at least for the time being, it would abandon the food, preferring to be safe rather than "sorry"? [1] Would experience in taking food and "riding out" a weak shock so condition a subject that it would later be undeterred by a stronger shock which, if used initially, would produce marked inhibition? These and many other intriguing questions can be asked—and, without too much trouble, answered (see, for example, Chapter 11); but the observations recorded are sufficient for our present purpose, which is simply to illustrate, in some detail, the essential features of so-called punishment and to indicate how this phenomenon can be accounted for by the fear-mediation hypothesis, in contrast to Thorndike's stamping-out notion.

III. Fear Conditioning and Active Avoidance Learning

Through historical accident and carelessness, the practice has grown up of speaking of "punishment" and of "avoidance learning" as if the former were, itself, not also a form of "avoidance." As seen in the preceding section, this practice is misleading and blinds us to the commonality of the principles involved. Hence it is here proposed that so-called punishment be termed *passive* avoidance learning (learning to "avoid" by *not* doing something) and that the contrasting form of avoidance (learning *to* do something as a means of avoidance) be termed *active* avoidance learning. It is with the latter that we shall now be especially concerned.

Imagine an elongated, narrow box, about three feet in length, a foot and a half high, and five or six inches wide or "deep." Imagine also that the box is divided into two compartments, by a partition in the middle with a small hole or "doorway" in it. In order to make the two compartments easily distinguishable, one—let us say the one at the

---

[1] Because the shock used in the demonstration was comparatively weak and the hunger fairly strong, there was not much general inhibition. The rat remained quite active between trials, but there was a tendency to "leave the field," as indicated by jumping behavior (attempted escape) which had not occurred previously. A more intense shock would have altered this general picture.

observer's right—is painted white and is illuminated by a small electric light, while the other is painted black and is unilluminated. Moreover, the floor of the black compartment is made of wood, while the floor of the white, or right-hand, compartment consists of a metal grill, through which an electric shock can be administered by the experimenter.

With a laboratory rat at hand, we are ready to start a simple demonstration of *active* avoidance learning. We put the rat into the apparatus and let it thoroughly explore for four or five minutes. The rat, which we can observe through a one-way mirror which acts as the front side of the apparatus, will move about sniffing, looking, and feeling with its vibrassae. It will thus explore first one of the compartments and then the other, passing back and forth between them until its "curiosity" (see below) has been satisfied. Then it will settle down, perhaps groom itself, and give the appearance of being just a bit bored with it all.

The following are notes from an actual demonstration of this kind.

1st trial: Rat soon came to rest, quite conveniently, in the white compartment. [Otherwise, after exploration, rat would have been placed in the white compartment.] When shock [same intensity as used in the punishment demonstration] was applied, rat churned its feet, squealed, circled about in the compartment, and, at the end of 6 seconds, escaped the shock by running through door into black compartment. But very soon the rat came back into the white compartment [see comments below] and had to be driven out with a second shock. This time the escape took less than 3 seconds.

2nd trial: When, after an interval of 2 minutes, rat was removed from black compartment and placed in white compartment, it promptly ran out of the white compartment into the black one. No shock applied. A little later the rat came and *looked through the door*, into the white compartment, but it did not enter.

3rd, 4th, and 5th trials: Fled from the white compartment into the black one within a second or two, without application of shock. Rat is now content to stay in the black compartment, some distance from the door. Demonstration ended.

In some ways this demonstration would have been neater if, on trial 1, the doorway had been closed after the rat ran into the black compartment, thus preventing its return to the white compartment. However, the demonstration, as actually conducted, revealed a side effect often noted in connection with punishment, namely, something which, for want of a better term, can be called the "curiosity" effect. One of the students in the seminar where the foregoing demonstration was made volunteered the information that he had once had a pet raccoon which was occasionally allowed to roam about in his family's summer cottage. On one occasion, the raccoon found a lamp cord on the floor and started gnawing into it. Shortly there was a flash of fire that caused the raccoon to bound away. But, almost immediately, the animal returned to the cord and started gnawing again. However, the second occurrence of a short circuit was enough for him, and he thereafter stayed a respectful distance from lamp cords. As will be observed in more detail later (Chapter 6), *slight* fear (of *uncertain* origin) may make an organism explore rather than avoid the stimuli or objects to which the fear is attached. Why this should be so has not been fully determined. But this fact in no way goes against the assumption that shock or other painful stimulation produces fear and that, in general, fear then makes the organism avoid the stimuli to which the fear is conditioned.

In a situation such as the demonstration just described, there is a tendency to say that the subject has learned to *avoid* the shock—hence the term, "avoidance" learning. But this is a rather inexact, abbreviated way of speaking. More precisely, what the rat has learned is (a) to *be afraid* in and of the white compartment and (b) to reduce the fear (and shock, when it is presented) by *running* into the black compartment. Strictly speaking, it is not the *avoidance* of shock that is rewarding to the animal and keeps the running response going. It is rather the fact that the white compartment arouses fear and the running provides a solution to, or *escape from*, this "problem" or drive. The *avoidance* of the shock is a sort of by-product—though, to be sure, a very important one. Action which thus appears to be teleological or "purposeful"—and which, in a sense, indeed is—can in this way be accounted for in a purely causal, or consequential, way. We do not have to say that the rat runs "in order to" avoid the shock; we can say instead that the rat runs *because* (or *by-cause*) of fear (see also Section Xb).

Now some readers may, at this point, ask: "But why introduce *fear* into the picture? A scientific hypothesis or explanation should always be as parsimonious as possible. And the most parsimonious explanation in the foregoing situation is to say, quite simply, that flight from the white compartment is a *reflexive reaction* to the shock which then, by classical Pavlovian principles, becomes connected to the stimulus constellation provided by the compartment itself, without shock. Thus, the flight reaction which later occurs immediately upon the animal's being put into the white compartment (before shock is applied) is interpretable as a straightforward *conditioned* reflex, without any reference to fear or similar subjective phenomena." This objection is entirely valid, as far as this particular situation is concerned: here, from the standpoint of sheer logic, it is indeed *not* necessary to introduce fear as an intervening variable. But the difficulty is that the classical Pavlovian theory, while adequate in this and in a narrow range of other situations, does not give us an explanation of broad applicability. It does not, for example, provide a satisfactory understanding of *passive* avoidance learning (ordinary punishment); and there are various other situations wherein it breaks down completely. This is why (see also Sections V and VII) it is incumbent upon us to introduce, at this early juncture, concepts with high generality, rather than knowingly limit ourselves to a type of explanation which, though valid in this particular situation—and, to be sure, simpler—would, however, soon stifle the development of a more inclusive, powerful explanatory system.

So our assumption will be that, in the situation under discussion, the shock initially produces two more or less concomitant responses, which are radically different: (a) the escape reaction of running (along with a number of other similar but ineffective reactions) and (b) the emotional reaction of fear. In principle, of course, either of these reactions would be conditionable, according to classical Pavlovian theory; and most Pavlovians would simply ignore (or deny) the fear reaction and assume, instead, that the running reaction becomes directly conditioned to the white compartment (or "CS," since it "precedes" the shock). But, as will be shown later, this interpretation, while appealingly simple, gets us into serious difficulties in other situations; and in light of these difficulties we shall make the very different assumption that it is not the overt, muscular action of running that gets conditioned in this situation but instead the emotional, autonomic reaction of *fear*. In fact, it will be our premise that ordinary behavioral ("voluntary") responses *in general* are not conditionable, in the strict sense of the term, and that the concept of conditioning applies only to emotional responses (rather broadly conceived). (We shall later—Chapter 7, Section IX; see also Mowrer, 1960, especially Chapter 5—have occasion to modify this statement in a special way; but for the present it can stand in this unqualified form.)

IV. Active and Passive Avoidance Learning Compared

The foregoing demonstration helps one to see the similarity between the principles involved in so-called punishment and what is commonly, though also too restrictively, known as avoidance learning. In both instances, there is fear conditioning; and in both instances a way of behaving is found which eliminates or controls the fear. The only important distinction, it seems, is that the *stimuli* to which the fear gets connected are different. In so-called punishment, these stimuli are produced by (correlated with) the behavior, or response, which we wish to block; whereas, in so-called avoidance learning, the fear-arousing stimuli are not response-produced—they are, so to say, extrinsic rather than intrinsic, independent rather than response-dependent. But in both cases there is *avoidance* and in both cases there is its antithesis, *punishment;* hence the impropriety of referring to the one as "punishment" and to the other as "avoidance learning." Obviously precision and clarity of understanding are better served by the alternative terms here suggested, namely, *passive* avoidance learning and *active* avoidance learning, respectively.

Perhaps the relationship, and also the distinction, between these two forms of learning is best expressed by noting that in active avoidance learning, there is first fear (produced by some external stimulus, or danger signal) and then overt response (which the fear produces), whereas in passive avoidance learning, there is first a response (produced by some other drive, such as hunger) and then fear produced by response-correlated stimuli). What the organism has to do, in the two cases, to *reduce* the fear is, of course, quite different, because of the difference in the nature of the stimuli to which the fear is conditioned: activity which eliminates (or removes the subject from) the external stimulus, in the one case, and cessation of the activity which is producing the response-correlated stimuli, in the other. But, as we have seen, the two phenomena involve exactly the same basic principles, of fear conditioning and of the reinforcement of whatever action (or inaction) eliminates the fear.

A student, after watching demonstrations of both these forms of avoidance learning, was once prompted to observe: "In passive avoidance learning the subject is *responsible* for what happens, while in active avoidance learning he is not. In the former situation, he gets into trouble only if *he* does something wrong, whereas in the latter, the next trial comes regardless of what he does." Intuitively, one senses what the student had in mind here. Yet there is a sense in which even this distinction is not entirely apt: one could say that in active avoidance the shock comes on because of something the subject has *not* done, whereas in passive avoidance it comes on because of something the subject *has* done. In active avoidance learning, the shock is, so to say, a way of *enforcing* or *ensuring* an action, rather than preventing one. So the subject is "responsible" for, or has control over, what happens in *both* cases in the sense that he can determine whether shock will or will not occur, by making or by inhibiting some specific response.[2]

But a difference in "responsibility" does exist with respect to the nature of the conditioned stimulus or danger signal: in passive avoidance the subject himself "makes" the stimuli which are associated with shock, whereas in active avoidance these stimuli are made by some other organism (or by "nature"). In the latter case, the danger signal is in the "imperative" mood: "*Do* this (or that), or pain will follow—so get along!" But in passive avoidance the mood is conditional: "*If* you do this (or that), pain will follow—so watch out."

The similarity and contrast between active and passive avoidance learning can be indicated in yet another way. By means of a noxious stimulus, such as electric shock, one can teach a rat (or other organism) either to do something it does not wish to do or not to do something it wishes to do. In other words, both situations imply conflict; but this phenomenon is usually more obvious in passive avoidance, where the subject, because of hunger or some other definite drive, is set to do something, which can be blocked only if a competing motive (fear) is introduced. In active avoidance, there may at first seem to be no competing motive; but there is always some inertia against movement (see Chapter 11); and there is at least this to contend with when an attempt is being made to coerce, or drive, an organism to *do* something, as opposed to *preventing* it from doing something. Hence, although conflict is not wholly absent in active avoidance (and may be relatively intense, in a fatigued or ill organism), in passive avoidance conflict—almost by definition—is always present and of an intensity proportional to the drive underlying the behavior which is being blocked.

Somewhat parenthetically it may be remarked that the foregoing is a fair exhibit of the integrating or "resolving" power of the type of theory systematically explored in this book. Many similar instances will be discovered as we proceed.

[2] In a paper by Dinsmoor (1954) which will be discussed in more detail later in this chapter, the distinction, in paraphrase, is made thus: In active avoidance, only one response is *rewarded* (by termination of the danger signal and reduction of fear) and all others are "punished," in the sense that they fail to avert shock; and in passive learning, only one response is *punished* and all others are "rewarded," in the sense, at least, of being safe and therefore in welcome contrast to the specifically punished response.

V. More Complex Instances of Fear, and Fear-Motivated, Learning

Though the practical differences between passive and active avoidance learning are important ones, we thus see that the theoretical distinctions are trivial: Both involve the conditioning of fear to specific stimuli or stimulus compounds, and the organism then behaves in a way calculated to reduce or control that fear. In the one case, the subject learns what *not to do* and in the other case what *to do*. Also, we see how unsatisfactory is the term, "avoidance learning," when used to imply a contrast with "punishment." In both cases there is an element of avoidance, pain avoidance; and in both, there is a possibility of pain infliction. Moreover, some measure of conflict is always present in both types of situation.

The procedure for demonstrating active avoidance learning with rats which has been described in the preceding section was developed and first reported by N. E. Miller (1948a). This investigator also extended the procedure in a number of ingenious ways, showing that once a rat has been conditioned to fear one compartment of the apparatus, it can be made to learn fairly complicated ways of getting out of that compartment and into the other, safer one. For example, if the opening between the two compartments is obstructed by a sliding door, the rat will learn to press a little bar located nearby or perform any of a variety of other "instrumental acts" if they cause the door to open and thus permit entry into the black compartment. On the basis of this and similar types of experiments, fear has been termed an acquired, or *secondary*, motive or drive. Once acquired, through conditioning, it evidently acts very much as do such primary motives as hunger, thirst, and cold, to "drive" the organism until a means of reducing or eliminating the motivational state is found.

It is also possible to exemplify active avoidance learning in another way. In the Miller-type demonstration, fear becomes connected to a complex of stimuli, i.e., to a *situation*. Fear can also be conditioned to a more delimited stimulus (Mowrer, 1950a; see also Chapters 3 and 4). Let us suppose that the apparatus described in the preceding section is modified, by removing the partition between the two halves, painting the whole interior the same color, and changing the floor so that shock can be administered on either side. Let us suppose, also, that there is a buzzer on or near the apparatus which can be sounded by the experimenter. The procedure will then be as follows. A rat is put into the apparatus and allowed to explore for 10 minutes or so. Then the buzzer, which initially produces only a momentary, "listening" reaction, is sounded for five seconds and the shock is applied to that half of the grill floor on which the animal happens to be located. As in the preceding demonstration, the rat will at first not "know" specifically what to do about the shock. Soon, however, it will escape by running to the opposite (uncharged) side of the apparatus, at which point the buzzer will also be turned off. At intervals of about two minutes, the buzzer and shock will be repeated, until the animal has had a total of, let us say, ten trials. The rat will then be returned to its living cage and allowed to "rest" until the next day, when it will again be taken to the apparatus and given another set of ten trials. This procedure will be continued until the rat has learned to run to the opposite end of the apparatus in response to the *buzzer alone.*

Under the circumstances just described, a rat may make one or two runs in response to the buzzer on the first day, or it may make none at all. However, shock-avoidance runs will almost certainly begin to occur on the second or third day, and by the sixth or seventh day the animal may be making six or eight such runs out of a total ten trials. By the end of 10 days, that is, 100 trials in all, most animals will be making 9 out of 10, or even 10 out of 10, runs to the buzzer alone (see Fig. 2–2).

Another interesting thing one observes in a demonstration of this kind is the appearance, and disappearance, of what may be called "spontaneous," or "interval," runs. About the time the animal makes its first runs in response to the buzzer alone, it will be seen occasionally to move from one side of the apparatus to the other, *between trials.* This is a sign that the animal has not yet distinguished between situation-with buzzer and situation-without-buzzer. It is the former and it alone that is dangerous; and as soon as the animal learns this, the interval responses drop out and the running occurs quite specifically to the buzzer.[3]

Watching the foregoing demonstration, one is likely to say that the learning is a good deal slower than that which occurs in the Miller-type experiment. A better way to put it is to say that the animal has a good

---

[3] Responses to situation alone, i.e., without buzzer, disappear because, in a procedure of the kind described, they perform no function: the next trial comes at precisely the same time, regardless of whether such "interval" runs do or do not take place (see Chapter 11). The interesting situation wherein between-trial runs are allowed to be functional, in the sense of postponing the next trial, will be considered in Chapter 12, Section X.

deal *more to learn* in the "shuttling" situation. The rat not only has to learn what to do about the shock and then about the buzzer; it also has to learn, as already noted, that the situation is dangerous *only* when the buzzer is present. In the beginning, the whole apparatus, being associated with shock presentation, becomes fear arousing; and before the animal's behavior can become smoothly adaptive and efficient, fear of the situation when buzzer is absent has to extinguish (Chapter 11). In other words, as already noted, the animal has to form a *discrimination* (see Chapter 12) between situation-with-buzzer and situation-without-buzzer. Because many so-called conditioning experiments have called for this type of learning, over and beyond the conditioning proper, "conditioning" has commonly appeared to be a more difficult and slower form of learning than it actually is. If the *solution* to the problem of acquired fear is kept *simple*, as it is in the Miller experiment, we see that the "conditioning" occurs quite rapidly, in a trial or two, instead of requiring upwards of a hundred trials, as is likely

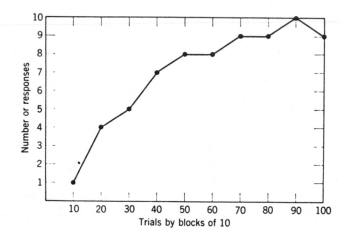

Fig. 2–2. Typical performance of a laboratory rat in shuttle-box avoidance learning. While comparing favorably with many other reported instances of "instrumental" conditioning, this learning is obviously rather slow and does not show conditioning in pure form, and at its best. Under optimal circumstances (see text), simple escape learning may require only two or three trials. The far greater number of trials required in the shuttle-box and similar experimental procedures is due to the fact that here conditioning is confounded with a high order of discrimination learning. Hence, the apparent slowness of "conditioning" —and the apparent "stupidity" of the subject.

where, in addition, a discrimination of some sort must also be formed (Mowrer & Lamoreaux, 1951).

In a demonstration of "shuttling" of the kind just described, the following stages or levels of learning must occur:

1. The rat has to learn what to *do* about the shock—how to get it turned off, how to *escape* from it.

2. Because shock is accompanied and slightly preceded by a buzzer, the buzzer alone (see below) becomes capable of arousing fear.

3. The rat now has a second, or secondary, problem or drive to deal with, namely, the fear which is now conditioned to the buzzer. In favorable situations, the subject now learns what to do as a means of *escaping* from it (and, in the process, avoiding shock).

4. However, for a considerable time the rat fails to discriminate between situation-with- and situation-without-buzzer and runs somewhat "indiscriminately." Only when the subject has reached the point of running to buzzer only is "avoidance learning" said to be clearly and unambiguously displayed.

Manifestly, the total learning task is here a good deal more complicated than it is in the simplest possible forms of fear conditioning and escape. In the latter (for example, the Miller demonstration), all the organism has to do is to associate fear with a given *place* (situation, or stimulus complex)—and to act accordingly; whereas, in the shuttle-box procedure, the fear has to become specifically connected with a *cue*, and more or less dissociated from the particular situation in which the cue occurs (see Section VI). It is useful to keep this difference clearly in mind.

VI. Generalization and Discrimination, Preliminary Considerations

Although the learning ultimately exhibited in the situation just described is a good deal more specific, and more difficult, than that involved in the Miller demonstration, it, too, is somewhat situation-bound. This point can be illustrated in the following way. Let us suppose that instead of teaching a rat to "shuttle" as a means of escaping from the shock and, thereafter, of terminating the fear-producing buzzer, we decide to teach it to leap into the air. This, as we have already seen, is a response which a rat is naturally disposed to make to electric shock; and if this response is rewarded by drive reduction, it will occur more and more promptly, first to the primary drive of shock and, then, to the secondary drive of fear, as aroused by situation-plus-buzzer.

After our subject has learned to jump in the manner described—and with a high degree of reliability—to the buzzer under these conditions, let us do the following. We take the rat out of the apparatus and put it on a table. Then, after the rat has had an opportunity to explore for a while, we sound the buzzer. The chances are very high that the rat will now *not* leap into the air. The reason is that the conditioning of fear to the buzzer has been *in a particular situation;* and when the specific buzzer stimulus is presented under altered conditions, there is comparatively little spread, or generalization (see Chapter 12), of the fear—thus showing that the fear has not become conditioned to the buzzer-as-such but to buzzer-in-a-given-situation.

The fact that a buzzer is a danger signal when heard in the box-like apparatus does not necessarily mean that it is dangerous, i.e., will be followed by shock, under *all* circumstances. As a consequence, the nervous systems of living organisms have evolved in such a way as to keep them from over-generalizing. In other words, conditioning tends to be specific to the situation in which it has occurred; and if the situation changes, the tendency for the conditioned reaction to occur, even though "*the* conditioned stimulus" remains the same, is considerably reduced. Hence, a rat that has been conditioned to buzzer-in-box will not react with the same degree of fear to buzzer-without-box. What this demonstration shows, therefore, is that although the shuttling or jumping response as it occurs in the apparatus seems to be caused quite specifically by the buzzer, "*the* conditioned stimulus" is really buzzer-in-a-particular-situation.[4]

A bright student, upon hearing the foregoing demonstration described, called attention to an inconsistency between it and the story of the boy (Section I) who taught the cats to stay away from his plate when he coughed, by associating cough with "punishment" in another situation. While valid in principle, the story is clearly at fault

[4] Earlier, reference has been made to the tendency which rats show, in the shuttle-box experiment, to make the running response in the interval between trials, i.e., the tendency for their fear to generalize from box-with-buzzer to box-*without*-buzzer. In the situation just described we tested to see to what extent a rat trained to react in a given way to buzzer-with-box would generalize to buzzer-without-*box*. As noted, generalization of the latter sort is less marked, suggesting that conditioning, without special training (see next paragraph), tends to be more to the situation-as-a-whole than to a particular segment thereof, i.e., to a particular "stimulus."

in that it presumed more generalization of fear than would, in fact, probably occur. What one would have to do, with both the buzzer and the cough, to get the fear to generalize widely, would be to "confirm," or "reinforce," such a stimulus in a variety of different situations. Then, in a new situation, where there had been no reinforcement, the fear might be expected to occur to the specific stimulus, full force. In other words, the "meaning" of the buzzer, or the cough, would have to be made *abstract*, i.e., independent of the situation. This is a state which has to be achieved with those stimuli which we call "words" before language can function at all efficiently. Although they continue to be somewhat modified, as we say, "by the context," yet the distinguishing thing about "words" is the stability of their "meanings," regardless of the situation or circumstances under which they are used (Mowrer, 1960, Chapters 3 and 4). Much the same observations can, of course, be made with respect to the medium of exchange known as *money*.

VII. Fear as an Intervening Variable

Thorndike's theory that punishment simply reverses or stamps out the learning involved in a "habit" is manifestly limited in that there is nothing in it which would also help us understand what happens when "punishment" is applied, not because of something done, but because of something left undone. As noted in preceding sections of this chapter, a far more satisfactory view is that both passive and active avoidance learning operate in much the same way and that in both cases a crucial fact is the conditioning of fear to formerly neutral (response-dependent or independent) stimuli.

Because this improved conception of the way "punishment" (in both its inhibitory and excitatory forms) operates is importantly dependent on the principle of conditioning, one may be inclined to infer that Thorndike was "all wrong" and that Pavlov had the answer. Neither assumption would, in fact, be valid. *Empirically*, Thorndike was entirely correct in his observations as to how punishment (in its inhibitory guise) operates; it was only in regard to the *theory*, or explanation, thereof which Thorndike offered that he was in error. Pavlov, it will be recalled, was a self-professed reflexologist and eschewed anything so subjective and mentalistic as fear; and although we find that this particular reaction is readily conditionable, in keeping with Pavlovian principles, the applications of fear conditioning made in this chapter are quite different from anything for which Pavlov was himself responsible. His attempt was to found a science of behavior which was based exclusively upon unconditioned (native) and conditioned (acquired) "reflexes," involving manifest movement of observable parts of the body and with no "intervening variables."

Actually, Pavlov did resort to intervening variables, or constructs, of a kind. As already noted, he was meticulous in avoiding any and all *psychological* constructs, such as fear obviously is; but he made considerable use of two purely hypothetical states of the central nervous system which he called *excitation* and *inhibition*. Under the influence of *positive* reinforcement, e.g., food presented to a hungry dog, "excitation" was supposedly generated in a localized area of the cerebral cortex, from which it then radiated out into adjacent cortical area. And, conversely, under the influence of *negative* reinforcement, e.g., weak acid injected into a dog's mouth or electric shock applied to some other area of the body, "inhibition" was supposedly generated in the appropriate area of the cortex and, like excitation, radiated out into surrounding parts of the brain.

From the latter way of thinking it is possible to derive a kind of indirect theory of punishment; but Pavlov's notion of cortical excitation and inhibition has itself never been empirically confirmed, and very little systematic effort has been made to apply it to the problem of punishment. (In fact, Pavlov himself did not make much use of his theory in this connection but used it mainly to explain the results of "experimental neurosis" in his dogs as it was produced by conflict situations. The impairment of function which sometimes resulted Pavlov attributed to the simultaneous presence and "clashing" of excitatory and inhibitory states in the same or adjoining areas of the brain.) The real difficulty, of course, was the fact that Pavlov tried to derive an explanation of inhibition and facilitation (or excitation) in purely *cortical* (central nervous system) terms, without making any systematic reference to the *autonomic* nervous system and the responses which it mediates, one of the most important of which is *fear* (cf. Chapter 6, especially Section IX). This neglect of the autonomic nervous system and of the *emotions* in general was to be a very costly mistake for Pavlov and his school (as we shall shortly see); and it seems all the more remarkable when one recalls that most of Pavlov's experimental work on conditioning was done with the response of salivation, which is itself mediated, not by the central nervous system, but by the autonomic nervous system and which (as we shall also see) also has emotional concomitants.

Inherent in Pavlov's basic conception of conditioning there is, actually, a somewhat better possibility of explaining punishment along quite different lines. Let us assume, for example, that a dog has been taught to make a "positive" or approach reaction to some conditioned stimulus: when a whistle is sounded the dog comes for food. Now we take the whistle and pair it with a *different* unconditioned stimulus, i.e., one that produces a different *response*. Suppose, for example, that every time the whistle blows the dog now gets shot with a small B-B gun. Flight rather than approach will be produced by this latter stimulus, so it would be a natural expectation that the dog would now begin to react to the whistle with *this* response, rather than with the original one of approach. Thus, by means of the same simple assumptions which constituted Pavlov's general theory of conditioning, it is possible to derive at least an oblique theory of punishment: that is, one which suggests how it would be possible to inhibit or reverse previously conditioned behavior. But at once we see that the example given does not typify punishment as we ordinarily think of it; and other considerations show that the Pavlovian approach is generally unsatisfactory.

Thus we arrive at the realization that whereas Thorndikian learning theory could account (at least formally) for punishment, it could give no explanation at all for active avoidance learning; and whereas Pavlovian theory could (again, formally) account for active avoidance learning (see last paragraph of Section III), it was, as we have just seen, quite unable to handle the problem of punishment. Therefore, we find each of these two major schemes inadequate in important, though different, ways. And, it so happens, when we look more closely at even the strongest features of Pavlov's and Thorndike's views in this area, they, too, are considerably short of satisfactory. In preceding sections it has been shown that the conflict or feedback theory of punishment (involving conditioned fear) is a good deal more plausible than Thorndike's stamping-out hypothesis; and we are now in a position to show that Pavlovian theory likewise does not give a really competent account of active avoidance learning. In other words, on close inspection, it turns out that neither Thorndike's nor Pavlov's theory, as originally formulated, can give a first-rate explanation of *either* active *or* passive avoidance learning.

So we now turn to a more detailed analysis of active avoidance learning, which superficially seemed to lend itself so readily to a classical conditioning interpretation but which, in reality, was to prove a great embarrassment to that theory.

VIII. The Classical versus Instrumental Conditioning Dilemma

Although it was Pavlov who gave the concept of conditioning widest scientific currency and who tried to make it explain all behavior modification, his own researches, as already noted, were very largely restricted to the conditioning of the salivary response; and although salivation has both an appetitive and an aversive or avoidance aspect (actually different glands are involved), it was another Russian physiologist, V. M. Bekhterev (1913), who pioneered the investigation of overt avoidance *behavior*, from the conditioned-reflex standpoint. This investigator found, with dogs as subjects, that if a buzzer or some other, originally neutral stimulus precedes an electric shock delivered, for example, to a dog's paw, the dog will at first lift his leg only to the shock but, after a few pairings of buzzer and shock, will then start lifting the leg "defensively," to the buzzer alone. Superficially, this exhibit of active avoidance learning looks like a pure instance of reflex conditioning, or simple stimulus substitution. If the leg flexion, made in response to shock, is thought of as an unconditioned reflex, then the same response, made to the buzzer, can be called a conditioned reflex, without reference to any sort of intervening, subjective factor such as fear. But it was soon to be discovered that even in this seemingly perfect example of classical avoidance conditioning, there was a serious flaw.

According to Pavlovian theory, learning is contingent upon the temporal conjunction, or contiguity, of a formerly neutral stimulus and one which, from the outset, is capable of producing the desired reaction. Thus, in the Bekhterev type of experiment, the conditioning of leg flexion is dependent upon the pairing of buzzer and shock; and, per theory, the more frequently these stimuli are conjoined the better will be the learning. But it is now well known that, in a situation of this kind, better learning is usually obtained if the CS (conditioned stimulus) is followed by the US (or UnCS, for unconditioned stimulus) *only* in the event that the subject does *not* respond in the expected way to the CS alone. If such a reaction does occur, the UnCS is omitted, so that the procedure is said to be "instrumental" in that the conditioned response prevents the occurrence of the noxious unconditioned stimulus. This is to be contrasted with the "classical" procedure of invariably pairing CS and UnCS. Schlosberg (1934), Hunter (1935), and Brogden, Lipman, & Culler (1938) were some of the first American psychologists to work on this problem; and the experiment by the last-named investigators gave especially dramatic and striking results. This experiment has been summarized by Hilgard & Marquis (1940) thus:

A guinea pig was placed in a [revolvable] cage and after a conditioned stimulus (buzzer) it was given a shock which evoked running behavior. One group of animals, trained according to the Pavlov procedure, were shocked whether or not they ran. Another group, trained according to the arrangements of avoidance learning, were not shocked if they ran. Learning began similarly in both groups but reached a much higher level of performance in the second group. The results are plotted in [Fig. 2–3]. Guinea pigs which were shocked whether or not they ran continued to show anticipatory agitation at the sound of the buzzer, but after the first few trials the tendency to run did not increase; those shocked only if they did not run developed the habit of running promptly at the sound of the buzzer. Learning in this situation appears to be based in a real sense on the avoidance of the shock (p. 58).

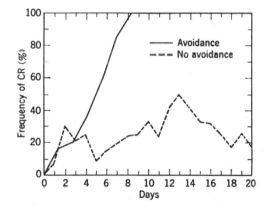

Fig. 2–3. Learning curves, reproduced from Brogden, Lipman, & Culler (1938, p. 110), showing the results of an experiment in which shock-avoidance and nonavoidance procedures were compared. The erratic lower curve is indicative of the conflict generated by the nonavoidance procedure.

Pavlov had held that in conditioning some response, initially elicitable only by an unconditioned stimulus, becomes capable of being elicited by some formerly ineffective stimulus, as a consequence of the paired presentation, in "temporal contiguity," of these two stimuli. This paired presentation of CS and UnCS was termed "reinforcement," and the more frequently such "reinforcement" occurred the stronger the tendency for the CS to elicit the response in question supposedly became. The results of the Brogden-Lipman-Culler experiment (and of various other investigations, see page 42, and the two following chapters) brought this assumption under grave suspicion. For here we see frequent (invariable) pairing of CS and UnCS leading

to extremely poor learning and decidedly less frequent pairing leading to extremely good learning.

In the passage quoted, Hilgard & Marquis remark that, "Learning
in this situation appears to be based in a real sense on the avoidance of
the shock." We now can be a good deal more explicit and say that
learning, in this situation, involves two different phenomena: (1) the
process whereby the subject learns to *be afraid* when the buzzer sounds
and (2) the process whereby the subject learns what to *do* about its
fear. The first is, to be sure, dependent upon the paired occurrence of
buzzer and shock; but once *this* learning has occurred, it is obviously
wise to .omit further CS-UnCS pairings on those trials when the
subject responds to its fear by *running* (since this is the response
which we supposedly wish the subject to acquire). For, as already
noted, if we *now* pair CS and UnCS we are creating conditions which
effectively *punish* the subject for running and thus set up a conflict:
between fear of the buzzer, which tends to evoke running, and fear
of the stimuli which running produces, which tends to inhibit running.

That the so-called instrumental conditioning procedure should give
better results in active avoidance learning than does a noninstrumental
(or "classical") procedure not only follows from considerations advanced in earlier sections of this chapter: it is the sheerest of common sense. In fact, the "classical" procedure, wherein the subject is
"punished" regardless of whether or not he does what he is "told" (by
the CS) to do, would seem no less absurd and "unfair" than would
a *passive* "avoidance" learning procedure in which the subject is
punished not only when he *makes* a certain "forbidden" response but
also when he, quite obediently, *refrains* from making the response.[5]

Recently Razran (1956c) has pointed out that the superiority of the
instrumental conditioning procedure, over the classical procedure,
was known in Russia considerably before it was discovered in this
country. He says:

Both avoidant and unavoidant conditioning were studied in Bekhterev's
"association-reflex" laboratory from its beginning in 1907. Protopopov (1909)
in his pioneer experiment on shock-conditioning used unavoidable shock with
five dogs, whereas Molotkov (1910) in conditioning four human adults used
avoidable shock. . . .

In 1926, Starytzin introduced avoidable shock with dogs. He compared
the conditionability of dogs under avoidable and unavoidable shock. His
results antedate those of Schlosberg's (1934) with rats by eight years. . . .
Starytzin found avoidable shock superior to unavoidable. . . .

Starytzin's procedure was modified and perfected by Petropavlovsky

---

[5] For further criticisms, of a different kind, of classical conditioning methodology, see Liddell (1944).

(1934), and since then Russian experiments have been using both avoidable and unavoidable shock with dogs and other animals (p. 127).

However, instead of allowing this finding to have the stimulating effect (on both theory and research) which it had in this country, the Russians have attempted to explain it away, in such a manner as not to disturb official Pavlovian doctrine. This is made clear in Razran's further comment:

> Despite the fact that the Russians have as a rule found avoidable shock more efficacious, they have not conceptualized it as a distinct form of conditioning. Conceptualization of avoidable shock began in this country with Schlosberg, who found avoidable shock, if anything, inferior to unavoidable shock. All the Russians seem to say about the superiority of avoidant conditioning is that it is "more natural," more "in line with animal evolution," that it results from partial reinforcement [see footnote 6], or, more exactly, from "non-overreinforcement" (pp. 127–128).

The concept of "over-reinforcement" is clearly *ad hoc* and improvised, and does not square with known facts. For example, if the inferior results produced by the classical conditioning procedure were indeed due to *too much* "reinforcement," the logical way to improve the situation would not be an instrumental procedure but one in which shock followed signal on every other trial, or every third trial, or every fourth trial, without regard for the subject's own behavior. This type of intermitted (fixed-ratio) reinforcement would, presumably, avoid "over-reinforcement," but it would still not produce nearly as good results as those which are obtained where the shock occurs only when the animal fails to respond to the signal and is withheld when the animal makes the expected response. There is nothing in the concept of over-reinforcement which can account for the superiority of the results of a truly instrumental procedure over those of a pre-arranged schedule of intermittent (*or* continuous) reinforcement.[6]

[6] Since intermittent reinforcement has commonly been found to result in greater "habit strength," as measured by resistance to extinction, than does continuous reinforcement (see Chapter 12), it has sometimes been argued that the so-called instrumental conditioning procedure gives better results simply and precisely because it involves intermittent reinforcement. There are several reasons for doubting this interpretation, among them these: (1) There is no evidence that intermittent reinforcement results in better *acquisition,* and this is where the advantages of the instrumental procedure are most apparent. (2) As suggested above, intermittency of reinforcement, programmed without reference to what the subject *does* on a particular trial, almost certainly will not give the same results as will instrumental reinforcement. And (3) there is current evidence for believing that intermittent reinforcement results in greater resistance to extinction, not because of greater "habit strength," but because such a training pro-

It has already been pointed out that the resolution of this and other dilemmas lies well within the scope of conditioning theory *provided* the theory is revised in certain crucial ways. If we assume that, in both active and passive avoidance learning, what happens, first and foremost, is that *fear* gets attached to a formerly neutral stimulus or stimulus complex, then all follows naturally enough. One can thus explain the *active* avoidance which occurs when fear is aroused by an independent stimulus; one can explain the *passive* avoidance which occurs when fear is aroused by response-produced stimuli; and one can explain the rather preposterous *conflict* which results from the use of a classical conditioning procedure, where fear gets attached *both* to an independent stimulus (e.g., buzzer), which says *do,* and to response-produced (e.g., proprioceptive, etc.) stimuli, which says *do not!*

Thus, somewhat paradoxically, we find that by *restricting* the concept of conditioning, we greatly *increase* its applicability and power. The reflexologists hoped, as we know, to account for *all behavior* in terms of native and acquired (conditioned) reflexes. But in thus being so ambitious for their principle, they actually robbed it of its true importance and value. In fact, they made a travesty of the concept. And what we are here trying to do is to show how, by limiting the concept of conditioning to emotional (autonomic) learning, we can develop an explanatory system of remarkable scope and consistency.

IX. Theories of Punishment and Common Sense

A recent technical paper by Dinsmoor (1954) on the psychology of punishment begins with these words:

A possible reason for the seeming neglect of the topic of punishment in contemporary behavioral research and in most of our handbook and textbook presentations may be found in the present entanglement of theoretical treatments. So confused is the current picture that Stone (1950), in a . . . review of the literature, was led to remark that "The task of resolving apparently conflicting results . . . is an all but impossible one" (p. 34).

Dinsmoor then goes on to say:

Actually . . . I feel that there is an available formulation which can handle the bulk of the data and which can incorporate it within a more general descriptive framework without requiring new explanatory principles (p. 34).

---

cedure reduces the effectiveness of the extinction process (Chapter 11). Thus, the attempt to account for the superiority of the instrumental conditioning procedure in a way which would by-pass the necessity of fear as an intervening variable falls short of its objective and will not be further considered (cf. Bitterman, 1957).

And the discussion which follows is very much along the lines explored in the preceding sections of this chapter (with certain exceptions which will be considered in Section Xa). Few would today deny that our understanding of both active and passive avoidance learning is much more systematic and unified than it was only a few years ago. But the remarkable thing is that, even now, our knowledge in this area cannot be said to represent much of an advance over common sense: anyone who ever drove a team of horses, or a yoke of oxen, had at least a *working knowledge* of all the principles reviewed in this chapter. What appears to be progress within the confines of scientific psychology is, therefore, little more than a recovery from the confusion into which the field was thrown by dramatic, but inadequate, earlier formulations.

As already noted (Chapter 1), Thorndike and Pavlov were both captivated by the idea that the way to have a true science of behavior was to base it upon observable correlations between stimulation and overt response; and in pursuit of this notion they both advanced appealingly simple (though otherwise quite different) suggestions as to how behavioral modification (learning) takes place.[7] The trouble was that their formulations, in striving for parsimony and objectivity, overshot the mark, and resulted in conceptual models which were much *too* simple to be "iconic" with respect to the actual phenomena in question. (Without this oversimplification, one is tempted to conjecture, they could not have been so different!) And so strong was existing dissatisfaction, around the turn of the century, with the obvious prolixity and disarray of explanatory concepts and categories in psychology that any promise of simplification and unification, if made with boldness and a modicum of empirical justification, was sure to have a favorable reception.

Science, of course, always aims at simplicity of explanation; and no great harm has been done by these efforts to reduce explanatory principles to the barest necessity. The difficulty is, they have not been *sufficient;* and much of the last twenty-five years has been devoted, in psychology, to the task of revising, expanding, and uniting these formulations. Today we have reason to be well pleased with what has been accomplished in this connection; and on this now presumably firm foundation we shall, in later chapters, examine other developments which take us from the so-called negative to the more positive aspects

[7] Psychologists who studied with Thorndike, especially in the early and middle stages of his career, say that he often remarked that every psychology laboratory should have a sign over the door which would read: STIMULUS and RESPONSE.

of behavioral adaption and learning. In view of the neglect of the problem of punishment alluded to by Dinsmoor and Stone, it may seem strange that this is the area chosen by the present writer as, so to say, the cornerstone of what purports to be an extended and systematic treatise on the psychology of learning; but it seems that, as in the story of the little girl who was told by the elves to "sweep under the rug," we too have found gold. However, there is still not a universal acceptance of the systematic position on which we propose, in this book, to build; and before proceeding with this undertaking it will be well to review and carefully appraise some of the misgivings and, in some instances at least, misunderstandings which thus exist.

X. Objections and Criticisms Considered

Central to the argument which has been presented in this chapter is the empirically derived assumption that there can be no adequate theory of behavior and behavior change which does not accept the reality and functional relevance of such subjective states as fear and (as later chapters will suggest) other emotions. In square opposition to this view is the behavioristic dictum that only observable, strictly "objective" events are proper data for a genuinely scientific psychology —or behaviorology. Gradually, over the years, much of the force has gone out of this stricture; but the position is still occasionally defended. It is the purpose of the present section to review some of the more energetic views thus expressed by latter-day behaviorists and other criticisms of the systematic premises on which later chapters of this book are founded.

(a) *Conditioned stimulus aversiveness versus fear.* In his 1953 book, *Science and human behavior*, B. F. Skinner states his position in this connection with stark simplicity. The chapter on "Emotion" begins with this sentence: "The 'emotions' are excellent examples of the *fictional causes* to which we commonly attribute behavior" (p. 160, italics added). Then the familiar, but highly debatable, assertion by William James is approvingly quoted to the effect "that we feel sorry because we cry, angry because we strike, afraid because we tremble, and not that we cry, strike, or tremble because we are sorry, angry, or fearful, as the case may be" (p. 160).

Rarely are theoretical issues (in psychology) so beautifully explicit and "clean." The present writer, in company with many others, takes the position that the emotion of fear *is* causal; that a one-step (simple S—R) psychology will not work; that, as a minimum, two casual steps are necessary to account for behavior; and that fear, in the case of

both active and passive avoidance behavior, is an essential intermediate "cause" or "variable."

By contrast, Skinner and those of like persuasion hold that this is
not at all the case and display great persistence in trying to suggest
alternative ways of dealing with the pertinent issues. One device commonly put forward in this connection is basically the same as what
early behaviorists termed "reflex chaining" (Hilgard & Marquis, 1940,
pp. 210, 226). Here the attempt is to get around certain subtle
problems of motivation and reinforcement by positing a purely "mechanical" (unmotivated and unreinforced) linkage of stimulus-response
(reflex) units (cf. Mowrer, 1960, Chapter 7). Or an attempt is made
to deal with the problem by means of a quite transparent logical sub-
terfuge: to deny the simple—and obvious?—assumption that, in
any avoidance-conditioning situation, the CS or danger signal arouses
fears and to affirm instead that the stimulus itself, in some rather
inexplicit way, becomes "aversive" and thus capable of motivating
and (at its termination) reinforcing behavior.

For example, in the otherwise highly cogent paper on punishment
by Dinsmoor, already cited, we find this strategy exemplified as
follows:

> Since the concept of aversive stimulus is fundamental to subsequent dis-
> cussion, I will begin by offering a definition. . . . I will use the word in a
> strictly functional or behavioral sense, with no reference to its subjective
> properties or to any assumed drive which might be said to be aroused or
> reduced by the presentation or removal, respectively, of the stimulus. . . .
> The critical observation is that *the reduction or elimination of the stimulus
> increases the frequency or probability of the preceding behavioral sequence*
> —that is, that it is reinforcing to the subject.
> For the naive organism, this classification apparently includes such stimu-
> lating events as immersion in water and certain intensities of light, sound,
> temperature, and electric shock (p. 35).

With the foregoing there need be no disagreement. The author
is here speaking of what others would refer to as extrinsic (as opposed to intrinsic or "metabolic") stimuli having inherent (as opposed to acquired) drive properties. The difficulty arises in the
next step, when Dinsmoor tries to explain "how neutral stimuli become aversive." He says:

> The main fact seems to be reliably established: that a neutral stimulus
> which is presented just prior to or overlapping with the administration of a
> primary aversive stimulus, like shock, acquires an aversive property in its
> own right and becomes what we may call a conditioned or secondary
> aversive stimulus (p. 36).

Such an assumption works well enough, up to a point, as Dinsmoor's paper demonstrates; the trouble, as in all behaviorism, is that the assumption is so disingenuous and, ultimately, nonfunctional. For some purposes it makes little difference whether one assumes that a danger signal elicits the "aversive" emotion of fear, which then acts to motivate and (through its reduction) to reward behavior, or instead assumes that the danger signal itself "becomes aversive," so that its appearance is directly motivating and its disappearance rewarding. Operationally, the two positions, in many situations, come to much the same thing. There are, however, limitations inherent in the Skinner-type approach which inhibit the kind of theory development with which we are especially concerned in this book. And there is, in addition, an absurdity in the position itself. Dinsmoor, with other members of the Skinner school of thought, says that the formerly neutral stimulus, as a result of its pairing with "a primary aversive stimulus, like shock, acquires an aversive property *in its own right*." [8] Can this, literally and actually, be true? If the expression, "in its own right" is to be taken seriously, it presumably means that the stimulus itself *changes;* and if this were to happen, it would subsequently affect *other* organisms aversively, and not just the organism which had, more or less adventitiously, been present when the formerly neutral and the primary aversive stimuli were "paired." An organism which is not present when, for example, a buzzer and electric shock are simultaneously presented to another organism (or, for that matter, in any empty box) does *not* subsequently find that buzzer to be aversive, "in its own right." The "aversiveness" is the property of the affected organism, not of the stimulus itself; and this fact is fully recognized in the hypothesis that the conditioned stimulus acts *as if* it had become "aversive" for the reason that the organism now reacts to it with an "aversive" emotion, *fear!*

Assuming that students of learning were themselves electronic robots, rather than members of the animal kingdom, they would still have to take the foregoing considerations into account; and if they operated at all logically, they would have to infer an intervening variable, *within the subject*, rather than a change in the stimulus. Being sentient creatures ourselves, we certainly know, first-hand, the phenomenon of fear; so it is not its postulation, but its systematic rejection, that is strange and unscientific.

(*b*) *Is shock avoidance rewarding?* A psychologist who read an

---

[8] Sidman & Boren (1957a) say that "The stimulus itself becomes aversive" (p. 282).

early draft of this chapter made a marginal comment to the effect that "Kamin has found evidence that, in [active] avoidance learning, it may not be just escape from fear, but also shock avoidance itself, that is reinforcing." The experiment here referred to was reported in 1956 under the title, "The effects of termination of the CS and avoidance of the US on avoidance learning." Kamin summarizes his experiment thus:

The effects of response termination of the CS and of avoidance of the US on avoidance learning were studied with a 2 x 2 factorial design employing 32 hooded rats as Ss in a shuttle-box. There were significant main effects of both factors, with no interaction. The avoidance of the US and response termination of the CS both resulted in more responding, and in shorter response latency. The effect of avoidance of the US was tentatively interpreted in S—R terms; no attempt was made to interpret the effect of response termination of the CS in cognitive terms (p. 423).

Kamin's results are here reproduced as Fig. 2–4. The performance of the eight animals in the "normal" group, wherein a response (running to the other end of the shuttlebox) made to the danger signal (buzzer) had the conjoint effect of terminating the signal and of preventing the occurrence of shock, is clearly superior to that of the other three groups. Here the procedure may be said to have been a *double* "instrumental" one: the running response not only provided immediate escape from fear (through buzzer termination) but also averted the shock (Mowrer & Lamoreaux, 1942). In contrast, the "classical" procedure, wherein response to the danger signal neither

Fig. 2–4. Results of a study by Kamin (1956, p. 422) suggesting that shock avoidance is reinforcing, quite apart from any reduction in fear. In the text reasons are given for believing that this interpretation is a mistaken one. Note how similar the top and bottom curves here are to those shown in Fig. 2–3.

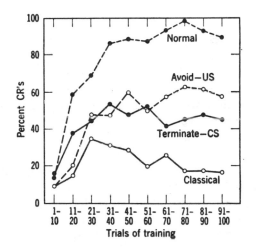

terminated the signal nor averted the shock, gave decidedly inferior results—consistent with other findings previously reported in this chapter (p. 43).

Thus far the results of the Kamin experiment tell us nothing new. But what we now note is that the subjects in the other two (intermediate) groups apparently benefited about equally from *each* of the two instrumental procedures, alone: shock avoidance and buzzer termination, with a slight advantage going to the shock-avoidance group (cf. an experiment by Traum & Horton, reported by Mowrer, 1950a, pp. 287 ff.). What does this finding mean?

As will be presently indicated, the Kamin experiment is somewhat confounded in design, or at least in interpretation, and its results cannot be taken at face value. But the study usefully serves to bring up an issue which has not yet been fully considered (cf. Section III). When it was becoming apparent, some years ago, that "instrumental" training procedures give better results than does the "classical" procedure, it was sometimes objected that this just could not be the case, for it would involve teleology, i.e., causation from the future rather than from the past (or present)—which is contrary to the basic assumptions of science. However, by the postulation of fear as an intervening variable the specter of teleology was effectively banished.

The finding that laboratory animals more readily respond to a danger signal if their response averts shock (or some other noxious stimulus) of which the signal is premonitory may well give the *appearance* of their behaving as they do "in order to" *avoid* the shock. This, of course, would be rank teleology. But if we assume, instead, that as a result of paired presentation of signal and shock, there is an associative shifting of fear from the latter to the former, then we see that, upon presentation of the signal, fear will be aroused and the subject will respond in a particular way *because* the signal produces the fear and the response in question gets rid of both. (This resolution of the paradox is today widely accepted, even by those writers who insist upon speaking of "conditioned stimulus aversion" rather than fear; see, e.g., Dinsmoor, 1954; Schoenfeld, 1950; Skinner, 1953a; etc.)

Now the Kamin experiment, in an ingenious but somewhat misleading way, calls this analysis into question. It implies, as the reader of this chapter pointed out, that there is, after all, something about shock avoidance *per se* that is reinforcing, quite apart from the fear reduction which termination of the danger signal provides. In Kamin's words, "While a combination of CS termination and US avoidance leads to the strongest responding, either of these factors alone adds substantially to response strength" (p. 422).[9] If valid, this is a serious complication and must be considered.

There is no problem, really, about the results reported by Kamin for the "terminate-CS" group. Here the procedure differed from that of the "classical" group only in that the CS was ended by the subject's response; and the fact that performance is superior in the "terminate-CS" group speaks *in favor* of the hypothesis that fear reduction, mediated by CS termination, is a reinforcing event although, obviously, CS termination here will not be *as* reinforcing as it is where it is never followed by shock ("normal" procedure).

The real issue hinges upon the interpretation given to the results for Kamin's "avoid-US" group. Here, ostensibly, the CS is not response-terminable, and only the avoidability of the US can account for the fact that performance of this group, while not so good as that of the "normal" group, is still reliably better than that of the "classical" group. The fallacy lies in the intimation that the danger signal, or CS, was *interminable*. Obviously this was not the case, for the author specifically says that: "With an avoid-US subject, a CR caused the US to be omitted for that trial but had no effect on the CS, which continued to act *until 5 sec. after its onset*" (p. 421; italics added).

The difficulty lies, of course, in the assertion that "a CR . . . had *no effect* on the CS." It is true that, in the "avoid-US" group, a response was not uniformly followed by *immediate* CS termination (and fear reduction), but CS termination did occur eventually, in fact fairly soon—after only five seconds; so that what is here involved, manifestly, is not a complete dissociation of response and CS termination but rather just a *delay* of reward. As will be shown in Chapter 10, it is now well established that rats and other laboratory animals can learn under conditions of delayed reward, where the response-reward interval is five seconds (or, for that matter, considerably longer), although such learning is not so efficient as it is with instantaneous reward. Therefore, it would seem that what Kamin has shown is not that US avoidance, as such, is reinforcing but merely that *delayed* CS termination (and fear reduction), following response, is less reinforcing than is immediate CS termination. This is quite different from purportedly proving that shock avoidance, as such, is reinforcing.[10]

[9] For a similar interpretation, see Woodworth & Schlosberg (1954).
[10] For a sequel to this study, see Kamin (1957a).

(c) *Avoidance learning and the "contiguity principle."* The experiment by Brogden, Lipman, & Culler (1938) has already been cited (p. 42) as providing one of the first and best demonstrations of the superiority of an instrumental training procedure in active avoidance learning. In 1948, Sheffield published a paper on "Avoidance Training and the Contiguity Principle" in which he criticized the interpretation commonly made of the Brogden-Lipman-Culler findings and advanced a different one. His first point is that too much has been made of the inability of the "contiguity principle" to account for results of this kind. As will be seen in Chapter 8, the term "contiguity principle," as it is employed by Sheffield and others who subscribe to a conception of learning put forward by E. R. Guthrie, has a somewhat elastic meaning. But *one* of its meanings is the reflexological notion that conditioning is simply a matter of a given item of overt behavior getting shifted, as a result of the contiguous presentation of a signal and an unconditioned stimulus, from UnCS to signal. Therefore, in the type of situation under discussion, if electric shock causes a guinea pig in a revolvable cage to jump forward or run, then this response should get directly connected to any stimulus which immediately precedes the shock-run sequence, without the necessity of positing fear or any other sort of intervening variable. But, in the experiment in question, this principle runs into the paradoxical fact that 100% (classical) reinforcement of the conditioned stimulus leads to decidedly poorer performance on the part of the subjects than does a procedure in which shock follows signal only part of the time, namely, on just those occasions when the subject does not respond to the signal.

Sheffield makes the observation that in the classical conditioning procedure, in the experiment cited, the shock often comes on, not while the animal is at rest, but (because of the action of the signal) *already running* and that, under *these* circumstances, the effect of the shock is sometimes that of causing the animal to *stop*. Hence, the contiguity principle would hold that on ensuing trials the signal would tend to elicit stopping, rather than running—which would then explain why 100%-shock-reinforced animals would not show a high incidence of *running* to the signal. This, of course, is a completely legitimate argument; but the facts admit of another—and more broadly applicable—interpretation. When an animal has been put into motion by the danger signal and is then shocked, obviously the effect, as far as the running response is concerned, is one of *punishment*, so that a condition of conflict (cf. p. 44) is thus generated: the danger signal arouses fear which says "go"; but the response-correlated stimuli aroused by "going" say "stop," with the highly erratic behavior indicated by the lower curve in Fig. 2–3.

Hence we may conclude that Sheffield's first point is apposite: that, taken alone, the results of the Brogden-Lipman-Culler experiment *can* be explained by the simple contiguity (Pavlovian) principle. But in other situations, some of which have already been mentioned in this chapter (but see also Chapter 3), the simple contiguity principle is manifestly inadequate. The alternative interpretation, which involves the concept of fear as an intervening variable, seems to apply equally well in *all* the situations cited. The formulation with the greater generality obviously has the advantage.

Sheffield's second point is based upon a rather common misconception. In referring to the Brogden-Lipman-Culler study and his own replication thereof, Sheffield says:

> The findings for avoidable shock offer no evidence for a strengthening effect of avoidance [compare the Kamin study] and follow the conventional result in Pavlovian experiments. Reinforcement by shock strengthened conditioned running; omission of shock led to extinction. The picture of alternate strengthening by shock and weakening by avoidance fits well Hull's (1929) theoretical analysis of conditioned defense reactions, and Schlosberg's (1936) description of his rats' behavior. The findings do not at all fit the alternative contention (Hilgard and Marquis, 1940; Mowrer and Lamoreaux, 1942; Schlosberg, 1937) that omission of shock strengthens the response rather than weakens it. For example, according to Hilgard and Marquis,
> "Learning in this situation appears to be based in a real sense on the avoidance of the shock. . . . In instrumental avoidance training the new response is strengthened in the absence of any such [noxious] stimulus; indeed, it is strengthened because of the absence of such a stimulus" (1940, pp. 58–59).
> The implication is that a learning curve rather than an extinction curve would be found during consecutive avoidances of shock. The present findings show the reverse to be true (pp. 174–175).

According to principles previously considered in this chapter, the resolution of this paradox is simple and straightforward. In a situation of the kind under discussion, on a trial when the subject responds to the danger signal and averts shock, *two* things happen: the trial is indeed an extinctive one for the *fear* which the danger signal produces, since the danger signal is not "confirmed" by the shock; *but* —and this is the main point—such a trial definitely involves reinforcement as far as the *behavioral* response is concerned, since its occurrence turns off the danger signal, with attendant fear reduction. It is, of course, entirely true that, in an instrumental avoidance procedure, the behavioral response will eventually stop occurring; but this is because the underlying *fear* reaction to the danger signal has extinguished, and not because the "habit" of responding *to* the fear has been exhausted. The "habit" may still exist in full force; but if the acquired drive which calls the habit forth is not present, either because it has not been stimulated or because it has extinguished, the habit will not be manifested—just as the habit of pressing a bar for food will not occur unless the subject is properly motivated, i.e., hungry.[11]

(*d*) *Is the present systematization "premature"?* Finally, we may consider a criticism from yet another quarter. Following an approach first used by Estes & Skinner (1941), Brady & Hunt (1955) have stressed the inhibiting, or "suppressing," effect of a danger signal upon on-going behavior—such as bar pressing, by a hungry rat, as a means of obtaining food. Here electric shock is used, not specifically as a punishment for bar pressing, but merely as an agency for imparting to a tone, a "clicking noise," or some other originally neutral stimulus the capacity to "disrupt or interfere with an organism's ongoing behavior" (p. 313). Nor does the danger signal occur, as a secondary punishment, just when the response occurs. Instead, the protracted presentation of the signal has a generalized inhibitory influence upon all overt behavior or, in short, the effect commonly termed "freezing." Can this effect be subsumed under principles already considered or does it go beyond or perhaps contradict them? Brady & Hunt conclude that:

> Many attempts have been made to order these diversities in behavior as a motivational construct mediating the establishment of instrumental behavior in such experimental situations (Miller, 1951b). The general orientation of the experiments summarized in this paper appear in rather clear contrast to this contemporary emphasis upon acquired drives and similar constructs. This more empirical approach . . . may clearly be seen to reflect some concern that such monolithic ordering, prematurely embraced, might serve to obscure important differences as well as significant similarities and relationships among behaviors which have in common some crucial dependence on what we conventionally regard as emotion (p. 322).

In this chapter what Brady & Hunt refer to as "such monolithic ordering" takes the form of the assumption that active and passive

---

[11] Lashley (1950) has made precisely the same point in these words: "Unless this affective element is aroused, the conditioned reflex does not occur. So-called extinction of the conditioned reflex is not a weakening of the specific association, but a waning of this affective reinforcement" (p. 474).

avoidance learning depend upon (a) the conditioning of fear to, respectively, independent and response-dependent stimuli and upon (b) the tendency of living organisms to develop, as a "habit," whatever form of behavior most effectively eliminates the fear thus aroused. In those instances where fear is conditioned to response-dependent stimuli (as in ordinary "punishment"), the effect is one of specific response interference or inhibition; and in those instances where fear is conditioned to an independent stimulus, the tendency is for the organism to be activated in whatever way will remove it from this particular stimulus or *vice versa*. Brady & Hunt are talking about an effect which is clearly different: the tendency for an independent, external danger signal which can be neither escaped from nor eliminated to have a nonspecific inhibitory effect upon *all* behavior. Such a stimulus makes the subject "cautious," yet highly "vigilant," in a way that probably has high biological utility.

Here there is no wish or need to deny the reality of the phenomenon about which Brady & Hunt are talking; but at the same time it in no way challenges the stated principles. This generalized "freezing" reaction to fear appears to be an instinctive device for ensuring care and circumspection in a *nonspecific danger situation;* whereas the mechanisms discussed in this chapter are relevant to those acquired adjustments to fear which have been here termed active and passive avoidance learning. We thus may assume that there is nothing demonstrably "premature" about embracing these principles, as will be still more apparent from the next section—and from ensuing chapters.

XI. Further Analysis of Instrumental Learning and the Increasing Acceptance of the Concept of Fear

As mentioned in the Preface of this volume, Dr. Janusz Reykowski, of the Department of Psychology of the University of Warsaw, was a Visiting Scholar at the University of Illinois during the early part of 1959 and at that time read the manuscript of this volume and its sequel. Among other perceptive questions which Dr. Reykowski raised was the following. The experiment of Brogden, Lipman, & Culler shows that in active *avoidance* learning an instrumental conditioning procedure results in far more efficient behavior than does the classical conditioning procedure. What now, Dr. Reykowski asked, would happen if the instrumental and classical procedures were similarly compared in an experimental situation involving *positive reward*, such as food, rather than escape from shock and fear of shock?

In the Brogden-Lipman-Culler experiment, the subject was in danger only when a specific cue stimulus or CS (compare Skinner's S^D notation, for "discriminative stimulus") was present. And if the correct response occurred when this stimulus was on, the subject was rewarded in the sense of averting the UnCS (shock), i.e., the response was "instrumental."

Now imagine a situation in which a hungry animal can obtain a bit of food by pressing a bar when a cue stimulus (S^D) is present. And, for sake of completeness, let it be added that if the animal presses the bar at other times, i.e., when the S^D is absent (Skinner calls this the S^Δ period or condition), nothing is accomplished, just as nothing is accomplished in the usual avoidance experiment if a response occurs before the CS, or "S^D", appears (but cf. Chapters 10 and 12). The question now is, what would constitute an instrumental as opposed to a classical training procedure in the type of situation just described? The answer would seem to go as follows. If, in the presence of the cue stimulus, the hungry animal is rewarded (with food) when it makes the prescribed response and not rewarded when it does not make this response, the procedure is "instrumental." That is to say, the procedure is instrumental if the food is *contingent* upon the occurrence of the response, which, of course, is the familiar, common-place procedure used in the establishment of "habits" in general.[12] Whereas, if the food follows the cue stimulus "unconditionally," i.e., without reference to any overt, behavioral act on the part of the subject, the procedure is "classical" and conforms to the situation so extensively employed by Pavlov and his followers in the investigation of the conditioned salivary response.

What, under the two conditions just described, would be the outcomes? The answer is clear: if reward is forthcoming when and only when the animal makes the prescribed *overt* response in the presence of the cue stimulus, the response will occur increasingly when and only when the stimulus is present. But if the reward follows the cue stimulus willy-nilly, the overt response will not be learned. The animal will, of

---

[12] This statement, without qualification, may be somewhat misleading. Two kinds of "habits" must be distinguished here, conveniently labeled by Skinner *free operants* and *discriminant operants* (habits which are under "stimulus control"). For example, a hungry rat can learn a bar-pressing habit either (a) in a situation where it is free to press the bar and obtain food *at any time* or (b) in a situation where bar pressing will produce food *only if* some special cue stimulus (S^D) is "on." Hence the above statement that habits "in general" are instrumental: i.e., reward appears only if response occurs. But the situation specifically under discussion is that wherein the habit is, in addition, under stimulus control, rather than being a so-called free operant.

course, learn to *expect food* following the appearance of the S^D or CS; and this state of positive expectancy (or *hope*) will be indexed, among other ways, by salivation (as Pavlov's experiments amply showed); but since the food is contingent only upon the occurrence of the cue stimulus and not upon the occurrence of any specific behavior, no such behavior will ordinarily be learned (but cf. Skinner, 1948; also Chapter 10).

The situation as regards instrumental and classical reward learning is thus parallel to what is known about instrumental and classical procedures in active avoidance learning. As the Brogden-Lipman-Culler experiment shows (Fig. 2–3), avoidance learning prospers under an instrumental procedure, just as does positive reward learning; and avoidance learning languishes under a classical procedure, just as does positive reward learning. In both cases, however, *autonomic* (emotional) conditioning can and does occur: fear (as indexed, for example, by the psychogalvanic reflex) in the first instance, and hope (as indexed by salivation; see also Chapter 5) in the second instance. But as far as overt (instrumental) behavior is concerned, the difference in the performance produced by the instrumental and classical training procedures is striking and crucial.

It goes without saying, presumably, that much the same picture also prevails as far as *passive* avoidance learning (punishment) is concerned. If an organism is punished "instrumentally," i.e., when and only when it performs a given action, the punishment is effective, i.e., the subject learns to inhibit this response (because the inhibition accomplishes something). But if a "classical" procedure is used, i.e., if the organism gets the noxious, painful stimulus (UnCS) regardless of whether it does or does not perform a given act, the punishment soon becomes ineffective, at least as far as the control of behavior is concerned. Here, as the common saying goes, "You're damned if you do and damned if you don't," so you might just as well go ahead and *do*, if you want to.

Thus the evidence is quite pervasive that as far as overt action in general is concerned, a so-called instrumental training procedure is decidedly preferable to the so-called classical procedure. This proposition is, in a sense, almost axiomatic and needs no special proof; for what it says, in effect, is simply that if behavior does not control what happens to an organism, the behavior is futile and just as well not occur. On the other hand, the same principle does not seem to apply to emotional reactions; here the classical procedure works very well. This is not the place to consider the question of what happens to such responses if an instrumental procedure is used with them, too (cf. Chapter 11). But what present considerations do show is that for all ordinary behavioral acts, the classical training procedure is contradictory, anomalous, and grossly inefficient. And as repeatedly indicated in this chapter, this state of affairs can be satisfactorily explained only if one posits a two-step theory of behavior, with certain internal reactions commonly known as *emotions* intervening between objective stimulation and overt, behavioral action.

Fear was the first emotion whose functional significance became clearly apparent in this context, and it is noteworthy how widely its reality and systematic importance are today accepted. There are, as already noted, a few American psychologists who are still reluctant to concede that fear is a necessary concept in the study and understanding of avoidance behavior. But common sense is clearly against them; and it is surely not without significance, also, that at the Nencki Institute of Experimental Biology, Warsaw, Poland—which has a strong reflexological (behavioral) tradition—there is today, under the leadership of Dr. Jerzy Konorski, a marked tendency to accept the two-step conception of avoidance behavior. For example, in a recent paper by Fonberg (1958), we read:

> The majority of the visceral and humoral reactions appearing [in the so-called experimental neuroses of dogs] (Gantt 1942, 1944, 1953, Gantt and Dykman 1952, Reese, Doss and Gantt 1953, Liddell *et al.* 1934, and others) are identical with the visceral and humoral reactions appearing to the defensive stimuli (Solomon and Wynne 1953, 1954, Dykman and Gantt 1954, 1956, Bersh *et al.* 1956, Wolpe 1952, 1954, and others). The appearance of these reactions in the defensive situation suggests that the above-mentioned visceral-vascular reactions form the basis of the anxiety state (Mowrer 1950, Solomon and Wynne 1954, Farber 1948). The fact that the pharmacological or surgical exclusion of the autonomic system (Wynne and Solomon 1955) weakens or even completely disperses the state of anxiety in the animal, handicaps the formation of defensive reactions, and causes their extinction, seems to favour this hypothesis (109–110).

> Thus the signals of the noxious stimuli—"imminent danger signals"— evoke a certain state in an organism, called the anxiety state, which consists mainly in a number of visceral and humoral reactions. The neurotic state which is a state of "emergency," heralding damage to the functioning of such an important organ as is the central nervous system, would also cause a state of anxiety similar to the state of expectancy for impending danger.

> The performance of an instrumental movement, a movement which always before removed the threatening danger, would reduce the anxiety state (Mowrer 1950, Solomon and Wynne 1953, 1954 and others), thus providing a positive reinforcement. Therefore the appearance of the anxiety state would always produce a tendency to its reduction, that is, a tendency

to perform a movement associated with the reduction or abolition of this state (pp. 109–110).

The congruence between the systematic position of the Nencki Institute workers (see also Beck, Doty, & Kooi, 1958) and the point of view represented in this book will be further indicated in Chapter 8. Although, to the best of the writer's knowledge, the Nencki group is not yet making systematic use of the concept of *hope*, it is believed that this concept is thoroughly consistent with their general theoretical position and that they will have no fundamental objection to the way in which its functional significance is elaborated in later chapters of this book. It now appears that hope is no less essential than fear to a genuinely adequate behavior theory; and, as later chapters will show, its empirical justification is no less abundant. However, before taking up this important strand of our story, it will be necessary to consider certain other developments, in the chapter which follows.

XII. Conclusions and Forecasts

But first, a sort of epitomizing statement. What our discussion in the preceding sections leads up to is the realization that living organisms make two radically different *kinds* of reactions: overt, behavioral, instrumental responses *and* emotional or "physiological" (autonomically mediated) reactions. The whole objective or function of the former is to *control* "what happens"—to prevent (avoid) undesirable happenings and to insure, or at least encourage, desirable ones. In other words, behavioral responses *must work*, or they are no good: they must be "instrumental" or they deteriorate. On the other hand, the "psychology" of the emotions is very different. They are not designed to control external events: they don't move us or other objects around, in the same immediate sense that contractions and relaxations of the skeletal ("voluntary") muscles do, and we don't expect them to be "instrumental" in the same way at all. They constitute our *feelings* and are clearly distinguishable from our *actions*, our *working* (workable, instrumental) responses.

So if our emotions do not help us control external events or happenings, what *do* they do? The answer is: they help us to know what to *expect* and to *prepare for* appropriate action. In other words, it is by means of the emotions that we internalize or "treasure-up," as Hume has said, a knowledge of the external world (see Mowrer, 1960, Chapter 8) and establish a sort of "isomorphism" between the world and our brains, between reality and mind. The emotions, so to speak, register, record, "accept" what is *out there;* but they don't *do* anything about it, at least not directly—that is the specialized task of our behavior responses. But, as we have seen, the emotions play a vital role in instigating, guiding, and directing behavior.

In other words, we have discovered that strict Behaviorism is not acceptable; that it is, in fact, grossly inadequate and has to be modified, at the very least, by admission of the concept of emotion. And when we thus acknowledge that there are two fundamentally different kinds of reactions, which serve two very different sets of functions or purposes, it is not in the least strange if we also seem to discover different laws of learning: *conditioning, classical* conditioning, that is—applicable to the emotions; *and* the Law of *Effect* (or "Instrumentality")—applicable to behavior proper. Behavior *has* to be instrumental if it is to be selected and retained (otherwise it would be quite worthless, even harmful), whereas emotions are learned, it seems, on the basis of the "sheer contiguity" of stimuli, without any reference to what these reactions "accomplish." (Actually, we find that the emotions "accomplish" a great deal—but not in the *same way* that behavioral reactions do.)

Thus, to many students of the problem, it has looked as if a *two-factor* conception of learning is essential. This view will be explored, at some length, in the next chapter. But the reader should, at this point, have a word of warning. In the end we are going to discover that all learning is reducible to conditioning; but it will be necessary for a few more chapters (four in fact) of the historical developments which we are here attempting to trace and understand to unfold before this hypothesis can be fully meaningful.

3

Two-Factor Learning Theory:
Versions One and Two

As a result of the line of analysis pursued in Chapter 2, we now have a relatively simple and self-consistent explanation of both active and passive avoidance learning; but this may not seem to bring us noticeably nearer to a unified and comprehensive conception of learning in general. When one looks away from the rather specific problems with which the preceding chapter is concerned toward the broader issues of the field, the picture may, indeed, seem obscured rather than clarified. However, things did not operate this way historically. Clarification of issues in the area of active and passive avoidance learning was followed by some notable developments, of far-reaching importance, and it is with some of these that we shall now be particularly concerned.

I. Two-Factor Theory, Original Version

The expression, two-factor learning theory, did not come into common use until about 1950; but it was merely the name, and not its referent, that was previously lacking. In the preceding chapters, we have seen the deep imprint made by the systematic views of both Pavlov and Thorndike. Although these views were diametrically opposite in their formal properties, there was an open question whether they were mutually exclusive or, perhaps, complementary. Their originators tended toward the former view. For example, in a paper entitled "The Reply of a Physiologist to Psychologists," Pavlov (1932) made conditioning the unmistakable cornerstone of his own theory building. He objected to the tendency of some to take conditioning as the model for all learning, without also acknowledging cognate processes which he and his co-workers had discovered; but there was no doubt as to the conception to which Pavlov gave cardinal emphasis. He said:

> The investigation of conditioned reflexes rests on the same three principles of the reflex theory: the principles of determinism, of gradual and successive analysis and synthesis, and of structure. . . . Thus there is opened up, so to speak, an unlimited possibility of studying the functions of the higher divisions of the brain, e.g., of the cerebral hemispheres, and of the adjacent subcortex with the most complicated fundamental unconditioned reflexes of the latter (p. 109).

In the same article there appears one of the few passages in which Pavlov ever took cognizance of response substitution or trial-and-error learning; and, as was to be expected, he here attempted (in a way which will be discussed in Section IV) to show how it could be derived from conditioning principles. Certainly he did not regard this form of learning as categorically different from or independent of the familiar conditioning process; whereas Thorndike, writing at about the same time (1931), took a very different position. He said:

> I must admit that the reported phenomena of the conditioned reflex are a mystery to me in many respects. Just what their relation to ordinary learning is I do not know, but I am not convinced that they show its fundamental pattern and most general principles (p. 113).

And again (1932b) he wrote:

> The C-R phenomenon seems much less general than ordinary learning. The phenomena of the conditioned reflex are probably not the archetype of learning in general. . . . They seem to be, on the contrary, a rather special case (p. 411).

Since stimulus substitution and response substitution both seemed to be real phenomena and since both, in different ways, have obvious biological utility, it was natural that less partisan investigators should gravitate toward the view that there are really two quite different, but complementary, learning processes. Each seemed to be useful in its own sphere, and certainly there is no inherent reason why they should not share the total task of organismic adjustment. Characteristically, R. S. Woodworth was among the first to see the possibility of such a division of labor here and, in a paper already cited in Chapter 1, approached the matter thus:

Little further would require to be said regarding selection [learning], if it were true that each stimulus were simply joined to one reaction, each reaction to a single stimulus, and if stimuli always came one at a time. As a matter of fact, none of these things is true. The same stimulus may have become linked with two or more reactions, and the same act with two or more stimuli; and the situation presented is always complex, containing a number of elements that are capable of acting as stimuli to different reactions (1918, p. 107).

When a response becomes "linked" to a new ("more than one") stimulus, we obviously have conditioning; and when a stimulus becomes linked to a new response, we have trial-and-error learning. Woodworth was thus arguing that *both* types of behavior modification are real and functionally important—a position which must have been rendered congenial to him by his earlier collaboration with C. S. Sherrington who, as early as 1906, had made a two-fold distinction between *consummatory* behavior and *anticipatory* behavior, which strikingly parallels the concepts of habit formation and conditioning.

Then, in 1935, B. F. Skinner, in a paper entitled "Two Types of Conditioned Reflex and a Pseudotype," proposed a fundamental distinction between behavior which is acquired on the basis of the Law of Effect and behavior which is acquired on the basis of the principle of conditioning. Two years later Konorski & Miller (1937) expressed their essential agreement with Skinner's distinction; and in the same year Schlosberg published a paper whose opening sentence read as follows:

The purpose of the present paper is to differentiate between two types of learning, namely, that involving simple conditioning and that involving the law of effect (p. 379).

In 1946 Tuttle, in an article on "Two Kinds of Learning," took the position that "an extensive and ever increasing mass of data points cogently and uniformly to the conclusion that there are two distinct kinds of learning" (p. 267), one of which he identified with Pavlovian conditioning and the other with the law of effect. And soon thereafter, Cowgill (1948) pointed with approval to a similar distinction which F. H. Allport had emphasized in 1924.

Thus it was apparent that, by mid-century, psychological thought was moving toward the view that Pavlov and Thorndike had both been right—right about different but complementary aspects of the total adjustmental process. However, in 1943 another way of regarding the matter was advanced, with great persuasiveness, by Clark L. Hull; and later developments with respect to two-factor learning theory cannot be appropriately reviewed until we examine Hull's alternative conception.

II. Hull's Attempted Synthesis of the Views of Pavlov and Thorndike

Attention has already been called to a stage in Thorndike's thinking when he seriously considered the possibility that reward strengthens S—R connections but that punishment does not weaken them. This view was most fully explored in a book, *The Fundamentals of Learning* (1932b), which Hull elaborately reviewed (1935) and which apparently made a deep impression upon him. From it he seems to have conceived the idea that *all* learning might be dependent upon a single, unitary process of reinforcement, namely, that provided by drive reduction (reward), and that such an assumption could be made to subsume under it both the Pavlovian and the Thorndikian forms of learning. With the strain toward parsimony always strong in science, it was only to be expected that, since neither of the theories which Pavlov and Thorndike had suggested had proved adequate to the needs of the situation, an attempt would be made to achieve a *synthesis* of the two which would replace the loose sort of "federation" implied by the conception of "two-factor" learning theory sketched in the preceding section of this chapter. Hull (1943) went about this task in the following way:

Because of the current differences of opinion concerning the relationship between selective learning and conditioned-reflex learning, an explicit and somewhat detailed comparison of them as types will now be made. In order to facilitate such a comparison, [Fig. 3–1] has been constructed to represent in considerable detail the dynamic factors here conceived to be involved in conditioned-reflex learning, in close parallel with the representation of the process of selective reinforcement (pp. 76–77).

Earlier in the same chapter Hull had postulated, in keeping with the positive half of Thorndike's Law of Effect, that if a response is made by an organism just before the termination of a drive such as that employed in the example shown in Fig. 3–1, that response will become more firmly connected with that drive, so that when the drive recurs, the response in question will tend to occur more promptly and more vigorously. In other words, it was here assumed that living organisms are so constructed that responses which "solve problems" (end drives) are "stamped in" and, in the future, will be more likely to recur. This was assumed to be the essence of selective learning or habit formation.

Fig. 3–1. Hull's diagram (slightly modified) for showing how selective learning and conditioning can be explained by a single set of assumptions. If a drive, such as that provided by electric shock, produces (in a dog) a response such as leg flexion and if the drive goes off shortly after this response occurs, the connection (solid arrow) between drive and response will be strengthened (selective learning). Likewise, it was reasoned, the reinforcement produced by drive reduction should also strengthen the connection (broken arrows) between any other contiguous stimuli (S_c, $S_{c'}$) and the response in question. When the latter connection becomes strong enough to cause R_u to occur in advance of the shock, "conditioning" is said to be manifested.

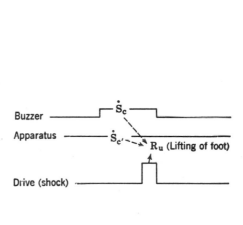

What Fig. 3–1 does then, in addition, is to suggest how the same sort of reinforcement, i.e., drive reduction, can also account for conditioning. If certain stimuli, such as S_c and $S_{c'}$, are present when the D—R_u connection is reinforced, it was argued that the same reinforcing event (at the termination of D) should likewise strengthen the connections between S_c and $S_{c'}$ and the response R_u. In other words, it was reasoned that if the termination of drive can strengthen the connection between the drive and R_u, the same event ought also to strengthen the connection between *other* stimuli, simultaneously present, and R_u. And when the latter type of connection gets strong enough, a "conditioned response" may be said to occur: i.e., R_u will occur to S_c and $S_{c'}$ or to S_c alone, *in advance of* D. R_u is then said to be a "defensive," or "anticipatory," response.

We may say, therefore, that in habit formation, or selective (Thorndikian) learning, the connection that is formed (or at least strengthened) is between some response and the stimulus ("drive") whose reduction provides the reward or reinforcement; whereas in conditioning (Pavlovian learning) the connection that is formed is between the same (unconditioned) response and some stimulus *other than* the one whose reduction provides the reinforcing state of affairs. In an earlier work, the writer (1950a, p. 89) suggested that the terms *intrinsic* and *parasitic* might be used, respectively, to indicate these two forms of reinforcement. The point of Hull's analysis was, of course, to explain *both* forms of learning with one and the same source of reinforcment—hence the common reference to his theory as *monistic*. Of his theory Hull said:

> These last considerations suggest that the differences between the two forms of learning [trial-and-error and conditioning] are superficial in nature; i.e., that they do not involve the action of fundamentally different principles or laws, but only differences in the *conditions* under which the principle operates. . . . On one critical point both cases are identical—the reinforcing state of affairs in each consists in the abolition of the shock injury or need, together with the associated decrement in the drive and drive receptor impulse, at once after the temporal conjunction of the afferent receptor discharge and the reaction. This is, of course, all in exact conformity with the law of primary reinforcement formulated above. . . .
>
> Pavlov differs from the law of reinforcement by regarding as the critical element of the reinforcing state of affairs the occurrence of S_u, in this case the *onset* of the shock.[1] On the other hand, the critical element in the reinforcing state of affairs by our own hypothesis is the reduction in the drive receptor impulse which accompanies the reduction of the need, i.e., reduction of the physiological injury of the feet, caused by the termination of the shock. . . .
>
> It is an easy matter to show the inadequacy of Pavlov's formulation as a general theory of learning. . . . It is not difficult to understand how Pavlov could have made such an error. His mistaken induction was presumably due in part to the exceedingly limited type of experiment which he employed (pp. 78–79).

This scheme of Hull's for explaining both response substitution and stimulus substitution in terms of the same principles can be perhaps most clearly portrayed by the type of diagram reproduced in Fig. 3–2. This is similar to the diagram in Fig. 3–1, except that no attempt is made to represent the experimental situation. Moreover, there is a further elaboration of the two kinds of learning supposedly in-

---

[1] Although, at an earlier point, Hull indicates that the experimental situation under discussion is more like the ones typically employed by V. M. Bekhterev (1913), he nevertheless felt that it fitted into the general theoretical framework of Pavlov (1927).

volved here. Response R_i, although instrumentally effective for dealing with the primary drive (lower line), in the beginning is slow to occur (see broken arrow from drive to R_i). But then, because it is "correct" and is consistently reinforced by drive reduction, it "moves forward" and eventually becomes the *first* response made after drive onset (see solid arrow from drive to R_i). Here we have response substitution in that responses (not shown in diagram) which are initially more strongly connected to the drive are eventually displaced and superseded by another, originally weaker response tendency.

Fig. 3–2. Schematic representation of Hull's monistic ("one-factor") reinforcement theory. Here both response substitution (lower line) and stimulus substitution (top line) were assumed to depend upon drive reduction. Drive induction, or onset, was assumed to have no reinforcing properties.

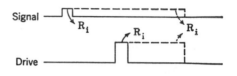

But while this trial-and-error learning or response substitution is going on, R_i is also becoming connected (according to Hull's theory) to the signal (see broken arrow from signal to R_i); and as this connection becomes stronger, R_i again "moves forward" and eventually starts occurring to the signal alone (see solid arrow from signal to R_i). Here we have conditioning, or stimulus substitution, in that a response which was originally capable of being elicited only by the drive (unconditioned stimulus) becomes "associatively shifted" (Thorndike's term) to a new, formerly ineffective stimulus. But R_i, as a conditioned response, is still "instrumentally effective": instead of merely terminating the drive stimulus after it impinges upon the organism, it now *prevents* the occurrence of this stimulus or otherwise *prepares* the organism for the stimulus (cf. Spence, 1951a, p. 262 ff.; Woodworth, 1958).

III. Difficulties Inherent in Hull's Theory

As theory, this is by no means a bad one in that, by means of one and the same principle, seemingly diverse phenomena are accounted for. But the theory involves a number of difficulties, some less serious, some more so. Several of these cluster around the problem of punishment. In one way this is not surprising, for punishment was a problem with which Hull never really attempted to deal. The term "punishment" does not appear in the index of any of the three books in which he developed his system; and he seems to have been curiously unconcerned with, almost unaware of, it.

Let us therefore begin by asking what might be expected to happen, according to the schematic version of Hull's basic theoretical concept shown in Fig. 3–2, if the "signal" which precedes the advent of drive consisted of stimuli which are response-correlated rather than independent. Suppose, for example, that a hungry rat makes some food-getting, hunger-reducing response R_{1h}, and that this response and its sensory consequences are followed by the onset of electric shock, which is terminated by a second instrumental response of some sort, R_{1s}. We know, empirically, that, if the shock is relatively strong, R_{1h} will be inhibited by two or three repetitions of this procedure. How, within the framework of Hullian theory, can this outcome be explained?

Hull has posited that learning occurs when and only when a drive is reduced (cf. Chapter 4, Section II). The onset of electric shock, in the example cited, would have no reinforcement significance (either positively or negatively), and learning would occur only when the shock went off, thus providing *positive* reinforcement. Therefore, one might expect that if, shortly before shock onset, the subject, under hunger motivation, had made some food-getting response, this stimulus-response connection would be *strengthened*, rather than weakened, by the advent of shock and shock reduction. Or it might be inferred, since the stimuli correlated with the occurrence of R_{1h} shortly precede (and their traces—see Chapter 10—overlap) shock termination, that response R_{1s} ought to get conditioned to these stimuli, so that whenever R_{1h} occurs it would cue off R_{1s}.

Both of these inferred outcomes are, of course, contrary to fact and might seem to count heavily against the Hullian formula. We know that if a response such as R_{1h} is followed by strong electric shock, that response will be inhibited rather than strengthened and that its occurrence will *not* cue off R_{1s}. Hence it might appear that here are two straightforward deductions from Hullian theory which are empirically refuted. However, the system has unexpected resiliency in this connection. We must remember that in the hypothetical situation described, hunger, though perhaps somewhat lessened by R_{1h}, is an on-going stimulus which overlaps shock and shock termination. Therefore, if the shock elicits R_{1s}, this response, by the principles represented in Figs. 3–1 and

3–2, will become conditioned *to the hunger drive;* and since R_{is} is probably incompatible with R_{ih}, the attachment of R_{is} to the hunger drive will make this drive *less likely* to elicit R_{ih}. *Q. E. D.*

Postulate 16, of Hull's system, 1943 version, specifically states:

When the reaction potentials ($_sE_R$) of two or more incompatible reactions (R) occur in an organism at the same time, only the reaction whose momentary effective reaction potential ($_s\dot{E}_R$) is greatest will be evoked (Hull, 1943, p. 344).[2]

Hence, given the conditions stated, a "theory of punishment" may be said to be implicit in the Hullian formulation. Since this formulation was not specifically designed to deal with the problem of punishment, it is much to its credit that it nevertheless appears to do so. However, further reflection will indicate that such an explanation of punishment is valid only under limited, rather special circumstances. In order for it to work it is necessary that there be some response made by the subject which consistently and promptly terminates the "punishment" (shock) stimulus. Suppose instead that this stimulus is of *fixed* duration. This would mean that there was no R_{is}, i.e., no response which would terminate the shock and therefore no response which would tend to get conditioned to the hunger drive, in competition with R_{ih}. Yet one would hardly doubt that, for these reasons, the shock would fail to have an inhibitory effect on R_{ih}. Results reported by Mowrer & Viek (1948) show that shock of fixed (uncontrollable) duration is *even more effective* as a punishment than is shock whose termination is dependent upon the occurrence of some specific response. Therefore, the explanation of punishment which follows, somewhat incidentally, from Hull's basic theoretical concept falls short of providing an entirely satisfactory explanation of punishment even under the special circumstances provided in the hypothetical example. And it appears that Hull, himself, did not think too highly of the capacity of his system to deal with the problem of punishment; for in an article published jointly with Livingston, Rouse, & Barker in 1951, on "True, Sham, and Esophageal Feeding as Reinforcements," Hull in effect repudiated the view that there is only one kind of reinforcement:

An incidental observation recorded by Bellows and Van Wagenen suggested at the outset that this deduction might be verified. One of their dogs (which were always esophageally fed) ceased to try to eat. "The temporal

[2] I am indebted to Dr. John D. Davis for calling attention to this postulate and its implications in the present context.

muscles became quite atrophic." It may be significant in this connection that the food surreptitiously seized by the dogs usually clogged "in the superior stenosed opening and caused retching." This clogging in the upper fistula presumably constituted fairly effective punishment in addition to a failure of normal nutritional reinforcement. This still further complicates the interpretation by suggesting the operation of *negative reinforcement* (punishment) as distinguished from experimental extinction (pp. 243–244; italics added).

The notion of *negative* reinforcement is foreign to the basic assumption in Hull's system that all reinforcement is positive (rewarding, drive-reducing) and can be articulated with his system only through the oblique device of relating it to the notion of reactive inhibition (or fatigue) which Hull employed to explain extinction. Therefore, immediately following the passage just quoted, we read:

A possible related observation made during extended sham-feedings is that our dog frequently showed "violent nervous shaking" (quoted from the laboratory notes), presumably from the fatigue of eating, which evidently was considerable. It seems likely that this, possibly coupled with the enormous incidental secretion of saliva, may have been an important negatively reinforcing (punishment) factor in causing the cessation from sham eating which we have tentatively labeled "experiment extinction." On the other hand, the Mowrer-Miller hypothesis (Hull, 1943) holds the I_R is based on a concept closely related to fatigue, which is akin to punishment (p. 244).[3]

Then there is yet another palpable defect in Hull's attempt to integrate the facts of conditioning and trial-and-error learning. As will be apparent from Fig. 3–2, his scheme will, in any case, work only where the response which becomes connected to a danger signal is the *same* as the response made to the stimulus thus signalized. It is well known that the response which becomes *anticipatory*, in a conditioning situation, may be radically different from the so-called "consummatory" or "unconditioned" response. For example, if a

---

[3] Earlier, in 1943, Hull had written somewhat equivocally on this score: While acknowledging the possibility that "there may be more than one mechanism of reinforcement," Hull took the position that the evidence that drive onset can provide reinforcement (of a negative kind) was meager and ambiguous. "Thus the only critical evidence now available seems to favor the reduction or termination hypothesis" (p. 82). "We shall proceed on the positive assumption that the termination of the need (or of its closely correlated receptor response) *is* a primary reinforcing factor; this hardly seems open to doubt. Even if the onset of the need, or of the correlated receptor response, proves to have genuine reinforcing capacity, the dynamics of behavior are such that it would not have much adaptive value" (p. 83). The latter assertion suggests, as do other considerations, that Hull never fully assimilated the implications of this problem into his system.

man discovers that his house is on fire, probably the most adaptive response for him to make is to call the local fire department. But suppose that this same man, after the fire is out (or even before it starts), becomes *afraid lest* his house catch fire. What would we *now* expect him to do? Taking the Hullian formula quite literally, we would expect this man to *call the fire department.* What we would actually expect instead is that such a person would get in touch with a good insurance agent—a response considerably different from the one appropriate to the fire itself.

Laboratory instances in which marked dissimilarity between the unconditioned and conditioned response has been noted, rather incidentally, are numerous; but at least one study has been published in which a successful effort was made to produce this effect deliberately (Mowrer & Lamoreaux, 1946). Let us imagine a rat in the type of shuttle box previously described (Chapter 2). After the usual period of free exploration, the buzzer is sounded for five seconds, followed by shock, which the animal can readily terminate by running to the opposite side of the box. Soon the rat scampers promptly to the other end of the box when the shock comes on; and a few trials later it starts making "avoidance" runs, to the buzzer alone. But, although running has been defined as the solution to the shock problem, it is not, in this situation, likewise the solution to the fear problem, created by the buzzer. The correct response, or solution, to the latter problem is now a response very different from running, namely a leap into the air. Consequently, when the animal runs in response to the buzzer-produced fear, this behavior does not terminate the buzzer or circumvent the shock; the buzzer continues for the full five seconds, the shock comes just the same, and the rat again has to run to terminate the shock.

The rat now becomes agitated and, particularly during the five-second period when the buzzer is on, just prior to the shock, will engage in quite a range of more or less "random" responses. Eventually, the rat is likely to *jump* while the buzzer is sounding. When this happens the buzzer is immediately turned off, and the shock is not presented. Jumping is thus reinforced, by fear reduction, and occurs with mounting frequency on ensuing trials.

It is naturally easier for an animal to master a learning situation in which the response which permits escape from the shock and the response which permits escape from fear (and avoidance of shock) are the same. But, with a little more time and effort, the rat can also learn to make one response as a means of escaping from shock itself and another, very different one as a means of escaping from the *fear* of shock (see also Keehn, 1959). Hull's system is unable to account for this type of learning.

How, then, must we appraise Hull's attempt to make all learning dependent upon what happens when a drive lessens or ends? We see that, although it can plausibly account for both trial-and-error learning and certain forms of conditioning, there is inherent in the theory most of the same weaknesses that were present in Thorndike's and Pavlov's original formulations. And it is, in addition, particularly inadequate as regards the phenomenon of punishment. Later (Chapter 8) we shall have occasion to examine Hull's work more minutely, but the present sketch will suffice for immediate purposes.

IV. Pavlov's Attempted Derivation of Trial-and-Error Learning

Hull's attempt to "integrate" the learning theories of Thorndike and Pavlov, which has been discussed in the two preceding sections, attracted much attention and, despite its palpable difficulties, the general reaction to it was favorable (for at least a considerable time). By contrast, an attempt which Pavlov made, in 1932, to account for trial-and-error learning in terms of conditioning principles has received almost no attention, at least in America; yet, in light of developments which will be traced in later chapters, this attack upon the problem, while in certain important ways incomplete and even obscure, had much to recommend it. Because this endeavor by Pavlov to deal with trial-and-error learning is so little known and because it comes so close to the systematic position which gradually evolves in this book, the pertinent passage from the 1932 paper will be quoted in full. It reads as follows:

When we were working out a method of feeding an animal from a distance at the time of the experiment [just discussed], we tried out many different methods. This among others: In front of the dog there was always an empty pan, to which a metal tube led down from a container above, which held the dried meat-powder and usually served to provide the food for our animals at the time of the experiment. At the junction of the container and the tube was a valve, which was opened at the proper moment by means of air transmission, so that a portion of the powder dropped down the tube and came out into the pan where it was eaten by the animal. The valve was not in good working order and if the pipe were shaken some of the powder from the container would drop into the pan. *The dog quickly learned to make use of this, of his own accord shaking out the powder.* And a shaking of the pipe took place almost continuously, when the dog was eating the portion of food which was given it and in doing so knocked up against the pipe. Of course this is exactly what takes place in *training a dog to give one his paw.* In our laboratory work, the conditions of life have in general done the teaching, but here, man forms part of the conditions. In the latter case the words "paw," "give," etc., the skin stimulation from the contact in lifting the paw, *the kinesthetic stimulation accompanying the lifting of the paw,* and finally the visual stimulation from the trainer, were accompanied by food, i.e., were bound to the unconditioned stimulus for food. It is absolutely the same in the instance cited: the noise of the shaking pipe, the skin stimulation from contact with the pipe, kinesthetic stimulation in jostling against the pipe, and finally the sight of the pipe—all these became similarly connected with the act of eating, with excitation of the feeding center. This of course occurred through the principle of simultaneous association, presenting thereby a conditioned reflex. And here, moreover, two additional distinctly physiological facts appear: In the first place, the *definite kinesthetic stimulation* in this case is probably linked up by a conditioned setting (in the lower parts of the central nervous system by an unconditioned setting) with the execution of those movements or the activity which produced it,—this kinesthetic stimulation. And second, when two centers in the nervous system are connected or joined, nervous impulses are set in motion *and pass from one to the other in both directions.* If we accept the absolute law of one-way conduction of nervous impulses in all points of the nervous system, then in the case cited one must assume an additional connection in the opposite direction between these centers, i.e., one must grant the existence of an additional neurone connecting them. When food is given on raising the paw, a stimulus undoubtedly runs from the kinesthetic center to the feeding center. But when the connection is established, and the dog, under the urge for food, gives his paw himself, obviously stimulation runs in the opposite direction. I can interpret this fact in no other way (Pavlov, 1932, pp. 123–124; italics added).

Despite the questionable neurologizing involved, this quotation contains a number of noteworthy suggestions. First and foremost, it makes explicit reference to a phenomenon which Thorndike (and Hull) largely ignored: *the proprioceptive and other forms of stimulation which are normally associated with the occurrence of the learned responses known as habits.* In Chapter 2 we have seen how crucial is the role of response-correlated stimuli in punishment; and, as later chapters will show, it is now apparent that response-dependent stimulation plays a no less important role in "positive" learning. Pavlov clearly adumbrated this perception, but many other events had to transpire before its full force could be appreciated, a quarter of a century later. Therefore, having noted this historically significant paper by Pavlov, we again pick up the threads of history and follow them as they lead to what may be termed the *second* version of two-factor learning theory.

V. Two-Factor Theory, Version Two

Those writers, cited in Section I of this chapter, who first adopted the two-factor position were relatively uncritical of the basic conceptions that had been set forth by Thorndike and Pavlov. The notions of response substitution and of stimulus substitution were, so to say, laid side by side and used, as the occasion demanded, to "explain" now one type of learning, now the other. However, as noted in Chapters 1 and 2, there were manifest weaknesses in both types of theory, even within their own spheres of special competence; and it gradually became apparent that, even when combined, they were not entirely satisfactory and required further modification. The crux of the difficulty, as it emerged during the fourth and fifth decades of the century, was that neither Pavlov nor Thorndike took the phenomenon of *fear* into sufficient account. In their attempts to be thoroughly "objective," they had ignored a vital aspect of behavior dynamics, and their theories suffered accordingly. Therefore, the present writer, in 1947, in an article, "On the Dual Nature of Learning—A Reinterpretation of 'Conditioning' and 'Problem Solving,'" attempted to show, on the basis of evidence and arguments that had been advanced by numerous other investigators (see p. 65), just how these two theories would have to be altered in order to be truly compatible and effectively complementary.

No attempt will be made here to give the details of this earlier analysis, but the main results thereof can be summarized as follows:

1. It is unrealistic and inaccurate (with a few unimportant exceptions) to speak of overt behavior as being learned on the basis of direct conditioning. Only emotions (and especially fear) are capable of being attached to new stimuli by the conditioning principle. They then operate as "intervening variables." [4]

2. Thorndike's analysis of habit formation (as opposed to habit elimination or punishment) was essentially sound but needs to be extended in the following manner. Thorndike limited his researches to situations wherein the subject was motivated by hunger, thirst, and similar primary, or "metabolic," drives. It is now clear that trial-and-

---

[4] The exceptions referred to are the so-called short-latency (skeletal-muscle) reflexes, such as the eyeblink and the knee jerk. These appear to be *directly* conditionable; but they are certainly not representative or typical of the responses which constitute behavior in general. And it is with the latter that we are here especially concerned. Cf. Chapter 10, Footnote 9 (p. 386).

error learning may also occur, with equal felicity, when the organism is motivated by an acquired, secondary drive, such as fear.

Thus redefined, conditioning and trial and error constitute two categorically different forms of learning, which may be termed *sign* learning and *solution* learning, respectively. They can be further distinguished in these ways:

1. Solution learning occurs when a drive is reduced, a problem solved; whereas sign learning occurs when a formerly neutral stimulus accompanies drive induction, or onset.

2. Solution learning is mediated by the central nervous system; sign learning, by the autonomic nervous system.

3. Solution learning involves the skeletal muscles; sign learning, glands and smooth muscles.

4. Solution learning involves voluntary responses (behavior); sign learning, involuntary responses (emotions).

Most learning situations are complicated and can be understood only by taking *both* of these forms of learning into account. Active avoidance learning is a case in point. Here, what occurs first is *sign* learning, whereby fear becomes conditioned to a formerly neutral stimulus or signal; then, with the organism now motivated by this secondary drive, trial-and-error behavior occurs and a behavioral *solution* to the fear problem is found. Thus, where Behaviorism restricted itself to the simple, one-step S—R formula, we are here confronted by the necessity of postulating, minimally, a two-step, *two-stage formula:* S—r: s—R, where S is the danger signal, r the response of fear which is conditioned to it, and where s is the fear, experienced as a drive, which elicits (after learning) response, R. Thus, what is elicited as the response to S, namely r (as an internal *response*), becomes the immediate (internal) *stimulus* for R. Miller & Dollard (1941) have usefully characterized fear as a response-produced drive. Fear occurs first as a response, but it is a disagreeable, "painful" response and so possesses motivational properties.

This is not to say that pure conditioning and pure solution learning may not, in some instances, occur, alone; the second two-factor position merely held that *both* are necessary to explain certain common instances of behavior change and that here they cannot be laid side by side but must be placed end to end.[5]

[5] For experimental evidence pointing to the contrary view, that emotional and behaviorial reactions to a danger signal are learned and occur simultaneously, see Dykman, Gantt, and Whitehorn (1956), but see also Gantt (1949, pp. 49–50).

This two-process conception of learning was summarized as follows:

> In summary, then, we see that there are many and highly diverse sources of evidence for the two-factor theory of learning which is here under consideration. Such a theory presupposes a delimitation of the term "conditioning" as it is usually employed and an extension of the traditional concept of "reward" learning. The term "conditioning" has commonly been used, erroneously as it now seems, to denote the process whereby a living organism comes to make any response, skeletal or visceral, immediate or delayed, to a stimulus which has "signal value." As we have seen, this usage is too broad for precise scientific purposes. It now seems preferable to apply the term "conditioning" to that and only that type of learning whereby *emotional* (visceral and vascular) responses are acquired. By contrast, reward learning has been previously conceived as applying mainly in those situations in which the motive, or "problem," is an unlearned biological drive, such as hunger, thirst, pain, etc. It is now clear that reward learning must be expanded to include those situations in which the motive, or "problem," is a *learned* drive, i.e., an emotion such as fear or an appetite. Many responses involving the skeletal musculature, which have previously been termed "conditioned responses," are, in the present conceptual scheme, not conditioned responses at all. Only those responses which involve visceral and vascular tissue and which are experienced subjectively as emotion are assumed to be conditioned responses. If an emotion, or secondary drive, causes the skeletal musculature to be activated and if such activity results in secondary drive reduction, then the overt response thus acquired is here conceived as an instance of reward learning, not conditioning (Mowrer, 1947, p. 121).

VI. Further Elaboration and Implications of the Two-Factor Position

By mid-century so much was known about the circumstances under which fear becomes attached to previously neutral stimuli and about the ways in which it can then function both to motivate and inhibit behavior that systematic learning theory had to take this knowledge into account. The consequences, some of which have been reviewed in preceding sections of this chapter, were numerous and far-reaching. For one thing, this acknowledgement of fear, as both a result and a cause of learning, sounded the death knell for primitive behaviorism. During most of the 19th Century, psychologists were preoccupied with the phenomenon of *consciousness*, and their principal method of investigation was introspection or "looking within." If we may use the letter, O, to represent the organism, the chief object of interest for these earlier researchers can be represented by the letter, c, located in the center of the O. But Behaviorism has changed all this, ushering in what Boring (1946) has called the era of "the *empty* organism," i.e., an O without c—in fact, even the O was commonly omitted and behavior was schematized in terms of stimulation and response only. In short, O disappeared and S—R took its place. But one could not talk about fear without rediscovering the organism and, indeed, restoring to it some of the internal, mediating functions which had traditionally been associated with the concept of consciousness.

In 1953 the present author described these developments as follows:

In writing a review of contemporary learning theory in the summer of 1952 for the *Journal of Educational Research*, it occurred to me that I had previously thought of conditioning, or *sign*, learning, and of habit formation, or *solution* learning, as essentially parallel processes whereas they were really *sequential*. The work of Miller (1948a), Brown and Jacobs (1949), and others had abundantly shown that if a formerly neutral stimulus, or sign, becomes capable, through conditioning, of eliciting a secondary drive, such as fear, the latter can then serve as the basis for trial-and-error, or instrumental, learning. However, almost no one had previously laid these two forms of learning *end-to-end*, diagrammatically; and I discovered that when one did so one was restoring to living organisms some of the internal operations which the behaviorists had so pre-emptorily dismissed.

In conventional diagrams for conditioning and habit formation, it is usually indicated that the stimulation and response represented by various S's and R's can be either external to or within the organism; but the "connection" between them is ordinarily represented by a very thin line and not much more. Woodworth, in 1921, suggested that this might be carrying scientific abstraction a bit too far and ventured to insert an "O," for organism, between stimulus and response, giving us the now familiar formula, S—O—R. McDougall (1938) made a related suggestion, and R. B. Cattell (1950) has proposed that the simple algebraic expression $R = f(S)$, be refined at least to the extent of positing that $R = f(S + O)$. The psychoanalysts had, of course, for many years been talking about all manner of interesting things that go on within organisms; but academic psychologists, once in full revolt against the consciousness idea, were loath to reacknowledge it or any equivalent. But many contemporary psychologists will feel comfortable with the notion of a two-step scheme of the kind shown [in Fig. 3–3] in contrast to and as a synthesis of the one-step conceptions of sign learning and solution learning taken separately (Mowrer, 1953b, pp. 164–165).

The particular notation and schematization employed in Fig. 3–3 were adopted in order to make them consistent with those employed in other figures in the paper cited to represent stimulus substitution and response substitution, separately. But an example of how Fig. 3–3 might work out in practice will perhaps be necessary to make this combined, two-step type of theory fully intelligible. Imagine that a rat, under the urgency of hunger (s) has learned to obtain food by making response R_1. Now let us suppose that the rat has been punished, by means of an electric shock (S_1), for performing this act. S_1 produces the fear reaction r, and since response R_1 arouses kinesthetic and other stimuli whenever it occurs, these stimuli (S_2) get conditioned to the fear response r. The result is that R_1 will be inhibited and R_2, R_3, or some other response which will also satisfy hunger (but not provoke shock) will take its place. Here, in a simple instance of trial-and-error learning, we see how conditioning, or stimulus substitution, also plays an integral and essential role.

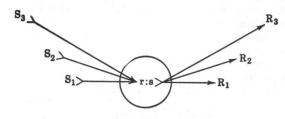

Fig. 3–3. Conditioning and trial-and-error learning put "end to end," thus providing a more complete and more realistic form of behavior theory.

Later this same type of relationship will be schematized in other, clearer terms; but enough has been said to indicate that, whereas in the first version of two-factor theory the two forms of learning were thought of as parallel or independent, in the *second* version thereof they were sequential and interdependent. And it will also now be apparent why it was that the latter schematization, so to say, revitalized the organism and revived interest in internal, as well as external, stimulus-response events.

VII. Empirical Support for the Two-Factor Position

Reservations concerning the two-factor conception of learning outlined in the preceding pages have come mainly from those followers of Hull who, with him, have held that there is really only one learning, or reinforcement, process and that that process is exclusively activated by or dependent upon drive reduction. For such a theory to be consistent it must take the somewhat paradoxical position that *even fear* is learned on the basis of drive reduction, or reward. In a symposium held in 1950 on "multi-process" learning theories, Miller put the issue squarely when he said:

In order to stick to a consistent drive-reduction theory of reinforcement, one is forced to assume that the reinforcement of learning to fear a painful event is not the onset of the pain, but its reduction. This seems to be a direct contradiction of all that is reasonable. . . . I agree that this application of the principle of drive-reduction goes against common sense; and I feel uncomfortable every time I am forced to make it. Once in a great while, however, when common sense is tested, it proves to be wrong; an utterly unreasonable assumption, like a ray of light being curved by gravity, or a light stone falling as fast as a heavy one, turns out to be correct. That is the reason for stubbornly insisting on conclusive experimental evidence (Miller, 1951a, p. 375).

In the meantime, new support for the view that fear is learned on the basis of incremental rather than decremental reinforcement has been provided by a number of studies. Let us consider the following experiment, carried out by Mowrer & Aiken (1954). Preliminary observations had shown that if hungry rats first learn to press a Skinner-bar as a means of obtaining a pellet of food and if the act of pressing the bar then causes a tone stimulus—which has previously been paired with electric shock—to come on, the resulting inhibition (secondary punishment) of the bar pressing provides a very sensitive

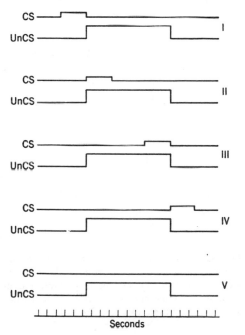

Fig. 3–4. Schematic representation of the five different arrangements of conditioned stimulus (CS) and unconditioned stimulus (UnCS) employed in experiment by Mowrer and Aiken (1954, p. 28). In Group V the conditioned stimulus (a blinking light) was not immediately associated with the unconditioned stimulus (electric shock) in any way, but was presented alone, in the middle of the 4-min. interval between trials.

index of the extent to which the tone has acquired the capacity to arouse fear. Accordingly, in the experiment proper, several groups of rats were exposed to tone and shock, presented in the various temporal relationships shown in Fig. 3–4. If fear conditioning is dependent upon what occurs when the shock comes on, then the best learning would be expected to occur in the group in which the tone stimulus immediately precedes shock onset. On the other hand, if fear conditioning is dependent upon what occurs when the shock goes off, then the best learning would be expected to occur in that group in which the tone was presented just in advance of shock termination. As the results shown in Fig. 3–5 indicate, the former rather than the latter predication was confirmed: A tone which had been paired with shock onset was much more effective in inhibiting bar pressing for food than was a tone which had been paired with shock termination.

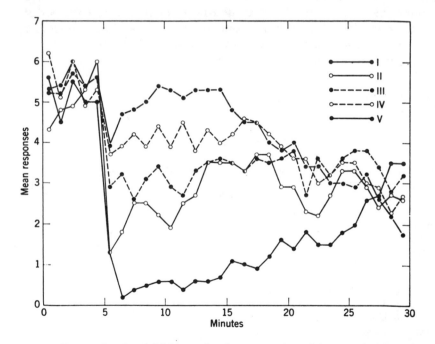

Fig. 3–5. Curves showing inhibition of a hunger-motivated bar-pressing response in rats. The inhibition was produced by a stimulus which had been associated with electric shock in the various ways indicated in Fig. 3–4. The stimulus associated with shock *onset* proved most effective as an inhibitor (secondary punishment), as revealed by the curve for Group I.

In a related experiment, by Mowrer & Solomon (1954), an attempt was made to get at the same issues in a somewhat different way. It is well known (see Chapter 10) that if a stimulus is immediately followed by reinforcement, conditioning is more effective than if the reinforcement is delayed. Moreover, Hull posited that the reinforcement provided by drive reduction is more effective if the reduction is abrupt rather than gradual. Therefore, it was decided to have a tone stimulus immediately followed by shocks of different durations and different rates of termination, as shown in Fig. 3–6. If the reinforcing event as far as fear conditioning is concerned is the conjunction of a signal with shock *onset*, one would expect roughly the same amount of learning in all four situations, since the relationship of the signal to shock onset is constant throughout. If, on the other hand, fear conditioning is dependent on what happens when the shock *terminates*, one would expect best learning in procedure I and less good conditioning in the other three procedures—less good in procedure II because drive reduction is temporally more remote from the signal, and less good in procedures III and IV because drive reduction is gradual rather than sudden.

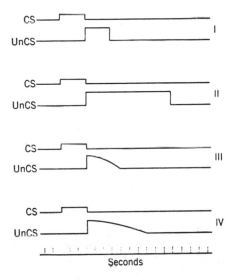

Fig. 3–6. Schematic indication of the four different forms of unconditioned stimulus (shock) employed in Mowrer-Solomon experiment (1954, p. 19). The conditioned stimulus was a blinking light of three seconds' duration, which was followed in each of the groups of subjects (rats) by a shock of the duration and form shown.

When the effects of fear conditioning were tested (using the procedure described in connection with the Aiken experiment), the results shown in Fig. 3–7 were obtained. They are exactly the reverse of what would be predicted on the basis of the drive-reduction theory of fear conditioning: Instead of procedure I giving the greatest amount of fear conditioning (because of the greater proximity and the more precipitous nature of drive reduction), it resulted in somewhat *less* effective conditioning (reliable at the .10 level of confidence).

The notion that fear conditioning is dependent upon the conjunction of a signal and shock onset, rather than shock termination, leads

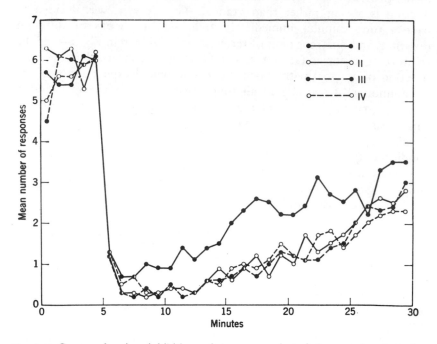

Fig. 3–7. Curves showing inhibition of hunger-motivated bar-pressing behavior in rats, produced by a stimulus which had been associated with the onset of the various forms of shock indicated in Fig. 3–6. The amount of inhibition manifested in Groups II, III, and IV is virtually identical; and the difference between these three groups and Group I, although probably representing a real trend (see text), is not highly significant statistically.

us to expect equally effective conditioning in all four experimental procedures. This prediction is well confirmed as far as procedures II, III, and IV are concerned; but, as we have just seen, procedure I was slightly (though probably reliably) *less* effective than the other three procedures. Re-inspection of Fig. 3–6 suggests a possible explanation. Let us posit that in all four situations exactly the same amount of fear was learned, because of the constancy of the signal-shock-onset relationship. But then the signal is followed, fairly promptly, by shock termination. It therefore might be expected to come to signify, along with fear, also some degree of anticipated "relief" or "hope." In what situation would the anticipation of relief, or escape from shock, be strongest? Clearly in procedure I, where drive reduction occurs relatively soon and also suddenly. To the extent that this opposite kind of conditioning occurred, it might be expected to counteract the fear aroused by the signal; and since the element of "hope" (see later chapters) would presumably be strongest in procedure I, the net effectiveness of the element of fear (presumably constant in all four procedures) would be least in procedure I. Such a deduction is constant with the findings shown in Fig. 3–7.[6]

VIII. More Evidence for the Two-Factor Position

It has sometimes been suggested that shock onset may appear to be the specific reinforcing event for fear learning because shock onset may be immediately followed by a subjective reduction in pain, even though the intensity of the shock stimulus remains the same. This possibility has been described by Miller & Dollard as follows:

Electrical recording of the responses of afferent nerves indicates that the sudden onset of a new stimulus produces at first a strong burst of impulses from the sense organ which rapidly diminishes in strength till a plateau of stimulation is reached (Adrian, 1928, pp. 67 and 116). This diminution is called adaptation. According to the principles which have been outlined, such a reduction in strength of stimulation should, if marked enough (as might be the case following the sudden onset of a relatively strong stimulus), act as a reward to any responses associated with it. Careful experiments may reveal that such a mechanism accounts for certain cases of learning which might superficially appear to be exceptions to a rigorous drive-reduction theory of reward (1941, p. 35).

In an ingenious experiment carried out recently by Davitz (1955), an attempt was made to test the foregoing supposition. Using an electric shock that came on very gradually but went off suddenly, Davitz presented a blinking-light stimulus to one group of rats just as the shock gradually came on, while another group of rats received the

---

[6] The essential reasonableness of the results shown in Fig. 3–7 can be seen in yet another way. Let the reader put himself in the place of a rat and ask: "Following the warning signal, which of those four patterns of electric shock would I dread or fear *least?*" There can be little doubt that the procedure-I shock form would be the one thus selected.

blinking-light just before the shock, at the height of its intensity, suddenly terminated. Since the shock came on so slowly, it seems unlikely that it produced any sort of Adrian "on-effect," yet it was found that the stimulus that had been associated with shock onset, gradual though it was, aroused considerably more fear (as measured by the capacity of the stimulus to inhibit free exploratory behavior in a standard test situation) than did the stimulus that had been associated with sudden drive reduction (Fig. 3–8). On the basis of common éxperience (and principles which will be considered later in this book), it would have been remarkable indeed if a stimulus which occurred just in advance of relief from the pain produced by the shock had become more fear-producing than a stimulus which occurred as the shock was just starting to come on.

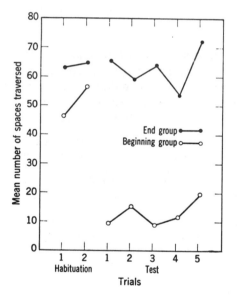

Fig. 3–8. Results obtained from an "open-field" test in an experiment reported by Davitz (1955, p. 153). In one group of subjects (rats), a stimulus was periodically presented which had been associated with the onset of a gradually mounting electric shock (Beginning Group); in the other group, the stimulus had been associated with the sudden termination of shock (End Group). The former was much more effective in inhibiting exploratory behavior, thus suggesting greater fear conditioning.

Some of Davitz's own observations concerning this experiment follow:

The purpose of this study was to determine whether or not a CS presented at the end of shock will acquire greater fear value than will a CS presented at the beginning of shock.

Hull (1943) has proposed a drive-reduction hypothesis to account for the learning of fear. In his discussion of secondary motivation he suggests that stimuli acquire secondary-drive value as a result of association with the "evocation of a primary or secondary drive" *and* the "abrupt diminution" of drive (p. 6). This suggests that the connection between a cue and a fear response evoked initially by the onset of pain is reinforced by a subsequent decrease of pain. "Abrupt diminution" of drive, or drive reduction, is the necessary condition of reinforcement; and, according to Hull's conception of the gradient of reinforcement, cues temporally closest to the occurrence of drive reduction are most strongly reinforced. If the beginning of shock increases drive and the end of shock decreases drive, a cue presented at the end of shock will be temporally closer to drive reduction than a cue presented at the beginning of shock. Therefore, the drive-reduction hypothesis suggests that CS at the end of shock will acquire greater fear value than CS at the beginning of shock.

In contrast to the drive-reduction hypothesis, Mowrer (1950a) has suggested that a cue acquires fear value as a result of contiguity with drive induction. Reinforcement in this case is a function of increased pain rather than decreased pain. Therefore, the drive-*induction* hypothesis suggests that CS at the beginning of shock will acquire greater fear value than CS at the end of shock (p. 152).

After briefly describing the Mowrer-Aiken study previously mentioned, Davitz says:

However, Miller (1951a) has suggested two other possible sources of drive reduction [other than the one provided when the shock was turned off]: (a) temporary escape from shock as a result of the animal's jumping off the grid soon after the beginning of shock; (b) rapid adaptation of afferent nerves and consequent reduction of pain after the initial burst of impulses at the beginning of shock [Adrian effect]. Thus, in Mowrer and Aiken's experiment, CS at the beginning of shock could have been contiguous with one of these sources of drive reduction and the results of the experiment may be accounted for by the drive-reduction hypothesis.

The present experiment was designed to minimize the effects of temporary escape and adaptation in order to permit the assumption that the end of shock was the primary source of drive reduction. To minimize the possibility of temporary escape from the grid, S, during the training period, was placed under a small inverted box which prevented it from jumping off the grid. To offset the effects of adaptation, a gradually increasing shock was administered for 5 sec. Although an animal may adapt to one level of shock intensity, it seems reasonable to assume that adaptation would be minimized by a steadily increasing level of intensity (p. 152).

The results of this experiment have already been reported; they may seem quite conclusive. Nevertheless, Davitz suggests two precautions in interpreting them.

In the present experiment, two possible sources of drive reduction, temporary escape and adaptation, were minimized; therefore, a drive-reduction hypothesis based on these two secondary sources of drive reduction was contradicted by the data. However, another possible factor was noted during the course of the experiment. The Ss exhibited extremely vigorous and apparently disorganized activity during the last part of the 5-sec. shock.

It is possible that Ss in the End group, preoccupied, in a sense, with the increasing pain of the shock, did not *attend to* presentation of the CS. Therefore, learning to fear CS when presented at the end of shock may have been mitigated by Ss' failure to perceive CS under the condition of strong drive at the end of shock.

A further consideration is based on the particular behavioral measure used in this study. Freezing is directly opposed to the *active* type of escape or avoidance behaviors used in previous studies of fear. Although it has been assumed that the "fear" underlying inhibition of behavior is essentially the same as that underlying escape or avoidance behaviors, it would seem appropriate to investigate this assumption experimentally (p. 154).

But in conclusion Davitz says:

Despite the considerations mentioned above, the results of the present experiment, as well as the results of a previous experiment by Mowrer and Aiken (1954), seem to be most parsimoniously accounted for by the drive-induction hypothesis. This hypothesis suggests that a cue acquires fear value as a result of contiguity with increased drive and that reinforcement of the fear is a function of drive induction (pp. 154–155).

Results similarly supporting the view that fear learning is contingent upon drive increment rather than drive decrement have been reported by Coppock & Chambers (1951) and also by Bitterman, Reed, & Krauskopf (1952). However, others, notably Sullivan (1950) and Zeaman & Wegner (1954), have reported evidence which they interpret to the contrary, so it is too early to say that the issue is absolutely settled. Nevertheless, it would now seem safe to proceed on the assumption that, in this particular instance, common sense has been right and that fear *is* learned on the basis of drive induction rather than drive reduction.[7] Since it is at the same time agreed that

[7] Since the above was written, the evidence on this score has become even clearer. Zeaman & Wegner, in the study cited, end with this statement: "The results are seen to favor the view that the mechanism of conditioning for this autonomically mediated response [heart rate] was that of drive reduction" (p. 354). However, Wegner & Zeaman (1958) treat the problem quite differently. They say, "N. E. Miller, for example, has stated that according to a strict drive-reduction theory of reinforcement '. . . other things equal, a signal followed by a brief noxious stimulus should acquire the capacity to elicit stronger fear than one followed by a prolonged noxious stimulus'" (Miller, 1951a, p. 375). And they conclude: "Despite the wide differences in Ss, procedures, and methods of inferring fear, the results of the Mowrer and Solomon study are in agreement with our own findings. . . . The discrepancy between Miller's theoretical statement and our own data can not easily be attributed to lack of control of shock intensity" (p. 240). "It is concluded that this proposition is either incorrect or not testable under the conditions provided" (p. 241). Miller himself has recently (1959) indicated that he is now "not

drive reduction is the reinforcing agent in other (ordinary trial-and-error) instances of learning, one is strongly tempted, on the basis of the evidence just reviewed, to adopt the two-factor position previously described in this chapter.

However, despite numerous attractions and advantages, the two-process, or two-factor, conception of learning—even in its two-step version—is not entirely satisfactory. In recent years, the present writer has felt and, on occasion, expressed growing discomfort with the conception of "habit" tacitly accepted in the original version of two-factor theory (Mowrer, 1953a, 1956). Moreover, the phenomenon of "secondary reinforcement" has come into increasing prominence in the experimental literature during the past decade or two, and even the second version of two-factor learning will not at all explain in this connection some of the reported and well-authenticated facts. It will therefore be our purpose, in the next chapter, to consider specifically the problem of secondary reinforcement. Doing so, we shall discover, leads (in Chapter 7) to a new interpretation of "habit" and to still further revision of the two-factor position.

IX. The Chapter in Review

In retrospect, then, we may say that the *first* version of two-factor learning theory came into existence because of the widespread conviction that neither Thorndike's Law of Effect nor the Pavlov-Bekhterev concept of reflex conditioning, taken alone, could provide a universal paradigm for learning but that, taken together, they were sufficient. Following an unexpected turn in Thorndike's thinking, Hull advanced the view that there is really only *one* type of learning (reinforcement), namely that provided by drive reduction (reward); and on the basis of this premise he tried to explain both trial-and-error learning and conditioning. However, Hull's theory, like the theories of Pavlov and Thorndike, could not adequately account for

completely committed to the drive-stimulus-reduction hypothesis" (p. 256); and, with characteristic candor, he adds: "I take this occasion to urge attempts to formulate and rigorously test competing hypotheses, and time permitting, may even join in that activity myself" (p. 257). And Spence (1956), another prominent exponent of Hull's system, has now taken a completely different position concerning the whole reinforcement problem (see also Chapter 8). So it may be said that the monistic thesis of Hull that drive reduction, and it alone, provides the conditions for learning has, in effect, collapsed.

all the facts of passive and active avoidance learning, so the search for a more adequate and inclusive conceptualization continued.

The *second* version of two-factor learning theory, like the first one, assumed that both conditioning and trial-and-error learning are real, and different, phenomena; but, unlike the first version, it made important changes in the way Pavlov and Thorndike had identified and explained them. It was assumed that Thorndike (and Hull) had been right in positing that trial-and-error learning (problem solving) is contingent upon drive reduction; but the conception of drive was extended to include fear, in addition to such primary drives as hunger and thirst. And it was further assumed that Pavlov (and Bekhterev) had been right in holding that instances of learning occur, through sheer contiguity of stimulation, without drive reduction; but whereas the reflexologists had been interested only in objectively observable responses, the revised two-factor position stressed the emotion of fear as the most important conditioned, or conditionable, response—which then motivates and when reduced reinforces, in a strictly Thorndikian way, many of the overt, behavioral acts which Pavlov and others had tried to interpret as examples of simple, direct conditioning.

Thus it was assumed that solution learning does indeed presuppose drive reduction but that sign learning, such as is involved in fear conditioning, depends upon the temporal conjunction of the sign with the *onset* of a noxious stimulus, such as electric shock. Here one is dealing, not with drive reduction, but with drive *induction*, i.e., with "punishment" rather than "reward." Therefore, in the second version of two-factor theory, not only were stimulus substitution and response substitution recognized as two different *forms* of learning; they were also assumed to involve two different types of *reinforcement*, drive induction and drive reduction, respectively.[8]

This formulation was highly efficient in accounting for active and passive avoidance learning. But it was by no means entirely satisfactory. In accepting, essentially unmodified, Thorndike's notion of habit as a stimulus-response connection or "bond," it was vulnerable to several telling criticisms that had been directed against this view (see Chapter 7; also Mowrer, 1960, Chapter 7). Moreover, it was also evident that fear is not the only emotion that can be conditioned and that some emotions are acquired in the context of drive reduction rather than drive induction. In other words, the assumption that there

---

[8] If the reader would find it helpful to see the first and second versions of two-factor theory represented graphically, he may consult the first four paragraphs of Section I, Chapter 8, and the accompanying illustrations.

was a neat and specific correlation between conditioning and drive induction was palpably false; and, as if in recognition of these conceptual difficulties, empirical research began to center more and more upon a phenomenon known as secondary reinforcement, which was to go far toward resolving them. So, once again, we follow history as well as logic and turn to this new topic.[9]

[9] While this book was in its first printing, experience suggested that a footnote could be usefully added here. In Behaviorism the great functional unit was the reflex or stimulus-response "connection." Here stimulation was *cause* and response was *effect*. However, over the years there has been a tendency for psychologists to take increasing account of response-stimulus relationships, i.e., situations in which response is cause and stimulation, effect; and such relationships have frequently been indicated in the preceding pages, not by an arrow or dash (as in stimulus-response relationships), but by a colon (:). Now we can further say that since there are two great classes of response, it follows that there are two corresponding categories of response-produced, or response-caused, stimulation: (a) stimulation produced by ordinary behavior (involving striated or skeletal muscles) and (b) stimulation produced by physiological reactions (involving smooth muscles, glands, etc.). In general, we see that type-a stimulation is *informational*, whereas type-b stimulation is *emotional*, or *motivational*. In other words, the sensory consequences of, or "feedback" from, what we commonly call "voluntary" responses constitute *cues*, and the sensory consequences of, or feedback from, involuntary, physiological reactions constitute emotions. Now, having recognized both stimulus-response and response-stimulus sequences, we see that the total activity of an organism has a continuous, on-going quality which we are likely to miss if we think only in stimulus-response terms. Behavior is not a succession of simple, disjunctive S—R sequences; instead, it involves S—R:S—R:S—R, etc. (it being understood that the "R" may be either behavioral or physiological and that the "S" may be either informational or emotional). Something of this sort was, of course, implied by the Behavioristic concept of "reflex chaining," in which the sensory consequences of one response supposedly produced the next response in the series, and so on. But this scheme had all the weaknesses of reflexology in general and some special ones of its own. Instead of assuming that the sensory consequences of one action produce (directly, reflexly) the next action in the series, we are here assuming that behavior is more complexly determined, along lines already indicated. Thorndike, of course, was aware of response-produced stimulation in the sense of the *effects* of responses which he called rewards and punishments; but his scheme remained seriously incomplete because he did not also take cognizance of the response-correlated stimuli which we are here calling cues and emotions. In a general way, the situation was more realistically appraised by Dewey, in the 1896 article which has already been cited, and by James in his *Principles of Psychology* (1890). But their ideas, to which we are now returning, were largely submerged for several decades by the passion for radical objectivity which was Behaviorism.

4 ————————

Two Conceptions
of Secondary Reinforcement

About 1940, the term "secondary reinforcement" began to appear with increasing frequency in psychological literature; and from the outset it had two, seemingly quite different meanings. The first of these, we shall find, is merely an extension of Thorndike's notion of *primary* reinforcement or "reward"; and the other interpretation, or meaning, of secondary reinforcement is likewise an outgrowth of primary, or "first-order," reinforcement as Pavlov conceived of it. Since these two investigators thought of primary reinforcement (i.e., of the conditions essential for the occurrence of rudimentary learning) in such very different terms, it is only natural that the correlative notions of *secondary* reinforcement should also differ.

These two conceptions will be separately examined in this chapter; and, in the chapter which follows, a formula will be proposed whereby they can both be accounted for in terms of a single, common set of assumptions. From this analysis the possibility then emerges of integrating and unifying Pavlov's and Thorndike's most basic and fundamental hypotheses, i.e., of formulating a conception of learning with high generality and "power."

I. Secondary Reinforcement as Fear Reduction

Since fear had, by 1940, been commonly recognized as an *acquired* or *secondary* drive, it was natural enough, as one group of writers held, to refer to the reinforcement of behavior through fear reduction as *secondary reinforcement, secondary reward,* or *acquired reward.* A paper which appeared in 1939, with the title, "A Stimulus-Response Analysis of Anxiety and Its Role as a Reinforcing Agent," reads in part as follows:

John B. Watson (1926) demonstrated experimentally that, contrary to the Jamesian view, most human fears are specifically related to and dependent upon individual experience. . . .

Freud seems to have seen the problem in this light from the outset and accordingly posited that *all* anxiety (fear) reactions are probably learned; his hypothesis, when recast in stimulus-response terminology, runs as follows. A so-called "traumatic" ("painful") stimulus (arising from external injury, of whatever kind, or from severe organic need) impinges upon the organism and produces a more or less violent defense reaction. Furthermore, such a stimulus-response sequence is usually preceded or accompanied by originally "indifferent" stimuli which, however, after one or more temporally contiguous associations with the traumatic stimulus, begin to be perceived as "danger signals," i.e., acquire the capacity to elicit an anxiety reaction. This latter reaction, which may or may not be grossly observable, has two outstanding characteristics: (a) it creates or, perhaps more accurately, consists of a state of heightened tension (or "attention") and a more or less specific readiness for (expectation of) the impending, traumatic stimulus; and (b), by virtue of the fact that such a state of tension is itself a form of discomfort, it adaptively motivates the organism to escape from the danger situation, thereby lessening the intensity of the tension and also probably decreasing the chance of encountering the traumatic stimulus. In short, *fear is the conditioned form of the pain reaction,* which has the highly useful function of motivating and reinforcing behavior that tends to avoid or prevent the recurrence of the pain-producing (unconditioned) stimulus (Mowrer, 1939, pp. 554–555).

What was being said here is, in effect, this: fear is acquired by conditioning and has the power not only to inhibit responses (if the unconditioned stimulus has followed these responses) but also, if the unconditioned stimulus has followed some external, environmentally produced stimulus, to motivate the subject to activity and to reinforce whatever response serves to eliminate the "danger signal" and thus reduce fear. Because of the great influence of Thorndike, there had been a tendency to think of a noxious, "punishing" stimulus as simply and directly weakening whatever response it followed (Chapter 2); and, because of the work of Pavlov and Bekhterev, there was also a tendency to think of a noxious stimulus as the "unconditioned stimulus" for some reflexive response (such as leg flexion in the example cited from Hull in the preceding chapter), which stimulus, if paired with a formerly neutral, incidental stimulus, would cause this response to become attached to that stimulus. These two highly influential conceptions are represented diagrammatically in Figs. 4–1 [1] and 4–2.

Although Thorndike, in his theory of punishment, was talking of something quite different from what Pavlov and Bekhterev were suggesting in their theory of defense conditioning, what is being said here is different from *both* these theories; and this different way of thinking was prompted by the fact that neither Thorndike's theory nor the

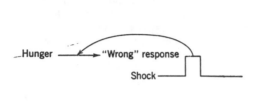

Fig. 4–1. Thorndikian conception of how punishment operated. If some drive, such as hunger, causes the subject to make some forbidden, "wrong" response and if this response is followed by a painful stimulus such as electric shock, then the connection between the hunger drive and the "wrong" response would, by virtue of the occurrence of the shock (see arrow), be weakened.

Pavlov-Bekhterev scheme was sufficient to the facts, as past chapters have indicated. The present position is that whenever a stimulus—be it response-produced (Fig. 4–1) or environmentally produced (Fig.

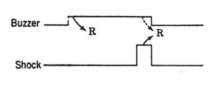

Fig. 4–2. The Pavlov-Bekhterev conception of defense-reflex conditioning. If an unconditioned stimulus, like electric shock, elicits some response R (solid arrow), and if some incidental stimulus, such as a buzzer, is present when R occurs, then the buzzer-response connection (broken arrow) will be strengthened and the response will tend to occur to the buzzer alone (solid arrow).

[1] Actually, since time is moving from left to right in this diagram, the shock should not be represented as weakening the Hunger—Wrong Response habit or "bond" by "acting backwards" in time (as suggested by the arrow). The true effect of the shock, or punishment, must clearly be upon the "bond" just as or just after the punishment occurs, which effect cannot, of course, be *observed* until the next time the punished response starts to occur. As already noted (Chapter 2), Thorndike, in speaking of his Law of Effect, often referred to punishments (and rewards) as "acting back" upon S—R bonds in the manner suggested by the arrow; but this practice almost certainly represented mere carelessness of speech, rather than real acceptance of teleology (backward conditioning).

4-2)—precedes marked drive increment, fear becomes conditioned to that stimulus and can then act either to produce response inhibition, if the signal is response-produced, *or* active avoidance behavior, if the signal is independent, i.e., environmentally produced. In both instances, doing whatever will eliminate the stimulus or stimulus constellation which is producing the fear will be rewarding and will reinforce whatever activity (or inactivity) is involved. In short, by positing fear conditioning—which Thorndike, Pavlov, Bekhterev, and Hull all eschewed—one can account equally well, and quite parsimoniously, for both response inhibition, as in "punishment," and response instigation, as in "avoidance learning." But this interpretation involves, in addition to the concept of fear conditioning, the notion that, once fear is attached to a stimulus or set of stimuli, fear reduction (or "relief") will reward and reinforce whatever behavior occurs in conjunction with this reduction: this, in essence, is what may be termed secondary reinforcement, *type-1*.

A decade after the publication of the paper cited at the outset of this chapter, Brown & Jacobs (1949) summarized this general point of view in the following words:

An important concept in a number of current theories of behavior is that the emotion of fear is (usually) a learned, anticipatory response to painful stimulation and that its significance as a behavior-determinant lies primarily in its motivational properties. The assumption that fear is a learned response stems from the fact that it can be elicited by (conditioned) stimuli which in the past have been closely associated with, or have been followed by, noxious (unconditioned) stimuli. The additional assumption that fear is (or produces) a drive, rests on the assumption that it exhibits certain of the major functional properties commonly attributed to primary drives such as hunger. Specifically, (1) the presence of fear is said to energize or motivate behavior, and (2) a reduction in fear is said to act as a reinforcement for the acquisition of new responses. Since the fear reaction is learned, the resulting drive is termed secondary or acquired to distinguish it from primary drives whose antecedent conditions are unlike those typically observed in learning situations.

This conception, which is essentially a translation of certain Freudian ideas (Freud, 1936) into stimulus-response terms was first proposed by Mowrer (1939). Subsequently, he and others have applied the notion to the interpretation of a variety of behavior and have carried out a number of experiments tending to support the hypothesis (Farber, 1948; May, 1948; Miller & Dollard, 1941; Mowrer, 1940a; Mowrer & Lamoreaux, 1946). A recent study by N. E. Miller (1948a), which apparently provides the most convincing confirmatory evidence, forms the point of departure for the present investigation (p. 747).[2]

[2] See also motion picture demonstration made by Miller & Hart (1948).

Brown & Jacobs then briefly describe the experiment, discussed in Chapter 3, in which Miller trained rats to run from the white compartment into a black one, under threat of shock, and then later showed that the rats would learn to perform various instrumental acts, under pressure of the fear drive, as a means of causing a door to open which initially blocked entrance into the black, or safety, compartment. Since the latter part of this experiment involved "frustrating" the animal (see Chapters 6 and 11) with respect to a "habit" previously learned, namely that of freely escaping from the white compartment into the black one, Brown & Jacobs reasoned that:

Although Miller's interpretation of his results in terms of fear and its reduction appears quite plausible, there are other interpretations that merit consideration. One alternative is to assume that frustration, not fear, is the important drive in the situation and hence that frustration-reduction is the significant reinforcing event. According to this hypothesis, the interruption or blocking of any strong, on-going response produces a state of frustration or anger which functions as a drive. . . . This drive, like that of fear, could lead to appearance of varied activity and, eventually, to the correct response of turning the wheel. Since the opening of the door would permit the resumption of the running response, there would follow an almost immediate reduction in frustration. As a consequence, the tendency to perform the wheel-turning response would be strengthened by this decrease in drive (p. 748).

Brown & Jacobs summarize their own experimentation and the results thus:

Two experiments have been described in which an investigation was made of the assumption that fear functions as a drive to motivate or energize behavior and that fear-reduction serves as a reinforcing event in the learning of new responses. In both studies, the methods employed in establishing the fear reaction and in measuring its reinforcing properties were designed to minimize the possibility of arousing some other emotional state such as frustration or conflict to which the results might be attributed instead of to fear. . . .

The general procedure of both studies involved a number of training trials during which rats were placed in an oblong box and given paired presentations of a conditioned stimulus and an electric shock. Control animals received the conditioned stimulus but not the shock. On subsequent learning trials the conditioned stimulus was presented alone to all animals and an opportunity was provided for them to perform a new response of crossing from one side of the box to the other by jumping over a central barrier. When the new response was made, the conditioned stimulus was immediately terminated.

The assumptions underlying this procedure were (a) that the paired presentation of the conditioned stimulus and shock, even though no specific escape response was systematically reinforced, would lead to the development of a conditioned fear reaction elicited by the conditioned stimulus alone; (b) that the conditioned fear would motivate the behavior of cross-ing the barrier; and (c) that the reduction in fear, occasioned by the cessa-tion of the conditioned stimulus following the new response, would act to strengthen the tendency to perform that response.

Since in both experiments the fearful animals learned the new response, whereas their comparable controls did not, the conclusion is drawn that fear-reduction functions much like other drive-reductions to reinforce new re-sponses (pp. 758–759).

In other words, during the original conditioning of fear to the signal (a high-pitched buzzer), there was nothing that the subjects could do to eliminate the fear (or avert the shock), so there were no well established fear-reducing "habits." Therefore, when the low bar-rier was introduced between the two ends of the rectangular compart-ment, the rats were in no way frustrated (as they might have been when Miller closed the door between the white and black compart-ments); and the motivation for learning to shuttle over the barrier when the buzzer was presented was clearly fear and fear alone. Brown & Jacobs did not, in their experiment, prove that frustration and anger were not operative in the Miller experiment; they simply fractionated out the possible frustration-anger element and showed that fear alone *can* motivate, and its reduction reinforce, a response such as is involved in the shuttling, on signal, from one side of this apparatus to the other.

Numerous other writers (Lichtenstein, 1950a, 1950b; Solomon & Wynne, 1954) have discussed the fear-reduction conception of sec-ondary reinforcement and have reported a variety of experimental confirmations. It is, of course—as the reader will have noticed—exactly the same conception that is presented in Chapter 2 as most adequately accounting for the facts of punishment and avoidance learning. It has been reviewed in the immediately preceding pages mainly as a means of providing additional historical perspective and of contrasting and comparing it with another conception of secondary reinforcement now to be considered.[3]

[3] Much new evidence for the centrality of fear in both active and passive avoid-ance learning has recently been accrued by studies involving the use of various tranquilizers and sedatives. Representative of these studies is one recently reported by Wenzel (1958). Here it was clearly shown that reserpine makes cats decidedly less responsive to a danger signal but only slightly, if at all, less so to a food signal. And Conger (1951), to take an earlier but no less interesting example, has reported a similar finding for alcohol in rats. Because of the known selective action of these and other chemical substances, such findings support, in a particu-larly convincing way, the thesis that fear is a decisive causal factor in avoidance behavior. This, of course, was never doubted by common sense; "proof" is needed only in a strictly behavioristic frame of reference. (See also Rutledge & Doty, 1957.)

II. Secondary Reinforcement as Conceived by Pavlov and Hull

A good many years ago, Pavlov (1927) and his students reported a type of learning from which a different conception of secondary reinforcement has evolved. As a means of illustrating "second-order," or "secondary," conditioning, as he termed it, Pavlov describes an experiment (performed by Frolov) in which the salivary reflex, first elicited (in a hungry dog) by food, was conditioned to the sound of a metronome (Fig. 4-3). Said Pavlov:

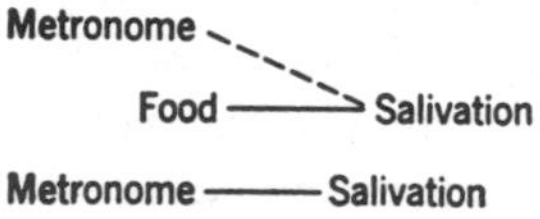

Metronome ⟍
⟍
Food ⟶ Salivation

Metronome ⸺ Salivation

Fig. 4-3. First-order conditioning of salivation to the sound of a metronome. The original, unconditioned stimulus for the salivation was food.

[Then a] black square is held in front of the dog for ten seconds, and after an interval of fifteen seconds the metronome is sounded during 30 seconds. . . .

Prior to these experiments the appearance of the black square had no secretory effect at all. As seen from the . . . table [not reproduced] the conditioned reflex of the second order is measured even at this early stage of its development [10th trial] by 5½ drops . . . (p. 34). [See Fig. 4-4.]

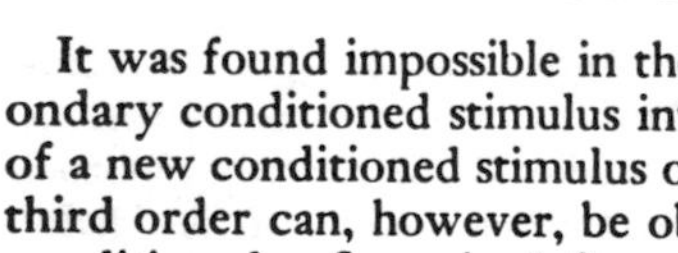

Black square ⟍
⟍
Metronome ⟶ Salivation

Black square ⸺ Salivation

Fig. 4-4. Second-order conditioning of salivation to the sight of a black square. The metronome, or first-order conditioned stimulus, here takes the place of the food as a means of eliciting the salivation in conjunction with the black square.

Pavlov then makes the following, more general comment:

It was found impossible in the case of alimentary reflexes to press the secondary conditioned stimulus into our service to help us in the establishment of a new conditioned stimulus of the third order. Conditioned reflexes of the third order can, however, be obtained with the help of the second order of conditioned reflexes in defense reactions such as that against stimulation of the skin by a strong electric current. But even in this case we cannot proceed further than a conditioned reflex of the third order (p. 34).

For Pavlov, "reinforcement" occurred whenever a formerly neutral stimulus was followed, or "confirmed," by an unconditioned stimulus or by a first-order (or higher-order) conditioned stimulus. Hence, if a second-order CS were followed by a first-order CS, which now functioned as a reinforcing agent (in place of the original unconditioned stimulus), it was logical to refer to this procedure as involving second-order, or "secondary," reinforcement. For Pavlov, reinforcement was, in any and all cases, a matter of pure *contiguity*, of a first-order CS occurring in conjunction with an UnCS, a second-order CS with a first-order CS, or yet higher-order pairings. In first-order conditioning, in the illustration given, there is, in addition to contiguity of stimuli, also drive reduction; i.e., the unconditioned stimulus (food) not only occurs conjointly with the metronome but also reduces hunger. Pavlov disregarded the latter function of the UnCS: thus one could say, as Hull subsequently did (see Chapter 3), that contiguity of CS and UnCS, while a necessary condition for first-order conditioning, is not a sufficient one; the reinforcement afforded by drive reduction may also have to be present.

But what is the situation as regards salivary conditioning of the *second* order? Here salivation is originally evoked, not by food, but by the metronome; and the clicking of the metronome could hardly be said to be a substitute for food and to reduce hunger (see Miles & Wickens, 1953, and Simons, Wickens, Brown, & Pennock, 1951, discussed in Chapter 6). Therefore, whatever the situation may be as far as first-order conditioning is concerned, we *seem* to have in second-order conditioning a form of learning which occurs *without drive reduction*. Here mere contiguity, or proximity, of stimuli appears to be both necessary and sufficient for learning. Let us now see how Hull approached and tried to handle this problem, within the framework of a monistic, drive-reduction theory.

While rejecting certain features of Pavlovian theory, Hull (Chapter 3, p. 68) was nevertheless much influenced by Pavlov's work on secondary reinforcement. In the beginning of Chapter VII of *Principles of behavior* (1943), Hull makes explicit reference to Pavlov's experiments on second-order salivary conditioning and concludes that "the metronome [in the demonstration previously described] had not only acquired the capacity to evoke the flow of saliva but had also acquired the capacity itself to act as a reinforcing agent" (p. 85). That is to say if, for example, after the metronome had become a CS and thus capable of mediating higher-order conditioning, it had been presented each time the subject made a particular movement, such as turning its head to the right, the tendency to make this movement would have been strengthened merely by the presentation of the metronome, without the accompanying presentation of food. From a common-sense standpoint this, of course, is not hard to understand: since the metronome was a stimulus which the hungry dog was "glad" to have occur (since it foreshadowed the delivery of food), naturally the dog would learn any action which produced this stimulus. In a later book, Hull (1951) cites several laboratory instances of this sort of thing:

The click of the food-release mechanism in Skinner's experiment served as the [secondary] reinforcing agent there involved. The sight of the grains of boiled rice in Grindley's experiment served to reinforce the locomotor re-action of his chicks even for a time when they received no food. The click of the food release mechanism in Bugelski's experiment yielded enough rein-forcement to delay the progress of experimental extinction. And Cowles' chimpanzees received secondary reinforcement from their possession of col·-ored tokens which would later be inserted into a vending machine and ex-changed for a raisin. Miller (1951b) has given an elaborate tabulated analy-sis of a dozen or more additional cases of analogous nature. . . . Since this indirect power of reinforcement is acquired through learning, it is called secondary reinforcement (pp. 27–28).

Thus we see that Pavlov and Hull were interested in two different aspects of the same phenomenon: Pavlov in the fact that a stimulus, once conditioned, could serve as the basis for still further (higher-order) conditioning; Hull in the fact that such a stimulus could be used to establish some entirely new "habit." Hull's views in this con-nection, as of 1943, are summarized in the following brief paragraphs, which are found near the end of the chapter on secondary reinforce-ment in *Principles of behavior:*

Our detailed findings concerning secondary reinforcement may be listed as follows:
    1. Perhaps the most striking characteristic of secondary reinforcement is that it is itself a kind of by-product of the setting up of a receptor-effector connection, in the first instance through primary reinforcement. Primary reinforcement, on the other hand, appears to be a native, unlearned capacity in some way associated with need reduction.
    2. Secondary reinforcement may be acquired by a stimulus from associa-tion with some previously established secondary reinforcement, as well as with a primary reinforcement. It would appear that transfer of this power of reinforcement from one stimulus situation to another may go on indefinitely, given the conditions of stable and consistent association. [Pavlov, 1927, on the other hand, put a limit on this process (cf. p. 98).]
    3. A receptor-effector connection ["habit"] involving any effector may be reinforced by a secondary reinforcing situation.
    4. Secondary reinforcement differs from primary reinforcement in that the former seems to be associated, at least in a molar sense, with stimulation, whereas the latter seems to be associated with the cessation of stimulation. . . . (p. 97).

In what way or ways, then, can the Pavlov-Hull conception of secondary reinforcement be said to differ from the other phenomenon, previously cited, to which this same term has also been applied? Secondary reinforcement type-1 refers quite simply, as we have seen, to the reward or satisfaction experienced when a danger signal *terminates*, thus indicating that some impending *objectionable* event has been averted; whereas secondary reinforcement *type-2* refers, it seems, to the reward or satisfaction experienced when a stimulus comes *on*, indicating the imminent occurrence of some *desired* event. Or, in completely nontechnical terms, secondary reinforcement type-1 implies *relief* (withdrawal of threat); and secondary reinforcement type-2 implies *hope* (presentation of a *promise*).

In some ways it is unfortunate that the same term should have come into use for both these phenomena, but in other ways it is perhaps an advantage. The common usage is certainly justifiable in the sense that both of these phenomena mediate learning without primary reinforcement; but, over and beyond this, the common usage also implies that the underlying process or mechanism is the same, which may or may not be the case. Those investigators who have been most interested in type-1 secondary reinforcement have been explicit in their assumption that drive reduction is involved, viz., reduction in the secondary drive of fear; whereas Hull, as the principal spokesman for those who have studied type-2 secondary reinforcement, has taken the position (see paragraph 4, p. 100) that this phenomenon involves *stimulation* rather than "cessation of stimulation." The latter premise has been stated even more strongly and explicitly by Seeman & Greenberg (1952), as follows:

The concept of secondary reinforcement is a highly significant construct in Hull's theoretical system. . . . It is Hull's view, further, that "the first secondary reinforcing stimulus acquires its power of reinforcement by virtue of having conditioned to it some fractional component of the need reduction of the goal situation, whose occurrence, wherever it takes place, has a specific power of reinforcement in a degree proportionate to the intensity of that occurrence" (Hull's *Principles*, p. 100). . . . All writers agree, or have until recently agreed, that the defining property of the concept lies in the acquisition of reinforcing properties by an initially non-reinforcing stimulus in consequence of its consistent proximity to a stimulus which is a primary reinforcer [drive reducer].[4] The essential point here, then, is that, although secondary reinforcement may operate jointly with primary reinforcement,

[4] This statement is not historically accurate: The use of the expression, secondary reinforcement, to denote reduction in a secondary drive such as fear dates back fully as far as does Hull's use of the term with what Seeman and Greenberg regard as its more legitimate connotation (see, for example, Miller and Dollard, 1941).

as it does, for example, in Denny's (1948) study, *it can operate in the absence of any such primary reinforcement once it has acquired secondary reinforcement properties. It can operate, that is, in the absence of any drive reduction of any kind* (pp. 1–2).

If one takes the position that secondary reinforcement type-2 does not involve drive reduction, it leads, as the following section will indicate, to a number of logical and psychological dilemmas; and if one takes the *reverse* position, i.e., the view that secondary reinforcement type-2 involves drive reduction no less than does secondary reinforcement type-1, there are important conceptual and empirical problems, which will be dealt with, at some length, in Chapters 5 and 6.[5]

III. Paradoxes in Hull's Treatment of Secondary Reinforcement

Hull has been more responsible than any other writer for stressing the general systematic importance of secondary reinforcement type-2, yet his conceptualization of this phenomenon leaves much to be desired; and because secondary reinforcement is so central to the argument developed in the present volume, it is essential that this phenomenon be understood as clearly and fully as possible.

For Hull, secondary reinforcement type-2 was, in fact, the *only* form of secondary reinforcement, properly speaking, since he tended to lump secondary reinforcement type-1 (whenever he referred to it), along with primary reinforcement, under the more general heading of so-called *primitive* reinforcement, i.e., any and all forms of drive reduction, regardless of whether the drive was biologically given (as in hunger and thirst) or derived (as in the case of fear). What then, in Hull's own frame of reference, was "secondary reinforcement"? His formal statement on this score reads as follows:

> Corollary ii: A neutral receptor impulse [stimulus] which occurs repeatedly and consistently in close conjunction with a reinforcing state of affairs, whether primary or secondary, will itself acquire the power of acting as a reinforcing agent (1952, p. 6).

This formulation is probably valid (cf. Chapters 5 and 6); but it involves two *logical* difficulties as employed within Hull's own system.

---

[5] It will perhaps be helpful at this point to remind the reader that two-factor theory (second version, see Chapter 3) involved a clear understanding of what has here been referred to as type-1 secondary reinforcement. It was in respect to secondary reinforcement *type-2* that the theory was "silent" and therefore incomplete and inadequate. It is, as we shall shortly see, the systematic exploration of this short-coming that makes possible the major theoretical advance with which later chapters of this book are specifically concerned.

The first of these is that it is logically identical with Hull's statement of the conditions for the acquisition of secondary motivation or drive, namely:

Corollary i: When neutral stimuli are repeatedly and consistently associated with the evocation of a primary or secondary drive and this drive stimulus undergoes an abrupt diminution, the hitherto neutral stimuli acquire the capacity to bring about the drive (S_D), which thereby become the condition (C_D) of a secondary drive or motivation (1952, p. 6).

In effect, what the first of these formal statements says is that if a formerly neutral stimulus occurs when some primary drive is reduced, that stimulus takes on the capacity to act as a secondary reinforcer; and what the second statement says is that if a formerly neutral stimulus occurs when some primary drive is reduced, that stimulus takes on the capacity to arouse secondary motivation. Now secondary reinforcement and secondary motivation are, at the very least, *different* phenomena and, quite possibly, even antithetical; yet Hull's two corollaries make them dependent upon identical conditions. Hilgard (1956), in discussing this paradox, says:

Despite the seeming formality of his exposition, Hull used many variations in wording when stating his postulates, so that precise meanings are sometimes hard to infer. I have restated the two corollaries in closely parallel form, which he did not do. Then it becomes evident that a neutral stimulus associated consistently with a reinforcing state of affairs acquires two functions (and both at once!): (1) the power to arouse a secondary drive (Corollary i), and (2) the power to reduce drive stimuli, and hence act as a secondary reinforcing agent (Corollary ii).
. . . The attempt to interpret the actual events in secondary reinforcement came late in Hull's theorizing, and he probably had not developed a theory fully satisfactory to himself (pp. 129–130).

This difficulty arises because of Hull's reluctance to admit the existence of two forms of *primary* reinforcement, namely what are commonly termed reward and punishment or decremental reinforcement (type-D) and incremental reinforcement (type-I). The difficulty in deriving fear conditioning (secondary motivation) from decremental reinforcement has been considered in Chapter 3 and need not be reviewed here. Suffice it to say that the contradiction implied by Hull's Corollaries i and ii is readily and satisfactorily resolved by the view that there are two basic, and basically different, reinforcement processes, rather than only one.[6]

But there is another difficulty in Hull's treatment of secondary

[6] For an attempt by Spence to justify Hull's treatment of secondary reinforcement, see Chapter 8, p. 261 ff. But see also McGuigan (1956) for further criticisms thereof.

reinforcement which is even more remarkable—and unnecessary. As already indicated (in the preceding section), Hull's formal system implied that secondary reinforcement involves an *increase* in stimulation, as opposed to the decrease in stimulation (drive) which is involved in primary reinforcement. This led to numerous problems, the most conspicuous of which was that it forced Hull's system beyond its avowed monism as regards the nature of reinforcement. As just noted, Hull refused to recognize the reality of incremental reinforcement; yet in conceiving secondary reinforcement as he did, there was no alternative but to grant that reinforcement sometimes involves drive reduction and sometimes not. If a secondary reinforcing agent can nevertheless mediate both higher-order conditioning and new habit formation, then the only principle of reinforcement which is left here is that of classical Pavlovian conditioning, namely, the mere temporal conjunction or "contiguity" of two stimuli.

It is true that Hull vacillated on this score. For example, at the end of the chapter on secondary reinforcement in his *Principles of Behavior* (1943), there is a long note entitled: "Are Primary and Secondary Reinforcement at Bottom Two Things or One?" And here he says:

> So far as our present knowledge goes, the habit structures mediated by the two types of reinforcement agents are qualitatively identical. This consideration alone constitutes a very considerable presumption in favor of the view that both forms are at bottom, i.e., physiologically, the same. It is difficult to believe that the processes of organic evolution would generate two entirely distinct physiological mechanisms which would yield qualitatively exactly the same product, even though real duplications of other physiological functions are known to have evolved (pp. 99–100).

It is true that later, as Hilgard (1956) has noted, Hull "was attempting to hold a consistent drive-stimulus reduction theory of secondary reinforcement (as well as of primary reinforcement)" (p. 130), as indicated by the following statement:

> It follows that any stimulus consistently associated with a reinforcement situation will through that association acquire the power of evoking the conditioned inhibition [of a drive-producing response such as fear], i.e., a reduction in stimulus intensity, and so of itself producing the resulting reinforcement. Since this indirect power of reinforcement is acquired through learning, it is called secondary reinforcement (Hull, 1951, pp. 27–28).

In subsequent chapters we shall see that the idea which Hull was exploring in the above quotation has considerable promise and power; but it is not the one which his followers have most generally accepted in this connection. Instead they have seized upon and utilized his conjecture that secondary reinforcement is mediated by a *fractional anticipatory goal reaction*, r_g, whose occurrence produces a distinctive stimulus, s_g which, in some way, carries the acquired, or secondary, reinforcement potential. This notion was stated differently from time to time by Hull; but the following formulation is selected here from the *Principles of Behavior* because it occurs in the same note, already cited. Having acknowledged the possibility that primary and secondary reinforcement are basically the same, Hull goes on to observe that since "the present development of neurophysiology is quite remote from such an achievement," the urgency of the problem calls for "an attempt at a workable first approximation," after which we read:

> These considerations suggest rather strongly that the first secondary reinforcing stimulus acquires its power of reinforcement by virtue of having conditioned to it some fractional component of the need reduction process of the goal situation (G) *whose occurrence, whenever it takes place, has a specific power of reinforcement in a degree proportionate to the intensity of that occurrence.*
>
> Let us represent this fractional component of the goal reaction by the symbol g [or $_g$] (1943, p. 100).

The following excerpt from K. W. Spence's recent Silliman Lectures at Yale University will provide one of many possible illustrations of the widespread use that has been made of this concept:

> The essential notion of this formulation . . . is that learning in instrumental reward sequences involves classical conditioning of the goal or consummatory response to stimulus cues throughout the chain as well as an increase in the habit strengths of the instrumental acts themselves. There is, of course, nothing new about this notion of the conditioned fractional anticipatory goal response. Indeed Hull introduced the concept in his early theoretical articles on maze learning (1930, 1931), although he never described its possible role in simple instrumental conditioning. The major difference between Hull's use of this theoretical mechanism and mine is that I have regarded it primarily as a motivator and have identified it with Hull's more recently formulated incentive motivational construct (Spence, 1951a, 1951b) (Spence, 1956, p. 126).

Here Spence is trying to evolve a theory of "habit" which will not be beset with the difficulties inherent in the S—R "bond" conception thereof, an objective which is of the upmost importance at the present stage of learning theory (see Chapter 7); but it is by no means certain that the particular approach suggested in the foregoing quotation is the most promising one (cf. Chapters 6 and 8). In the following chapter an alternative formulation will be suggested, on which the validity of the rest of this volume will depend; but first it will be desirable to take a more detailed look at secondary rein-forcement itself, not logically but empirically. If, after all, there should be any question about its reality, *qua* phenomenon, there would be little point in belaboring its theoretical significance.

IV. Experiments Exemplifying Secondary Reinforcement Type-2

As will be seen in Chapter 10, there were a number of early experiments on delayed primary reward which, inadvertently, involved the operation of secondary reinforcement type-2. But here we shall consider instead some of the outstanding attempts which were made to investigate this phenomenon as such. One of the earliest and best of these was reported by B. F. Skinner in 1938. After alluding to Pavlovian higher-order, or "secondary," conditioning (which Skinner termed "secondary conditioning of Type S," to stress the *stimulus* or *sensory* elements in the situation), this writer went on to say:

There is, however, a process that might be called secondary conditioning Type R [for *response*]. It does not involve a conflict with the process of discrimination because it is a response rather than a stimulus that is reinforced. The process is that of adding an initial member to a chain of reflexes without ultimately reinforcing the chain. In the present example, the sound of the magazine acquires reinforcing value through its correlation with ultimate [primary] reinforcement. It can function as a reinforcing agent even when this ultimate reinforcement is lacking. Its reinforcing power will be weakened through the resulting extinction, but considerable conditioning can be effected before a state of more or less complete extinction is reached. The maximal result to be obtained from a given amount of previous conditioning of the sound of the magazine is shown in the following experiment.

The usual preliminary procedure [preliminary, that is, to the rat's learning to press a bar as a means of obtaining food] was carried out with four rats, as the result of which they came to respond readily to the sound of the magazine by approaching the food tray. Sixty combined presentations of the sound and food were given. On the day of conditioning the magazine was connected with the lever but was empty. For the first time in the history of the rat the movement of the lever produced the (hitherto always reinforced) sound of the magazine, but no responses were ultimately reinforced with food. The four resulting curves are given [in Fig. 4-5] (Skinner, 1938, p. 82).

In going over the galley proof of this book with a class in the summer of 1959, the author was interrupted at this point by a student who asked a very pertinent question, one which indicated that she was beginning to grasp and apply the general theoretical system which is here evolving. In paraphrase, what she said went something like this. During the training stage of the experiment just described, Professor Skinner periodically pushed a key which caused the food delivery mechanism to click and to deliver to a hungry rat a pellet of food. And when the experimenter's key was replaced by one (the bar) which the rat could operate, the rat proceeded to push it and make the delivery mechanism operate several (about 50) times, even though it was now

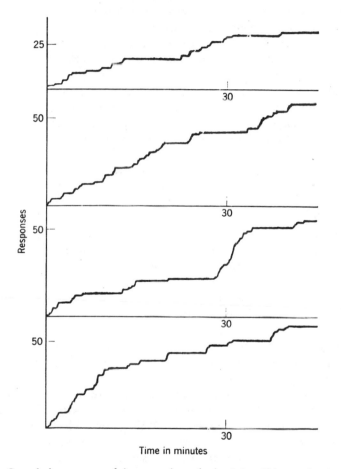

Time in minutes

Fig. 4–5. Cumulative curves of bar pressing obtained by Skinner (1938, p. 83) from four rats which received secondary reinforcement only. The latter consisted of the sound produced by the operation of a (now empty) food-delivery mechanism. Previously this sound had been associated 60 times with the delivery of food.

completely empty. In other words, all the rat got for his efforts, during this testing phase of the experiment, was the click. Now, said the student, let us train a rat in a different way. Again we are going to have click and food associated 60 times during the training period; but instead of Professor Skinner pushing the key that makes the food-delivery mechanism operate, we will require the rat to do it. In short, we will set up an ordinary bar-pressing *habit*, with 60 rewarded training trials. Now, in the test period (when bar pressing still produces the click but no food), how many times will *this* rat press the bar? Fewer or more times than will a rat trained in the other way?

Immediately another student rephrased the question, thus: In other words, both training procedures will cause the click to take on secondary-reinforcement properties—which will give it the most? The one procedure (arbitrary pairing of click and food) involves the classical conditioning procedure; the other procedure is clearly instrumental (click is followed by food *only if* the bar is pushed). So the question is, Does the one procedure work better, in this situation, than the other?

Here still another student entered the discussion and said she thought the second rat would press the bar more often following withdrawal of primary reinforcement than would the first. And the reason she gave was this. The rat for which food follows click (during training) only if the bar is pressed will be producing a lot of *other stimuli* besides the click (sight and touch of the bar, proprioception, etc.) which will acquire secondary-reinforcement properties (or S^r, to use a notation happily introduced by Skinner), whereas in the case of the other rat the click will be the *only* stimulus produced by bar pressing which will have S^r properties at the beginning of the test (or extinction) period. This inference has far-reaching implications, which will not be further elaborated until Chapter 7. But the reader can use it here to test himself on how well he has assimilated the discussion up to this point.

Then, observed a fourth student, one could do something else. One could test the strength or resistance to extinction of a bar-pressing habit under two different conditions: extinction with click and no food, and extinction with neither click nor food. This procedure, he said, would show us how much S^r potency had been acquired by the click and how much by the *other* response-correlated stimuli. This suggestion now leads us back to the experiment which was to be discussed next in the galley proof, immediately after the description of the 1938 Skinner experiment.

About the same time, Bugelski (1938) demonstrated secondary reinforcement in a related way, by showing that, following acquisition of a bar-pressing habit with regular primary reinforcement, rats will continue to press the bar *longer*, after the withdrawal of primary reinforcement, if the bar pressing continues to activate the (now empty) food-delivery mechanism and thus makes the accustomed sound, than if the bar and delivery mechanism are disconnected. Here we see that a stimulus which is produced by the subject's own actions and is then followed by primary reinforcement takes on secondary reinforcement capacity, just as does a stimulus which is produced *by the experimenter* without reference to the subject's behavior, as in the example quoted from Skinner.[7] And this same general type of phenomenon was further exhibited in studies by Wolfe (1936) and Cowles (1937), in which it was shown that if a chimpanzee learns to obtain food by inserting poker chips into a sort of "vending machine," the chips themselves take on unmistakable secondary reward value, as indicated by the subject's readiness to "work" to obtain them.

Earlier it had been shown by Katherine Williams (1924) that a small box from which food had been repeatedly received by rats in a different situation could, if placed in the goal compartment of a maze, be used to fixate performance therein. But this experiment was complicated by the fact that the subjects had been allowed to explore the maze extensively before the empty food box was introduced, so that the procedure was more like that employed in latent-learning experiments involving primary reward (see Mowrer, 1960, Chapter 2) than like the conventional type of maze-learning procedure. Therefore, in 1949, Saltzman reported a study which he introduced with this comment:

> In order to study the topic of secondary reinforcement learning in the maze situation, it seemed advisable first to establish the fact that rats can solve a maze problem on the basis of secondary reward. Williams' success with a latent-learning technique suggests, but does not prove, that rats are able to do so. She points out that when a conventional learning technique was used the rats did not show any improvement in their maze scores. Also, studies by Anderson (1941a) on externalization of drive [see Chapter 5] offer evidence that such learning can occur. However, the nature of the secondary reinforcement in these studies is not clearly defined (p. 162).

[7] The parallelism should be noted between these two examples of secondary reinforcement and active and passive avoidance learning, as previously considered. In the Skinner example, secondary reinforcement is conditioned to an independent, experimenter-produced stimulus, just as fear is in active avoidance learning; whereas, in the Bugelski example, secondary reinforcement is conditioned to a response-dependent, response-correlated stimulus, just as fear is in passive avoidance learning.

What Saltzman did, in essence, was to teach rats to travel down a short, straight alley to obtain food in a distinctively painted (e.g., black) goal compartment, entry into which also involved distinctive kinesthetic stimulation. Then, in a modified T-maze, he tested the capacity of this compartment, at the end of one wing of the maze, to cause the rats to go to it instead of to a visually and kinesthetically different compartment at the end of the other wing of the maze. But Saltzman knew, of course, from earlier studies that secondary reinforcement tends to be evanescent, so he tried a variety of procedures aimed at increasing its stability and durability. His investigation was divided into two major parts, the first of which involved the use of four groups of rats. Group 1 was given "consecutive reinforcement" in the runway training, i.e., on each and every entry into the goal compartment, the subjects found food. Group 2 was given "alternative reinforcement," meaning that "a rewarded trial always preceded and always followed a non-rewarded trial" (p. 164). And Group 3 was given "differential reinforcement," as follows:

> The rats in this group received the same treatment as those in Group 2, with the exception that on the non-rewarded trials, the goal box was not the same one that was used for the rewarded trials. The rats receiving food in the black goal box, found the white goal box at the end of the runway on the non-rewarded runs, and those receiving food in the white box, found the black box on the non-rewarded runs (p. 164).

In other words, the Group-3 procedure was one in which the color (and kinesthetic properties) of the goal compartment, instead of being always the same and therefore ambiguous (implying reward on some trials and nonreward on others), was consistently correlated with the presence or absence of food on any given trial.

A control group of animals, Group C, received the same runway training as did the Group-1 animals; but when tested in the T-maze the Group-C animals continued to receive primary reinforcement (food) for the correct choice. In contrast to this procedure, the other three (experimental) groups got no food in the T-maze, only the "satisfaction" of entering the goal compartment in which they had previously received food, in the straight alley.

All animals received 15 runs in the T-maze, so that, if chance alone were operating, they would on the average make 7.5 turns to the right and 7.5 turns to the left, in a random order. The animals in Group 1 went to the correct side 8.3 times; those in Group 2, 9.0 times; and those in Group 3, 10.7 times. Considering that the animals which received primary reinforcement in the T-maze (Group C) made only 10 correct choices out of the possible 15, the secondary-reinforcement groups made a surprisingly good showing. In fact, the Group-3 animals were actually *superior* to the Group-C animals (10.7 compared with 10.0) by an amount statistically significant at the .01 level of confidence; and *all* groups were significantly different (at the .05 level of confidence or better) from the hypothetical chance expectation of 7.5.

Thus we see that even *continuous* primary reinforcement of subjects in the straight alley led to a statistically reliable secondary reinforcing effect in the T-maze, that alternate (partial) reinforcement increased this effect, and that so-called differential reinforcement produced the best result of all, even exceeding that obtained from the use of primary reinforcement. Said Saltzman of this part of his investigation:

> The experiment establishes the ability of the rat to learn a simple maze when correct choices are followed only by stimuli previously associated with food, and probably enhances the possibilities of secondary reinforcement as a general principle of learning. Inasmuch as the distinctive aspects of the goal boxes were at least several, including kinesthetic as well as visual components, it is impossible to say which of them was the most effective. Taken together, however, they were at least as effective, or slightly more effective than food. This last fact challenges a re-interpretation of the whole problem of the relative effectiveness of rewards in learning (pp. 168–170).

The second part of Saltzman's study, being less directly relevant to our present concerns, can be described very briefly. Its purpose was given as follows:

> If the failure to show [highly efficient] learning with the Consecutive Reinforcement Method was due, as was suggested in Part I, to the extinction of the acquired reward value, and not to its absence altogether, then by merely preventing or retarding the extinction during the actual maze learning, we should be able to show that learning can occur with this method. The procedure that was employed for retarding the extinction was one of interpolating rewarded runway trials between the maze trials during the learning tests (p. 169).

Part II was an exact replication of Part I as far as runway training was concerned, i.e., one group received consecutive reinforcement, one partial (alternate) reinforcement, and one so-called differential reinforcement. The difference came in the T-maze test procedure: "The procedure differed from that used in the first study in only one respect: each of the maze trials, except the last one, was followed by a rewarded runway trial" (p. 169). The result was a dramatic increase in the effectiveness of the runway goal compartment as a secondary reinforcer in the T-maze situation: the Group-1 animals now making 11.5 out of 15 possible correct choices; the Group-2 animals making 10.4 correct choices; and the Group-3 animals making 11.6 correct choices—all of which exceed the performance of Group C (the same in both Part I and Part II) of only 10 correct choices out of a possible 15. Said Saltzman: "The effect of the interpolated runway trials [which involve primary reinforcement] is to prolong the effectiveness of the secondary reinforcing agent, and thereby make possible a successful measurement of learning" (p. 171).

Saltzman's over-all conclusions run as follows:

1. Rats are able to learn a simple maze when the only reward is an acquired or secondary one.

2. Secondary reward may be as effective as the primary reward of food in influencing the choices made in a maze.

3. Of the three methods studied for establishing secondary reward value, the most effective was the differential rewarding of positive and negative cues.

4. The effectiveness of acquired rewards for promoting learning may be prolonged by continuing the process of establishing reward value during the actual learning tests (p. 173).

One of the most significant things about the Saltzman experiments is that they not only give clear indication of the reality of secondary reinforcement, type-2, but that they also suggest an affinity between this phenomenon and "habit." As will be shown later, a so-called habit proves more resistant to extinction (Chapter 11) if it has been reinforced intermittently rather than continuously (Chapter 12); and the Saltzman results show a similar effect with respect to the acquisition by previously neutral stimuli of the capacity to act as secondary reinforcers. As will later be indicated (Chapter 7), this similarity has far-reaching implications; but these cannot be confidently developed until there is further exploration of secondary reinforcement *qua phenomenon*.[8] This task will continue to occupy us in this and the immediately succeeding chapters.

[8] That Hull had no intimation, as of 1943, of the possible identity of the phenomenon called secondary reinforcement and "habit" is suggested by the fact that, although he knew that a habit can be made more resistant to extinction if established by means of intermittent reinforcement (p. 337), he thought that the most effective secondary reinforcement was established by associating the secondary-reinforcement stimulus "repeatedly and *consistently*" with primary reinforcement (Corollary ii, quoted on p. 102). However, Hull, writing in 1951, showed a very good appreciation of the other view. He said, "The strength of a secondary reinforcing stimulus developing in essentially the same manner that the strength of a habit ($_sH_R$) develops might be a possible explanation of

V. Secondary Reinforcement Type-2, Doubt and Confirmation

Despite the very substantial evidence for the kind of secondary reinforcement here under discussion, misgivings concerning its reality and importance are still fairly prevalent. For example, Spence (1956) and McClelland *et al.* (1953) have expressed doubt concerning its systematic significance in psychology; and Razran (1955), in a paper entitled "A Note on Second-Order Conditioning—and Secondary Reinforcement," has written as follows:

Now, if second-order conditioning is difficult to obtain and maintain in animals, and it seems to need cognition to be set up in human beings, what about secondary reinforcement per se, conceived independently as the capacity of a stimulus to reinforce more or less permanently another reaction? In the writer's opinion, the answer is essentially the same. True, the laboratory evidence for secondary reinforcement in animals—while never too critically appraised—seems, to date, to be more consistent than that for second-order conditioning. Yet, as an isolated force, secondary reinforcement is, too, as any mere inspection of the data of its several experiments reveals, very impermanent, very extinguishable, and quite ancillary and immediately dependent upon primary reinforcement. Thus there is here, too, a far cry from the results obtained (several experiments) to the phenomena (the vast area of man's cultural behavior) which are purported to be explained—and lots of room is left for supplementary accounts (p. 330).

Fortunately, work just completed by D. W. Zimmerman, at the University of Illinois, goes far toward dispelling doubts of the kind here expressed and establishing, beyond peradventure, the empirical validity and potency of this phenomenon. Although somewhat complicated in detail, the procedure employed by Zimmerman is, in principle, simple. As the preceding sections of this chapter indicate, the study of secondary reinforcement (type-2) normally involves two successive learning procedures, or stages: (a) association of a formerly neutral stimulus with the occurrence of some form of primary reinforcement and (b) the establishment of some new form of be-

---

the operation of secondary reinforcement"; and the same writer observes that "intermittent primary reinforcement should increase the strength of a secondary reinforcing stimulus more than consecutive primary reinforcement" (p. 247) and cites Saltzman (1949) in support of this surmise. While Hull was almost certainly right in suggesting an intimate relationship between secondary reinforcement and the phenomenon of habit, it would seem that it is secondary reinforcement that *explains habit*, rather than the other way 'round (see Chapter 7).

havior (habit) on the basis of the acquired, or secondary, reinforcement now provided by the formerly neutral stimulus, alone. As already noted, Saltzman has shown that a formerly neutral stimulus (or stimulus compound) acquires greater secondary-reinforcement capacity if associated with primary reinforcement intermittently rather than unfailingly; and various other workers (see Chapter 12) have shown that habits which are established with *primary* reinforcement are likewise more resistant to extinction if acquired on the basis of intermittent rather than invariable reinforcement. But apparently no one, prior to Zimmerman, had thought of the possibility of using a *double* intermittent-reinforcement procedure, i.e., intermittent association of the formerly neutral stimulus with primary reinforcement *and*, subsequently, intermittent presentation of this stimulus upon the occurrence of the, so to say, test response or new "habit." [9] Because the potency of secondary reinforcers had, at best, seemed slight and very susceptible to extinction, earlier workers were impelled to give the secondary reinforcer for each and every occurrence of the test response. But this, reasoned Zimmerman, only "uses up" the capacity of the secondary reinforcer that much *faster*, so that the economical and effective thing to do is to employ the secondary reinforcer sparingly, i.e., intermittently. The result of thus combining the advantages of intermittency, at both the primary and secondary levels of reinforcement, has been to create a sort of multiplicative rather than merely summative effect. That is to say, by means of the double intermittent-reinforcement procedure, Zimmerman has succeeded in obtaining secondary reinforcement effects that are roughly 40 times as great as those previously reported. His procedure is exemplified in a study recently reported in the *Psychological Review*. Because of the special importance and novelty of this paper, we shall quote extensively from a section thereof entitled, "A Two-Stage Intermittent Reinforcement Procedure which leads to powerful secondary reinforcement."

With the experimental procedure to be reported here, it has been found possible to give a secondary reinforcer such strength that it could, if desired, be used as a class demonstration of the Law of Effect, much in the manner of such primary reinforcers as food and water. The method whereby such stable secondary reinforcement can be established is as follows:

[9] As a partial qualification of the above statement, it should be noted that Clayton, in 1952, had reported use of double intermittent reinforcement; but because she had employed only very low ratios of reinforcement nonreinforcement, this investigator failed to obtain the dramatic effects reported by Zimmerman. (See also Kelleher, 1957a, 1957b.)

A. *Training.* A thirsty rat is put into a small (11″ x 11″ x 11″) box fitted with a motor-driven water-delivery mechanism. After the animal becomes habituated to the situation, a formerly neutral stimulus is given secondary reinforcement potential in this way: A two-second buzzer, followed by operation of the water delivery dipper, is presented at approximately one-minute intervals. Buzzer presentations are programmed independently of the behavior of the animal with the exception that the buzzer never sounds while the animal hovers over the water-delivery aperture.

After the approach response has been firmly established, water reinforcements are omitted following the buzzer, at first on alternate presentations, then successively in longer runs. The ratio of rewarded to non-rewarded presentations varies somewhat randomly, the mean number of reinforcement omissions, however, moving upward. A 1:10 ratio is finally stabilized, with the longest single non-reinforced run being 1:14. What is involved here, then, is a *variable ratio* of water-rewarded to non-rewarded S^r (secondary-reinforcement stimulus) presentations, this ratio being gradually increased. During this training the vigor with which the animal leaps to the water delivery aperture following the buzzer does not lessen, in spite of the fact that the frequency of "pay off" is progressively decreasing.

During this type of training what happens is that the buzzer becomes a signal "that water *may* now be available." Water is received at no time except *when the buzzer sounds,* so the animal soon learns to "pay attention" to the buzzer—to, as it were, "jump at the chance" which it affords. But the buzzer is not a sure sign of water.

B. *Testing.* Following the training procedure just described, the buzzer is tested for its secondary reinforcing properties by presenting it as a consequence of the rat's pressing a small bar which is now available. The buzzer (S^r) alone is thus used to strengthen this response, no further water reinforcements being given. However, instead of having the buzzer invariably follow bar pressing, the procedure again involves intermittent reinforcement. Here various options regarding the detailed procedure that may be used are open to the experimenter. The one that produced the results shown [in Fig. 4–6] went as follows. On the first day of testing, the bar-pressing behavior was established by reinforcing (with the buzzer) the first six responses (segment A). Thereafter S^r was given following a response only when at least a minute had elapsed since the preceding reinforcement (segment B). When the buzzer was discontinued entirely, a typical extinction performance followed (segment C). Reconditioning, with secondary reinforcement only, was possible on a second day, without intervening primary reinforcement of the secondary reinforcer. Various fixed-ratio schedules have also given satisfactory results (Zimmerman, 1957a) (pp. 373–374).

Although the results thus obtained by Zimmerman are dramatic enough, he has since devised a procedure that produces effects that are still more striking. "By means of this procedure," he says, "instrumental behavior which appears to be virtually inextinguishable can be established on the basis of secondary reinforcement alone" (1957b p. 1). The details are presented as follows:

Apparatus. The apparatus can best be described as a conventional straight-alley runway, the starting box of which is a Skinner box. The Skinner-box segment is separated from the runway segment by a guillotine door of the usual kind. Food pellets can be delivered in the goal box through a small chute. One wall of the Skinner box is removable in such a way that a new wall, fitted with a bar, can be inserted.

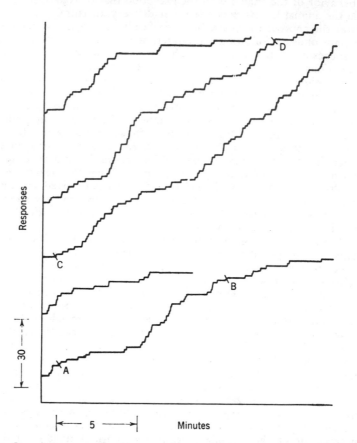

Fig. 4–6. Cumulative records of bar pressing obtained by means of unusually powerful secondary reinforcement (Zimmerman, 1957a, p. 374). The two lower curves (which are continuous) were obtained on the first test day, whereas the three upper curves (also continuous) were obtained on the second test day. From the origin of the lowest curve to A, the subject (a laboratory rat) received the secondary reinforcer each time it pressed the bar. From A to B, a one-minute fixed-interval schedule of reinforcement was used. No reinforcement occurred on the first day after B. At C (second day), the fixed-interval reinforcement procedure was resumed. Reinforcement was withdrawn at D. For further details, see text.

Training. The training which the animals [rats] first receive is in many respects similar to that involved in the usual kind of runway acquisition. The animal is placed in the starting box, and several seconds later a buzzer sounds briefly and the gate lifts. This event (the buzzer in combination with the lifting of the gate) is what will here be referred to as the "secondary reinforcer." Following this event, obviously, it is possible for the animal to run quickly to the end of the runway and receive food in the goal box. This event thus qualifies as a secondary reinforcer in the usual sense: it is an event which is closely and consistently associated with the consumption of food in the goal box. And, as will be shown, it becomes itself capable of strengthening instrumental behavior. But, it should be noted, the buzzer and gate-raising is not the sort of thing which is usually considered as a secondary reinforcer in runway experiments. Ordinarily cues such as the color of the goal box are studied. The event here studied precedes (and "releases") the whole instrumental behavior chain of moving along the runway and entering the goal box.

The runway training is continued [for 15 or 20 trials] until the running times are near asymptote. At this point *intermittent* reinforcement is introduced, according to the scheduling procedure previously described (Zimmerman, 1957a). At first food is omitted in the goal box on alternate trials; then successively longer and longer sequences of non-reinforced trials are interspersed between the reinforced ones. This kind of intermittent scheduling is distinctive in that (a) it is programmed randomly, in such a way that there is no regular pattern or sequence of reinforcement and non-reinforcement and (b) it is built up gradually, rather than being introduced "all at once" from the beginning. The training is continued until a *terminal* ratio of approximately one reinforced trial to every 8 non-reinforced trials is reached.

This intermittent scheduling is used so that the animal will run without primary reinforcement. If at any time the behavior begins to extinguish it is necessary to drop back to a lower ratio and begin working up anew. After such training we have a situation in which a rat will reliably and predictably respond to the opening of the gate by running to the goal box, where, however, food is found only occasionally.

Testing. At this point a novel feature is introduced in that the animal can now cause the gate to lift by pressing a bar which is inserted into the starting box. Primary reward in the goal box is, however, discontinued at this point; and the secondary reinforcing properties of the buzzer and gatelifting are relied upon, exclusively, to strengthen the bar-pressing behavior.[10]

As far as the bar-pressing is concerned, in other words, *acquisition* now

---

[10] To the thoughtful reader a relationship will be apparent between the procedure just described and some of the ideas expressed in the quotation from Skinner, p. 106. Especially relevant here is the statement: "The process is that of adding an initial member to a chain of reflexes without ultimately reinforcing the chain." In other words, Skinner is saying that once a sequence of actions has acquired a modicum of "habit strength" (or response momentum), a new action can be added as an "initial member" of the chain *after* the chain has ceased to lead to (primary) reinforcement. This can only mean, presumably, that stimuli inherently associated with the action sequence have taken on secondary-reinforcing (hope-

begins; but with respect to the running behavior the procedure at this point becomes one of *extinction*. But because of the previous intermittent-reinforcement training, the non-reinforcement condition which now holds with regard to running is not clearly demarcated, for the rat, from the foregoing acquisition. In common sense terms, we would thus say that the animal is "fooled" or "tricked" into working for a chance to execute behavior that is actually futile [see Chapter 12].

As soon as the bar-pressing behavior "catches hold"—after five or six runs —it, in turn, is only intermittently reinforced (secondarily). This further prolongs the effect. The final stable performance which is obtained, then, is this: the animal presses the bar in the starting box over and over again; and occasionally the gate lifts, releasing a run toward the empty goal box. Then the animal is returned to the starting box again, and the cycle is repeated (Zimmerman, 1957b, pp. 1–4).

Preliminary results with this technique show that animals can be made to emit as many as 2,000 bar-pressing responses, with secondary reinforcement only, and that even then the buzzer and gate raising have not entirely lost their secondary-reinforcement potency. This figure, of 2,000-plus responses, is to be compared with the 15 T-maze runs reported by Saltzman and the 30 to 60 bar pressings obtained by Skinner (Section IV). There thus remains no question that secondary reinforcement, given the proper conditions, can be exceedingly persistent and powerful (see also Zimmerman, 1958, 1959).[11] This fact is of crucial importance for the on-going argument of this volume as a whole; but before that argument can be systematically developed, it will be necessary, in the two succeeding chapters, to assimilate some of the more immediate implications thereof.

———

arousing) capacity, which persists for a time after primary reinforcement has been withdrawn. From this the notion, which is to be developed more fully in Chapter 7, it follows that "habit strength" *is* secondary reinforcement, and not a connection or bond of the type posited by Thorndike and Hull. The genius of the Zimmerman experiment, it may be added, lies in its use of intermittent reinforcement (at both the primary and secondary levels) as a means of keeping secondary reinforcement (hope) from extinguishing (see Chapters 11 and 12).

[11] In the passage previously cited (p. 113), Razran has held that the evidence, as of 1955, suggested that second-order conditioning (as conceived by Pavlov) and for secondary reinforcement (as conceived by Hull) was equally sparce and unimpressive. Since a method has now been reported for establishing extremely powerful secondary reinforcement, the interesting possibility is opened up that, by the same basic methodology ("double" intermittent reinforcement), higher-order conditioning could also be made more effective, i.e., capable of being carried to "orders," or levels, well beyond the second (or, in the case of "defense" conditioning, the third) order. This is a possibility which would seem to warrant immediate investigation.

VI. Special Implications of the Experiments of Culler and His Students

Too late to be systematically integrated into this chapter, a number of highly pertinent observations have been discovered in a paper published in 1941 by Eccher & Culler. These will be presented in the order in which they are mentioned by the authors and will be articulated with various aspects of the argument which has just been concluded. First of all, Eccher & Culler say:

Finch and Culler (1934), using paw-withdrawal in dogs as the response, succeeded in conditioning to it stimuli of first, second, third, fourth, and fifth order successively by the simple expedient of applying a shock to the left thorax whenever the subject failed to respond. They ascribed the failure of Frolov (Pavlov, 1927, p. 33) and of Foursikov (Pavlov, 1927, p. 34) to surmount the second or third order as due to inadequate drive or activation of the animal (p. 223).

This excerpt bears upon the phenomenon of higher-order conditioning (discussed in Section II) and throws further doubt upon the argument that classical conditioning theory can be made to account for active avoidance learning (Chapters II and III). Here is active avoidance learning, long maintained, without any recourse whatever to the specific, unconditioned stimulus for leg flexion, namely, shock to the foot or paw. However, the stimulus actually used (namely, shock to the "left thorax" or lateral chest area) *is* an adequate (unconditioned) stimulus for the emotional response of *fear;* and Finch & Culler show that by keeping *it* alive, they were able to keep their subjects responding to various formerly indifferent (conditioned) stimuli without (after initial conditioning) subsequently presenting shock to the dog's paw.[12] Although not commonly cited in this connection, the Finch-Culler experiment thus clearly argues against the classical conditioning interpretation of active avoidance learning and constitutes yet another line of evidence in favor of fear as an intervening variable. The authors are, of course, in error in thinking of these experiments as showing higher-order conditioning. If we think of fear as the conditioned reaction in these experiments (and of paw lifting as an instrumental habit or adjustment made thereto), then shock to the chest could serve as an unconditioned or reinforcing stimulus for *fear* quite as well as shock to the leg or paw of the dog.

[12] Actually, as the Mowrer-Lamoreaux experiment suggests (p. 73), one could probably even *start* the defensive leg-retraction response with the thoracic shock.

Eccher & Culler next report:

Brogden (1939), instead of punishing the animals upon failure to react in successively higher orders [as Finch & Culler had done, by mea.is of thoracic shock], rewarded them with food when they did respond. He was thus able to extend conditioning as far as the fourth-order (p. 223).

Here again there is a question of interpretation. It is certainly true that one cannot legitimately think of food as an unconditioned stimulus for paw retraction, but neither is it legitimate to speak of the results which Brogden obtained as representing higher-order conditioning. As is now well known, food can readily and directly impart secondary re-inforcing power to any stimulus associated therewith; and this is all that is needed to keep alive a bit of behavior such as leg retraction. This statement follows in part from considerations advanced in this chapter; but will be more completely amplified in Chapter 7.

Then Eccher & Culler say:

In the course of further experimentation with higher-order motor con-ditioning in cats, we noted quite by accident and much to our surprise, that the first order CR (bell-flexion) showed no sign of impairment when used as the conditioning agent in second-order (tone + bell). The bell-response alone, when not supported by shock reinforcement, quickly extinguished in the usual way; but when used for second-order conditioning, it became if anything increasingly vigorous and stable (p. 223).

The unusual curves shown in Fig. 4–7 record systematic evidence on this score. The curve extending from 0 to 10 along the baseline depicts the incidence of paw retraction in 24 cats in response to a bell which, if not responded to, was reinforced by electric shock to the paw. The curve which then extends downward shows the progressive extinction of this response (in two animals) when the bell was presented and *not* followed by shock if there was no leg flexion. The continuously ascend-ing curve, on the other hand, shows what happened when 11 animals were subjected to higher-order conditioning, involving tone and bell (but no shock). And the final descending curve (for one animal) shows the extinction of the paw-retraction response to the second-order conditioned stimulus (tone) when this stimulus was no longer reinforced by the first-order conditioned stimulus (bell).[13]

Here it does indeed appear, as Eccher & Culler state, that when a first-order conditioned response (bell-response) is "used for second-

---

[13] The animals not otherwise accounted for in this experiment (from the 24 which received initial training) were used for other purposes which are of no immediate interest.

order conditioning, it becomes if anything increasingly vigorous and stable." But there were some very interesting features of this experiment which might easily escape one's attention. It should be noted, first of all, that in the second stage of this experiment, wherein 11 animals received a combination of tone and bell, the bell followed the tone *only* on those trials when there was no response to the tone. ("The reader is reminded that in group III the bell is sounded only when subject *fails* to react to the tone," p. 228.) So the procedure used here, in this second-order conditioning, involved intermittent rather than continuous reinforcement; or, said differently, the conditioning procedure was instrumental rather than classical. This procedure, it seems,

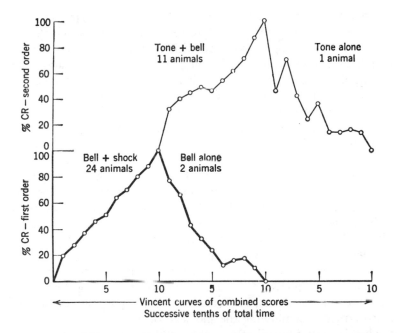

Fig. 4-7. Curves reproduced from Eccher & Culler (1941) showing the results of two forms of conditioning and two forms of extinction. In the curve extending from 0 to 10 (along the baseline), bell was paired (instrumentally) with shock to cat's forepaw; and when shock was discontinued, leg flexion to bell alone extinguished as shown. But during the intermediate third of the experiment, tone and bell were paired instrumentally (in second-order conditioning), with the results shown. When bell was discontinued, leg flexion to tone also extinguished. The somewhat unusual units along the baseline result from the combining of data from several animals into so-called Vincent curves.

had two distinct advantages: (a) it meant that the reinforcing potential of the bell was "used up" less rapidly than it would have been in a classical-reinforcement procedure; and (b) the defensive reaction of paw-lifting was also learned more readily than it would have been if bell had followed tone willy-nilly.

Eccher & Culler put it this way:

> The CR to bell, which is now used as the conditioning agent, becomes both more brisk and more vigorous; hurried instead of deliberate. The cat gives every appearance of "fearing" the bell even more than the shock. Instead of delaying as in first-order it now seems anxious to get the foot out of the danger-zone with utmost dispatch. We hesitate to introspect for the cat or to speculate upon its experience; but the increased force of the CR is undeniable (p. 230).

Although it was Brogden, Lipman, & Culler who, in 1938, reported the experiment with guinea pigs in the revolvable cage which did so much toward discrediting classical conditioning theory, at least as an explanation of active avoidance learning, and so strongly suggested the concept of fear as an essential intervening variable, yet it is apparent that in their 1941 paper Eccher & Culler were still hesitant and apologetic in their use of the fear concept. As we have seen near the beginning of this section, they would have been on much sounder grounds if they had been more daring. What they needed to recognize was that a stimulus, for example the bell, which precedes shock—*any* shock, tends to acquire the capacity to arouse fear and that the reduction of this fear can then be used to reinforce any given item of behavior, for example, leg flexion. And fear, of course, has aversive properties in its own right, so that once acquired as a regular response to bell, an organism will do what it can to prevent its occurrence. Thus, if tone precedes bell, it is not surprising if some fear gets conditioned to it; but this fear will be less strong than that which occurs to the bell, so there is a net gain if the animal responds to the tone rather than allowing the bell to occur (just as there is a gain, in first-order conditioning, in responding to the bell rather than allowing the shock to occur).

But what is most immediately pertinent about the experiment described by Eccher & Culler is their introduction of a procedure which is a sort of forerunner or counterpart of the methodology developed and employed by Zimmerman to such dramatic advantage (Section V). Skinner, in the experiment described in Section IV, found that if he associated the click of the food-delivery mechanism 60 times with the delivery of a small pellet of food, this click alone would serve to reinforce rats for 30 to 60 bar-pressing responses (without food). Now what Zimmerman did, in effect, was to repeat the Skinner experiment but to use intermittent reinforcement both in the training (click, food) and the test (bar-press, click) phases of the experiment. In other words, in the first part of the experiment he used an intermittent classical conditioning procedure, and in the second part he used an intermittent instrumental. What Eccher & Culler did was to use two instrumental *avoidance* training procedures in succession, the one involving first-order, the other second-order, conditioning. But the very fact of instrumentality meant that the procedure also involved intermittency; so that one may say that here, too, in the Eccher-Culler experiment, was a procedure involving double intermittent reinforcement—but with certain differences, prominently including the fact that the Eccher-Culler experiment involved the conditioning of fear (or secondary motivation), whereas the Zimmerman experiment involved the conditioning of hope (or secondary reinforcement). In both instances remarkable resistance to extinction was observed, the fuller understanding of which will have to be postponed to Chapters 11 and 12. But they indicate clearly that both fear and hope can have considerable potency and, if properly handled, also great persistence.

Now it will be useful, in the next section, to take our conceptual bearings and see, more precisely, where we are and where we are going.

VII. The Argument Summarized [14]

In previous chapters we have seen that, by the turn of the century, Pavlov and Thorndike had advanced two quite different (though equally behavioristic) conceptions of the learning process, the one stressing conditioning or stimulus substitution and the other stressing trial-and-error learning or response substitution. Hull attempted, unsuccessfully, to "integrate" these two theories; and many psycholo-

[14] One of the learning-theory experts who read and criticized the original manuscript of this book found the use of these recurrent, cummulative summaries tedious. Others may have a similar reaction. However, from extended experience in teaching this material, it is apparent that students profit from and are grateful for this arrangement. Even the professional psychologist will not find these summaries to be sheer repetition of an unchanging refrain or "chorus," after each new "verse" (chapter). Instead, the summaries attempt to remind the reader of the general context or over-all argument and to show how the just preceding discussion logically fits into it. If, however, a reader finds the summaries genuinely nonfunctional, he can, of course, easily omit them.

gists continued to assume that Pavlov and Thorndike had identified two distinctly different forms of learning. This is what may be called the *first* two-factor, or two-process, conception of learning.

But then it gradually became apparent that punishment does not "stamp out" stimulus-response bonds (or habits) in the direct way which Thorndike had supposed and that so-called defense or avoidance behavior is likewise not directly conditioned, as Pavlovian theory implied. In the latter connection, *fear* was soon introduced as an essential intervening variable; and the same phenomenon was used to derive a new (conflict) theory of punishment.

On the basis of these developments, two-factor theory was then modified in the following way (to become version *two*). Conditioning continued to be accepted as a real phenomenon, but it was redefined so as to apply only to the acquisition of new *emotional* reactions, of which *fear* was taken as the prime example; and the acquisition of fear was assumed, more specifically, to be dependent upon the conjunction of a formerly neutral stimulus with the *onset* of some noxious stimulus or drive (such as electric shock). By contrast, the termination or *reduction* of such a drive was assumed to provide the conditions necessary for habit formation (and secondary reinforcement type-1). Emotional learning (conditioning) was thus identified as *sign* learning and habit formation (trial and error) as *solution* learning. In the acquisition of active and passive avoidance behavior, it was assumed that *both* forms of learning are involved: fear becomes conditioned to some formerly neutral (independent or response-dependent) stimulus and the organism develops, as a "habit," whatever response will eliminate the danger signal and reduce the attendant fear. Thus, whereas sign learning was *restricted* to emotional conditioning, solution learning was *extended* to include learning where secondary, as well as primary, drives are concerned.

This revised version of two-factor learning theory had numerous advantages and strengths, but it also had two major weaknesses: it continued to accept, essentially unmodified, Thorndike's conception of habit ("bond") formation; and it did not adequately recognize or explain what has been referred to in this chapter as secondary reinforcement type-2. Here we have seen that a stimulus with type-2 secondary reinforcement capacity can exhibit this capacity in either of two, quite different ways: (a) it can produce higher-order conditioning or (b) it can set up a new "habit" of some sort. In the one case, the type-2 secondary reinforcer precedes and *produces* the response which is to be associatively shifted (conditioned) to the new stimulus;

whereas in the other case it *follows* the new response which is to be selectively strengthened. Thus, one and the same stimulus, if it has type-2 reinforcement capacity, can serve these two distinctive functions. Pavlov, as we have seen, was especially interested in the first, Hull in the second.[15]

Although both of the effects of type-2 secondary reinforcement have been repeatedly reported in the experimental literature, the evidence suggested that these phenomena were, at best, transitory and unstable; and some investigators even questioned their reality altogether. In the present chapter new and dramatic proof of the existence and potency of secondary reinforcement type-2 is reported; so we are justified (in the following chapters) in making a careful and searching analysis of this phenomenon from a more theoretical and interpretative standpoint. In the end we shall find that type-2 secondary reinforcement is probably destined to bring about a change in our thinking about habit formation as radical and as important as the change which secondary reinforcement type-1 produced in our thinking about punishment and active avoidance learning.[16]

[15] As implied earlier in this chapter (Section IV), the distinction between these two functions of a secondary reinforcer (S^r) is not so great as it at first appears to be. For example, a careful re-analysis of the Zimmerman (or any similar) experiment will reveal that when an S^r is used to establish a new habit, it actually achieves this effect by means of higher-order conditioning. If we assume that the secondary reinforcer itself produces a "response" of some sort (see Chapter 5), and if we further assume that any given bit of behavior which we wish to make habitual (such, for example, as bar pressing) regularly produces a distinctive pattern of sensory feedback as it occurs, i.e., response-correlated stimuli, then the S^r, in effect, serves as the "unconditioned" stimulus for getting its "response" (of secondary reinforcement) shifted, or conditioned, to the stimuli which the to-be-habituated action produces. This, as already remarked, is higher-order conditioning, pure and simple. But the cogency of this way of thinking will not be fully apparent until the new conception of habit which is emerging as our discussion proceeds becomes fully explicit, in Chapter 7. This footnote is therefore, in a sense, out of order; but it will help prepare the reader for this new conception of habit when it is later presented. (See also Chapter 12, Section V.)

[16] Too late for a textual revision (p. 103), it was realized that Hull's Corollaries i and ii are *not* strictly identical in their implications. Cor. ii says that a formerly neutral stimulus which occurs "in *close* conjunction" with drive reduction will become a secondary reinforcer; whereas Cor. i says that a formerly neutral stimulus, if it is associated somewhat *less* closely (in time) with drive reduction, will become a secondary motivator. After examination of Chapters 5 and 9, the reader will see that this distinction, though real, is trivial and cannot bear the explanatory load which Hull placed upon it.

5

Secondary Reinforcement: A Unifying Theory

In light of the very substantial evidence reviewed in previous chapters, there can be no reasonable doubt as to the reality of either type-1 or type-2 secondary reinforcement. The question is now no longer one of fact but of interpretation, explanation, *theory*. When behavior terminates a danger signal (either an independent or a response-correlated one) and, as a result, becomes increasingly likely to occur in the presence thereof, we are justified in inferring that the reinforcing agent is the fear reduction which presumably occurs when the danger signal ends. An occasional attempt is still made to explain such learning in terms of classical conditioning or in some other ultra-objective way; but the evidence clearly favors the notion that secondary reinforcement, of the type-1 variety, is here involved. By contrast, although secondary reinforcement type-2 is now also firmly established as an empircial fact, there is little or no agreement as to how it is mediated. The purpose of the present chapter is to put forward, and cite evidence for, a theory of type-2 secondary reinforcement which will bring this phenomenon into a consistent and systematic relationship to secondary reinforcement type-1.

I. Type-2 Secondary Reinforcement as Decremental Fear Conditioning or "Hope"

Perhaps the best way of beginning this discussion will be to revert to the conceptual scheme suggested in Chapter 2 to account for fear conditioning, of the incremental variety. For convenience of reference, Fig. 2-1 is reproduced here as Fig. 5-1. This diagram involves an assumption which invites further consideration and suggests some interesting possibilities. The present writer had originally taken the position that fear is a "conditioned form of the pain reaction" (Mowrer, 1939; see also Chapter 4, p. 93). If, for example, electric shock is thought of as an unconditioned stimulus and pain as the unconditioned reaction, then the fear reaction elicited by a formerly neutral stimulus, which has been paired with the shock, would be the *conditioned reaction*. But N. E. Miller (1948b) was probably closer to the truth when he suggested that fear is instead a part of the total response innately produced by a painfully intense stimulus, such as electric shock, and that, in conditioning, this particular response component (unlike the pain component, which is not conditionable, or only weakly so) gets shifted from the UnCS to the CS, in the manner of classical Pavlovian theory.[1]

Fig. 5-1. Commonly used conceptual scheme for indicating the circumstances under which the emotion of fear, initially aroused by an "unconditioned" stimulus like electric shock, becomes conditioned to a formerly neutral stimulus which has been paired with onset of shock.

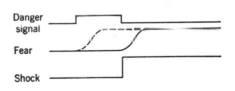

In other words, Miller argued that fear occurs to shock, along with various other reactions (including pain), but that it alone is readily conditionable; whereas the view previously suggested was that pain is the principal reaction to shock and that when it becomes conditioned, it is transformed into and experienced as fear. As far as fear (as a conditioned, or anticipatory, response) is concerned, these

[1] Miller's notion here is analogous to the r_g concept advanced by Hull in his discussion of type-2 secondary reinforcement. If the *total* reaction to electric shock is represented as R_g, then fear, as a "fractional component" thereof, may be denoted as r_g. However, the "g," it will be recalled, stands for "goal"; and one cannot very meaningfully speak of fear and the other responses aroused by a painful electric shock as a "goal reaction." Because we are here attempting to develop a way of thinking that will encompass both type-1 and type-2 secondary reinforcement, Hull's r_g notation thus lacks the desired generality. A preferable notation would be R_i, to refer to the total reaction elicited by incremental reinforcement, and r_f, to indicate the conditionable (fear) component thereof. In like manner, R_d can be used to denote the total reaction to decremental reinforcement (reward) and r_h, as the conditionable (hope) component (see below).

two ways of thinking come to much the same thing. But they have quite different implications when one turns to a consideration of the reactions or states of mind which are aroused by the noxious stimulus itself. It is with the latter that we are now especially concerned; and here we find that Miller's formulation lends itself quite ideally to our purposes.

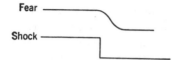

Fig. 5–2. Schematic indication of the probable relationship between termination of a noxious stimulus, such as electric shock, and the accompanying emotion of fear.

If, as Miller suggests, fear is aroused by the onset of a noxious (unconditioned) stimulus, we may reasonably infer that *fear continues to be experienced (in some degree) as long as this stimulus is present.* The question which then arises is: What happens to the fear when the unconditioned stimulus terminates? Since studies involving the galvanic-skin-reaction technique show that, following shock onset, the fear reaction builds up rather slowly (as indicated in Fig. 5–1), it is reasonable to suppose that it subsides, following the end of shock, roughly in the manner shown in Fig. 5–2. If this be true, then the next question to suggest itself is whether fear reduction, *following* shock reduction, can be conditioned to an antecedent stimulus, just as fear induction following shock onset can be. If so, we are justified in showing, in Fig. 5–3, at the right, what is essentially the mirror image, or counterpart, of Fig. 5–1 reproduced here at the left.

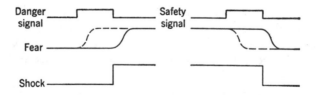

Fig. 5–3. Composite of diagrams shown in Figs. 5–1 and 5–2, with two added features. As will be seen, a "safety signal" has been added to the diagram at the right; and the broken lines suggest how the drop in fear that occurs after the end of shock may become anticipatory.

If this schematization is valid, then we may assume (a) that secondary reinforcements types 1 and 2 *both involve fear reduction* but that (b) the fear which is reduced in the two instances is at least operationally different: in secondary reinforcement type-1, it is aroused by and terminates with a mere *danger signal;* whereas, in secondary reinforcement type-2, fear is aroused by some inherently noxious stimulus—which is "already present"—and is reduced by the appearance of what is in effect a *safety signal*, indicating that the noxious stimulus will soon end. Thus, we may say that in secondary reinforcement type-2 the subject will learn whatever behavior *gets* the safety signal; whereas in secondary reinforcement type-1 the subject will learn whatever behavior *gets rid* of the danger signal. Superficially, these two learning situations are antithetical, getting and getting rid of a signal of some kind. But *getting rid* of a danger signal is dynamically (hedonistically) equivalent to *getting* a safety signal; and this is why we may now speak of these two forms of secondary reinforcement as being much the same in principle.

The reader must, of course, bear in mind that the ways in which a danger signal and a safety signal, as here defined, acquire their *meanings* are indeed antithetical: a danger signal, by association with *onset* of some noxious stimulus; and a safety signal, by association with the *offset* of such a stimulus. And it is precisely because of this difference in meaning that the appearance of one type of signal is functionally equivalent to the disappearance of the other. As we shall later see, the "integrative," or "resolving," power of this formulation is considerable; [2] but it involves a logical complication which was first pointed out to the writer by Mr. Murray S. Miron.

If the reader will again refer to Fig. 5–3, he will be reminded that we are here accepting Miller's notion that fear is an "unconditioned" response to a painfully intense stimulus, such as can be provided by electric shock, and that if such a stimulus is preceded by a signal, fear may become attached to it as a *conditioned* response. And there is, of course, nothing enigmatic about the hypothesis that if fear is aroused, as a conditioned response to a signal, it can also be allayed by termination of this signal. If the signal *causes* the fear, its termination should also be a sufficient condition for cessation of the fear.

But in going beyond this point, we encounter a complication. In

[2] More or less independently, a number of writers seem to be moving toward this general point of view. For example, Jourard (1958) writes as follows: "It is convenient, and perhaps valid to think of the liking-response as a conditioned response, or more precisely, as the affective component of an expectancy. The object which induces the liking-response has, in the past, produced satisfaction, or is related to something which produced satisfaction. The liking-response is a sort of *preparatory set* for something satisfying to occur, just as anxiety is a preparatory set for something painful to occur" (p. 195). Cf. also Henle (1956), McGuigan (1956), and Olds (1954, p. 232).

the right half of Fig. 5–3 we are assuming that, if a signal precedes the *end* of shock, the reduction in fear which follows shock termination can also be conditioned to that signal and will, on later occasions, take place *before* shock termination. The crux of the dilemma posed by Mr. Miron, then, is this: How can fear be an *unconditioned* response to shock and yet be capable of anticipatory (learned, conditioned) reduction, on the basis of the occurrence of a *mere signal* of shock termination? Or, in different words, if shock is a sufficient and necessary cause of fear, how can the addition of another stimulus eliminate the fear, while the shock is still present?

This is obviously an important question. There are, however, two plausible and mutually compatible answers.

For a number of years it has been known that a primary drive, such as an electric shock, may have, in addition to drive properties, also signal or *cue* properties. This can be readily demonstrated in the following way. Suppose that a "naive" (i.e., previously unshocked) rat is put on a grill and that an electrical charge is gradually imposed on the grill, starting at zero intensity and building up, progressively, to a relatively high intensity. Suppose, also, that after reaching this intensity, the shock is suddenly turned off and that after a rest interval of two or three minutes, the shock is again gradually built up. On the second or, at most, third presentation of shock in this way, it will be observed that the rat starts "churning" its feet, running, jumping, and squealing at a considerably *lower intensity* of shock than was necessary to produce these reactions on the *first* trial.

How is one to explain such an observation? It does not seem likely that the animal has become literally "more sensitive" to shock, so that a weaker intensity "hurts" just as much as a stronger intensity originally did. The usual effect of repeated exposure to and experience with electric shock, short of actually damaging intensities, is to make one somewhat "adapted" to it. More likely is the possibility that, under the circumstances described, the shock, at the weaker intensities, becomes a "conditioned stimulus," or *signal*, for the stronger intensities of shock *which are to follow*. This would mean that, though the shock, as a primary drive, does not become subjectively any stronger at the low intensities, these intensities of shock *cue off* relatively strong fear, which in turn helps to motivate, more quickly now, the various forms of agitated behavior which, on the first trial, are eventually produced by shock alone.[3]

[3] Observation of a parallel effect, with hunger drive, has been reported by Mandler (1958). Here rats which had previously, and repeatedly, been subjected

Taking this demonstration as a paradigm, we may therefore reason that, especially with drives which gradually mount in intensity (as primary drives often do) but even with drives of relatively sudden onset and continuous intensity, there is a tendency for fear to occur in response thereto, both on a conditioned and an unconditioned basis. Hence, to return to the Miron paradox, we conjecture that it would be possible for *at least the conditioned portion* of the fear produced by a drive such as electric shock to undergo anticipatory reduction in response to a signal of impending shock termination. The unconditioned portion would, of course, by definition persist until the shock itself terminated; but since it appears that the conditioned portion of the total fear elicited by a primary drive (or "unconditional" stimulus) may be considerable, there is still ample latitude for secondary reinforcement, as fear reduction in advance of primary drive reduction, to operate in the manner hypothesized.

II. The Miron Paradox Further Considered

If what has thus far been said, in the preceding section, is clear and convincing to the reader, he should perhaps go at once to Section III. If not, he may profit from the following additional discussion.

One of the things that may make the foregoing analysis somewhat obscure is the fact that in the example given, of a gradually mounting electric shock, both the conditioned and the unconditioned stimuli for fear (i.e., different intensities of electric shock) impinge upon the organism through the same sensory modality. Ordinarily, in fear conditioning, we produce the fear, on an unconditioned basis, by a painfully intense shock and pair with it, for example, a light or sound of some sort. However, in principle, there is nothing different in using a faint shock (which just "tickles") as a conditioned stimulus and a more intense shock as the UnCS. Perhaps all this is clearer if we use, not a continuous, gradually increasing shock, but two discrete intensities of shock, as shown in Fig. 5–4. Here the weak shock is completely innocuous and, if the subject is "naive," has no tendency to arouse fear. If, however, this intensity of shock is followed a few times by

---

to severe food deprivation later reacted to *mild* deprivation by *eating more* than did control animals. "In both experiments the experimental Ss exhibited accelerated and more frequent consummatory behavior. . . . Within a Hullian framework this finding suggests that the definition of drive (D) in terms of hours of deprivation alone is inadequate: Previous deprivation experience of the animal must be taken into account" (pp. 516–517).

the higher intensity shown, it would be very surprising if the subject did not soon start reacting to the weak shock with fear, in anticipation of the strong shock to follow. To the best of the writer's knowledge, no one has performed an experiment of precisely this kind, with either mice or men; but the outcome is pretty much a foregone conclusion, especially since it has been observed, as previously noted, that with recurrent presentation of a gradually mounting shock of the kind described, evidences of fear occur sooner and sooner. *In principle*, there is no difference between the two situations.

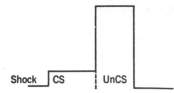

Fig. 5–4. Suggested scheme for making a faint electric shock serve as the conditioned stimulus, and a much higher intensity of the same stimulus serve as the unconditioned stimulus, in fear conditioning.

Or, let us consider a different, though not incompatible, solution to the Miron dilemma. If the idea of the fear, reflexly aroused by strong shock, being conditioned to a weak intensity of the same stimulus which precedes it does not seem very attractive, we may think about the problem in the following way. If a rat experiences protracted shock in a given experimental situation, that situation will become "fear-charged"; which is to say, the fear aroused by the shock will become conditioned to the preceding and accompanying constellation of stimuli which we call the "situation." Therefore, when our subject is put into this situation, he will experience considerable fear, in advance of the shock being turned on; and when the shock is applied, the animal, having previously suffered protracted shock here, will again "expect the worst." In other words, to the unconditioned pain and fear produced by the shock is now added the conditioned fear produced by the situation.

If, now, after such training, the rat were given, let us say, a tone for two or three seconds just before the shock terminated and the animal got out of the apparatus, the tone could easily acquire secondary reinforcing capacity in the following sense. When the shock is on, the situation-without-tone is *dangerous*, i.e., the situation is one in which shock may continue for an unpredictable period of time. On the other hand, the situation-*with*-tone (even though shock is still present) is *not* dangerous, in the sense just suggested, because the subject will soon be delivered from shock *and* situation. Therefore the tone will be heard with a feeling of "hope," which is what we mean here by "secondary reinforcement."

At first it may appear that this resolution of the Miron paradox is no different from the one first proposed. But the assumption here is that the fear which is capable of being "turned off" by the safety signal is not (necessarily) conditioned to the shock stimulus itself, but to the *situation* in which that stimulus has been experienced. And when the safety signal occurs, it *changes the situation*, from one in which shock may be experienced indefinitely to one in which it "will be over in a moment." Hence we do not here have to assume either that a conditioned stimulus relaxes an unconditioned response (the Miron dilemma) or that it relaxes a component of fear that has become conditioned to the unconditioned stimulus. We may assume instead, simply, that there are *two* situations: situation-with-shock-but-no-tone and situation-with-shock-and-tone, the one being quite ominous, the other much less so. And the specific stimulus, the tone, which makes the *difference* may be thought of equally as a *cue*, for making a "discrimination" between the two situations (see also Chapter 12), and as a *secondary reinforcer.*

As already noted, the nice thing about the two possible resolutions of the Miron dilemma advanced above is that they are not in any sense opposed to one another. Either could be correct (or incorrect) without necessarily prejudicing the validity of the other; and, what seems most likely, they may *both* be valid and operate simultaneously. Thus we happily escape from what at first seemed like a formidable difficulty and, in so doing, derive some new ways of thinking which will stand us in good stead at several later stages in our analysis.

By way, then, of summarizing the discussion in this and the preceding section, let us suppose that a shock of *moderate* intensity is suddenly applied to the grill on which a rat is sitting. Assuming the rat to be naive with respect to such stimulation, the shock will be immediately felt as "painful" and the rat will show "surprise" and mildly agitated behavior; and if the shock continues, with nothing to be *done* about it, we see the rat gradually become more and more "worried." To the pain and unconditioned fear caused by the shock at any given moment is now added a *conditioned* fear, i.e., fear of *more* pain. (One can conjecture that there would even be, not just a fear of more pain, but also fear of *more fear*, i.e., the fear to follow. This, presumably, is what William James and, later, F. D. Roosevelt meant by "fear of fear.") Thus, although the *pain* caused by the shock remains about the same, the *total discomfort* presumably mounts—and may eventually result in a sort of "frenzy" or "panic." Eskimos, it is said, in the old days sometimes committed suicide because of a protracted toothache. It is not that the ache at any given moment is so unbearable, but rather that the *fear of continued pain* (and continued fear?), cued off by the present pain (and fear?), becomes intolerable. It is then, presumably, this *conditioned* element in the total experience of discomfort that can be lessened by "reassurance" in human beings, or by a "safety signal" in rats, and provides the basis for *hope*.[4]

III. Empirical Evidence for Proposed Theory of Secondary Reinforcement Type-2

More than a decade ago Mowrer & Viek called attention to a commonplace example of type-2 secondary reinforcement, as follows:

One of the commonest yet most dramatic illustrations of this phenomenon is the relief experienced when a physician is consulted. One is ill and suffering from pain and inconvenience. The physician arrives, diagnoses the difficulty, prescribes treatment, and intimates that in a day or two one will be quite hale again. It is unlikely that the examination or the ensuing exchange of words has altered the *physical* condition of the patient in the least; yet he is likely to "feel a lot better" as a result of the doctor's call. What obviously happens in such instances is that initially the patient's physical suffering is complicated by concern lest his suffering continue indefinitely or perhaps grow worse. After a reassuring diagnosis, this concern abates; and if, subsequently, the same ailment recurs, one can predict that it will arouse less apprehension than it did originally (provided, of course, that the physician's reassurances were valid and his treatment effective) (Mowrer & Viek, 1948, p. 193).

Or one might consider a group of desert travelers who, almost dead from thirst, catch a glimpse of an oasis in the distance. Immediately they will feel relieved, hopeful. Their thirst will not as yet have les-

---

[4] A thoughtful student, with considerable background in Gestalt psychology (especially as taught in schools of education) has remarked upon the similarity between the foregoing ideas and the Gestalt conception of *closure,* in the sense of "completion." This term is used, particularly in the area of perception, to indicate the act of mentally completing a physically incomplete figure so as to give it a "good gestalt," a familiar form, a definite meaning. But it seems that the term is also used, more informally, to imply completion in the sense of consummation of a need, the satisfaction or reduction of a drive. Thus, a type-2 secondary reinforcer may be said to give promise of "closure" or drive reduction; and the reduction of drive thus forecast *is* the closure. This interpretation is unobjectionable so long as one remembers that the secondary reinforcer, in predicting primary drive reduction (closure), itself mediates a form of drive reduction, namely *secondary* drive reduction. (See also Chapter 9.)

sened, but the fear engendered thereby will be reduced. The oasis is a "safety signal," and its appearance would undoubtedly be powerfully reinforcing, albeit only secondarily so.

Intuitively compelling as they may be, such commonplace illustrations are not, however, the stuff of which an exact science is made. Therefore, it is fortunate that evidence of a more rigorous kind is available. In his review of the evidence for secondary reinforcement already alluded to, Miller (1951b) writes:

> Spragg (1940) showed that morphine-addicted chimpanzees will strive to get the syringe and other objects they have learned to associate with an injection. Sometimes the use of morphine may be reinforced by a reduction in fear like that described for alcohol, but in this experiment it seems probable that the motivation was produced by physiological withdrawal symptoms and hence was not a learned drive. Furthermore, the animals worked for the syringe only when they had withdrawal symptoms. Later in the experiment, however, incidental observations suggested that temporary relief from withdrawal symptoms could be produced by injections of physiological saline. Such relief must have been the product of learning and would be expected to give reward value to the cues involved in the injection (p. 462).

This observation provides an excellent paradigm for the conception of secondary reinforcement here under discussion. It is to be inferred that the morphine withdrawal symptoms, being severely painful, not only aroused a certain amount of reflexive fear but also a good deal of conditioned or anticipatory fear—fear based upon the possibility, born of past experience, that the present suffering might be followed by more and, quite possibly, worse suffering. An injection of morphine had, in the past, brought relief; so it is understandable, if the present line of thought is sound, that the mere *prospect* of such relief (at the physiological level) would be somewhat relieving (emotionally). This supposition seems to be confirmed by the observation that the animals were calmed (at least on the first few times it was tried— and then the familiar extinction problem arises) by an injection, not of morphine, but of an inert saline solution.

Here, obviously, is an instance of the well-known "placebo effect," as manifested at the human level [5]—and an illustration of the general principle of *suggestion*. This term has not been previously used in this book; and, to the writer's knowledge, it has not previously been discussed by others in the context of contemporary learning theory. But, from the foregoing considerations, it will be clear that so-called

[5] Cf. J. S. Brown's (1955) comment: "Wolff and Goodell (1943) have found that the administration of a placebo falsely described as aspirin can produce an actual increase in a subject's threshold for pain" (p. 175).

suggestion (of at least one kind) is but another name for the effect produced by a type-2 secondary reinforcer: it arouses hope or, equivalently, relieves apprehension and in so doing makes the individual *feel* better without, in a more fundamental sense, really *being* "better." This effect may be termed *positive* suggestion, to distinguish it from the opposite situation, wherein an individual is made to feel *worse* without, for the moment at any rate, really being any the worse off. In the latter case we speak of the arousal, not of hope, but of fear—to which, in like manner, we might apply the term, *negative* suggestion.

More systematic evidence for the phenomenon here under discussion is reported by Elithorn, Piercy, & Crosskey (1955) in a paper entitled "Prefrontal Leucotomy and the Anticipation of Pain." These investigators pose the problem thus:

> Since our own observations and those of others suggested that the frontal areas [of the human brain which are] damaged by leucotomy contain no primary vegetative centres, an attempt was made to devise a test which would measure autonomic changes which could be interpreted in terms of the psychological effects of leucotomy. A typical effect of a prefrontal destructive lesion, whether therapeutic or accidental, is an apparent reduction in the patient's feelings of anxiety. Further, an early paradoxical observation was that patients who suffered from severe pain, organic in origin, might be relieved of their suffering although their perception of pain remained unimpaired (Chapman, Rose, and Solomon, 1948). With a view therefore to analysing further the changed attitude to pain which follows prefrontal leucotomy the following test procedure was devised (p. 34).

It is not necessary to give the details of this study; but the relevant facts are contained in the summary, which reads as follows:

> In order to test the hypothesis that prefrontal leucotomy relieves painful conditions by reducing the anticipatory element of fear, a pain-expectancy test was devised. The relative disturbance caused by a painful shock and by a preceding warning light was estimated by measuring the ratio of the psychogalvanic responses aroused by these two stimuli. Twelve of the 13 patients examined showed post-operatively an increase in this ratio, which indicates a relative reduction in the autonomic disturbance caused by the warning signal. It was shown that this reduction in the anticipatory fear associated with a painful stimulus was not due to an alteration in the perception of pain or to a reduction in the amount of pain tolerated during the test.
>
> One subject, who had been relieved by leucotomy of a totally incapacitating preoccupation with a post-herpetic neuralgia, is reported in detail (pp. 42-43).

The fact that the painful electric shock continued to produce a vigorous psychogalvanic reflex indicates that the reflexive, or unconditioned, response of fear to pain is still intact after leucotomy; but the fact that a *signal* that shock is imminent produces, in leucotomized individuals, a diminished psychogalvanic response suggests, as the authors note, that "this reduction in the anticipatory fear" is a rather specific effect of the operation. In other words, it appears that the relief produced by leucotomy in cases of intractable pain is achieved by reducing the patient's capacity to "worry," i.e., to experience *conditioned* fear, rather than by reducing either reflexive fear or sensitivity to the noxious stimulation (pain) itself.

If, therefore, the element of discomfort (or "motivation") added by purely emotional factors in intractable pain is great enough to justify so radical an interventive measure as leucotomy, we are here dealing with no purely hypothetical construct, invented solely for purposes of theory construction. Put another way, what leucotomy apparently accomplishes is this: in cases where pain itself cannot be controlled and where the patient, as a result, has developed a state of chronic apprehension and hopelessness, this operation destroys the capacity to experience apprehension, or "anticipatory fear," and thus spares the patient one important element of his otherwise unavoidable suffering. Here we presumably see, *in extremis*, the mechanism whereby conditioned fear and its antithesis, hope, normally operate.[6]

Psychologists have only recently begun to explore the possibility that secondary reinforcement type-2 involves fear reduction no less than does secondary reinforcement type-1. Writing in 1954, Farber summed up the status of this argument as of that date, thus:

Another way in which these problems have been met has been to suppose that these latter events, usually designated as "secondary reinforcers," do somehow operate by reducing a drive. Mowrer, in discussing Estes' results, has speculated that ". . . when an organism is subjected to strong primary drive, there is commonly added to this the secondary motive of *anticipated* continuation of the primary drive" (Mowrer, 1950b, p. 149). It is this drive, according to Mowrer's view, that might be reduced by secondary reinforcers. [And] Whiting, in personal communication, has suggested that this hypothetical drive of "insecurity" might be regarded as an acquirable portion of drive states resulting from deprivation, just as fear or anxiety is regarded as an acquirable portion of the drive state resulting from noxious stimulation (Dollard & Miller, 1950).

A somewhat different conjecture with respect to a possible drive-reducing

[6] Further evidence for this view is provided by Hill, Belleville, & Wikler (1954) when they say, of an experiment with rats, "The results are analogous to those of the earlier studies on human subjects and support the hypothesis that reduction of anxiety associated with anticipation of pain is one necessary action of a potent analgesic" (p. 183). See also Barber (1959).

mechanism for secondary reinforcers has been discussed by Osgood (1953). Pointing out that there is evidence that specific hormones are associated with satiation as well as with hunger, he suggests that stimuli associated with drive reduction might serve as conditioned stimuli, releasing the hormones that accompany satiation.

It is probably not necessary to observe that these suggested mechanisms are hypotheses to be investigated, rather than conclusions drawn from empirical evidence. But I believe most psychologists would agree that the drive-reduction hypothesis has not been so unproductive that the investigation of these possibilities and their implications is unwarranted (pp. 7–8).

And even Hull, who did so much to popularize the r_g—s_g conception of secondary reinforcement as a form of *stimulation* rather than drive or stimulation *reduction* (see Chapter 4, also Chapter 6), in his 1952 book, *Essentials of Behavior*, took a position with respect to secondary reinforcement basically similar to the one presently under discussion. Hull said:

We must now observe that in a behavior sequence such as that of a rat passing from a compartment where its feet are receiving electric shocks on its way to a non-shock goal or compartment, there occurs a cessation not only of the shock stimuli but of the proprioceptive stimuli arising from the running. This major reduction in stimulation constitutes, of course, the concrete substance of the [primary] reinforcement of the running or escape activity, quite as ordinarily aroused. But it also constitutes much more, and this is the main point to observe: the cessation of the shocks not only brings the locomotor escape [sic], but also a general relaxation of the autonomic activity called *fear*. This relaxation process appears to become attached, much as positive activity would, to the stimuli active at the time, together with the traces of earlier stimuli. As a result, on later repetitions of the objective conditions in question this relaxation generalizes forward on those traces, and gives rise to conditioned inhibition. This has appropriately been called by Miller (1951b), *anticipatory relaxation* (pp. 26–27).

This is one of the very few occasions when Hull ever made formal reference to the concept of fear; and his infelicity in dealing with it here attests its unfamiliarity to him. However, it would be unfair (after the treatment of Hull's theorizing in Chapter 4) not to make reference to this gesture on his part in the direction of another kind of thinking.[7] The passage quoted serves, also, the useful purpose

---

[7] Although the passage just quoted can hardly be squared with the view that secondary reinforcement type-2 involves stimulation *increase* (as Hull elsewhere stipulated), one can, however, reconcile it with the notion of r_g. If one thinks of R_g as the totality of responses which occur to shock termination, then "anticipatory relaxation" of fear is a component thereof, representable as r_g. But here one stops with r_g and does not extend it to include the notion of r_g—s_g (cf. Chapter 8; also footnote 1 of this chapter).

of leading up to the problem which is to be discussed in the next section. First, however, it is instructive to note some observations reported (personal communication) by Dr. Richard D. Walk, of Cornell University. He says:

> Recently I have been working on a paper tentatively titled, "Some parameters of fear." This paper is based on material collected at Fort Benning, Georgia, in 1953. . . . I asked the trainees, at the conclusion of their first five parachute jumps, to do the following: "In your own words, describe some of your fear reactions during parachute jumping." Their reports refer to the feeling of fear at many points in the sequence, when the parachute was fitted on, the wait in the sweat shed for the plane, etc.
>
> Looking at the data one gets the impression of a period of anticipation which is turned into intense fear at the command, "stand up, hook up." This is analogous in many respects to the *conditioned stimulus*, in ordinary laboratory conditioning. Where should fear diminish? All of the most feared events —jumping from the door, the parachute opening, the opening shock—occur within 3 to 8 seconds; and many say that relaxation comes, as might be expected, when the parachute opens. However, the interesting thing is that many report relaxation and lack of fear *as soon as they stand in the door.* This is not logical. None of the most feared events has been experienced and yet the trainee relaxes. This puzzled me greatly until it occurred to me that the door had a special function—as a CS for "hope of relief," hence relaxation. As a matter of fact, one trainee even reported that he was in a high state of fear until the command, "stand up," and then he was unafraid. For him, "hope" had moved forward even further in the sequence.

Here, then, is a situation in which anticipatory relaxation occurs *before* the traumatic event itself occurs. In earlier pages we have been discussing situations where the traumatic (painful, noxious) stimulus is present but relief is in sight. However, in parachute jumping, the "shock of opening" is the only really painful incident; and it is so brief that apparently the thought, "It will soon be over now," can intervene *in advance* and produce a drop in fear. Because standing in the open door of the plane is shortly followed by the jump, the door apparently arouses, as Dr. Walk suggests, some of the relief reaction which, on past jumps, has shortly followed. Dr. Walk pertinently adds:

> Since my data were collected at the end of five parachute jumps, I have no way of knowing whether the door was feared on the first jumps and acquired fear-reducing properties on the later ones, or whether it was a function of the individual. Some interesting experiments and some very practical implications are suggested by these findings.

(Too late for extensive discussion here, a fuller report of Dr. Walk's investigation has become available as a purple-duplicated monograph entitled, "Fear and Courage: A Psychological Report" (Walk, 1959).)

IV. Shock Termination and Secondary Reinforcement

It would seem that electric shock should, in many respects, be quite ideal for use in the establishment and study of secondary reinforcement type-2, just as it has proved to be in the investigation of secondary reinforcement type-1. It can be turned on and off at will, at any desired intensity, and in other ways is extremely convenient and effective. However, as regards the use of shock for the study of secondary reinforcement type-2, the results have been highly inconsistent. In an earlier draft of this chapter, a number of experiments which have been carried out in this connection (Barlow, 1952; Coppock, 1950; Smith & Buchanan, 1954; Nefzger, 1957; Goodson & Brownstein, 1955; Montgomery & Galton, see Solomon & Brush, 1956; Gleitman, 1955; Littman & Wade, 1955; Lee, 1951; and Mowrer & Aiken, 1954) were reviewed in detail; but this no longer seems necessary or desirable, for it is now evident that these investigations involved a number of misconceptions and artifacts which render them far from crucial. Moreover, in the meantime Beck (1957) has done a particularly thorough review of these studies and from them draws the following conclusions:

1. Several contemporary behavior theories clearly predict that it should be possible to establish secondary reinforcement by pairing a neutral stimulus with the termination of shock.
2. There is no clear-cut positive evidence in support of this prediction, and there are a number of experiments with negative results.
3. The shock-termination experiments have not been ideally suited for demonstrating [type-2] secondary reinforcement insofar as they have not met the conditions most adequate for demonstrating secondary reinforcement with other forms of primary reinforcement (food and water) (p. 57).

One of the commonest reasons for failure to demonstrate that stimuli associated with shock reduction acquire secondary reinforcement capacity is this. In the study of this phenomenon in relation to other primary drives, such as hunger and thirst, it has been common practice to test the efficacy of the secondary-reinforcing stimulus *with the primary drive still operative.* Thus, if a given stimulus has been associated, for example, with hunger reduction, the secondary-reinforcing power of this stimulus will be tested while the subject is *hungry.* It is, after all, only reasonable that a promise of hunger reduction will be most effective when the subject is, here and now, experiencing this particular drive. And this conjecture has been re-peatedly confirmed in the animal laboratory. For example, Miller (1951b) says:

> Wolfe (1936) reported that an animal [chimpanzee] satiated on bananas will not beg for tokens and does not seem interested in them. When hungry, the same animal is very much interested in getting tokens. Similarly Bruce's (1932) experiment suggested that an increase in the hunger drive raises the reward value of the sight and the smell of food that rats are prevented from eating by the presence of a screen [cf. also Schlosberg & Pratt, 1956; Wike & Barrientos, 1958]. . . .
> In Wolfe's experiments the chimpanzees' motivation to secure tokens seemed to disappear, or at least it was not clearly demonstrated, when the hunger drive was satiated (p. 460). [But see also Section VI.]

Typical of those studies in which the secondary-reinforcing power of a stimulus associated with shock reduction could not be demonstrated in the *absence* of shock is that of Littman & Wade (1955), which these writers summarize as follows:

> A major deduction of the drive-reduction hypothesis of reinforcement was tested. A light which follows the termination of shock coincides with a condition of drive or need reduction. If drive reduction is a sufficient condition for reinforcement, then the light should become a secondary reinforcing agent by virtue of its association with the drive-reduction event. If it becomes a secondary reinforcing agent, it should be able to reinforce an instrumental act.
> This sequence of deductions was tested by placing rats in a stock, giving them a brief shock upon the termination of which a light was flashed for one second. After sixty such pairings, subjects were then placed in a Skinner box under operant test conditions; when they pressed the bar a light flashed on.
> Animals subjected to this training program were compared for rate of bar pressing with animals subjected to a variety of control conditions. No significant differences were found among the groups, and it was concluded that in so far as the deductions from drive-reduction theory were correct, the theory was not substantiated (p. 56).

Much the same sort of finding was obtained by Lee (1951), as reported by McClelland *et al.* (1953):

> In addition to these two basic aspects of motivation [success and failure], there is at least the logical possibility of two other types which would result from other kinds of affective change. Thus the two types we have already mentioned might be thought of as resulting primarily from, first, an increase in pleasure (an approach motive) and, second, from an increase in pain (an avoidance motive). But, at least theoretically, cues may also be associated with a decrease in pain or with a decrease in pleasure. One would expect the former to lead to approach behavior and the latter to avoidance behavior of a sort. At the present writing, however, there is very little evi-

dence for the existence of either of these aspects of motivation, despite the current popularity of the notion that stimulus reduction is particularly important in motivation theory. Thus in a preliminary experiment Lee (1951) has shown that a cue paired with *onset* of shock will lead to intense avoidance behavior when presented in a new situation, whereas a cue associated with *offset* of shock will not lead to approach behavior, as it should, but to a somewhat less intense avoidance behavior (pp. 74–75).

In both the Littman-Wade and the Lee experiment the stimulus previously associated with shock reduction was tested, for secondary-reinforcement properties, in a *"new* situation," i.e., one in which shock had never been experienced; and the results were consistently negative. In Chapter 3 (p. 81), reference has already been made to an experiment in which it was shown that a stimulus just preceding or accompanying shock *onset* acquires the capacity to act as a secondary punisher, whereas a stimulus just preceding or accompanying shock termination took on no capacity to act as a secondary reinforcer; and here the test occurred in the *same* situation where the training had taken place. However, as in the other two studies cited, the test for secondary reinforcement was likewise made in the *absence* of shock, which is presumably the crucial consideration.

Hence we may say that the group of studies cited, of which the Littman-Wade investigation is prototypical, do not really test the hypothesis (here proposed) that a stimulus associated with primary drive reduction will manifest secondary-reinforcing properties when it again occurs *in the presence of the primary drive*. Instead, they test —and disconfirm!—Hull's original view that secondary reinforcement is mediated by the r_g—s_g mechanism, independently of concurrent drive or drive reduction of any kind (see quotation from Seeman & Greenburg, Chapter 4, p. 101). This type of finding is also consistent with the well-known finding that a conditioned salivary response will occur only when the subject is hungry (Zener & McCurdy, 1939).

The illogic of testing for the secondary reinforcing properties of a stimulus which has been associated with shock reduction, in the *absence* of shock, has been pointed out (personal communication) by Dr. D. J. Mason in the following way. A stimulus, for example a buzzer, which has been associated with shock termination in one experimental situation will not have any very positive appeal to the subject in another, neutral situation (where no shock has ever been experienced) for the reason that it will "remind" the subject of the original experimental situation and make him less rather than more comfortable. Or, put in more precise terms, the buzzer makes the second situation *more like* the first one and thus promotes the *generalization of fear* from the one to the other. The notion here involved can be further clarified by the following illustration. Suppose that one is sitting in a restaurant having an enjoyable, relaxed meal with friends and someone comes and whispers into his ear: "Don't worry! Now just take it easy, everything is going to be all right." Under other circumstances these words might have a strongly reassuring effect, but under the conditions described they would almost certainly *arouse*, rather than allay, apprehension. Here they would suggest, not that everything is indeed all right, but that "something *must* be wrong," because they have been heard before in situations where something indeed *was* wrong.

The tendency to suppose that one might reasonably test for the effectiveness of a secondary reinforcer in the absence of the primary drive whose prior reduction has imparted this capacity is traceable in large part to Hull's suggestion that secondary reinforcement is mediated by the hypothetical r_g—s_g mechanism, which could presumably operate *without* the presence of drive and drive reduction. Here, then, is at least further indirect evidence of the untenability of this interpretation of secondary reinforcement.

Another reason why shock termination has commonly failed to impart secondary reinforcing properties to stimuli associated therewith is this. In situations where hunger or thirst (instead of shock) is the primary drive, the subject has to *do something*, after the appearance of the associated stimulus, before drive reduction can be experienced, i.e., the subject has to *eat* or *drink*. Thus, a stimulus may indicate that food or water is now available, but the primary drive reduction does not follow forthwith. The stimulus becomes, that is to say, a *cue* for the appropriate consummatory response. But where electric shock is being used, the situation is different: a "safety signal" may appear and the shock can then go off forthwith, without the subject himself having to do anything whatever about it. In this situation the signal has no necessary meaning or function for the subject. It is not the cue for some shock-terminating response and may very well never be noticed or "attended to," since the shock itself, by contrast, is so much more prepotent as a stimulus. Zimmerman (1957b), in discussing this problem, has made the following comment:

There is a common-sense justification for the notion that a secondary reinforcer, in order to be effective, must be a means to an end. The color of the wallpaper in a restaurant where we eat does not ordinarily possess much in the way of reinforcement value, i.e., it has little "meaning" for us. On the other hand, the taxi which we use to get to the restaurant, or the money which we use to pay the taxi fare, does possess reinforcement value, in the sense that we will work to get them (p. 9).

Therefore it would appear that better results would be obtained if the stimulus which is associated with shock reduction operates as a cue, releasing some specific action which is instrumental in terminating the shock. In fact, some writers (see Chapter 12) have generalized this line of thinking and have maintained that cue function and second-ary-reinforcing function are inseparable, if not identical. In any event, it seems that, in the future, it will be desirable to require the subject to do something, on cue, as a means of terminating the shock, instead of simply pairing some stimulus with shock termination which occurs without respect to the subject's behavior (see Beck, 1957). Also it would seem desirable, in future experimentation with shock-reduction reinforcement, to take advantage of some of the procedures which Zimmerman (1957b) has found so effective in maximizing secondary reinforcement where hunger or thirst is involved (see Chapter 4). At the present time, a number of investigators are working on this problem, with improved techniques; and there is good reason to believe that results will soon be forthcoming which will be less ambiguous than those obtained in the recent past.[8]

[8] Since the above was written, Crowder (1958) has reported a series of studies in which the secondary-reinforcing potency of a stimulus associated with shock reduction was tested *in the continued presence of shock*. Here, for the first time, unambiguously positive results were obtained, with *p*-values of the order of .01 and lower. Also, in 1957 Carlton and Marks, using a "low ambient temperature" of 0° Centigrade to motivate rats, found that a tone associated with a quick rise in temperature (provided by means of radiant heat lamps) took on unmistakable secondary-reinforcement properties; but here, again, the testing was done with the aversive drive (coldness) present, rather than absent. Hence it appears that the procedural difficulties previously encountered in this type of research have now been overcome and that we may, with considerable confidence, accept the validity of the foregoing discussion. This is of more than ordinary importance, for the following reason. It has, of course, long been known that a *response* which is contiguous with shock termination is very quickly learned and occurs with in-creasing alacrity with recurrence of the shock. In short, shock termination can be used, with great effectiveness, to establish instrumental responses or habits (Chapters 2 and 3). Now as already indicated, we are here working toward a conception of habit in which type-2 secondary reinforcement is crucial (see Chapter 7); and if it had turned out that shock termination could *not* be used to impart S^r properties to a stimulus or stimulus compound associated therewith, this finding would have materially weakened the argument. As it is, the evidence is entirely as it should be, if the new conception of habit is valid; and there is no cause for embarrassment or hesitation on this score.

V. Fear Conditioning with Hunger or Thirst as the UnCS

On the basis of evidence already reviewed in this book, it is well established that an originally neutral stimulus, associated with the onset of a noxious stimulus such as electric shock, acquires the capacity to arouse fear; and it is now equally clear that a stimulus associated with the termination of a metabolic drive such as hunger or thirst will acquire secondary reinforcement properties. In the immediately preceding section, the question has been explored as to whether a stimulus associated with the termination of a noxious drive stimulus, such as shock, can likewise acquire secondary-reinforcement potency. The answer, while still somewhat indeterminate, seems to be that as soon as truly comparable experimental procedures are devised, it will be found that stimuli associated with shock termination take on this capacity, no less than do stimuli associated with hunger or thirst reduction (see footnote 8). For purposes of logical symmetry, the remaining question is: Can the *onset of a metabolic drive* be used to condition a fear reaction to some formerly neutral stimulus or situation, in a manner comparable to the fear conditioning that can be obtained, for example, with shock onset?

Perhaps the first study that should be cited in this connection is one reported in 1953 by Calvin, Bicknell & Sperling. These writers pose the problem which they wish to investigate in the following manner. They say:

A reinforcement theory of behavior assumes that a complete behavior cycle may be described as instigated by a motive, or drive, and terminated by a reward, or reinforcement. This notion is suggested [in Fig. 5–5], which depicts a motive-reward cycle; this is drawn to represent a gradually increasing motive, like the hunger drive, and its rapid reduction under the presentation of a reward, like food.

This cycle can be divided into two phases: (a) the *motivating phase*, covering the period during which the drive is building up; and (b) the *reinforcing phase*, covering the period of the reward, during which the drive is falling off.

If a previously neutral stimulus is presented during the reinforcing phase of the cycle, this stimulus will acquire reinforcing properties. This is the phenomenon of secondary reinforcement (Hull, 1943), and there have been many experiments demonstrating its existence, and experimental inquiry into its empirical determining variables (Bersh, 1951; Hall, 1951) has begun.

Comparable investigations for the other phase of the cycle—the motivating phase—are fewer in number. Miller (1948a) has shown that a previously neutral stimulus presented during existence of a pain drive can acquire motivating properties. He used the term "fear" as a name for this secondary motive based on pain.

The present investigation was designed to determine whether a sti.nulus situation will acquire motivating properties if it is repeatedly presented during the motivating phase of the cycle shown [in Fig. 5-5]. Strength of drive is relatively high at point SD and it is relatively low at point WD. Will a stimulus situation repeatedly presented at point SD acquire stronger secondary motivating properties than the same stimulus situation repeated presented at point WD? (p. 173).

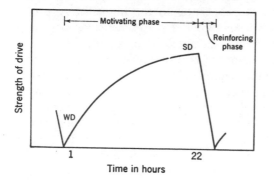

Fig. 5–5. Motivation-reward cycle, from Calvin, Bicknel!, and Sperling (1953, p. 173). The subjects in this experiment were tested at a point about midway between WD and SD, after 11 1/2 hours of food deprivation.

Later, the writers summarize the procedure which they employed thus:

Two groups of rats were placed in striped boxes 30 min. a day for 24 consecutive days. Group SD [strong drive] received this daily experience under conditions of 22 hr. food deprivation; for group WD [weak drive], the deprivation period was 1 hr. Following this procedure, the food consumption of each group was measured [in the striped box] under 11½ hr. food deprivation (p. 175).

The results show that the rats which had been under *strong* hunger when placed in the distinctive box during the 24 training days ate reliably more when later tested, after 11½ hours of food deprivation, than did rats which had been under *weak* hunger when previously exposed to the striped box. The authors interpret their findings thus:

The results of this experiment indicate that a neutral stimulus [striped box] can acquire motivating properties if it has been associated with a primary drive [hunger] state (p. 174).

The results of the Calvin-Bicknell-Sperling study thus seem to be clearly confirmatory of the notion that a mounting metabolic drive, such as hunger, can be used as the unconditioned stimulus for at least a mild conditioned-fear state which, in the present instance, is indexed by eating. But in 1954 Siegel and MacDonnell carried out an essentially similar experiment, with completely negative results: "Our findings do not agree with those of Calvin, Bicknell, and Sperling. We can offer no explanation for the disagreement" (p. 251).

In 1955, Solomon & Swanson reported a related type of investigation, in which rats were deprived of water in their home cages for 23 hours and were then put (individually) into small "water boxes," with free access to water for one-half hour. They were then put into another type of compartment, quite different in shape and appearance from the first two. This may be termed the "neutral compartment," since the animals experienced neither thirst nor thirst reduction in it. After spending one-half hour in such a compartment, the rats were put back into their living cages, there to begin another period of 23 hours of water deprivation. The nature of this "circuit," which the rats negotiated every day for 10 days, is shown diagrammatically in Fig. 5–6. It should be added that *food* was always available to the animals in the home cage and in the water box. However, during the 10 days of training, water was available *only* in the "water box."

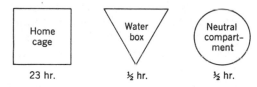

Fig. 5–6. Schematic version of the training procedure employed in the Solomon-Swanson study of thirst-fear conditioning.

On the eleventh day of this investigation the subjects were randomly divided into two equal groups and were *tested* as follows. The animals in one group, which we shall call Group E (experimental), after drinking to satiation as usual in the water box, were placed directly back in the home cages, where water was now, *for the first time* since the start of the experiment, available. The animals in the other group, which we shall call Groups C (control), after drinking to satiation as usual in the water boxes, were put into the neutral compartment, where water, likewise for the first time, was available.

If the assumptions which we have been exploring in this chapter are true, how should these two groups of animals behave under the test circumstances just described? As a result of repeatedly experiencing prolonged and relatively intense thirst in their living cages, all animals should have developed thirst fear as a conditioned reaction to these cages. Therefore, when the animals in Group E were put into these cages *without thirst, thirst fear* should nevertheless have been aroused in them; and if the rats were thus afraid of *being* thirsty in this situation, it would be reasonable for them to drink still more water. This is what they did. After having just drunk, in the preceding half hour, an average of 13 cc. of water, these rats, in the half hour following their return to the home cages, drank on the average an additional 5.8 cc. of water. On the other hand, the animals in Group C, when placed in the "neutral" compartment, each drank an average of only 2.5 cc. of water during the same period of time. This finding is, of course, in conformity with the logic set forth in the Calvin-Bicknell-Sperling experiment; but like that of the writers just cited, this finding has not been confirmed by subsequent (unpublished) repetitions thereof.

In yet another, and somewhat different, attack upon the problem, Swanson (1955) conducted an experiment in which rats were put on the following 24-hour training cycle. As in the Calvin-Sperling-Bicknell experiment, the rats were deprived of food for 23 hours and were then fed to repletion. However, they were randomly divided into two groups and, during the training period, were treated differently in one respect. Half of the rats were put into a distinctive box one hour after having been fed and were left there for one hour. They were then returned to their living cage. The other half of the animals were put into this box, also for an hour, but much later in the food-deprivation cycle (21 hours after feeding), when their hunger was relatively intense. They were then returned to their living cages. At the end of 23 hours of food deprivation, the animals in *both* groups were trained as follows. In still another box, different from both the living cage and the hunger-fear conditioning box, the rats were individually given a brief tone, followed by a bit of food. There were 10 pairings of tone and food, after which the animals were returned to the living cage and fed as much as they could eat, thus completing the 24-hour deprivation-feeding cycle. This procedure was followed for 12 days, at the end of which time all animals were put on full feed for two days and then tested in the manner indicated below.

Having enjoyed 48 hours of unrestricted feed and having thus gained back any weight that they may have lost during the preceding 12 days, the rats, now fully satiated, were put into the hunger-fear conditioning box with a small bar available, depression of which would cause the tone, previously associated with food, to sound. In keeping with the prediction generated by antecedent assumptions, the animals that had been quite hungry when previously in the box pressed the bar and produced the tone *three times as much* as did the animals which had been satiated, or only very slightly hungry, when in the box. As a result of its prior association with hunger reduction, the tone had presumably acquired the capacity to reduce hunger fear. This was demonstrated by the fact that when hunger fear was aroused in the one group of animals, not by their being made hungry, but by being placed in a situation which "reminded" them of being hungry, these animals engaged in behavior that produced the tone 300% more than did those animals which, in the same situation, were *not* reminded by it of being hungry. (Parenthetically, Swanson had a control group of animals which showed that the greater bar pressing in the one group was not due merely to heightened activity and exploratory tendency in that group.)

The rats in the Swanson experiment, though satiated when tested in the hunger-fear conditioning box, became somewhat afraid, presumably, that they were going to *become hungry;* and the tone was therefore a welcome sound because it said, in effect, "If you become hungry, you will be fed." In short, the box reminded them of hunger pain and aroused fear thereof, while the tone "recalled" hunger reduction and the ensuing diminution in hunger fear.[9]

It is not yet known whether the procedure used by Swanson will or will not be substantiated by other studies. Perhaps here, too, we are dealing with a tenuous, unstable sort of phenomenon. A metabolic drive in comparison with a noxious stimulus, such as shock, is, after all, of very gradual onset and rather feeble intensity. It may therefore be that, in light of these circumstances, the conditioning of fear with a metabolic drive as the UnCS is, at best, ephemeral and sometimes so slight as to elude detection. However, with more refined methods, the phenomenon may be found to be more substantial than the findings to date would indicate. Certainly it has good logical justification; and incidental

---

[9] Mr. Neal M. Burns, when a student in a course taught by the writer, suggested the following notion which is instructive in this connection. Primary drives may be thought of as *physiological* "death warnings." They say to the organism, in effect, "If you expect to remain alive, you are going to need a supply of this or that (or, to change this or that condition)." Therefore, reasoned Mr. Burns, primary drives are pretty serious, and it is not surprising that living organisms become "exercised" about them. Fear, as a learned or conditioned response, is a sort of *psychological* warning, not of impending death, but of impending primary drive (discomfort); and being a discomfort in its own right, i.e., a secondary *drive*, the fear can stimulate the organism to more or less appropriate behavior while still, so to speak, one step removed from death danger. As fear, i.e., primary-drive danger, undergoes higher-order conditioning, behavior becomes still more self-preservative and "foresightful."

observations, to be reviewed in the next section, lend rather impressive en.pirical support, of a different kind.[10]

By way, then, of summarizing this section and the preceding one, we may note, first of all, that experiments involving *shock onset* have been especially successful in the conditioning of *fear* (and the study of type-1 secondary reinforcement) and that in our attempts to condition *hope* (and to study type-2 secondary reinforcement), experiments involving the reduction of *metabolic drives* have been most satisfactory. Although, if our over-all scheme is sound, it is logical (indeed, incumbent upon us) to suppose that shock offset could also be used to condition hope and that fear could be conditioned by means of the induction of metabolic drives, these two inferences were not immediately confirmed. However, as we now know, shock termination *can* be used to attach hope to a stimulus or situation associated therewith (see especially footnote 8); and there is evidence, just reviewed, which at least suggests that metabolic-drive induction can likewise be used to condition fear. In principle, it should be possible to use the onset and offset of *any* primary drive (if sufficiently intense) to condition, respectively, fear and hope to formerly neutral stimuli. The difficulty in using shock offset for the conditioning of hope now seems to have arisen from the fact that we at first were not testing for this effect under appropriate conditions. And it may develop that some similar oversight is responsible for the difficulties which have been encountered in using metabolic-drive onset to condition fear. But here the problem may be more intrinsic, stemming from the simple fact that metabolic drives normally mount *slowly*, so that one cannot make any particular stimulus or situation signal drive onset in the same dramatic way that this can be done with shock, since the shock can be turned on quite suddenly. Considering the great gradualness with which metabolic drives normally arise, it is perhaps a triumph for our theory that even moderate indications of fear conditioning have here been obtained.

With this consolidation of theory, we are now in a position to extend our analysis to the phenomena discussed in the next section.

[10] In this connection Miller (1959a) has reported that he has "repeatedly failed to establish experimentally any appreciable learned elicitation of drive on the basis of primary drives such as hunger or thirst" and cites a study by Myers and Miller (1954) as an example. "Although this failure has not caused me to abandon completely the attempt to apply the fear-elicitation paradigm to appetitive drives, it has caused me to shift the emphasis in a new direction," namely, in the direction of the possibility that "the primary drives themselves may be profoundly modified by learning" (p. 263). It remains to be seen what fruit this new hypothesis will bear.

VI. Hoarding, Externalization of Drive, and Related Phenomena

The experiments cited in the two preceding sections, prompted as they were by contemporary theoretical formulations, have all been carried out and reported quite recently. There are, however, a number of older observations and laboratory researches recorded in the literature which can now, in light of these formulations, be more satisfactorily explained than was formerly possible.

Let us consider, first of all, the phenomenon of *hoarding*. Here rats, though food-satiated, will nevertheless continue, sometimes for a surprisingly long time, to go for pieces of food at some distance and carry them back to the home cage.[11] This phenomenon has been extensively studied in the laboratory, and various instinctual and physiological types of explanation have been put forward to account for such behavior (Morgan, 1947), all with some measure of empirical support. However, the interpretation which seems most natural in light of the preceding discussion goes as follows. Even though well filled with food and thus free from hunger, a rat may nevertheless be in the presence of certain stimuli which cue off hunger fear (or some other fear; see Section VII); and the latter, rather than hunger proper, may motivate the characteristic hoarding pattern, because the stimuli involved in such behavior have hunger-fear reducing (secondary reinforcement) properties. This point of view has been most fully and ingeniously developed in a paper by Marx (1950).

Or, in order further to suggest the relationship between food hoarding and the type of thinking developed in other parts of this chapter, let us revert to the Solomon-Swanson experiment. Here rats, after being repeatedly deprived of water in a particular cage, were satiated and, upon being returned to this cage, drank still more water. In a sense, it would be fair to say that they were *hoarding water*. They were, we infer, afraid that they were going to *become* thirsty; and water drinking, as we have seen, would have a tendency to reduce such

[11] An apparently similar phenomenon has been cited by Miller (1951b) as follows: "Brogden (1942) trained hungry dogs to lift their paws to get food. When the dogs were satiated he found that they continued to respond longer if he kept giving them food (which they did not eat) than if he disconnected the food-delivery mechanism. Presumably some learned drive must have been present to make the sight of food effective as a learned reward in the absence of hunger" (p. 461; cf. also Myers, 1949).

fear. Rats with hunger fear (but no real hunger) can either eat or store food in a corner of their cage or nest, whereas the only place the rats with thirst fear can "store" water is—in the manner of the desert camel—in their stomachs.[12] However, the underlying mechanisms in the two situations seem to be basically similar.

Thus we see how the *motivation* for hoarding behavior presumably arises; but are we equally clear as to how such behavior gets reinforced? For this form of behavior to *persist*, it must be in some way uniquely satisfying; i.e., it must make the animal *feel better* than anything else it can do. How is such an effect achieved? Following a line of reasoning developed earlier (see especially Section II), we may assume that rats are familiar with *two* "situations" or "conditions" which may prevail in their home cage (or, in a state of nature, in their den or nest): cage-with-food-present and cage-without-food. Strong hunger is never experienced in the first situation; whereas it may well be experienced in the second one. Hence we may assume that hunger fear tends to get conditioned to *empty* cage, whereas no such emotion is aroused by cage-with-food. Now let us suppose that a rat, though not immediately hungry, is in an empty cage. Our assumption is that here he may well experience hunger fear. Suppose, also, that a supply of food is available at a little distance from the home cage through a runway connected to the cage. By going and fetching food from this remote supply and putting it in the home cage, the animal manifestly *changes* empty-cage into cage-with-food and, in the bargain, reduces his conditioned hunger fear. The resulting diminution of fear presumably reinforces (rewards) the food-fetching behavior which we call "hoarding."

This interpretation gains support from the following statement by Stellar (1951):

(1) Rats do not carry any appreciable amount of food into their cages until after they have been kept on a food deprivation schedule for a number of days, and (2) once started, hoarding does not stop until after rats have been allowed continuous supplies of food for several days. Both of these findings have been amply substantiated (Morgan, 1947). They make it clear that hoarding does not depend upon simple hunger or on any other acute effects of food deprivation. Rather, hoarding seems to be the result of some effect produced by repeated deprivation and rectified only by fairly long periods of satiation (p. 290).

[12] Bindra (1947), interestingly enough, has shown that, under certain conditions, rats will hoard cotton balls soaked in water, though not at the moment thirsty. His conclusion is simply that rats will hoard anything which they are likely to need.

Although some more basic physiological mechanism may be involved here, certainly the facts cited by Stellar are congruent with the notion that hoarding is based upon hunger fear and the reinforcement provided by the mere presence of food (cf. Lowney, 1958).

Wike & Casey (1954) have reported a study the purpose of which was "to determine whether or not a secondary reinforcing agent [sight, smell, and touch of food] will facilitate runway performance when the primary drives of hunger and thirst are satiated" (p. 441). And in conclusion these investigators say:

> Since the experimental Ss, traversing a runway to an end box containing food, ran more rapidly and consistently than the control Ss running to an empty goal box, it was concluded that the sight of food has reward value when the primary drives of hunger and thirst are satiated.
> The learned reward value and its observed persistence were attributable to the historical and contemporary association of the learned reward with drive reduction (p. 443).

Here, too, was a kind of "hoarding." But instead of the subjects going and getting food and returning it to a nest box, they *took themselves* to a place where there was an abundance of food, rather than remain in a place where there was none.

Do human beings show similar tendencies? Rather obviously they do. They insist, if it is at all possible, upon having "food stores" as well as various other kinds of "stores." True, these stores, or supplies, or "hoards," are usually *common* stores, i.e., several different families will use them. But we want such a store to be regularly available, not just in the sense of a building, but as a store or reserve supply of the commodity in question. When, during a war, there is a shortage of certain "goods" (drive reducers, reinforcers) in common, public stores, there is a tendency for families to try to establish their own private "stores." This, of course, is also called "hoarding" and is officially discouraged, since more of the commodity is now needed to stock the many private stores than one common store; but "hoarding" is of a piece with the normal situation, the main difference being that in the one case the reassuring reserve is private, in the other shared, common. As long as an abundance of food is *in sight*, either in a public or a private "store," there is no hunger fear; but if there is food in neither place, the individual, though not immediately hungry, may still be worried about where his "next meal is coming from."

Over the years there has been a good deal of interest in, though apparently some misunderstanding of, a phenomenon known as the "externalization of drive." A classical example of this sort of behavior was reported by E. E. Anderson (1941c). First of all, this investigator gave 20 hungry rats one trial per day for 73 days in a 14-unit T-maze, which he called Maze-A. A "rest period" of two weeks, on full feed, was then provided, after which the subjects were again put "on drive" and divided into four different groups, of five animals each. Group 1–HR (hungry, rewarded) was given one trial per day for 37 days in a six-unit T-maze (with a pattern different from that found in Maze-A). The results are indicated in Fig. 5–7 by the solid curve. Since the maze was so short and simple, these subjects, "normally" motivated (by hunger) and rewarded (by food), learned Maze-B quickly and well.

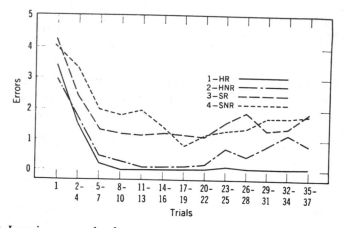

Fig. 5–7. Learning curves for four groups of rats, run through a maze under four conditions of motivation and reward described in text (Anderson, 1941c, p. 402).

The animals in Group 2–HNR (hungry but nonrewarded) were treated just like the animals in Group 1–HR, except that they received no food in the goal box, at the end of the maze. The Group 3–SR animals (satiated but rewarded) and the Group 4–SNR animals (satiated and nonrewarded) were treated just like those in Group 1–HR and Group 2–HNR, respectively, except that they were not hungry (having been fed shortly before the daily maze run). The performance of the animals in Groups 2–HNR, 3–SR, and 4–SNR are also shown in Fig. 5–7.

These findings make sense. The animals (1–HR) which were rewarded, on completing the maze, by reduction in both hunger and hunger fear, learned best. The next-best learners were the animals

(2–HNR) which were motivated both by hunger and by hunger fear but which were rewarded only secondarily, by hunger fear reduction. And, as the secondary reinforcing potency of the goal-end of the maze extinguished, their performance tended to deteriorate, as one would expect.

Elimination of hunger as a primary drive caused the performances of the animals in Groups 3–SR and 4–SNR to be decidedly inferior to those of the first two groups. The satiated animals were, presumably, motivated largely or perhaps exclusively only by such hunger fear as had become conditioned to the maze (see Section II); and, quite understandably, it did not matter much under these circumstances whether the subjects did or did not get a bit of food (which they did not especially need) at the end of the maze. These two groups, in other words, ran and learned Maze-B, to the extent that they did run and learn it, on the basis of secondary motivation and secondary reinforcement alone (see also Fig. 5–8).

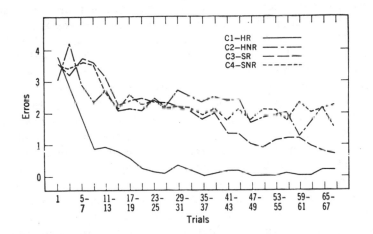

Fig. 5–8. Learning curves for four groups of rats intended as "controls" for the four curves shown in Fig. 5–7 (Anderson, 1941c, p. 408).

There is a good deal more to the Anderson study than here reported, and it should be examined in the context of two earlier papers by the same author (Anderson, 1941a, 1941b) for a full appreciation of the very methodical and logical way in which it was carried out. However, the empirical aspects of the Anderson study need not be further reviewed here, since it has been dramatically confirmed, in a different sort of study reported, by Danziger (1951).

The only question, it seems, is one of interpretation. Both Anderson and Danziger spoke in terms of the "externalization of drive"; and, by implication, they were thinking of the hunger drive. The alternative assumption here favored is that hunger, like strong primary drives in general, arouses fear and that this reaction can become conditioned to stimuli or situations which have been associated with the onset (or augmentation) thereof. Thus, instead of speaking of the "externalization" of the hunger drive, one may refer more appropriately to the subsequent arousal of hunger fear (which, of course, is an internal state) by an external stimulus or situation. And, of course, the elimination of such stimulation would be expected, in keeping with principles already elaborated, to have a (secondary) reinforcing effect (cf. Denny & Behan, 1956).

Earlier in this chapter (Section IV) we arrived at the conclusion that secondary reinforcement type-2 can be demonstrated only if the relevant primary drive is currently present. Now it seems that, in the present and immediately preceding sections, we have a good deal of evidence to the effect that this phenomenon can be found in situations where there is complete satiation as far as primary drive is concerned. Fortunately, this paradox is easily resolved by our theory. This theory holds that secondary reinforcement can be demonstrated either if the primary drive is present *or* if there is fear of the recurrence thereof. If, for example, hunger fear is being stimulated by hunger itself, then a stimulus which promises hunger reduction will reduce the hunger fear; but, similarly, if hunger fear is being aroused on a *conditioned* basis, in the absence of hunger, the elimination of the conditioned stimulus or situation will likewise act as a secondary reinforcer. The first is clearly an instance of type-2 secondary reinforcement, whereas the latter qualifies as secondary reinforcement type-1. Our assumption is that type-1 secondary reinforcement occurs when a fear of drive *increase* (of any kind) is disconfirmed and that type-2 secondary reinforcement occurs when there is a prospect of drive *decrease* (see also Sections I and II).

VII. Drive Fear and Drive Equivalence

The fact that a response learned under the motivation and reward provided by one source of drive may later "crop up" when the organism is ostensibly motivated by quite a different drive has occasioned a good deal of interest and at least mild perplexity. And Estes (1949) has reported an experiment in which it was shown that a stimulus which had been associated, in thirsty rats, with thirst reduction could be used to reinforce a Skinner-type bar-pressing habit when the rats were not thirsty but *hungry*. Estes concludes from this finding that "since the effectiveness of a secondary reinforcer clearly is not specific to the original drive, it will not be profitable to define the concept of reinforcement in terms of drive reduction" (p. 294). The present writer has previously suggested the following alternative interpretation:

It will be remembered that the subjects [in the Estes experiment] which were tested when satiated with water were strongly motivated by *hunger*. Thus, although there was no fear of thirst in them, there was, presumably, now *fear of hunger instead*. It is by no means far-fetched to assume that a stimulus which has become capable of reducing thirst fear will also be capable, through generalization, of likewise reducing hunger fear. Granted these inferences, there is nothing inexplicable about the fact that a stimulus which had previously been associated with thirst reduction was later capable of providing secondary reinforcement, even though the subjects were, at the time, water-satiated (Mowrer, 1950, p. 149).

The assumption here is that the "equivalence" sometimes observed between different primary drives stems from the element or component of fear that is *common* to these drives. This thought is obviously related to Hull's notion of "a generalized drive state" or drive generality. Summarizing the relevant experimental literature, Grice & Davis (1957) have recently written as follows:

The generalized response-activating character of drive (*D*) which has been hypothesized by Hull (1943) and Spence (1954) has received a fairly substantial amount of empirical support. Amsel (1950) found that rats will perform a running habit motivated by fear more vigorously when they are also hungry. Amsel and Maltzman (1950) found that the presence of emotionality will, under certain circumstances, increase the amount of drinking. The Iowa studies of anxiety in human Ss have been based on this assumption and, in general, have yielded results in accord with prediction (Farber and Spence, 1953; Montague, 1953; Taylor, 1951) [See also Spence, 1958]. In the case of purely appetitional drives, Webb (1949) trained rats on a panel-pushing response under food deprivation for food reward and conducted extinction trials under various degrees of water deprivation with the hunger drive satiated. He found that the number of extinction responses was an increasing function of the number of hours of water deprivation. This result was confirmed by Brandauer (1953) in a similarly designed experiment employing a bar-pressing response (p. 347).

However, one complicating consideration to which Grice & Davis point is that there is some evidence that in a number of laboratory animals, and notably rats, thirst and hunger appear to be somewhat interdependent: i.e., a hungry animal will not *drink* as much as a non-hungry one and a thirsty animal will not *eat* as much as a nonthirsty one. The possibility therefore exists that the satiation of either of these drives while the other one is strong is questionable. When special provisions were taken to control for this sort of interdependence, Grice & Davis (see also Ellis, 1957) failed to confirm the Webb findings, cited above.

However, there are other studies of drive interaction or summation where the same mechanism can hardly be suspected of operating. For example, Braun, Wedekind, & Smudski (1957) have studied the summational tendencies of hunger and discomfort produced by immersion in water (rather than thirst). They preface their study with this theoretical statement:

Hull (1943) has made the assumption that response strength is a multiplicative function of learning or cognitive factors and motivational or drive factors. Drive factors are designated by the hypothetical construct, drive strength (D), which comprises the total effective drive strength operating in S at any given moment. In any experimental situation, both relevant and irrelevant needs or motivations are assumed to summate to contribute to the value of D. A relevant need is one which is reduced by the response under consideration; irrelevant needs encompass all other primary and secondary needs in S when the response occurs but which are not reduced by the response (p. 148).

And these investigators summarize their empirical findings thus:

This study investigated the learning by the rat of a modified Lashley Maze III adapted for swimming as a function of the combination of a relevant drive —escape from water—and an irrelevant drive—hunger resulting from food deprivation. Two levels of relevant drive were produced by using water temperatures of 35°C. (high) and 15°C. (low). The irrelevant drive was induced by o-hr. and 22-hr. deprivation. The addition of a high irrelevant drive to both high and low levels of relevant drive results in an increased total drive strength as measured by swimming time and error elimination (p. 151).

Even more striking is an experimental finding reported by Ullman (1951). In this study,

Eight female rats were taught to eat small pellets of food in an apparatus whose floor was capable of being electrified. After four days of 20-minute experimental sessions during which the time when each pellet of food was eaten was recorded, electric shock of moderate intensity was introduced for five seconds of each minute. This led to a reduction in eating for the first two days, followed by an increase in eating especially during the five seconds when shock was on. Then the intensity of shock was increased for four more days. During this period, eating activity increased markedly, with a very large increase during shock. For the last four days of the experiment, the animals were satiated prior to being placed in the apparatus, and the procedure was carried out as before. During this time, total eating activity decreased, but most of the eating was done during the time when electric shock was on (p. 581).

Before experimentation proper was begun (as a sort of control), all eight subjects were allowed a period of 20 minutes of "free eating" each day for a period of four days. Hunger was standardized, with animals being held at 80% of normal body weight. Figure 5–9 shows a composite bar diagram for the total number of pellets eaten, by five-second intervals, during the free-eating periods on these four days. As was to be expected, about the same number of pellets were consumed during each of the 12 five-second periods. In all, the eight rats ate 2,305 pellets during the four 20-minute periods.

Figure 5–10 shows the eating pattern for the eight rats used in this study when a mild electric shock was put on the floor grill during the first five-second interval in each minute. (When the rats were first put into the apparatus, instead of being shocked immediately, they were allowed each day a one-minute orientation period without shock.) Hunger was held at the same level as before, each subject had 20 minutes each day in the apparatus, and this part of the investigation again lasted for four days. As will be noted in the bar diagram, the number of pellets eaten during the five-second shock interval was slightly, but not markedly, greater than during any other five-second period. It should also be said that the total number of pellets consumed during the four 20-minute periods was 3,049, as compared to 2,305 for the preceding four periods of free (as opposed to "forced") eating. This increase of 744 pellets may have been due to unidentified causes (e.g., greater familiarity with the apparatus, or increased hunger despite constancy of body weight). But it could also be interpreted as arising from the fact that the introduction of the shock increased the subjects' total motivation by making them somewhat fearful. This suggestion is given further credence by the next phase of the study.

Because the increase in eating produced by the shock was so slight (in comparison with results obtained in a pilot study), shock intensity was somewhat increased during another four-day experimental period. The results are shown in Fig. 5–11. Here we see that the number of pellets eaten during the shock interval was more than twice as great as the number eaten during any other comparable interval. Moreover, the total consumption of pellets rose to a new high of 3,630.

The next and final phase of the experiment consisted of four daily

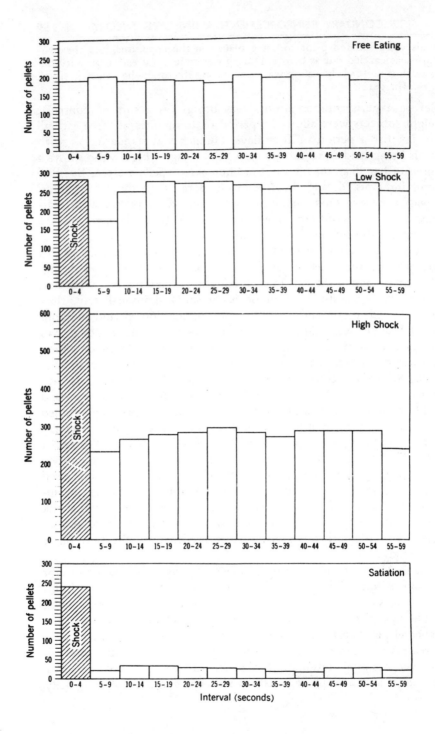

20-minute sessions in the apparatus after "complete" satiation of the subjects on wet mash (a preferred food) in their living cages, just prior to being put into the apparatus. The very interesting results thus obtained are shown in Fig. 5–12. As was to be expected, there was a marked over-all drop in the number of pellets (530) consumed; but it is noteworthy that shock still caused a great augmentation in eating and that, in the eleven five-second intervals between shocks, there was still some eating, despite the immediately prior "satiation" of the animals. The presumption is that this eating was motivated, purely and simply, by fear.[13]

Ullman gives an astute analysis of his findings in these words:

The salient feature of the experiment can immediately be seen from the results described above. The introduction of an extraneous stimulus, electric shock, after a brief depression in pellet-taking behavior leads to an increase in this activity, an increase which is particularly marked in that 5-sec. interval during which the electric shock is on.

In analyzing what occurred in the experiment, we see that along with the two sources of primary motivation, hunger and pain, from electric shock, two derived drives can be posited. These may be called "hunger-fear" and "shock-fear." The assumption is here made that any primary drive has a coexistent emotional component. Perhaps this emotional drive takes the form of fear of more of the primary drive; thus, not only are the rats hungry, but they have learned that they may go on being hungry. It is as if hunger were a conditioned stimulus for more hunger. In the same manner, a fear of

[13] It would have been interesting if Ullman had preceded the shock with a five-second warning signal. Eating during this period would presumably have been considerably higher than in the rest of the inter-shock interval, though not so high as when the shock itself was on.

LEGEND for Fig. 5–9.
Fig. 5–9. Bar diagram showing uniform eating, on the part of eight hungry rats, during each 5-second interval in one-minute cycles. The data (taken from Ullman, 1951, p. 578) were obtained during four 20-minute test periods on successive days.

LEGEND for Fig. 5–10.
Fig. 5–10. Bar diagram of eating during four 20-minute daily test periods involving mild shock during the first five-second interval in each one-minute cycle.

LEGEND for Fig. 5–11.
Fig. 5–11. Bar diagram of eating during four 20-minute daily test periods involving a somewhat stronger shock during the first five-second interval in each one-minute cycle.

LEGEND for Fig. 5–12.
Fig. 5–12. Bar diagram of eating during four 20-minute daily test periods under same conditions as described for Fig. 5–11, except that the subjects were not hungry.

shock may be developed. The entire stimulus situation, the apparatus, the experimenter, etc., may be considered a conditioned stimulus which becomes paired with electric shock (p. 580).

Ullman then considers various ways in which this complex motivational structure may have operated in his experiment but concludes in favor of the following interpretation:

What probably happened was that the animals had learned to reduce hunger-fear by eating and that this behavior, through generalization, was elicited when pain-fear was created. The only adjustive act available to the animal was eating, and this act served to reduce the entire burden of tension or drive from all sources except pain. Thus, three of the four ongoing drives were being reduced by eating: hunger, hunger-fear, and pain-fear. This point of view is consistent with the results obtained in the satiation procedure during which one of the two primary drives, hunger, is absent, and it is presumed that its emotional component, hunger-fear, is also eliminated [cf. next experiment to be described]. Then, when the animal eats to shock, it is reducing only pain-fear, something it learned to do in the earlier procedures of the experiment (pp. 580–581).

The Ullman experiment is reminiscent of a clinical phenomenon sometimes referred to as "ice-box neurosis." Here individuals, when they become anxious or tense, use *eating* as a way of dealing with this emotional state (see, for example, Bruch, 1943; Greene, 1939; and *Science Illustrated*, 1946). Perhaps, for reasons which will be considered in Chapter 6, the stimulation of the taste (and olfactory) receptors acts in such a way in these individuals as to directly assuage fear; but there is also the possibility that food, which by long experience has been found to reduce hunger and hunger fear, now also, by generalization, is used to reduce *other* fears.[14]

It is, of course, only to be expected that when an "irrelevant" drive exceeds a certain intensity, it will have a disruptive rather than facilitative effect upon behavior appropriate to the so-called relevant drive. And there is now considerable laboratory evidence for this supposition. Recently it has been shown (Chapter VI) that anxiety in human subjects, if too intense or if the task at hand is delicate and complex, may impede rather than expedite performance. A similar relationship is also known to exist with respect to what was formerly termed "dynomogenesis" (Morey, 1933; Brown, 1955).

And Eroféeva, working in Pavlov's laboratory, reported that an electric shock of gradually mounting intensity could be successfully

---

[14] An overweight character on a recent TV program put the theory well when she said: "Whenever I get upset, I *always* have to nibble." (Cf. Miles, 1958a).

used as a stimulus for conditioned salivation, *until* a certain point was reached, at which the dog's behavior became completely disorganized—or, more exactly, *re*-organized and directed toward the shock, rather than toward food (Pavlov, 1927, pp. 289–290).

So what, then, is to be inferred, systematically, from this large and heterogeneous mass of research findings and commonplace observations? The fact of drive interaction, generalization, equivalence, or summation seems unmistakable; and it is consistent with the facts to suppose that this phenomenon is achieved by virtue of the element of fear which seems to be common to all primary drives, when they reach moderate to great intensity. A special application of this supposition is made elsewhere (Mowrer, 1960, Ch. 10); its more general implications will be developed in Chapter 7. Alternative interpretations of drive equivalence and summation are, of course, possible and even plausible; but the interpretation of greatest generality and systematic power seems to be the one here outlined.[15]

VIII. Hope and Disappointment: A New Kind of Secondary Punishment

Inherent in the foregoing discussion is an implication of no little theoretical, and even some practical, interest. In this and the preceding chapters we have seen how, step by step, it has been necessary to modify a strictly behavioristic approach to the psychology of learning by the introduction of intervening variables. The first of these was the concept of *fear* and the attendant concept of fear reduction, *relief*, or

[15] A particularly significant line of developments has just been reviewed by Malmo (1958). Noting the unprecise and generally unsatisfactory nature of most operational definitions of drive, Malmo (on the basis of a now growing literature) suggests that degree of *emotional arousal* (as indexed by the PGR or other physiological measures) may yet turn out to be the best measure of the intensity of any given primary drive. He says: " 'Drive' . . . has traditionally been inferred from conditions such as hours of deprivation, strength of shock, and other such antecedent conditions. . . . It appears that what we have been calling 'arousal' comes very close to being identical with the concept of general drive, or *D*." And in his reference to a particularly relevant study by Freeman (1940), Malmo says: "In other words, palmar conductance appeared to serve in place of conventional conditions (e.g., time since last eating, or drinking) as the independent variable in this experiment" (p. 245). In short, Malmo is proposing that what we have in this book described as *drive fear* (or "emotional arousal") is not only a real phenomenon but may, in fact, be our most direct and reliable index of drive itself. If this way of thinking is substantiated, it will provide powerful additional support for our general position.

what has here been termed secondary reinforcement type-1. In the preceding and present chapters we have also seen how essential it has become to acknowledge the reality of type-2 secondary reinforcement, which is clearly equivalent to what is ordinarily called *hope*. The latter step, as we have seen and shall further see, resolves a great many otherwise vexing problems and lays the basis for a new conception of habit which has great generality. But, in passing, attention should likewise be called to the fact that just as fear implies relief, so also does hope imply *disappointment*, a concept familiar enough in common speech and experience but only just beginning to be recognized scientifically (see Chapter 11).

Clearly enough, if a signal has acquired the capacity to arouse hope, i.e., promises relief from some primary discomfort, and if such a signal is presented and then withdrawn before it is confirmed, there will be a recrudescence of fear, dismay, hoplessness. The individual, as one may say, "loses hope," feels disappointed. And this, it would seem, is precisely what happens when a type-2 secondary reinforcer is presented and then withdrawn, without fulfillment. And from this reasoning yet another inference follows. If fear induction, produced by appearance of a danger signal, can act as a secondary punishment, then the fear induction mediated by *dis*appearance of a so-called safety signal should likewise have punishing properties. Said otherwise, *disappointment is punishing*, as common experience amply confirms. But the only attempt which has apparently been made to date to bring this inference to experimental demonstration is a study briefly reported by Morse & Herrnstein (1956) under the title: "The Maintenance of Avoidance Behavior Using the Removal of a Conditioned Positive Reinforcer as the Aversive Stimulus." Unfortunately, the procedure employed in this investigation is intricate and its full understanding would presuppose knowledge of several matters which will not be considered until later. However, Professor William E. Kappauf (personal communication) has suggested an experiment which is both simple and clear. For a thirsty rat the appearance of a small tube from which water can be slowly drunk acts, in effect, as a promise (of thirst reduction) and its withdrawal (before thirst is eliminated) presumably produces disappointment. Now suppose that for a second or two before the tube is withdrawn a tone or some other distinctive stimulus is presented. Certainly the still thirsty rat will not "like" to hear this tone, signifying as it does the imminent disappearance of the water tube; and it seems likely that if, during the period while the rat is waiting for the original appearance of the tube, it could produce the tone by pressing a little bar, it would make a point of *not repeating* such an action, once it had occurred. In other words, the tone would very likely *punish* any action which preceded it, just as a hope-arousing signal has the reverse effect (cf. Zbrozyna, 1957, 1958; Ferster, 1957, 1958).

A new systematic relationship thus comes into view: just as there are two forms of secondary reinforcement, which we have designated types 1 and 2, so also are there, apparently, *two forms of secondary punishment*. In an earlier chapter it has already been pointed out that an action which is followed, not by primary punishment, but merely by a "warning," produces what may be termed type-1 secondary punishment; and now we may appropriately designate so-called disappointment as secondary punishment type-2. Thus, type-1 secondary punishment is the antithesis of secondary reinforcement type-1; and type-2 secondary punishment is the antithesis of type-2 secondary reinforcement. Or, one may say, there are two types of secondary *decremental* reinforcement and two types of secondary *incremental* reinforcement.

In *Science and human behavior*, Skinner (1953a) considers the effects on behavior of presenting and removing positive and negative reinforcers—a sort of four-fold contingency table. The effects of some of these operations are well-substantiated experimentally, especially those which serve to define positive and negative reinforcers (Morse and Herrnstein, personal communication).

The suggestion is strong that positive secondary reinforcement figures in the explanation of "joys"—like the joy of revisiting "the scenes of our childhood." Apparently the source lies in the reinforcements connected with familiar places, people, things, and actions. The loss or absence of old secondary reinforcers, on the other hand, seems often to be at the heart of our "sorrows." . . . Indeed, the tie-up of secondary reinforcement and "feelings" seems to pervade our whole lives as social organisms. . . .

The changes in rat behavior resulting from stimuli that have been regularly associated with electric shock often lead observers to attribute *fear* to these animals. The sudden burst of bar-pressing and biting responses at the beginning of an extinction session is frequently said to show *anger*. We now see that the use of these two terms is justified in some degree. *Sorrow* and *joy*, on the other hand, are seldom imputed to the rat in any situation, even by persons who regularly employ such terms in connection with the behavior of dogs, chimpanzees, and human beings. Are there operations, different from those we use to define anger and fear, which are related to special changes in reflex strength? (Keller & Schoenfeld, 1950, p. 256 and p. 344.)

You will recollect that Shand (1914) named an important group of human emotions, e.g., hope and disappointment, "prospective emotions of desire," and that to these McDougall (1919) added a group of retrospective emotions, e.g., regret and remorse. Few psychologists except Stern, who included a chapter on "The Temporal Reference of Feeling" in his *General Psychology* (1938), have paid much attention to the Shand-McDougall Scheme. Yet explanations in terms of physiological concomitants and expressive movements have not taken us far in the understanding of the more complex human emotions. Temporal reference may, after all, hold the key to a more fruitful interpretation (Hearnshaw, 1956, p. 18).

I say there be four perturbations of the mind, desire, joy, fear, sorrow; and whatsoever I can dispute thereon, by dividing each into its subordinate species, and by defining it, in my memory find I what to say, and thence do I bring it (St. Augustine, 399, p. 31).[16]

Our "rediscovery" of phenomena which, it seems, are as old as mammalian life itself may not seem like much of an accomplishment; and certainly there is every reason to be appropriately modest about it. But in one respect, there is real progress here: these phenomena are now being identified in a *systematic conceptual framework* and their definition is in terms of *clear-cut, empirical operations*. In this small but not insignificant way only does the present type of analysis represent any very substantial advance over common sense.

IX. The Situational Definition of Emotions

Since the preceding sections of this chapter were written, a particularly relevant paper by Hunt, Cole, & Reis (1958) has appeared which calls for special comment. These writers begin by listing several criteria which have been used in the past for identifying the emotions: "(1) the overt responses or expressions, (2) the inner organic, neural, and visceral changes or indicators, (3) the arousing situations, (4) the emotional experiences, and (5) the motivational effects" (p. 136), of which the third is singled out by these authors as the most valid and useful. They say:

Arguing in this same direction, Sherman (1927) has found that judges attempting to name the emotions expressed by young infants show very poor agreement when they see only the overt behavior of the infant, but the percentage of agreements jumps sharply when they are shown moving pictures which include the situation. Moreover, when the judges base their naming upon movies in which stimuli and the expressions have been transposed, it is the names based upon the situations which prevail (p. 137).

W. A. Hunt (1941) has advocated standardizing the stimulus-situations for all emotions investigated in a manner similar to that done for the startle-response. Before this excellent suggestion can be implemented, however,

---

[16] Cf. also passage quoted from McClelland *et al.*, pp. 141–142.

more must be known about the general charactristics of the situations which
serve as cues for the various complex emotions. The burden of this paper is
to present two hypotheses concerning the characteristics of the relationship
between the reacting individual and his environment which differentiate the
three unpleasant emotions commonly termed *fear, anger,* and *sorrow,* and to
describe several tests of these hypotheses (p. 138).

The details of the procedures employed by Hunt, Cole, & Reis
cannot be reviewed here; instead, we are primarily concerned with the
fact that these investigators point the way so clearly to the importance
of using a situational, or *operational,* definition of emotion, which is
what has been tacitly done in the preceding discussion, in this and
earlier chapters. All emotions—fear, relief, hope, and disappointment
—have been identified in terms of the situations that presumably
evoke them, and not in terms of subjective descriptions, physiological
concomitants, or the like. Thus, Hunt, Cole, & Reis, on quite independent grounds, justify and support this approach and give us added
confidence in its general validity.

Although ostensibly concerned only with "the three unpleasant
emotions commonly termed *fear, anger,* and *sorrow,*" these investigators nevertheless discovered that the research methods they employed also directed attention to the emotion of *hope,* thus providing, once again (see Section VIII), a four-fold classificatory system.
However, as is immediately evident, the emotions thus identified are
not exactly the same as those previously stressed in this chapter; but
the discrepancies are easily explained. *Fear* and *hope* are, of course,
clearly common to both systems; and the writers cited would presumably have no objection to the emotion of *relief.* The important
difference hinges upon the presence of *anger* and *sorrow* in their system, as opposed to *disappointment* in our own. The latter we have defined as the emotion which occurs in a situation where a promise (hope-
arousing stimulus) has been withdrawn; and now we see that such a
withdrawal may carry either of two implications: irretrievable loss,
leading to *sorrow;* and provisional loss, leading to *anger.* Thus we
return to the original classification of fear, relief, hope, and disappointment, with the latter now bifurcated into sorrow and anger. As we
shall see in Chapter 11, this added distinction is operationally important, in accounting for the appearance, in the face of disappointment, of aggression in some cases and extinction in others. But for the
present no further reference will be made to this distinction. Instead
we turn to what is perhaps a more fundamental disagreement with
the Hunt-Cole-Reis analysis.

These writers assume that *frustration* is the key to the understanding and identification of the negative emotions of anger, fear, and sorrow. They then say:

The cues for these three emotions have been formulated in two ways. In one formulation, upon which the first study to be reported was based, the cues were conceived to derive from the *perceived timing* of the frustration. The notion of *perceived timing* served to describe on one continuum the nature of the relationship among person, obstacle, and anticipated goal-response. In one case, the obstacle may be evident without actually interfering with the goal-response, *i.e.*, it may be threatening. In the second case, the obstacle may be evident and blocking the behavior-sequence or course of action. In the third case, the blocking already has occurred, and the goal is lost irrevocably. The three cases were described as *future, present,* and *past* perceived timing. The finding of the first study prompted a change in the formulation, and the reformulation was then tested in the second study to be reported (p. 140).

Discrimination of fear, sorrow, and anger would, in terms of the revised formulation, depend in general upon S's perception of his relationship in a frustrating situation to the goal being sought and to the presence of an obstacle. *Fear* should be named when S perceives a threat to his goal and uncertainty of achieving it. *Sorrow* should be named when S perceives the goal as irretrievably lost, and when his concern is limited to the loss of the goal. For either of these two emotions, it is important that the concern with the frustrating agent or obstacle be minimized. *Anger* should be reported when this frustrating agent or obstacle is of central concern to S. (p. 146).

Would it not be preferable to make *threat*, rather than frustration, the common basis for these emotions? And to assume that they are all *future*-oriented? *Fear* is thus identifiable as the prospect of the situation *getting worse* (drive increment); *anger* as the prospect that something hoped-for *may* be lost; and *sorrow* as the prospect that something hoped-for is definitely lost. *Hope*, by contrast, is the prospect of the situation *getting better* (drive decrement), although there is always a possibility that it will not, which presumably explains why hope and fear, being mirror images of the same phenomenon, are dynamically always so intertwined. In this connection, Hunt, Cole, and Reis say:

Situations intended to evoke fear brought out a new fact, namely, a relationship between *hope* and *fear* which was poorly recognized by the judges or sorters. For instance, only 5 of the 20 sorters put *hope* into the *fear*-category, while 2 put it in the *anger*-category as a first choice and 6 as a second choice. *Hope* was even put into the *sorrow*-category once as a first choice and once as a second choice by sorters. A much closer relationship between *hope* and *fear* is suggested by the fact that they were the two predominant names for the emotions evoked by the situations intended to arouse fear. Hope and fear also were given in response to seven of the equivocal situations, but these situations also clearly contain threats to the goal along with other cues. On the other hand, the *hope*-response came only three times from the situations intended to evoke *anger* and never from the situations intended to evoke *sorrow*. It would thus appear that *fear* and *hope* are alternative responses to a situation in which the goal is threatened.[17] This suggests that which term is used predominantly may be a function of the degree to which S is inclined toward pessimism or optimism. If S is pessimistically inclined, the predominant response to be expected may be *fear,* but if he is optimistically inclined, the predominant response to be expected may be *hope.* This finding and these considerations suggest that a battery of paragraphs like our descriptions of intended-fear situations might possibly serve as a useful projective device to assess the degree to which individuals are inclined toward pessimism or optimism (pp. 149–150).

Perhaps the picture will be clarified if we think about the emotions in the context of *prospective gains and losses.* Losses are, roughly, of two kinds: a rise in primary drive (e.g., shock) or a rise in secondary drive (e.g., fear). And, in like manner, gains may take either of two forms: a drop in primary drive or a drop in secondary drive. A stimulus which signals a *loss* is said to arouse *fear;* and a stimulus which signals a *gain* is said to arouse *hope.* When a hope signal appears and then disappears, the reaction is one of *disappointment* and, more specifically, may take the form of either anger or sorrow. Properly speaking, *relief* should perhaps not be termed an "emotion"; but if our earlier analysis in this chapter is correct, this is the essence of hope (type-2 secondary reinforcement) as well as of the experience which occurs when a danger signal disappears (type-1 secondary reinforcement).

Especially important, here, is the fact that it now seems possible to develop a relatively inclusive "theory of the emotions" around the basic notion that every strong primary drive is accompanied by an undifferentiated "arousal state" (cf. Chapter 6) and that the four main emotions thus identified—fear, relief, hope, and disappointment—can all be interpreted as some aspect or phase of this basic state, situationally defined.

There are, obviously, still unsolved problems in this area, but enough now is known that we can nevertheless proceed with the tasks immediately at hand. Certain of the problems raised in this chapter will be considered again, in different contexts, in Chapters 6 and 11.

---

[17] May (1950) quotes Spinoza as saying, with "astute psychological insight," "Fear cannot be without hope, nor hope without fear" (p. 6).

6 ═══════════════

Secondary Reinforcement:
Reservations and Complications

Because the theory of secondary reinforcement which has been presented in the preceding chapter is so central to much of the argument that is to follow, it will be useful, at this juncture, to examine some of the criticisms which have been directed against this approach and to determine in what ways it is most questionable or incomplete.

I. Harlow's Criticisms of the "Homeostatic" Model

Perhaps the most scintillating skepticism with respect to the fear-reduction interpretation of secondary reinforcement has been expressed, in a series of experimental reports and theoretical papers, by H. F. Harlow. Fortunately, for our purposes, these have recently been admirably set forth in a compact, highly readable paper (Harlow, 1954) which will form the basis of the present discussion.

After some preliminary remarks, Harlow comes to the heart of his thesis, thus:

Motivational theory and research have in the past put undue emphasis upon the role of the homeostatic drives—hunger, thirst, sex, and elimination —as forces energizing and directing human behavior. There are, indeed, some psychological theorists who would have us believe that all or most of our adult human motives are either directly dependent upon these homeostatic drives, or are second- or third-order derived drives conditioned upon visceral needs. The fact that derived drives based on homeostatic needs are unstable and transient, the fact that the conditioned drive stimulus does not apparently reinstate the unlearned drive state (Miles & Wickens, 1953;

Simon, Wickens, Brown, & Pennock, 1951), and the fact that human beings learn and live for days, weeks, or months without or in spite of a particular homeostatic need state do not disturb such psychological theorists in the least. It is, of course, the privilege of theorists to look at man from the point of view of the pylorus or to look at the pylorus from the point of view of man.

Recently, some psychological theorists, including Mowrer (1950a) and Brown (1953), have emphasized another area of motivation—pain and conditioned pain or anxiety—and some psychological theorists have argued that these motivational mechanisms could directly or indirectly underlie much human learning and could be extremely powerful forces in shaping human personality structure. No psychologist will underestimate the importance of conditioned pain (or anxiety, if it is so defined), because this derived drive appears to be far less susceptible to experiment extinction than are the derived drives based on the visceral need states. But lest the role of conditioned pain and fear be overestimated, it should be pointed out that common sense tells us that the greater part of our energies are motivated by positive goals, not escape from fear and threat (pp. 37–38).

In what has just been said it is implied that the secondary drives derived from primary drives other than pain are qualitatively, and usually also quantitatively, different from fear. In the preceding chapter, we have proceeded on the opposite assumption, apparently supported by a good deal of empirical evidence, that every drive, of considerable intensity, arouses some degree of fear and that it is this reaction which is most readily conditioned to formerly neutral stimuli that precede sudden drive onset or accompany drive of mounting intensity. Hence the supposition is that all secondary drives acquired in this way are, basically, the same: they are presumably all species of the fear response. Somewhat later in this chapter, this generalization will be slightly qualified (Section V); but the point is, this approach integrates what Harlow calls "positive goals" and "escape from fear and threat" into a unified system.

Furthermore, on the basis of the experimental findings reported by Zimmerman and others (Chapter 5), we now know that Harlow overemphasized the "unstable and transient" nature of "derived drives based on homeostatic needs." However, in light of much of the previous evidence, this misinterpretation was a very natural one.

Harlow's argument against the homeostatic view continues:

Furthermore, we would emphasize that intense emotional states are theoretically unsatisfactory motives for many learned activities of a moderate or high degree of complexity. It has been recognized for subhuman animals from the time of the formulation of the Yerkes-Dodson law (1908) that an inverse relationship exists between the intensity of motive and the complexity of task that can be efficiently learned (p. 38).

In the preceding chapters our assumption has been that many instances of secondary reinforcement are provided by a reduction or termination of relatively *mild* fears or fear-like tensions, and we have not at all assumed that "*intense* emotional states" are in any way prerequisite to the occurrence of this phenomenon. Diminutions in the level of intense and less intense secondary drives are assumed to be qualitatively similar and to differ, in their capacity to provide a reinforcing state of affairs, only in a quantitative sense. It is well known, of course (see, for example, Young, 1949a; Taylor & Spence, 1952; Montague, 1953; Spence & Farber, 1953; and Gordon & Berlyne, 1954), that intense fears or anxieties can have a markedly disorganizing effect upon problem-solving behavior, presumably because, when intense, they tend to distract the subject from the problem at hand and make him respond to and attempt to resolve the anxiety itself. But short of this threshold of distraction and disorganization, fear states seem quite capable of acting as suggested (cf. Chapter 5).

But the foregoing is a comparatively minor consideration, and we return again to Dr. Harlow's presentation.

It is certainly not our desire to underestimate the importance of either visceral drive states or emotional conditions as motivating forces underlying learning and influencing personality formation. Visceral drive states are important motivating mechanisms in children, and they become important motivational mechanisms in human adults under deprivation. Furthermore, the appetitive mechanisms [see pp. 196 ff.], innate and acquired, which are associated with (even though not of necessity derived from) the visceral need states are important and persistent human motivational mechanisms. Emotional conditions including pain, fear, anger, and frustration are also important and persistent human motivational mechanisms.

But above and beyond the visceral need-appetitive motivational mechanisms and the emotional motivational mechanisms there is, we believe, a third category of motives, a category of motives which are elicited by external stimuli and which have been described by such names as manipulation, exploration, curiosity, and play (p. 38).

Lest Harlow's "third category" appear more distinctive than it actually is, let us recall some of the assumptions made in the preceding chapters. In Chapters 2 and 3 it is posited that fear (secondary motivation) can be conditioned either to response-produced stimuli (as in punishment) *or* to independent stimuli (as in avoidance learning); and in Chapters 4 and 5 it is posited that fear reduction (secondary reinforcement) can, likewise, be conditioned either to independent *or* to response-produced stimuli (see also Chapter 7). Hence, if the third-category motives mentioned by Harlow are cued off by external stimuli, this fact alone does not set them apart from other secondary motivators and reinforcers. Moreover, it will be noted that the descriptive terms used to identify this third-order drive—"manipulation, exploration, curiosity, and play"—refer to *forms of behavior*. Though there is much precedent for it, the identification of drives in terms of behavior patterns is precarious, for the reason that a given drive can produce many different types of behavior and the same behavior may be produced by a variety of different kinds of drives. For example, to illustrate the latter point, it is perfectly possible to have two rats, both of which will leap into the air when placed in a demonstration apparatus of the type described in Chapter 2; but one of them will be doing so because it is afraid of being shocked and the other because it is hungry, as a means of "begging" for food. It would be most unwise, on the basis of the behavior of these two animals, to infer the presence of a "jumposity" *drive*. Various earlier writers (e.g., Murray, 1938) have explored the possibility of naming drives after characteristically recurrent actions or action patterns, somewhat in the way, at a still earlier time, psychologists used to spend a good deal of their energy—not very fruitfully, it now appears—drawing up "lists of instincts." A more dynamic approach to behavior theory seems to require that motives and the motions they produce be carefully differentiated (see Brown, 1953, pp. 11–18; Farber, 1954, pp. 24–25; Miller, 1951b, p. 467). Although there is a certain limited sense in which motivation and "habit" become almost synonymous (Chapters 8 and 12), only confusion results from inferring specific drives from behavior rather than identifying them by some *independent* criterion.[1]

[1] It will perhaps be helpful at this point to call attention to a similarity between the position which Harlow is here advocating and the general stance of Progressive Education. Under the leadership of John Dewey, the latter movement was in rebellion against the fear and coercion that characterized many 19th-century classrooms and stressed instead the importance of the child's *own* "needs and interests." The older approach was said to be "negative," the newer one, "positive." And since it is currently fashionable to "accent the positive," any recourse to "negative" methods is regarded as somewhat immoral. Two considerations are in order here. In the systematic conception of motivation and reinforcement which has been delineated in Chapter 5, we have made theoretical provision for *both types* of motivation and learning—(a) motivation aroused by a danger signal and secondary reinforcement (type-1) provided by the reduction thereof and (b) the motivation (fear, "interest") aroused by some *already present* drive or need and the secondary reinforcement (type-2) which a safety signal or promise produces. What the Progressive Educators, in effect, do is to stress the greater desirability in the classroom (and in child training generally) of the second of these situations. We do not in the least claim that the two situations are identical, or that

II. "Curiosity" and Fear

It is well known that the concept of imitation was weakened by the circular way in which it was commonly used, i.e., as both a description and as an explanation of behavior (Mowrer, 1960, Chapter 3). And it now appears that "curiosity" suffers from the same abuse: it is either a phenomenon which is to be explained, or it is itself a force or drive that can produce certain specific effects, but it is not both. Said otherwise, it is not simultaneously cause and effect. The position we shall here adopt is that "curiosity" is an effect, which may take the form of either physical or visual exploration of the environment (or both), and that fear is a common cause thereof.

Speaking for what he believes to be a different and more legitimate conception of curiosity, Harlow (1954) says:

The denial of the existence or importance of the externally elicited motives is amazing because at the common-sense level of humor and aphorism there are many references to the operation of the external-drive mechanisms. It is recognized that all primates, including man, spend a large amount of time just "monkeying around" and that monkeying around is an activity often leading to invention and creativity. There are countless cartoons bearing on the theme that the monkeys in the cage stare at the people outside

---

they do not have differential consequences. For example, a teacher (or any other person) who is constantly emitting danger signals will tend to drive students *away* from her (and from the school situation in general), whereas a teacher who emits safety signals and promises (which are confirmed) tends to *attract* them. And this is important, educationally. But our approach makes provision for both forms of "motivation and learning" and shows that, in the final analysis, they are not so very different, theoretically. Such *practical* differences as there are hinge mainly upon the question of what arouses the fear (or "interest"): a danger signal from the environment or a primary drive (or "danger") within the individual himself. The by-products of the two methods or situations are often very different indeed; but there is, it seems, no great difference in theory or scientific principle. Moreover, it now appears that even the practical advantages of the "progressive" approach are not so great as early enthusiasts believed, in that some children are so secure and "well-fed" that there are no secondary motives or interests on which the would-be educator can build; and, in addition, there are some things which human beings have to learn which apparently have to come from external, "imposed" authority and cannot be handled entirely on the basis of "indigenous" or "intrinsic" motivation. This line of thought cannot be further pursued here (cf. Mowrer, 1960, Chapter 10). But it may be useful to the reader, in evaluating the following discussion, to keep in mind that the issues which are here under scientific scrutiny have broad and, very often, emotionally loaded "philosophical" implications. It is hoped that our analysis will reduce the emotion and increase mutual understanding.

and are just as amused by what they see as are the people. Kohler reported staring through a peephole to see what a chimp was doing and found that it was staring at him! Visual exploration drives in subhuman primates are clearly recognized by the saying "Monkey see, monkey do." Yet, in spite of the obvious existence of the external drives psychologists have persisted in limiting themselves to endlessly repeating with insignificant variations, experiments designed to show the allegedly overwhelming importance of the homeostatic, internal drives. . . .

Every comparative psychologist who has adapted rats for maze experiments knows that the rodents frequently run down the straight-away path used in the adaption procedure, ignore the food, and continue to explore the environment. Frequently, the rat will refuse to eat until exploration and curiosity are sated, although it may have been deprived of food for 23 hours previously (p. 39).

But two other psychologists have previously interpreted similar observations quite differently. They say:

Preliminary observations had indicated that if animals [rats] were placed on [an elevated] maze without prior habituation, they showed considerable anxiety. This was first indicated by great cautiousness of movement and excessive urination and defecation. Later there was a period of feverish exploration, during which the animals ignored food even though they had not eaten for 24–36 hours. These observations suggest that "curiosity" is perhaps more closely related to anxiety than is ordinarily supposed (Whiting & Mowrer, 1943, p. 236).

Here the assumption is that hungry rats in an unfamiliar maze may, quite understandably, want to make sure that they are safe before they attempt to sate their hunger. Only after they are "satisfied" that there is *nothing dangerous* in the new situation are they able, it seems, to respond to their nutritional needs. And although the fear is here, to be sure, elicited by stimulation external to the organism, there is no reason for assuming that it is any the less internal than is the metabolic drive of hunger. Yet some writers show a persistent tendency to reject fear as the cause of "curiosity," although the facts are completely congruent with such an interpretation. For example, Montgomery (1955) begins a much-cited experimental paper as follows:

The purpose of the present investigation is to determine whether novel stimulation evokes the fear drive as well as the exploratory drive. A growing body of evidence indicates that novel stimuli evoke the exploratory drive (Butler, 1953; Harlow, 1950; Montgomery, 1951b, 1953; and Thompson & Heron, 1954). Qualitative observation has repeatedly suggested to the author that such stimuli may also evoke the fear drive. In the psychological and zoological literature the same suggestion has been made a number of times, and scattered and unsystematic evidence supporting it can be found (e.g., Hebb, 1946; McDougall, 1923; Melzack, 1952; and Rand, 1941) (p. 254).

What this writer neglects is the possibility that fear and the "exploratory drive" are one and the same thing. This oversight apparently occurs because of the assumption "that the exploratory drive leads to approach behavior (Berlyne, 1950; Montgomery & Monkman, 1955) and that the fear drive leads to avoidance behavior (Miller, 1951b; Montgomery & Monkman, 1955)" (p. 254). The latter proposition is clearly gratuitous. It is true (as already seen in Chapter 2) that if a source of discomfort has been clearly and definitely localized in space, the resulting fear leads to avoidance; but it is also well established that a vaguer, less-well-identified threat can cause vigorous generalized activity and even specific tendencies to *return* to the place where some painful experience (such as electric shock) has occurred. Rats shocked in one of two adjacent compartments and thereby driven into the other show an almost irresistible tendency to go back to the first compartment (cf. Chapter 2). And Hebb & Thompson (1954) report that:

. . . the dog that is frightened by a strange object is nevertheless apt to return to look at it again, balanced between closer approach and flight (Melzack, 1954). The same thing can be observed in chimpanzees, and Woodworth (1921) and Valentine (1930) have described the behavior of young children who ask to be shown again—at a safe distance—the object that has frightened them (p. 551). [2]

The biological utility of such a tendency is clear: it is important for living organisms to know whether a given event is accidental or is associated in some orderly and predictable way with a particular place or action. Therefore, a certain amount of "exploration" (or "reality testing") is necessary and useful as a means of more definitely "structuring" a situation, i.e., freeing the individual from what might otherwise be needless inhibitions (or "superstitions") or confirming a specific and reliable source of danger. And fear—diffuse, nonspecific fear—can serve as an adequate motivation for such behavior; there is no need to posit a special (and tautological) "exploratory" or "curiosity" drive.

This tendency for organisms to re-expose themselves to rather nonspecific dangers has suggested to some the possibility that the "ego likes

[2] On the basis of extensive experience in breeding and training horses, Miss Gertrude Hendrix reports that "Young colts are afraid of everything that is strange. But breeders and trainers know that colts react in two different ways to strange situations: some of them just *avoid* them—others *investigate* them. Only the latter are regarded as good candidates for training" (personal communication). Cf. Welker (1956), "Effects of Age and Experience on Play and Exploration of Young Chimpanzees."

to precipitate anxiety in manageable amounts" and that this tendency is the basis for masochism. However, such speculations have not received laboratory confirmation. For example, Eriksen and Zimmerman, at the University of Illinois, taught rats to press a bar as a means of turning off a danger signal and averting an electric shock. Then they made it possible for the subjects, by means of another manipulation, to turn *on* the danger signal, which they could, of course, immediately terminate by means of the bar. Suffice it to say that the rats showed no inclination to turn the danger signal on, because it "felt so good" to turn it off. Apparently, at this point, it was perfectly clear to the rats that the danger signal was something they wanted as little of as possible; and there was no tendency to try to "master" (extinguish) their fear of it or to "explore" it. Here, it seems, the situation was already too highly structured (perceptually) for the rats to have any "curiosity" about it whatever: they definitely knew that the danger signal was bad and that the less they had of it the better. Only, it seems, in situations which are in some way ambiguous do exploration and curiosity manifest themselves. Whiteis (1955, 1956) has shown that rats will continue to give themselves a brief shock as a means of escaping from a fear situation; but this phenomenon has been rather thoroughly analyzed in other terms (Mowrer, 1950a) and has no special relevance here (see Sidman & Boren, 1957b; also Chapter 12).

III. The Problem of Visual Exploration

But what of another type of observation reported by Harlow? This involves putting a monkey into a small light-proof box and rewarding it, for manipulative or discrimination behavior, merely by a brief "look" out of the box (see Fig. 6–1; also Butler, 1953). Of the results of this kind of experimentation and as a summary of his general point of view, Professor Harlow says:

We are convinced that the externally elicited motivational systems are as fundamental and as innate as are the hunger-appetite and thirst-appetite systems. By this we do not mean that learning does not operate as a component in the externally elicited motivational systems of the adult animal; we merely mean that the learning component here is probably no larger than it is for the hunger-appetite motivational system. We firmly believe that externally elicited motivational systems interact with the hunger-appetite and thirst-appetite systems, but we do not believe, and there is no evidence to support the position, that any of these systems is derived from the other, or that any differential degree of dependence exists among them.

Recently, motivation theorists and personality theorists have shown some

motivational obsession about anxiety. No one will deny that anxiety, or
many other emotional states, serve as motives—but any assumption that
anxiety has some special, prepotent motivational role has yet to be established [cf. Chapter 5, footnote 15]. At best, anxiety is a motive for avoidant
behavior [cf. Section II], and the greatest part of human motivation is
positive searching toward goals, not mere avoidance. In spite of our faith
in the importance of positive, forward-oriented motives such as curiosity,
manipulation, and exploration, we do not wish to put any constraints, in
research or theory, upon the anxious psychologists. We merely wish to
insist, however, that even if some psychologists are scourged to their experimental dungeons like quarry slaves, the remainder of the population
will continue to be motivated by pleasant and positive incentives (1954, p. 52).

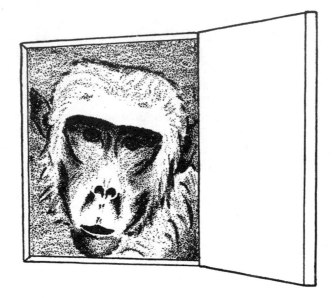

Fig. 6–1. Sketch indicating a portion of the research set-up developed by Harlow
(1954) for the study of visual motivation and reward in the monkey. When the
door is closed, the subject readily learns to solve puzzles and make complex discriminations as a means of getting the door to open for a few minutes. The opportunity to "look out" is the only reinforcement received for such activities. A
theoretical analysis of this type of learning is suggested in the text.

    Harlow is, of course, right in saying that many psychologists have
stressed the "negative" side of motivation and neglected the "positive"
side. As indicated toward the end of Chapter 2, there is, however, a
historical, if not logical, reason for this; and the two immediately

preceding chapters show the extent to which psychologists have, more recently, concerned themselves with the "pull" rather than the "push" side of the motivation and learning problem. Nevertheless, one wonders if it is not a contradiction in terms to speak of "pleasant and positive" motives or drives. A good many years ago, in a very thoughtful paper, Muenzinger & Fletcher (1936) took the position that *all* motivation is, almost by definition, "negative," in that it involves a state of affairs which the organism is striving to alter, correct, terminate. In order to reduce hunger, for example, the organism must, to be sure, behave "positively" with respect to certain substances or objects in its environment; but this "adient" behavior, to borrow E. B. Holt's terms, is *basically* "abient." In other words, the organism tries to get *more* of certain stimuli (food) as a means of having *less* of certain other stimuli (hunger). In this frame of reference, hunger is the *motive* and food is the *incentive*, and one wonders if Harlow's discussion is not misleading in the way it involves an easy, seemingly uncritical use of one as virtually synonymous with the other (see also Chapter 8).

But perhaps all this can be made more specific by looking carefully at the methodology which Harlow, in the paper under discussion, stresses most: the work-for-look procedure. Harlow has steadily argued that the privilege of peering out of the little cell-like box for a few minutes cannot reasonably be thought of as involving reward or reinforcement in the sense of any kind of drive reduction. Pretty obviously, there is no primary drive gratification, such as hunger or thirst reduction; but he has equally held, with less clear justification, that there is likewise no reduction in any sort of secondary drive, such as fear. At the International Congress of Psychology, held in Montreal in 1954, N. E. Miller, in response to a presentation by Harlow, pertinently observed that "solitary confinement" is one of the most dreaded methods of disciplining human prisoners; and, being only a little less social, the monkey probably finds it equally odious.[3] If

___

[3] This point has been elaborated by Myers & Miller (1954) as follows: "We believe it possible that confinement produces anxiety, restraint is frustrating, or monotony arouses a drive of boredom. Indeed, the observation of small children who are required to sit absolutely still, the reports of prisoners subjected to solitary confinement, and the difficulty of Bexton, Heron, & Scott (1954) in retaining Ss in their experiment on the effects of decreased sensory variation would indicate that such conditions can produce strong motivation [see also Lilly, 1956; Heron, Doane, & Scott, 1956]. Therefore, we suggest that drive produced by homogeneous or montonous stimulation, enforced inaction, etc., may be reduced by sensory variety, freedom of action, etc., and that such drive reduction is the *reinforcement* involved in learning for 'exploratory,' 'manipulatory,' and

visual isolation is objectionable, then even a brief period of visual freedom would be rewarding and could be used to facilitate, perhaps quite powerfully, learning of various kinds (see Miller, 1954).

It has long been known among bird trainers that one of the best ways to motivate a bird to "talk" is to cover its cage so that it cannot see "what is going on." Having thus been deprived of visual contact with its environment, the bird tends to concentrate upon the oral-aural channel of communication and will listen more attentively to the voice of the trainer and will, itself, be more likely to vocalize.

Even more dramatic and more recent evidence comes from the psychology laboratories at McGill University (Bexton, Huron, & Scott, 1954) of the disturbing effects produced upon human beings by cutting off, as nearly as possible, all sensory contact with their environment. In a dark, silent room, with even cutaneous and tactile stimulation greatly reduced, human subjects, in the course of three or four days, often find themselves having experiences which, under ordinary circumstances, would certainly be regarded as psychotic. These experiences, fortunately, are transitory and lift with a return to normal experience; but they show how disagreeable and disorganizing sensory deprivation can be. The box employed in the Harlow experiments is presumably a sort of miniature version of the isolation room used in the McGill experiments; and one would predict that monkeys would not only learn to do whatever would temporarily end the visual isolation, but would also show great alacrity in leaving such a box, when given the opportunity, and also reluctance to re-enter it.

Nor is it difficult to see why exclusion of visual stimulation should make for apprehensiveness. In terms of orientation and movement in space, vision is by all odds our most valuable sense; and one can quickly gain a nice appreciation of it by attempting for a few minutes to carry on, blindfolded, his routine activities. Everyone has vivid memories of falls and assorted bumps and bruises received when moving about in darkness; and vision is perhaps even more useful in the social, interorganismic world. Being able to see, to "lay eyes" on,

---

'exercise' rewards. For the present, we choose the more parsimonious alternative of trying to analyze such concepts as exploratory drive along the same lines as conventional drives" (p. 435). Cf. Miles (1958b) who, in a paper on learning "in kittens with manipulatory, exploratory, and food incentives," says: "The results support the thesis that manipulatory and exploratory activities are rewarding in their own right and that the postulation of a derived-incentive function is unnecessary" (p. 41)

friends and loved ones is a very comforting experience, at both the human and subhuman levels. And when enemies are about, it is even more desirable, for different reasons, to be able to "watch out" for them. An organism which has reason to attack another one which is without vision has, in effect, the advantage, often mentioned in tales of fantasy, of invisibility. How terrifying to think of the assassin's knife or the tiger's fangs brought to one's throat without possible visual foreknowledge! Or, imagine the predicament of a blind boxer. Small wonder, then, that children openly confess to a fear of or, more accurately, fear *in* the dark and that even adults tacitly avoid "dark places." So great, in fact, is our dependence upon vision that we commonly equate the ability to comprehend or understand something to being able to *see into it* (insight); and in the field of electroencephalography it is known that vision, more than any other modality, influences the frequency and pattern of brain waves. Closing one's eyes is more often suggestive of sleep or even death than is the blockage of any other sensory avenue. So the Creator, as portrayed in Genesis, apparently had the right idea when, preparatory to getting the world going, he said, "Let there be light." Light is proverbially associated with freedom, security, understanding, and happiness—darkness with insecurity and fear.[4]

Moreover, Myers & Miller (1954) make a nice point when they say:

> We . . . would not put a drive in a special category simply because it is elicited by external stimuli. We prefer the drive-reduction hypothesis of Hull (1943) and Miller & Dollard (1941), which treats externally elicited drives (such as pain) in the same way as other drives. Furthermore, as Brown (1953) has pointed out, in some of the Wisconsin studies on the "visual exploration drive" the novel stimuli to be explored are not present at the time the animal begins working to secure them. If the novel stimuli elicit the drive, this would mean that the drive is produced *after* the animal has performed the response the drive is supposed to be motivating.
>
> If, as Harlow seems to imply, the same novel stimuli elicit an exploratory drive and *simultaneously* serve as an exploratory reward, a strict drive-reduction theory would be unable to deal with these phenomena (p. 435).

Stimulus-response psychology, with science in general, assumes that the *cause* of an action must be present, here and now, and cannot lie at some future point in time. Thus, as Myers & Miller indicate,

[4] Rhoades & Wyers (1958) have reported that experimentally blinded rats consume more than twice as much saccharine water as do normal controls. It is not readily apparent why this should occur, unless it is that the loss of vision increases the animals' insecurity and the drinking of a sweet solution is somewhat reassuring (see Section VI; also "ice-box neurosis," p. 162).

logic would seem to require that in Harlow's experiments the *drive* be in the monkey, in the box, *before* the little window is opened and that what is then seen, on the outside, is *rewarding*, not "motivating" (except in so far as a reward always sets up an incentive system or "habit"—see Chapter 7).

Dr. Harlow has certainly reported some interesting and important observations; and he has, in addition, performed a valuable service in alerting us against the danger of a too ready acceptance of the "homeostatic" conception of motivation and reinforcement. However, it can scarcely be said that any of his experimental data constitute crucial, or even very strongly presumptive, evidence against such a view. In fact, an examination of these experiments, at a little deeper level of analysis, seems to provide support for the very position which Harlow so vigorously (though charmingly) rejects.

IV. Illumination as Reinforcement and the Concept of Optimal Stimulation

Closely related to Harlow's researches is a study by Kish (1955) on the use of a moderate increase in illumination as a source of reinforcement. This study was suggested by another (Kish & Antonitis, 1956), in which it was found that "a class of events that appears neither to be need-reducing nor previously associated with need reduction [such as] microswitch clicks, relay noises, and stimuli produced by a moving platform exerted what appeared to be reinforcing effects on the unconditioned operant behavior of mice" (p. 261). These investigators were disposed to think of these events as "reinforcers," and in a certain special sense they were: they reinforced, or strengthened, general exploratory activity, but they seem to have done this by continually introducing novel stimuli into the environment, thus keeping the mice "interested," aroused, stimulated, curious, apprehensive, motivated (cf. Walker, Dember, Earl, & Karoly, 1955). There is not, so far as one can see, any indication here that the mice were reinforced in the sense of being rewarded or relieved by these stimuli: quite the reverse. But the experiment to which these observations led was of a different order: it involved putting laboratory mice into a dark box and then making it possible for them, by means of a "bar-touch response," to turn on "dim illumination." After seven daily habituation sessions (of 25 minutes each) in the box, the subjects, on the eighth day, found that the bar, which had been previously available but "dead," now caused the box to be briefly illuminated: the number of contacts with the bar, per session, now increased from about 70 to 160. And on five subsequent "extinction" days the incidence of bar pressing was considerably higher than it had been in the preceding habituation sessions, thus indicating that this response had acquired considerable "habit strength" on the one day it had been reinforced (i.e., had turned on the light).

Kish is therefore obviously on sound grounds when he says:

The data clearly demonstrate that the onset of dim illumination occurring as the consequence of the response, leads to behavioral effects which correspond to those noted as the criteria for the occurrence of reinforcement (p. 263).

But the justification is less good when he goes on to say:

These results, therefore, appear to support the hypothesis that a perceptible environmental change, which is unrelated to such need states as hunger and thirst, will reinforce any response which it follows (p. 263).

The hypothesis does not specify whether the process involved here is one of primary or secondary reinforcement. Several considerations, however, would appear to indicate that this process is not one of secondary reinforcement. . . .

Apparently, the process involved in this experiment is that of primary reinforcement [although] the term is not used here to denote the process defined by Hull (1943) as involving the reduction of a need (p. 264).

For some time now, human beings have been striking matches and lighting candles and, more recently, pressing electric-light switches, as a means of converting darkness into visibility; but no one has previously made much of a mystery of it. The advantages of being able to "see what you are doing" and of not having to be "in the dark" have already been noted (Section II). Darkness characteristically produces feelings of apprehension ranging from vague uneasiness to panic, so it is puzzling that the investigator cited insists that "there is no evidence for any drive or need that could be reduced by the onset of light" (p. 264). When one wishes to go to sleep, one commonly retreats from or eliminates light; but whenever one has "something to *do*," illumination is usually an enormous asset. And laboratory evidence to this effect is now available. For example, Davis (1958) has recently shown that *satiated* rats press a bar that provides illumination no more than they press one that does not; but if they are deprived of food for only two hours, interest in having "light on the subject" increases markedly and is even more striking after 24 hours of deprivation. The moral seems to be: If you are not "going anywhere," it doesn't matter too much whether you can see or not; but if you are "looking for something," either good or bad, ability to see it is of the essence (see also Mowrer, 1960, Chapter 5).[5]

That the value of light to laboratory animals under the conditions just described is that it enables them to *see*, rather than providing some inherent "primary reinforcement" of the kind posited by Kish, is clearly suggested by observations recently reported by Hurwitz (1956b). With rats as subjects, this investigator says:

> When the light is kept on [by means of bar pressing] for extended periods, the animal vigorously surveys the box, making rapid, scanning-like head movements. The rate of pressing was not regular. Responses tended to be bunched, each "burst" being separated by periods of "silence." During a response burst the animal would stand on its paws on the lever, the head held at right angles pointing to the light source (p. 33).

Since it is thus so apparent that the rats were here using the light as a means of scrutinizing the environment, it is somewhat surprising that Hurwitz goes on to comment, thus:

> The above results are relevant to the controversy about the importance of homeostatic mechanisms in animal learning which continues to feature prominently in the literature on the psychology of learning. Some writers (Hull, 1943) hold that the conditioning of responses is only possible in the presence of stimuli representative of need stabilization. So far, at least, it has been extraordinarily difficult to adduce evidence inimical to this theory. However, since it is not obvious how light—in the case of rats—is instrumental to the stabilization of organic needs, it seems that the experiments reported here, as well as those reported by Girdner (1953), Henderson (1953) and Marx et al. (1955) call for an alternative approach to the central problem of conditioning (p. 33).

Any paradox which may be apparent here is resolved by the assumption that every primary drive has an affective component and that the latter can be either heightened or lowered by external conditions that are, respectively, unfavorable or favorable to the prospect of primary-drive reduction. Also, it is to be remembered that affect can be aroused in the absence of strong primary drive (but in anticipation thereof) and that it, too, is a potential source of secondary reinforcement which can be mediated by environmental cues or circumstances.

---

[5] The possibility should be explored that *familiarity* with a situation will influence a rat's interest in illumination. If the size, shape, floor texture, and smell of a compartment were well known, a rat might immediately identify where he was and, especially with the aid of vibrissae, be able to get around in the situation quite well without light, hence show less tendency to perform an act which would turn light on than would be evident in a strange situation.

Experiments by Keller (1942) and others have shown that *intense* light (like electric shock) can be used (a) to motivate and reinforce laboratory rats in the development of *escape* responses and (b) as the unconditioned stimulus for the development of anticipatory, *avoidance* reactions. Therefore, since the work of Kish and others shows that when in total darkness (and otherwise properly motivated) laboratory animals will also strive to *get* illumination, it is not surprising that the concept of "optimal stimulation" should have occurred to some writers. For example, Leuba (1955), after reviewing the work of Harlow, Montgomery, Kish, and others, comes to the conclusion that:

Tension reduction would not seem to be a general or the only principle of learning. It may be only one aspect of a more general principle, a principle which might be called one of optimal stimulation: the organism tends to learn those reactions which will produce an optimal level of *total* stimulation. Hebb writes "animals will always act so as to produce an optimal level of excitation" (Hebb & Thompson, 1954, p. 552). That level is often higher than the one present at the moment (p. 28).

Both the experimental evidence now available and general observations seem to indicate that the concept of optimal stimulation may have wide applicability in human development. *The organism tends to acquire those reactions which, when over-all stimulation is low, are accompanied by increasing stimulation; and when over-all stimulation is high, those which are accompanied by decreasing stimulation* (p. 29).

This, certainly, is not a point of view that can be summarily dismissed; at the same time it is not one to be uncritically accepted. As we have seen, situations which at first seem to violate the homeostatic model often prove, upon further analysis, to conform to it very acceptably. Furthermore, the principle of optimal stimulation proves hard to test because it "cuts both ways" and can "explain" anything that happens, *post hoc*, but is weak on prediction. Also it should be remembered that few theorists would today, in any case, hold that "tension reduction [is] the only principle of learning." As repeatedly noted in this volume, learning also occurs in connection with drive increase; but this learning is *different* from that associated with drive decrement. Therefore, many instances where organisms *seem* to be (and, at a superficial level, *are*) seeking stimulation turn out to represent attempts to *reduce* a more fundamental type of stimulation (fears or tensions) acquired on the basis of prior learning of the incremental-reinforcement variety.

Yet another consideration that is relevant here is that the *physiological* principle of optimal state does not necessarily provide a valid analogue of *psychological* functioning. Mammals, for example, must maintain a given bodily temperature, within rather narrow limits, or die; and when this state goes either above or below optimum, steps are taken to correct it. However, from a psychological and motivational standpoint, temperature deviations both above and below "normal" function in similar ways; *each* makes the organism uncomfortable and so, basically, may be said to drive it in only *one* direction: toward *reduced*, rather than heightened, stimulation. Even though seeking a higher temperature physiologically, what the organism is trying to do *motivationally* is to *get rid* of the noxious feeling of coldness, or hotness, as the case may be.

Despite these negative indications, however, one should not completely exclude the concept of optimum stimulation or tension. Beyond a certain point of relaxation or tensionlessness, living organisms do, after all, cease to function in the behavioral (psychological) sense and go to sleep (a purely physiological state). And waking is now commonly thought to involve an "arousal reaction" (Delafresnaye *et al.*, 1954). Even a steam engine, an electric motor, or an internal-combustion engine must have a minimum of internal "strain," pressure, or torque to operate. And the McGill University studies (already cited) suggest that after human beings, in an environment of abnormally constant and low stimulation, have "caught up" on their sleep, they find such an environment strangely uncomfortable and disconcerting. The issue is therefore by no means a closed one; but it seems that there are still unexploited possibilities in respect to drive-reduction (homeostatic) theory which should be carefully considered before one resorts to the notion that drive induction can be rewarding (rather than punishing).

V. Affectivity, Drive, and Need: The Views of P. T. Young

Over a period of some years now the researches and writings of Professor P. T. Young have generated considerable interest in the general area of motivation and learning. Fortunately, these studies have recently been summarized in two papers, which will form the basis of the present discussion. The most salient conclusions reached at the end of these two papers read, in part, as follows:

Affective processes exist in the rat as truly as in man. When the head receptors, especially those of taste and touch and smell, come in contact with a food there is an affective arousal which we have designated as enjoyment. . . . Distress produced by deprivation and the relief of distress through food ingestion are also affective processes which are importantly related to food acceptance.

An hedonic theory of drive is proposed. Specific food-seeking dete.:-minations are organized within the nervous system to preserve the enjoyment of foods and to relieve organic distress produced by dietary deprivation. In general, rats develop drives to run to foods which they *like* (find enjoyable) rather than to foods which they *need* (require nutritionally). There is, however, a positive correlation between what rats *like* and what they *need* but not a one-to-one relation (Young, 1949b, p. 119).

The sign (positive or negative), intensity, and duration of affective processes are of prime importance in the organization of behavior, especially in the organization of approach and avoidance patterns. Current stimulus-response psychology is completely inadequate as an explanation of the many facts considered in this paper. American psychologists, dominated by the S—R principles, have followed Watson in rejecting affective processes on grounds of subjectivism and the inadequacy of introspective methods. But a wholly objective approach to problems of affective arousal is now possible and, moreover, such an approach is necessary. The S—R approach has marked limitations in the analysis of preferences, optimal acceptance of foods, acquisition of attitudes and motives and related problems. This S—R approach must be supplemented by a theory that recognizes the central importance of affective processes in motivation and learning and that supplements S—R principles by sound hedonic theory (Young, 1955, pp. 232–233).

Before attempting to comment more specifically on these excerpts from Young's writings, it may be helpful to provide some background material. Young received his graduate training as a psychologist at Cornell University, under the great Structuralist and introspectionist, E. B. Titchener. Remnants of phrase and concept from the Titchenerian school are still common in his writings; but, unlike most students who came under Titchener's influence, Young went into animal research; and, lacking the then common Watsonian orientation, he was able to interest himself in problems which the strict Behaviorist felt he must eschew.

Taken in their entirety, Young's writings are involved, terminologically difficult, and somewhat inconsistent. Yet, they call attention to some commonly neglected but manifestly important problems. In order to appreciate the full importance of Young's reasoning with respect to one of these, it will be necessary to go back to the body of the 1955 paper. Here we read:

Affective processes are positive or negative in sign. If an animal in a novel situation takes a sip of sugar solution and returns for another sip, I would assume that a positive affective process has been aroused by the sweet taste. If an animal in a novel situation receives an electric shock and then avoids the place where the shock was received, I would assume a negative affective process. In both situations the affective process is inferred as a cause or source of behavior and as a factor that sustains or terminates the pattern aroused. The acquisition of approach and avoidance patterns proceeds according to the hedonic principle of maximizing positive affectivity (delight, enjoyment) and minimizing negative affectivity (distress). The hedonic processes thus regulate behavior in a very fundamental sense. They underlie the *direction* that is characteristic of many acquired motives (p. 194).

In terms of revised two-factor learning theory, we would interpret Young's two illustrations in terms of the following principles: Responses, stimuli, or situations which are associated with incremental reinforcement (punishment) take on the capacity, themselves, to arouse a form of discomfort (fear); and responses, stimuli, or situations associated with decremental reinforcement (reward) take on the capacity to reduce discomfort (arouse hope); and, as a result, living organisms tend to be guided away from punishing situations and toward rewarding ones.

The point of difference, it seems, is this: Young takes the position that "a sip of sugar solution" is capable of acting as a "positive" reinforcer without any necessary drive decrement. In support of this position he cites an experiment in which:

Rats were fed *ad libitum* upon a standard diet and an unlimited supply of tap water. There was never any deprivation of food or water; no known dietary deficiency existed; there was no initial drive to be reduced. The rats were healthy and active throughout the experiment. Motivation came solely from contact with the sweet-tasting fluid; the rats ran to get a taste just as a child runs to get a piece of candy (p. 196).

Young is here assuming that the actions and situation associated with the sip of sugar solution were positively reinforced merely because the solution *tasted good*, and not because it reduced any drive. This is the essence of his theory of "palatability" or "positive affectivity." First let us examine possible weaknesses in this interpretation and then a supporting consideration.

The passage just quoted contains some very bold and questionable assumptions. For example, it completely ignores the possibility of *specific hungers*. It assumes, quite unjustifiably, that because rats have no nutritional drives which water or some bulk food like Purina chow can satisfy, they have no nutritional drives at all. It is entirely possible, indeed probable, that certain types of hunger can be appeased while others remain unappeased (see Young, 1955, p. 229). And this assumption is made all the more plausible by the fact of satiation: rats *do* satiate on sugar solution. This fact strongly suggests that some sort of drive reduction, rather than mere palatability, is here involved. (In the experiment cited, the rats received "only one sip per day," so that the possibility of satiation was carefully avoided; see also Smith & Duffy, 1957).

As pointed out in the preceding chapter, living organisms will sometimes eat (or engage in other consummatory behavior) in the absence of the appropriate, relevant primary drive; but analysis of these situations indicates that such behavior tends to be drive reducing in the sense of lessening some form of fear or other tension state. Although there is no very compelling reason to believe that the rats in the experiment cited sipped the sugar solution because it "pacified" them, yet this is a possibility which cannot be categorically excluded. Certainly if the rats were for any reason fearful, it would not be at all surprising if they showed a predeliction for a source of stimulation that is sweet and "soothing" (see footnote 4).

Yet Young's general argument cannot be dismissed. The alternative view, as it stems from "homeostatic-drive" theory, would have to take some such position as this concerning the problem of palatability. It would have to hold that tastes are palatable in proportion to the extent to which foods with which they are associated are drive reducing. In general, there does indeed seem to be a correlation here, although not a perfect one. Of all ordinary foods, the sugars provide the most quickly available form of energy—and they also are "most palatable." Inert, nutritionally useless substances tend to taste flat, bland; and harmful substances tend to be extremely bitter, sour, or putrid. However, the question remains whether this correlation is learned or innate. It might be either. Substances whose ingestion leads to hunger reduction ought to come to taste *good;* those which are ineffective in reducing hunger ought to taste *neutral;* and those which are harmful if ingested ought to come to taste *bad.* Such would follow from the conception of learning being elaborated in this book.

But the question is: Can living organisms afford to be dependent upon individual experience for guidance concerning the acceptability of a substance as food *or* would they do better with a built-in set of "palatability" values or guides? It could well be that a very young mammal would sometimes starve before learning, on the basis of conditioning, that milk is "good"; or, equally unfortunate, it might poison itself before learning that some other substance is "bad." *Innately given affective reactions,* of both a positive and negative nature, might therefore provide an organism with an important advantage over one that had no such racially derived "knowledge." [6]

What are the facts? There is a good deal of evidence that newly born mammals react differently, without prior learning, to sweet and bitter (Pratt, Nelson, & Sun, 1930). And certainly common sense suggests that we ordinarily taste things in order to see if they are "fit to eat," not that they taste good because they have, in the past, appeased our hunger. Yet it would obviously not be biologically useful for our food likes and dislikes to be completely and irrevocably fixed by instinctive mechanisms.[7] Laboratory facts seem to suggest that they are not. In the 1955 paper previously cited and discussed, Young reviews a number of experiments in which food preferences have been altered. It has been found that, as common experience would suggest, satiation on one distinctive type of food (say sugar) may reverse the normal preference of that food for another (say protein). Such alternations in apparent palatability are, of course, transient. But chronic deprivation of animals with respect to a particular type of essential food may produce, as Young has shown, relatively enduring changes in the relative acceptability or palatability of foods (see also Brown, 1955).

In sum, then, what do we really know about the question of whether

[6] These considerations can be given added cogency by thinking of taste, and smell too, as a kind of *preliminary chemical analysis* (or physiological "sampling") that is quickly made of substances as they enter the body, through the mouth or nose. These are the two normal intake portals of the body; and because it may be "too late" after a substance gets inside, it must be "checked" before being allowed "admission." A less refined, second-stage checking also goes on, in the lungs and stomach, to be followed by ejection if the results are not good; but the greatest sensitivity and discernment is in the special receptors which are more peripherally located. Considering how much is here at stake, biologically, it is not surprising that there should be considerable "excitement" ("affective arousal," in Young's terms), of either a positive or negative kind, as the reports of such analyses flow to the central nervous system. (A good "poison," obviously, is one which gets by both levels of censorship and is taken, from the stomach, or lungs, into the bloodstream.) For another dimension of this problem, see also Chapter 10.

[7] Murray, Wells, Kohn, & Miller (1953) have recently shown that sodium sucaryl, a substance which tastes sweet to human beings, is rejected by rats. "This difference," they say, "indicates that the taste mechanisms of the two species are different" (p. 137). And they imply that the difference is inherent rather than experientially determined. "The affective value of taste stimuli is a little-explored area with important implications for a theory of taste (Pfaffman, 1951). Furthermore, species differences in behavioral measures of taste receptivity may be a strategic point of departure for the analysis of the mechanism of taste" (p. 134).

taste values are derived from the extent to which they have been associated with physiologically nutritious or injurious substances or whether taste values are given, more or less completely, at birth? While it is apparently quite possible for an organism to *learn* to like or to dislike a particular kind of food (on the basis of specific experiences therewith), there can be no doubt that some tastes are innately agreeable or disagreeable; and Young has done a real service in keeping this fact from being overlooked in an age of extreme (and quite possibly excessive) empiricism. However, it is still a mystery how the nativistic attitudes of acceptance or rejection toward particular foods are achieved, neurologically speaking; and, as already indicated, these "affective" (palatability) reactions do not operate in complete independence of homeostatic mechanisms. In general, a food "tastes good" only when there is a hunger for it, and the odiousness of a substance also seems somewhat related to whether the organism is hungry or satiated. But even though particular tastes have a biologically given capacity to elicit positive or negative affectivity (to use Young's terms), the fact seems to be that this arrangement is not the *most general* one: more common, apparently, is the tendency for stimuli to be originally "neutral" as far as the organism is concerned, and thus capable of acquiring sign function in terms of the organism's individual experiences.[8]

Moreover, even in the realm of taste there is a logical problem which has not been adequately resolved. In one of the passages previously quoted, Young says: "Motivation came solely from contact with the sweet-tasting fluid; the rats ran to get a taste just as a child runs to get a piece of candy." The difficulty here is the familiar one of teleology. Everyone, from time to time, lapses into teleological language, because of the simplicity of statement it permits; but in a sound theoretical system, such loose expressions can be restated in more rigorous terms. The trouble with hedonism, in general, is that it is *necessarily* teleological. In denying motives and drives as the prime movers or cause of behavior, it *must* take the position that living organisms behave as they do "in order to attain pleasure and avoid pain." The difficulty is that the pleasure or pain can be experienced only *after* a given action has taken place and therefore cannot operate causally (cf. Section III; also Smith & Duffy, 1957).

[8] Cf. Olds' 1956 book, *The Growth and Structure of Motives,* in which it is argued "that any neutral object can become the goal of an approach motive, that is, an object of desire, depending upon controllable aspects of the subject's experience with the object" (from the jacket).

In a paper published in 1948 Young himself recognized this problem:

> We had previously assumed that the rate of running depended directly upon the stimulation of the head receptors. Just as painful stimulation of the skin releases energy and heightens the activity level of an animal so, we assumed, stimulation of the tongue with sugar releases more energy in behavior than stimulation with casein.
>
> This interpretation is probably incorrect. On every run in the present experiment the direct stimulation of the tongue came *after* the approach to food had been completed. If any effects of such stimulation could modify the time of approach to food, that effect would have to appear 24 hours later during the next run. It is highly improbable that the excitatory effect of stimulation of the head receptors could be revealed 24 hours later, more or less, in the speed of approach to and acceptance of food (p. 282).

The resolution of this dilemma which Young proposed brings his thinking into general proximity with the over-all position of the present volume (see also Young, 1959). However, it will be necessary to postpone further discussion thereof to Chapter 8.

VI. The Effects of Saccharine, Sham Feeding, and Stomach Loading

Here we shall consider a variety of experiments centering on a common problem: Is consummatory behavior, such as eating or drinking, reinforcing from a learning standpoint only if it results in primary drive reduction or is such behavior, somehow, reinforcing in its own right? In the preceding section it has been shown that the mere *taste* of food may be reinforcing to a hungry animal, through some presumably innate mechanism; but this does not at all exclude the possibility that learned processes (involving so-called secondary reinforcement) are also prominently involved. Although the evidence is by no means yet complete, enough is known to state with some confidence that there are purely "habitual" elements in consummatory actions, which means that these actions may be reinforcing without necessarily involving primary-drive satiation.

Because a solution of sugar water is highly palatable and nutritious to rats and because a saccharine solution tastes much the same but is not at all nutritious, there is here an interesting opportunity to fractionate out the influence of hunger reduction from the total eating-ingestion constellation. Therefore, in 1950, Sheffield & Roby carried out a series of experiments with saccharine (rats served as subjects) which led them to draw the following inferences:

1. A non-nourishing but sweet-tasting substance [saccharine] was shown in three successive learning situations to be effective reward for instrumental learning, its reward value depending on the state of hunger present.

2. The possibility that the sweet taste was an acquired reward rather than a primary reward was shown to be extremely unlikely.

3. The findings demonstrate the expected limitations of Hull's molar "need reduction" theory of reinforcement and the necessity of exploring indirect reduction of striped-muscle tension as a drive-reduction factor in Miller and Dollard's theory of reinforcement. The results are consistent with Guthrie's last-response theory of reinforcement, and demonstrate that a sweet taste is "reinforcing" in Skinner's system, "satisfying" in Thorndike's system, and "demanded" in Tolman's system.

4. It is suggested that elicitation of the consummatory response appears to be a more critical *primary* reinforcing factor in instrumental learning than the drive reduction subsequently achieved (p. 481).

By way of amplifying these statements and of relating them to the theories and research findings of others, Sheffield & Roby say:

The experiments prove that a non-nourishing but sweet-tasting substance served as a reinforcement for instrumental learning. Hunger was presumably in no way reduced by the saccharine solution, yet hungry animals clearly demonstrated acquisition in the three different learning situations in which the reward was a saccharine solution (p. 479).

In conclusion the question should be answered as to whether any novel hypotheses concerning the reinforcement process are indicated by the results. The chief suggestion the authors have to make is that stimulation and performance of a consummatory response appears to be more important to instrumental learning—in a primary, not acquired, way—than the drive satisfaction which the consummatory response normally achieves. The present experiments were essentially sham feeding experiments in which the animal was innately stimulated to ingest a substance which did not change his state of hunger, and the result was acquisition, without extinction, of the instrumental responses. Thus it would appear that *eliciting* the consummatory response of ingestion was the critical factor. This suggestion is in line with Wolfe & Kaplon's (1941) finding that with total food intake held constant, the reward value of eating is a function of amount of consummatory activity required to ingest the food (pp. 480–481).

A more recent study by Sheffield, Roby, & Campbell (1954) sub- stantiates, these writers believe, the findings and theoretical position described earlier by Sheffield & Roby:

The results strengthen the interpretation that the vigor of the consum- matory response is the final determining factor in the reinforcing power of a reward for instrumental learning. In the present experiments nourishment per se was apparently irrelevant to learning. Reinforcement was in propor- tion to calories ingested in the dextrose solutions, but the saccharine controls indicate that this is an artifact of the confounding of calories and sweetness. The position taken here is that sweet stimulation innately elicits ingestion and that this reinforces instrumental learning in proportion to the strength of the ingestion response (p. 353).

As Sheffield & Roby have indicated, the saccharine technique amounts in effect to sham feeding (cf. Miller, 1958a, pp. 257–258); but they are on less firm ground in insisting that no form of secondary reinforcement is involved. They argue that the saccharine itself could not have had secondary reinforcing properties (on the dubious grounds that the rats had never before tasted anything as sweet as the saccharine which had led to hunger reduction, i.e., real food) and that its reinforcing effect upon instrumental behavior must, therefore, be in some way innately determined. However this may be, the fact is that there were *many other* sources of stimulation accompanying the saccharine consumption which *had* been followed, often and powerfully, by hunger or thirst reduction or both: notably those stimuli produced by the act of ingestion itself. And if these response-correlated stimuli had thus acquired secondary-reinforcement power, the consummatory act (and the attendant stimuli) could easily reinforce behavior antecedent thereto. Stated less rigorously, the idea is that just so long as the rats *"thought"* they were consuming something that would allay their hunger, hope would be aroused and would reward the behavior that had led up to such consummatory action.

The older, and more radical way, to carry out sham feeding in a laboratory animal is to let it masticate real food but then to have the esophagus fastened to a fistula in the neck so that the masticated food, instead of passing into the stomach when swallowed, is ejected through the fistula. Pavlov (1927) showed that salivary conditioning can be set up in a sham-fed dog just as readily as in a normal one; and in an experiment reported in 1951 by Hull, Livington, Rouse, & Barker, it was found that sham feeding can similarly be used to reinforce maze or other forms of instrumental learning. But here, as in the saccharine experiments, one could not be sure whether it was the *taste* of the food or the consummatory activity as such that carried the reinforcing capacity—or, what is more likely, both of them. What obviously needs to be done now is an experiment where, in addition to being prepared for sham feeding, the subject also has its taste receptors deafferenated. If the subject still ate and seemed to be rewarded by the reception and mastication of food, it would be clear that it is response-correlated stimuli other than taste which are providing the secondary reinforcement for antecedent acts and the momentum or "habit strength" for the eating behavior itself. The fact that human beings often complain that food is "tasteless," but still eat it, suggests that positive results might be obtained in such an investigation.

That the artifical injection of food into the stomach (stomach loading) is rewarding has recently been demonstrated by N. E. Miller and co-workers.

> In chronic operations little plastic tubes were sewn into the stomachs of rats, threaded under the skin, and allowed to project from the back of the neck. . . . A control solution of normal saline injected directly into the stomach had relatively little effect on rate of working for food or amount consumed. Food injected directly into the stomach promptly reduced hunger, and food taken normally by mouth produced an even greater reduction (Miller, 1954, p. 151; see also Berkun, Kessen, & Miller, 1952, and Kohn, 1951).

Here we see further evidence that normal consummatory behavior is reinforcing quite apart from primary drive reduction; and O'Kelly (1954) has obtained similar results in rats motivated by thirst rather than hunger. This investigator reports that rats which have been deprived of water for 23½ hours will normally consume an amount of water equivalent to about 7% of their predrink body weight, but that if this amount of water is injected (under light anesthesia) directly into the stomach (through an esophageal catheter), the rats will not be satisfied and will drink another two or three cc. As O'Kelly says, "The animals consistently overshoot the volume that would be predicted on the basis of their non-loaded [normal] intake" (p. 8). Control experiments indicate that this effect is not produced by the anesthesia (see also Miller, Sampliner, & Woodrow, 1957).

There is a common saying to the effect that "eating is just a habit," and there is a well-known (but rather feeble) joke about a man who said he believed he could train a horse to go without food, except that he seemed to have bad luck when he tried it: the horse always died. Food, obviously, is a life necessity; and no matter how it gets there, a full stomach is a generally rewarding experience. In fact, Coppock & Chambers (1954) have even found that rats are rewarded by *intravenous* injections of glucose (but not by saline solution). Yet it is clear that in eating there is also an element of "pure habit" in the sense of secondary reinforcement (cf. Neff, 1953). What this means, presumably, is that hunger, like other primary drives, is often accompanied by an element of apprehension which can be allayed without hunger reduction (as in saccharine ingestion and sham feeding), just as hunger (or thirst) can be reduced without necessarily allaying the apprehension (as in stomach loading). If, at noon, a healthy human being could be made to believe (perhaps by hypnosis) that he had eaten a hearty lunch, it is quite possible that he would not be unusually "hungry" during the ensuing afternoon; and if, contrariwise, a human being (under anesthesia) could be given a good meal without knowing it just before his lunch time, he would very probably eat lunch again. If asked if he were hungry, he might well reply that he was not, at the moment, but was "afraid" he might be in the afternoon if he did not eat as usual.

Further substantiation of this point of view has been advanced by Ashby (1952):

Thus it has been shown that dogs with an esophageal fistula, deprived of water for some hours, would, when offered water, drink approximately the quantity that would correct the deprivation, and would then stop drinking; they would stop although no water had entered stomach or system. The properties of these mechanisms have not yet been fully elucidated; so training by reward uses mechanisms of unknown properties (p. 113).

It is believed that we are now approaching an improved understanding of these mechanisms.

VII. The Problem of Motivation, Activity, and Appetite

At this point in our analysis we come to what is probably the most important and difficult issue in this entire volume. If it can be resolved satisfactorily, the rest of the chapters follow almost as a matter of course; if not, the ensuing discussion is fraught with ambiguity and uncertainty.

Already a number of writers have been cited who have hinted at this difficulty, and it has probably become even more explicit in the reader's mind. The dilemma, briefly put, is this: The present analysis assumes that type-2 secondary reinforcement (hope) consists of a reduction in drive fear, cued off by some stimulus or situation which has commonly been associated with primary-drive reduction, whereas common observation suggests that the appearance of such a stimulus or situation often produces in the subject, not a relaxation (as the notion of drive-fear reduction would seem to require), but a state of *excitement and heightened activity*.[9]

The problem may, in part, arise from a misconception: because

[9] For a presentation of the general background of this discussion, see Brown's (1955) paper, "Pleasure-seeking behavior and the drive-reduction hypothesis."

there is, in general, a positive correlation between motivation and activity, it is easy, but perhaps nevertheless unwarranted, to assume that any increase in activity implies increased motivation and that quiescence necessarily implies an absence of motivation. That the latter inference is not valid is dramatically indicated in the case of a deeply depressed psychiatric patient. For hours he may sit virtually motionless; but he would tell you, upon questioning, that far from being unmotivated and comfortable, he is the most miserable and tortured of living mortals. If then asked why he does not *do* something about his discomforts and problems, he will reply (if he bothers to reply) that there is nothing that he *can* do, that he is in utter despair, and that he has no hope of *ever* being able to resolve his difficulties and feel well again. Here the term *hopelessness* is the key to the situation: it is not that the individual is unmotivated, driveless; it is rather that so far as he can see no action he can take will better the situation. So he just sits, immobile and miserable!

In like manner, the mere fact that a formerly quiescent individual suddenly goes into action does not mean, necessarily, that there has been a corresponding rise in motivation: he may have just thought of something he can do about his problems; and, far from being more "motivated" (in the sense of over-all discomfort), he may actually feel considerably better (i.e., relieved in the sense of hopeful). In other words, the *release* of an activity that promises to be rewarding may be accompanied, not by more "drive," but by *less*. So we must not, it seems, equate motivation and motion; they need to be independently conceptualized and measured. High motivation, if correlated with despair and disorganization, may result in low activity; whereas, if the individual suddenly "clicks" and becomes goal-oriented (hopeful), heightened activity *may* mean an actual lowering of the total drive or tension state.[10]

These thoughts are, of course, largely speculative and anchored in only the most general kind of empirical evidence. Fortunately, there is more solid justification for them. In a much-cited study by Munn

---

[10] Independently, Malmo (1958) has advanced precisely the same argument: "As Brown indicated, amount of overt skeletal activity does not appear a promising measure of drive (1953, p. 4). Rats showing signs of fear (e.g., defecation and urination) in a new situation may be less active than usual, and we know that a man immobilized by terror is enormously more aroused than someone doing his setting-up exercises. Even hunger does not necessarily lead to appreciable increase in 'spontaneous' activity (Campbell & Sheffield, 1953). It is therefore essential to distinguish physiological indicants of drive from overt skeletal activity (p. 250)." Cf. Chapter 5, footnote 15.

(1950), it was found that rats performed at a higher level in an activity wheel when hungry than when not hungry; and this, among similar observations, has led to the widespread inference that activity and drive are, of necessity, covariant. But Sheffield & Campbell (1954) have made a more detailed analysis of the situation, along the following lines:

In a previous study (Campbell & Sheffield, 1953) it was shown that in a highly constant environment food deprivation for even 72 hr. produces only a very slight increase in activity compared to the increase during 10-min. periods in which the visual and auditory environment is altered. Moreover, the magnitude of the increase in activity produced by the environmental change was related to hours of deprivation in a much more pronounced way than was the so-called "spontaneous" activity. These results are . . . interpreted by the authors as evidence that hunger does not function as a stimulus to activity but instead is a state in which thresholds of normal activity responses to internal and particularly to external stimuli are lowered. The purpose of the present study was to investigate [these suppositions] under controlled conditions (p. 97).

In summarizing their study, Sheffield & Campbell say:

Using stabilimeter-type activity cages, the increase in activity in hungry rats produced by sudden change in an otherwise constant environment was recorded once each day for a 5-min. period of the environmental change. For one experimental group and one control group the environmental change consisted of shutting off a masking sound and turning on lights in normally dark environment; for a second experimental group and control group the change consisted of turning off the sound and turning off the lights in a normal lighted environment. For the experimental groups the 5-min. of change in the auditory and visual fields were always followed immediately by automatic dropping of the daily food ration into the activity cages. For the control groups the change was unaccompanied by food —their daily ration was dropped at a different time.
Experimental animals showed a progressive rise over a 12-day period in the amount of activity during the 5-min. stimulus change leading to food [Fig. 6–2], while control animals showed a decline over the 12 days. Also, when the activity during the 5-min. interval was plotted minute by minute in the experimental groups, it was found that the acquisition of increased activity during the last 3 days of training was greater in later portions of the interval—shortly before food arrived (p. 100).

Nothing, it seems, could be empirically clearer or logically neater than these results. They show, quite unambiguously, that hunger, *per se*, is not a drive to activity but that a stimulus or situation change which forecasts the arrival of food releases a very marked increase in activity. Here, manifestly, a discrimination is being established (although Sheffield & Campbell interpret the situation otherwise): the rats learn that most of the time there is no point in moving about (in search of food), and during this period they are, relatively speaking, "hopeless" and "depressed"; whereas, when the situation changes, thus giving promise of food, the subjects become hopeful and active—although it is still a question as to whether we can say they are also "more motivated." Certainly there is no reason to infer that they are now hungrier; the most that one might assume is that there is a rise in *secondary* motivation of some sort. It would not, of course, make sense to assume that this increment in secondary motivation involved

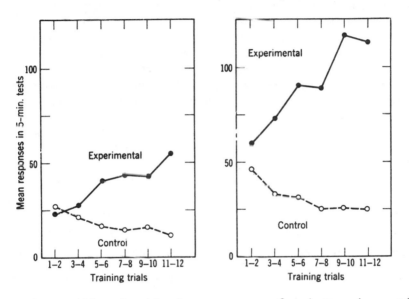

Fig. 6–2. "Acquisition of activity in response to a five-minute environmental change that regularly precedes daily feeding (experimental group) compared with adaptation to the change when it does not precede feeding (control group). The environmental change for the results on the left was cessation of a masking sound and a shift from darkness to light; the results on the right are with cessation of the sound and a shift from light to darkness" (Sheffield and Campbell, 1954).

a rise in hunger fear, for the change in situation is definitely promising, not threatening. Whatever the nature of the motivation change thus produced, it is almost certainly a "pleasant" one, since the animals would presumably themselves bring it about if they could; so it is entirely reasonable to suppose that it is hope which is involved here and that it is predicated upon a *drop* in secondary motivation rather than a rise.[11]

[11] Miller (1959a) has made a somewhat different analysis of the Sheffield-Campbell results, but one which is thoroughly consonant with present assumptions:

However, there are purely subjective grounds for supposing that the problem is not so easily disposed of as the foregoing discussion might suggest. Appetitive excitement, or "passion," in the region of a goal is a universal experience and is particular striking in the realm of sex (where the primary drive is comparatively weak and the "arousal" element prominent). However, in order to keep the discussion as simple and clear as possible, let us take as a paradigm the appetitive or excitement reaction as it occurs in connection with the act of urination. An individual may be for some time vaguely aware of bladder pressure (primary drive); and when, at length, he finally decides to "relieve" himself, he may experience a sudden and quite powerful accretion in the "need." As he approaches the act itself, the over-all motivation may become highly impelling and the thought of not proceeding almost intolerable. Here, it seems, is a *bona fide* instance where stimuli (and actions) previously associated with primary-drive reduction acquire the capacity to elicit an unmistakable rise in total motivation, under circumstances which ought, at the same time, to invest them with the power of secondary reinforcement. This, then, is the type of evidence which makes some writers hesitant to accept the view that secondary reinforcement involves drive decrement. Spence has already been quoted (Chapter 5) as favoring an excitatory (rather than relaxation) theory of secondary reinforcement; and Seward (1956b) has recently put the predicament thus:

Drive reduction seems to be a sufficient condition for response selection. But rewards apparently do more than reduce drive; as incentives they appear to heighten excitement as well as activate instrumental responses. This

---

"Although these experiments show that drives do not inevitably goad the animal into activity, they do not rule out the possibility that drives are strong stimuli. . . . It will be remembered that my definition of drives says nothing about activity, but rather deals with increasing the performance of responses *rewarded* by the offset of the drive or by the goal objects that produce satiation. . . . Suppose that at unpredictable intervals, without providing any stimulation, the experimenters had introduced food alternatively at opposite sides of their activity apparatus throughout the test session. Then the animals would have been reinforced for shuttling on a variable-interval schedule. We would expect this shuttling, which would be recorded as activity, to increase with increasing hunger just as does the rate of bar-pressing. . . . In short, we can only predict that the subjects will be active to a pattern of stimulation including strong drives whenever activity has been reinforced to that pattern. The situation used by Sheffield & Campbell involve long periods during which activity was not reinforced to the pattern of drive stimulus plus apparatus without the sound of the food-delivery mechanism" (pp. 255–256). The only question in this discussion would seem to hinge upon the definition of "stimulus." This problem will be reverted to at various points later in this book.

poses a problem: How can drive reduction and incentive *induction* both produce the same result, i.e., strengthen a concurrent response? (p. 202).

In an effort to resolve this paradox (one wonders how long it took Nature, in the course of organic evolution, to resolve it!), Seward (1950) has suggested that (a) primary reinforcement involves a reduction in primary motivation, that (b) secondary reinforcement type-1 involves a drop in secondary motivation, but that (c) secondary reinforcement type-2 involves an *increase* in what he calls *tertiary* motivation. While this formulation seems to fit the raw facts rather exactly, there is the difficulty (which Seward himself well recognizes) that it takes one away from the homeostatic mode of thought (which has otherwise proved so useful) toward a type of theory that is conceptually far from neat and satisfying. A sort of "last-ditch" attempt will be made in the next section to suggest how the phenomenon of appetite arousal can be accommodated within the general homeostatic framework.

VIII. A Possible Resolution of the Basic Dilemma

A few years ago the present writer made some preliminary suggestions concerning the "tertiary-motivation" paradox which will be used as the basis for the more detailed analysis that is to follow shortly:

Since homeostasis, or self-regulation, is one of the essential characteristics of living organisms, it will be immediately evident that many of their activities have the properties of *negative* feedback, as just defined [see Mowrer, 1960, Chapter 7]. These activities or functions serve to hold certain states or qualities within fairly narrow limits of variation. *Positive* feedback, when the concept is applied to living organisms, sounds as if it would be pathological, to say the least, and, in the extreme case, lethal. Actually, we find some very instructive instances of it in living organisms.

We have already seen that there is a general tendency for incidental stimuli which have been associated with primary-drive reduction to produce secondary-drive reduction and for such stimuli as have been associated with primary-drive induction to produce secondary-drive induction. These two types of contiguity learning, or conditioning, unquestionably tend to produce (indirectly, through the integrating function we call consciousness) responses which have biological utility—notably, flight or immobility in the face of danger and approach to objects or situations with rewarding potentialities. However, there is one crucial respect in which this general scheme is inadequate, non-biological. The world's good things do not always remain conveniently at rest, waiting to be claimed and consumed. Sometimes these goal objects, especially when they are other organisms, have a way, at the critical moment, of eluding their pursuers. Therefore, an organism that became more and more confident and *relaxed* as it approached a quarry might find itself slowing up at just the point when a final "push" was needed for success. It is therefore interesting and altogether understandable that we should find the phenomenon of *appetite*. Its outstanding feature is an *increase* in secondary motivation just as consummation is imminent, thus giving to behavior at this crucial moment a peculiar urgency and "oomph."

Here, it seems, is an instance of *positive* feedback: "The nearer you get, the more you want it" carries the proper connotation here. Certainly such an arrangement is biologically intelligible, but it is nonetheless enigmatic. Neal Miller (1951b) has put the matter this way. We have reason for thinking that stimuli associated with consummatory states take on contradictory capacities: a tendency to cause a decrement in secondary drive (secondary reinforcement) and a tendency to cause an increment in secondary drive (which we call, not punishment, but appetite). As Miller points out, if these two tendencies occurred simultaneously, they would be self-cancelling, mutually neutralizing; so his proposal is that they may alternate, producing intermittent bubbles of pleasurable anticipation (relaxation) and surges of intensified (appetitive) drive. This is frankly a speculation and, even if true, leaves many unanswered questions. However, consideration of the problem in the cybernetics setting illuminates and usefully sharpens it (Mowrer, 1954, pp. 86–87).

Granted that the evidence on this complicated issue is not yet all in, at least a provisional resolution seems possible. A stimulus which has secondary reinforcing properties is one which, per hypothesis, is capable of reducing some sort of secondary drive, most commonly drive-produced fear. Now fear reduction presupposes a lessening of activity on the part of the *sympathetic division* of the autonomic nervous system. But we know that stimuli associated with primary drive reduction may be not only reassuring and relaxing but also exciting, stimulating, motivating. How are these seemingly contradictory effects possible? May it not be that stimuli which in the past have been associated with consummatory states acquire the capacity *first* to allay fear, i.e., quiet sympathetic arousal, and *then* to activate the parasympathetic nervous system, which mediates the appetites?

It has often been remarked that the sympathetic and parasympathetic divisions of the autonomic nervous system are antagonistic or reciprocal in their actions; and it is certainly true that fear must subside before one can react appetitively and that one has to stop being appetitively aroused before one can become very fearful.[12] However, there is a good deal more that can be said about this relationship, if it is

---

[12] Brown (1955) cites Gantt (1949) for the observation "that anxiety symptoms in neurotic dogs are completely inhibited by sexual stimulation even prior to orgasm" (p. 175). See also Section VII, Chapter 5.

schematized as indicated in Fig. 6–3. Here it is suggested that there is not only a "vertical" (quantitative) but also a "horizontal" (qualitative) dimension of function. This means that a rise or fall in either sympathetic or parasympathetic activity involve a rise or fall in motivation. But—and this is the point especially to be noted—"movement" along the functional course indicated in Fig. 6–3 is never directly up or down; there is always a *lateral* component, such that the individual, in becoming either more or less fearful or more or less appetitively aroused, is also moving either from left to right (away from privation toward consummation) or from right to left (away from consummation toward privation). Therefore, although a *decline* in fear and a *rise* in appetite are, from one point of view, antithetical, in another way they represent a *continuous* function: they are two successive steps or stages in the organism's progress from privation to consummation. And, of course, the same holds true, in reverse order, of the relationship between a decline in appetite and a rise in fear.

Classical hedonic theory (see Section V) tended to assume that stimuli are inherently pleasant or unpleasant, quite apart from any factor of intensity; whereas, in homeostatic theory, the tendency is to equate pleasure to drive reduction and the opposite quality to drive increase. It may be that these two systems, in appearing to be contradictory, are really complementary, each referring more particularly to one rather than to the other of the *two* different, but related, dimensions implied in Fig. 6–3.

Hence we conclude, if this analysis is sound, that a secondary reinforcer, when it *first* impinges upon an organism in a state of strong drive and drive fear (privation), causes a relief (fear reduction) reaction and *then*, very probably, an appetitive (excitement) reaction, as a sort of *detour* which the organism has to pass through, for reasons already indicated, on its way to a state of consummation and satiation. This is not to deny that appetitive arousal is motivating and, in a sense, even punishing. If, for example, an individual in a state of complete satiation and comfort could, merely by wishing (or by pressing a button), suddenly transport himself back to a condition of appetitive arousal (without the normally attendant primary drive also being present), it is unlikely that he would do so. Why, then, when a hungry, thirsty, or otherwise deprived organism is at point X on the curve shown in Fig. 6–3, does it not *remain* there, instead of moving on through appetitive arousal to consummation? This may, in fact, be exactly what happens in individuals who are said to be *shy*. But the more confident, more experienced individual is willing to tolerate appetitive arousal because it promises to lead, ultimately, to consummation; whereas the rise in motivation which is produced by fear points in the reverse direction, toward further privation (Chapter 11). Or, to put the matter a little differently, movement in either

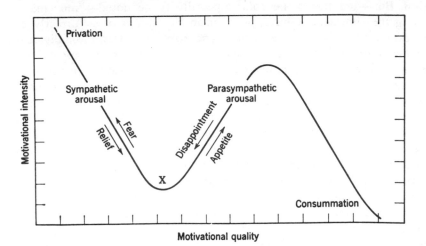

Fig. 6–3. Diagram suggesting a hypothesis concerning the relationship between secondary reinforcement, conceived as fear reduction, and appetite. It is true that fear reduction (lessening of sympathetic activity) represents a *drop* in motivation and that appetite induction (parasympathetic arousal) represents a *rise* in motivation. Therefore, in one important sense, the two processes are antithetical. However, both fear reduction and appetite induction represent *lateral movement* in the *same direction*, namely to the right. Further implications of this scheme are discussed in the text.

direction from point X on the curve involves a form of "loss," i.e., drive increase; but appetitive arousal also involves a form of "gain," i.e., movement toward consummation, whereas fear arousal involves a "loss" in *both* dimensions.[13]

What then, in simplest terms, may one say of the concept of sec-

[13] In like manner one may ask: Should not disappointment be experienced as rewarding, since it presumably involves a drop in motivation. Again, for *shy* individuals it may be perceived in somewhat this way: "I am really *glad* I didn't get it." But, in the more usual situation, disappointment is not perceived in this way for this reason: Just as appetitive arousal, while mildly "punishing" in its own right, is at the same time premonitory of good things to come; disappointment, while mildly "rewarding" in its own right, is premonitory of *bad* things (want, privation, etc.) to come, thus more than cancelling out such indigenous reward value as it may have.

ondary reinforcement type-2, or of hope? One may say: (a) that whenever an otherwise strongly motivated organism is moving to the *right*, along the curve show in Fig. 6–3, that organism is in a state of hope or hopefulness; and (b) that such movement may involve either drive fear decrement (first phase) or appetitive arousal (second phase), followed by the attainment (normally) of a state of consummation, with a general drive level well below anything achieved beforehand, at point X.[14]

It is to be regretted that this hypothesis is somewhat intricate; but so, apparently, are the facts. As of the present, this hypothesis fits the facts rather well and will be accepted as the basis for further theoretical analysis until revision is clearly indicated.

IX. Homeostasis, Hedonism, and Brain Stimulation

Although already long, this chapter cannot end without reference to an experimental phenomenon which has recently challenged homeostatic theory in a particularly dramatic way. Electrical stimulation of the central nervous system for experimental purposes has, of course, a relatively long history. And the classical question which underlay such work has been this: If stimulation is applied at a particular point,

[14] It will perhaps be helpful to suggest that, in the movement of an organism from left to right along the continuum shown in Fig. 6–3, there is what may be called a *qualitative* change that occurs at X. Fear is the normal accompaniment of strong drive when no prospect of consummation is in sight (equals, no hope). But then if circumstances change and the organism sees itself moving toward consummation, its fear diminishes and reaches a low point at X. However, in order to avoid the let-down in total motivation which could be so disastrous at this crucial point (see above), it is as if a second or *auxiliary* motivational mechanism of a different (appetitive) kind goes into operation. Hence, the reference to a "qualitative" change in the nature of affective arousal at X. In trying to make this point with a class, the author once took the example of a hungry dog which, in the beginning, was not only hungry but "worried." Then he spied a rabbit, started chasing it, gradually gained on it, and, as his hunger fear dissipated, began to anticipate how good the rabbit was going to taste. Here, presumably, is the qualitative change in emotional arousal alluded to. But then a student asked: "What was happening to the rabbit during this same time?" This side of the story is, of course, a sad one. Since the rabbit was "moving," not toward consummation but consumption, his fear was presumably rising and would terminate in terror. Any reader who likes rabbits better than dogs may therefore supply a different ending: just in the nick of time the rabbit got to a safe hole in the ground and the dog didn't have him for dinner after all (relief for the rabbit, disappointment for the dog)!

what response (or sensation) will it produce? However, in 1954, Olds & Milner reported an investigation in which they had, in effect, asked this question in reverse: If an organism has *already made* a response of some sort, how will brain stimulation *then* affect the organism's subsequent tendency to repeat or inhibit this response? Because electrical stimulation (shock) applied to the cutaneous receptors of the body (and to the underlying muscles) has a tendency to inhibit responses which it follows, it was natural to assume that electrical stimulation, centrally applied, would have the same effect. But such was not found to be necessarily the case. If rats with electrodes chronically implanted in the septal area of the brain were given an opportunity to press a small bar and thereby "shock" themselves, centrally, they would do so with astonishing regularity and persistence. Here, obviously, was a first-rate enigma—and one whose resolution may prove highly instructive.

One of the most immediate effects of the Olds-Milner discovery has been to prompt a careful reconsideration of the question: What, precisely, *is* "pleasure," "reward," "reinforcement?" As previously indicated in this chapter, there have been, in general, two types of answers, with hedonism holding that this phenomenon occurs whenever certain distinctive *sensations* are aroused, and the homeostatic type of theory holding that it occurs only when there is a major *diminution* in stimulation or drive ("adjustment") of some sort. At first blush, hedonism fares better than does homeostasis when reexamined in light of the Olds-Milner effect: If reward is simply a matter of certain types of sensation, this phenomenon should, reasonably enough, be reproducible by artificial stimulation of either the appropriate peripheral (afferent) nerves or by appropriate *central* stimulation; whereas, since reward, homeostatically considered, involves a *reduction* in stimulation, it is less readily conceivable how it could be recreated *by stimulation*.[15] However, as we shall see, there are some other interesting and plausible possibilities in this connection which, in view of the general difficulties in hedonistic theory already delineated in this chapter, are well worth considering.

One of these possibilities has recently been explored by N. E. Miller (1959b). He points out that if any drive of natural origin is present when septal brain stimulation occurs, the latter might well produce its demonstrated reinforcing effect by at least briefly obliterating the central representation of the drive—or, as Miller says, by "temporarily

[15] Olds & Milner's own comment in this connection is: "The 'Clinical impression' of the [experimenters is] that the phenomenon represents strong pursuit of a positive stimulus rather than escape from some negative condition" (1954, p. 426).

blocking out motivational sources of stimulation. Such a functional elimination of motivational stimuli might occur during unconsciousness produced by a petit mal seizure" (p. 2; cf. Brady, 1958a).

And this surmise has received quite specific support from a paper recently published by Nielson, Doty, & Rutledge (1958). Addressing themselves to the "reasons why central stimulation should be rewarding" (p. 427), these writers conclude:

All procedures in these experiments necessary to induce sustained self-stimulation of the caudate nucleus suggest that the apparently rewarding effect for the animal could be based on excessive, seizure-like neural action. . . . One cannot say why such excessive neural action, if such it is, should be rewarding; but this element is present in the phenomenon of orgasm, and the self-induction in children of petit mal attacks by photic means (Robertson, 1954) is not unlike the behavior of self-stimulating cats (p. 432).

The reason why Nielson, Doty, & Rutledge regard the electrical stimulation involved in the Olds effect as "excessive" is that they have demonstrated that the intensity of the stimulation here required is considerably greater than is necessary to produce a central "sensation," as detected by the conditioned-response technique. They say:

The intensity [required to produce the Olds effect] must be far above that required for perception as CS and the stimulation must be prolonged or available in rapidly succeeding bursts. High intensity stimulation appears to be a common factor in other experiments of this type (Olds & Milner, 1954; Olds, 1956c; and Brady, Boren, Conrad, & Sidman, 1957) and rapidly repeated bursts of self-stimulation of structures of the limbic system are sought in monkeys (Lilly, 1958). The wide distribution of the neural structure from which such effects can be obtained and their concentration in the limbic system which is known to be seizure-prone, certainly suggests that some non-specific, convulsion-like effect forms the basis of this behavior (p. 432).

In discussing the Olds effect, Miller (among others) has also pointed to a probable relationship between it and the presence of specific primary drives. Miller (1959b) says:

In Dr. Olds' paper [Olds, 1958] we have just seen that, as we might expect from the drive-reduction hypothesis, the rate of bar-pressing reinforced by central stimulation in at least some locations can be manipulated by changing the intensity of certain drives. The fact that the effect of certain drives is at least partially specific to the reward effect of stimulation in certain locations opens up the possibility for further experiments (p. 2).

But there is another equally plausible possibility. One can reasonably assume that, somewhere in the central nervous system, the cessation of drive (which homeostatic theory identifies with reinforcement) becomes translated from mere stimulation termination over into a more "positive," more "active" state of some kind and that it is the latter which, in the final analysis, is the agent that fixates response tendencies. This being true, the Olds-Milner effect becomes not in the least surprising: all that is necessary is that a part of the brain be found in which the final, active reinforcing state can be aroused, not by cessation of natural stimulation, but by an artificial electrical stimulus. Since reward, in the homeostatic sense, can of course be experienced as a result of the satiation of many different forms of drive and discomfort, it follows that there may well be many different sites in the brain where this sort of transformation takes place. Say Olds & Milner:

> There are numerous places in the lower centers of the brain where electrical stimulation is rewarding in the sense that the experimental animal will stimulate itself in these places frequently and regularly for long periods of time if permitted to do so. It is possible to obtain these results from as far back as the tegmentum, and as far forward as the septal area; from as far down as the subthalamus, and as far up as the cingulate gyrus of the cortex (1954, p. 426).

When J. Konorski, of the Nencki Institute of Experimental Biology (Warsaw), was in this country early in 1958, he described unpublished experiments recently conducted in Sweden in which it has been found possible to stimulate the "thirst center" of goats electrically (Andersson & Wyrwicka, 1957). A normally thirsty goat is first trained to push a treadle with one of its front feet as a means of obtaining a small amount of water. After the habit is well established, the animal is allowed to drink to satiation and then the thirst center is stimulated. The immediate result is that the animal starts pushing the treadle as a means of obtaining water (see also Miller, 1957). This shows that the subject is being made genuinely thirsty, rather than that some "drinking reflex" is merely being stimulated. If the experience of thirst can be thus artificially aroused, it is by no means improbable that the experience of thirst (or other drive) reduction can be likewise produced.

In the literature there has already been some speculation about the possible existence of a "joy center," which, quite unjustifiably, has been interpreted as being more congruent with the presuppositions of hedonism than with those of homeostasis. If the notion advanced in the preceding paragraph should be valid, such a center or centers would follow as a matter of course. Relief or reward, as *centrally* registered, need not at all be the mere absence or cessation of excitation but a decidedly active state of affairs which might be tripped off by just the procedure which Olds & Milner have hit upon.

Ziegler (1957) summarizes prevailing opinions in this connection as follows:

> As might be expected, the discovery of positive reinforcement produced by intracranial self-stimulation has aroused considerable interest and a great deal of speculation. This speculation ranges from Delgado's concept of "attractive" and "unattractive" cerebral areas (Delgado & Burstein, 1956), to Olds' tentative conclusion that "stimulation in these areas might excite some of the nerve cells that would be excited by satisfaction of the basic drives − hunger, sex, thirst, and so forth" (Olds, 1956b). The analysis of neural and behavioral mechanisms mediating the reinforcing effects of intracranial self-stimulation has hardly begun. Indeed, it has not yet been conclusively demonstrated that we are dealing with "pleasure centers" or "a system within the brain whose function it is to produce a rewarding effect upon behavior" (Olds & Milner, 1954) (p. 373).

Inspired by the work of the investigators cited, N. E. Miller (1957) has recently reported the localization of a *distress* or "*alarm*" center in the cat brain, stimulation of which operates precisely as does the onset of strong peripheral drive or "punishment." Miller says:

> The foregoing experiments have shown, point by point, that the particular emotional reaction elicited by electrical stimulation of the cat's brain has all of the functional properties of externally elicited pain and fear: (i) its evocation can motivate and its termination can reinforce the learning and performance of an instrumental response; (ii) it can be used to establish a conditioned response; (iii) it can be used to condition an emotional disturbance to a distinctive test compartment; and (iv) it can act as a punishment to teach hungry cats to avoid food (p. 6).[16]

The existence of centers of relief, joy, or delight, as posited above, is only slightly less probable than pain centers; and it is perhaps no accident that Miller, Richter, Coons, & Berman (unpublished research; see also Miller, 1957) report that central stimulation which produces ejaculation also will reinforce antecedent behavior.

Yet another possibility of interpreting the Olds-Milner effect within the bounds of homeostatic theory is one which Miller (1959b) again has suggested:

> It is possible that in some cases, the reward phenomenon [produced by cortical stimulation] may be analogous to addiction, with the effects of one stimulation tending to remove the unpleasant after-effects of the preceding one (p. 3).

---

[16] These findings have been confirmed and somewhat amplified by Cohen, Brown, & Brown (1957).

Moreover, an experiment recently reported by Sidman, Brady, Boren, & Conrad (1955) calls attention to the possibility that the Olds-Milner effect is highly anomalous and not at all the same as that involved in normal reward learning. At least they find that a Skinner bar-pressing habit which is established under the influence of reward provided by food or water is typically inhibited by a tone which has previously been associated with electric shock administered to the surface of the body, whereas a bar-passing habit established by the Olds-Milner method is not so inhibited. And Miller has shown that although rats and other laboratory animals will develop habits if *briefly* stimulated by the Olds-Milner method, they will also learn to make a response which *turns off* this form of stimulation if it is appreciably extended.[17]

In light of these varied and not entirely consistent experimental findings, suffice it to say, for the present, that the exact import of the Olds-Milner effect is not yet known; certainly there is nothing in the now-known facts which argues compellingly against the general biological and psychological principle of homeostasis (Stagner, 1951; Dempsy, 1951; R. C. Davis, 1958). One might well wish that the whole matter were less up in the air than it presently is; but since homeostasis accounts for such a very wide range of behavioral data and since the apparent exceptions involve many ambiguities, it seems that the systematic theory builder, as of this writing, has no choice but to proceed on the assumption that this model is basically sound and will, at most, be refined and corrected in minor ways rather than totally invalidated.

On the whole, it can be said that recent studies of the reticular mechanisms lend *strong support* for the systematic position which this book is attempting to portray. For example, Samuels (1959) concludes a long review on "Reticular Mechanisms and Behavior" as follows:

> Studies of the reticular formation indicate that its structural complexity and functional plasticity override the conceptual limitations inherent in more static, reflex-like neural mechanisms. These characteristics permit it to exert facilitatory and suppressive effects which have a time-course of seconds and even minutes on the activity of central nervous system structures. This span is comparable to that of many behavioral events.

[17] Penfield (1954), Heath (1955), and others have extensively stimulated various areas and surfaces of the brains of locally anesthetized human beings and have obtained elaborate introspective reports (see also Mowrer, 1960, Chapter 7). It would seem that the information thus derived could be used to clarify the issues discussed above. To date, apparently, no systematic effort has been made to collate knowledge obtained by the two different approaches.

The neurophysiological distinction between "specific" and "nonspecific" systems is particularly relevant to psychological theory. Constructs such as attention, perception, motivation, drive, reward, and punishment possess *a common factor of nonspecific reticular activation in addition to their specific properties.* This general factor of nonspecific activity has effects which are lawfully related to the timing and intensity of its application. It is essential, therefore, that psychological constructs be critically evaluated in an attempt to determine the extent to which they are a function of "nonspecific" as well as "specific" factors. Conceptual reassessment may well indicate that categories now regarded as independent and mutually exclusive in terms of operational criteria *are functionally interrelated on the basis of a common factor of reticular activation* (p. 20, italics added).

The foregoing is eminently consistent with our assumption that every "specific" drive state of considerable intensity activates a relatively "nonspecific" affective state (of tension, arousal, apprehension) which is also capable of being conditioned (both as regards onset and offset, arousal and relaxation) to formerly neutral stimuli. From this assumption we can derive (as shown in Chapter 5) *fear, relief, hope,* and *disappointment* (including grief and anger). And when these states are related to both response-dependent and independent stimuli, we have a remarkably flexible and comprehensive explanatory system.

At this point, Conant's (1947) famous dictum comes to mind, that a theory is never overthrown by facts, only by *another (better) theory!* It must be admitted that there are some facts which do not, at present, accord perfectly with *our* theory. Such facts, it is hoped, will stimulate this theory toward further expansion and refinement; and one can only be grateful to those who insistently call attention to them. But we hold, with Conant, that it takes a theory to "kill" a theory; and, as of the moment, there seems to be no other theory which, in comprehensiveness and power, is comparable to the one here espoused. So, on this note, we stop probing the weaknesses of homeostatic conceptions (but see also Chapters 8 and 11) and turn again to the task of systematically developing implications which seem to be inherent in our schema.[18]

[18] Too late for systematic discussion in this chapter, two works have appeared— Malmo's (1959) article, "Activation: A Neuro-physiological Dimension," and Berlyne's (1960) book, *Conflict, Arousal, and Curiosity* (see also Chapter 11)— which are highly pertinent to and, on the whole, supportive of the general position here adopted. It is believed that these studies will go far toward resolving some of the perplexities delineated in this chapter.

7

Revised Two-Factor Theory
and the Concept of Habit

In some ways, the present chapter is the most important one in this book. In it a hypothesis will be made explicit which is central to the book as a whole. The six preceding chapters have been stepping stones for the development of this hypothesis; and the chapters which follow are, in the main, merely amplifications or applications thereof. But for the thoughtful reader, this chapter is almost certain to be anticlimactic: he will already have anticipated at least the essence of the point of view which is now to be presented, for it is broadly implicit in what has gone before. However, before entering upon the discussion of the conception of "habit" which will constitute most of this chapter, it will be useful to review, in highly synoptic form, the argument as it has developed up to this point.

I. Recapitulation and an Inference

Although the foregoing chapters have topical, or logical, headings, the reader will have noted that they are also organized historically, chronologically. In order to make both of these principles of organization more explicit and to indicate more clearly how and why this type of analysis generates a special way of viewing the phenomenon of habit, the high lights of the preceding discussion are presented in Table 7-1.

TABLE 7–1

Historical and Logical Antecedents of Present Version of Two-Factor Learning Theory

Two-Factor Learning Theory, Original Version

Conditioning (Pavlov, Bekhterev)	Habit formation (Thorndike)
Positive and negative unconditioned stimuli	Reward and punishment
Stimulus substitution	Response substitution

Hull's Drive-Reduction Theory

A monistic theory of reinforcement purporting to explain both conditioning and habit formation. Did not deal adequately with avoidance behavior (active and passive) or with secondary reinforcement.

Two-Factor Learning Theory, Version Two

Sign learning (fear conditioning)	Solution learning (habit formation)
Autonomic nervous system and visceral and vascular tissue	Central nervous system and skeletal musculature

Showed that avoidance behavior, to be adequately explained, must involve both sign learning and solution learning. Theory did not, however deal adequately with secondary reinforcement (type-2) or with the concept of habit.

Present Version of Two-Factor Theory

Incremental reinforcement (punishment)	Decremental reinforcement (reward)
Primary reinforcement	Primary reinforcement
Secondary reinforcement	Secondary reinforcement

Danger signal on (fear)	Safety signal off (disappointment)	Danger signal off (relief)	Safety signal on (hope)

Here it will be noted that *all* learning is (by implication) conditioning, so that the theory remains "two-factored" only with respect to the forms of reinforcement involved, i.e., incremental and decremental. Since each of these may involve primary drive or either of two forms of secondary drive, there are thus, in effect, *six* operationally distinguishable forms of reinforcement; and each of these may be associated with either independent or response-dependent stimulation. Therefore, if this classification is so defined as to include the nature of the associated stimuli, there are *twelve* "kinds" of reinforcement. The reader is encouraged to test this classification for exhaustiveness.

As previous chapters have indicated, there is now widespread agreement concerning the nature of avoidance learning, both active and passive. As suggested in Table 7–1, there are three ways in which *active* avoidance, and three ways in which passive avoidance, learning can occur. If an independent, environmentally produced stimulus is followed by (a) primary-drive increment, by (b) secondary-drive increment (fear type), or by (c) secondary drive increment (disappointment type; see Chapter 5, Section VIII), then that stimulus will acquire the capacity to drive and keep the subject *away* from it. That is to say, active avoidance learning can occur on the basis of ordinary punishment (infliction of pain), threat (warning), or disappointment. And if response-correlated stimulation is followed by any of these three forms of incremental reinforcement, *passive* avoidance learning (i.e., response inhibition) will ensue. Here theory seems to be adequate to the facts, and the facts logically exhaust the theory.

In like manner, if an independent, environmentally produced stimulus is followed (a) by primary-drive decrement, (b) by secondary-drive decrement (relief type), or (c) by secondary-drive decrement (hope type), then that stimulus will acquire the capacity to *attract and hold* the subject to or near it, thus accounting for the known forms of active approach behavior. *But what happens if any of these three forms of decremental reinforcement is associated with response-correlated stimulation?* Here is an area of the total system which is manifestly undeveloped and unexploited. Can our surmise be correct that therein lies the possibility for an advance in the understanding of habit as radical and as far-reaching in its implications as has been the change from Thorndike's "stamping-out" conception of punishment to the present view thereof?

II. The Phenomenon of "Habit" Reinterpreted

Perhaps the best way to move forward with this discussion is to recall what has been said in Chapters 4 to 6 about what happens when a stimulus, or signal, which is *external* to the organism, immediately precedes primary-drive reduction. We know that such a stimulus itself soon becomes capable of serving as a so-called "secondary" reinforcing agent. It can be used to produce higher-order conditioning, of the type studied by Pavlov in his salivary experiments; and it can be used to fixate a particular bit of so-called instrumental behavior, as in the Saltzman and Zimmerman experiments (Chapter 4). And more than this, we know (or at least suspect) that a stimulus with secondary-reinforcement potency is effective as a reinforcer by virtue of its own capacity to produce drive reduction, i.e., reduction in some species of the secondary drive of fear (Chapters 5 and 6).

Now against the background of this knowledge, let us ask: What would happen if a stimulus, or stimulus pattern, which is to be followed by primary-drive reduction, instead of originating in the external environment, were *response-produced?* In other words: What would happen if secondary-reinforcement properties got attached to the tactile, proprioceptive, and other stimuli characteristically associated with the occurrence of a given response? A commonplace example provides an instructive answer. All boys who ever lived in the country (and even some city boys) know how to teach a dog to "shake hands." You do not wait until the dog "just happens" to make the response in question and then reward its occurrence; that would be too slow and uncertain a procedure. Instead you take the dog's right forepaw in your right hand and flex the leg acutely. At the same time, you give the dog a morsel of some preferred food. If the dog is at all bright and friendly, you soon have the satisfaction of seeing him spontaneously "offer" to "shake hands" with you. What has happened? You have taught the dog a "habit." And he has learned it, not by "doing" anything, but by having something *done to* him. It is not that the dog's hunger initially prompted him, in the course of trial-and-error, or "random," behavior, to lift his foot in such a way as to prompt you to reward him: You lifted it *for him.* In other words, you did not reinforce an S—R connection, or "bond," between hunger (S_d) and paw lifting (R_1). What happened instead, it seems, is that the training procedure established a "connection" between certain stimuli, aroused by passively moving the dog's leg, *and secondary reinforcement*, type-2, i.e., the hope or expectation that food would be along shortly. And what is the result? Soon the dog is "doing it himself," making the response as a means of "begging" for (showing he *wants*) food. The dog thus acts *as if* there were a bond, connection, or "reflex" connecting hunger with paw lifting; but the circumstances under which the learning has occurred give us pause.

That the example just cited is in no way exceptional is indicated by the fact that human language behavior, at least in its beginnings in the infant, is similarly learned (Mowrer, 1960, Chapter 3). But perhaps this sort of "passive" learning, this "baiting" of a response with secondary reinforcement, so that the subject will be disposed to make it, is still a sort of trick and does not exemplify "habit formation" in its most general and most typical form. Perhaps something else, quite different, is involved when the correct response is made initially *by* the subject himself, rather than *for* him. How can we get evidence on this important issue?

First of all, it should be noted that both passive and active performances of a given response characteristically produce certain stimuli; and when such a response is, as we say, rewarded, ideal conditions are provided for those stimuli to take on secondary reward capacity. In other words, the conditions which are supposedly conducive to the formation of a "habit," as a putative "bond" between some drive stimulus S_d and some instrumental response R_i, are precisely those which will also give the stimuli produced by R_i the capacity to act as secondary reinforcers. Thus we arrive at the interesting possibility that "habits" arc not dependent at all upon a change in the resistance or conductivity of S_d—R_i connections but, rather, involve increased conductivity between the stimuli which response R_i produces and the phenomenon of secondary reward, or "hope." In other words, just as response inhibition through punishment has been shown to depend, not upon a *weakening* of some S_d—R_i neural bond, but upon the conditioning of fear to the stimuli which R_i arouses, so would the facilitation of a behavioral tendency which we loosely refer to as "habit formation" depend, not upon the *strengthening* of some S_d—R_i connection, but upon the conditioning of a different type of "feedback," namely *hope*, to the stimuli which R_i arouses.[1]

Perhaps the plausibility of this interpretation of so-called habit formation will be increased if we approach it a little differently. If the theory which has just been sketched is valid, it would follow that

---

[1] I am indebted to Dr. Norman Ginsburg for the suggestion (personal communication) that this altered way of thinking about "habit" might be applied, with equal cogency, to the concept of "instinct." Like habit, instinct has been commonly regarded as a *complex reflex* which, however, is innate rather than acquired. Dr. Ginsburg's suggestion is that perhaps what is innate or nativistic about an instinct is not certain sensory-motor connections but rather connections between certain stimuli (sensations) and *certain emotions.* Behavior would then be modified as a matter of course—but more flexibly than if S—R reflexes were directly involved. Cf. Tinbergen's (1950) statement: "We begin to realize now that the fact that an animal may use various behaviour patterns in order to attain one special |instinctive| end does not necessarily mean that this plastic behaviour is not dependent on nervous mechanisms, but that it might also, and certainly does, mean that the underlying nervous mechanisms are much more complicated than was expected before" (p. 305). Perhaps the way of conceiving instincts which has been suggested by Ginsburg will serve to reduce this complexity. For a review of current thinking about the concept of instinct, see also Tinbergen (1953).

just as responses can be facilitated, i.e., made *more* likely to occur, without their ever having been made by the subject, so can responses be inhibited, i.e., made *less* likely to occur, without their being made by the subject (cf. Section VI and Chapter 11). In other words, if traditional habit theory says that an act can be learned only by occurring and being rewarded, it also says that an act can be unlearned or inhibited only by occurring and being followed by punishment. But if we now assume that learning can occur, as in the hand-shaking illustration, without an act occurring, in the active, voluntary sense of that word, so should we infer that an act can be inhibited likewise without occurring. This inference could be tested as follows. Suppose that a dog's right foreleg was passively flexed and that there followed, not a reward, but an electric shock (either to the leg or to some other part of the body). What would we expect the result of a few repetitions of this procedure to be? We would expect that any tendency on the part of the dog to make this movement voluntarily would be considerably depressed, rather than augmented—and that the dog would thereafter *resist* having the leg moved passively. This inference follows not only from the altered conception of habit which has just been suggested, but also from what we have now known for at least two decades about the psychology of punishment. In fact, it was the discovery that punishment is basically a matter of acquired "negative" (fear) feedback which has led us to conjecture that reward similarly operates to set up a feedback, not of fear, but of fear reduction and hope (see also Mowrer, 1960, Chapter 7).

III. The Neurological Correlates of Learning

For simplicity of exposition, traditional habit theory has been represented up to this point as involving the assumption (which it logically implies) that learning, or habit formation, involves the modification of the neural pathway between some drive stimulus and some instrumental response so as to reduce the "synaptic resistance" of this pathway and increase the likelihood that S_d will be followed by R_1. And the postulations of Thorndike have been especially cited in this connection. However, such an imputation is not entirely fair and needs to be slightly modified. It is true that most of Thorndike's statements sound as if they implied this kind of neurologizing, but in 1931 Thorndike made an explicit disclaimer on this score. He said:

I hope that the sort of connection-system which I have described is more acceptable than the kind against which configurationists . . . direct their criticisms—criticisms from which I have profited and with which I often agree . . . (p. 130).

The connectionist welcomes the factual criticisms of an over-simplified conduction system. The connectionist indeed realizes the difficulties of explaining human nature as a system of connections between neurons . . . The word *connection* has been used without prejudice concerning what physiological event or condition parallels it. It is so far simply an expression of the probability that a certain S will be followed by a certain R, *bond*, or *link* or *relation* or *tendency*, or any still more colorless word may be put in its place (p. 7).

For Thorndike, at least as of 1931, habit was therefore simply a word for the *increased probability* of a response's recurrence when its prior occurrence has been followed by reward. But there is ample evidence that others have taken the terms "connection," "bond," and "association" more literally, i.e., have, quite reasonably, thought of them in specifically neurological terms. For example, Wolpe, in a paper published in 1950, in a section headed "Reinforcement as a Neural Process," says:

If it is presumed that the stimulus-response sequences set up by learning depend, just as maturationally established sequences do, upon the development of functional neural connections, then the *process* of establishing such connections is the essence of what is called *reinforcement*, and an individual event that has the effect of initiating or strengthening a functional neural connection is *a reinforcement* (pp. 19–20).

And two years later, in a second article along similar lines, Wolpe (1952) re-affirmed this view by saying: " . . . learning depends upon the formation or strengthening of synaptic connections at points of anatomical apposition of neurones, a synapse being a functional point of contact between neurones" (p. 194).

Hull, also, was a connectionist in the neurological sense of the word; but Spence, though in some respects a follower of Hull, has himself been careful to avoid making any commitment on this score and has said of Hull's neurological "entanglements":

Just why Hull, after formulating his mathematical theory of *habit*, found it necessary to elaborate a neurophysiological model of receptor-effector connection, has always been a puzzle to me. Actually he does little more than identify or coordinate this concept of receptor-effector connection with his mathematical construct of habit. I doubt whether a single one of the deductions with respect to learning in his *Principles of Behavior* would be lost or changed in any way if it were eliminated. These implications follow exclusively from his mathematical theorizing and not at all from the superfluous physiological model. The same is true for Thorndike's theory about the alteration of synaptic conductances" (Spence, 1950, pp. 163–164).

Birch & Bitterman (1949) likewise observe: "anyone who has read Hull knows that he makes use of supporting physiological data." To which they then add this pertinent comment on the tendency of others to avoid making any commitment regarding the neurological substructure of learning:

But irrespective of Hull's practice, the present writers hold that since the material substratum for learning is the nervous system, a fruitful theory is one that yields inferences of a neurological kind, which in turn yield testable hypotheses crucial for the theory. A non-reductive approach indicates theoretical weakness rather than theoretical strength (pp. 302–303).

For an extreme nonreductivist position, the reader is referred to B. F. Skinner (1953b), who, for example, says:

Frequency of response is emphasized by most of the concepts which have foreshadowed an explicit recognition of the probability of a datum. An organism possesses a "habit" to the extent that a certain form of behavior is observed with a special frequency—attributable to events in the history of the individual (p. 69).
The basic datum in analysis of behavior has the status of a [mathematical] probability (p. 78).

And Spence (1951a) takes the position that:

In the case of those events (that is, rewards) that are known to result in an increased likelihood of occurrence of the response, the theorist holding to a general reinforcement theory assumes that "rewards" operate in some *unspecified* manner to strengthen the functional connection of the response to its eliciting stimulus. So long as the properties of this class of events (rewards) are not specified, other than that they lead to increased response strength, a theorist may be said to be supporting a general [and, unfortunately, thoroughly circular] reinforcement interpretation (p. 245).

It is easy to see why some habit theorists have, in the past, been reluctant to take a definite position concerning the neurological correlates of learning: To assume that a "habit" involves the lowering of synaptic resistance between S_d and R_1, where R_1 consists of activity which would ordinarily be termed "voluntary," is to imply a rigidity and fixity of so-called "habitual" behavior which goes contrary to common experience and observation.

Now we must ask where revised two-factor theory stands on this question of learning and neurology. The answer is quite simple: This theory assumes that learning does indeed involve "the formation or strengthening of synaptic connections at points of anatomical apposition of neurones" (Wolpe's statement). But there is an important difference here as to *which connections*. Traditional habit theory has stated or at least strongly implied that learning involves a strengthening of synapses between neurones connecting some drive and some behavioral act, whereas revised two-factor theory assumes that so-called habit formation involves a strengthening of synapses between the neurones *connecting stimuli produced by some behavioral act and the emotion of hope* and that punishment involves a similar conditioning of fear. In other words, the assumption here is that learning is related, exclusively, to the connections involved in the *informational feedback* from a response or response "intention" (i.e., a partial or perhaps symbolic occurrence of the response), and that it involves no change in what may be called the "executive" (brain-to-muscle) pathways in the nervous system (see Mowrer, 1960, Chapter 7). In this way we avoid the dilemmas which have dogged habit theory for these many years: such a view leaves behavior—even so-called habitual behavior—free, flexible, and uncommitted while at the same time it does not hedge on the question of the neurological correlates of learning.

The issues here at stake can be summarized as follows. The S—R bond conception of habit formation has to assume (a) that learning consists of an increase or a decrease in the conductivity of the neural connection between drive and behavior or (b) that no such neurological modification occurs and that the change in response probability is mediated in some *other* (usually unspecified) way. Neither alternative is logically attractive. The position here suggested is that learning, clearly and unambiguously, involves the strengthening or weakening of neural bonds (Chapter 11) but that these bonds are between formerly neutral stimuli and "conditioned responses" (notably the emotions; but see also Mowrer, 1960, Chapter 5). Learning thus alters what the individual *wants* and wants *to do* (and does) but not what he *can* do. The *capacity* for executing behavior is assumed to be innately given and (probably) not alterable through learning. Some of the factual support for this statement, summarized by Sperry (1951), runs as follows:

Adaptation in the timing of the central discharges is not achieved by the learning process. If limbs [of mature amphibia] are transplanted to dorsal positions such that their movements are of no value to the animal, the central-peripheral adjustments occur in the usual systematic manner. This is true even when the limbs are transplanted to the contralateral side and reversed in such a way that the movement of the limbs tends to push the animal backward when it attempts to go forward and vice versa. Similar effects are obtained when the limb transplantations are made in prefunctional stages, showing that these relations are patterned initially through developmental forces and not through any kind of functional adjustment. Furthermore it has been shown that these motor patterns develop in the same systematic way in the absence of sensory innervation and that they persist after de-cerebration and cord transection down to levels of the cord just rostral to the limb segments. The possibility that learning or any type of functional adaptation might be responsible has thus been excluded. The motor neurons must somehow be distinguished from one another in the centers according to the muscles they innervate. . . ." (pp. 257-258).

However, Sperry goes on to point out that:

Motor reorganization of this kind occurs readily in the limbs of amphibian larvae. It goes more slowly during and shortly after metamorphosis and evidently does not occur at all in full-grown anurans. In the phylogenetically more ancient oculo-motor system of amphibians the capacity for reorganization seems to be lost at a very early larval stage in both anurans and urodeles. . . . In the rat the relations of the limb motor neurons has been found to be already irreversible at, or shortly after birth. The newborn oppossum has yet to be investigated in this respect. Where adjustment fails to occur, it may be attributed to the fact that either the motor neurons in postem-bryonic and postlarval stages are no longer subject to respecification, or else that such respecification no longer causes a breakdown in the existing synapses" (p. 260).

And Carmichael (1946), more than a decade ago, made the logical point that in so-called trial-and-error learning, the response has to be *made before* "learning" can begin. Therefore learning (as already indicated) must be more a matter of control, of coming to *want* or *not want* to make a particular response, than of capacity. It is only the relative *attractiveness* of the response, it seems, that is altered by learning; and *this* alteration is unequivocally assumed to be neurolog-ically based. This point of view, as we shall see in later chapters, calls for some changes in our thinking about psychology in general; but these readjustments seem not to be in any sense stultifying but instead liberating and creative (see also Mowrer, 1960, especially Chapter 7).

Since the above was written, a paper by the Polish neurophysiologist, J. Konorski (1958), has appeared which throws additional light upon the issues here under discussion. This writer's thesis is briefly this: C. S. Sherrington (1906) provided a satisfactory conceptual model for the operation of the spinal cord and the reflexes which it mediates, but no one has given us a satisfactory model for the operation of the "higher nervous centers," viz., the *brain*. Here is where learning manifestly occurs; and because the reflex model has proven seriously inadequate in this connection, there has been a widespread tendency on the part of the students of learning to abjure and reject neurology altogether, with the results that only *formal* or *mathematical* statements, in the last analysis, remain. Konorski says:

According to my own view, purely formal behaviourism is in the long run sterile. In fact, if we make the decision to refuse to accept psychological interpretations of animal behaviour, we are bound sooner or later to substitute physiological ones; otherwise we are doomed to remain on a purely empirical level without any possibility of creating a causal system of the facts observed. Therefore I consider that the gradual "physiologisation" of behaviouristic psychology is an "historical necessity," and we are now witnessing the acceleration of this very process (p. 1107).

Pavlov's theory of cortical processes could not play the part of a framework in the physiology of the brain, as did Sherrington's concepts—developed at about the same time—as regards the functioning of the spinal cord; thus, the physiology of higher nervous activity failed to become "assimilated" by neurophysiology as an important new branch. This involved two important consequences. On the one hand, the behaviourists, though representing a trend quite close to that of the physiology of higher nervous activity by which they were greatly influenced, declined to assimilate Pavlov's theory of cortical processes (even in spite of their not infrequent good will), and turned away altogether from the physiological approach to the problems of behaviour, going the way of formalism. On the other hand, contemporary neurophysiology became mainly "analytical" in character, dealing primarily with the architecture of the connections between particular parts of the brain, and caring but little for their functional significance (p. 1110).

The speculative brain physiology of Pavlov has thus collapsed under its own dead weight; and by its own inherent logic and evidence, behavioristic research has shown the inadequacy of the "brainless" (spinal) model of Sherrington. So where do we stand today? The two positive facts in the situation are these: (a) Behavioristic researches have led to a new and different (nonreflexive) conception of behavior control and selection; and (b) neurophysiology, with its numerous recent improvements in technique, has given us a far clearer picture of the course of pathways in the brain than had ever before existed. It seems likely that these two facts will soon be brought together in a fruitful, creative way. In later chapters we shall, indeed, see indications that just such a development is, as Konorski intimates, already in progress (see also Chapter 6, Section IX).

IV. An Earlier Statement of the Hypothesis

The intriguing, but also rather disconcerting, possibility that "habit" is simply a matter of secondary-reinforcement feedback was first explored by the present author (1953a), in an unpublished paper with the title: "Is 'Habit Strength' Merely Secondary Reinforcement?" [2] The idea has also been considered, in a preliminary way, in two other papers (Mowrer, 1953b, 1956). In the first of the three papers cited, the basic notion and some of its implications were developed as follows:

Among the graduate students in our department, there is a bit of common folklore to this effect: If an instructor asks, "What is wrong with this (or that) learning experiment?" the correct answer is: "The experimentor did not properly control 'secondary reinforcement.'" And as we become practiced in thinking about this phenomenon, we can see its subtle and insidious operation in every maze and memory drum. So far researchers, more commonly than not, have regarded secondary reinforcement as a process which ubiquitously frustrates their efforts to get at the "real thing," namely the basic process of learning whereby habit formation, or S—R bonding, occurs [see also Chapter 11]. Here we shall explore the possibility that secondary reinforcement is itself the *real thing*, with "habit" as one of its derivatives.

Let us approach the matter as follows. Recently we have been preoccupied with a number of animal experiments on secondary reinforcement in one of which the basic procedure is as follows. A blinking light is presented, twenty times per day on four consecutive days, for a few seconds before the subject (a rat) is fed. On the fifth day, the subject is put into a different situation, with a "Skinner bar" available, depression of which produces the blinking light—but no food. As might be expected [see Skinner, 1938; Jenkins, 1950; also Chapters 4 and 10], the subject soon "learns" to press the bar, solely on the basis of the secondary reinforcement provided by the blinking light. Of course, the *performance* of this response presently ceases because the secondary reinforcement extinguishes. But for a while

[2] Sometimes new ideas have to be expressed, for a time at least, in old—and inappropriate—terminology. For example, there is an implied contradiction in saying that a response has "habit strength" in proportion to the extent to which stimuli which are produced by the occurrence thereof have acquired secondary reinforcing capacity. Capacity to "reinforce" *what?* In the older frame of reference, the answer would be: reinforce ("thicken," "open") the stimulus-response bond which mediates the response. But if we repudiate the bond conception of habit, then the notion of "reinforcement" must be reconsidered. As will be shown in Chapter 8 (see especially Section IV), it is from one point of view more accurate to speak here of "motivation" rather than of "reinforcement"; but in another sense, the term reinforcement is still valid, as referring to an agent which produces new learning. Any stimulus which has acquired so-called secondary reinforcement capacity has, in addition to the "motivating" (behavior-releasing) function just mentioned, the capacity to act as the "unconditioned" (conditioning) stimulus in higher-order conditioning. In this book, we shall continue to use the term "secondary reinforcement" with these qualifications in mind; but eventually a terminology will have to be found which more precisely reflects the present state of our theoretical understanding (see also Chapter 12, Sections III and IV).

we have, purely on the basis of secondary reinforcement, a fine little "habit."

This simple demonstration suggests the following line of thought. By having associated the blinking light with food (i.e., with hunger-drive reduction), we caused it to acquire secondary reinforcing properties, and this was enough to give our subject the "habit" of pressing a bar which produced the blinking light [see also Section V].

But this, we may be told, was a special, rather tricky habit, not a real one. Let us, then, set up a "real" one. To do this we put a naive hungry rat into an experimental situation with the Skinner bar arranged so that it produces, not a blinking light, not a mere *promise* of food, but food itself, i.e., so-called primary reinforcement. Again we get a bar-pressing habit— this time a "real" one. But wherein does it differ, basically, from the "habit" first described? In both cases we see habit strength manifested by resistance to extinction, i.e., by a tendency on the part of the rat to perform the response after food ceases to be forthcoming—and, one may suppose, for the same reason: In the one case the animal gets secondary reinforcement from the blinking light which bar-depression produces, while in the other case the secondary reinforcement derives *from the proprioceptive, tactile, visual, and other stimuli inherently associated with the response.* How did these latter stimuli acquire secondary reinforcing properties? Presumably in the same way the blinking light did—by having occurred contiguously with the reinforcement provided by food and hunger reduction!

Recently the writer was trying to explain this line of reasoning to a colleague at another university, and when he had finished the colleague said: "But the rat, in the first case, did have to *learn* to press the bar; he did not just start doing it all of a sudden."

While acknowledging the reality of secondary reinforcement, this psychologist was so steeped in the tradition that habit formation represents a growth in the neural connection between drive and response that he could not understand what the writer was saying. And, more interesting still, the writer himself was so unaccustomed to this other way of thinking that it was not until several hours later that he realized (too late, alas, for a direct rejoinder!) how he should have replied. What he should have said (obviously, now) is this: "Yes, the rat did have to *learn* to press the bar. But there is this difference. You are assuming that this learning, this habit formation, consisted of the rat's learning *how* to press the bar. I am suggesting rather that the habit formation consisted of the rat's learning to *want* to press the bar.[3] Pretty clearly the rat, when put into the situation with the Skinner bar, *already had* the necessary know-how, or skill, to perform this simple act, in a dozen different ways. But at first the rat just didn't particularly *want* to. Why should it? It preferred to "explore" [see Chapter 6]. In the course of its exploration, the rat eventually got around to pressing the bar—and when it did so, something special happened: the blinking light came on. This one, initial performance of the bar-pressing response shows that the rat already "knows *how*." The result was that the various stimuli inherently associated with the bar pressing now began to

[3] "Traditional experiments in learning have usually been concerned with changes in the character of behavior. The organism learns *how* to do something; it acquires new behavior" (B. F. Skinner, 1953, p. 70). Cf. the following excerpts from

take on secondary reinforcing powers [4]—and, as this occurred, the bar pressing "habit" became manifest.

In other words, having been once paired with the blinking light, the stimuli indigenous to the act themselves acquire some "reinforcing" capacity and thus increase the likelihood of the act's being repeated. And with each repetition of the act, the indigenous stimuli will be temporally associated with the blinking light and will acquire further reinforcing properties. This transfer of reinforcement from the extrinsic stimulus (blinking light) to the intrinsic (proprioceptive, tactual, visual, and other) stimuli continues, then, with each occurrence of the bar-pressing, light-producing response, until both the extrinsic and intrinsic stimuli lose, through extinction, their reinforcing potency—at which point we say the "habit" is gone.

What we thus arrive at is a conception of "habit formation" which is based upon sign-learning, or conditioning, and which, as we shall later see, is not encumbered by the difficulties which beset both the stimulus-response bond conception of habit and the simple conditioned-reflex approach to behavior modification (Mowrer, 1953b, pp. 5–10).

V. Supporting Evidence:
(a) The Bugelski-Miles Experiments

With the conception of habit which has just been elaborated in mind, it is surprising how many experimental facts—some of them not previously explicable—now drop neatly into place. In this section we shall review a number of empirical findings concerning "habit strength," as measured by *resistance to extinction,* which lend them-

---

a paper by Seward (1950): "Thorndike points out that in maze experiments 'there is a mixture of learning to be able to go quickly to a certain place and of learning to wish to go there' (Thorndike, 1932b, p. 458). Tolman . . . distinguishes between acquiring field expectancies and positive cathexes; the corresponding distinction in maze learning would be between field expectancies and 'subgoal cathexes.' A similar distinction is conceivable between learning any response and acquiring a need to perform it. The most economical solution, and the one here recommended, is to subsume 'learning to wish' and 'learning to do' under a single inclusive principle" (p. 371) [see Chapter 8].

[4] A note on terminology is in order here. We have spoken above of response-produced stimuli taking on secondary reinforcing capacity by virtue of their association with the blinking light, which also possessed this capacity. Strictly speaking, one should perhaps refer to secondary reinforcement only with respect to stimuli which have been associated with primary reinforcement, to tertiary reinforcement with respect to stimuli which have been associated with secondary reinforcement, etc. But it is a growing practice, and a well-justified one, to speak only of primary reinforcement and secondary reinforcement, the former referring to a reduction in a primary drive and the latter referring to a reduction in a secondary drive, or emotion, without reference to how far removed, in terms of stimulus pairings, it is from primary reinforcement. In this discussion, we shall follow the latter usage.

selves particularly well to interpretation within this new theoretical framework.

Reference has already been made (Chapters 4 and 5) to Bugelski's discovery that a Skinner bar-pressing habit "extinguishes" more rapidly if its occurrence is not accompanied, during the extinction period, by stimuli which accompanied it during the acquisition period. Because this discovery is so basic to the present analysis, it will be useful to read a part of Bugelski's own account of this now twenty-year-old experiment, as given in his 1938 paper, "Extinction with and without Sub-goal Reinforcement." It begins:

In recent theoretical papers Hull (1932, 1937) has posited sub-goal mechanisms as of major importance in serial behavior acts. White (1936) has based his *completion* hypothesis on the reality of the anticipatory goal reaction functioning as a behavior-directing stimulus; he adds, however, that "this has not yet been widely accepted or supported by crucial experiments." The Skinner (1932) bar-pressing technique, as currently used in the study of learning problems, provides an example of such a sub-goal mechanism operating in a concrete laboratory situation.

A common practice in the preliminary training of rats by the Skinner method is to deliver to the animal a series of uniform pellets of food. Upon the closing of an electric circuit one pellet of food is delivered to the animal automatically by an electro-magnetic vending device placed outside the partially sound-shielded experimental box. The falling of the hard pellet down the chute into the metal food cup produces a distinct rattle and the action of the magnet is transmitted mechanically through the walls of the box as a click. Under these conditions rats very quickly acquire the habit of running to the cup to get the pellet as soon as the sounds occur. After this associative connection has been set up the rat is trained to operate the food-delivery mechanism himself by pressing downward on a short horizontal bar. The preliminary training to the rattle and click presumably hastens the learning of the bar habit by insuring that whenever the animal accidentally presses the bar this action shall be followed very closely by the reinforcement associated with the eating of the food. Such close temporal relationship between act and reinforcement has long been known as a condition favorable for rapid learning.

Once the bar-pressing habit has been set up, it is plausible to assume that in some sense the click becomes a significant subordinate goal, the attainment of which, according to White's hypothesis (1936), should have reinforcing properties. On the other hand, the absence of an accustomed reinforcing state of affairs normally tends to produce experimental extinction. On these assumptions, then, if experimental extinction of the bar habit is carried out in such a way that each act of the animal is followed by the magnetic click but no food, it is to be expected that extinction would take place at a slower rate than it would if performed in the same way except without the magnetic click. The present experiment was designed to test this hypothesis (pp. 121–122).

There then follows the conventional description of subjects, apparatus, procedure, and results—after which there is this summary:

Sixty-four albino rats were trained to press a bar to obtain a food reward. Operation of the bar was accompanied by a sharp distinct click. After the animals had received 30 reinforcements of this habit they were divided into two groups and extinguished to a criterion of five minutes without a response. Half the animals were extinguished under the original learning conditions which included a sharp click. The other animals did not hear the click during extinction.

The results indicate that the animals who heard the click during extinction responded to the bar more often than did the animals who did not hear the click. [An average of 77.60 extinction responses as compared with an average of 54.06.] The difference between the mean number of responses was over 30% in favor of the rats who heard the click. These results correspond with deductions drawn in advance of the experimental work.

After the first extinction the rats were divided into groups of 16; 32 rats now extinguished under reversed conditions of "click" or "no click." The remaining 32 rats extinguished a second time under the original conditions. The same general results followed; those animals who heard the click made more responses than those animals who did not hear the click. The results again corresponded to theoretical deductions drawn in advance of the experimental work.

On the basis of the results it appears fairly certain that the presence of the click during extinction was a partial or "sub-goal" to the animals and that its absence added more frustration to that resulting from the absence of the food reward [see Chapter 11]. These findings offer an experimental demonstration of the sub-goal principle advanced to explain certain features of serial acts and the satisfying nature of an anticipatory goal response (pp. 132–133).

Bugelski's paper is doubly useful for present purposes. First of all, in describing the method employed by Skinner for quickly setting up the bar-pressing habit, it provides a nice illustration of the point that learning is not necessarily dependent upon *doing*. The click of the delivery mechanism and the sound of the pellet tumbling into the food trough are two stimuli which will follow the response one wishes the subject to perform when the bar is made available. They, in other words, will be response-correlated with respect to the bar-pressing "habit." What the Skinner training procedure does, therefore, is to give these particular stimuli secondary-reinforcement potency by a special, preliminary training procedure. Then, when an opportunity is provided for the rat itself to produce these effects, by pressing the bar, there is a strong predisposition to do so.

There is a tendency to interpret the effect just described by saying that the click and the drop of the pellet provide *immediate* secondary reinforcement of the connection between the stimulus of seeing the bar and the response of pressing it, instead of allowing the strengthening of this "bond" to depend entirely upon the necessarily somewhat delayed primary reinforcement provided by ingestion of the food. The alternative interpretation which our particular conception of "habit" suggests is that, by "baiting" some of the stimuli which are naturally associated with bar pressing, the Skinner method is, in effect, a sort of latent-learning procedure (Mowrer, 1960, Chapter 2) in which the bar-pressing habit is partially learned in advance of ever occurring. Just as the boy who flexes his dog's right forepaw and then gives the dog food is predisposing the dog to make this response himself, so does the Skinner method of "pretraining" tend to create a habit without the subject's engaging in trial-and-error behavior or otherwise exerting himself. The present assumption is that if *all* the stimuli normally associated with the occurrence of a particular response could be produced thus "artificially," i.e., without the occurrence of that response, a "habit" could be established which would have just as much "strength" as if the response had itself occurred and been rewarded.

What, now, may we say of Bugelski's study of *extinction*, with and without the noise normally made by the operation of the (empty) delivery mechanism? The more conventional interpretation of the Bugelski findings has been that the bar-pressing habit, properly speaking, consisted of an S_d—R_1 neural connection which, when primary reinforcement was withdrawn, stayed alive and active (experimental group) longer than it otherwise would (control group) because of the strengthening, sustaining effect of the secondary reinforcement provided by the sound of the food-delivery mechanism. According to revised two-factor learning theory, this finding is taken as showing that instead of the "strength" of a "habit" being maintained or reinforced by stimuli with so-called secondary reinforcement capacity, habit strength *is* stimuli with secondary-reinforcement capacity and that a "habit" is strong or weak, not as a function of the S_d—R_1 "bond," but as a function of *how many* of the stimuli produced by a response possess *how much* of this so-called reinforcing potential. If this potential is extinguished *or* if the stimuli which a given response usually arouses are, by whatever means, prevented from occurring, it is assumed that the "habit" will be obliterated forthwith, whatever the state of the S_d—R_1 connection.

Recently an experiment was reported by Dr. Raymond C. Miles (1956) which further clarifies and empirically supports this type of thinking. In the first part of this study, laboratory rats learned to press a Skinner bar as a means of obtaining food and were then subjected to extinction, with and without *two* external sources of secondary reinforcement. During the acquisition or training period, each bar depression was accompanied by a flash of light and the click made by the food-delivery mechanism. In the case of some animals, the bar-pressing habit was extinguished with the light and click occurring at each depression of the bar (but no food); and in the case of other animals, the habit was extinguished with the light and the click both "disconnected" (and again no food).

Up to this point, our description of the Miles experiment does not differentiate it, in principle, from the experiment by Bugelski, previously discussed. The distinctiveness of the Miles experiment lies, first of all, in the fact that the procedure was replicated with wide variation in the number of food-reinforced bar-pressing responses which were permitted during the period of training, prior to extinction. In all, 240 animals were used in this part of the study; and they were randomly divided into six groups, of 40 animals each. These six groups were given an opportunity to press the bar and receive food the following number of times: 0, 10, 20, 40, 80, and 160. After this training, each of the six groups of 40 animals was divided, again randomly, into two subgroups, of 20 animals each; and these twelve subgroups were tested for resistance to extinction under the two conditions already mentioned. The results are shown graphically in Fig. 7–1. Here it will be seen that the decrement produced in resistance to extinction by withholding the light and click was relatively constant for the various

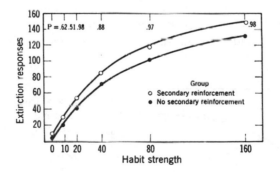

Fig. 7–1. Median number of extinction responses made by 12 groups of animals described in text. Note the parallelism between the smoothed curves. This and the five following figures are reproduced from Miles (1956).

groups which received different amounts of original training in making the bar response. The stability of the ratio between resistance to extinction with and without the two external secondary reinforcers, regardless of amount of original training, is shown in Fig. 7–2.

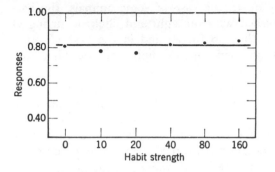

Fig. 7–2. Values derived by dividing scores for No-Secondary - Reinforcement Groups by corresponding scores for Secondary-Reinforcement Groups, as shown in Fig. 7–1. As will be seen, the resulting quotient is very nearly a constant.

What do these results mean? Miles suggests that they may offer a basis for partialing out the extent to which the resistance to extinction shown by the bar-pressing response was due to external, secondary reinforcers and the extent to which it represented habit strength, properly speaking. But there is a suggestive fact to be noted here: It turns out that both habit and secondary reinforcement develop, with progressive reinforcement, according to what appears to be *exactly the same function*. This is shown, first of all, by the curves in Figs. 7–1 and 7–2. It is further indicated by a comparison of the lower curve in Fig. 7–1 and the curve in Fig. 7–3. Miles constructed the latter by taking the successive differences in amount of resistance to extinction for the various groups shown in Fig. 7–1 and plotting these differences independently. He reasoned that these differences ought to show the growth of secondary reinforcement, as opposed to habit strength

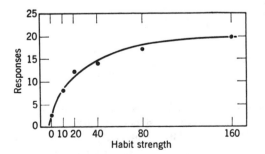

Fig. 7–3. Curve showing the increasing discrepancy between corresponding values shown in Fig. 7–1, as a function of amount of antecedent primary reinforcement. The curve has much the same shape as the typical learning curve.

proper, in his investigation. The shape of the growth function for secondary reinforcement, as revealed in this curve, is the same as obtained, typically, for habit formation itself.

The other part of the Miles experiment involved the following procedure. Again 240 animals were used; but instead of receiving various amounts of bar-pressing training, they all received the same number of reinforced trials: namely, 80. However, these animals were tested for resistance to extinction, under the two described conditions, after having been deprived of food for *varying periods of time*. In the first experiment, it will be recalled, all animals were tested for resistance to extinction after having been without food for 20 hours. In the second experiment, the animals were again divided into six groups of 40 animals each but were tested for resistance to extinction after 0, 2½, 5, 10, 20, and 40 hours of deprivation, respectively. The results, analyzed as were those for the first part of the study, are shown in Figs. 7–4, 7–5, and 7–6. The implications are highly similar: resistance to extinction with and without the click and light varies in *direct proportion* to the intensity of the motivation prevailing at the time of extinction. In other words, the secondary reinforcement behaves exactly as does the "habit" itself.

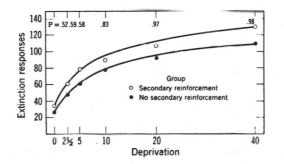

Fig. 7–4. Median number of extinction responses made by 12 groups of animals, as a function of the inferred intensity of their hunger when tested. Here, again, the parallelism of the two curves suggests that habit strength and secondary reinforcement, so-called, are the same phenomenon.

In short, then, the Miles investigation shows (a) that "habit" and "secondary reinforcement" gain in strength, in a strictly parallel way, with the number of primary reinforcements and (b) that "habit" and "secondary reinforcement" vary in a strictly parallel way, when tested for resistance to extinction, under varying amounts of primary drive, i.e., hunger. Here, it seems, is about as compelling evidence, of at least an indirect nature, as one could ask for the hypothesis that "habit strength" and "secondary reinforcement" are one and the same thing, the main difference between them being that when secondary reinforcement is connected to internal, response-produced stimuli we call it—for no very apparent reason—"habit."

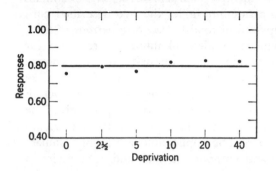

Fig. 7–5. Values derived by dividing scores for the No-Secondary - Reinforcement Groups by corresponding scores for Secondary-Reinforcement Groups, as shown in Fig. 7–4. As in the case of the values shown in Fig. 7–2, the resulting function is apparently a constant.

From the text of the Miles paper, it is clear that the author himself, at the time this paper was written, was of two minds as to the meaning of his very systematic and empirically beautiful findings. He was, on the one hand, inclined to differentiate between what may be called inherent habit strength, i.e., the established "thickness" of the S_d—R_i "bond," and the capacity which *external* stimuli acquire to impart additional strength to such a habit or bond through the action of secondary reinforcement. At the same time, Miles gives careful consideration to the possibility that so-called habit strength is exactly equal to the so-called secondary reinforcing capacity possessed by all response-correlated stimuli, be they external or internal as far as the organism is concerned. Certainly the results obtained by Miles and by other investigators whom he cites suggest that habits lose their "strength" *pari passu* as response-produced stimuli, which have been

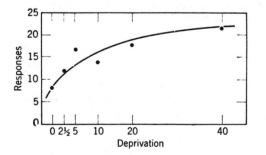

Fig. 7–6. Curve showing the increasing discrepancy between corresponding values shown in Fig. 7–4, as a function of hunger intensity. The curve, like that shown in Fig. 7–3, has much the same shape as the typical learning curve.

previously associated with primary reinforcement, are excluded (or "extinguished"). Present theory holds that a response which arouses *no* stimuli with secondary reinforcing properties possesses, ergo, *no* "habit strength."

VI. Supporting Evidence:
(b) Further Indications that "Habit" Is
"Secondary Reinforcement"

In addition to the results of the two studies cited in the preceding section, there are many other laboratory findings, both formal and informal, which support the view that "habit" is nothing more nor less than the secondary reinforcement, so-called, which has become attached to response-correlated stimulation. For example, in a personal communication, Professor L. I. O'Kelly has reported the following observation. In an exploratory experiment conducted for a different purpose, several white rats, motivated by thirst and housed in individual compartments, learned to press a bar and cause a drinking tube to become briefly accessible. Extinction was then conducted under two different conditions: (a) bar pressing caused the motor which had previously delivered the drinking tube to make its customary sound but without producing the tube; and (b) bar pressing caused the motor to sound and to deliver the tube but with no water in it. Professor O'Kelly reports that animals with which the second of these procedures was used were "about *12 times* as resistant to extinction" as were the other animals. He says there was virtually "no over-lap at all in the scores for the two groups." Although there are perhaps other acceptable ways of interpreting this observation, it is clearly consistent with the view that the more completely the stimulus consequences of a nonrewarded response approximates those prevailing under the antecedent conditions of primary reinforcement, the greater will be the resistance to extinction. This observation and interpretation thereof are congruent with the facts previously cited (Chapter 6) in connection with the discussion of sham eating. The O'Kelly procedure is, in effect, an instance of at least quasi-sham-drinking since the subjects went through most of the motions of drinking—lapping, etc.—in the tube's presence.

If the foregoing hypothesis is sound, it would follow that a response which calls for a given amount of muscular *effort* during acquisition would be more resistant to extinction if that response continued to call for this, rather than some other, amount of effort. The assumption is that the "habit" thus acquired consists largely of the secondary reinforcement which has become attached to the proprioceptive feed-back from (or "feel" of) a given amount of effortfulness and that if the response is made either *more* or *less* effortful during extinction, its habit strength will be forthwith diminished. Although no attempt has apparently as yet been made to test this inference, directly and specifically, results reported by Stanley & Aamodt (1954), in a paper entitled "Force of Responding During Extinction as a Function of Force Requirement During Conditioning," are consistent with expectations generated by this inference. In a personal communication, Dr. Stanley expresses the opinion that although, in the article cited, the obtained results were interpreted somewhat differently, they are nevertheless consistent with the notion of "proprioceptive scanning, as mentioned in your recent *Review* article" (Mowrer, 1956; cf. also Chapter 11). And Wyckoff (1959), in a recent paper, says:

> The profound effects which may result from subtle similarities and differences in stimulus conditions between acquisition and extinction have been brought to light in the context of studies on the influence of intermittent reinforcement (Crum, Brown, & Bitterman, 1951; Schoenfeld, Antonitis, & Bersh, 1950; Spence, 1947; and Tyler, Weinstock, & Amsel, 1957) [see Lawson & Brownstein, 1957; also Chapter 12] (p. 2).

Also relevant, and even more directly so, is a study by Melching (1954), the results of which are summarized in Table 7-2. The procedure was as follows:

> Six groups of 10 rats each were conditioned to press a bar for food. For one pair of groups [C and D] a buzzer sounded on half the occasions the bar was pressed. For a second pair of groups [A and B] a buzzer sounded each time the bar was pressed. For the final pair of groups [E and F] the buzzer did not sound at all during conditioning. In extinction, the buzzer sounded when one group in each pair pressed the bar. The buzzer did not sound when the other group in each pair pressed the bar (p. 373).

TABLE 7–2

Total Extinction Scores of Groups Conditioned under Three Schedules of Buzzer Presentation and Extinguished under Two Schedules of Buzzer Presentation (Melching, 1954)

Group	Frequency of Buzzer in Conditioning (%)	Frequency of Buzzer in Extinction (%)	Number of Extinction Responses
A	100	100	755
B	100	0	574
C	50	100	719
D	50	0	727
E	0	100	402
F	0	0	637

As will be seen in Table 7-2, if animals received the buzzer during each and every acquisition bar press, they were more resistant to extinction if the buzzer continued to sound (Group A vs. Group B); whereas, if animals received no buzzer during acquisition bar pressing, they were more resistant to extinction if the buzzer did *not* sound during extinction (Group E vs. Group F). In other words it was found that a response is more resistant to extinction (i.e., has greater "habit strength") if, during extinction, it continues to produce *exactly the same* rather than a different pattern of stimulation. This finding has been independently confirmed by Hurwitz & Cutts (1957) and is in line with the view that habit is merely the secondary reinforcement which has been conditioned to the stimuli associated with the response during acquisition. (The results reported by Melching for Groups C and D lend themselves to no simple interpretation—cf. Chapter 12— and will not be discussed here.)

Thus far in this (and the preceding) section, we have considered only the effect of withholding, during extinction, previously relevant— or adding previously irrelevant—stimuli. And the findings are strictly in accord with the hypothesis under examination. Even more striking is the finding that a habit can be depressed, not only by the procedures just mentioned, but also by what may be termed the "pre-extinction" of relevant stimuli. At the outset of the preceding section, a passage is quoted from Bugelski (1938) describing the procedure previously developed by Skinner for establishing a bar-pressing habit more rapidly than would be possible on a strictly trial-and-error basis. Here response-relevant stimuli were, so to say, "preconditioned," i.e., given secondary-reinforcement potency prior to their "natural" occurrence in conjunction with the habit-to-be. The procedure now to be described is a logical corollary of that procedure, and is reported by Bugelski (1956) as follows:

One of the writer's students, R. T. White (1953), designed an experiment to discover the possible role of the click in the Skinner box. He trained several groups of rats in the manner previously described so that they were efficient bar-pressers. When all the rats were trained they were given different *pre-extinction* training. Some rats were placed in the box without a bar present and were presented with a click at an average interval of 30 seconds. The click was followed ordinarily by an approach to the food cup, now empty. As the clicks continued the fruitless trips began to decline until they stopped altogether (usually within a period of 30 clicks). It would appear that the food-cup approach was extinguished as far as the click was concerned. The next day the rats were replaced in the box with the bar present and underwent ordinary extinction (that is, no food was dropped to them after the bar-presses). Allowing for "spontaneous recovery" and for the probable short-circuiting of the behavior so that the click might not be particularly important if food were present, we could expect the rats to make some food-cup approaches, which they did. However, an interesting chain of events began to unfold. The rats began to cut down the number of trips to the food cup after bar-pressing, compared with a normal (non pre-extinguished) group. Their behavior toward the food cup became less regular, frequently they failed to reach it at all, and frequently they failed to "search" for food [see Fig. 7–7]. As the food-cup behavior began to break down, the entire pattern of return to the bar also weakened and broke down. . . . The pre-extinction rats met an extinction criteria sooner than did the control animals (pp. 91–92).

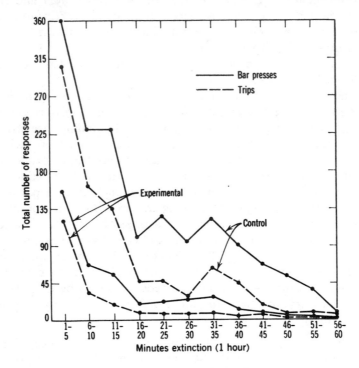

Fig. 7–7. Extinction of a bar-pressing response (and trips to food trough) in rats as a function of whether the secondary-reinforcing value of an associated "click" had (Experimental Group) or had not (Control Group) been independently extinguished. It appears that the secondary reinforcement provided by the "click" was an important component of the bar-pressing "habit." The graph is reproduced from Bugelski (1956, p. 92).

Bugelski himself interprets this finding according to an ultra-objective theoretical model which has been discussed elsewhere (Mowrer & Keehn, 1958) and will not be further considered here (cf. Chapter

12, Section X). What is more immediately important is the way in which such an outcome coincides with expectations generated by the present view of habit. Here we see that the strength of a habit can be lessened, precisely as this view would predict, without either non-rewarded or punished occurrences thereof: all that is necessary is to rob the response-correlated stimuli (by extinction or counterconditioning; see Chapter 11) of their power to arouse secondary reinforcement —and the "habit" vanishes forthwith. This is hardly to be expected on the assumption that habit is a drive-behavior neural bond. This type of finding has, of course, important implications for the general subject of "latent learning" (and extinction) (Mowrer, 1960, Chapter 2) and for the question of the relationship between secondary reinforcement and discrimination (Chapter 12). For immediate purposes, however, its bearing is sufficiently clear and needs no further elaboration.[5]

VII. Supporting Evidence:
(c) The Loucks Experiment

Reference has already been made to the "trick" of teaching a dog to "shake hands" by passively flexing the right foreleg and then administering food, approval, or some other primary or secondary reward. By this procedure, secondary reinforcement is presumably attached to the stimuli associated with leg flexion, with the result that presently the dog begins "voluntarily" making this response, because

---

[5] The foregoing discussion may remind the reader of the "sensory deprivation" experiments already alluded to in Chapter 6 (Section III) in which young men were temporarily deprived of normal visual, auditory, and tactile stimulation (Lilly, 1956; Heron, Doane, & Scott, 1956; Heron, 1957), with resulting "acute disturbance of the normal personality . . . swings in motivation . . . periods of apathy . . . desire to get back to a normal environment . . . handsome visual hallucinations, disturbances of perception of the self, impairment of intelligence" (Hebb, 1958, pp. 110–111). Whatever else this type of "isolation" involved, it certainly constituted an interference with normal sensory feedback from the subject's ordinary behavior. Here, with the exception of proprioception, *most* of the sensory feedback was, in fact, eliminated; and if our present analysis is correct, it is not surprising (especially since the condition was maintained for many hours, or even days) that there were disorganizing effects. Just imagine what it would be like if *all* sensory feedback from action were eliminated, so that one could not tell if he had or had not performed a given action, whether he was in one bodily position or another, and so on! Frightening, isn't it? As the experiments cited suggest, we are here apparently dealing with variables which not only control specific "habits" but also one's very sense of identity and self-awareness. (This matter is further discussed, from a still different standpoint, in Mowrer, 1960, Chapter 7).

of the secondary, or *autistic* (Mowrer, 1960, Chapter 3), satisfaction mediated by the stimulation produced by the occurrence thereof.

Now the leg of a dog can be caused to flex and thus produce a characteristic pattern of stimuli by various means other than the one just described. One of these (see also Chapter 8) involves so-called faradic (electrical) stimulation of the dog's brain in the area of the cortex that controls this movement. In an article published by Loucks, in 1935, and entitled, "The Experimental Delimitation of Neural Structures Essential for Learning: The Attempt to Condition Striped Muscle Responses with Faradization of the Sigmoid Gyri," the author tried to "condition" the response thus elicited to a buzzer which immediately preceded the faradic stimulation to the brain, with highly instructive results. Loucks begins his report by pointing out that:

> In a typical, striped muscle conditional reaction experiment, a signal such as a light is flashed for a second or so and then the unconditional stimulus, e.g., a faradic shock at [sic] the skin of the leg, is administered. This results in a prompt movement of the limb. After a number of repetitions of the signal light and cutaneous shock in combination, the light unaccompanied by shock evokes a movement of the leg. This lifting of the leg at the flash of the light in the absence of, or preceding the shock, is designated a conditional response.
>
> The question arises as to whether or not all the various neural elements involved in such modifications of behavior are indispensable (pp. 5–6).

Before we proceed with the further analysis of this investigation, two comments are in order. It will be noted, first of all, that Loucks speaks of *conditional*, rather than of condition*ed*, reactions. This is a usage which has a good deal to recommend it (Mowrer & Lamoreaux, 1951); but it is not the common one and is not adopted for general use in this volume. However, no misunderstanding will result if the reader simply keeps in mind that the two words, as far as their technical denotations go, are strictly equivalent.

The other point to be noted is that Loucks, following the practice generally accepted at the time of writing, here speaks of leg flexion as a conditioned, or "conditional," response. We would now assume that, in the example given, the emotion of *fear* was, strictly speaking, the response that had been conditioned and that flexion of the leg was a "voluntary" or "habitual" act, motivated *by* the fear. However, again no difficulty need arise if one remembers that in referring to leg flexion, when it occurs to the flash of light, as a conditioned (or "conditional") response, Loucks was merely conforming to an oversimplified way of speaking.

In a section headed, "Conditioning with Faradization of the Sigmoid Gyri as the Unconditional Stimulus," Loucks then goes on to say:

In the first of the experiments to be reported at this time, the objective was the stimulation of the motor cortex to see if the limb response thus elicited could be conditioned to an auditory signal such as a buzzer. . . . This cortical faradization may be regarded as the unconditional stimulus inasmuch as it produces an involuntary and reflex-like movement of the limb. It is analogous, in a sense, to the cutaneous shock at a limb in the usual experimental procedure. An obvious difference between this and the customary routine is that in directly stimulating cerebral motor elements the investigator, in effect, short-circuits the afferent limb of the reflex pathways that would normally be activated by cutaneous shock—disregarding for the moment secondary proprioceptive stimuli from the movement of the limb. This particular phase of the project was taken as a starting point because of its technical simplicity and because it was hoped that the role of the secondary proprioceptive stimuli, from movement of the limb, would be clarified (p. 7).

Here the author is saying that in eliciting leg flexion by direct stimulation of the brain, the sensation of *pain* which is experienced by the dog when movement of the leg is prompted by peripheral shock is "in effect, short-circuited," but that "secondary proprioceptive stimuli from the movement of the limb" will, on other hand, be normally experienced.

Loucks continues:

The method of chronic faradization of unanesthetized and intact animals has been described by the writer in another place. . . . Briefly, it involves the embedding of a collodion-coated coil beneath the skin [of the head] and leading insulated wires from the coil to the point to be stimulated [in the brain]. No wires penetrate the integument [body surface]. Subsequently, this buried coil will absorb energy by induction from the activated primary "field" coil external to the animal. The experimenter can thus produce an excitation at the bare tips of the buried electrodes by pressing a button which causes current to flow through the field coil external to the animal (pp. 7–8).

Loucks describes the results of his attempt to cause the buzzer to elicit leg flexion through paired presentation of buzzer and brain stimulation thus:

In a project to determine what structures are essential for learning, an attempt was made to condition a movement of the right hind limb to an auditory signal, with faradization of the *sigmoid gyri* as the unconditional stimulus. A conditional reaction of the hind limb failed to be established in any of three dogs receiving approximately 600 trials each (p. 42).

There could hardly be a more dramatic substantiation of the view that active avoidance behavior involves fear arousal and relief, rather than just the temporal conjunction of a formerly neutral stimulus with the occurrence of some reflex reaction to a second stimulus. Here, in the Loucks experiment, the latter condition is fully met, yet there is not the slightest indication of the development of avoidance behavior; and the reason presumably is that the stimulus for the leg reflex is put into the nervous system in such a way that it can cause no pain. Without pain there is no possibility that fear will get attached to the signal; and without such a reaction to the signal, there is nothing to motivate and reinforce the occurrence of the specific leg movement (or any other overt act). As already noted in Chapter 4 (Section I), Solomon & Wynne (1954; see also 1950) have shown that sympathectomizing an animal seriously impairs its capacity to react with fear and that an animal so treated shows a correspondingly impaired capacity for developing avoidance behavior. And in the same context, several other investigators are cited who have shown that sedatives and tranquilizers also depress avoidance behavior. But the Loucks experiment made the point, back in 1935, most convincingly of all: a reflex response made to a stimulus which cannot arouse pain (and fear) is utterly incapable of occurring anticipatorily, to a signal. A signal or "conditioned stimulus," to be effective, must, it seems, be a *danger* signal. And if there is nothing noxious or "dangerous" about the unconditioned stimulus, avoidance behavior simply does not develop, even after "approximately 600 trials."

Woodbury (1942), in "A note on 'passive' conditioning," likewise reports failure of "conditioning" in a situation wherein dogs were given a signal and then one of their legs was gently lifted by mechanical means. This writer refers to a 1928 experiment by Miller & Konorski in which it was found that a signal which was followed by passive lifting of a dog's leg did acquire the capacity to elicit this response. Woodbury repeated their procedure, with minor modifications, and failed to get conditioning. "In the course of 350 trials . . . there was no sign of such a change, either in the form of active flexion in response to the buzzer, or in a decrease in pressure on the treadle in preparation for the active lifting" (p. 360). Woodbury suggests that Miller & Konorski may have gotten anticipatory leg flexion in their experiment because they yanked the leg up, roughly, by means of "a cord attached directly to the ankle, instead of lifting the surface on which the foot rested." The yank on the string may therefore have caused pain; and subsequent leg movement in response to the signal may have been simply an ordinary avoidance reaction, which would not have developed if the leg had been lifted more gently.

Thus we have, in the Woodbury experiment, a confirmation (in normal, unoperated dogs) of the Loucks finding that leg flexion which is produced by a stimulus which is in no way painful does not occur "avoidantly"—and why should it? If, on the other hand, a response were to be elicited in this manner (or by the method employed by Woodbury) and followed by a *positive* reinforcer (such as food), one might anticipate a quite different outcome (Section II). We now turn to the second part of Loucks' investigation, which he reports as follows:

> The three dogs in the preceding group were given biscuits at irregular intervals of four to ten trials [presumably as a means of making them content to stay in the conditioning stand, without struggling]. The routine for the two remaining animals differs from that described above in that food was given at the end of every trial. In other words, the buzzer was sounded for approximately one second, the shock being added during the last tenth of the second, and then after a second or so, the animal would receive one or two biscuits (p. 16).

Fig. 7–8. Schematization of the procedure used in Loucks' second experiment: The buzzer was presented for one second, during the last one-tenth of which there was faradic stimulation of the *sigmoid gyri*. Food was present (X) about one second after these two other forms of stimulation and leg flexion.

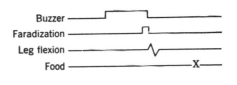

The procedure just described is shown diagrammatically in Fig. 7–8. In summarizing his findings, Loucks says of this part of his investigation:

> Lifting the hind limb to cortical shock was an adequate basis for conditioning if each movement was rewarded with food. This was shown to be based upon a mechanism of backward association, since once the response to the buzzer was extinguished, the animal failed to re-establish it if the food was omitted (p. 42).

In light of revised two-factor learning theory, a different way of interpreting Loucks' findings suggests itself. This investigator infers that the subject "formed the conditional response upon the basis of a *backward association* with the food reward." Just how this would occur is not entirely clear (see Chapter 10). But a different type of explanation makes the experimental facts readily comprehensible. According to present theory, we would see in this experiment, not an instance of backward conditioning at all, but rather a straightforward case of forward conditioning. Loucks speaks of the "centripital volleys of proprioceptive impulses to the higher somesthetic nuclei" which were excited by each flexion of the leg by means of faradic stimulation. And each of these "volleys of proprioceptive impulses" was followed by food, eating, and hunger reduction. Therefore, the proprioceptive stimuli produced by the leg flexion caused by cortical stimulation would take on secondary reinforcement, which would then generalize, probably quite strongly, to the proprioceptive stimuli produced by normal, "voluntary" leg flexion (see Fig. 7–9). In short, the procedure described by Loucks is analogous to that used to teach a hungry dog to "shake hands" with one of its forepaws and, in light of our earlier discussion, would be beautifully calculated to establish a "habit."

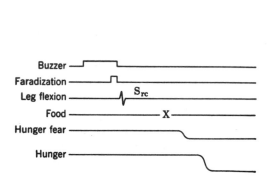

Fig. 7–9. A more complete analysis of the procedure depicted in Fig. 7–8. Here is shown, by means of the spike, the leg flexion produced by the faradic stimulation. This response produces certain response-correlated stimuli, S_{rc}. Also shown are the reduction in hunger and the reduction in hunger fear produced by the food. The crucial learning here consists, presumably, of the reduction in hunger fear (or secondary reinforcement, decremental type) becoming conditioned to the response-correlated stimuli, S_{rc}. Per hypothesis, these conditions meet the requirements for the establishment of a leg-flexing "habit."

There is only one complication in the foregoing analysis: If the procedure employed by Loucks produced a regular "habit," motivated by hunger and reinforced by hunger reduction, why did it occur, seemingly quite specifically, *in response to the buzzer?* Our surmise would be that in this situation the buzzer really functioned more as a *cue* than as a signal. During training the dog would have found that voluntary flexion of the leg would produce food *only if* the buzzer had just sounded; so the dog would accordingly form a discrimination between experimental-situation-without-buzzer and experimental-situation-when-buzzer-has-just-sounded, the former being "negative" and the latter being "positive" as far as response effectiveness was concerned.

If this interpretation is correct, one would expect the dog, in the process of forming such a discrimination, to have made a goodly number of wrong or false responses, in the sense of often flexing the right hind leg *between* trials, when the buzzer cue was *not* present. Loucks makes no reference in the text of his paper to such intervening or "spontaneous" leg flexions; but the legend of one kymographic record reads:

First phase of training where dog was fed crackers between each trial [i.e., immediately after each cortically elicited leg flexion]. Definite conditional movement in right hind leg at each buzzer signal. Conditional lifting a sustained movement, whereas unconditional response to cortical shock a relatively brief swing of short latency. A further difference between the conditional and unconditional movements is that the latter was obviously a lifting of the limb, the former a swing or kick (p. 12).

And in this record one not only sees the "conditional" leg flexions which occurred when the buzzer came on, but also relatively frequent interval, or "spontaneous," flexions. Here, then, is direct support for the assumption that the response ostensibly made *to* the buzzer was actually motivated by hunger and that the buzzer was just a cue, indicating when the response would and would not be rewarded. One can predict with considerable confidence that as training proceeded, the interval (wrong) responses diminished in frequency of occurrence while the "conditional" (right) responses increased in frequency—and specificity (cf. Chapter 12).

It is not clear how traditional habit theory would explain the results reported by Loucks; and in order to interpret them in terms of traditional conditioning theory, one has to posit the highly questionable phenomenon of backward conditioning. But the findings, as just shown, are "made to order" as far as revised two-factor theory is concerned.

In a third and final part of this study, which is of only incidental interest to us here, Loucks found that faradization of the sigmoid gyri, in addition to eliciting a movement of the dog's hind leg, also produced a conscious sensation of some kind, as indicated by the fact that this form of stimulation could be made to act as a signal, or CS, for flexion of one of the dog's *front* legs, as a result of its being paired with ordinary cutaneous shock to that leg. There was, of course, a possibility that it was not the direct perception of brain stimulation as such that was here acting as the conditioned stimulus but instead the proprioceptive "back-lash" from the resulting flexion of the hind leg. In order to check this possibility, Loucks simply deafferentated the hind leg, so that the dog had no sensations of touch or movement therefrom; but still the brain stimulation acted as a CS for foreleg flexion, under threat of ordinary electric shock to this leg (cf. Nielson, Doty, & Rutledge, 1958).

The over-all import of Loucks' ingenious researches is therefore to show the necessity of secondary reinforcement, in one form or another, for the development of a "habitual" response. In the experiment just described, secondary reinforcement type-1 was provided for the occurrence of foreleg flexion by reduction in the fear aroused by the "buz" produced by sigmoid gyri stimulation; this, therefore, was simply an instance of ordinary active avoidance learning. And, in the earlier part of Loucks' study, the dogs learned to lift the *hind* leg, on cue, because the proprioceptive, cutaneous, and other stimuli produced by this response had come to signalize secondary reinforcement type-2, i.e., hope of receiving food. The result was an ordinary discriminative habit.

An excerpt from Loucks' own discussion of his experimental findings follows:

One of the most striking facts arising from these experiments is the inadequacy of mere repetition, as such, for learning. Although the dogs were given hundreds of trials in which an auditory stimulus was associated with a limb response, the repetition of these two events, in quick succession, was inadequate to bring about learning. This would seem to necessitate a reinterpretation of the Law of Exercise as usually formulated in the psychology of learning. It indicates the serious inadequacy of those formulations of learning or conditioning built solely upon the principle of association by contiguity. It would appear that mere repetition, as such, is not enough. Contiguity is not enough (pp. 34–35).

And, in conclusion, Loucks says:

Various experiments in which conditioning has taken place when only limited portions of the normal, reflex pathways were functioning were reviewed to show that conditioning is established upon the basis of certain primitive urges, impulses, appetites—probably subcortical in character—and that it is the feeling of pain, hunger, nausea, *etc.*, which is the significant factor rather than the reflex response which is merely one component in a complex pattern (p. 42).

It would thus appear that Loucks' empirical findings are completely congruent with expectations generated by revised two-factor theory and that this theory is a logical culmination of interpretative trends to be noted in the passages last quoted.

VIII. Supporting Evidence:
(d) Delayed Auditory Feedback and Related Phenomena

Writing in *The Scientific Monthly*, for February, 1953, Stanton and Sylva Cohn, drew the following cogent distinction:

> The nineteenth century was the "Age of Power." It saw the development of the machine, and concomitant with it there arose a mechanistic philosophy of life and a mechanical interpretation of life processes. . . .
> Science has advanced beyond the mechanistic stage, however. Just as the nineteenth century was the Age of Power, the twentieth century is the Age of Communication and Control. It is not enough to make a powerful machine, having the ability to do many times the work of man. There must be an intelligent application of this energy—it must be controlled (p. 87).

Nineteenth-century *power* machines were typically what are now being called *open-cycle* control systems: a button was pushed or a lever thrown here and an effect (considerably magnified in terms of energy) appeared there. And this was the model of stimulus-and-response functioning which tacitly underlay the classical conceptions of the reflex and of habit, as they have existed in physiology and in psychology. By contrast, the twentieth century has produced, in increasing profusion, machines which operate as *closed-cycle* systems, i.e., which are *self*-regulatory (cf. Mowrer, 1960, Chapter 7). Manifestly, the latter provide a much more realistic model for the behavior of living organisms, which are so exquisitely self-regulatory and "homeostatic" (Chapter 6), than did earlier mechanical conceptions. But only now, at mid-twentieth century, is a conception of "habit" evolving which makes living organisms, per theory, as intelligent as they manifestly are in action and, for that matter, as intelligent as are some of the machines which man himself has recently perfected.

The following is a portion of a paper by the present writer which reviews some of these developments, with special reference to the dramatic effects produced by delayed auditory feedback.

> What this line of evidence seems to add up to, then, is the inference that responses become "habitual" by virtue of the proprioceptive and other stimulation associated therewith having acquired secondary reinforcement value. This formulation, paradoxical as it sounds, seems to apply with equal cogency regardless of whether we are speaking of a "habit" (a) which is initiated by

the learner, as in trial-and-error behavior, (b) one in which the subject is "put through" a given performance, passively, or (c) one which is first executed by *another* organism with resulting stimulation which the subject, on the basis of secondary reinforcement, subsequently tries to reproduce [see Mowrer, 1960, Chapter 3]. A conception which thus accounts, economically yet adequately, for the learning involved in trial and error, in passive "putting through," and in "imitation" has, it seems, some claim to serious consideration.

If we assume that a "habit" or "habit strength" depends, not upon the degree of neural connectedness between a given drive and a drive-reducing response, but upon the amount of secondary reinforcement that has been built up by association of incidental stimuli with other reinforcing states of affairs, it follows that a "habit" will be more seriously disturbed by interference with the sensory "feed-back" therefrom than by interference with specific stimulus-response bonds. Certainly brain ablation experiments have not given results which look much like what would be expected if habits were just acquired reflexes. Especially pointed are the results obtained by means of various forms of peripheral interference. In an early series of experiments, Lashley & McCarthy (1926) showed that one can radically impair the locomotor facilities of a rat without impairing a maze "habit." And it is also known that if, on the other hand, the *sensory return* from the bodily members involved in behavior is eliminated, habitual performances are seriously disorganized. For example, Light & Gantt (1936) have shown that a leg-flexing, paw-lifting habit can be taught to a dog while the limb in question is completely paralyzed. Under these conditions, what the dog learns is that a given signal is likely to be followed by an electric charge upon the grill on which the paw is resting; and when voluntary control of the limb recovers and the signal is presented, the animal makes an adaptive flexion response—a response which will now occur "habitually" despite the fact that occurrence of the response was not involved in the acquisition of the so-called habit.[6] And it is well known that locomotor habits in human beings

[6] Superficially, these observations appear, in one respect, to go *against* the present view of habit. To be sure, they indicate that "performance" is not essential to this kind of learning; but they also seem to show that *neither* is the sensory feedback from behavior (cf. Beck & Doty, 1957). However, this misleading impression is easily corrected. In the Lashley-McCarthy experiment, although the subjects' mode of locomotion—and hence the kinesthetic and tactile feedback therefrom—was radically disturbed without serious impairment of the maze "habit," it must be remembered that the visual, olfactory, and possibly other associated forms of stimulation were *not* affected and that the "habit" could easily have been carried, or retained, by *these*, rather than necessarily by the kinesthetic and tactile stimuli. Response-correlated (response-produced) stimuli, as here conceived, are by no means restricted to stimuli of the latter kinds. But what of the Light-Gantt study? Here it was found that an avoidance habit could be *established* without occurrence (or even "putting through") of response. The issues here involved are clarified by an earlier study reported by Crisler (1930). This investigator found that a conditioned salivary response could be established with morphine as the UnCS even though, during conditioning, the salivary response was prevented from occurring by the use of atropine (for a

are spectacularly disorganized in *tabes dorsalis*—a condition in which the motor nerves to the legs are fully intact but one in which the proprioceptive return therefrom is lost.

There is, however, a different, and even neater, type of observation. If a normal human being is asked to speak, he can do so with little or no distortion even though all air-borne feedback is cut off. This feat is accomplished, presumably, on the basis of bone-conducted sound and proprioceptive stimulation from the throat, tongue, lips, and jaw. But now let us re-introduce the air-borne feedback, on which the subject ordinarily places greatest reliance in monitoring his speech, and see what happens if we *delay it* by a fraction (e.g., $\frac{1}{4}$) of a second, as can be done by "storing" the speech momentarily on a magnetic tape before allowing it to get back to the speaker. Experiments by Lee (1950), Black (1951), Fairbanks (1954, 1955), and Fairbanks and Jaeger (1951), and others reveal a very dramatic result: Despite its highly practiced, "habitual" nature, under these circumstances human speech is immediately and almost invariably distorted, often quite ludicrously, and sometimes becomes so disorganized as to be utterly chaotic! [7]

On the basis of the traditional S—R interpretation of habit, this remarkable effect has been quite incomprehensible. Can it be that in our re-examination of habit theory we have stumbled upon its true explanation? This effect is very possibly a better test of our hypothesis than would be any effort to exclude all sensory feedback from a habitual response system by means of

------

review of other related studies, see Morgan & Stellar, 1950, pp. 453 ff.). However, far from being evidence against the present over-all conception of learning, this finding neatly supports it. We are here assuming that *habit* involves the conditioning of hope to certain response-correlated stimuli. Conditioning itself is *not* assumed to operate this way: it is dependent solely upon the pairing of the conditioned and unconditioned stimulus (cf. Chapter 11, Section V). Therefore, what presumably happened in the Light-Gantt experiment was this. The dog, as a result of past experience, had undoubtedly already learned what to do when its foot was being hurt (or was in danger of being hurt) by the surface on which it is resting, i.e., to *retract* it. Thus, one may say that all that happened in the Light-Gantt experiment was that an already existent "habit" was *energized* by the specific training procedure but could not be manifested until the motor nerve had regenerated. It seems likely, therefore—in fact, virtually certain—that no such effect would be obtained with respect to a response which had had no prior practice, or "habit strength." However, even here success could very likely be attained by (a) pairing a signal with shock (in order to give it fear-arousing potency) and (b), while the motor nerve was still severed, using the putting-through technique for associating certain response-correlated stimuli with signal termination and fear reduction. Upon recovery of the motor nerve, such a "habit" might very well make its appearance *de novo!*

[7] A 10-inch L-P recording of this phenomenon, with explanatory comment, may be obtained free of charge (through courtesy of John Wiley & Sons) by writing to the author of this book. An extensive bibliography (Sutton, Chase, & First, 1959) can be obtained from Dr. R. A. Chase, Biometrics Institute, New York City. Dr. Chase and associates are also studying delayed feedback in other sensory modalities.

anaesthesia, nerve sectioning, or the like. In this procedure, with the subject in an otherwise completely normal state, we can mask out, apparently quite effectively, all (or certainly most) subsidiary sensory feedback by the trick of slightly delaying, or throwing "out of phase," the major sensory return from the activity in question. Anyone who has experienced the effect is impressed, not to say appalled, by it, as pure phenomenon. And in the present context we are likewise struck by how satisfactorily this otherwise baffling result is accounted for by what is to us an unaccustomed, but intriguing, conception of the mechanism of 'habit.'

In conversation Professor Fairbanks has reported that with the same set-up mentioned above, observations have been made with persons playing musical instruments, rather than speaking: e.g., a violinist is asked to play but with the only auditory feedback occurring *via* a microphone, the "delaying" mechanism, and a set of headphones which exclude all other (i.e., the direct) auditory stimulation. Under these conditions, the habits involved in performing on a musical instrument are disorganized in much the same manner as are speech habits. Dr. Donald J. Mason has suggested another interesting possibility: namely that of switching the out-put of an electronic organ from its loudspeaker to the tape delayer and then connecting the speaker to the output of the delayer. This would give the desired asynchronism and yet would eliminate the necessity of having the performer wear headphones, thus making the situation more "natural." The only direct, immediate feedback from the movements involved in playing the organ would be kinesthetic and, to a lesser extent, visual. With the major feedback, i.e., the auditory one, out of phase, the organist would almost certainly find it impossible to play normally on the basis of proprioceptive and visual cues alone—particularly if the composition were a rapid one. Chimes players and public-events announcers using a public-address system with one or more remote loudspeakers also report "habit interference" because of the (acoustically) delayed feedback (Mowrer, 1953b, pp. 12–15; see also Chase, 1959.)

The facts reviewed in this and the preceding sections of this chapter by no means exhaust the evidence that can be adduced in support of what, for want of a better term, has here been called the revised two-factor conception of habit. And in later chapters further evidence, of both a direct and indirect nature, will in fact be extensively cited (see also Mowrer, 1960). But the theory itself has now been sufficiently delineated and enough empirical justification for it presented to warrant using the next two chapters to show its relationship to other conceptual schemes. The success or failure of the present theory, in one important respect, will hinge upon how well it articulates with and unifies the view of others.[8]

---

[8] Upon reading a typescript copy of this chapter, Dr. D. W. Zimmerman made the following comment: "Relevant to the argument in this chapter are Ritchie's (1954) criticisms of the S—R model. His argument, advanced from a somewhat different standpoint, has much the same import. The revised conception of habit

IX. Summary and Comment

In this chapter we have "rounded out," in at least one phase of its development, the extensive program of research and logical analysis which has been traced in the preceding chapters. As it gradually became apparent that neither of the two great behavioristic conceptions of learning (classical Pavlovian conditioning and habit formation in the manner of Thorndike) was satisfactory, special interest developed in *active avoidance* learning, with the resulting discovery that *fear* (which had previously been barred from consideration as too subjective and unscientific) must be posited as an intervening variable. This done, a new conception of *passive avoidance* learning (punishment) emerged, which quickly superseded (or, rather, integrated) the views of both Pavlov and Thorndike in this area. And it was at this stage that the second version of *two-factor learning theory* came into currency.

But while an advance over the original formulations of Pavlov and Thorndike (which, in conjunction, constituted the *first* version of two-factor theory), this schematization also had its troubles, among them the fact that it paid so little attention to "positive" *approach* behavior. As this and related phenomena have been investigated (especially in the past 10 or 15 years), we have come to distinguish systematically between secondary reinforcement *type-1* (as it occurs in active and passive avoidance learning) and secondary reinforcement *type-2* (as it occurs in approach behavior). And at this point we discovered that a new and vastly improved conception of *habit* had suddenly dropped

---

developed in this book, one might argue, also leads to the necessity of re-examining the *logic and methodology* of psychological theory. Spence's classic description of psychological 'laws,' as $R = f(S)$, is no longer adequate as a model for the kind of behavior dynamics developed here. Ritchie's position, however, is more congruous with what would seem to be needed." The present author is not sufficiently certain that he understands Ritchie's argument to endorse Zimmerman's evaluation, but it is reproduced here as suggestive. This much, however, is certain: The view that *a* stimulus "causes" *a* response must be replaced with the notion that what we have previously called a "response" can, in most instances, be better termed an *act*, which is composed of a great many S—R sequences in which "S" is produced by the just preceding "response" or *segment* of the total act. The reader can easily demonstrate all this for himself as follows. Take a straight-edge and draw a line, A-B, one foot long. Then, starting at A, quickly *trace* A-B freehand. From the many slight deviations from A-B and returns thereto which the tracing will show, it will be evident that the total act of tracing A-B consists, actually, of a *succession* of "responses." For further discussion of this problem, see Mowrer (1960, Chapter 7).

into our hands. It is the latter, of course, which has been elaborated in the present chapter, with considerable array of both old and new lines of supporting evidence.

However, despite the logical fit of this conception of habit and its widespread empirical justification, it has, thus far, received little formal recognition. For example, it is not even mentioned in Kendler's review of "Learning" in the 1959 *Annual review of psychology*—although a great deal of research is therein described which fairly cries for this type of interpretation, and new findings are constantly appearing in the literature which quite specifically support it. Kendler refers to "the stark inadequacies and limitations of existing learning theories" (p. 43) but makes no use of what would now appear to be the most powerfully integrative system of all. His concluding remarks are nevertheless instructive:

Learning psychologists are still groping with methodological problems (both in the philosophy of science as well as in the experimental sense) that they hope will lead to a major breakthrough in understanding behavior. Some believe a breakthrough is now occurring. But nobody is willing to recognize anybody's breakthrough but his own. [Cf. our efforts to achieve a functional and comprehensive *synthesis*.]

However, the gropings of the past year do suggest a pattern. The major features of this pattern will now be given in a modestly pontifical fashion.

(*a*) The range of empirical phenomena that learning theorists are now trying to handle is becoming wider and wider with motivation and perception (at least orienting acts) playing a larger and larger role. Truly, learning theories are behavior theories. [See Chapters 8 and 9; also Mowrer, 1960.]

(*b*) S—R psychology dominates the psychology of learning. The success of S—R psychology is partly due to the fact that it forces its user to think in terms of manipulable experimental variables and observable responses. [Cf. Chapter 5, Section IX.]

(*c*) Yesterday's physiological models of the learning process have failed to pay off in generating research. Physiology, however, is not becoming less important, but rather more important to the psychology of learning. The great advances that are now taking place in experimental psychology are, and will continue, establishing a true rapprochement between learning theory and physiology. [Cf. Chapter 6.]

(*d*) Learning theories are paying more and more attention to the S's response. The dream that behavior could be simply related to such independent variables as delay of reinforcement [Chapter 10] or amount of reward [Chapter 8] has been shattered. It has been demonstrated (Spence, 1956) that it is not the delay which is the important variable but what the S does during the delay. The consummatory response is probably more important than the amount consumed (Wike & Barrientos, 1957). Guthrie should be given credit for emphasizing this point many years ago [Chapter 8].

(e) Skⁱnnerian experimental techniques are becoming more widely adopted [Chapter 8]. The rate of response measure seems to be at times (Miller, 1957) a more sensitive measure than traditional measures of behavior.

(f) Complicated experimental designs involving complex statistical procedures seem to be offered at times in lieu of theoretical notions.

(g) In general, learning theorists understand each other much better than did their ancestors of two decades ago. Neobehaviorists, S—R functionalists, and statistical learning theorists can communicate easily with each other. Skinnerians also find it easy to communicate among themselves.

(h) Progress is being made! (pp. 78–79).

In view of the widespread confusion which Kendler finds in contemporary learning theory and research, it is all the more remarkable that he makes so little reference to the scheme we have found so useful (only in d is there tangential allusion to it). But perhaps there is, after all, a reason! In advancing a feedback conception of both response inhibition (punishment) and response facilitation (habit), we have emancipated behavior theory from what may be called the "bondage" of Thorndike's scheme and also liberated it from the crass reflexology of Pavlov. However, in one respect this "revolution" may appear to have gone *too far*. Once a response which has previously been rewarded or punished is in progress (either actively or symbolically—see Mowrer, 1960, Chapters 2–6), we readily see how it can be facilitated or inhibited, respectively, by hope or fear. But if we thus put all learning (i.e., the conditioning of hopes and fears) over on the side of the sensory consequences of an act, we seem to be left without any explanation whatever as to how it is that certain responses rather than others do, after all, manage to *get started* in, i.e., apparently become "connected with," a given situation. Why, in other words, are *these* particular responses, rather than hundreds or even thousands of other possible reactions, selected and initiated?

Thorndikian connectionism had the very considerable merit of avoiding this problem, since it assumed, quite simply, that a habit is a stimulus-response bond, in the sense of a (neural?) connection between a given drive or situation (when it occurs) and a particular response tendency. But now, for good and sufficient reasons, we have been forced to abandon this theory; and, as we have seen, the one we have put in its stead has all the advantages that could be asked—except for the critical question of *response selection and initiation!*

At this point we face an expositional dilemma. The writer believes there is an eminently satisfactory solution to the problem just posed; but it has been arrived at in a rather circuitous and unexpected manner and cannot be convincingly described at this juncture without a major digression. Therefore, what we shall do is deliberately postpone full discussion of this problem until later (Mowrer, 1960, see especially Chapters 6 and 7) and proceed in the remainder of this volume with the analysis of various other problems which more naturally articulate with what has already been said and which do not depend, in any critical manner, upon the resolution of this dilemma. The strategy, therefore, will be to ask the reader to take it "on faith" that a solution to this basic problem *is* available, with only the briefest intimation here of what it specifically involves.

As we have now seen, the whole history of Behaviorism has been in the direction of liberalization (cf. Miller, 1959a), so much so, in fact, that Kendler, in his review, hardly refers to it at all, preferring instead to speak of "neobehaviorism" and "S-R functionalism." These latter movements readily accommodate concepts, such as fear and hope, which pristine Behaviorism would not countenance. Moreover, as also intimated by Kendler, these movements are now even beginning to acknowledge "perception (or at least orienting acts)." In other words, the relevance of *cognitive* as well as *affective* processes is being recognized in systematic theory; and the solution to the problem of response selection and initiation hinges, quite specifically it seems, upon the reality of *imagery* (or *memory*), which is a cognitive phenomenon, pure and simple. If, however, we now plunged into a full-scale consideration of cognitive (and symbolic) processes, we would by-pass topics of real importance, to which we would then later find it difficult and somewhat artificial to return. Therefore, as already indicated, our plan will be to hold discussion for the balance of this volume at a level such that cognitive considerations can be side-tracked and then, subsequently, returned to for detailed treatment.

With this explanation, we now proceed, in the next chapter, to further development and defense of what—for want of a more graphic term—may be called Two-Factor Learning Theory, Model III or, simply, revised two-factor theory.

8

Other Theories,
and Some Further Evidence,
Compared

Thus far, an effort has been made to present a particular conception of learning in as explicit and distinctive a manner as possible. This conception has been carefully contrasted with the views of other writers, in the hope of eliminating ambiguity and of posing logical and empirical issues with maximal clarity. Now, however, the time has come to look for agreements and congruences. And since one of the avowed aims of this book is to delineate a position which "integrates" seemingly diverse theories of learning, then naturally, the *more* agreements that can be found the better!

Sometimes it has been said to the author, "But isn't your theory a lot like that of Dr. X or Prof. Y?" Two disclaimers are in order here. The author very much hopes that the position which is being set forth in this book will not be regarded as "his," since it is specifically aimed at finding the *common ground* toward which the thought and research of *many* workers have for some time been moving. Moreover, in light of this objective, the fact that there are similarities between the position here adduced and that of other learning theorists is decidedly to the good. Prevailing disparity of views is not the hallmark of a great science; and it will now be our purpose to show the very substantial unity which has already been reached in this area and to suggest the even larger and more rigorous integrations that may be achieved in the future. First, however, it will be useful to make an explicit, summary statement of just how the present position differs from earlier versions of two-factor theory.

I. The Three Successive Versions of Two-Factor Learning Theory

Thorndike's Law of Effect, as formulated around the turn of the century, is schematized in Fig. 8–1; and Pavlov's conception of conditioning is represented in Fig. 8–2. Each alone, according to its proponents, was capable of accounting for the basic facts of learnings; but many others felt that *both* conceptions were necessary for a well-rounded account of behavior dynamics. Thus, what we may call the *original* two-factor learning theory assumed that conditioning and problem solving played equally useful, complementary roles in the total adjustmental economy of living organisms and that each alone was inadequate, conceptually and practically, without the other.

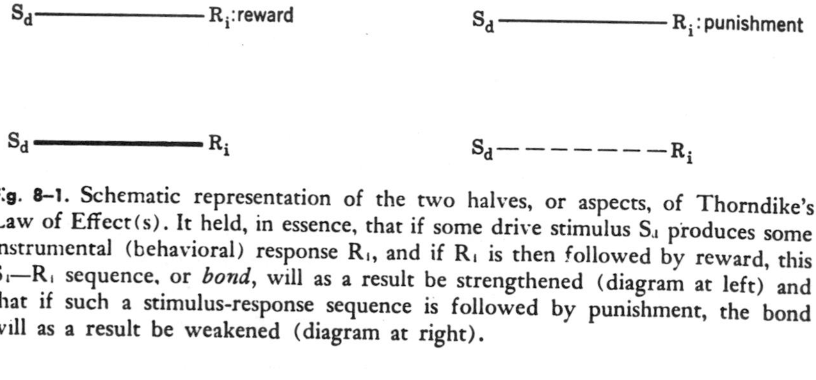

$$S_d \text{———————} R_i : \text{reward} \qquad\qquad S_d \text{———————} R_i : \text{punishment}$$

$$S_d \text{———————} R_i \qquad\qquad\qquad S_d \text{— — — — — —} R_i$$

Fig. 8–1. Schematic representation of the two halves, or aspects, of Thorndike's Law of Effect(s). It held, in essence, that if some drive stimulus S_d produces some instrumental (behavioral) response R_i, and if R_i is then followed by reward, this S_i–R_i sequence, or *bond*, will as a result be strengthened (diagram at left) and that if such a stimulus-response sequence is followed by punishment, the bond will as a result be weakened (diagram at right).

$$S_c \text{————————} R$$

Fig. 8–2. Schematic representation of conditioning, as conceived by Pavlov. S_c is a stimulus which, initially, is not capable of eliciting response R, but which as a result of contiguous occurrence with S_u (above, left), acquires this capacity (above right). The subscripts c and u are used to designate, respectively, what Pavlov termed the "conditioned" and the "unconditioned" stimulus.

The *second* version of two-factor theory (actually the first one to which this special nomenclature was applied) accepted, essentially unmodified, the "first half" of the Law of Effect, which held that reward strengthens habit; but it departed therefrom in holding that *punishment* achieves its action, not simply by reversing the effects of reward, but by causing fears to become attached (conditioned) to stimulation associated with the occurrence of the punished response. This version of two-factor theory is shown in Fig. 8–3. Here habit formation, or solution learning, is conceived essentially as Thorndike suggested; but punishment is seen in more complex terms. Instead of reversing the effect produced by past reward, punishment is here thought of as providing the basis for the conditioning of fear to response-correlated stimuli, which, when the response starts to recur, produces conflict and, if the fear is strong enough, response inhibition.

The details of this interpretation of punishment are shown at the right in Fig. 8–3. Here a problem situation or drive, S_d, produces an overt, instrumental response, R_i. R_i is followed by punishment, which is here represented as S_p. The punishment elicits a response R_p of which r_f, or fear, is a component. But when R_i occurs, it not only elicits the extrinsic stimulus, S_p; it also produces a number of other stimuli, s, s, s, which are inherently associated with the occurrence of R_i. The result: a part of the reaction produced by S_p, namely fear, gets conditioned to these response-produced stimuli, s, s, s. Consequently, when S_d recurs and the organism starts to perform R_i, the resulting stimuli "remind" the organism of the antecedent punishment, i.e., cue off r_f, which tends to inhibit R_i (cf. Chapter 3, Section V).

Two-factor learning theory, second version, thus accepted Thorn-

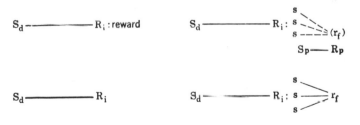

Fig. 8–3. Schematic representation of the second version of two-factor learning theory. According to this formulation, habits were made by reward, as shown at the left, in essentially the way suggested by the Law of Effect. However, punishment was assumed to involve fear conditioning, as shown at right, with ensuing conflict and probable inhibition (see text).

dike's conception of habit formation (essentially unmodified) but derived the phenomenon of punishment from fear conditioning, rather than attributing it to a process which simply reversed the effects of past reward. As we have shown, this theory of punishment (or *passive* avoidance learning) involves the same principles that have been found most satisfactory for explaining avoidance learning (of the *active* variety). In both instances, fear becomes conditioned to stimuli, either external or response-produced; and the organism then makes whatever type of adjustment will most effectively eliminate these stimuli and reduce the attendant fear.

The present-day version of two-factor theory is diagrammed in Fig. 8–4. Here it is assumed that habit formation is a matter of conditioning no less than is punishment. If a stimulus S_d produces a given response R_i, and if R_i is followed by reward S_r, then it is assumed that a part of the total response R_r which is produced by S_r will become conditioned to the stimuli inherently connected with R_i. Here the conditionable component of R_r is r_h, the "hope" (secondary reinforcement) reaction; and it becomes connected to stimuli, s, s, s, just as fear does in punishment. The result is that whenever R_i starts to occur, it is facilitated rather than blocked. This, it is assumed, is the essence of "habit," as opposed to "inhibition." Parenthetically, it is interesting to discover, from *Webster's Unabridged Dictionary*, that "habit" and "inhibition" both come from the same Latin root, *habare*, meaning to have. It is good to have a theoretical conception of these two phenomena which sees them as closely related as the etymology of these words would thus imply. This is not the only occasion on which wisdom has been found deeply imbedded in the very structure of language!

The second version of two-factor theory was "two-factored" in two

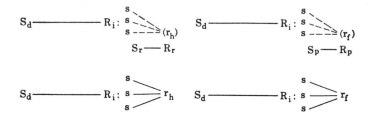

Fig. 8–4. Schematic representation of current two-factor theory. Here the changes produced in behavior by reward, as well as those produced by punishment, are derived from conditioning plus the feedback principle.

different ways: it distinguished between sign learning and solution learning *and* between incremental reinforcement and decremental reinforcement, sign learning being associated, presumably, with incremental reinforcement and solution learning with decremental reinforcement. Now the present version of the theory is two-factored in only *one* way: namely, with respect to the *two types of reinforcement*, incremental and decremental. With respect to the other principle of classification employed in the second version, the theory is now decidedly one-factored; that is, it assumes that all learning is sign learning and that solution learning (as well as response inhibition) is a derivative thereof.

In short, then, as far as "types of learning" are concerned, the revised version is "one-factored"; but it remains two-factored as regards type of reinforcement. This is perhaps not a very good basis for deriving a *name* for the theory; but, for the time being at least, this designation can perhaps serve as well as any other, provided that it is taken as implying two kinds of *reinforcement* but *not* two kinds of learning as well.

II. Early Adumbrations of the Present Position

The debt of the present approach to the conceptions of E. L. Thorndike and I. P. Pavlov has already been indicated. Although much time has been spent in suggesting how these conceptions have to be modified or refined in order to be maximally useful, the fact remains that the principle of conditioning is no less central to the emerging theoretical position than is Thorndike's Law of Effect. As Carr (1938), McGeoch (1942), and others have repeatedly observed, the latter is virtually incontestable, at a grossly descriptive, empirical level and, as such, is completely incorporated into present thinking. In fact, Thorndike himself can even be said to have been a "two-factor" theorist of sorts; for the so-called Law of Effect is really a Law of *Effects*, since it deals with *two kinds* of consequences which may follow a given action. It is true that Thorndike thought of these two effects as reciprocal, in the sense of one making and the other unmaking habit "bonds," instead of each being capable of producing its own brand of "forward" learning. However, as we shall see in Chapter 11, there is a limited sense in which Thorndike's views are correct even in this respect. Our principal departure here from the views of Thorndike is that we take explicit account of some of the more *immediate* effects of behavior which he overlooked (i.e., various forms of sensory feedback; cf. Chapter 9) and incorporate, rather than exclude, the concept of conditioning, thus arriving at a notion of habit which supersedes his "bond" conception thereof.

Pavlov, also, was a kind of early two-factor theorist. He acknowledged that some unconditioned stimuli (or reinforcers) are "positive" and others "negative"; and, as indicated in Chapter 3, he even made a preliminary effort to derive the phenomenon of "habit" from much the same basic principles as are employed in the present approach. The difficulty was that Pavlov was such an inveterate objectivist that he could not "see" certain of the "intervening variables" which a sophisticated behavior theory requires.

There were, of course, even earlier adumbrations of the present position. For example, in the famous chapter on "Habit" in his *Principles of Psychology* (1890), William James wrote as follows: [1]

> In action grown habitual, what instigates each new muscular contraction to take place in its appointed order is not a thought or a perception, but the *sensation occasioned by the muscular contraction just finished.* A strictly voluntary act has to be guided by idea, perception, and volition, throughout its whole course. In an habitual action, mere sensation is a sufficient guide, and the upper regions of the brain and mind are set comparatively free. A diagram [see Fig. 8–5] will make the matter clear:
>
> Let *A, B, C, D, E, F, G* represent an habitual chain of muscular contractions, and let *a, b, c, d, e, f* stand for the respective sensations which these contractions excite in us when they are successively performed. Such sensations will usually be of the muscles, skin, or joints of the parts moved, but they may also be effects of the movement upon the eye or the ear. Through them, and through them alone, we are made aware whether the contraction

---

[1] This is not to say, of course, that there were not still earlier, *much* earlier adumbrations of the present view, both in common sense and in scholarly speculation (cf. Chapter 2). But in the interest of time and space conservation, no systematic effort is made in this volume to cite earlier thinking. Moreover, between 1850 and 1900 a whole new "universe of discourse" was introduced which marks a sort of natural hiatus between the past and the present. There is, however, a definite "line of descent" leading to contemporary learning theory from the "association movement" as it appeared (primarily in England) during the two preceding centuries—for the details of which see a book such as Boring's *History of Experimental Psychology* (1929). David Hartley (1705–1757), as the official "founder" of this movement, held that learning consists of the "association of *ideas*" (cf. also Aristotle); and an idea was, basically, an *image* or, as we might say today, a conditioned sensation (Boring, p. 199; cf. also Mowrer, 1960, Chapter 5). Thus the association of *stimuli*, which since Pavlov has been taken as a crucial condition for learning, is really just a more objective way of talking about the association of sensations, images, ideas. The connectionism of Thorndike, on the other hand, was much more directly an outgrowth of the thinking of the utilitarians (hedonists), such as Alexander Bain (1818–1903) (see Boring, pp. 223 ff.).

has or has not occurred. When the series, A, B, C, D, E, F, G, is being learned, each of these sensations becomes the object of a separate perception by the mind. By it we test each movement, to see if it be right before advancing to the next. We hesitate, compare, choose, review, reject, etc., by intellectual means; and the order by which the next movement is discharged is an express order from the ideational centres after this deliberation has been gone through.

In habitual action, on the contrary, the only impulse which the centres of idea or perception need send down is the initial impulse, the command to start. This is represented in the diagram by V. . . . (pp. 115–116).

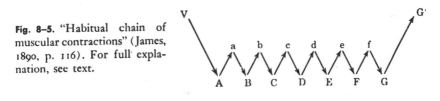

Fig. 8–5. "Habitual chain of muscular contractions" (James, 1890, p. 116). For full explanation, see text.

Whether James meant this analysis to apply only to a response *chain*, of more or less discrete acts, or thought of it also as germane to any given act or movement *while in progress* is not entirely clear. But this much is evident: he had a clear conception of the phenomenon of sensory feedback from on-going behavior as the cue and guide for further behavior. Our assumption is that behavior is thus guided by the hopes and fears which have been previously conditioned to these stimuli, emotions which produce, respectively, the right amount of facilitation and inhibition of specific movements for the accomplishment of certain "acts." James, of course, speaks more mentalistically, less "dynamically" about the process; but the similarity is obvious.

In the latter part of Dewey's 1896 paper, on "The Reflex Arc Concept in Psychology," there is an even closer approximation of present thinking. However, Dewey's comments on this score are discussed at length in another connection (Mowrer, 1960, Chapter 7—where further reference is also made to James' ideas) and will not be considered here.

Although Sigmund Freud spoke rarely of "learning" and apparently never of "learning theory," yet his imprint on contemporary thought in this area is unmistakable. In an era when organic theories of personality disturbance were very much in vogue, Freud boldly challenged them by holding that "neurosis," far from being an "osis" of the nerves, is actually *learned* (cf. Mowrer, 1960, Chapter 10). And he incorporated into his systematic position certain ideas which have quite specifically influenced subsequent developments in learning theory in its more technical aspects. In holding that a neurotic "symptom" is essentially a way of "defending against" or "binding" anxiety, Freud (1936) definitely foreshadowed later work on avoidance learning (see Chapters 2 and 3). And in his contention that much personality change occurs on the basis of *identification*, Freud showed, by implication, the gross inadequacy and incompleteness of the then current "mechanical" learning schemata. As will be seen elsewhere (Mowrer, 1960, Chapter 3), Freudian thinking has directly stimulated recent laboratory work on imitation (especially as it relates to the development of language) which, in turn, has been highly important in fostering the general interpretation of habit which has been made explicit in the preceding chapter.

Freud's concepts of "cathexis" and "countercathexis" are definitely related to what we here designate as hope and fear; and even in respect to the role of sensory feedback from activities in progress there is a most interesting allusion. Writing on Freud and Hull in a recent issue of the *American Scientist*, McClelland (1957) put it thus:

In the proposition which is basic to his whole system, Hull postulated that the reduction in need automatically strengthens the connection between the stimulus and response preceding it, a statement of the well-known "law of effect," which is usually thought to have been formulated first by Thorndike in this country. It is interesting to observe, however, that Freud, thinking along very similar lines, had come to an identical conclusion in the 1890's: "When this [the process of satisfying a desire] occurs, associations are forged . . . with the perceptual image of the satisfying object on the one hand, and on the other hand, the information derived from the motor activity that brought that object within reach" [Jones, 1953, p. 392]. In Hull's terms, he is saying that need reduction forges a connection between the "stimulus" and the response-produced stimulus, a conception quite similar to Hull's in most respects. It is probably because the basic "model" of how the organism functioned is so similar for the two men that it was so easy to incorporate certain Freudian notions into Hull's system. Both men were essentially natural scientists, who had been strongly influenced by the theory of evolution, and who tended, therefore, to think of the organism as responding and adapting to changes in the environment so that it could survive or maintain its equilibrium (pp. 108-109).

The important and salient point here is the reference to "the information derived from the motor activity" or, as McClelland says, "the response-produced stimulus." Here Freud takes cognizance of those *immediate* "effects" of behavior which Thorndike consistently overlooked, and relates them, albeit rather inexplicitly, to the phenomenon of habit formation. Freud, as we have seen, also had the idea that when a stimulus is associated with a pleasurable state it takes on "positive cathexis" and when associated with a painful state it takes on "anticathexis." Therefore, if he had merely gone a step further and had certain response-produced stimuli giving rise to positive and others to negative "cathexis," he would have anticipated present theory quite perfectly.

Hull also was aware of the stimulation which invariably results from behavior and even went so far as to refer to "pure-stimulus acts" (see Mowrer, 1960, Chapter 2), i.e., acts which are performed precisely for their stimulus- or cue-producing value. But because of his aversion to including affective states in his formal system, Hull never made maximal use of the possibility which here lay clearly within his reach.

A search of the literature between 1890 and 1920 would unquestionably reveal many other interesting forecasts of present developments in the field of learning theory; but those cited will suffice to show that the position with which we are currently concerned is broadly based and historically deeply rooted.

III. Incentive Motivation:
Hull, Crespi, and Spence

It is one of those paradoxes in which the history of science so abounds that although Clark Hull took a leading role in exciting interest in what we have here termed type-2 secondary reinforcement, he never fully saw its implications for general behavior theory. As has just been indicated, Hull repeatedly indicated his awareness of the reality of response-correlated stimulation; and he was also aware that independent, environmentally produced stimuli can take on the kind of "positive charge" which Freud termed "cathexis." But he never seems to have seriously asked the question, What happens when it is response-correlated stimuli, rather than independent ones, that take on such a "charge" or, in his own terms, acquire the capacity to act as secondary reinforcers? It is, we assume, this phenomenon, coupled with that of fear-mediated inhibition, which shapes behavior into those characteristic modes of action which are known as "habits" or, equivalently, "voluntary acts."

The nearest Hull came to this conception was in what he referred to as "incentive motivation" and which he symbolized by the notation K. Spence (1951a, p. 252), one of Hull's chief expositors, has interpreted this feature of his theoretical system thus:

Incentive motivation (K). The properties of the reinforcing stimulus also appear to determine the strength of the response being learned. In the case of classical conditioning involving food as the US, and in instrumental learning problems involving positive goal objects such as food, water, and so on, the magnitude of the reward has been shown to affect the response measure, for example, to lower or increase response latency, increase or decrease running speed, and so forth (Crespi, 1944; Zeaman, 1949). Delay of the incentive has also been shown to determine the level of performance attained in any simple learning situation (Harker, 1950; Perin, 1943a, 1943b; Perkins, 1947). With these facts in mind, Hull has postulated an incentive motivational factor (K) that is assumed to be a function of the magnitude of (G) and the time of delay (T_G) of the reward following the occurrence of the response to be learned.

$$K = f\,(W_a, T_G)$$

In many ways the incentive-motivation concept was redundant in Hull's system (cf. Bolles, 1958, p. 109; and Bevan & Adamson, 1959, p. 2). Pavlov, much earlier, had referred to what he termed "natural" conditioned reflexes, by which he meant the tendency for living organisms to salivate or make other appropriate anticipatory response to the mere sight, or sound, or smell of objects such as food, sex partners, and other sources of primary gratification—unconditioned stimuli he called them. These *natural* conditioned reflexes Pavlov contrasted to the *artificial* ones which are set up in the laboratory for experimental purposes. And, on a purely common-sense basis, one would expect a living organism to react, for example, to the *sight* of food in very much the same way as to any other stimulus (e.g., a buzzer) which, by special arrangements, indicates that food is "near." And since a secondary reinforcer was for Hull essentially the same as what Pavlov called a (positive) conditioned stimulus, it seems remarkable that Hull felt it necessary, in order to deal with the facts cited in the Spence quotation, to resort to the seemingly superfluous concept of "incentive motivation." The trouble, apparently, arose from Hull's addiction to the idea that a secondary reinforcer, so-called, achieves its efficacy by strengthening some "habit" in the sense of a stimulus-response bond.

Almost immediately after the appearance of Hull's first full-length statement of his system (1943), Crespi (1944) took strong exception to the way in which Hull conceived and employed his K variable. He said:

The object of the present paper is to subject Hull's treatment of quantitative variation of incentive and performance to criticism and amplification in the light of a recent series of experiments by the writer (Crespi, 1942). On the basis of this appraisal the writer will be led to reject Hull's strength-of-conditioning explanation of the effects of incentive variation upon action. Suggested in its stead will be a theory grounded upon emotional drive (p. 341).

And later in this paper Crespi expands his argument thus:

The writer wishes to present the thesis that *emotional drive* has been varying among the groups of animals running to the different amounts of incentive [in experiments cited], and this factor rather than simple learning is
the major determinant of differences in levels of performance. With varying
incentive amounts, after they have been experienced of course, there arise
among the groups of animals varying amounts of anticipatory tension or
excitement at the prospect of their acquisition. This is a differential of what
may be termed *eagerness*. The differential of eagerness, of emotional tension
or anticipatory excitement for the various amounts of incentive, generates,
according to this hypothesis, the differences within each trial in the obtained
curves of performance. The larger the incentive amount for which an animal
is performing the more eager he is to attain it, i.e., the more emotional drive
is summating with his hunger drive to motivate his response. Eagerness is
related to learning only in the sense that the animal must find out how much
incentive he is obtaining before he exhibits a corresponding amount of eagerness (p. 352).

The relevance of all this to our present way of thinking hardly
needs emphasis. The concept of "eagerness," as Crespi here employs
it, is manifestly equivalent to *hopefulness* (cf. also appetite, Chapter
6), as we have conceived it. Crespi is similarly assuming that this
phenomenon is basically *emotional,* as do we; and he is further assuming that the resulting modification in behavior is less a change
in "habit strength," i.e., less a change in what the organism *can* do,
than it is a change in what it *wants* to do. As Crespi puts it,

The comparison just completed and the preceding arguments make plausible the hypothesis that variations of amount of incentive operate to influence
performance through the agency of variation of emotional drive or anticipatory eagerness. . . . The differences in levels of action . . . cannot be
looked upon as caused by differences in habit strength or learning alone, but
must be understood as owing also to differences in drive strength (p. 354).

This statement, as it stands, is entirely congruent with the present
conception of secondary reinforcement—a change or "difference in
[secondary] drive strength." Because it results in intensified activity,
Crespi assumes that this change involves an *increase* in emotional or
secondary drive; this, as we have seen (Chapter 6; see also Section IV
of this chapter), is by no means certain; but Crespi's insistence that
"incentive motivation" or "*natural* secondary reinforcement" is an
emotional phenomenon was a major step forward and a real advance
over Hull's more indefinite, quasi-mathematical variable, K.

Hull, as we have seen, seems never to have assimilated completely
the implications for systematic behavior theory of considerations such
as those advanced by Crespi; but Spence (1956) has taken up the

challenge and in his recently published Silliman Lectures, delivered at Yale University, shows how profoundly shaken is Hull's system when one comes to grips with the now available facts and arguments. Hilgard (1956) has prepared an excellent précis of Spence's current thinking, and we shall follow this in the present discussion. First we note that "the r_G—s_G mechanism [see Chapter 4, Section III] becomes identified in Spence's theory with Hull's incentive motivation (K) rather than with habit strength (H)" (p. 416). This, as previously noted, is a thoroughly logical and long overdue development. And Spence goes on to replace Hull's definition of E (excitatory potential) with the simple formula: $E = H(D + K)$, where D is drive. And Hilgard concludes his exposition thus:

> How can Spence's theory best be characterized, in relation to other reinforcement theories? Let us quote his own words:
> "This theory is, then, a reinforcement theory so far as excitatory potential is concerned; that is, the presence or absence of a reinforcer, and differences in its properties when present, do make a difference in the strength of the instrumental response. It is not, however, a reinforcement theory in the traditional sense of the term, for the habit or associative factor is not assumed to vary with variations in reinforcement" (p. 419).

The implications of this statement are numerous and far-reaching. The statement is, first of all, an abandonment of the classical S—R bond conception of "habit." It says, in effect, that changes in "reaction potential" or, more simply, "performance" are *not dependent* upon the previously assumed "strength of association" between stimulus and response but upon "the presence or absence of a reinforcer," by which is presumably meant a *secondary* reinforcer or "incentive" motivator.[2]

This move has been foreshadowed for some time by Spence's repeatedly expressed dissatisfaction with the classical conception of reinforcement. His chariness about making any kind of neurological commitments has already been noted (Chapter 7); and he has been equally reluctant to commit himself to Hull's hypothesis that reinforcement occurs when and only when a drive is reduced. For example, we read:

[2] "Having decided (with Hull) that *H* is unaffected by magnitude and delay of reinforcement, the author (unlike Hull) considers that he |Spence| has joined the 'contiguity camp,' at least insofar as 'instrumental reward conditioning' is concerned. (This is a surprising development, since earlier in the same lecture the possibility of a 'crucial experiment on the reinforcement-contiguity issue' is denied on the ground that it is 'impossible to conduct an experiment without some form of motivation and reinforcing event')" (Bitterman, 1957, p. 142).

Because Hull's concept of secondary reinforcement does not involve drive reduction, it has been claimed that he is not a consistent reinforcement theorist. This criticism fails to note, however, that Hull does not abandon a reinforcement position in the case of secondary reinforcement, but only the special hypothesis that reinforcement always involves drive reduction" (Spence, 1951b, p. 709).

But if the term "reinforcement" is not to be purely *circular*, i.e., equated to learning itself and thus incapable of "explaining" learning, some independent criterion thereof *must* be specified. If it is not drive reduction, then, what *is* it? If the definition of reinforcement is left indefinite—Spence has often spoken of himself as accepting "a theory of *general* reinforcement"—it can hardly avoid being circular. However, by means of the radically new position, Spence, by means which will presently be indicated, at last escapes from this dilemma.

What the new view says is that performance changes as a result of change, not in S—R bonds, but as a result of changes in the incentive (secondary-reinforcement) value of particular stimuli. And that is also the view which we are here espousing. There is, however, this salient divergence. As indicated in a passage quoted earlier in this book (Chapter 4), Spence takes the postion that "the K factors (based on anticipatory goal response) act as drive" (Hilgard, 1956, p. 417); whereas our supposition is that an incentive or secondary reinforcer is, basically, a stimulus which mediates a *reduction* in (secondary) drive. Although the latter view is not without complications which remain only tentatively resolved (see Chapter 6), they seem less serious than do those attendant upon the assumption that secondary reinforcement, conceived as the "r_g—s_g mechanism," is a form of drive increase or excitation.[3] Recently, on an examination an advanced graduate student put the matter thus: "This intervening variable is hard to index, and again it is used in theory in a way which is not particularly clear—e.g., the same fractional anticipatory goal response explains both secondary drive *and* secondary reinforcement. I never know where in a behavior sequence the drive function ends and the reward function begins." The conception of secondary reinforcement (type-2) developed in Chapter 5 and given special application to habit formation in Chapter 7, whatever its other weaknesses may be, does not suffer from this form of ambiguity.

[3] "The value of K is determined by the 'vigor' of the 'classically conditioned' fractional goal-response, r_g, which is regarded as its underlying 'mechanism.' (The theory thus is tied to a consummatory interpretation of reinforcement. . . .)" (Bitterman, 1957, p. 142). See also Spence's (1951b) equating of the r_g mechanism and secondary reinforcement.

Hilgard also points out the following interesting development in Spence's thinking:

Because reinforcement may be necessary for classical conditioning and is not decisive for instrumental learning, Spence toys with the notion (without committing himself to it) that he may have a two-factor theory just the opposite of Mowrer's:
"It is interesting to note that *if* one were to adopt a theory that reinforcement (e.g., need reduction) plays a decisive role in the acquisition of habit strength of classical conditioned responses but not in the case of instrumental conditioned responses, one would have a two-factor theory that is exactly the opposite of the well known two-factor theory espoused by Schlosberg, Mowrer, and others" (p. 416).[4]

Implicit here is the assumption that incentive motivators or secondary reinforcers acquire their potency as a consequence of temporal contiguity with primary drive reduction. This, too, is *our* assumption (see Chapter 5). And it is our further assumption that so-called "instrumental" conditioning or habit formation is dependent upon this kind of conditioning (Chapter 7). But instead of this state of affairs implying the *reversal* of the two-factor position (version two) which Spence suggests, it, more logically, implies (a) that *all* learning is in the nature of "classical conditioning" and that so-called instrumental conditioning is derived therefrom and (b) that there are, however, *two kinds* of classical conditioning: that which occurs when a drive is reduced (decremental reinforcement) and that which occurs when a drive is induced (incremental reinforcement). Spence's system, as it presently stands is, like Hull's, seriously deficient in its lack of reference to the latter fact.[5]

Incidentally, in passing it is interesting to note the following excerpt from Hilgard's résumé:

Spence indicates two reasons why, over the years, he was not actively interested in the mechanism of reinforcement. The first was his interest in quantification, which he repeatedly pointed out did not require a theory of

[4] "Reluctance to renounce the necessity of reinforcement for *classical* conditioning leads then to the tentative statement of a kind of inverted 'two-factor' position—'that reinforcement (e.g., need reduction) . . .'—the implications of which do not seem to have been thought through very clearly" (Bitterman, 1957, p. 143).

[5] "Spence repeatedly emphasizes the narrowness of the 'boundary conditions' within which his theory is intended to apply. . . . Although here and there in the book passing reference is made to a troublesome fact, the uninitiated reader might never guess that the overall empirical fit of the theory is far less impressive than the lack of it" (Bitterman, 1957, p. 144). It must be admitted that although some of Bitterman's structures upon Spence's views also apply to our own, the charge of "narrowness" would be less well justified.

reinforcement. The second was the difficulty that showed up in experiments on latent learning of ever finding an experimental situation totally free of reinforcing effects. It was the effort to explain the various things happening in latent-learning experiments that led to an interpretation of reinforcement important to Spence's contemporary theorizing (pp. 415–16).

As indicated elsewhere (Mowrer, 1960, Chapter 2), our present conception of learning meshes nicely with the facts of so-called latent learning; and it is presumed that as Spence's thinking develops along these new lines, the degree of congruence which is already evident will become greater still.

IV. Seward on "Tertiary Motivation"— and a Recapitulation

Also indicative of the confluence of contemporary thinking with respect to the psychology of learning is the work of J. P. Seward. As early as 1950 this writer had moved a long way toward the position which is presently under discussion. He said:

There is a third possible alternative [to possibilities suggested by Wolpe (1950) and by Meehl (1950)] that does not confine the term [reinforcement] to the learning process. Increase in response strength does not necessarily mean increase in strength of S—R connections; it may mean simply that when a situation is repeated the response is more likely to occur. As we shall see, there are other ways than learning by which the probability of a response may be increased . . . (p. 363).

What Seward meant by this provocative statement becomes clear from the following discussion:

The question before us is how a reinforcer increases response strength. Does it do so by strengthening S—R connections for future use, or does it help *on that future occasion* to bring about the response? In other words we are facing that much debated issue, is reinforcement a matter of learning or performance? (p. 365).

And then Seward says:

Our theory may be restated in the following nutshell: A reinforcer, in the case of positive cathexis, gains its potency through its ability, native or acquired, to arouse a consummatory response in the presence of the relevant need. In a learning situation this becomes conditioned to stimuli associated with the preceding instrumental act. When these stimuli recur they therefore arouse tertiary motivation, which in turn *facilitates the act in progress* (p. 372, italics added).

Particularly noteworthy in the foregoing is Seward's very explicit reference to the role which "stimuli associated with the preceding instrumental act" (so-called response-produced or response-dependent stimuli) presumably play in the development of a "habit." Indeed, his formulation differs from the present one only in one regard: instead of positing that it is "secondary reinforcement" that gets conditioned to such stimuli (in the process of habit formation), Seward refers to what he called "tertiary motivation." [6] What does this imply? In a footnote Seward gives this important part of the answer:

> Although the definition of tertiary motivation here proposed, as due to facilitation of a goal set, is confined to positive demands, a three-component theory of motivation is intended to apply to aversion as well. Thus pain may be considered a primary drive, fear a secondary drive, and anticipated fear reduction (or a fractional antedating escape reaction) a tertiary drive (p. 370).

Here, obviously, what we have called *hope* Seward is calling tertiary motivation and tertiary drive. But whereas our system requires us to think of hope ("anticipated fear reduction" in Seward's terms) as itself involving secondary-drive reduction, Seward sees a drive or motivation *increment* in the situation. This, obviously, is the heart of an important matter. We have already seen (Chapter 6) that subjectively there is considerable evidence for believing that at least at a particular stage of "hoping" there may indeed be an increment in motivation of the kind commonly termed appetite; but considerations previously advanced suggest that appetite is a special aspect of the more general problem of hope and that we obscure the larger truth if we focus on the drive-increment rather than the drive-decrement aspect of such situations.

There is, of course, the thoroughly objective observation that the appearance of a stimulus with secondary-reinforcing, or "tertiary-motivating," properties often results in augmented activity on the part of the subject. What better evidence, one might ask, of a correspond-

---

[6] It is possible that more is here being "read into" Seward's 1950 statements than is legitimate. It may be that by "stimuli associated with the preceding instrumental act" he means, not response-correlated or response-*produced* stimuli, but merely those stimuli which are *present*, more or less incidentally, when the response is (otherwise) instigated and occurs. If this is true, then Seward's position is, in at least this particular respect, more similiar to that of Hull (or perhaps Guthrie, see Section VIII) than to the present formulation. Seward nevertheless makes statements such as this: "When these stimuli recur they therefore arouse tertiary motivation, which in turn facilitates the act *in progress*" (p. 372; italics added), which can certainly be interpreted as referring to stimuli which are, in fact, *produced by* "the act in progress." If *this* is the intended meaning, then the parallelism is great (see also Chapter 9).

ing increase in "motivation"? But attention has already been called to the fact that motivation and motility are by no means perfectly correlated; and still further evidence on this score will be taken up early in the next section. In the meantime, a few further words will bring Seward's thinking in this area more fully up to date. In a paper published in 1956 this writer makes a number of assumptions which are completely congruent with the present analysis. He posits that "mediating or response-produced stimuli" may have conditioned to them either "instigators" or "satisfiers." The former are conditioned when response-produced stimuli are followed "by certain disturbers of homeostasis, whether external (e.g., pain and pain signals) or internal (e.g., metabolic deficit)," and the latter are conditioned when response-produced stimuli are followed "by removal of the disturbing stimulus or by replacement of the deficit" (1956b, p. 200). This language corresponds to our assumption that, as a result of being followed by either primary punishment or primary reward, response-correlated stimuli take on the capacity to arouse, respectively, fear or hope and that these emotional forecasters of things to come then guide the subject, more or less reliably, away from actions (or places) that are likely to be harmful and into actions (or places) that are likely to be helpful. For this process, commonly but not entirely appropriately termed "habit formation," Seward suggests the very apt term, *response selection.*

Only in one respect is the Seward position importantly different from our present one (or, perhaps more accurately, ours different from his)—and even here Seward admits to being "on the fence":

> My own attempts to solve this problem, starting five or ten years ago, reflect its stubbornness. In retrospect I find I have vacillated between the two viewpoints here brought face to face—between considering [secondary?] rewards as satisfiers and as incentives (p. 199).

Seward still seems to favor the latter possiblity; but he himself refers to his formulation as "only a fragment of theory," and perhaps as it becomes more explicit the dissimilarities will still further dissolve themselves. Certainly Seward has been an indefatigable investigator and an intrepid thinker in this area; and much of the movement in recent years toward unifications has undoubtedly been a reflection of his experimental ingenuity, logical astuteness, and complete candor and fair-mindedness.

This and the preceding sections can now be summarized as follows. As we have seen, there is today a decided tendency among major learning theorists to abandon the S—R bond conception of habit and to stress instead the notion of "incentive (tertiary) motivation." But we are now in a transitional period, with some writers holding that, because incentives "produce" activity, they must involve motivation increase; whereas others incline to the view that incentives (secondary reinforcers) achieve their effects upon behavior through a *decrease* in motivation (conceived as pure drive rather than an "urge to act"). Take the question of why human beings drink alcoholic beverages, i.e., why they engage in responses which lead to their becoming intoxicated (in whatever degree). The present analysis suggests that when an individual drinks he does so, not just because he is tense, anxious, depressed, but because when he *merely thinks* of drinking, his tensions drop somewhat—and come right back up again when he thinks of *not* drinking! It is, we hold, this *token* relief of tension that "drives" the individual to drink—and to do all the other things he "habitually" does.[7] It seems most unlikely that a person would "habitually" drink if each time he *thought* of it he got *more* tense. In fact, one well-known method of treating alcoholism consists of deliberately conditioning a specific drive (nausea) to the stimuli associated with alcohol consumption. The only way, apparently, that one can consistently hold to a drive-increment conception of the role of "incentives" is to assume that *some forms* of drive are inherently "pleasant," whereas most are admittedly not. This position involves *many* difficulties, not the least of which is that it provides no independent (and noncircular) criterion of what drives are and are not "pleasant." All things considered, a thoroughgoing homeostatic position seems most defensible here.[8]

Some readers may be troubled by the appearances of teleology in the foregoing discussion. From one point of view *our* assumptions *are* teleological, and frankly so. We assume that behavior *is* governed by its anticipated ends and consequences. But the underlying mechanism which mediates the process is thoroughly cause-and-effect. Our hypothesis says, quite simply, that the alcoholic *drinks* because he is "drunk." In other words, because the *anticipation* of drinking produces some of the effects of liquor itself, the alcoholic is powerfully propelled toward consummation of the act. The anticipatory satisfac-

[7] See Lillian Roth's, *I'll Cry Tomorrow* (1954), for a highly sensitive and illuminating account of the psychology of alcoholism, especially her discussion of what just the *thought* of having or not having alcohol available means to an alcoholic. See also Hull's (1931) paper on "Goal Attraction and Directing Ideas Conceived as Habit Phenomena."

[8] For a survey of empirical studies on "incentive motivation" which cannot be discussed here, see Mason (1956) and Dyal (1957).

tion is, of course, short-lived unless the individual actually *moves forward* in the sequence of actions which on past occasions has led to drinking. If, at any point in this sequence, the individual stops or turns about, then his anxiety and despair return in full force; and this is how it is that he is led forward (activated) by what is effectively a *reduction* rather than increase in motivation, He, like "habituated" organisms in general, is, properly speaking, driven by the tension and discomfort that lie "behind" and is, simultaneously, tempted by the "path of least resistance" which lies ahead. With, so to say, one's "back against the wall," there is only one direction in which one can move.

Thus are we able to resolve the dilemma posed by what Seward has called "tertiary motivation" or, alternatively, the "motivating [rather than relaxing] function of reward" (Seward, 1951). Reward brings hope into existence, and hope leads to action. This way of thinking will be developed further in the next section.

V. "Motivation" versus "Reinforcement": The Views of McClelland and Collaborators

In Chapter 6 some of the researches and theorizing of P. T. Young have already been alluded to, in some detail, and will be briefly considered again presently. In the meantime it will be instructive to review a systematic position, advanced by McClelland, Atkinson, Clark, & Lowell (1953), which has recently attracted much attention and interest. In many respects this system is remarkably similar to the one under discussion. Reference has already been made (Chapter 5, Section VIII) to the virtual identity between the "ecology of emotions" derived by these investigators and the one developed in preceding chapters. And McClelland *et al.* are likewise skeptical of the assumption that drive, in the sense of organic need or discomfort, can necessarily be inferred from an organism's level of overt activity. They say:

> The idea that motives are esesntially "tensional" in nature and energize organisms certainly has its difficulties which vary somewhat according to the way in which the tension is conceived. Hebb (1949) has objected vigorously and effectively to the notion of a motive as an *energizer*. . . . The same point has been made by Brown and Jacobs (1949), who state that one should abandon "the rather limited assumption that drives, when functioning as energizers, always lead to more vigorous overt or random action" (pp. 8-9).

And by way of making the point that a drop in drive may actually *release* rather than depress behavior, these same writers go on to quote from Hebb as follows:

"A behavioral excitation, an increase in some bodily activity, is not necessarily a sign of increased neural activity either in the brain as a whole or in some part of it. The point is well illustrated by the process of getting drunk. A small amount of alcohol may be an excitant—socially, and in its immediate net effect on behavior—but this, of course, does not prove that alcohol is a neural excitant" (p. 209).

In concluding their discussion of this issue, McClelland *et al.* say:

Thus the idea behind the stimulus intensity model, that strong afferent stimulation leads to strong, central neural activity which leads to strong response activity, appears to be much too simple. . . . We are not arguing that there is *no* connection between amount of activity and motive level but only that the relationship is complex and that therefore some other measure of motive strength may be preferable. It is perhaps because of such considerations that Miller (1951b), as well as Brown and Jacobs, argues for learning, rather than increased activity, as the chief criterion for inferring the existence of a drive (p. 21).

The relevance of all this is, first of all, that it calls into question the inference that because a secondary reinforcer or incentive stimulus *releases* activity it necessarily involves stimulation or drive increase (see preceding sections). If, as Hebb observes, alcohol (which is chemically related to ether and which likewise has *anesthetic* properties) can, in the process of *relaxing* the person, also heighten activity, there is nothing paradoxical about the assumption that an organism is most likely to go into action when it is *hopeful*, which is to say, under somewhat *less* drive or tension than when hopeless. The point is that an anticipation of more basic satisfaction which itself is somewhat satisfying may release, organize, or focus behavior and thus give the appearance of "increased drive" when, in fact, it is just the reverse phenomenon. The trouble, apparently, is that in both common speech and in more scientific discourse we do not always distinguish carefully between drive (as pure discomfort) and "drive" as activity, industry, organization, busy-ness. The key to the latter connotation is whether the individual has "received the word," i.e., gotten the *cue*, the "go-ahead," or is unfocused, aimless, hopeless.[9]

[9] Indicative of the generality of the revolt against primitive S—R psychology is the number of writers who are now disputing the assumption of a one-to-one relationship between drive and activity. The following excerpts are typical. "The problem of drive arises because on some occasions an animal will respond in a given situation while on other occasions it fails to respond" (Bolles, 1958, p. 22). "Brown's review makes it very clear that merely because a stimulus is physically intense is no assurance that it will raise the drive level. . . . This is probably the same point that Skinner (1938) is making when he says that drive is not a stimulus" (Malmo, 1958, p. 230). "It may be because I have been steeped in 'drive' psy-

McClelland *et al.* then make an inference which, if the present writer fully understands it, is most intriguing. They assume, in effect, that the so-called primary drives are *not motives*. "In our system," they say, "all motives are learned" (p. 28). And by this they mean, apparently, that a primary state of drive or tension leaves the organism essentially inert, until and unless certain "affective states" have become conditioned to independent or response-correlated stimuli. These stimuli then become capable of "affective arousal," which brings *motivation and activity* into being (cf. Skinner, 1958, p. 98).

Psychologists have for some time now followed the practice of speaking of *primary* and *secondary* motives and reinforcers as if they functioned in essentially the same ways, except that the latter are acquired and the former are innate. Perhaps the time has come to make a more radical distinction. If, as now seems likely, there is no necessary relationship between intensity of primary drive and overt activity, then it may indeed be desirable to speak of hopes, fears and other emotions as the true "motivators," in the sense of controlling, organizing, and directing behavior. But at the same time we know that the so-called primary-drive states are in some way important; and a moment's reflection reminds us that they serve as primary "reinforcers," on the basis of which our specific hopes and fears are themselves learned. Hence we may say that the biologically all-important events of primary-drive increments and decrements provide the basis for the acquisition of those behavior selectors which we called fears and hopes; but, strictly speaking, only these emotions (or affects) *motivate*, whereas primary-drive increments and decrements *reinforce*, i.e., mediate learning.

Only one complication arises here, in making this distinction between (secondary) motivators and (primary) reinforcers: Although we thus conceive the motivation function in such a way as to restrict it

---

chologies that I have begun to consider the drive concept as the current villain of this warfare among dynamic schools of thought. I hope you will not write me off as a reactionary if I answer my initial question, 'Are there drives?' in the negative" (Monroe, 1956, p. 25). "Although these experiments [by Campbell & Sheffield, 1953, and Sheffield & Campbell, 1954—see Chapter 6. p. 198] show that drives do not inevitably goad the animal into activity, they do not rule out the possibility that drives are strong stimuli. . . . It will be remembered that my definition of drives says nothing about activity, but rather deals with increasing the performance of responses *rewarded* by the offset of the drive or by the goal objects that produce satiation" (Miller, 1959a, p. 255). Here, in different words, Miller is making the same point as is stressed in the text above: that drives may have *reinforcing* functions without necessarily acting as "motives."

to the emotions and see the primary drives solely as reinforcers, the fact is that the emotions can also act as reinforcers, in the sense of providing the basis for *higher-order* conditioning. But aside from this, the distinction seems to stand. So the conclusion with which one would thus emerge would go like this: primary (biologically given) drives do not directly "motivate" behavior at all—their chief function is to provide the basis for the conditioning of hopes and fears to independent or response-dependent stimuli; whereas the hopes and fears thus acquired have a *double* function—they motivate (direct) behavior and *also* provide the basis for further (higher-order) conditioning.

Another way of putting this same general point of view is to say that the primary drives cannot "motivate" behavior in the sense of *directing* it because they, themselves, are not capable of being conditioned to either independent or response-dependent stimuli. In other words, moving toward or away from a given object or performing or inhibiting a particular act can alter the hope or fear that an organism feels; but such behavior will *not*, of itself, cause hunger, thirst, or any other primary drive to vary in a similar way. This is why it was previously remarked that the primary drives are essentially "inert," nondirective, nonmotivating. They serve only *reinforcing* functions, as explained above. This way of thinking, obviously, can emerge only when one has abandoned the S—R connection notion of habit and embraced the feedback idea. As long as one is thinking in terms of S—R bonds, then *any* stimulus, *any* drive can be said to "motivate," or *cause*, a particular response.[10] But when one adopts the view that we behave as we do because we are constantly trying to get from "regions" of emotional tension to "regions" of emotional comfort, then we see that the primary drives are not, directly and immediately, "motivating" but *are* responsible for the original *development* of our hopes and fears, in terms of the principles of learning, or reinforcement, already delineated.

[10] Here another comment by Miller (1959a) is apposite: "Stimulus-response psychologists have concentrated on determining the laws governing the connections of response to stimuli. Thus, stimulus-response psychologists may be said to know and care relatively little about either stimuli or responses; they are specialists at the hyphen between the capital S and capital R and could more aptly be called 'hyphen psychologists,' or to use Thorndike's term, 'connectionists.' While admitting our ignorance, I trust it is not necessary to point out that we have made considerable progress on this basis. Unfortunately it is also true that other theorists are not far ahead of us in solving these particular problems" (p. 242; see also Lashley, 1950).

That this conclusion is congruent with the views of McClelland and collaborators is indicated by the following quotation:

We have decided to base motives on affective arousal, following Young's lead (1949b), for several reasons. In the first place, it seems apparent that the motive concept will be useful only if it has some kind of limited base. That is, if all associations are motivating, then there seems no particular reason to introduce the concept of motivation to apply to a particular subclass of associations. And we have chosen affective states as the basis for motives rather than biological needs or strong stimuli because of the limitations of those concepts already discussed. A more positive reason for choosing affective states as primary is that they are "obviously" important in controlling behavior, at least at the common-sense level. The hedonic or pleasure-pain view of motivation is certainly one of the oldest in psychological thinking and can be traced at least to Plato's *Protagoras*. Furthermore, in order to get motives in the laboratory we commonly pair cues with affective states resulting from shock, saccharine in the mouth, food deprivation, and the like. Operationally we manipulate states which we know subjectively will produce pleasure and pain when we work with motives (p. 30).

VI. Hedonism or Homeostasis?
The Views of Young and McClelland Compared

The paper last cited by Seward in Section IV of this chapter begins by pointing out that the Law of Effect as originally formulated by Thorndike was at one and the same time both hedonistic *and* homeostatic. Initially Thorndike spoke of "satisfiers" (rewards) and "annoyers" (punishments), thus implying both the pleasure-pain relationship and the dimension of drive reduction and drive induction. But Thorndike, under pressure of the times to be more behavioristic (and less subjective), abandoned his former terminology; and the Law of Effect has since been thought of mainly in the context of biological (physiological) gain and loss, i.e., in terms of the homeostatic model, which implies that pleasure (if this term be used) is correlated with drive reduction—and pain, with drive induction.

However, Young (in keeping with an older precedent) has insisted upon a purely "hedonic" element in the picture, i.e., the tendency for some stimuli to be *inherently* pleasant or unpleasant, agreeable or disagreeable, without reference to any necessary correlation with drive reduction or induction. And here he cites particularly the case of *tastes* and *odors*. They too, he insists (and with some reason), are capable of producing "affective arousal" and of controlling behavior. But how, precisely, can this occur?

Perhaps the most promising answer is one that derives from considerations already suggested in Chapter 6. Living organisms are apparently constructed so that some foods will *taste* good (or bad) because it is *such a long way* (both physically and temporally) between ingestion and digestion. The ultimate benefit (or harm) can come only from digestion; but in order to bridge this gap, little "sentinels" are put in the mouth and nose which predict, with fair reliability but by no means perfectly, what will be good for us and what will not be. Later (in Chapter 10) we shall see how useful *learned* affects (of fear or hope) can be in bridging the gap between instrumentally appropriate behavior and *delayed* primary reward or punishment. Now in connection with tastes and odors (and certain other forms of sensory stimulation), it seems that there are innately given, built-in provisions for "affective arousal" which function in a similar way (as "warnings" or "approvals") whenever learning would be too slow and hazardous. As indicated, such "instinctive" provisions are by no means perfect: some substances (e.g., saccharine) may taste good and be biologically useless or even poisonous, whereas other substances may taste bad but be very good for us, as in the case, for example, of certain medicines. However, the correlation is, in general, a valid one between how things taste and smell and how they affect us physiologically. And it also appears that just as drive reduction and induction provide one basis for "affective arousal" and conditioning, so also may what Young calls *palatability* provide another such basis. In other words, the mere experience of something tasting good (without reducing a drive) can apparently provide the basis for the conditioning of secondary reinforcement (or hope); and the mere experience of something tasting bad can similarly provide the basis for the conditioning of secondary motivation (or fear, aversion, disgust), without any increase in the primary hunger drive.

Thus, rather than seeing any necessary opposition between hedonism and homeostasis, we see that *both* mechanisms are real and important, but with hedonism, in the final analysis, being the handmaiden of homeostasis. The present writer's assumption is that in the broad evolutionary scheme of things, pleasure is important, i.e., has survival value, *only if* it is correlated with homeostatic adjustment. Somewhat inexplicably, McClelland and Young take the reverse position that drive decrement and increment are but "special cases of a more general theory" (McClelland *et al.*, p. 53).

Perhaps sexuality will provide an instructive example here. Certainly it seems to offer the best case for hedonism, for sexual gratification is in no way physiologically necessary, i.e., an individual can apparently *live* just as long (perhaps even longer) without sexual gratification as with it. Thus, the homeostatic model seems to break down completely; but, taking a larger view, we see homeostasis still at work. In the domain of sexuality it is the survival of the *race*, rather than of the individual, which is at stake; and because the *delay* between relevant behavior and the biological result is here not a matter of seconds or minutes (as in the case of food ingestion and assimilation) but of *weeks* or *months*, no simple "homeostatic" mechanism would work and so must be supplemented by a hedonic one. But the *ultimate* consideration, it seems, is still biological, homeostatic, survivalistic.[11]

At the one extreme, electric shock and the learning associated therewith provides an example of pure homeostasis. Here drive induction and pain and drive reduction and pleasure are perfectly correlated. And at the opposite extreme is sexuality, where the hedonic principle is striking and homeostasis discernible only as a background factor. But there is no basic incompatibility. Where it is feasible for action-related stimuli to acquire "affective" value on the basis of primary reinforcement (type-I or type-D), this occurs; but where there is biological hazard in such an arrangement, learning seems to occur also on the basis of a hedonic mechanism of the kind described. We are still far from knowing how to talk about these matters with satisfactory precision; but even the present state of uncertainty here is an advance over former certainty born of gross over-simplification of the kind involved in primitive stimulus-response psychology and in classical hedonism.

VII. "Sensory Integration" as Conceived by Woodworth and by Birch & Bitterman

A distinction is commonly drawn between three forms of learning theory: (a) S—R reinforcement, (b) S—S contiguity, and (c) S—R

---

[11] Useful as such a mechanism is in some situations, it can also operate in a distinctly maladaptive way. At the present time, with the world population of human beings fairly "exploding," we see this mechanism operating *in reverse*, as far as biological survival is concerned. Because of the powerful immediate pleasure connected with the sexual act, it has a tendency to out-compete the very legitimate, and urgent, concern with eventual world-wide want and—literally—starvation, because of the constant increase in numbers and, alas, equally constant decrease in natural resources. We know that other species have, in the past, multiplied themselves right out of business; and there is no reason—except reason (see Mowrer, 1960, Chapter 5)—why it should not happen to us (cf. Huxley, 1958).

contiguity (Spence, 1951a; Seward, 1956a). There is, evidently, a growing conviction in the field that none of these conceptualizations, alone, is entirely adequate and that in order to match reality something of a *composite* theory is needed. This is what we are presently attempting to develop.

A major division of opinion among learning theorists is the one concerned with the conception of the nature of the hypothetical learning changes. Thus one group of theorists, the associationists (Thorndike, 1935; Hull, 1943; Guthrie, 1935) has employed the notion of a functional connection of some kind of linkage becoming gradually established or strengthened with successive practice occasions. Within this point of view one may find different preferences with respect to whether physiological concepts (for example, receptor-effector connections in the nervous system) or nonphysiological ones (for example, associations, bonds, habits) are employed (Spence, 1951a, p. 241).

Already much attention has been given to the reasons for doubting the adequacy of S—R reinforcement theory, i.e., the notion that learning is a question of strengthening or weakening stimulus-response bonds by means of reward or punishment. The situation is obviously more complicated; and as we recognize this greater complexity, we come into proximity with what has been commonly termed S—S contiguity theory, which Spence (1951a) has characterized thus:

The cognition theorists, on the other hand, appear to be much more thoroughly committed [than the S—R associationists] to the view that learning involves establishing relations (organizations) between sensory or perceptual processes. Certainly all of them have taken a definite and explicit stand on the matter. Thus the Gestaltists, and such other psychologists in this group as Lashley, Adams, Zener, Lewin, and Tolman, conceive of learning in terms of the formation of cognitive patterns in which are organized the successive perceptual processes occurring in a behavior sequence (p. 243).

What, more precisely, does the S—S contiguity theory imply and how does it articulate with or differ from present theory? Fortunately, in 1947, R. S. Woodworth published a paper which not only delineates the S—S contiguity position but also brings it into relationship with the concept of reinforcement. It was entitled, "Reinforcement and Perception," and begins with the observation that there is "no obvious incompatibility of [these] two factors, and the thesis of this paper is that both of them are essential in any process of learning" (p. 119).

It should be said that reinforcement in the S—R bond sense does not imply or logically demand any subjective concomitant whatever. But reinforcement, as Pavlov used the term, does lead to such a relationship. This does not occur, of course, as long as one speaks of the (classical) conditioning of overt items of behavior, i.e., of behavior in terms of "conditioned reflexes." But with the shift of emphasis from overt behavior to *emotions*, which has been previously traced in this volume, the basis for a liaison emerges very naturally. To say, for example, that an organism is *afraid* or *hopeful* almost axiomatically implies a state of consciousness and *perception of* objects and relationships. And the learning thus implied manifestly has to do with expectancies rather than with the execution of particular acts or movements. Says Woodworth, in similar vein:

> What I am struggling to say, all empathy aside, is that there is something present in the organism from the first trial on that is capable of reinforcement, and that this something *belongs to the receptive and not to the efferent part of the organism's total behavior.* "Registration" fits the facts better than "perception," for the human subject, at least, must perceive the sequence of events very quickly, while it may take many trials for the sequence to strike home enough to produce the appropriate motor or glandular response.
>
> As to connections, several may be established before the conditioning is complete, but the primary one connects *the conditioning stimulus with the meaningful character it acquires* as the first event in a regular sequence (pp. 121–122; italics added).

Here, clearly, is a quite explicit anticipation of present thinking. Woodworth, with the present analysis, is implying a two-step rather than a simple S—R paradigm for learning and is moreover suggesting that "learning" occurs in the *first* of these two steps rather than in the second and that it consists basically of conditioning conceived as the development of certain perceptions, expectations, anticipations, meanings, emotions—these terms all being more or less equivalent (cf. Mowrer, 1960).

For Woodworth, habit formation or response selection becomes a derivative of the more basic (sole?) form of learning just described. He says: "In experiments that offer alternatives and demand a choice, what has to be learned is a distinction between stimulus-objects and not between motor responses" (p. 122). Woodworth does not indicate what a "perception" *is,* dynamically, or precisely *how* it can eventuate in one action rather than another. But the important thing is that he makes conditioning the primary (only?) form of learning and derives response selection therefrom.

A somewhat similar approach was independently developed in a paper published in 1949 by Birch & Bitterman under the title, "Reinforcement and Learning: The Process of Sensory Integration." The upshot of this study is that there are *two* forms of learning, conditioning and trial-and-error, which are at least superficially different but that, in the final analysis, conditioning, conceived as "sensory integration," is the more basic. And they cited Maier & Schneirla (1942) for the statement "that association by contiguity is more primitive than selective learning" (p. 304). Birch & Bitterman further anticipate the present analysis by noting that:

> Many of these changes in behavior apparently require the direct reorganization of afferent-efferent relationships. Since there is no reason to believe that proprioceptive stimuli cannot participate in the integration process, we may assume that the specific proprioceptive consequences of the correct response may also come to acquire food properties (Grice, 1948b) (p. 306).

What these writers are here saying, if we understand them correctly, is that so-called habit formation or response selection may be derived from the fact that response-correlated stimuli, if followed by primary reinforcement, take on the capacity to provide secondary reinforcement, which will subsequently cause this response to be selected, in preference to others, and not because an S—R bond has been strengthened but because the feedback from the R is "positive" and facilitative. Inhibition or response rejection (as opposed to selection) can be comparably explained. They say: "Evidently one can account for avoidance if one assumes that stimuli contiguously related to the *onset* of shock acquire the functional properties of shock" (p. 297).

Up to this point the parallelism with the present analysis is very striking. However, something of a divergence develops as Birch & Bitterman go on to suggest that "sensory integration" can occur on the basis of sheer contiguity of stimuli, without the second of these having reinforcing properties in the sense of implying either drive decrement or increment. They say: "The results of the sensory preconditioning experiments require us to postulate a process of afferent modification (sensory integration), the essential condition for which is contiguity of stimulation, and which takes place independently of need reduction [or induction, presumably]" (p. 302).

As long as learning is assumed to involve an S_2—S_1—r sequence, the question of the conditions necessary for reinforcement has an operational basis: in order for learning to result from the pairing of the two stimuli, S_2 and S_1, S_1 must be capable from the beginning of producing r. And since the r's which, in the present frame of reference, are most easily and most commonly conditionable are those of fear and hope and since these are, respectively, the correlates of primary drive onset and primary drive reduction, it is obvious that the latter events are ultimately necessary for learning to occur. On the other hand, Birch & Bitterman seem willing to think of learning as also occurring in situations where there *is* no r and where, therefore, the sheer coincidence of stimuli suffices to produce new "sensory integrations."

To the present writer it is not at all clear what a "sensory integration" is apart from a response of *some sort*. The response certainly need not be one involving overt, voluntary behavior; in fact, the whole force of our argument up to this point has been to show the error of conceiving of such behavior either as the result of S—R bonds or of simple, direct conditioning. More commonly, the R or r which is learned as a result of stimulus pairing is in the nature of an *emotion*. And it is even probable that in "purely cognitive" learning there is a "response" of some sort within the central nervous system.

The pertinence of this assumption can be illustrated by reference to the phenomenon of "sensory conditioning" or what is sometimes also known as "preconditioning." Since this phenomenon is cited by Birch & Bitterman as crucially supporting their S—S contiguity theory and since it is not elsewhere discussed in this book, it should be given some notice here. Osgood (1953) presents the problem well, in these words:

> Brogden (1939) reported that he had obtained evidence for "sensory conditioning" in dogs. A bell and a light were presented simultaneously two hundred times. When one of these stimuli was later made the CS for conditioned forelimb flexion, with shock serving as US, tests with the other stimulus, which had never been paired with shock, showed that it, too, had become capable of eliciting the new response. Certain controls were applied: pretests with both stimuli showed that they did not initially elicit this reaction; animals treated identically, except for the original *pairing* of tone and light, gave no evidence of transfer. This was a highly significant experiment because it bore directly upon this fundamental issue of psychology: *Is the modification that takes place in learning a central, cognitive event (S—S) or must some behavior (S—R) be involved?* The results of this experiment made it appear that the simple contiguity in experience of purely sensory events was sufficient for learning (p. 461).

Osgood goes on to review a number of subsequent studies, some of which confirm the Brogden findings and some of which do not. But the evidence is predominantly positive—and substantial enough to be taken seriously. As has already been intimated (Chapter 7, Section IX), a comprehensive conception of the psychology of learning seems to require that conditioning be thought of as applicable, not only to affective processes (emotions), but also to so-called cognitive responses, in the sense of *images*. This hypothesis again shows its cogency here.

In order to clarify the discussion, let us suppose that in the "preconditioning" phase of the Brogden experiment, the bell and light, instead of being presented simultaneously, are given in the order, bell-light. Later, then, the light is paired with shock (which produces fear and leg flexion); and when the bell is then presented, it too produces fear and leg flexion. On the basis of evidence that will be reviewed elsewhere (Mowrer, 1960, Chapter 5), we may confidently assume that the light used in this experiment produces a light *sensation* (a "reaction" in the dog's head) which is conditionable in the form of a light *image*. Such a reaction, to be sure, is central or "cognitive," rather than overt, behavioral; but emotions also are covert, nonbehavioral, yet we have not refused (at least not in recent decades) to admit them to our theoretical system. And if we grant that sensations *are* conditionable in the form of images, then the mystery of sensory conditioning is solved: The bell, after pairing with the light, arouses an *image* of the light; and after light itself has become capable of arousing fear and leg flexion, we would expect the latter reactions to generalize (Chapter 12) from light itself (sensation) to the conditioned image thereof, as elicited by the bell. In other words, if, after the conditioning of fear and flexion to light, the bell merely "reminds" the subject of light, this alone may suffice to produce (or mediate—see Mowrer, 1960, Chapter 2) the defense reactions.

The principal difficulty about postulating this type of "purely sensory" conditioning is that it is not at all clear when such conditioning occurs and when it does not. Not *every* stimulus that precedes another serves to remind us of it, even though the association has perhaps occurred many, many times.[12] Something valuely known as "attention" is undoubtedly in some way relevant here, but as yet we have no operational definition thereof (but see Mowrer, 1960, Chapter 5) and cannot, therefore, employ it systematically.

Hence, in the present writer's judgment, it is misleading and unrealistic to talk about "S—S contiguity" learning. What we have instead, it seems, is always S—S—R or, more exactly, S—S—r learning; and for this the term "conditioning" seems generally adequate and preferable to such expressions as "perceptual reorganization," "sensory integration," "afferent modification," and the like; although, in many other respects, the kind of thinking developed both by Woodworth and by Birch & Bitterman is entirely congruent with our own and

---

[12] This is perhaps why the phenomenon of sensory conditioning, or preconditioning, is erratic: sometimes you get it and sometimes you don't, depending upon variables which we have not yet clearly identified and are not yet well able to control. For a recent literature review, see Seidel (1959).

importantly supplements and supports it (see also Birch & Bitterman, 1951).

VIII. S—R Contiguity Theory

The group of theories which are to be discussed in this section have always been hard for the present writer to "understand." Perhaps it is the fact that they are, as one may say, "antitheoretical" theories that creates this difficulty. Skinner has been very frank to declare his aversion to formal theorizing; Guthrie has said that his views "really do not constitute a system or complete theory, just a prejudice in the direction to be taken" (personal communication—cf. Hilgard, 1956, pp. 78–80); and Estes is concerned with essentially statistical rather than psychological variables. Nevertheless, the writings of these three men have attracted interest, inspired research, and stimulated others very much as one might expect *bona fide* theories to do. We shall therefore have to give them careful attention, hopefully with the view to finding ways in which they articulate with present thinking.

Let us begin with the following summary by Spence of Guthrie's position:

> The main principle governing the development of association between stimulus and response movements is *association by contiguity*. This principle states, "*A stimulus pattern that is acting at the time of a response will, if it recurs, tend to produce that response*" (Guthrie, 1942, p. 23). The essential and sufficient condition for learning, according to this principle, is simultaneity of stimulus pattern and responses. Motivation, in the form of a drive state, such as hunger, and the US serve merely to assure that the response to be conditioned will occur. Their function is that of a "forcer" of the response rather than that of a "reinforcer" of a connection (Spence, 1951b, p. 703).

In Guthrie's own hands and in those of some of his students this formulation (together with some supplementary assumptions) can be made to give the appearance of accounting for a wide range of behavioral phenomena. But it is hardly a theory of learning in any very conventional sense of that term. Ordinarily one thinks of behavioral *change* as the hallmark of this process, whereas Guthrie's principle is really more logically related to the prediction of behavioral *constancy* or *continuity*. This can be illustrated by the kind of experimental evidence which Voeks (1948) has adduced in support of Guthrie's position. A corollary of the principle already quoted is that the response *last made* to a given situation or stimulus pattern will be the response most probably made when that situation or stimulus pattern recurs. And Voeks analyzes data reported by Peterson, Yoshioka, and herself to show that what she calls the "principle of postremity" (lastness of response) is highly prognostic. She says, for example:

> Of those occasions when the postreme response had been the "right" response, 73.0 per cent of the time it was made on the next trial. Of those occasions when the postreme response had been the "wrong" response, only 63.9 per cent of the time was it made on the next trial. Therefore, it appears that if postremity tends more toward preserving one set of responses rather than another, it tends more toward preserving the correct response rather than the incorrect. . . . Thus it is found that contrary to Peterson's conclusions, his data indicate that postremity may be a significantly accurate basis for prediction and is not negative in its effect (p. 497).

But the question is, What does one *wish* to predict? It is probably true that the statistically safest prediction that one can make about behavior is that "next time" it will be the same as it was last time. If, in other words, a given response tendency *exists*, the chances are it will *persist*.[13] But while this premise may have a 64%–85% accuracy (Voeks, 1948), it is still 100% *useless* as far as giving us any way of predicting or producing change.[14] In reply to criticisms of his theory advanced by O'Connor (1946), Guthrie (1946a) has himself said:

> I am interested in the laws of movements as determined by stimuli. The effect psychologists are interested in the end results of action. . . . I am interested in the prediction of such particular movement series (p. 289).

From this one might infer that Guthrie's theory is useful only for predicting behavior constancy, not change. But this writer goes on to say: "My own interest has been in the question: under what circumstances do responses to stimuli change and what constitutes such change." The postremity principle, at least as interpreted by Voeks, would seem to require simply that living organisms always do what they did "last time," thus precluding the possibility of change except as the environment itself may change. Yet there is a sense in which

---

[13] In weather forecasting, it is well known that a prediction of "more of the same" will be correct well over 50% of the time.

[14] Hilgard (1956) has voiced the same objection: "The postremity principle cannot predict when the first CR appears, because its appearance *always* violates the principle (at least, so far as the *recorded* responses are concerned)" (p. 74). And Miller (1958a) has similiarly said: "I have been unable to see . . . why it [Guthrie's theory] should not predict that a thoroughly learned response to a momentary stimulus will never extinguish. . . . There is also the problem of why the stimulus-change produced by the *onset* of a painful stimulus does not protect preceding responses from retroactive inhibition" (p 261).

Guthrie's thinking seems to provide for genuine learning, i.e., of at least a limited kind. In the passage already quoted from Spence, it is pointed out or at least implied that if a particular stimulus occurs and "forces" a particular response, *other* stimuli will have a tendency to produce the response.[15] But this is nothing but the "redintegrative" theory of *conditioning* which Hollingworth (1928a, 1928b; see also Thorndike 1913, 1932) has advanced long since.[16] Therefore, at this point Guthrie's theory ceases to be an S—R contiguity theory and becomes simply an instance of S—S—R contiguity, or conditioning. It is, moreover, a particularly primitive, unelaborated version thereof, subject to all the objections and difficulties so extensively explored in earlier chapters.

Yet on more than one occasion other psychologists have reported seeing a similarity between Guthrie's position and the one delineated in this book. Perhaps the key to this impression is the emphasis in both upon response-produced stimuli. Hilgard (1956) gives a good summary of Guthrie's position in this connection as follows:

One of the standard experiments in the literature of conditioning is that showing the importance of the time interval between the conditioned stimulus and unconditioned response. The empirical results suggest a gradient, with a most favorable interval and less favorable intervals on either side of this optimal interval [see Chapter 10].

Guthrie is able to hold out for strict simultaneity of cue and response in the face of these data by proposing that the true cue being conditioned is not the stimulus as measured. An external stimulus may give rise to movements of the organism. These movements in turn produce stimuli. When associations appear to be made between stimuli and responses separated in time, it is because these intervening movements fill in the gap. The true association is between simultaneous events.

There is a strong preference for *movement-produced stimuli* as the true conditioners in Guthrie's system. They permit the integration of habits within a wide range of environmental change in stimulation, because these stimuli are carried around by the organism. It appears that some of this preference dates from the early emphasis of Watson (1907) on kinesthesis as the basis of control of the maze habit, a position no longer tenable. Such covert movement-produced stimuli provide ever-present explanations for conduct which cannot be inferred from external stimulus-response relationships (p. 54).

Despite Hilgard's observation that it is "movement-produced stimuli" which are the "true conditioners in Guthrie's system," the

[15] "The stimuli present as the response occurs are the future cues for the response" (Voeks, 1950).

[16] In the revised edition of his book Guthrie (1952) himself uses the term "redintegrates" and hails Pierre Janet as its principal early exponent.

fact is that the resulting similarity to our own position remains very faint.[17] When Hilgard speaks of intervening movements "which fill in the gap," it is clear that the mechanism here posited is the old, familiar, and relatively barren one of *reflex chaining*. This is a notion which was popular in the heyday of Behaviorism but which finds few contemporary advocates (cf. Keller & Schoenfeld, 1950). The present theory stresses movement-produced stimuli for quite a different purpose.[18]

Reverting now to Guthrie's suggestion that a response is "conditioned" to the total situation or stimulus "population" present at the time of its occurrence, we find that two interesting implications flow from this. One is that it leads directly to Estes' "statistical" theory of learning, which will be considered shortly. The other is more closely concerned with present theory. In Chapter 7 evidence is cited for believing that if a previously rewarded response, when it recurs, produces all or most of the stimuli which it has previously produced when the response has been followed by reward, that response, owing to the secondary-reinforcing or incentive power of these stimuli, will have maximal "habit strength" and that habit strength will be progressively less as the number of response-produced stimuli is reduced. Thus, in both Guthrie's system and in ours, the likelihood of a previously reinforced response's occurring is a function of the "similarity" of the "situation" in which the response was reinforced and the now prevailing situation. *But* there is a silent difference: For Guthrie the "situation" that is important is made up of that pattern or population of stimuli which is said to initiate or "cause" the response, whereas in revised two-factor theory the "situation" that counts is that pattern or population of stimuli which is the *consequence of* the response *as it occurs* (or is symbolically "contemplated"; see Mowrer, 1960, Chapter 6). Whether a response will or will not occur thus depends, not especially upon the similarity between present and past objective situations, but rather upon whether it produces response-related stimuli which have "cathexis" relevant to the organism's current *needs*. Thus, "habit strength" is made to depend crucially upon the feedback from a re-

[17] Professor Guthrie has himself stated: "The differences between our positions are very profound" (personal communication).

[18] Guthrie's special interest in movement-cued behavior chaining arises for the reason that delayed reinforcement constitutes a very difficult problem in his system. Holding that it is always the *last* response made to a given situation that is "learned," it is hard to explain how a reward (or punishment) can, so to say, act at a distance (see O'Connor, 1946; Guthrie. 1946a). The way the delay of reinforcement is handled in the present system is described in Chapter 10.

sponse, rather than upon familiarity or similarity of the initial situation. Hilgard quotes Guthrie thus:

"Drinking or smoking after years of practice are action systems which can be started by thousands of reminders. . . . I had once a caller to whom I was explaining that the apple I had just finished was a splendid device for avoiding a smoke. The caller pointed out that I was at that moment smoking. The habit of lighting a cigarette was so attached to the finish of eating that smoking had started automatically" (p. 56).

Does this incident represent the adaptive capacity of living organisms at its *best*, or quite otherwise? The reality and high psychological relevance of *cues* will be given special consideration later in this volume (Chapter 12); but the hypothesis which is currently regnant is that it is the *expectations* which response-produced stimuli arouse, rather than stimuli that have previously *produced the response*, that are most highly relevant here. As Rogers (1956) has observed in a recent review of George Kelly's (1956) book on clinical psychology, for living organisms the *future* is more important than the *past:* ". . . a theoretical system which looks forward, not backward—which sees behavior as anticipatory, not reactive" (p. 357).

IX. The Views of Estes and Skinner

Estes' (1950) *statistical theory* of learning is a direct and natural outgrowth of Guthrie's formulations. In fact, Estes regards his hypotheses as essentially mathematical equivalents of "Guthrie's (1946b) verbal analyses" (p. 107). With Guthrie, Estes assumes that "on each occurrence of a response, R_1, all new elements (i.e., elements not already conditioned to R_1) in the momentarily effective sample of elements, s, become conditioned to R_1" (p. 97). And the likelihood of R_1's being subsequently elicited is determined by the extent to which a later situation contains the same or different stimulus elements (cf. Chapter 7, p. 234). The way in which Estes converts this hypothesis into mathematical terms is ingenious; and his attempt thus "to overcome some of the rigidity and oversimplification of traditional stimulus-response theory without abandoning its principal advantages" (p. 106) is very much worth while. The question is: Can even the most elegant of mathematical transformations redeem stimulus-response theory from its basic *disadvantages?* Following Guthrie (and Skinner), the particular brand of stimulus-response theory which Estes accepts as the logical basis for his equations is behaviorism in its most extreme and dubious form. For this writer, the independent variable (cause) is the "environment" of the organism and the dependent variable (effect) is the organism's "behavior." And the "connection" is direct and uncomplicated by intervening variables. Thus, S—R is the basic paradigm, without so much as an allusion to the more intricate S—r: s—R formula which previous chapters have shown to be minimally essential.[19] Prototypical of the inherent weakness of such an approach is the dilemma suggested by the following quotation:

> In the familiar buzz-shock conditioning experiment, for example, S_c would represent the population of stimulus elements emanating from the sound source and R would include all movements of a limb meeting certain specifications of direction and amplitude; typically, the R to be conditioned is a flexion response which may be evoked on each training trial by administration of an electric shock (Estes, 1950, p. 98).

Here it is assumed that the "R to be conditioned" is the same as that produced "on each training trial" by the unconditioned stimulus, or shock. But we know (Chapters 2 and 3) that the "conditioned" response is often *radically different* from the unconditioned response; and the only satisfactory way of accounting for this fact involves the postulation of *fear* as an intervening variable. Although it is a good thing to have psychologists (like Hull and Estes) who have the ability and the motivation to translate "purely verbal" hypotheses into mathematical form, the resulting derivations and inferences will be no better than the assumptions that have gone into them. The writer is not aware of any instance where the formalization of a theory of learning in mathematical terms has importantly advanced our understanding and knowledge (see Chapter 7, Section III). More commonly, such formalizations have merely produced a deceptive appearance of a finality which has fixated thought at an immature stage of development. The writer recalls having once heard Clark Hull recount a conversation with Max Wiertheimer, in the course of which the latter had maintained, to Hull's evident consternation, that the formalization of psychological theory was then (in the 1930's) "premature." The fact is that all Hull's equations did not keep his theoretical system from being inadequate, nor did the absence thereof prevent Tolman's speculations from containing a more generous segment of truth (see Chapter 9).

A few years ago Spence wrote that, in his opinion, "as Tolman's theory is developed, the essential similarity of its formal structure to that of Hull's theory will become more and more apparent" (Spence, 1951b, p. 706). Since it remained for two admitted "fifth columnists" (MacCorquodale & Meehl,

---

[19] For some recent examples of the theory in action, see Brody (1957), Estes, Burke, Atkinson, & Frankman (1957), and Anderson & Grant (1957).

1953, p. 63) to "formalize" Tolman's theory, such an outcome would not be too surprising. More surprising, it appears that Spence would have predicted better if he had interchanged Tolman with Hull in the above quotation (Seward, 1956b, p. 111).

With this admission of skepticism about the utility (to date) of mathematical formalizations of learning theory, we turn to an even profounder form of doubt, namely B. F. Skinner's (1950) questioning of the fruitfulness of theory itself. This, as one might guess, is a qualified kind of skepticism, it being admitted that "it would be foolhardy to deny the achievements of theories . . . in the history of science" (p. 194). Skinner's objections, such as they are, can be said to be these: (a) "Much useless experimentation results from theories, and much energy and skill are absorbed by them" (p. 194). When Hull's theories are criticized, they are sometimes obliquely defended by the rejoinder: "But look at all the *research* they have stimulated!" The question is whether this research has any *value*, other than as its confirms or refutes the theory. Suppose, as now seems probable, that the net effect of the research which Hull inspired is to show the basic unsoundness of his system. Does this mean that both the theorizing and the research were a waste of "energy and skill?" Skinner is inclined to think so. And (b) "It might be argued that the principal function of learning theory to date has been, not to suggest appropriate research, but to create a false sense of security, an unwarranted satisfaction with the *status quo*" (p. 194)—and, one might add, a tendency among those who have found their sense of security in *different* theories to dispute rather than experiment. Certainly Skinner's own professional career, in terms of its productivity and its scientific and practical impact, has been such as to command respectful consideration of the alternative which he proposes and exemplifies.

His programmatic "platform" is relatively simple. We need to do many more experiments, make many more observations of a purely empirical kind, obtain more "data showing orderly changes characteristic of the learning process" (p. 215). Theories are, admittedly, "fun," but, says Skinner, we are not "ready" for them. And we are especially far removed from the time when we can fruitfully cast our theory into mathematical form:

> At the moment we make little effective use of empirical, let alone rational, equations. A few of the present curves could have been fairly closely fitted. But the most elementary preliminary research shows that there are many relevant variables, and until their importance has been experimentally determined, any equation that allows for them will have so many arbitrary constants that a good fit will be a matter of course and a cause for very little satisfaction (p. 216).

Skinner even distrusts so rudimentary a statistical device as the use of averages: Let us, for the moment, stick to the detailed observation of individual subjects, he says. And, above all, let us avoid that selectivity of observation and attention that permits us to "prove" diametrically opposite assumptions, depending on our vantage point.

Why, then, should Skinner be discussed in the context of the highly mathematical work of Estes and the highly speculative (if not "theoretical") formulations of Guthrie? Like the two investigators just cited, Skinner is, in the first place, a radical Behaviorist, a thoroughgoing empiricist, and essentially an operationist. It would hardly be fair, in view of his explicit repudiation of theory, to call him an S—R contiguity theorist; but he is at least one "by association," in terms of those who have been attracted or influenced by his work. Nor would we have him be other than what he is. In terms of behavior-control techniques, methods of qualification, and ingenious "schedules of reinforcement" (Skinner, 1953b; Ferster & Skinner, 1958), Skinner has shown himself extraordinarily resourceful and creative. Would that there were more of his ilk. But this is not to say that his "dust-bowl empiricism" brand of science is alone sufficient. As the very title of this book implies, the present writer believes, with others, that some sort of *balance* between theory and observation is desirable; and it is not surprising that Skinnerians feel that they have to take an *extreme* position if they are to counteract the dead weight of the all-too-numerous "pure thinkers."

The present writer regrets that he is not able to make a more extended comparison of Skinner's "system" with the one under review in this book. This limitation comes in part from the somewhat enigmatic nature of Skinner's work, which Verplanck (1954) has succinctly summarized thus:

[Here] we are concerned with a theorist who now espouses no theory, a systematist whose system is still developing, and a constructive thinker some of whose most important contributions have been those of a critic (p. 268).

In his review of current research and theory in the field of learning, Kendler (1959) has been particularly thorough in covering and appraising the work of Skinner and his followers (he also gives a great deal of space to Estes' "statistical learning theory"); and here we read:

Skinner is an enigma. His attitudes, and those of many of his partisans toward facts, theories, statistics, and science itself are incongruous. But in spite of this his work, as well as that of his rapidly growing legions of adherents, is fascinating and creative, and has much of permanent value (p. 59) [cf. Mowrer, 1960, Chapters 8 and 9].

This "option-play" (or "playing-by-ear") type of research generates a mass of data that is most difficult to analyze systematically. Each experimental article contains many more variables than subjects. The knowledge obtained, as well as the interpretation offered, is that some variables, in conjunction with other variables, result in changes in behavior (p. 61).

Where does the Skinnerian formulation go from here? At present the Skinnerians have been able to generate an enthusiasm and conviction among themselves resembling a quaint mixture of that found in a revolutionary party, a revival meeting, and a homecoming football gathering. Can this enthusiasm and conviction maintain itself on such a skimpy diet of theoretical notions? This writer thinks not . . . (p. 65).

And Hilgard's (1956) evaluation of Skinner's strategy reads, in part, as follows:

Skinner's "fresh start" approach to psychology has made it difficult for him to use the data collected by others, and, on principle, he rejects their concepts. His role in reference to the theories of others—insofar as he has paid any attention to their claims—has been chiefly that of a trenchant critic. He has felt no responsibility for the task of inter-investigator coordination. In his book, *Science and human behavior* (1953), written as a textbook, he used no literature citations, and he mentions by name, among writers with some place in learning theory, only Thorndike, Pavlov, and Freud (p. 116).

Keller & Schoenfeld (1950), while remaining within Skinner's "system" (i.e., his conception of what is psychological science), have been somewhat more eclectic. And Schoenfeld (1950), writing alone, has a bibliography of 42 items following a comparatively short paper. Here, in good Skinnerian tradition, he sets out to "recast the anxiety-reduction hypothesis" as it pertains to "avoidance conditioning" (p. 77), with results that seem to retard rather than advance the general level of our understanding in this area (see Mowrer & Keehn, 1958). But in one important respect, Schoenfeld's discussion breaks new ground: it explicitly calls attention to the probable role of response-correlated stimuli in the control of behavior, in a way almost exactly parallel to the emphasis upon this phenomenon in present theory. Schoenfeld says:

In addition to the termination of aversive stimulus compounds [Schoenfeld's circumlocution for *fear*], it is possible that another source of reinforcement comes into play. The proprioceptive stimuli produced by the avoidance response may, because they are correlated with the termination of noxious stimuli, become secondary positive reinforcers and hence strengthen the tendency to make the response which generates them (p. 88).

And again:

It is argued that the avoidance response terminates stimulus compounds in which proprioceptive and tactile stimuli are important components. Recent experimental data, cited to support this formulation, are interpreted as indicating that proprioceptive stimuli generated by the organism's own movements can act as secondary negative or positive reinforcers and thus control the movements producing them (p. 97).

Although we would not at all agree with Schoenfeld in his "sanitized" (and essentially circular) definitions of "secondary negative and positive reinforcers," the fact that he sees and stresses the implications of their being conditioned to the *"proprioceptive stimuli generated by the organism's own movements"* constitutes one more important indication of the extent to which investigators of the most diverse conceptual backgrounds are today arriving at a basically similar position. All roads do in truth, it seems, "lead to Rome."

X. Konorski's Version of Two-Factor Theory

An unsympathetic reader of this chapter might be tempted to observe that the theory here under review has drawn much of its support thus far from the "soft-" rather than from the "hard-headed" wing of psychological science. Certainly we have not been excessively impressed by the pretensions of the ultra-objectivists in the domain of learning theory; and we have not hesitated to listen respectfully to those who admit to employing both concepts and data of a frankly subjective kind. But this is not to say that support does not also accrue from some extremely sober and empirical kinds of inquiry. In an earlier chapter the internationally known physiologist, Professor J. Konorski, has already been cited as an advocate of an earlier version of two-factor theory; and it will now be our purpose, within the remaining limits of space in this chapter, to show that, quite independently, his laboratory researches in recent years have moved along lines very similar to those we are exploring here. This parallelism becomes especially evident in a paper published in 1950, which reads in part as follows:

In 1928 we succeeded in separating out a new form of conditioned reflex, different from the Pavlovian conditioned reflex, which we called the "conditioned reflex of the second type" (Miller & Konorski, 1928). On the basis of our experimental work concerning this type of reflex (vide Konorski, 1948, Chapter xi) the principles of its elaboration can be generally formulated as follows:
If we subject to conditioning procedure of the first type (i.e., reinforce by an unconditioned stimulus) a compound of stimuli consisting of an exteroceptive and a proprioceptive stimulus, in which the proprioceptive stimulus constitutes an indispensable complement to the conditioned compound, then the exteroceptive stimulus begins to evoke either the movement

generating the proprioceptive stimulus or the movement antagonistic to it,
which depends (1) on whether the conditioned reflex, first type, to the com-
pound is excitatory or inhibitory, and (2) on whether the reinforcing stimulus
is positive or negative. By positive unconditioned stimuli we denote such
agents as food, an individual of other sex, etc., and by negative unconditioned
stimuli we denote such agents as the introduction of acid into the animal's
mouth, the electric shock, etc.

Thus we obtain four varieties of conditioned reflexes, second type. They
are as follows (s denotes an exteroceptive stimulus, s_r proprioceptive stimulus,
r corresponding movement, ∼ r antagonistic movement, → evokes):

(1) If the compound $s + s_r$ is reinforced by a positive unconditioned
stimulus, stimulus s alone not being reinforced, then stimulus s begins to
evoke the movement r ($s → r$).

(2) If the compound $s + s_r$ is not reinforced by a positive unconditioned
stimulus, while stimulus s alone is reinforced, then stimulus s begins to evoke
the movement antagonistic to r ($s → ∼ r$).

(3) If the compound $s + s_r$ is not reinforced by a negative unconditioned
stimulus, while stimulus s alone is reinforced, then stimulus s begins to evoke
the movement r ($s → r$).

(4) If the compound $s + s_r$ is reinforced by a negative unconditioned
stimulus, while stimulus s alone is not reinforced, then stimulus s begins
to evoke the movement antagonistic to r ($s → ∼ r$) (p. 418).

Near the end of Chapter 7, an experiment by Loucks has been described which nicely exemplifies the first of the four learning situations
here listed by Konorski. In that experiment, it will be recalled, a
buzzer and proprioceptive stimuli produced by cortical excitation of
leg flexion, in the dog, were followed by food; and soon the subject
was flexing the leg whenever the experimenter sounded the buzzer.
This procedure corresponds, obviously and exactly, to the circumstances described in (1) above.

Now let us suppose that in the Loucks experiment buzzer and cortically induced leg flexion had been followed, not by food, but by a
punishment of some sort. Thereafter, when the dog heard the buzzer,
if it started to lift its leg, other "danger signals" (i.e., proprioceptive
stimuli) would be introduced; and the dog might very well make the
reverse movement of leg extension, because this would eliminate the
proprioceptive stimuli associated with leg flexion. This procedure
would correspond to the one described in (4) above—and is reminiscent of an effect long ago reported by Pavlov (1927).

But what of procedure (3)? How are we to interpret or identify
it? Perhaps its implications will be clearer if we describe it a little
differently. Suppose we say:

If s alone is followed by a negative unconditioned stimulus (such
as shock or some other disagreeable experience) and if the compound

s + s, is not followed by the negative unconditioned stimulus, then s begins to evoke the movement r (s → r).

What the dog discovers here is that by lifting his leg and producing S_r he can, so to say, "nullify" the s alone and prevent the negative unconditioned stimulus from occurring. In other words, the dog finds that s is a danger signal but that s + s_r is not. Thus, the fear aroused by s is reduced by the occurrence of s_r. Hence the dog will be rewarded, by secondary reinforcement (type-1), for making the leg flexion response. It will therefore tend to occur, promptly and specifically, whenever s is presented (cf. Mowrer & Keehn, 1958; Sidman, 1953; and Chapter 12).

Thus Konorski's situations (1), (4), and (3) are readily understandable in terms of principles already established in our preceding discussions. What, now, of situation (2)? Here again a restatement may be helpful.

(2) *If a stimulus s alone is reinforced by a positive unconditioned stimulus (e.g., food) and if the compound s + s_r is not reinforced, when the subject gets the stimulus s it will be careful not to make response r and thus nullify the reinforcement, and one way to guard against the occurrence of r is for the subject to make the movement antagonistic to r.*

With this reformulation Konorski's situation (2) becomes quite as intelligible as the other three.

It is apparent that *discrimination* (see Chapter 12), as opposed to simpler learning, is involved in all four of the above situations. In all of them, what the animal has to learn is the difference between what happens if s alone occurs and what happens if s + s_r occurs. In situation (1), s will be followed by primary decremental reinforcement (food) *only if* s_r accompanies it; therefore the animal has a strong incentive for making r. In situation (3), s will be followed by primary incremental reinforcement (shock) if s_r does *not* accompany it; therefore, again, the subject has a strong incentive for making r. In situation (2), s will *not* be followed by primary decremental reinforcement (food) if it is accompanied by s_r, so that the subject has reason for seeing to it that r does *not* occur (and to this end may instigate the reciprocal of r). And in situation (4), s *will* be followed by primary incremental reinforcement (shock) if it is accompanied by s_r, so that the subject again has reason for making sure that r does not occur (and to this end may instigate the reciprocal of r). In two of these situations, s_r is, in other words, a *positive* cue in the sense that it

o

ensures decremental reinforcement (1) or prevents incremental reinforcement (3); while in the other two situations, s_r is a negative cue in that it prevents decremental reinforcement (2) or produces incremental reinforcement (4).

From an intuitive, common-sense point of view, we can see why, in situations (1) and (3), r is positively motivated and why, in situatoins (2) and (4), r is negatively motivated (and its reciprocal positively motivated). But how, from the standpoint of revised two-factor theory, do these facts look? At once we see that in situation (1) the stimuli which are correlated with the occurrence of r take on secondary-reinforcement properties (of the *hope* variety), thus providing the conditions for "voluntary" ("habitual") performance of this response. And we see that in situation (3) the stimuli which are correlated with the occurrence of r likewise take on secondary-reinforcement properties (but of the *relief* variety), again providing the conditions for the performance of this response. In situation (2), the stimuli which are correlated with the occurrence of r acquire secondary motivation properties (of the *disappointment* variety) and provide conditions for the inhibition of this (performance of the antagonistic) response. And in situation (4), the stimuli which are correlated with the occurrence of r acquire secondary motivational properties (of the *fear* variety) and provide conditions for the inhibition of this (and performance of the antagonistic) response. Thus, we have exemplified all four forms of secondary reinforcement, two decremental and two incremental, as shown in Table 7-1, with intrinsic stimulation.

These four experimental situations may be very simply presented in four verbal injunctions to the subject:

(1) "Now (when the buzzer sounds) if you lift your foreleg, you will get food"—hope.

(2) "Now if you lift your foreleg, you will *not* get food"—disappointment.

(3) "Now if you lift your foreleg, you will *not* get shocked"—relief.

(4) "Now if you lift your foreleg when the buzzer sounds, you *will* get shocked"—fear.

We are accustomed, in so-called discrimination situations (Chapter 12), to having the experimenter present one of two or more possible cues which will cause the subject to follow one rather than another course of action. In all four of the situations here described, the situation is similar, except that the roles of command and obedience are, in a sense, reversed: Here the subject *causes the experimenter* to follow one or another course of action (present food, not present food, not present shock, present shock) according to a cue which the subject *gives to him* (and to himself) in the form of a particular response. As in trial-and-error behavior generally, the subject is "responsible" for what happens, in the sense that, by responding or not responding in a particular way, he can ensure favorable consequences (reward) or incur unfavorable consequences (punishment). In one way, the experimenter is, of course, controlling the behavior of the dog; but in another way the dog is controlling the behavior of the experimenter.

What, then, is the role of the buzzer? It seems to serve mainly as an alerting or readying signal. It says, in effect, "*Now* is the time for . . . ." It is a constant in all four conditions, with the meaning that gets attached to the leg-lifting varying systematically. In situations (1) and (3) hope and relief, respectively, become attached to the proprioceptive stimuli produced by this response and thus facilitate it, whereas in situations (2) and (4) disappointment and fear, respectively, become attached to these stimuli and inhibit the response that produces them or instigate an antagonistic response.

The four situations discussed above are not hypothetical ones: Dr. Konorski and his associates (and others) have reproduced all of them experimentally. And they illustrate, almost as if made to order, our hypothesis that behavior is controlled (or, in McClelland's terms, motivated) by two "positive" and two "negative" affective states—hope and relief, on the one hand, and fear and disappointment, on the other. When the stimuli which mediate these four states are response-produced, the results reported by Konorski are obtained. And, in the event that these stimuli are *not* response-produced, what then? Already we know that the result is so-called approach or avoidance behavior, in the *spatial sense*. In the next chapter we shall examine these phenomena more carefully.

XI. Further Indication of the Role of Proprioception in Habit

As an illustration of the kind of research which is now issuing from Konorski's laboratory, let us examine a paper recently published by Stepien & Stepien (1958). Because the report is compact and clearly written, we shall reproduce its essential parts in the authors' own words:

Experiments were performed on 9 dogs. In all the animals instrumental (type II) alimentary conditioned reflexes were established. The dogs were trained to lift the right foreleg to various acoustic stimuli (bell, metronome, buzzer, tone, etc.), and put it on the food-tray in front of the animal. [In other words, a discriminant operant (see Chapter 12, Section IX) was established, i.e., a habit which was under stimulus control: the leg movement would "work" only when the cue stimulus, or S^D, was present.] The performance of this movement in response to the conditioned stimulus was reinforced by food. Each daily experiment consisted of 8–9 trials. Usually, after several days, the dog learned to perform the required movement in response to the conditioned stimuli. After 2–3 months conditioned reflexes were firmly established.

In some of our dogs a number of additional tests were performed in other situations. The dogs were trained to run to a given signal through a very simple maze, each run being reinforced by food (locomotor instrumental reflex). Further, tests were made of their ability to secure food by climbing onto a table, or going over a barrier.

After all test responses had been established, and the conditioned reflexes had become stable and regular, more or less extensive ablations of the sensory cortex were performed. In two dogs, only the sensory area of the left hemisphere was removed; in six dogs, bilateral sensory lesions were performed; in one dog, first the left and after some time the right sensory cortex was ablated (pp. 309–310).

Results—After bilateral ablations of total sensory areas I and II, the general behaviour of the animals was unchanged. No tendency to hyperactivity or to stereotyped movements was observed; the dogs found their way easily to the experimental room, they reacted normally to calling, and so on.

In contradistinction to their general behaviour, proprioception was very much impaired. Very often they put the dorsal aspect of the foot to the ground, they slid on the smooth floor, they crossed their legs, etc. All these defects were gradually compensated, but only partially. The placing reaction [not to be confused with the response of "placing" the forepaw on the food-tray—see below] was permanently abolished. Their ability to go over a barrier and to climb onto a table was greater impaired, but improved gradually.

When brought to the experimental chamber, the dogs behaved quite adequately; they stood correctly on the stand awaiting the conditioned signals. They manifested a very clear and prompt general alimentary reaction to the conditioned stimuli consisting in turning towards the food-tray and salivation, but they were completely unable to perform the movement of putting the leg on the food-tray.

This lack of instrumental conditioned reflexes lasted in various dogs from 16 to 78 days. Then conditioned reflexes "spontaneously" reappeared, either gradually, through a series of abortive movements, or suddenly. 2–3 months after operation the movement of the leg was hardly different from that before operation.

On the other hand, the locomotor conditioned reflexes were totally preserved and the animals easily found their way to the goal (p. 311).

Discussion—The problem arises, what is the cause of the abolition of the instrumental conditioned reflexes after sensory ablations, and why they reappear spontaneously after some time without any additional training.

There is a vast body of evidence showing that, in all instrumental ("voluntary") behaviour, the feed-back from the performance of movement and the posture of the extremity plays a very important or, maybe, quite indispensable role. By removal of the sensory cortex a great part of the sensory feed-back connected with tactile and postural stimuli is destroyed, and this may be the reason why the animal is unable to perform the required movement. On the other hand, the general reaction towards food and the locomotor conditioned reflexes are preserved because they are chiefly based on visual and labryinthine reception. As proprioception of the extremities is also represented in the so-called motor cortex, the animal probably relearns in his normal life, outside the experimental chamber, to perform "voluntary" movements by means of his partially reduced feed-back, and when this has been achieved he is also able to perform the instrumental movement trained in the experimental situation.

Which parts of the central mechanism connected with proprioception are indispensable for performing the so-called "voluntary" movements is not quite clear. In particular, it remains to be elucidated whether sufficiently extensive cortical ablations, destroying all cortical representation of proprioception, would lead to the permanent and irreversible loss of instrumental conditioned reactions (pp. 311–312).

Observe how neatly these findings, and the authors' interpretation thereof, parallel our own assumptions concerning the role of response-correlated stimulation in the establishment of so-called habits. Note also the tendency of these authors to equate habit and voluntary action, thus tacitly repudiating the older idea that a habit is a relatively fixed connection or bond between a given stimulus and response which operates automatically, involuntarily, without involvement of the rest of the nervous system. And it is likewise instructive to compare the findings of Stepien & Stepien with Lashley's (1934) conclusion that habits could not be localized at all, neurologically; that they were dependent upon "mass action," of the whole central nervous system. Here, in the work of Stepien & Stepien, we find that something a good deal more complicated than a stimulus-response bond, or one-way transit, is involved in a habit; but we also see how specifically important are the centers for the sensations aroused by performance of the response in question.

Stepien & Stepien pertinently remark that when a habit can be executed mainly on the basis of visual feedback, impairment of proprioceptive sensation produces little or no effect. Also interesting are their observations concerning *labyrinthine* stimulation. Ordinarily behavior theorists do not think of the sensations generated by excitation of the semicircular canals and otoliths of the inner ear as participating in the feedback from and control over behavior. But it is well established that in all movement and postural changes involving the organism's *head*, this type of stimulation can be highly important: it is a part of the total response-correlated stimulation resulting from movements of the head and body as a whole, no less than are visual, kinesthetic, tactile, and other forms of stimulation. This fact is well attested by the effect upon postural adjustments and general locomotion which removal of the labyrinthine organs is known to have (Geldard, 1953). Although feedback from the organs of sense which are located directly in the muscles (i.e., the proprioceptors) is especially important in the control of movement, it is clear that various other sensory modalities play a concomitant role in this connection and can, if necessary, often "take over" quite satisfactorily. We are here dealing with what is, in effect, a servo-mechanism (Mowrer, 1960, Chapter 8); and information from one source is just as good as another, provided it is equally prompt and precise.

Somewhat anachronistically Stepien & Stepien continue (because of the Pavlovian background of their work) to speak of the habits which they studied as "instrumental alimentary conditioned reflexes" (type-II, to distinguish them from type-I, or classical, conditioned reflexes); but the reaction mechanism with which they are dealing is obviously something a good deal less simple than a one-way S—R connection. Actually, it is now known that even the purest of so-called motor, or motoric, reflexes are also dependent upon the intactness of sensory feedback therefrom; for if this is destroyed, the "reflex," no less than a "habit," becomes highly incoordinate. Thus, even the reflex (except when mediated by the autonomic nervous system) is no simple, single bond. So how much less plausible is it to conceive of *habits* in this artificial, unrealistic way!

XII. A Dissonant Note: The Views of Woodworth, Hunt, and Others

In general, the theory of learning and behavior adaptation which has been described in this book is like a symphony, with many variations and complementary developments, but with a basic form and style. However, we must now take cognizance of a contrapuntal theme currently running through American psychology, like a discordant obligato. It has many individual advocates, no one of whom seems to quite agree with any other; but two noteworthy attempts have recently been made to capture the essence of this movement and to give it succinct statement, which we shall here examine.

In 1958 R. S. Woodworth published a book entitled *Dynamics of Behavior* which, curiously, rejects "dynamics" in the customary sense of this term and places central emphasis instead on cognition—or what one might call "cognitics." The book, says the author, is an elaboration—both as regards theory and scope—of those parts of his *Experimental psychology* (Woodworth, 1938) which dealt with "motivation, perception, and learning." And it was also foreshadowed by the 1947 article cited earlier in this chapter. The thesis of *Dynamics of behavior* is that what living organisms learn, primarily, is not the solutions to problems (in the homeostatic sense); instead, says Woodworth they *learn their environments!* When one recalls that Woodworth was one of those psychologists who were responsible for reintroducing *the organism* into the S—R formula, thus making it read S—O—R, it is surprising how little attention he is now disposed to give to the organism, as such. Part of the trouble arises, he says, from the fact that "Fundamental laws of learning and motivation have been obtained from the animal laboratory" (p. 12); and these need to be re-examined in the light of what we know from the study of human sensation and perception.

It is not easy to get hold, quickly and firmly, of the ideas which Woodworth would present as a substitute for prevailing theory; but the following quotation is perhaps as close to a résumé as one can find:

Without going back far into the history of the subject we shall consider two opposed theories—one of which is accepted by many psychologists at the present time; the other is emerging and deserving of a radical presentation and support. The first may be called the *need-primacy* theory and the other the *behavior-primacy.* The need-primacy theory holds that all behavior is motivated directly or indirectly by the internal needs of the organism, such as hunger and thirst. Sex is regarded as a need to escape from certain internal tensions, and the need to escape from pain and external injury must also be included. The behavior-primacy theory holds that all behavior is directed primarily toward dealing with the environment. Even eating and drinking, which certainly rid the organism of needs, can be regarded as ways of dealing with the environment and securing positive benefits and satisfactions; i.e., as forms of behavior which secure positive good rather than merely escape from harm. No matter which of these theories has the greater emotional appeal to the reader, the scientific question is which has more predictive value. Which one better covers the ground and is more systematic and parsimonious? At first sight the need-primacy theory would be the more parsimonious and systematic if it could possibly be stretched to cover the play motives of children and the absorbing interests of adults. We should have to show how these motives and interests could possibly be derived from the primary needs; thus we could "explain" the motives. But could we *predict* them for the individual or for the social group without assuming additional primaries besides the organic needs?

Two systems which clearly belong in the need-primacy class are the psychoanalytic system of Sigmund Freud and the behavioristic system of Clark Hull (pp. 101–102).

In one sense, the whole of the present book is an answer to Woodworth's challenge to the predictive capacity of homeostatic theory; and many of the problems which he raises have been dealt with specifically in Chapter 6 (see also Mowrer, 1960, Chapter 10). Moreover, the present writer has elsewhere (Mowrer, 1959) reviewed the Woodworth book and pointed out some of its palpable weaknesses. These need not be re-examined here. Instead, let us attempt an over-all appraisal, in the form of two major points:

1). Despite many sallies against it, Woodworth knows that homeostasis cannot be totally disregarded in the analysis and explanation of behavior. This point is implied or expressed in various places: e.g., "We are not pretending that the organic needs are derived from the tendency to deal with the environment. The organic needs are autonomous" (p. 128). But perhaps the most interesting elaborations of the relationship between homeostasis and learning occur in the following passage:

Hull's system has the advantage over Freud's of taking much more account of the effects of learning. What he calls primary reinforcement is the satisfaction of a primary need such as hunger for food. More exactly, it is defined by Hull as the cessation or reduction of the need. . . . When an act leads promptly to such primary reinforcement, learning occurs. The act that is reinforced becomes conditioned to the need and to the external situation so that when the same need and situation occur again, the same act is likely to be made in response. Consequently, by repetition with reinforcement, a habit or mechanism is built up which deals with the situation in such a way as to satisfy or reduce the need (p. 110).

Here, surely, is an excellent statement of Hull's scheme for accounting for both Thorndikian learning ("the act that is reinforced becomes conditioned to the need") and Pavlovian conditioning ("and to the external situation"), which we have considered at length in Chapter 3 and also earlier in this chapter. But then Woodworth makes this additional comment, as if by way of further exposition of Hull's views, which is more accurately an extension of Woodworth's own earlier (1918) thinking:

More than that—the mechanism itself acquires some secondary incentive value. Suppose the mechanism consists in going to a certain place where food is found; this place and the act of going there will serve as reward for a number of trials even if no more food is found there. Or, if the drive is changed from hunger to thirst, the animal will go there for water which he has never found there. This place has become a "good" place. Similarly, a place where an animal has been shocked has become a bad place, a place to be avoided; the place to which he goes and where he gets no shocks has become a good place. (Our way of stating the facts is somewhat different from Hull's). There are many similar results from the animal laboratories. A stimulus that just precedes the obtaining of food—like the click of the pellet-delivering machine in the Skinner box—becomes something worth working for even after the primary reward has ceased (pp. 110–111).

Woodworth obviously concedes these (homeostatic) "facts." And he casts them in such a way as to bring his statement of them very close to our position (cf. also his discussion of "sensory feedback," p. 139, in his chapter on "The Control of Movement"). But he then, so to speak, throws it all away by citing some very incomplete and antequated research on secondary reinforcement which he believes enables him to devaluate the importance of this type of analysis.

2). From the strategy just described, Woodworth goes on to make his main point: that learning is essentially cognitive, a learning "of the environment," rather than of specific responses of any kind (be they behavioral *or* emotional). Chapters 9, 10, and 11 of *Dynamics of Behavior* are all entitled "Learning the Environment" (with appropriate subtitles), and the first of these epitomizes his argument thus:

> In accordance with our general definition of behavior as a "dealing with the environment," several chapters on "learning to deal with the environment" would be expected, for certainly a great deal of learning is necessary. If, instead, this series of chapters is headed *learning the environment*, some explanation and justification are in order. Such a phrase as "learning a person or thing or place" has an unfamiliar, awkward sound, though the awkwardness is gone if we say "getting acquainted with" instead of "learning." No one can deny that getting acquainted with the environment and with the objects in it is a form of learning and should be included in any general investigation of the learning process. Our choice of chapter headings is influenced by the conviction, several times expressed already, that the motor behavior of human beings (at least) is guided by the perception of objective facts. Accordingly, learning to deal with the environment depends on exploration and perception of the environment, with enough retention of what has been perceived to influence later behavior (p. 221).

Here, in a somewhat round-about way, Woodworth is pointing to a real problem. We have previously indicated (Chapter 7, Section IX) that whereas our system is very satisfactory for explaining the *guidance* of behavior once it is selected and initiated, it leaves open the question of how one act rather than another *gets started*. And it has also been pointed out that the phenomenon of conditioned sensations, in the form of *imagery* (or *memories*), is probably intimately associated with the answer. This conjecture will not be discussed in detail until later (Mowrer, 1960, Chapters 5–7). Now it is obvious what Woodworth has in mind in the above quotation: learning to *know* a person, surely, is learning to have an image or memory of some sort *of that person* when his name or some other identifying characteristic is mentioned. This, as we have already noted, is a real phenomenon; but we see it as supplementing rather than supplanting the process of affective conditioning, as it relates to reward and punishment (or homeostasis). In stressing the *primacy* of cognition, Woodworth seems to be reverting to pre-behavioristic psychology, with its emphasis upon consciousness and conscious states, per se. If one *starts* with an objective, behavioral base and then, as occasion demands, introduces first affectivity and *then* imagery, one has, it seems, a far sounder and more systematic conceptual scheme than if one instead *starts* "at the top."

In the next chapter we shall consider the theoretical position of E. C. Tolman, which Woodworth regards very highly—and so shall we! But it is now generally recognized that although Tolman has usefully indicated where a behavior system ought to "come out," he has not been very helpful in showing exactly how to *get there*. The same criticism is also applicable, it seems, to Woodworth's approach. Professor Woodworth undoubtedly does us a substantial service in noting the neglect of cognitive processes in prevailing behavior theory; and as a critique of that theory his work is highly valuable. If, however, his views are presented as a *substitute* for existing behavior theory, their value and validity are considerably less certain.

For some time, now, J. McV. Hunt has been scrutinizing the field of motivation and learning with special reference to human developmental psychology; and he has recently summarized his impressions (Hunt, 1959) as follows:

According to our dominant theory, it is claimed, first of all, that "all behavior is motivated," and that the aim or function of every instinct, defense, action, or habit is to reduce or eliminate stimulation or excitation within the nervous system. . . . Organisms are driven, first, by those so-called primary, inner stimuli which arise from homeostatic imbalances or needs. . . . Organisms are driven, second, by various forms of intense and painful external stimulation (2–3).

It is also assumed, as the proposition that "all behavior is motivated" implies, that the organism would be inactive unless driven by either inner or outer stimuli (p. 4).

The dominant theory has been a conceptual edifice of large demensions and considerable detail. It has provided a plausible account of both personality development and social motives. The experimental facts of homeostasis and of conditioned drive and fear are sound. Nevertheless, it has become more and more evident in the past 10 years that some of the explanatory extrapolations contradict facts and call for reinterpretation (p. 7).

The first of the assumptions to be called into question is the one that all behavior is motivated and that organisms become inactive unless stimulated by homeostatic need or painful stimulation or conditioned stimuli for these (p. 7).

Elsewhere in this volume we, too, have advanced reasons for believing that there is no one-to-one relationship between drive and activity (see especially Chapter 6 and Section V of the present chapter). But our reservation has taken the form of merely noting that drive can be present without activity. Hunt maintains that the *reverse* also is true. He says:

Let us note that such observations do contradict our assumption that organisms will become inactive unless driven by homeostatic needs and painful stimuli, and give up this ancient Greek notion that living matter is inert substance to which motive must be imparted by extrinsic forces. We can then embrace the thermodynamic conception of living things as open systems of energy exchange which exhibit activity upon which stimuli have a modulating effect, but not an initiating effect (p. 9).

The point of mentioning these evidences of spontaneous activities of organ systems is merely to help inter for good the notion that activity of living systems requires homeostatic need or painful external stimulation and to foster the idea that to live means to be active in some degree.

This idea of activity being intrinsic in living organisms has implications for our conception of reinforcement. It makes it unnecessary to see all activity as a matter of either reducing or avoiding stimulation which is implied in the assumption that organisms become inactive unless stimulated (p. 10).

The difficulty is that when one leaves the homeostatic model and averts to organisms which behave "spontaneously," one also leaves the realm of orderly principle, prediction, and control. Perhaps this is as it *should* be. Perhaps the science of behavior is, at best, severely circumscribed and that the *fact* of spontaneity is the reason for such a state of affairs. Yet this is not what Hunt, Woodworth, and related writers seem to be saying. They seem to be implying, instead, that some sort of orderliness or lawfulness is possible *within* this realm of "spontaneity." This remains to be demonstrated. On the other hand, the homeostatic model already has a long record of substantial accomplishment, as Hunt (as well as Woodworth) readily grants:

There is still a place for drive reduction. It is clear that under conditions of homeostatic need and painful stimulation, and perhaps under circumstance when the conditions of stimulation are changing with too great rapidity, both animals and persons learn techniques and strategies leading to gratification or reduction in external stimulation. The evidence that led Thorndike to formulate the "law of effect" is as convincing as ever. Moreover, in association with reductions in homeostatic need, animals and men may also learn cathexes or emotional attachments. The facts referred to are those highly familiar in secondary reinforcement (Pavlov, 1927; Hull, 1943) (p. 11).

The objections and reservations with respect to the homeostatic principle which Hunt then proceeds to cite constitute important and useful challenges to this principle; but, as noted in the present writer's review of Woodworth's book, "they have neither unhorsed it nor led to a rival conceptual scheme of comparable cogency" (p. 130). Granted that homeostatic theory is presently laggard in its treatment of cognitive functions, this is not to say that the thing to do is to *scrap* the theory, simply because it is in this one respect undeveloped. Cognition and "spontaneity," unless anchored in the good bedrock of homeostasis, seem incapable of generating anything more than scattered, unsystematic observations and data. They do not give us a comprehensive, powerful, unified *theory*. Our faith is that the homeostatic model can and indeed *must* be extended to include cognitive phenomena, not only because of their independent reality, but also because the homeostatic model has itself reached a stage of development where cognitive processes are logically demanded. This is a major task and objective of *Learning Theory and the Symbolic Processes*, the sequel to the present work. However, in the remaining four chapters of this book, we shall make no further attempt to deal with this aspect of the problem (see, however, Chapter 9, Section V [20]) but will instead proceed on the assumption that the best way to make progress is to continue to build on the substantial foundation which homeostasis already provides, rather than launch off on some seemingly easier but, in the long run, abortive form of analysis.

[20] See also Chapter 6 for reference to recent studies of the reticular formation ("arousal center") and its bearing on the question of behavior spontaneity (also Mowrer, 1960, Chapter 7).

9 ═══════════

Hope, Fear, and Field Theory

Reflexology and psychological "field theory" have represented polar extremes; and controversy, not infrequently heated, has often occurred between the proponents thereof. Revised two-factor theory takes an intermediate position designed to effect, not merely a compromise and uneasy peace, but a true synthesis and logical integration.

We shall here consider, first of all, the more radical version of field theory developed by Kurt Lewin and his students and will show how naturally it articulates with the systematic views which are presently under discussion. We shall then survey some of the forerunners of field theory, with special reference to the work of E. C. Tolman and his students on the subject of place versus response learning, as it has been called. We shall consider current researches on the problem of behavior variability in a more or less "open-field" situation and examine some of the systematic implications thereof. And finally, we shall see that in his last book Clark Hull, throwing pride and past objections to the winds, himself attempted a kind of behavioral analysis which is manifestly "field theoretical."

Were it not that the principles which make this emerging synthesis possible derive mainly from the stimulus-response tradition, the contemporary situation might seem to constitute quite a victory for the field theorists. Perhaps, as is so often the case, an important part of the truth has existed on both sides of this argument.

I. Recapitulation

However, before proceeding with this chapter, it will be well to pause for a moment, in our upward "climb," and look back and about us to see what may have come clearly into view which we have previously seen only dimly or perhaps not at all.

We now see how essential it is to distinguish between *metabolic* (or primary) drives and those conditionable reactions which we call *emotions*. We see, indeed, that it is *only* by acknowledging the latter that we can have anything remotely like an adequate psychology of learning and performance.

Thorndike had little or nothing to say about the emotions; undoubtedly he felt he did not need them in his system. He dealt instead in terms of hypothetical bonds supposedly established (by reward) or destroyed (by punishment) directly between the metabolic drives (hunger, thirst, etc.) and successful or unsuccessful consummatory (instrumental) behavior. Elegant in its simplicity, this scheme nevertheless had some fatal defects.

Pavlov likewise had no use (literally) for the emotions; but he differed from Thorndike in holding that biological adaptation occurs, not because of changes in the "strength" of drive-response (or UnCS—R) bonds, but because of changes in the connection or bond between the response in question and some *new* stimulus (CS). Again elegantly simple, Pavlov's system also had certain crucial shortcomings.

Hull, as we know, tried to "integrate" Thorndike and Pavlov, but his scheme was basically Thorndikian. While he sometimes acknowledged the reality of secondary drives or emotions (viz. fear), he assumed, here again, that learning was a matter of bonds being formed between these drives and drive-reducing overt actions.

Our assumption, by contrast, is that the emotions play a central, indeed an indispensable, role in those changes in behavior or performance which are said to represent "learning." The emotions are involved, first of all, in that they are, strictly speaking, *what* is learned. Fear, hope, relief, and disappointment—these we assume are the reactions which are most readily and importantly conditionable; and once conditioned, to independent and/or response-dependent stimuli, they then guide and control performance in a generally sensible, adaptive manner.

Thus far, major attention has been given to the changes in behavior that occur when emotions get conditioned to response-correlated stimuli. The reason for this is that our principal objective has been to develop (as a counterpart to the "new" theory of punishment—see Chapters 2 to 4) a new, and improved, way of thinking about the phenomenon of "habit." But, in the present chapter, we shall discover that the foundation thus laid is also highly satisfactory for accounting for so-called *place* learning or "field" behavior.

Here it remains only to be said—or, rather, re-emphasized—that, whatever its virtues and strengths (which were considerable), Behaviorism's rejection of emotions was a major stumbling block. If the present conceptual scheme is valid, the emotions are of absolutely central importance to a theory of learning and behavior modification and control. This position contrasts radically with the teaching of one of the writer's early teachers to the effect that emotions are "wasted reactions" (Meyer, 1922, 1933).

There has been a widespread tendency in Western civilization to look upon "the emotions" with a certain distrust and contempt and to elevate "the intellect" (reason, logic) high above them. If the present analysis is sound, the emotions are of quite extraordinary importance in the total economy of living organisms and do not at all deserve being put into opposition with "intelligence." The emotions are, it seems, themselves a high order of intelligence. The full meaning and justification of this statement will unfold gradually in this and later chapters (see also Mowrer, 1960).

II. Field Theory as Developed by Kurt Lewin

As Deutsch (1954) and others have pointed out, field theory, as developed by Lewin and associates, is largely an outgrowth of the theorizing of 19th century physicists. Instead of thinking of a discrete cause producing a correspondingly discrete effect, these men—including Maxwell, Faraday, and Hertz—found that they could formulate more inclusive laws and write more powerful equations if they made reference to *fields*, notably gravitational and electromagnetic fields.

One of the first impacts of field-theoretical thinking in psychology was to produce a conception of behavior antithetical to that of reflexology. Instead of seeing behavior as made up of isolated S—R bonds, either native or acquired, the field theorists (including Gestalt psychologists) took the position that the individual always reacts as a totality, as a more or less well-organized entity in response to a total situation in so far as it is perceived and interpreted by the individual. Moreover, as Deutsch observes:

The [field-theoretical] explanation of behavior assumes that all behaviors have directional characteristics. Hence, it is concerned with the purposes which underlie behavior and the goals towards or away from which behavior is directed. There is little direct interest in tools or mediating processes *per se* apart from the interest in how they are learned or acquired and in how desirable and effective they are considered to be by the individual (p. 183).

In other words, an act or action is not something which is automatically "run off," once the adequate stimulus has set a given cause-effect sequence in motion; an action is something which is being continually guided and corrected by additional stimulation or "information" which is impinging upon the organism. Passing reference has already been made (Chapter 7) to the concept of "feedback," and it is considered more fully in another connection (Mowrer, 1960, Chapter 7). Suffice it to say here that it is closely related to field theory. In both cases it is assumed that a given behavior sequence, once set in motion, is not ineluctably determined but is, rather, subject to continuous modification on the basis of the "meaning of the situation," as it is sensed or perceived moment-to-moment. In other words, behavior is a continuous, on-going function of the informational feedback from *all senses*, internal and external; it is, in a word, a function of the total *psychological field*.

Furthermore, as already implied, the effects of a given constellation of stimuli, a "situation," or a "field," upon an individual cannot be predicted or even understood without knowledge of the individual and what he *brings to* the situation. To quote Deutsch again:

Lewin's point is that to develop psychological laws we must deal with psychological processes—the perception of the external event, not the event itself; behavior, and not its effects by themselves. Thus, we ought to be concerned with the psychological impact of a "reward," e.g., whether it is perceived as a "bribe" or as a "sign of accomplishment," rather than simply with the external situation of reward. In essence, one has to deal with what *exists psychologically*, what is real for the person being studied (p. 184).

That is to say, even though one has taken the total situation into account, at least as far as its stimulus aspects are concerned, one must, in addition, consider what Tolman (see Section IV) has aptly called *intervening variables*. External events or stimuli influence and determine behavior, not in a direct, physicalistic sense, but through the intervening action of the *meanings* they have acquired for the individual as a result of prior experience, i.e., through learning, either immediate or vicarious (see Krechevsky, 1932; also Mowrer, 1960, Chapter 6).[1]

Enough has now been said about psychological field theory, partic-

---

[1] For further discussion of what he terms the "cognition versus association issue" in psychology, see Spence (1951b, pp. 241 ff.).

ularly as developed by Kurt Lewin and his students, to make possible a comparison with revised two-factor learning theory. The congruences are striking. Both are agreed that a rigid S—R, reflexological interpretation of the *behavior* of higher organisms is not feasible. And both are also agreed that, at the very least, one must have a two-step conception of situation-behavior sequences; stimuli, purely environmental and response-produced, elicit meanings, motives, interpretations which (along with organically given drives) are then the immediate determiners of overt action, not the "raw" stimuli themselves.

But two-factor theory differs from field theory in this respect: it does not find the concept of reflex and conditioned reflex entirely useless. It agrees that these concepts, applied to overt, behavioral responses, are misleading and inadequate. It holds, however, that the meanings, emotions, secondary motives, and interpretations which, as a result of learning, become attached to particular stimuli or situations *are basically reflexive* (involuntary, autonomically mediated) and that the best paradigm for the learning here involved is that of conditioning, or sign learning. Associationistic psychology, including both conditioning and habit theory, has in the past often seemed to be diametrically opposed to field theory. Two-factor theory offers a possible avenue of reconciliation.[2] It agrees with field theory and disagrees with associationism in holding that the concept of reflex, be it in the guise of "habit" or conditioned reflex, does not give anything like an adequate general explanation of behavior. But it disagrees with, or at least goes beyond, field theory and espouses reflexological thinking in holding that it is precisely through conditioning, or associative shifting, that stimuli take on their inner meanings for the individual, that signs and situations acquire their significances. Meanings, it is held, constitute for the individual a sort of *inner, subjective field;* and it is this on-going, ever-changing motivational state which, moment by moment, modifies, controls, and directs behavior.

[2] As if anticipating the possibility of such a reconciliation, Estes (1954) has observed: "During recent years reviewers and text writers, if not theorists themselves, have come to characterize, or dramatize, the psychology of learning in terms of a conflict between two camps, the one commonly called stimulus-response or stimulus-response-reinforcement theory and the other gestalt, cognitive or, most generally, field theory. The lines of demarcation are not entirely distinct" (p. 317). "[But] there is no reason to expect that direct comparison of learning theory and field theory will be easy . . ." (p. 318). And Estes concludes that "it did not seem possible to clear up this disparity at a level of broad generalities" (p. 341). It is believed that the present theoretical framework provides the basis for an integration at just such "a level of broad generalities."

At least at one stage, Lewin's work took a different turn. He attempted to organize his theorizing around a sort of geometric, or spatial, model called *topology*. "Vectors" and "valences" were supposed to articulate the individual with his "psychological space" or environment; and these, according to their intensity and sign (positive or negative), constituted the "field" in which the individual reacted and behaved.[3] Two-factor theory also sees signs and situations as having meanings which can properly be interpreted as positive or negative: if a sign is "negative" it produces an increment in emotional tension, and if it is "positive" it produces a decrement in emotional tension. But beyond this the agreement with topology is tenuous. Lewin, despite his acknowledgment of meanings, seemed to give considerable potency to external, environmental, or field forces as the actual determiners of behavior. In contrast, two-factor theory emphasizes an *internal*, rather than an external, "field" as the dynamic, energy-producing, causally effective source of behavior. Ordinarily, the amount of energy involved in the stimuli impinging upon living organisms from without is miniscule and can be detected only by the most refined and sensitive types of physical apparatus. But, somewhat in the manner of a radio receiving set, living organisms take these minute and, as such, causally ineffective stimuli and convert, or *amplify*, them into forms of *psychological energy* which are quite powerful. A stimulus which is very weak in its own right—for example, a whispered or written word—may bring either overwhelming fright or joyous relief to an individual; but it is surely the "amplified," interpreted, conditioned inner reaction *to* the stimulus and not the stimulus itself that produces these important motivational consequences.[4]

Perhaps, for the reasons just cited, we can see why the topological formulation of field theory was not very successful. Says Deutsch:

Although Lewin's "topological" and "hodological" concepts are not much more than diagrammatic representations of his brilliant theoretical and experimental insights, it would be foolish to neglect the suggestive value of his imaginative attempt to develop a geometry suitable for psychologists. He pointed out the need for a new mathematics based on axioms different from those of the mathematics developed for the physical sciences. He indicated

[3] The term *valence*, borrowed from chemistry, here implies a direct force of attraction or repulsion; *vector*, on the other hand, comes from mathematics and was used by Lewin to imply the net effect, algebraic summation, or resultant of two or more valences simultaneously impinging upon the individual.

[4] Lewin himself (1942), in an article on "Field Theory of Learning," acknowledged that valences "change with experience" thus implying that it is not the stimulus itself that supplies the "valence" but a learned reaction thereto.

some of the properties that would be required of a geometry adequate to handle psychological space and he stimulated a more widespread interest in the development of such a geometry (p. 199).

More relevant to and compatible with two-factor theory are some of Lewin's earlier hypotheses concerning *tension systems*. These are internal to the organism and were thought of as producing (1) locomotion or movement *away from* stimuli or situations that augment tension and (2) locomotion or movement *toward* stimuli or situations that diminish tension. This mode of thought, which is wholly compatible with two-factor learning theory, prompted Lewin and his students to do some of their most ingenious research: the study of completed and uncompleted tasks (Zeigarnick effect), detour behavior, satiation, frustration, substitution, levels of reality, and so on. Much of this research, it is believed, can now be more felicitously interpreted in the terms of two-factor theory than in those characteristically employed by Lewin; and in making such a translation one relates these investigations to other psychological systems, from which they originally seemed quite remote.

Because this book introduces the concept of "hope," presumably for the first time, into stimulus-response theorizing, it is interesting to discover how freely it has already been employed in field-theoretical considerations. Says Deutsch:

An emphasis on the psychological explanation of psychological events in contrast to an explanation in terms of physical or neurophysiological processes has several important consequences. The scientist who works with the assumption that psychological phenomena are realities, even if they cannot be expressed in physical terms or located in physical space, is more apt to investigate them. Recognizing that people in everyday affairs use such concepts as "hope," "desire," "action," "ability," "ought," etc., to characterize others as well as themselves (and acknowledging that these phenomena have reality in their own right), he is more likely to feel that the concepts of this everyday psychology are legitimate and important objects for investigation by a scientific psychology (Heider, 1953). That is, he will want to know under what conditions a person with given characteristics will say he is "hopeful" and under what conditions this person will say that another person is "hopeful." In other words, he is more apt to concern himself with the psychological phenomena which occur in everyday life, including the concepts of everyday psychology, than is the scientist who feels that he is not being scientific unless he can either say "hope" is really a specified pattern of neural excitation in a certain region of the brain or that "hope" is really a certain pattern of bodily movements which can be expressed in physical terms. This is not to assert that the psychologist who employs a psychological approach in theorizing will be content to stop at the level of description of the phenomenal properties of psychological events.

He will want to know how "hope" can be characterized in terms of the constructs of a psychological theory. Lewin, in his writings, continuously stresses that the understanding of causal relationships requires one to proceed from the more accessible, phenomenal properties of psychological events to their underlying dynamic or geno-typical properties (pp. 183–184).

Chapter IV of Lewin's *Dynamic Theory of Personality* (1935) is entitled, "The Psychological Situations of Reward and Punishment"; and it might be expected that here Lewin himself would have established points of contact between his thinking and that of Thorndike, Pavlov, and others whose writings have provided much of the background for two-factor theory. However, the chapter is largely devoted to showing how reward and punishment are interpretable in topological terms; and there is no reference to Thorndike, Pavlov, or Hull or to the major ideas with which they were concerned.

In two other papers, "Field Theory of Learning" (1942) and "Field Theory and Learning" (1951), Lewin more nearly articulates his particular concepts with those of stimulus-response theorists. Here he indicates two types or forms of learning: learning as it relates to changes in *cognition*, or "cognitive structure," and learning as it related to *motivation* (cf. Mowrer, 1960, Chapter 5). But even here a language is used which is foreign to most learning theorists, and not much of an integration is achieved. However, as indicated in the preceding pages, Lewin's formulations are by no means unrelatable to a modified stimulus-response psychology; and it appears that the two types of system can now be merged into a theoretical structure which is both more comprehensive and stable.

In his recent review and critique of Lewinian theory, Bronfenbrenner (1951) has made some summarizing statements which can be usefully quoted. He says:

Lewin emphasizes that personality can be understood only if it is viewed, not in isolation, but in relation to the field in which it operates. This leads directly into the most familiar aspect of Lewin's theory—his emphasis on the importance of the environmental field in terms of physiomathematical concepts—such as *valence, vector, barrier, detour,* and the like (p. 211).

[But] even such a concept as valence, which upon first consideration appears to be an attribute of the object, is seen upon analysis to arise from needs or tensions within the perceiving organism—the person:

"The close connection . . . between the perceptual field and the course of the process must not let us forget that the forces which control the course of the process remain without effect or simply do not arise when no psychical energies are present, when there exists no connection with tense psychical systems which keep the process in motion" (Lewin, 1935, pp. 50–51) (p. 212).

We are told that there are systems of forces acting within and between the individual and his environment, but what these forces are, whence they come, and whither they impel, remain unanswered questions. . . . "The place for a more comprehensive discussion of the internal structure of personality" was evidently not in this world (pp. 214–215).

It is believed that the concepts of *hope* and *fear*, as developed in the present volume, provide the "internal structure" that Bronfenbrenner is calling for and, at the same time, articulate the organism with the stimulus environment, or "field," which was of such special interest to Lewin and which he studied so productively.

III. Adumbrations of Psychological Field Theory and Two-Factor Theory (Freud and Craig)

As already indicated (in Chapter 8), Sigmund Freud could hardly be called a learning theorist, in any formal sense of that term, yet one finds in his writings two concepts which are more than a little reminiscent of "hope" and "fear," as employed in this and preceding chapters. Although Freud hardly ever used the term "learning," he frequently referred to *cathexis* as a form of "interest" which is attached to or invested in a given object or activity because that object or activity has been associated with pleasure; and he referred to *anticathexis* as the state of mind engendered toward a given object or activity as a result of its having been associated with frustration, disappointment, or pain. A cathected object was one which an individual tends to seek or approach, and an object with anticathexis is one which an individual tends to retreat from or avoid. Similarly, a cathected activity is one which an organism tends to repeat; and an activity which has taken on anticathexis is one which an organism tends not to repeat. Freud was never very explicit about these concepts, beyond saying that cathexis involves a "charge of energy" and that anticathexis involves a "counter-charge" (1935, pp. 314–315). But without doing violence to his thought, one can interpret them as representing, respectively, conditioned tension decrement and conditioned tension increment, i.e., secondary reward and secondary motivation. With such a translation, Freudian theory is readily relatable to the integrated version of field theory and habit theory which is represented by two-factor learning theory.[5]

[5] For a more detailed discussion of Freud's influence upon contemporary learning theory, see Hilgard (1956, Chapter 9).

Also of considerable historical importance and influence is a paper, entitled "Appetites and Aversions as Constituents of Instincts," which was published in 1918 by Wallace Craig. Tolman (see Section V) has repeatedly acknowledged a debt to this paper, and in it we see one of the first stirrings of dissatisfaction with the reflexology introduced by Behaviorism and a clear intimation of the concepts of hope and fear. The gist of Craig's thesis is given in the opening paragraph of his paper:

The overt behavior of adult animals occurs largely in rather definite chains and cycles, and it has been held that these are merely chain reflexes. Many years of study of the behavior of animals—studies especially of the blond ring-dove (*Turtur risorius*) and other pigeons—have convinced me that instinctive behavior does not consist of mere chain reflexes; it involves other factors which it is the purpose of this article to describe. I do not deny that innate chain reflexes constitute a considerable part of the instinctive equipment of doves. Indeed, I think it probable that some of the dove's instincts include an element which is even a tropism as described by Loeb. But with few if any exceptions among the instincts of doves, this reflex action constitutes only a part of each instinct in which it is present. Each instinct involves *an element of appetite, or aversion, or both* (p. 91; italics added).

One observes, both from the title of Craig's article and from the foregoing quotation, that his interest is centered upon "instincts," rather than upon "habits"; but it should be remembered that at the time Craig was writing the former term was often used very broadly; and on a later page (p. 94) Craig indicates that, in his own thinking, "instincts" often include learned elements. (Others—Holt, 1931; Wheeler, 1928—have of course held that "instincts" are largely or wholly the products of learning). Therefore, it is of interest to explore Craig's paper somewhat more thoroughly. He continues by saying:

An appetite (or appetence, if this term may be used with a purely behavioristic meaning), so far as externally observable, is a state of agitation which continues so long as a certain stimulus, which may be called the appeted [compare Freud's term, cathected] stimulus, is absent. When the appeted stimulus is at length received it stimulates a consummatory reaction, after which the appetitive behavior ceases and is succeeded by a state of relative rest.
An aversion is a state of agitation which continues so long as a certain stimulus, referred to as the disturbing stimulus, is present; but which ceases, being replaced by a state of relative rest, when that stimulus has ceased to act on the sense-organs (p. 91).

And later Craig adds:

Appetitive behavior in vertebrates is evidently a higher development of what Jennings (1906, p. 309) calls the positive reaction in lower organisms; aversive behavior in vertebrates corresponds to what Jennings (p. 301) calls negative reactions (p. 95).

Craig is obviously caught in a dilemma: he wishes to remain within a behavioristic framework, indexing his concepts by means of behavioral activities; but at the same time the terms "appetite" and "aversion" suggest subjective, internal, emotional phenomena. His use of the term "aversion," despite its behavioral implications, can be equated without much trouble to fear (or perhaps fear and anger). But the term "appetence" is more ambiguous. It can, of course, be roughly equated to "hope"; but as we have seen, hope itself is ambiguous and bidimensional in that it implies both the relief and the excitement which are occasioned by stimuli previously associated with satisfying states of affairs. (A provisional resolution of this difficulty has been proposed in Chapter 6.)

We may conclude our consideration of Craig's article with a final paragraph in which he says:

In the theoretically simplest case, which I think we may observe in doves to some extent, these states [of activity] bring about the appeted situation in a simple mechanical manner. The organism is disturbed, actively moving, in one situation, but quiet and inactive in another; hence it tends to move out of the first situation and to remain in the second, obeying essentially the same law as seen in the physical laboratory when sand or lycopodium powder on a sounding board leaves the anti-nodes and comes to rest in the nodes (p. 92).

It is interesting, in passing, to note the implied references to electricity in both Freud's concept of cathexis (as a "charge") and in Craig's concept of appetite. As indicated elsewhere (Mowrer, 1960, Chapter 7), the influence of electronic and "servo" devices upon contemporary theory is also very marked.

IV. The Work of L. T. Troland Re-examined

In scanning the history of American psychology over the past half century, one's eye is also caught by Troland's concept of "retroflex action," which has interesting parallels with both field theory and two-factor learning theory. In a book published in 1928 and entitled *The Fundamentals of Human Motivation*, this author gives the gist of his theory in a chapter headed "Nociception, Beneception and Retroflex

Action", and it is this chapter, and more particularly the latter half, with which we shall now be concerned.

In summarizing the earlier part of the chapter, Troland says:

Thus, the neutroceptors may be regarded generally as recording the environment, and the relation of the organism thereto; whereas the noci- and beneceptors transmit to the cortex constant reports concerning the effect of these factors upon the welfare of the individual or species (p. 215).

One might expect this author then to equate neutroceptive stimuli to those which, through conditioning, become signals and to equate no-ciceptive and beneceptive stimuli to the so-called unconditioned stimuli. But this does not occur. Instead, Troland follows a different line of thought. He says:

We must now consider more in detail how the cortex can be assisted by such "welfare reports." If they are to be of any biological value, they must help in removing the organism from environmental relationships which are detrimental, and in establishing or maintaining such relationships as are beneficial. Now, thus far we have intended our classification of receptive mechanisms—as nociceptive, beneceptive or neutroceptive, respectively—to be of a purely formal biological character. In other words, we have laid down no physiological criterion which would enable us to detect a noci-ceptive or a beneceptive system by a mere examination of the neural mecha-nisms. Their definition has been formulated in terms of the status of given nerve channels or activities with respect to the total biological situation. However, we have already stated the principle that the action of noci-ceptors upon the nervous system is such as to *inhibit* cortical processes, whereas that of beneceptors has a facilitative effect upon what the cortex is doing (p. 215).

We may now generalize this proposition in the following way. *Noci-ception is accompanied by a decreasing of the conductances of operating cortical adjustors; whereas beneception is accompanied by an increasing of the conductance of operating cortical adjustors.* We may assign to the process which is thus described the general name: *retroflex action.* This term is selected because the action in question is a kind of "back-kick" of organic effects into the cortex. The cortex, by its principle of trial and error, or random activity, initiates a certain line of response. This, in turn, produces certain actual or incipient organic changes which are reported back to the cortex via the beneceptive or nociceptive channels, and the ex-citations of these channels modify the cortical tendency. If the "report" is beneceptive or favorable, the tendency in question is enhanced, whereas if it is nociceptive or unfavorable, the tendency is reduced. These actions can be regarded as being determined quite mechanistically, without reference to any accompanying pleasantness or unpleasantness, or any "intelligence" on the part of the cortical process. Facilitative retroflex action, based upon beneception, may be characterized as *positive* because it increases the given cortical conductance; while the nociceptive consequences may be charac-terized a negative (p. 216).

Psychologists of the introspective era had taken the position that stimuli always, or at least commonly, have what they referred to as "hedonic tone." By this they meant, simply, that stimuli tend to be inherently pleasant or unpleasant (see Chapters 6 and 8). While rejecting the subjectivism of such concepts as pleasantness and unpleasantness, Troland was still only one step removed from this tradition in that he argued that stimuli, if not "neutral," are *inherently* harmful or helpful to the organism in its struggle for existence and that the principle of retroflex action operates in such a way as to make responses which lead to nociceptive stimulation *less,* and responses which lead to beneceptive stimulation *more,* likely to recur.

In the hope of making his theory more tangible, Troland gives the following illustrations:

As examples of these two processes, we may consider the familiar cases of the "burned child" and the child with candy. In the first case we may suppose the child to be indulging in the form of random response which is known as "play." One of the objects to which it responds is a candle-flame, and the reaction happens to consist in placing a finger in the flame. As a consequence, the pain nerves are violently stimulated, and the cortical adjustor process which is associating the afferent flame-pattern nerve current with the outward thrust of the finger, is abruptly reduced in conductance. The consequence of this, in turn, is that the flame-pattern currents cease to pass through this particular junction, and pick out the next most conductive path, which will probably set off a sufficiently different reaction to liberate the finger from the singeing effect of the flame. If it should happen that the next most conducting adjustor does not bring about a sufficient change of posture, this adjustor will also be reduced in conductance in the same manner, the process continuing in this way until an escape is effected. Along with these changes in the cortically controlled reactions there will also be a complex group of reflexes, which may in themselves assist in the withdrawal of the finger. The sympathetic nervous system will be aroused, the child will cry, etc.

Now the important point about this process, so far as learning is concerned, lies not in the immediate effect of the nociceptive excitation upon the cortically controlled behavior but in the fact that a permanent alteration has been made in the tendencies of cortical adjustment. The flame-finger-thrust adjustor has had its conductance decreased, and, hence, is permanently less liable to recur. The next time the flame image is presented to the child's eyes, this particular path of response will be found sluggish, and some other reaction will probably occur. Thus, physiological nociception, as we have defined it, has a lasting learning effect. In some cases, the original nociceptive operation will be inadequate to put the particular adjustor, which is concerned, out of action; but it follows from our general formula that successive operations of this kind will have a cumulative influence, each decrease of conductance starting where the other one left off (pp. 217–218).

In the case of the child and the candy, we may suppose him to respond by a movement which places the candy in his mouth. Thereupon the beneceptive sugar excitation is set off. This increases the conductance of the operative adjustor, which is responsible for the presence of the candy in the mouth. Consequently the candy remains, or is swallowed as a consequence of the deglutition reflex which is aroused; and thereafter, the child shows a greatly increased tendency to seek and eat sweetmeats. In this case there is positive learning, or a real enhancement of the conductance of given nerve paths over and above the original values. The enhancement will also be greater than would be effected by the principle of exercise. . . . The behavior of the individual under these circumstances should consist in a repetition of the movements, or a maintenance of the postures which bring about the beneceptive process (p. 219).

Clearly, Troland was attempting to formulate a psychology of reward and punishment but one which would by-pass the difficulties which arise when these concepts are defined as involving, respectively, the subjective experiences of pleasantness and unpleasantness. Thorndike (1913) had tried to resolve this problem by operationally defining unpleasantness as an experience which the organism tries to *avoid* and pleasantness as an experience which the organism does nothing to avoid or *seeks to repeat*. But there is an element of circularity here: in studying the effects of reward and punishment what one is endeavoring to do, precisely, is to explain *the fact* of avoidance or approach.

More recent thinking has taken still another turn. Now the emphasis is neither upon pleasantness or unpleasantness nor upon biological welfare or injury, but upon drive reduction and drive induction. In general, drive reduction is both pleasant and beneficial to the organism and drive induction is unpleasant and actually or potentially harmful; and their use in defining the conditions of learning avoids any suggestion of circularity in that they can be defined and identified, in most instances, without reference to the facts we are attempting to explain, notably approach and avoidance, facilitation and inhibition *of behavior*. Drive reduction, if shortly preceded or accompanied by a formerly neutral stimulus, can give to that stimulus the capacity to arouse hope (secondary reinforcement); and drive induction, if shortly preceded or accompanied by a formerly neutral stimulus, can give to that stimulus the capacity to arouse fear (secondary motivation). And these two emotions, as they become attached to both external and response-produced stimuli, "structure" (constitute) the individual's "total psychological field," which is assumed, in revised two-factor theory, to control and guide overt behavior.

It is interesting that Troland speaks of the "back-kick" of the "organic effects" produced by beneceptive stimulation (reward) and nociceptive stimulation (punishment)—a concept certainly suggestive of the notion of "feed-back." But the parallelism is a limited one. Troland is assuming, in a manner reminiscent of Thorndike's first formulation of the Law of Effect, that beneception lowers the "resistance" of S—R bonds and that nociception increases their resistance. In revised two-factor theory the assumption is that "motor pathways," i.e., pathways leading from the cortex to muscles, are not modified by learning and that all change in "conductance" so produced occurs between formerly neutral stimuli and internal meaning reactions, such as those of "good" and "bad," right and wrong, hope and fear. This, too, is a kind of "back-kick" theory in the sense that it assumes that behavior is constantly checked or encouraged by these "foretastes" of probable consequences; but the influence and control thus achieved are presumed to depend upon dynamic, motivational factors rather than upon simple changes in stimulus-response conductivity. Another, by no means trivial, advantage of two-factor theory is that in seeing reward and punishment operate through the principle of here-and-now *conditioning*, one escapes from the paradox of retroaction, such as was commonly attributed to Thorndike's position and which was implied by Troland's terms, retroflex and retroflexion.

Obviously, therefore, Troland was still "wide of the mark." But in his emphasis upon *two kinds* of stimuli, he was coming closer to a field-theoretical system than some of his strictly behavioristic predecessors had been. A somewhat parallel development, of about the same era, was Holt's conception of *adience* (stimuli which the organism tries to approach or "get more of") and *abience* (stimuli which an organism tries to avoid or "get less of"). Holt's (1931) book, *Animal Drive and the Learning Process*, may be usefully consulted in this connection; but it has not contributed in any otherwise distinctive way to major developments in the area of learning theory (but see Section X).

V. The Theoretical Formulations of E. C. Tolman

The conception of learning which, by all odds, has done most to relate Behaviorism and field theory and which represents perhaps the closest approximation, so far, to the position here termed revised two-factor theory is that advanced by Edward Chase Tolman. Yet it is not easy to give an accurate and adequate summary of Tolman's views concerning learning. They have undergone change and repeated revision over a period of some thirty years, as new experimental facts and logical contingencies have emerged. Perhaps the main difficulty is that Professor Tolman was "ahead of time" in that he had, from the beginning, high standards for what behavior theory ought to be and do, long before such theory was at all fully developed. From the outset Tolman has insisted that he is a "Behaviorist" of sorts, but he has also expressed lively dissatisfactions with what has traditionally passed as Behaviorism. It would be an interesting task to start with his 1922 paper, "A New Formula for Behaviorism," and follow down through the years his unremitting efforts to develop a theoretical system which would not have the limitations of other neater, but manifestly oversimplified, schemes. Instead, we shall try to pick from his writings a set of propositions that capture the spirit as well as substance of his endeavors and which will highlight both the similarities and differences between his thought and the point of view presented in preceding chapters. We shall attempt to do this in two stages: first a mere outline of his position and its relation to two-factor learning theory as presently formulated, then a somewhat more detailed and analytical presentation.

Perhaps most central to and most characteristic of Tolmanian theory is the view that all learning is *sign* learning. Although behavior is altered as a consequence of learning, this is not because there has been a change in the synaptic resistance of neural pathways leading from particular stimuli to particular muscles, but because certain stimuli, or signs, have become integrated with, or into, certain "sign-gestalt expectations." The latter Tolman defines as a belief or conviction or "hypothesis" on the part of the learner that "such and such performances or behaviors (if carried out) would be successful in reaching such and such a goal" (1945, p. 237). "These expectancies fundamentally are merely sets in the nervous system aroused by environmental stimuli" (p. 237). And, he adds, "goals" may be either positive (desirable and to be sought) or negative (objectionable and to be avoided).

To sum up [says Tolman elsewhere], it appears that it is the actual leadings-on or not-leadings-on,—including such sub-varieties of this function as "obstructing," "being an alternate to," "being a shorter way than," or "a longer way than," or "farther off than," and the like, which constitute the means-end relations; and it is the aroused preparatory sets in the organism for such possible leadings-on, or not-leadings-on, and their various sub-varieties which constitute what I would call the means-end expectations (1933b, p. 402).

In other words, Tolman has held that learning leads to *knowledge*, to *cognitions*, instead of specific, stereotyped performances, or "habits." And with this statement of the essence of his position we are ready to compare it, at least in a preliminary way, with revised two-factor learning theory. The latter agrees completely that learning is sign learning and that it does not fix or stereotype performance. It also agrees that learning results in a change in "intervening variables," rather than in altered resistance in stimulus-response connections. The difference between the two positions lies primarily, it seems, in the nature of the assumptions made concerning the intervening variables themselves. In both systems these can be characterized, at least loosely, as anticipations or expectancies. But for Tolman these phenomena are "purposive" and "cognitive," whereas in two-factor theory they have a somewhat less mentalistic, more corporeal, more dynamic quality. One writer—E. R. Guthrie (1952)—has observed, somewhat facetiously but not irrelevantly, that a Tolman-type rat, after learning, would never *do* anything about it. He would, this writer suggests, be perpetually "lost in thought" at the choice point, unmotivated and unmoved by his altered cognitions. Thus, in Guthrie's own words:

The form of association theory which Tolman has adopted does not use the association of stimulus with response, but the association of cues, which he first called "sign gestalts" and later called "field expectancies," with a mental event. The early parts of the maze (Tolman, 1933a) act not as cues for action, but as signs that the goal is to come, cues for the rat to expect the goal. By "expect" in this sense Tolman does not mean action or preparation, but a mental awareness of some kind. His "sign-gestalt" formula leaves quite untouched the problem of what a rat will do with a sign, or of how signs are translated into action. "These sign-gestalt expectations," he says (1933a, p. 249), "I assumed would be to the effect that the earlier parts of the discrimination apparatus would have become a sign or a set of signs to the rats that the encountering of the food-compartments was to be achieved by running through this discrimination apparatus." Signs, in Tolman's theory, occasion in the rat *realization*, or *cognition*, or *judgment*, or *hypotheses*, or *abstraction*, but *they do not occasion action*. In his concern with what goes on in the rat's mind, Tolman has neglected to predict what the rat will do. So far as the theory is concerned the rat is left buried in thought; if it gets to the food box in the end that is its concern, not the concern of the theory (p. 143).

As we have already seen, a purely "objective" S—R psychology of learning (whether of the Pavlovian or Thorndikian variety) runs into many paradoxes and difficulties; and Guthrie has put his finger on a seemingly crucial weakness in Tolman's theorizing. Incorporating certain features of *both* lines of thought, revised two-factor theory takes a middle ground, which seems to be sounder than either of these more extreme positions. Reflexology (used here to include Thorndikian habit theory as well as Pavlovian conditioning) and cognition are, in some ways, poles apart—one being *behavioristic* and the other *mentalistic*—but two-factor theory represents an effort to bring about a creative synthesis thereof. We discard the notion that *behavior itself* is learned, whether as habit or as conditioned reflex; but we retain the concept of conditioning and, with Tolman, use it to explain how certain *internal events* get attached to new (extrinsic or intrinsic) stimuli. But whereas Tolman identified these interval events as "pure cognitions," we see them, simply but more dynamically, as *hopes and fears.* And these then *guide, select,* or *control* behavior along lines which are, generally speaking, adaptive—a phenomenon which both Thorndike and Pavlov, in their different but equally oversimplified ways, were also attempting to account for.[6]

Two-factor learning theory does not, of course, *exclude* the notion of cognition, perception, knowledge; it simply makes these "intellectual" phenomena part and parcel of a more inclusive type of reaction, which importantly involves emotional—and therefore motivational—factors (cf. Mowrer, 1960, Chapters 5 and 6). Our assump-

---

[6] In a paper entitled "Principles of Performance," Tolman (1955) has himself amended his earlier formulations so as to attempt to take account of Guthrie's charge that he could not predict or explain *actions*, only "cognitions." Here Tolman makes more explicit reference than previously (but see also his concept of positive and negative "demands"—Spence, 1951a, pp. 260 ff.) to "drives and incentive-values within a drive-incentive-value system" (p. 315), thus introducing a more dynamic element and somewhat diluting the purity of his prior emphasis upon cognitive factors alone. Although he by no means completely accepts the particular psychology of hope and fear set forth here, he thus comes appreciably nearer our position and makes brighter still the prospect of a true and basic unification of the field. Incidentally but not unimportantly, in this paper Tolman even acknowledges that some readers may feel that, in at least certain respects, "my formula and Hull's are not significantly different. And, if you do, so much the better. It would indicate that there has been really much common agreement between us in spite of differences of words, phrases, and slogans" (pp. 321–322). And, in like manner, Hull (1952) only a short time before had said that "the fractional goal reaction (r_G) . . . molar foresight or foreknowledge of the not-here and the not-now . . . is probably roughly equivalent to what Tolman has called 'cognition'" (p. 151). For an early effort to compare the systems of Lewin, Tolman, and Hull, see White (1943).

tion is that when signs are followed by *negative* consequences ("effects" for Thorndike, "significates" for Tolman, "unconditioned stimuli" for Pavlov), they acquire the capacity to arouse fear and that when they are followed by *positive* consequences, they acquire the capacity to lessen fear, arouse hope, and (in a manner not yet fully understood, see Chapter 6) to "whet appetites." Thus the organism is internally conditioned, or dynamically structured, so as to make certain behaviors more probable and other behaviors less probable. In this scheme, the organism not only *knows* (believes) but also *goes* (behaves).

VI. Tolman's Theory Made More Explicit and Further Compared with Two-Factor Theory

Because Tolman sometimes employs an esoteric terminology and because his concepts are inherently recondite, it will be useful now, after a once-over-lightly review of his position, to examine it more thoroughly. For this purpose we turn to a paper entitled "Theories of Learning," published in 1934 as a chapter in Moss' *Comparative Psychology*. Here Tolman begins the statement of his own position by referring to it as a "variety of the field theory" (p. 392). He says:

> The present writer starts from the doctrine of Adams and Lewin, but asserts that, for the problem of learning, the important relations in the "psychobiological fields" are "sign relations." "Learning" he would describe as the new formation, or the reformation, of "sign-gestalts" within the larger psychobiological fields. The theory is therefore to be designated a "sign-gestalt" theory.[7]
>
> Sign gestalts are to be conceived as having three parts: a *sign*, a *significate*, and a *behavior-route leading from sign to significate*. A sign-gestalt is equivalent to an "expectation" by the animal that "this" (that is, the sign),

[7] It may help the reader to think of the expression, sign-gestalt theory, as follows. With Lewin, Adams, and others, Tolman, in the passage cited, was saying that organisms "live, move, and have their being" in *fields* (situations, patterns of stimuli, *Gestalten*)—hence the latter half of the modifying expression "sign-gestalt." But he was also saying, somewhat in opposition to the view of more "orthodox" field theorists, that the stimuli which comprise any given field, or situation, have positive or negative potency ("valence," in Lewin's terminology), not because of any inherent properties or physical force they exert upon the organism (in the manner of gravity or electromagnetism), but because they have taken on *sign value* or sign-ificance—which, in the final analysis, is something *inside* the organism—see Section IX. And here enters the first term in the expression "sign-gestalt." Learning is then, in part, the process whereby objects in the field take on meaning or sign value. What *else* learning is was, as we shall see in the next paragraph, less explicit in Tolman's system.

"if behaved to in such and such a way" (that is, the behavior-route), will lead to "that" (that is, the significate). A sign-gestalt sets the animal to "expect" that when he actually behaves, "this" field-feature will lead, "by such and such a behavior-route," to "that" field-feature. And learning, according to the theory, will consist in the making or the remaking of such expectation-sets under the hard tutelage of the outcomes experienced as the result of the actual behaviors that are tried (pp. 392–393).

In order to understand and appreciate Tolman's position, it is necessary to realize that he was aiming at a theory of high generality, one that would reconcile and integrate the facts of conditioning, trial-and-error learning, and the so-called higher learning processes. As he remarked in a still earlier paper, "this new formula for behavior which we would propose is intended as a formula for *all* psychology—a formula to bring formal peace, not merely to the animal worker, but also to the addict of imagery and feeling tone" (1922, p. 3). The relationship between his theory and conditioning is, of course, implicit in the terms *sign* and *significate*, corresponding, as they do, to the Pavlovian terms, conditioned stimulus and unconditioned stimulus. Tolman himself develops this relationship as follows:

The sign-gestalt theory and conditioned reflexes. The sign-gestalt theory asserts that the conditioning of a reflex is the formation of a new sign-gestalt. It asserts that a conditioned reflex, when learned, is an acquired expectation set on the part of the animal that the feature of the field corresponding to the conditioned stimulus will lead, *if the animal but waits,* to the feature of the field corresponding to the unconditioned stimulus (p. 393).

The sign-gestalt theory and sign learning. It is obvious by now that what the sign-gestalt theory does is to reduce all learning to the pattern of sign learning. Sign learning is taken as the prototype for all learning. In sign learning, one field-feature becomes the sign for another field-feature, and the response that appears as a result is appropriate to the temporal and other characteristics of this sign relationship. Such a description has been shown to hold for the conditioned reflex. And, obviously, it holds for the cases that we have specifically labelled sign learning: the dog's response to the sound of my approaching automobile, the "flutter" response of Wever's (1930) cat, and the gentle dropping-off response of Warner's (1932a) rats (p. 396).[8]

Tolman's theory thus articulates readily enough with conditioning theory, provided one is willing to concede that, in the most typical and important instances, what gets conditioned is not a reflex but an *expectation* of some sort. In two-factor theory, "expectations" are of

---

[8] This position has been elaborated and empirically supported in a study reported by Zener (1937), who goes perhaps even further in anticipating present developments by advocating "a sign-urge conception [of learning] in which both reorganization of a perceptual system and its relation to an urge or tension system are essential features" (p. 403).

two major varieties: hopes and fears, representing, respectively, anticipations of good and bad events (significates) to come. But how can
mere sign learning explain changes in behavior of the kinds noted
in trial-and-error learning? At least a provisional answer to this question has already been given, in an earlier chapter, for two-factor
theory. Let us now study Tolman's way of dealing with this problem:

> Trial-and-error learning consists, according to this [sign-gestalt] theory,
> in learning "what" each of the initially alternative responses "leads to."
> Thus, given the situation shown in [Fig. 9–1], the theory says that what
> the animal learns is that the initial field situation F_a, responded to by the
> response R_1, will lead to the resultant field-feature f_1; responded to by
> R_2, will lead to the field-feature f_2; etc. The result of its learning is, thus,
> that F_a becomes the sign for all the different alternative significates f_1, f_2,
> f_3, and so on. Or, in other words, it learns the whole array of alternative
> sign-gestalts, F_a—R_1—f_1, F_a—R_2—f_2, and so on. But the animals's final
> taking of R_3 (the correct response) rather than any of the others is some-
> thing not part of this learning *per se*. It indicates the further fact that under
> the motivation conditions of the moment, the one significate f_3 is more de-
> manded by the animal than are any of the other alternative significates
> f_1, f_2, f_4, and so on (pp. 396–397).

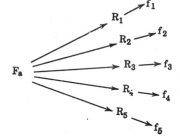

Fig. 9–1. Schematization of trial-and-error learning in terms of sign-gestalt theory (Tolman,
1934, p. 397).

This schematization has some very interesting and suggestive features. First, it will be noted that it differs from the usual fan-shaped
diagram used to represent trial-and-error learning in that, instead of
showing merely a hierarchy of S—R bonds, it attempts to indicate,
in addition, *the effects*, or consequences, that follow any given response. And here we see where the principle of sign learning, or conditioning, may be said to be involved even in trial-and-error, selective-
response learning. Although Tolman speaks of "sign-gestalts" in a
somewhat more inclusive way, it is clear, from the diagram and the
text, that a given response R_1, for example, which is followed by
consequence or significate f_1, will become, in some sense, a *sign* of f_1.

Ordinarily, in conditioning theory, we think of a sign as a stimulus, not as a response; but when we recall that virtually all responses are stimulus-producing, then we can see how the significance, or meaning, of f_1 can become connected, through what may be called *stimulus mediation*, to the response R_1 (see Mowrer, 1960, Chapter 2).

Tolman has already been quoted as saying that "a conditioned reflex, when learned, is an acquired expectation-set on the part of the animal and that the feature of the field corresponding to the conditioned stimulus will lead, *if the animal but waits*, to the feature of the field corresponding to the unconditioned stimulus" (p. 393). In trial-and-error situations, the picture differs in one, and perhaps only one, important respect. Here the animal does not *wait* for the significate or UnCS; instead the animal *produces the UnCS, by its own behavior.* Then, depending upon whether the UnCS is good or bad, the stimuli associated with this behavior take on the capacity to arouse, respectively, hope or fear, and the tendency for the response to recur will be correspondingly increased or decreased.

In order to make more specific the notion that trial-and-error learning is, in the final analysis, dependent upon conditioning, let us take a single "sign-gestalt" segment, or sequence, from Tolman's diagram: e.g., F_a—R_1-f_1. As already noted, in a typically Thorndikian depiction of trial-and-error learning, only the F_a—R_1 part of the sequence would be represented, although R_1-f_1 would be implied (as the *effect* of the R); and learning would be assumed to involve *strengthening* of the F_a—R_1 (S—R) bond. Tolman makes a different assumption, as does revised two-factor theory. Tolman, using a highly molar language, says simply that a total sign-gestalt expectation, F_a—R_1-f_1, is formed. Figure 9–2 shows a more molecular way of thinking about the problem. Here, certain additional details, omitted in Fig. 9–1, are filled in.

Fig. 9–2. A Tolman "sign-gestalt" (top line) made more explicit (below). F_a is a drive (Tolman calls it a "field-feature") which produces some instrument response R_1. This produces certain response-correlated stimuli S_{rc}, shortly followed by f_1, an effect (or "field-feature") which produces some molar response R, of which (r) is the conditionable (hope or fear) component. According to the nature of this "meaning" reaction, one would expect subsequent performance of R_1 to be facilitated or inhibited.

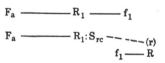

Significate or effect f_1 produces some total response R, of which (r) is the conditionable component. And on the basis of now abundant evidence, it has already been posited that R_1 has certain immediate stimulus consequences, which are represented by S_{rc} (response-correlated stimuli). Therefore when the response-correlated stimuli, S_{rc} are followed by the significate f_1 (unconditioned stimulus), which produces a total reaction R, we expect r to "associatively shift" from f_1 to S_{rc}. The result is that if f_1 is of such a nature as to elicit an r reaction of fear, then the response which produces S_{rc} will tend, subsequently, to be inhibited; whereas, if f_1 is of such a nature as to produce an r reaction of hope (or appetite), then the response which produces S_{rc} will, on future occasions, be facilitated, strengthened. In this way, following leads provided by Tolman and in a manner consistent with assumptions previously made in this book, we *deduce so-called trial-and-error learning from conditioning principles*. Or, said differently, when we make Tolman's sign-gestalt notion $(F_a—R_1-f_1)$ more explicit, we arrive at precisely the same conception of habit acquisition and inhibition as has been delineated in Chapter 7.[9]

At this point there is a temptation to digress and review another paper in which Tolman (1933a) approaches the same problem from a somewhat different angle; however, this paper will be referred to, more appropriately, in another connection (Mowrer, 1960, Chapter 2). Instead, let us conclude our synoptic review of Tolman's thinking with a final quotation from the document under discussion. Here, in reference to "the sign-gestalt theory and the higher forms of learning," Tolman says:

The higher forms of learning were classed, at the beginning of this chapter, as cases in which the final correct response is controlled, at least in part, by temporally absent or by unique, previously unreacted-to features of the field. It now further appears, however, that we must really distinguish between two subclasses. First, there are the delayed reaction type of problem and the double alternation type. In such problems, the situation

[9] Some years ago Youtz (1938) showed that in respect to "reinforcement, extinction and spontaneous recovery," both Pavlovian and trial-and-error learning behave in much the same ways. And recently Miller (1959a), in referring to Youtz's work, has said: "These laws seem to be the same for classically conditioned autonomic as well as for trial-and-error somatic response reinforced by either escape from electric shock or rewarding a hungry animal with food. . . . Proponents of multiple factor theories of learning [see Chapter 3] can attract more serious attention if they can rigorously specify differing laws associated with supposedly different types of learning" (p. 261). If, as we now suppose, conditioning is the primal form of learning and if trial and error is a derivative thereof, the Youtz findings would follow as a matter of course.

is primarily one of *temporal absence*. And, secondly, there are the "reasoning" and "insight" sorts of experiment, in which the situation is both one of temporal absence and one where an important controlling feature has not, *as such*, been experienced as a result of the given behavior but has to be "inferred" (pp. 399–400).

But what, finally, are the new laws, if any, involved in such higher forms of learning? We do not know. We can merely say that these higher forms certainly involve all the laws of mere trial-and-error learning plus some new ones. And the new laws, whatever they may eventually prove to be, will be concerned with the ability to build up sign-gestalts that, on the one hand, include in the sign field features that are temporally past and, on the other hand, include in the significate field-features that are creatively inferred.

Are symbolic processes necessary for building up these sign-gestalts? This is a question that we shall not here attempt to answer. We human beings know from our own experience that such symbolic processes would undoubtedly be helpful. But whether the logic of the situation absolutely requires them, the sign-gestalt theory will not at present attempt to say (pp. 401–402).

Some of the problems referred to in the immediately preceding quotations will be discussed in later chapters, where, with the aid of recent research findings, more satisfactory solutions may be forthcoming (see also Mowrer, 1960). But these passages serve usefully to indicate the wide range of problems with which Tolman has been concerned for more than a quarter of a century and to show his unwillingness to be satisfied with a too simple and manifestly incomplete type of conceptual scheme. Here we should, however, look at one more type of problem to which Tolman has directed attention and which will point up further the similarities and differences between sign-gestalt theory and two-factor theory.

VII. The Problem of So-called Place Learning versus Response Learning

Tolman's theorizing has given rise to a considerable literature on what is known as "place learning" as compared with "response learning." Thorndike, Hull, and others have held that learning is largely a matter of "habit formation" and that "habits" consist of specific S—R bonds, which determine that when a given situation or motivation (S) is present certain responses or response patterns (R) will occur. By contrast, Tolman has stressed cognitions, knowledge—knowledge of certain "means-end relationships," which are purposive and goal-oriented, but which do not involve a stereotyped, fixed form of behavior of any kind. Once a situation has been learned, i.e., "cognitively mapped" (1948), then an organism, according to Tolman, can reach its goal by any of a variety of specific response routes, without prior rehearsal or practice. Having once learned *where* a given goal object is located, the question of *how* to get there presents little or no problem, assuming, that is, that there are not insurmountable physical barriers.

Stimulus-response theories, while stated with different degrees of sophistication, imply that the organism is goaded along a path by internal and external stimuli, learning the correct movement sequences so that they are released under appropriate conditions of drive and environmental stimulation. The alternative possibility is that the learner is following signs to a goal, is learning his way about, is following a sort of map—in other words, is learning not movements but meanings. This is the contention of Tolman's theory of sign learning. The organism learns sign-significate relations; it learns a behavior route, not a movement pattern. Many learning situations do not permit a clear distinction between these two possibilities. If there is a single path with food at the end and the organism runs faster at each opportunity, there is no way of telling whether his responses are being stamped in by reinforcement or whether he is guided by his immanent purposes and cognitions (Hilgard, 1956, pp. 191–192).

No attempt will be made here to review the many studies on this problem of place versus response learning which have now been published. In fact, we shall not even attempt to describe, in exact detail, any one of these studies. But for our purposes it will be useful to consider a simplified or, one may say, "idealized" version of a study reported in 1946 by Tolman, Richie, & Kalish.

Let the reader imagine an elevated open maze forming a perfect cross or "X," with each arm thereof measuring, let us say, six feet in length. Now further imagine that the four arms of the maze are made to point in the cardinal directions of the compass and that a hungry rat is placed at the end of the East arm, with food (not visible at a distance) in a little hole at the end of the North arm. After a few trials, the rat will, of course, go promptly and directly from the East arm to the North arm, and there obtain and eat food. Clearly the rat has thus acquired a "habit," but we cannot say whether this "habit" represents place learning or response learning. However, the issue can be put to the test in the following manner. Suppose that, instead of being released onto the maze from the end of the East arm, the animal, after training of the kind described, is released from the end of the *West* arm. If the "habit" which has been acquired is a matter of *response* learning, the rat will, as before, turn *right* at the choice point, which will take it out onto the *South* arm of the maze. But if the "habit" is a matter of *place* learning, then, at the choice point, the animal will turn *left* and enter, as usual, the North arm of the maze.

On the assumption that, in a situation of the kind described, the rat's initial learning involves the conditioning of hope to *both* place-correlated and response-correlated stimuli, a reasonable surmise would be that when tested in the manner indicated the rat would show (by hesitation and vacillation) some *conflict* at the choice point but might very well decide in favor of the place-correlated stimuli (see also Mowrer, 1960, Chapter 7). If *many* rats were trained and tested as indicated, some of them might persist in turning right at the choice point (and thus moving spatially away from the goal of food); but most of them would probably act more "sensibly" and abandon the "correct" response in favor of the "correct" place. This, in point of fact, has been the common empirical finding (see, for example, Galanter, 1955; Waddell, Gans, Kempner, & Williams, 1955; but see also Scharlock, 1955, and Grice, 1948a, and Bugelski, 1956, pp. 94 ff.); and there has been some tendency to infer from such results "that the disposition to orient toward the goal is simpler and more primitive than the disposition to make right turns (Tolman *et al.*, 1946, p. 228).

But, as is at once evident, one could easily alter the situation so that response learning would predominate. Suppose, for example, that the X-maze were tubular (tunnel-like) rather than open, thus excluding all extra-maze stimuli. It is now likely that place learning would be much less stable than response learning (see Aderman, 1957, 1958). As Tolman, Richie, & Kalish themselves observe, "place-learning is simpler than response-learning [only] in situations where there are marked extra-maze cues" (p. 229).

A strict stimulus-response psychology would seem to demand that the only form of learning which is possible is response learning; whereas a strict "field theory" would perhaps insist that all learning is place learning. But *our* position suggests an intermediate interpretation which squares quite nicely with all the facts: Normally, in so-called habit formation, hope is conditioned *both* to place- and to response-produced stimuli and whether, in case of conflict, one or the other will gain the ascendancy depends upon a number of considerations, including the relative intensity and numerousness of each (cf. Campbell, 1954; Restle, 1957; Robinson & McGill, 1958).

As will now be clear, Tolman and co-workers have been more interested in and have tended to give greater theoretical importance to place learning than to response learning; but, inherently, sign-gestalt theory does not demand that conditioning occur only to environmental stimuli, any more than does revised two-factor theory; conditioning can, and apparently does, occur to proprioceptive and other internal, response-produced stimuli, as well as to environmental, place-produced stimuli. The former type of learning was rather dramatically illustrated, a few years ago, in the following situation. A graduate (Harold Underwood) was teaching several rats to "shuttle," from one compartment to another, by means of a mild electric shock delivered from the floor grills of the compartments. By some coincidence, one rat, on the first occasion when shock was presented in one compartment, escaped from it by *backing* through the little door leading to the other compartment. On the second trial, it so happened that the rat was again facing away from the door and, as before, backed through it. And on the third trial, although this time facing *toward* the door when the shock was presented, the rat nevertheless carefully turned around and *backed out* of the one compartment and into the other one (cf. discussion of Guthrie's theory of learning, Chapter 8). Only on the fourth trial did the rat get the "idea" that *where* he was going was more important than *how* he got there; this time he quickly ran through the doorway head first. Thus we see that *both* place- and response-produced stimuli, if associated with drive reduction, became positively "cathexed" and cause an organism, when subsequently in the same situation, to seek to reinstate them.

It is particularly instructive to consider this issue of place versus response learning in the context of incremental rather than decremental reinforcement. Here it becomes particularly clear that it is not at all a question of either-or but of *both*. Who would seriously debate the question of whether a rat, as a result of going to a particular place two or three times and getting shocked there, would thereafter avoid the place *or* the action that took him there? Obviously, fear would become conditioned both to the *place* where the shock was experienced *and* to the stimuli produced by the antecedent response or response sequence. Having abandoned, once and for all, the bond-stamping-in and bond-stamping-out conception of habit, one sees no point to the question of whether fear gets connected, or connected more strongly, to stimuli associated with a response or with a place. Circumstances will almost certainly alter cases; and since the *principle* involved in both instances is the same, there is no theoretical problem at stake whatever. Here again, then, we see how completely revised two-factor theory dissolves the apparent differences between so-called reinforcement theory and so-called field theory.

In Chapter 8, attention has already been called to some striking similarities between the present approach and that suggested by Mc-Clelland, Atkinson, Clark, & Lowell (1953). This parallelism becomes even more apparent in the following passage:

> The terms *approach* and *avoidance* must not be understood simply as "going towards" or "away from" a stimulus in a spatial sense. Thus "rage," when it goes over into attack, is an "avoidance" response, even though it involves "going towards" something. *Avoidance* must be defined in terms of its objective—to discontinue, remove, or escape from a certain type of stimulation and not in terms of its own characteristics. Attack has, as its objective, removal of the source of stimulation in the same sense that withdrawal does. *Approach* must also be defined functionally—i.e., it is any activity, the objective of which is to continue, maintain, or pursue a certain kind of stimulation (p. 35).

Whether approach activities ultimately have an "avoidance" (abient) motif need not be debated (cf. Chapter 6). What is more immediately to the point is that McClelland *et al.* are saying, apparently in complete accord with what has gone before, that "approach" (in the sense of producing or getting more of a particular stimulus) may involve either movement through space *toward* some stimulus object or mere *bodily* movement with which now desired stimulation is inherently associated. And the same for "avoidance"—it involves either movement through space *away* from some stimulus object or the *inhibition* of bodily movement with which now *un*desired stimulation is inherently associated. Conceived in this way, the issue of place-versus-response learning has only practical interest, and no theoretical importance whatever.

VIII. Place versus Response Learning Further Analyzed

In an earlier mimeographed version of this book, the preceding section of this chapter appeared very much as it does here, and to the writer it seemed quite clearly and fully developed. But as a result of classroom use and discussion, it became apparent that this material had many implications which the writer had not previously explored. Moreover, the students seemed to attach to it special importance and to be unwilling to leave it until their perplexities and interests were fully satisfied. From this reaction to the preceding section, the following additional considerations emerged.

Let us begin by paraphrasing one of the points made in the preceding section. Ordinarily, in a controlled experimental environment, the "right" *response* takes the organism to the "right" *place*. In other words, response learning and place learning coincide. But now, as becomes evident in the Tolman-Richie-Kalish experiment with the X-maze, conditions can be altered so that this is no longer the case. Now, in the test situation, the correct response (a right turn at the choice point) takes the animal to the wrong place; and in order to get to the right place (end of the North arm), the animal has to make the "wrong" response (i.e., has to turn left, rather than right, at the choice point). Or, put otherwise, the place cues now say "do this" whereas the response cues say "do that," and the individual experiences a conflict which will be resolved one way or the other, depending upon whether the place or the response cues are predominant (cf. the Wickens experiment of 1938, cited in Chapter 1; also Gibson & Mowrer, 1938, as discussed in Mowrer, 1960).

But what this analysis overlooks is that in the test situation, the "wrong" response at the choice point (i.e., a turn to the right) might *still* be right, correct. Suppose that on trials when the rat is started from the end of the West maze arm, food is now, in point of fact, at the end of the South arm. If, under these conditions, the animal went to the end of the North arm of the maze, not only would the response be wrong; so also would be the place. And by continued training of this kind, it should be but a short time until the animal would always and unhesitatingly *go right* at the choice point, regardless of the arm on which the animal was introduced to the maze. Here we would have, so to say, an instance of "pure" response learning; just as we would have an instance of "pure" place learning if the animal found that, for example, the food were always in the North arm, regardless of where it was put onto the maze.

Here, perhaps more clearly than before, we see that in theory there is no "opposition" between place and response learning whatever. Both are possible, and each may be uniquely useful, depending upon the circumstances. Fortunately, we have an over-all conception of the nature of learning from which these two "phenotypically" different forms of learning can be equally well derived. "Genotypically," they are the same, i.e., both are dependent upon the conditioning of hopes (or fears) to place-produced and/or response-produced stimuli.

At the risk of perhaps elaborating the obvious, let us look again at the rat which first *backed* from one compartment to the other of the shuttle apparatus and then abandoned this behavior and started running *forward*. Superficially, it looks as if this was a situation calling mainly for place learning; and we are inclined to be amused by the rat's behavior on the first few trials, for the reason that he was making what might seem to be a rather silly mistake. He was "assuming" that *how* he got to the other side of the apparatus was important, when, in point of fact, it made not the least difference—just so long as he got there. And since moving forward is normally, by all odds, a superior form of locomotion as compared with moving backwards, our lowly subject seemed pretty ludicrous.

But as Tolman himself has reminded us (see Mowrer, 1960, Chapter 2) we must not be too "lofty" or hasty in such situations. Here, for all the rat knew, it was entirely possible that the *nature* of the locomotion, as well as its *direction*, was important. And we, as experimenters, could easily have made it so by simply deciding that we would turn the shock off when the rat "shuttled" *only* if he did it backwards. If *this* "rule" had been in force, then the behavior of this particular rat would have been highly efficient—and not funny at all. In other words, response learning is by no means inherently inferior to or more stupid than place learning: it all depends, as we have seen, upon the circumstances; and it is fortunate indeed that living organisms have good potentialities for *both*.

In the preceding section attention is called to the fact that place and response learning may occur either with decremental or incremental reinforcement, i.e., with reward or punishment. We may now note, in addition, that in the latter case, response learning corresponds to what we have previously termed inhibition or *passive avoidance behavior;* and that the corresponding place learning would be, surely, a species of *active avoidance behavior*, i.e., the subject, if put in a *place* where it had previously been shocked, would be strongly instigated to "get out of here." But, we must now ask, is the picture equally clear as far as decremental reinforcement is concerned? Clear, yes, but also a little complicated. If, as a result of such reinforcement, an organism comes to make a particular response, this, manifestly, is response learning. And if he regularly goes to a particular place, regardless of how he gets there, this, equally clearly, is place learning. But we cannot, it seems, here make a distinction between active and passive *approach* behavior, in the same way we have found it possible and convenient to distinguish between active and passive *avoidance* behavior. Instead it seems that the counterpart of passive avoidance behavior is what is here termed *response* learning and that the counterpart of active avoidance behavior is what is here termed *place* learning.[10] Later, in

[10] The "symmetry" of these four situations can be made somewhat more apparent as follows: If, after a series of movements, an organism arrives at a particular place and is there punished, the organism, if at a distance will subse-

connection with our analysis of *discrimination* learning, we shall find that this four-fold classification does not quite exhaust the logical and, indeed, psychological possibilities; but for present purposes it will suffice (cf. also the quotation from McClelland *et al.* appearing at the end of the preceding section).

Here it need only be added that the students referred to at the outset of this section were quite right. This matter of the distinction between place learning and response learning is indeed important. It is, so to say, the "battleground" between stimulus-response bond ("reinforcement") theory and field theory; and if one sees, clearly and fully, how it is that revised two-factor learning theory handles and resolves the attendant issues, then one has a firm and insightful hold upon that theory itself.

IX. Behavior Variability in a More or Less "Open" Field

Psychologists, when studying the so-called trial-and-error behavior of animals under laboratory conditions, have usually employed either a maze or a problem box in which there is *only one* "route" or behavior sequence leading to the goal. Occasionally they have, however, employed situations involving two (or more) equally good ways of reaching the goal. Suppose that on the first trial, in the simple maze shown in Fig. 9–3, a rat (or other laboratory animal) takes the right-hand pathway from the starting box to the goal box. This means, presumably, that the animal had, to begin with, a stronger tendency to take this pathway than to take the other one; and, moreover, he gets reward for having done so. One might expect, therefore, that the animal would immediately *fixate* on this pathway and never try the alternative, left-hand pathway. But this is not what happens. Despite reinforcement for having taken the initially preferred pathway, the rat alternates irregularly from one route to the other.[11]

---

quently refrain from returning thereto (passive avoidance) and if passively placed in the setting where the punishment previously occurred, the organism will strive to escape therefrom (active avoidance). If, on the other hand, after a series of movements, an organism arrives at a particular place and is there rewarded, the organism, if at a distance will subsequently strive to get to this place and if passively placed in the setting where the reward previously occurred, will tend to stay there.

[11] For a somewhat different set of facts and a quite different way of interpreting them, see Guthrie & Horton (1946). These investigators report a considerable degree of stereotypy in cats in a situation involving alternative means of solving a given problem.

Mowrer & Jones (1943) have advanced the suggestion that behavior variability of the kind just described might arise from what Hull (1943) was to term "reactive inhibition." The basic notion here was this: Every activity involves effort, and effort produces fatigue, and fatigue is at least mildly punishing; therefore, even though a behavior sequence is consistently rewarding, it is also somewhat punishing; so that one might expect the stimuli associated with that response to take

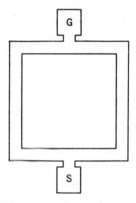

Fig. 9–3. A simple maze with equally satisfactory alternative routes to the same goal. The starting box is labeled S, and the goal box G.

on ambivalent meanings for the subject—"good" because the response leads to a desired goal, "bad" because it involves work (see Chapter 11). This would involve conflict and, conjecturally, would prompt the organism to vary its activities. And from this it was inferred that, other things equal, the greater the expenditure of effort involved in reaching a given goal the greater would be the tendency toward response variability. However, several experiments failed to confirm this inference.

Then it was hypothesized that response variability, at least in a maze situation, might come from the "anticipatory intrusion," early in the maze, of responses (turns) which, on previous runs, have been strongly rewarded (because nearer the goal). A specially designed H-maze seemed to offer a good test of this notion; but the results were again negative (Mowrer, 1950a, pp. 171–173).

Pretty clearly, then, in a situation involving more than one equally (or even unequally—see Whiting & Mowrer, 1943) satisfactory routes to a given goal, there are factors operating other than those which, from the experimenter's point of view, are goal-relevant. Or perhaps we have not as yet grasped some very basic principles of motivation and learning. Of course, the fact that an organism has one drive or motive, such as hunger, does not preclude the possibility that it may simultaneously have other motives: fear, fleas, sex, and so forth. These competing motives would act as "distractions" and, hence, could account for deviations from that type of behavior which might seem, again to the experimenter, to be most efficient and business-like (see Bijou, 1958). Hull (1943), on the other hand, has approached this problem along the following lines:

> At this point we must introduce a factor to be taken up in detail a little later—that of the spontaneous oscillation or variability in habit strength. It will be sufficient here to say only that there is reason to believe that the effective strength of all habits when functioning as reaction potentials is subject to continuous uncorrelated interferences, presumably mainly from processes arising spontaneously within the nervous system, and that the magnitudes of these disturbances are distributed approximately according to the "normal" law of probability. On the assumption that the oscillations in habit strength are largely uncorrelated, it follows that the weaker of two competing habit tendencies will frequently be depressed only slightly when the stronger chances to be depressed relatively much, with the result that the weaker habit will dominate on that occasion (pp. 149–150).

Whether the above is merely *ad hoc* neurologizing or the beginnings of a real explanation is not easy to say. In any event, this approach to the problem has not been generally accepted; and other psychologists have continued to search for more strictly psychological solutions.

Some experiments, largely unpublished, which have been carried out at the University of Michigan promise to shed new light upon this perplexing matter. These have been briefly reviewed by Dr. William N. Dember in a seminar report, given in 1954, which reads in part as follows:

> The general problem I am going to discuss is, essentially, the problem of choice. It concerns the prediction of what an organism will do when faced with two or more alternatives. This is really the basic question of motivation—which alternative will the organism take? Is there some order with respect to the alternatives it will choose? Can you predict from one choice to the next? I'll be forced to talk about overt, observable choice, i.e., motor response, but contained in what I'm saying will be implicit the notion that at least some of it refers to cognitive events—the sequence of ideas and percepts which are not directly observable.

After referring to the "reactive inhibition" theory of behavior variability and to certain related experiments (cf. Glanzer, 1953; Montgomery, 1951a, 1954), Dember goes on to say:

> There is a set of experiments by Dr. C. R. Brown of this department which I thought you should all become familiar with. Dr. Brown was in-

terested in the exploratory behavior of rats in simple, unstructured situations. He built an enormous round table which would just about fit into this room. The rat finds himself sitting in the middle of this table—and Dr. Brown is up by the ceiling looking down and recording what the rat does. And it turns out to be some of the most consistent behavior ever observed.

Suppose the rat makes a little excursion to the east. It is predictable with almost perfect certainty that the rat will return to where he started from: if he walks away from the place where he first found himself, he will return there. That is one of the main principles that comes out of Dr. Brown's work. [See references in Chapter 6 to exploratory behavior and its probable relation to fear.]

What does the rat do next? He makes another excursion, this time to the west—that is, in the opposite direction from his previous excursion. On this second trip he'll venture a little farther than he did on the first. And again he'll return. The rat makes another excursion; this time I don't think it's possible to predict the direction, except that it will *not* be east or west. Let's say the rat goes north on the third trip. On the fourth he'll travel south. From rat to rat and day to day this pattern shows up perfectly.

Now let us return to the original problem. How do you modify what seems to be such a basic pattern of behavior? What can you do to the environment that will change this nice sequence of east-west, north-south? This Dr. Brown has also answered.

Suppose you put a little wooden box somewhere on the table. And the rat is again placed in the middle of the table. At first you will get the pattern previously described, if the box is far enough from the rat so that he can't see it clearly. When, however, in the course of his excursions the rat comes upon the box, the pattern of his behavior is markedly changed. The rat spends most of his time sniffing around this object. If there is another object somewhere else in the field, he'll spend a lot of time exploring one and then move over to the other, play around with that for a while and return to the first one. In short, what the rat now does is to orient his behavior around these objects. Again, it seems that the presence of differential complexity in one portion of the environment disrupts the basic pattern of alternation.

This is the principle that Robert Earl and I were interested in when we built the infinity-maze. One of the things we wanted to find out was whether we could manipulate the visual environment of the rat with respect to this variable of complexity in such a way as to modify the general alternation of pattern. We didn't want to use objects as Dr. Brown has done, because this might lead to problems of interpretation. We searched for visual patterns that would work as his objects had (pp. 9–11).

More recently, an account of the research just described (with the "infinity maze") has been published by Dember, Earl, & Paradise (1956) in a paper entitled, "Between- and Within-Stimulus Alternation; the Response to Differential Stimulus Complexity," which begins:

Krechevsky (1937a, 1937b) has shown that under certain conditions normal rats tend to select the more variable of two paths to similar goals. Butler

(1953), Montgomery (1954), and Myers and Miller (1954) have demonstrated that animals will perform specific acts if the acts are instrumental in providing the animals with interesting environments.

The present experiments, on the empirical level, fit well into such a context. Abstractly, they derive from the authors' concern with the particular problem of alternation and the more general problem of choice-behavior. Both of the experiments presented in this article involve the following procedure. Naive, "satiated" rats are given access over extended periods of time to two contiguous circular pathways. The animals can move freely within and between paths. The walls of one circle are lined with a simple pattern. The pattern in the adjacent circle is relatively more complex. That aspect of choice-behavior which is of primary concern here is *the relative amount of time spent responding to each stimulus* (p. 1).

And the authors state, in summary:

In both experiments the records were analyzed using three arbitrary time units. Data were presented for only one of these analyses, since all three yield substantially the same results. In both experiments the results closely conformed to prediction [that more time would be spent in the visually complex portion of a "maze" than in the visually simple portion] (p. 13).

What is one to make of findings such as these? And how do they bear upon the particular type of thinking which is being explored in this volume?

In Chapter 1 (cf. also Sears *et al.*, 1957) a tentative distinction was made between "learning theory" and "behavior theory," the latter being presumably more inclusive than the former. Perhaps, in the studies just cited, the question is less one of what is *learned* than it is, given a particular set of circumstances, of what will an organism *do?* The answer to the latter question presupposes a knowledge of what has been learned, but something more: a knowledge of prevailing environmental conditions. Still, we try to be objective in our study of learning, i.e., we are inclined to use *performance* criteria of learning; and with this we are back at the point of having to be able to predict and explain *behavior* in order to talk meaningfully about *learning.*

Certainly, in the objective study of learning, we have to take primary, metabolically produced drives into account and we also have to acknowledge the secondary drives that are cued off by various forms of stimulation. But perhaps we have been, even so, too narrow in the variables which we have noted and on the basis of which we seek to make predictions. As already suggested, the mere fact that a rat (or a college student) is hungry does not, forthwith, prevent him from being "interested" in things other than food. And if interests—i.e., an organism's hopes and fears—vary in a somewhat uncontrollable manner, it follows that behavior will also have considerable fluidity. Such a view lacks the systematic rigor which one ideally seeks in science, but we do not want a theory which is more "rigorous" than the reality to which it applies. Perhaps, as we go from highly to less highly structured situations, the degree of predictability necessarily drops. Or, as the Dember work suggests, it may be that behavior remains predictable but that we must take other, previously neglected variables into account: e.g., visual complexity. Eventually, as we move from highly structured to unstructured, or "open," situations, the number of variables one has to take into account becomes unmanageably large and precise prediction breaks down, and all one can do is to speak in terms of tendencies or probabilities (see Mowrer, 1960, Chapters 8 and 9).

It is possible that, even in such controlled environments as those provided by mazes, some of the so-called "errors" made by an organism are, from its point of view, not errors at all but instead represent behavior relevant to motives and goals which, for the moment, are of transcendant importance to the organism, though nonexistent for the experimenter. Ideally, rats in a maze are all monomaniacs; but, in practice, they probably have a number of things "on their minds" at any given time, and it need not surprise us if their behavior sometimes shows this multiplicity of motivation.

Elsewhere (Mowrer, 1960, Chapter 6) an attempt is made to relate the main body of revised two-factor learning theory more specifically to the problem of response selection and "choice"; but, in passing, reference should be made to a parenthetical comment appearing in the paper by Dember previously cited, to wit:

> The distinction between stimulus and response is not a useful one; what we mean by response, at least in the present context, is response-feedback, which is no different in formal properties from any other source of stimulation (p. 5).

This statement agrees well with one of the basic assumptions involved in revised two-factor theory, and suggests the direction in which the integration of habit theory and field theory can most felicitously move. As Dember implies, a response is most accurately and meaningfully defined in terms of the stimulation it produces; and our assumption is that responses are reinforced, positively or negatively, and subsequently repeated or restrained on precisely the same basis. Thus, psychologically speaking, responses *are* stimuli; but obviously, there can be stimuli other than those which are response-produced. The total "field," psychologically speaking, therefore consists of both extrinsic and response-correlated stimuli and their attendant meanings; and these meanings are being constantly collated, compared, and organized into "choices," i.e., specific actions and inactions. But more detailed reference to this process should be reserved for a later discussion of the role of consciousness (Mowrer, 1960, Chapter 7).

X. Hull on the Problem of "Behavior in Relation to Objects in Space"

As I see it, the moment one expresses in any very general manner the various potentialities of behavior as dependent upon the simultaneous status of one or more variables, he has the substance of what is currently called field theory. My habit-family hypothesis is presumably a field principle in this sense. It is probable that my equation expressing the goal gradient hypothesis (gradient of reinforcement) and even the one expressing the generalization gradient (gradient of irradiation of Pavlov) might also qualify as bits of field theory. On the other hand, some might object to this usage on the ground that equations of this nature are not peculiar to gravitational or electromagnetic fields but are almost universal in natural science theory. Moreover the variables and the constants, together with their inter-relationships, which have so far appeared in equations expressing behavior theories, seem to differ radically from those which appear in the equations of physical field theories. The notable lack of such equations in current Gestalt field formulations, while paradoxical, is probably symptomatic. For such reasons I prefer to be rather sparing in my use of the expression "field theory"; if one has the substance, the use of the term is scientifically unimportant however valuable it may be for purposes of propaganda. But if one means by field theory what I had indicated, I am all for it and I see no inherent disagreement on this point between stimulus-response theory and Gestalt theory (Hull, 1943, p. 287).

Finally, a word about Hull's remark on the poor way in which such field theorists, as I, are handling field theory. I suppose that Mr. Hull will understand that even the cry "Let's take field theory away from the field theorists" would be sweet music for the latter. I am even optimistic enough to believe that, in time, Hull and I will agree as to the main characteristics of field theory, in particular that this is a method of analyzing causal relations and constructing theories and concepts rather than a "theory" in the usual sense of the term. In the meantime what counts is that after a decade of refutation, psychology is turning more and more toward field theory (Lewin, 1943, p. 290).

If he could have lived until 1952, Lewin would have had the satisfaction of seeing his prophecy fulfilled; for in that year Hull published a book containing a chapter with the title appearing in the heading of the present section. Here he attempted to articulate his own systematic views with some of the problems with which field theory has been particularly concerned. As he points out in the beginning of this chapter, "All behavior must necessarily occur in space [but] students of behavior have for the most part not explicitly recognized approach and avoidance behavior as a division of psychology requiring special and distinctive treatment" (p. 215). Instead, they have been largely preoccupied with the process whereby an organism comes to make a specific response to a specific stimulus or situation. Here the emphasis is upon what Murray (1938) has called "actones," i.e., specific muscular contractions and movements, as opposed to *acts*, which are defined more in terms of the attainment of a particular goal than in terms of the exact behavioral elements involved.[12]

In his approach to this problem, Hull makes extended use of Holt's terms, "adience" and "abience," but defines and systematizes them in his own way. Here it is not possible to give a complete summary of Hull's chapter, because of its complexity and length; but there are a few paragraphs near the end which give the historical context of the problem as Hull saw it and the gist of his own mature thinking about it:

> The facts of adience and abience are so obvious in animal behavior that they cannot be overlooked. Adience has been widely employed by animal psychologist as an indicator of the results of learning in the greatest variety of situations. Unfortunately this has been done with little or no explicit recognition of the inherent complexities involved in the process itself. It is believed that this is the reason for some of the theoretical confusion regarding maze learning.
>
> The first important publication in the field of behavior of organisms toward objects in space was by Lewin in 1933. An amplification of substantially the same material was published as a book in 1935. These works presented an exceedingly valuable analysis of the general field, and raised at a qualitative level a large number of problems concerning behavior toward objects in space which have occupied the attention of subsequent workers, even

---

[12] As opposed to the general disposition on the part of American psychologists, during the past several decades, to think response-wise rather than "spatially," we may cite a remark made in 1938 by Woodworth: "Since neither chain reflex nor motor pattern accounts for the rat's behavior in the maze, we ask once more what it is that the animal learns. The most obvious answer, which has been given repeatedly by investigators in describing the rat's concrete behavior, though avoided in their theories, is simply that the rat learns the place. By place we mean a concrete situation containing *objects in spatial relations*" (p. 135). It is hoped that we now have a theory that accommodates both forms of learning with equal felicity.

though Lewin himself seemed not to have been much interested in the spatial problems as such.

In 1938 the present writer published a manuscript written in 1934, which attempted to apply a quantitative mathematical analysis to some of these problems, in particular to those involving the goal gradient hypothesis. Since the manuscript was already written on the basis of the by-then-abandoned logarithmic formulation of the goal gradient, this form of the hypothesis appears in the published study. This article gave what is believed to be the first quantitative mathematical derivation of the problem of adient-abient equilibrium. It also gave quantitative analyses of several forms of the barrier problem. The author's present view is that these latter analyses are defective in that the principle of afferent stimulus interaction and stimulus patterning was not employed (Hull, 1943, pp. 349 ff.).

Around the year 1940, Neal E. Miller, in association with Judson S. Brown and several others, began an exceedingly sagacious and ingenious experimental attack on this series of problems, employing albino rats as subjects. Fortunately as early as 1942 Brown published in detail a part of this experimental work, together with the important germinal idea that the goal gradient principle is not the only factor operating in open space. He says:

"It can be shown, however, that a number of these facts are also in accord with the concept of the *spatial generalization of conditioned responses*" (Brown, 1942, p. 209).

In the opinion of the present writer, the principle just quoted constitutes the most important single advance recently made in this field. As the reader has already seen, it has been exploited on a large scale in the foregoing chapter. While much of the work of Miller and his associates had not been published, owing to the participation of both Miller and Brown in the war effort, Miller was able in 1944 to include a summary of much of it in his chapter, "Experimental Studies in Conflict," which appeared in Hunt's *Personality and the Behavior Disorders* (Miller, 1944, pp. 431 ff.). Miller's theoretical analysis is essentially behavioristic in nature and while technically qualitative in form, clearly advances the subject to a new high level. The experimental results are admirably quantitative (Hull, 1952, pp. 270–272).

From this last quotation we see that, in his final work, Hull, who was in some way the most outstanding habit theorist of his generation, was moving toward common ground with the field theorists. It is believed that this confluence of two great streams of psychological thought is faciltated by revised two-factor learning theory and that further unification and strengthening of this area of psychology can be confidently expected in the years immediately ahead.

10

Gradients of Reinforcement (Type-D and Type-I) and Temporal Integration

It has long been known that learning occurs most readily when a stimulus or response (which produces stimuli) is followed immediately by reward or punishment; but it is also well established that a reinforcing state of affairs (type-D or type-I) can be somewhat delayed and still have an effect. These facts have given rise to the notion of a declining *gradient* in the effectiveness of a reinforcement as its occurrence is more and more removed in time from the stimulus or response with which it is associated (Fig. 10–1). The purpose of the present chapter is to examine this phenomenon in the context of revised two-factor learning theory. And because a stimulus that is *spatially* far or near with respect to an organism is likely also to be temporally remote or proximate, the topic of reinforcement gradients follows naturally upon the discussion, in the preceding chapter, of field theory.

I. The Question of Backward Conditioning

Before proceeding with the main business of this chapter, it will be useful to consider a side issue: namely, the question of whether conditioning can occur only in the *forward* direction or can also occur "backwards." The Polish neurophysiologist, J. Konorski (1950), has treated this problem in a particularly trenchant manner. He begins with this definition of conditioning:

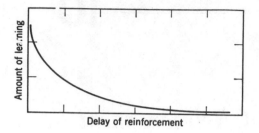

Delay of reinforcement

Fig. 10–1. Learning as a (hypothetical) function of the interval between the occurrence of a stimulus S (or a response R which produces stimuli) and the occurrence of reinforcement (decremental or incremental). The resulting curve is commonly called the *gradient of reinforcement.*

If two stimulus s_1 and s_2 are applied in overlapping sequence, the stimulus s_1 being antecedent, then, with repetition of such combination, a plastic change in the nervous system is formed, consisting in the stimulus s_1 acquiring the ability to elicit the response of the same kind as [that made to] the stimulus s_2 (p. 413).

Then Konorski says:

In our definition we have introduced two statements which need a more detailed examination.

The first is the assumption that the "direction" of conditioning is determined by the sequence of the stimuli applied, i.e., that the antecedent stimulus is always conditioned and the subsequent stimulus is conditioning. This assumption is based on the vast experimental evidence collected both in Russia (cf. Konorski, 1948, p. 19) and in America (cf. Hilgard & Marquis, 1940, p. 174). It goes to show that if a "neutral" stimulus is preceded by an unconditioned stimulus the conditioned reflex to the neutral stimulus either fails to be established at all or is insignificant and evanescent. It has been claimed that "backward conditioning" (as it is called) *can* be successfully elaborated (Schnirman, 1925; Switzer, 1930; Nezdanova, 1940), but as the experiments yielding the negative result are abundant and unequivocal while those yielding the positive result contain some possibilities of error, we deem that the hypothesis concerning the sequence of stimuli in the process of conditioning is well substantiated (p. 414).

Quite a different type of evidence for believing that conditioning is normally and predominantly (if not exclusively) in the forward direction has been advanced by both Pavlov and Hull. In the introductory chapter of his famous book, *Conditioned reflexes,* Pavlov (1927) says that one can, in fact, speak equally of *signal* reflexes; and in support of this basic notion he says:

Let us return now to the simplest reflex from which our investigations started. If food or some rejectable substance finds its way into the mouth, a secretion of saliva is produced. The purpose of this secretion is in the case of food to alter it chemically, in the case of a rejectable substance to dilute and wash it out of the mouth. This is an example of a reflex due to the physical and chemical properties of a substance when it comes into contact with the mucuous membrane of the mouth and tongue. But, in addition to this, a similar reflex secretion is evoked when these substances are placed at a distance from the dog and the receptor organs affected are only those of smell and sight. Even the vessel from which the food has been given is sufficient to evoke an alimentary reflex complete in all its details; and, further, the secretion may be provoked even by the sight of the person who brought the vessel, or by the sound of his footsteps. All these innumerable stimuli falling upon the several finely discriminating distance receptors lose their power for ever as soon as the hemispheres are taken from the animal, and those only which have a direct effect on mouth and tongue still retain their power. The great advantage to the organism of a capacity to react to the former stimuli is evident, for it is in virtue of their action that food finding its way into the mouth immediately encounters plenty of moistening saliva, and rejectable substances, often nocuous to the mucuous membrane, find a layer of protective saliva already in the mouth which rapidly dilutes and washes them out. Even greater is their importance when they evoke the motor component of the complex reflex of nutrition, i.e., when they act as stimuli to the reflex of seeking food.

Here is another example—the reflex of self-defense. The strong carnivorous animal preys on weaker animals, and these if they waited to defend themselves until the teeth of the foe were in their flesh would speedily be exterminated. The case takes on a different aspect when the defense reflex is called into play by the sights and sounds of the enemy's approach. Then the prey has a chance to save itself by hiding or by flight.

How can we describe, in general, this difference in the dynamic balance of life between the normal and the decorticated animal? What is the general mechanism and law of this distinction? It is pretty evident that under natural conditions the normal animal must respond not only to stimuli which themselves bring immediate benefit or harm, but also to other physical or chemical agencies—waves of sound, light, and the like—which in themselves only *signal* the approach of these stimuli; though it is not the sight and sound of the beast of prey which is in itself harmful to the smaller animal, but its teeth and claws (pp. 13–14).

Thus we see that the fundamental and most general function of the hemispheres is that of reacting to signals presented by innumerable stimuli of interchangeable significance (p. 15).

What Pavlov did *not* see, of course, was the motivational and mediational significance of conditioned responses. He took no cognizance whatever of the fact, as we now perceive it, that signals of danger arouse *fear* and that signals of safety and satisfaction arouse *hope* and that these two powerful inner forces then largely determine and direct external, objective behavior. Pavlov, along with the other reflexologists, completely by-passed these phenomena and, in so doing, prevented his theorizing and experimentation from having the maximal generality and power which they might otherwise have attained. But Pavlov saw some things with great clarity, and among these was certainly the fact that conditioning, in order to be biologically meaningful and useful, must be a forward- rather than backward-occurring process.

Hull, similarly, in a paper which was published in 1929 with the title "A Functional Interpretation of the Conditioned Reflex," stressed the "biological utility" which arises, "blindly but beautifully," from the circumstance that living organisms, through the mechanism of conditioning, can react to signals adaptively, in advance of the occurrence of the event signified. Stimuli which come *after* a significant event (either "positive"—helpful, or "negative"—harmful) obviously cannot function as *signals* of such an event; and there would therefore be no reason why such stimuli should become capable of eliciting any part of the response made to the event itself. On the other hand, as has been abundantly demonstrated, a stimulus which characteristically occurs in advance of a significant event can be extremely useful if it becomes connected to some part of the reaction called out by the event itself. Hence the theoretical assumption and the empirical evidence that conditioning is a *forward*, rather than backward, process. Therefore, in the present chapter, in speaking of *gradients* of reinforcement, we shall consistently assume that we are speaking of variation in learning as a function of the time interval between some stimulus or response and an *ensuing* reinforcement, decremental or incremental.[1]

[1] Thorndike (1933), Muenzinger *et al.* (1936), and a few other writers have entertained the idea, on the basis of certain research findings, that the gradient of reinforcement, at least as far as reward is concerned, may be "bidirectional." This possibility is discussed and evaluated in Hilgard & Marquis' volume, *Conditioning and Learning* (1940). Because later research and theory have not supported this notion, it will not be further considered here. The reader will likewise find no consideration here of Hull's early postulations concerning the so-called "goal-gradient" (1932), also discussed by Hilgard & Marquis. Later work has shown that it is a derivative rather than primary phenomenon and of less importance than was formerly supposed. A somewhat related notion will, however, be discussed in Chapter 12. For further evidence that conditioning occurs only in the forward direction, see Perkins (1955), who says: "This interpretation is strongly supported by recent work (Borasio, 1952; Fitzwater & Reisman, 1952; Mowrer & Aiken, 1954; Spooner & Kellogg, 1947) which rather clearly indicates that effective conditioning occurs only when the CS precedes the US. Instances of apparent backward or strictly simultaneous conditioning can all be explained as special cases of pseudoconditioning. Pseudoconditioning, in turn, appears to be only a special instance of the operation of stimulus generalization (Wickens & Wickens, 1942)" (p. 345). And Deese (1952) cites Spooner

II. Delayed Reinforcement Type-D, Intrinsic Stimuli

Experiments on delayed reinforcement may be expected, on the basis of revised two-factor learning theory, to fall into *four* major categories. In the first place, they may be classified according to whether they employ decremental reinforcement or incremental reinforcement, i.e., reward or punishment; and, in the second place, they may be cross-classified according to whether the stimulus or stimuli which the reinforcement follows is extrinsic (environmentally produced) or intrinsic (response produced). It so happens that one or more experiments of each of these four types have been reported in the literature, with results that conform very acceptably to what one would expect on the basis of theory.

The type of delay-of-reinforcement study which happens to have the longest and largest history is that involving decremental reinforcement of intrinsic, response-produced stimuli, i.e., the so-called delayed-reward type of experiment (not to be confused with the delayed-*response* type of experiment; see Mowrer, 1960, Chapter 6). It will be recalled, from Chapter 2, that Thorndike, in his 1913 formulation of the Law of Effect, explicitly recognized that reward and punishment are effective in proportion to their proximity to antecedent behavior. He said:

The strengthening effect of satisfyingness (or the weakening effect of annoyingness) upon a bond varies with the closeness of the connection between it and the bond (1913, p. 4).

In fact, more than a decade earlier, Thorndike (1898) had made at least passing reference to the phenomenon, as follows:

Now the process of learning here consists of the selection, from among a number, of a certain impulse to act in connection with a certain situation. And our first business is to discover the cause of that selection. The result of such discovery was dogmatically stated in the previous lecture. "Any impulse to act which, in a given situation, leads to pleasurable feelings, tends to be connected more firmly with that situation; . . . I say *tends* because the pleasurable feelings must follow the act with certain limits of time . . . (p. 71).

& Kellogg (1947) for the observation "that the percentage of backward conditioned responses is initially high, but *decreases* during training" (p. 82), thus suggesting that it is an artifact due to some sort of sensitization. The only writer who has, within recent years, seriously questioned this view is Razran (1956a).

And, on a later page of the same study, Thorndike remarked that "the pleasurable feeling may not be contemporaneous with the act, but may come considerably later, and the act itself and impulse thereto may not be in the least pleasurable" (pp. 79–80).

Although the term, "gradient of reinforcement," was apparently first used by Miller & Miles in 1935, it is thus evident that the facts denoted by this expression had been recognized in technical psychological literature since the turn of the century; and one would suppose that they had been known, on the basis of common observation, for thousands of years. It is therefore surprising to discover that, in 1916, John B. Watson, then president of the American Psychological Association, published a paper in which he questioned the reality of this phenomenon on theoretical grounds and, stranger still, reported experimental observations tending to support his skepticism. More extensively reported elsewhere (Watson, 1917), this experiment was summarized, in the *Psychological Bulletin* (Watson, 1916a), as follows:

The purpose of this experiment was to throw light upon the factors which govern the stamping in of successful movements and the stamping out of unsuccessful movements. According to Thorndike the resulting *pleasure* from a successful act stamps in the reaction. Other investigators hold that the stamping in of a successful act depends upon the principles of *recency* and *frequency* and is not dependent upon the pleasantness or unpleasantness resulting from the activity.

A small experimental beginning was made upon this problem. Two groups of animals (rats), closely similar in age, docility, body weight, etc., were chosen. The problem box used was a modification of the sawdust box. The animal had to learn to scratch under a bank of sawdust, find a small hole an inch and a half in diameter, crawl under the sawdust box, and mount through an opening to a raised floor. Screwed to the floor of the problem box was a small metal food dish covered by a perforated metal disc. The metal disc could be opened from the outside. The experiment was conducted as follows: The animal was put into the restraining cage and allowed to work until the problem was solved. With one group the metal disc was raised immediately upon the entrance of the animal and the animal was allowed to feed until his appetite was appeased. In the other group the metal disc was not raised until thirty seconds *after* the animal had entered the problem box. During those thirty seconds the animals in this group were very active, biting and tearing at the metal food dish, running around the cage, etc. At the end of thirty seconds the metal disc was raised and the animals allowed to appease their hunger.

The learning curves for the two groups of animals were almost exactly identical (p. 77).

Any student of modern behavior theory can at once suggest why Watson failed to obtain a difference in the learning of the immediate-reward and delayed-reward groups in the experiment just described: the delay of feeding delayed primary reinforcement, but it did *not* delay secondary reinforcement (cf. Chapters 4 and 5). Sight of the food container and, very possibly, odors from the food itself could easily have mediated the latter effect and thus "bridged the gap" between the instrumentally effective digging behavior and the primary reinforcement provided by the food when consumed, somewhat later. However, it was a good many years before this explanation was forthcoming.

In the meantime, in 1927, Warden & Haas performed an experiment somewhat similar to that of Watson and obtained similar results. These writers stated the objective of their investigation by asking:

Does the fixation of a pattern response, such as a maze habit, proceed more effectively and speedily wnen the reward immediately follows the performance? What, in fact, are the results of a progressive series of intervals of delay upon the rate of learning? The present study is a preliminary report of a systematic investigation of this general problem (p. 108).

Instead of the problem box which Watson used, Warden & Haas used a multiple (eight-unit) U-maze, at the end of which was located a food box approximately 18 inches square. A small metal food dish was screwed to the floor of this box; and an inverted funnel, heavily weighted with lead, was suspended above the dish so that, by means of a cord, it could be let down over the dish and then, after a time, lifted. Say the authors: "Perforations in the funnel permitted normal olfactory stimuli during the period of delay" (p. 111).

In this experiment, with one group of rats the funnel was lifted, thus giving access to the food, as soon as the food box was entered. With a second group there was a delay of one minute; and with another group, a delay of five minutes. All three groups were closely comparable in terms of three criteria of maze mastery: "trials, errors, and time." Say the authors:

We must conclude that a 5-minute interval between the pattern response to be learned and the feeding activity has no disadvantageous effect upon the fixation of the maze habit. In fact, the value for both trials and errors are —in most instances—slightly lower than those of the control [no delay] group, although this difference in favor of the 5-minute group is in no case significant. . . . The average total time spent within the maze was, however, somewhat greater for the 5-minute group . . . (p. 112).

This latter result must be considered as so much evidence against the law of effect, insofar as the latter insists that the value of the "satisfying state" is a function of its "nearness in time" to the act, or series of acts to be fixated (p. 116).

Even more striking are the results of an experiment, evidently not known to Warden & Haas, which had been reported by Simmons in 1924. For 10 days prior to the experiment proper, rats were fed in a particular cage. The animals were then divided into two groups and required to run a maze as a means of getting to this cage. One group received food immediately upon getting into the cage or goal box; the other group had to wait for food *one and one-half hours*. Even with so long a delay as this, there was no clear difference in the maze performance of the delayed- and the immediate-feeding groups.

In 1929, Hamilton (née Haas) again attacked the problem of delayed reward but with procedures which were rather different from those employed in the preceding studies. First she made a study of the effect of delayed reward (food) upon the willingness of rats to cross a lightly charged grill. Once having crossed the grill, the rats, instead of being admitted immediately into the eating compartment and being delayed there, were delayed in a sort of "anteroom." Under these circumstances, it was found that a delay-of-reward of as little as *15 seconds* was sufficient to reduce the willingness of rats to cross the electrified barrier; and the effect was even more marked with a group of animals which were delayed three minutes, after crossing the grill, before being allowed to enter the food compartment.

In a second study, Hamilton required her subjects to learn to run a maze, with the same arrangement for delaying reward: i.e., the animals, after getting through the maze, were either admitted immediately to the food compartment and fed or were delayed, in a "restraining compartment," for one minute, three, five, or seven minutes. "After the period of delay was over, the animal was permitted to enter the food box . . . as in the control group" (p. 175). All groups learned to run the maze, but the no-delay group learned it most readily. There was, however, no very clear difference between the four delay groups, though all were clearly inferior to the no-delay group.

Mrs. Hamilton has the following to say by way of explaining the difference between her own findings and those of the study previously carried out by her and Warden:

The previous study differed from the present one in one important respect: the animal was delayed in the same compartment with the food. That is, in the former experiment the animal was directly stimulated by the presence of the unobtainable food, whereas in the present case the direct stimulation of the food could occur only after the animal was released from the delay compartment into the food box. In the present experiment the matter of place of delay was much better controlled—the delay compartment was entirely separated from the food compartment. Evidently the situation of being delayed in the same place with the food, even though the latter be inaccessible, has little or no effect on the fixation process (p. 195).

By way of interpretation, Hamilton continues:

It would seem to be impossible to relate our findings in any very important way to the law of effect as formulated by Thorndike. . . .

As a corollary to the law of effect, Thorndike develops the principle that the strength of the bond is determined by the temporal closeness of the response and the satisfying of annoying state which follows. If we assume, as Thorndike seems to, that the incentive (food) produces a satisfying state, then our results would suggest that very definite restriction must be placed upon the value of the temporal factor in this type of learning. For, while any interval, within the limits investigated, cuts down very markedly the efficiency of the learning process, the longer intervals were hardly more effective than the shorter. Our results do not afford us a basis for conjecture as to whether delay operated as a positive "punishment" or merely as a distraction from the incentive situation in a purely negative sense, nor do they offer any clues as to the physiological (or neurological) processes underlying the behavior called out (pp. 197–198).

With present-day knowledge, it is now possible to see why there was little or no differentiation in the learning of the various delayed-reward groups used in the Hamilton maze study: the stimulation provided by the delay compartment was associated, each time a subject was released into the food compartment, with primary reinforcement, and so acquired secondary reinforcement potency. Therefore, getting into the delay compartment, although not so satisfactory as being allowed to pass directly through it into the food compartment, was still somewhat rewarding; and this satisfaction was experienced immediately upon entering the delay compartment and apparently in about the same degree, regardless of the length of time (within the limits used) that the animal was retained therein. Thus, although the use of a delay box represents an advance over the types of procedure used by Watson, by Simmons, and by Warden & Haas, it still did not provide an entirely satisfactory way of demonstrating the diminishing effectiveness of progressively delayed reward.[2] This problem was,

[2] The Simmons study, previously cited, apparently failed to reveal a gradient of primary reinforcement for the following reason. Although no food was in the feeding compartment during the delay period, the fact that the compartment had been previously associated (during the preliminary training) with eating seems to have given it, from the outset, considerable secondary reinforcement potency and to have caused entry into it to be about as effective in rewarding maze learning as was immediate primary reward. Cf. the Saltzman study discussed in Chapter 4.

however, largely solved by a different procedure employed in a study reported by Roberts, in 1930.

The apparatus used in the Roberts study is shown in Fig. 10–2. Hungry rats were released, individually, from the starting box shown at the right into the "problem box" (center). The correct response for gaining access to the feeding compartment, at the left, was touching the small strip of wood which can be seen suspended by a string

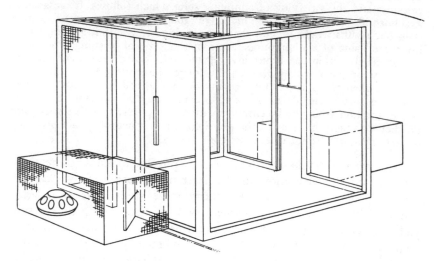

Fig. 10–2. Sketch of apparatus used by Roberts (1930, p. 36) in one of the first experiments which adequately controlled secondary reinforcement in studying the gradient of primary reinforcement. The compartment at the right is the starting box, the one at the left the goal box.

from the ceiling of the main compartment. Four groups of rats, 10 to the group, were used as subjects. The rats in one group, upon touching the piece of wood, were given immediate access to the food compartment, while in the other three groups, there was a delay of 5, 10, and 30 seconds, respectively. Learning, on successive trials, was measured in all groups by recording with a stopwatch the time elapsing between release from the starting box and the occurrence of the correct, or "key," response. The results are shown in Fig. 10–3. Of them the author says:

The "learning curves" for the different groups showed distinctly the effect of the different periods of delay. The longer the delay, the slower was "learning" and the less prompt and stable the behavior pattern at the conclusion of the experiment.

It should be noted that a variation of procedure led to results quite at variance with those published by Watson in 1917 and by Warden & Haas in 1927 (p. 36). [Because of its recency, the Hamilton study was evidently not known to Roberts.]

Although Roberts makes no attempt to construct a reinforcement gradient on the basis of his results, he regards his findings as clearly supporting Thorndike's assumption that reward becomes progressively less effective as it is removed in time from the occurrence of a specific instrumental act. Why earlier investigators, using different procedures, had found no evidence for such a gradient was not entirely clear to Roberts; but in the following remarks he shows a good, intuitive understanding of the concept of secondary reinforcement.

In any such *serial* action, each stage must in itself be a "reward" for the immediately preceding activity [compare Skinner's later (1938) concept of "response chaining"]. To be in the chamber, close to the food box and subject to olfactory stimulation [as in the Watson experiment] was a very large part of the consummatory situation. In anthropomorphic terms, the animals *knew* where the food was and were only puzzled by the apparently irrational

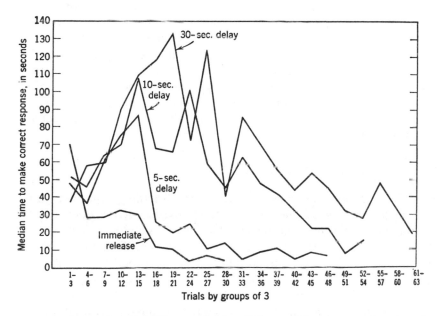

Fig. 10–3. Curves showing differences in the efficiency of learning as a function of the time interval between the relevant act and the occurrence of primary reinforcement (Roberts, 1930, p. 46).

manner in which they were restrained from feeding as soon as they arrived at it (p. 50).

While the experimental procedure employed by Roberts represented an advance over earlier procedures, it was in one respect not ideal: it was conducive, in the delay groups, to a certain amount of "mislearning," which accounts for the "hump" in the early part of the learning curves for these groups. Because contact with the wooden bob or pendulum was probably not the last, or most "recent," response which a delayed animal would have made before being admitted to the food compartment, there was a tendency for these more recent *but irrelevant* responses to be reinforced more powerfully than the relevant response. These responses would then take precedence over the right response and would have to be extinguished, one after another, until the slight but consistent reinforcement of the correct response would finally "win out."

During the two decades following Roberts' experiment, numerous other studies were reported which tried to attack the problem of delayed-reward learning by still more refined and exact techniques. It will not be possible here to review or even cite a good many of these. Suffice it to say that in 1943 Perin, working under the direction of Clark Hull, published a study, in which he empirically derived the gradient shown in Fig. 10–4. And a few years later Perkins (1947) carried out a different sort of study from which he derived the reinforcement gradient shown in Fig. 10–5. The evidence was thus substantial for believing that primary reward may follow an instrumental act by as much as 30 or 40 seconds and still have some reinforcing effect thereon.

III. The Spence-Grice Hypothesis

At this stage of developments a rather peculiar thing happened. Just as a point had been reached at which it looked as if the gradient of reinforcement for delayed reward had been established with some stability, Spence introduced a notion which was little short of a "bombshell." In a paper entitled "The Role of Secondary Reinforcement in Delayed Reward Learning," which appeared in 1947, Spence noted that with increasingly adequate control of the influence of secondary reinforcement, what had appeared, on the basis of early studies, to be an almost infinitely long gradient of reinforcement had been progressively shortened to a duration of something over 20 and probably less than 60 seconds. Then said Spence:

But more crucial evidence supporting the notion that delayed reward learning is in part a function of secondary reinforcement from differential internal (proprioceptive?) cues is the experimental finding of Gulde (1941) and Riesen (1940) that when care is taken to delay the consequence of both correct and incorrect response as little as four or five seconds, animals (rats and chimpanzees) are unable to learn in a discrimination learning situation (p. 6).

Fig. 10–4. Gradient of reinforcement empirically derived by Perin (1943b, p. 107).

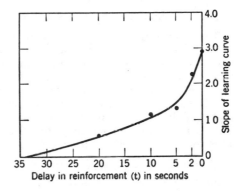

It is thus clear in what direction Spence's thoughts were moving: since the control of secondary reinforcement had resulted in a progressive contraction of the gradient of primary reinforcement, perhaps still more refined investigation would show that this gradient is simply nonexistent. As if extrapolating from such evidence, Spence continues:

The fact that no learning occurs with delays as short as five seconds in the discrimination situation suggests that the primary gradient of reinforcement, if there is such a thing at all, is much shorter than the 20 or 30 seconds inferred by Hull on the basis of the Perin studies. Indeed, it would not seem

Fig. 10–5. Gradient of reinforcement empirically derived by Perkins (1947, p. 389).

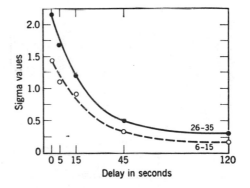

unreasonable to hypothesize that there is no primary gradient of reinforcement, but that all learning involving delay of the primary reward results from the action of *immediate* secondary reinforcement which develops in the situation. Factors affecting the development of this secondary reinforcement would then be considered as responsible for all gradients found with delay of reward. Such a hypothesis, it will be observed, eliminates the necessity of explaining how the reward seemingly acts backward over time to influence something which occurred earlier (p. 7).

And, in summary, Spence says:

The interpretation that learning under conditions of delay of primary reward involves a backward action of the goal object on the preceding stimulus-response event is rejected. The hypothesis suggested as an alternative to this conception is that all such learning occurs as the result of the development of secondary reinforcement, the action of which is conceived to take place immediately upon the occurrence of the response. A prominent aspect of this theory is the concept of *differential secondary reinforcement* based either on cues from the external environment or inner cues such as proprioceptive stimulation provides (pp. 7–8).

This line of argument received what might appear to be strong support in a paper later published by Grice (1948b). In his summary, Grice wrote:

Groups of white rats were run on a black-white discrimination problem with delays of reward of 0. 0.5, 1.2, 2.5, and 10 sec. [Fig. 10–6]. A very steep delay of reinforcement function was obtained within this range, with no learning by three of five Ss in the 10 sec. group (p. 15).

These findings are congruent with those of Gulde and Riesen, previously cited by Spence, and seemed to confirm the latter's supposition that "the primary gradient of reinforcement, if there is such a thing

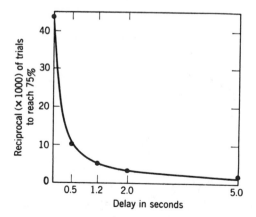

Fig. 10–6. Gradient of reinforcement empirically derived by Grice (1948a, p. 9); using discrimination learning task.

at all, is much shorter than the 20 or 30 seconds inferred by Hull."
Moreover, a supplementary experiment by Grice showed that:

When immediate secondary reinforcement was introduced by allowing
the animal to eat in a goal box of the same color as the positive stimulus,
learning with delayed reward was greatly facilitated.

When animals were forced to make characteristically different motor responses to the black and white stimuli, they learned at a significantly faster
rate than [did] animal which received equal delay, but made no such characteristically different motor adjustments (p. 16).

Fig. 10–7. Gradient of reinforcement as conceived by Hull in
1952 (p. 131).

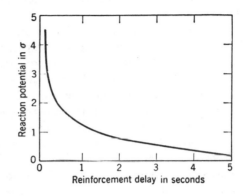

These findings appear to provide striking confirmation of Spence's
surmise that "differential secondary reinforcement based either on
cues from the external environment or internal cues such as proprioceptive stimulation" are of crucial importance in accounting for
learning which involves a delay of primary reinforcement.[3]

Grice's own comments on this score follow:

The data are consistent with a theory which assumes no "primary" delay
of reinforcement gradient, but accounts for learning under delayed reward
conditions in terms of some type of immediate secondary reinforcement
(p. 16).

[3] Here Spence came extremely close, at least in terminology, to the revised
theory of habit set forth in Chapter 7 and amplified and compared with the views
of others in Chapters 8 and 9. All he would have had to do to enunciate that
theory quite explicitly was to modify his statement to read: "*All* learning [in-
volving so-called habits, regardless of whether the primary reward is immediate
or delayed] results from the action of *immediate* secondary reinforcement which
develops in the situation, such reinforcement being provided either by cues from
the external environment or by inner cues such as those produced by proprioceptive stimulation." This conception was missed, however narrowly, because the
author was still thinking of "secondary reinforcement" as *reinforcing* a habit (in
the connectionistic sense) rather than as *being* the "habit." See also Section IV.

On the basis of the evidence and logic just reviewed, Hull, in his *Behavior System* (1952), took the position that the gradient of primary reinforcement probably does not exceed, at best, five seconds and that it declines according to the function shown in Fig. 10–7. But there are a number of reasons for thinking that this abandonment of the longer type of gradient, such as suggested by the experimental findings of Perin and by Perkins, was premature. One point to be considered in this connection is the rather special nature of discrimination learning, from which much of the evidence for the Spence-Grice argument is derived.

It should be recalled that the type of gradient under discussion is that which represents the decreasing effectiveness of a reward as it is made more and more remote in time *from a particular response*. A little reflection will reveal that the discrimination experiment, as ordinarily carried out with animals, does not meet these conditions. Here, typically, an animal has to learn to go *either* to the right or to the left at a choice point, depending upon *where* the so-called "positive" cue is located. Thus the correct response, i.e., the one which will lead to reward, will sometimes involve turning right at the choice point, sometimes left. Hence, if one studies the effect of delaying reward in a situation of this kind, it is not the same as studying the effect of delaying reward for the performance of a single, specific response which is *always* correct. In the discrimination experiment, the animal does not learn either to make a particular response or to go to a particular place (see Chapter 9 for a discussion of response versus place learning). What it learns instead is to be *guided* in what it does and where it goes by a cue or sign which, so to say, "moves around" (cf. Mowrer, 1960, Chapter 3, Section VIII). This, as we shall see later (Chapter 12), is a relatively complex and difficult order of learning; and for this reason it may not provide a very sensitive method for studying the delay of reinforcement. Other things being equal, place learning is probably easiest, response learning next most difficult, and discrimination learning most difficult—and "abstract"—of all. For this reason, then, we may question the typicality of the results reported by Riesen, Gulde, and Grice and the interpretation placed upon them by Grice and Spence. Simpler and presumably more sensitive learning tasks give evidence of a primary gradient of reinforcement of more extended duration (Sections VI through IX).

However, before this evidence is examined, it will be desirable to consider certain issues which have implications for learning theory in the broadest sense of the term.

IV. Some Logical Difficulties in the Connectionist Notion of Habit

Spence says that his hypothesis "eliminates the necessity of explaining how the reward seemingly acts back over time to influence something which has occurred earlier." This difficulty, at least as stated, is a somewhat fallacious one, stemming from a certain looseness of terminology for which Thorndike was largely responsible. In stating his Law of Effect, he was sometimes given to saying that an S—R "bond" or "connection" *occurs* and is *then strengthened* by an ensuing reward. Superficially, this statement implies retroaction, but not necessarily. More precisely Thorndike's statement means that an organism, motivated by some drive S_d, makes some instrumental response R_1, which is then followed by reward, presumably a reduction in S_d. Then, *at the time of reward*, the organism—or, more specifically, the neural pathway between S_d and R_1—is modified (as the Law of Effect, or habit theory, would have it) in such a way as to make S_d still more likely, *on future occasions*, to elicit R_1. Such reasoning involves no assumption or implication of retroactive causation.

But there is still a problem. In order to get out of the retroaction dilemma by the logical device just suggested, one has to assume that rewards always occur *immediately after* a given connection has been active (or activated) and, indeed, while the connection is in some sense *still active*, so that the reinforcing effect of the reward can act *selectively* upon *this* connection rather than any of innumerable other "connections." However, we know that such perfect simultaneity of response and reward is, in reality, not necessary; and Spence was therefore quite correct in supposing that the facts of delayed-reward learning constitute a special problem for habit theory.

On the basis of evidence which will be reviewed in the next section, it has been suspected for some decades that a stimulus typically produces a "reverberation" in the nervous system which continues for some little time after the physical excitation of the sensory organ has ceased. But apparently no one has been able to adduce anything more than the most speculative kind of evidence for believing that "connections" in some sense also "reverberate" and thus remain capable of reinforcement "at a distance." Therefore, an advantage of the revised conception of habit which is suggested in this volume, which was in no sense anticipated, is that in reducing all learning to conditioning (as opposed to bond "stamping in"), the effects of delayed reinforcement are easily derivable. Let us represent the situation, with maximal generality, in the manner suggested in Fig. 10–8. Let S_n represent any originally neutral stimulus or stimulus complex. Such an S_n may, by prior assumption, be produced either by the environment (extrinsic stimulation) or by some behavioral act S_d—R_i (intrinsic stimulation). And the diminishing wavy line following S_n is its *trace*. The delayed primary reinforcing situation, Sit_r, which may be either decremental or incremental, will produce some total reaction R, of which r is the conditionable component (hope, in the case of decremental reinforcement; fear, in the case of incremental reinforcement). S_n, through its trace, is thus rendered strictly contiguous with Sit_r and R; and we have no difficulty in thinking of r (a component of R) becoming conditioned to S_n, provided we are willing to think of r "generalizing forward" on the S_n trace. The latter assumption is inherently plausible for the reason that a weak trace of S_n is very much *like* a strong trace of S_n; and if r becomes conditioned to the trace at a weak (later) point, it should tend to transfer to a stronger (earlier) point on the trace (see Mowrer, 1960, Chapter 2). (This, of course, leaves unanswered the question of just *how* conditioning, whether to an immediate or to the delayed effects of a stimulus, occurs *neurologically speaking*. On this issue no one has any very clear notion as yet. What we are at present trying to do is simply indicate, with as great precision as possible, just what the *conditions* for the occurrence of learning may be. Cf. Mowrer, 1960, Chapters 5 and 6.)

In short, then, we may say that the Spence-Grice hypothesis, although radical, was not *sufficiently* radical. It continued to presup-

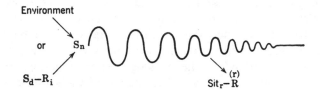

Fig. 10–8. Diagram showing delayed reinforcement where learning is thought of as conditioning rather than habit formation. S_n is a formerly neutral stimulus, produced either by the environment or by some instrumental response R_i, and the wavy line is the "trace" of this stimulus. Learning here consists of r, the conditionable component of the total reaction R made to the reinforcing situation (Sit_r, which may be either decremental or incremental) becoming attached to the trace of S_n and then "generalizing forward" and, on later occasions, occurring relatively soon (though in diminished form) after the presentation of S_n.

pose an essentially connectionist conception of habit and attempted to resolve the problem of delayed reward which such a conception unavoidably encounters by proposing that all reinforcement at a distance is mediated by secondary reinforcement. In the present analysis we surmount or rather circumvent this problem by completely abandoning the connectionist view of habit and assuming that *response selection* in any given situation is mediated by the hopes and fears which are conditioned to the various stimuli inherently associated with the occurrence of different responses. And because the concept of stimulus trace is well authenticated (see next section), there is no problem about the occurrence of *conditioning* where there is a sizable time interval between the conditioned and the conditioning (reinforcing) stimulus (cf. O'Connor, 1946).

As already indicated, Hull was inclined, in his later writings, to accept the view that the gradient of primary reinforcement, if there be such a thing at all, is much shorter than he had formerly supposed, and to accept also the notion that most instances of delayed primary reinforcement are really mediated by concurrent secondary reinforcement. Because it may still not be fully apparent just how this position differs from our own, it will be useful to examine Hull's position in somewhat greater detail. In his book, *A Behavior System* (1952), Hull said:

Since the detailed quantitative theory of the delay in reinforcement of a single response is both very new and very complex, we proceed to its elaboration with considerable uncertainty. . . . Spence first proposed the basic notion that the fractional antedating goal reaction [which has secondary reinforcing power] would generalize on the continuum of the stimulus trace. From this the present theory has been developed (p. 127).

But there is a basic problem, previously cited, which Hull never squarely faced: How can an "S—R connection" (Hull's term, p. 126) be reinforced by the conditioning of the so-called "fractional antedating goal reaction" to a *stimulus* trace? The "stimulus" here is presumably the cause of, and therefore antecedent to, the "response." And since a reward has to *follow* the S—R connection which it is to reinforce, how can secondary reinforcement which is conditioned to S be said to function in this way? Here the reward or reinforcement occurs with S and therefore *before* R, not after it. In at least an oblique effort to deal with this problem, Hull gives the following example:

Let it be supposed that a hungry albino rat is presented at hourly intervals with a response-bar in a Skinner-box situation, and that each time the animal makes a bar-pressing response (R) to the smell of food on the bar a delay of 4″ elapses before it receives the food reward (K′). Simultaneously with the animal's reception of the food the goal reaction of eating (r_G) occurs and becomes primarily reinforced to the stimulus trace left by the apparatus and response stimuli (p. 127).

The critical phrase here is "the stimulus trace left by the apparatus and response stimuli." If Hull had made further use of the notion of "response-produced stimuli," he would have been moving at least in the general direction of a satisfactory solution to this problem; but instead he makes no further reference to this concept and concentrates upon the stimulation provided by the apparatus and produced by the response in question:

Now since s_G [the experienced consequences of r_G] is intimately associated with primary reinforcement, i e., eating, it will acquire the power of secondary reinforcement. But the greater the delay in reinforcement, the weaker will be the generalized r_G, the weaker the s_G, and consequently the weaker the secondary reinforcement between S, the apparatus stimulus, and R, the response. . . . This is a rough qualitative outline of the theory of the present gradient of reinforcement of a response as a function of its delay (p. 128).

V. Delayed Reinforcement and Stimulus Trace

One must certainly agree with the characterization of this hypothesis as "rough." Otherwise the statement has little to recommend it and only goes to show, once again, the sort of logical impasse to which S—R connectionism seems inevitably to lead. Revised two-factor theory does not encounter this problem because it assumes that learnning is *always* in the nature of conditioning (rather than S—R bonding); and the question of how a response (r) produced by the UnCS gets attached to a CS, despite a temporal interval between CS and UnCS, is resolved quite specifically and adequately by the notion of a persisting "trace" from CS which provides the necessary contiguity with the UnCS and r.

If a stimulus, be it environmentally produced or response-produced, occurred but aroused within the nervous system no perseverating trace or after-effect of any kind, it would presumably be impossible for it to become connected to responses, of either fear or hope, if that stimulus and such responses were not strictly contiguous. However, we have reason to believe that learning can and does occur when the CS and the UnCS—r sequence are separated by relatively long intervals; and there is further evidence that this is made possible by the fact that stimulus events do "live on," for at least a short time, after their occurrence. That stimulation continues to "echo" in the nervous system is suggested, first of all, by the common experience (Lashley, 1950, p. 473) of *immediate memory*, as it has been called (in opposition to permanent memory or learning proper). For example, a telephone number will be "remembered," without rehearsal, for a short time after it is seen in a directory (or heard spoken), but will then usually be lost quite completely. This, it seems, is the subjective aspect of what is otherwise known as stimulus trace. Neurological evidence for this sort of phenomenon is found in the so-called reverberating neural circuits, which have been demonstrated both historically and functionally by Lorente de Nó (1933) (see Fig. 10–9).[4]

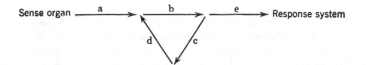

Fig. 10–9. Diagram of a neural "after-discharge" circuit. An impulse, originating in a sense organ, travels over neuron a, activating neuron b (but not d, because of the principle of "one-way" conduction). When the impulse reaches the end of the neuron b, it there activates, or excites, impulses in both neuron e and neuron c. The former travels to some response system, while the latter stimulates neuron d, which in turn causes b to fire again, and so on. In other words, every time an impulse travels around the circuit comprised of neurons b, c, and d, it "shoots off" an impulse through neuron e to the response system, thus keeping that system in action long after impulses have ceased to arrive, over neuron a, from the sense organ. Eventually, of course, neurons b, c, and d will fatigue, their "refractory phase" will become longer and longer, and the impulse in the circuit will be lost. An actual after-discharge system consists of hundreds, perhaps thousands of individual circuits of the kind shown; and since these circuits presumably "go out" successively rather than simultaneously, one can deduce the gradual "decay" typically observed in a stimulus trace.

It is, of course, not surprising to discover that the concept of stimulus trace was suggested by Pavlov (1927) to account for the learning which manifestly occurs when there is a brief interval between the CS and UnCS. But Hull likewise, though for somewhat

[4] Although the concept of the reverberating neural circuit is a comparatively new one, the corresponding psychological phenomenon has long been known. For example, Boring (1929) cites Hartley (1705–1757) for the notion that "After the object of sensation has been removed, the sensation and its vibrations persist briefly, but become fainter the while" (p. 199). For an extended discussion of the concept of immediate memory, with special reference to reverberating circuits, see Overton (1958).

different—and not wholly apparent—reasons (see Section IV), has stressed this phenomenon. In one place in his 1943 book he says:

The first [principle] to be observed is that after the stimulus (S) has ceased to act upon the receptor, the afferent impulse (s) continues its activity for some seconds, or possibly minutes under certain circumstances, though with gradually decreasing intensity. This *perseverative stimulus trace* is biologically important because it brings the effector organ *en rapport* not only with environmental events which are occurring at the time but with events which have occurred in the recent past, a matter frequently critical for survival. Thus is effected a short-range temporal integration (Postulate 1, p. 47) (p. 385).

Earlier in the same chapter from which Postulate I comes, Hull says:

Certain molar behavioral observations render it extremely probable that the after-effects of receptor stimulation continue to reverberate in the nervous system for a period measurable in seconds, and even minutes, after the termination of the action of the stimulus upon the receptor. Apparently the receptor after-discharge . . . is much too brief to account for the observed phenomena. Lorente de Nó (1933) has demonstrated histologically the existence of nerve-cell organizations which might conceivably serve as a locus for a continuous circular self-excitation process in the nerve tissue. Rosenblueth (1934) has presented experimental evidence indicating that neural after-discharges affecting the heart rate may persist for several minutes. This is shown graphically in [Fig. 10–10.] Such bits of evidence as these tend to substantiate the *stimulus trace hypothesis* of Pavlov (1927, pp. 39–40) which is utilized extensively in the present work. Indeed, were it not for the presumptive presence of stimulus traces it would be impossible to account for whole sections of well-authenticated molar behavior, notably those involving the adaptive timing of action (pp. 41–42).

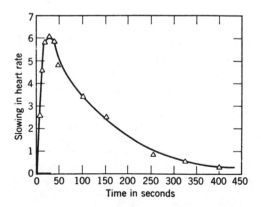

Fig. 10–10. "Graphic representation of the reflex slowing down of the heart rate of a cat and its recovery after cessation of the stimulus. Left vagus and depressor stimulated centrally; right vagus cut; accellerators intact. Ordinate: slowing of the heart per 10 seconds. Stimulation was at the rate of 7.8 per second during the period indicated by the heavy portion of the base line. (Adapted from Rosenblueth, 1934, Fig. 6A, p. 303.)" (Hull, 1943, p. 43.)

That Hull realized that the phenomenon of stimulus trace does not, however, resolve the problem of delayed primary reinforcement of a "habit" as conceived in his theoretical system is indicated by the readiness with which he accepted the Spence-Grice inference that there is no such thing as a gradient of primary reinforcement or that it lasts, at most, for only four or five seconds. Hull was well aware of the fact that stimulus traces may last for a considerably longer time; and if he had seen learning as dependent upon conditioning rather than the strengthening of S—R "habit" connections, it would have been apparent to him that there is no theoretical reason whatever for dismissing the possibility of correspondingly long gradients of primary reinforcement.

In passing, one additional observation is in order. The immediately preceding discussion indicates that for living organisms "time" in the sense of "the present" is not instantaneous but, through the agency of stimulation traces (and immediate memory), has some considerable "thickness" or duration. With this tendency for objective stimulus events to persist briefly in the nervous system, the possibility of conditioning is, as we have seen, enormously increased; and conditioning, or learning, thus gives us both memory of the past and vision into the future.

So again we see the critical importance of the phenomenon of stimulus trace, as the basis, among other things, for gradients of primary reinforcement. We turn now to a review of further evidence for such gradients.

VI. Delayed Reinforcement Type-D, Extrinsic Stimuli

Let us examine, now, experimental results which have been obtained by varying the interval, not between a response and an ensuing reward, but between some external, environmental *stimulus* and a rewarding state of affairs. In the paper by Roberts, already cited in this chapter, passing reference is made to an early investigation of this nature which was carried out by Thorndike. Says Roberts:

Thorndike's (1911) classical experiments reported in *Animal Intelligence* are so familiar that the briefest mention will suffice. One group of these, however, seems to have failed to attract the attention that it deserves or to have been given its proper weight in the discussion of theories of learning. . . . Professor Thorndike would say in a firm tone, "I must feed those cats." Ten seconds later he would feed them. The words came in time to stimulate the cats to energetic activity. As to whether or not this indicated the presence of "ideas," the investigator apparently could not feel quite certain (p. 49).

Then, some years later, Pavlov (1927), using dogs as subjects, reported observations of a similar kind. Here the procedure was to present a stimulus, such as a buzzer or light, for one-half to one minute and then, after an interval of one to three minutes, present food. Says Pavlov:

It is found that after several repetitions of this routine the stimulus will not itself evoke any reaction; neither will its disappearance; but the appropriate reaction (salivation) will occur after a definite interval, the after-effect of the excitation caused by the stimulus being the operative factor. We have to distinguish this type of reflex from the type described previously, in which the unconditioned stimulus coincided for part of its duration with the conditioned stimulus. The type described in this paragraph is termed *a trace conditioned reflex* (pp. 39–40).

Pavlov then reports an experiment by Feokritova in which a dog was fed regularly at 30-minute intervals. After training, it was found that, despite omission of feeding at the established interval, "a secretion of saliva with a corresponding alimentary motor reaction is produced at about the thirtieth minute, but it may be one or two minutes late" (p. 41; cf. Liddell, 1950, p. 194).

Interesting and suggestive as the experiments just described are, the data obtained were not very extensive or systematic; and for purposes of determining the full extent and shape of the complete gradient of reinforcement in this type of learning, it is necessary to turn to other workers. One of the seemingly best-controlled studies reported to date is that carried out and published, in 1950, by W. O. Jenkins. After briefly alluding to some of the studies already discussed in this chapter, Jenkins says:

Separate from these problems but related to them the question arises as to the operation of temporal factors in the acquisition of reinforcing properties. That is, how close to primary reinforcement in time must a stimulus occur in order for it to acquire the property of maintaining the response by itself. The present experiment dealt with the acquisition of reinforcing properties by a discrete, formerly-neutral stimulus as a function of the time-interval between its presentation and that of an established reinforcing agent. The action of the derived reinforcing agent was measured in terms of learning and performing a new response (p. 238).

Preliminary training of the subjects (rats) consisted in putting them, individually, into a small compartment something less than a foot square, sounding a buzzer for three seconds, and then following it, after an interval, by food. The subjects, before training, were divided into five groups (ranging in number from 10 to 15 rats per group), and the buzzer-food interval, or delay, for these five groups was, respectively, 1, 3, 9, 21, and 81 seconds. The rats were maintained at 85% of normal body weight throughout the investigation. The testing procedure is described as follows:

On the day following completion of conditioning, the food magazines [used, after the appropriate interval, to deliver food following occurrence of buzzer] were disconnected and the levers inserted in the boxes. Depression of the levers produced the buzz and activated the recorders. A total of 6 hr. of bar-pressing was given with a half-hour session per day at the usual time of experimenting. Food was never presented in the experimental boxes after the lever had been inserted (p. 239).

Fig. 10–11. Gradient of secondary reinforcement, Type-D. The curve shows bar pressing (in rats) which was reinforced by a buzzer that had been previously followed by food at the temporal intervals indicated. (Reproduced from Jenkins, 1950, p. 240.)

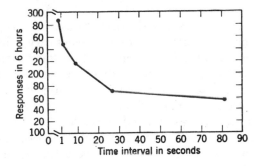

The results are shown graphically in Fig. 10–11. The function thus obtained is quite similar to that obtained, on the basis of superficially very different experimental procedures, by Perin and Perkins. In discussing his findings, Jenkins says:

This study has demonstrated a pronounced and significant temporal gradient of derived reinforcement generated by pairing a neutral stimulus with primary reward in conditioning. Responses for the derived reinforcement differed by nearly a factor of two from close to distant temporal association of the two stimuli [see also Bersh, 1951].

During the training it appears that there were two stimuli to which responses had to be learned: the noise of the food-machine and the buzz. An attempt was made to bring the rats of all groups up to an equal level as regards responding to the magazine prior to buzz-food training by giving 20 preliminary trials. The latency data at the end of training suggest approximate equality in response to the magazine. [It was necessary, of course, to have some signal which would announce the appearance of food in, and which would bring the rat to, the food trough; for otherwise, the interval between buzzer and delivery of food might be quite variable, since the rat would not then "know" exactly when food became available. The sound of the food-delivery mechanism served this purpose.] The learning of the response to buzz presumably differed according to the time-interval. For the short-interval groups, it came to serve as a cue for approaching the food-magazine. Although the rats in the longer-interval groups also approached the magazine after buzz, it seems reasonable to assume that further training would have produced a greater differentiation of behavior. A factor that probably made the response to buzz more difficult to learn was the similarity of the buzz and the presentation of the food magazine. Both were noises although the latter lasted less than 0.5 sec. The noise of the magazine presumably acted by way of generalization to maintain approach responses when buzz occurred even for the long-interval groups (p. 242).

If the Jenkins experiment may be said to have had a weakness, it was this: the stimulus which was paired with primary reinforcement (food) at various intervals was somewhat similar to the stimulus which announced the arrival of food and was therefore, in all groups, immediately associated therewith. As Jenkins points out, there was probably some generalization of secondary reinforcement from the latter sound to the former one; and this may account for the relatively high level of responding, with buzzer as sole reinforcement, in the long-delay groups. It would have been preferable to use a visual stimulus, such as a blinking light, in place of the buzzer, as a means of cutting down on this type of generalization. Otherwise the experiment appears to have been admirably designed; and even with this defect, it still yields a curve which is very similar to what appears, on the basis of experiments previously described and also those to be discussed shortly, to be the "true" gradient of delayed primary reinforcement.

VII. Delayed Reinforcement Type-I, Intrinsic Stimuli

.At the outset of this chapter, we considered some of the many experiments that have been carried out on the effect of delayed decremental reinforcement following the performance of some instrumental response; and in the immediately preceding section, we have seen that a very similar gradient, or function, is obtained when the delay is varied between some extrinsic stimulus and a reward. Let us turn now to a consideration of results obtained in situations where the interval between a particular response and a *punishment* has been systematically varied. Here the index of learning will, of course, be response inhibition rather than response strengthening or facilitation.

In an experiment which Mowrer & Ullman (1945) carried out several years ago, for a somewhat different purpose (see Section IX), it was found that the particular bit of behavior on the part of rats (i.e., eating) which was under investigation could not be much influenced by a comparatively weak shock if the latter was delayed by as much as nine seconds. However, the competing motivation (hunger) was fairly strong in this situation, so that the experiment did not provide a very sensitive indicator of the extent to which the stimuli produced by this particular behavior became conditioned to fear as a result of the occurrence of the ensuing shock.

More recently, another and more specifically relevant experiment has been carried out in collaboration with Peter Viek (Davitz, Mason, Mowrer, & Viek, 1957). In this study 28 Lashley-strain female rats, about four months of age were reduced to and held at 15% below normal body weight (i.e., the weight of the animals when on a full and unrestricted diet). The animals were then randomly divided into seven groups, of four animals each. On the first day of the experiment proper, each animal was put into a box-like compartment approximately 12 inches square. The sides and top of each compartment were made of wood, and the floor consisted of a metal grill which could be electrified. A small electric lamp illuminated the interior of each of these compartments (of which there were seven), and there was a small observation window in the top of each compartment.

After each animal had been in a compartment of this kind for three hours, a bit of mash (made of Purina Laboratory Chow) was offered to it on the end of a stick, which was projected upward toward the animal from beneath the grill. On the first day, each of the 28 animals immediately ate the food, and the conveying stick was promptly withdrawn. The animals, upon eating the food, were then given a two-second electric shock (130 volts, a.c., with a limiting resistance of 200,000 ohms), after a delay of 0, 2, 5, 10, 30, 120, or 600 seconds, depending on the group to which a particular animal has been assigned. One presentation of food and shock constituted a "trial," and only one trial was given per day. After a trial all animals were left in the apparatus again for three hours; then they were returned to their home cages and fed sufficiently to hold their weight at the desired level. Seven animals, one for each of the seven delay intervals, were run concurrently, for a total of 15 days. The experiment as a whole therefore consisted of four replications of this procedure.

The reason for leaving the animals in the experimental compartments for such a long period before and after each trial was this. The object of the experiment was to see to what extent the subjects were deterred from taking the food as a function of the proximity or remoteness of the punishment. Therefore, it was most important that

the subjects be thoroughly habituated to the experimental compartments, i.e., not afraid of the compartments as such. If the rats had
been put into the compartments and immediately offered food and
then shocked at the various intervals, it is likely that they would become afraid as soon as placed in the compartments and thus inhibited
from eating, regardless of the interval by which punishment of the
specific act of eating was delayed. However, having them in the compartments for a total of six hours each day ensured extinction of the
fear reaction to the compartment itself and guaranteed that fear of
eating would be specifically related to the nearness or remoteness of
the shock.

There are obviously two ways of summarizing the data obtained
from this experiment. It can be done in terms of the "number of inhibitions," i.e., the number of times during the course of the experiment that each animal refrained from eating (for as much as 10 seconds, after which the food was withdrawn and the "trial" ended). Or
one can summarize the data in terms of the total delay shown by
each animal on all trials. Both of these methods have been used, and
the results are shown graphically in Fig. 10–12. As will be seen, the
gradients thus obtained compare favorably, in shape and extent, with
those of Perin, Perkins, and Jenkins, already discussed.

There was, however, a possible source of weakness in this experi-

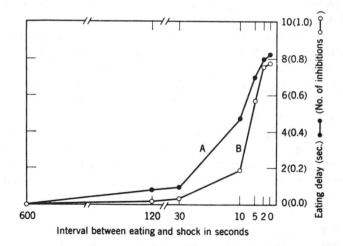

Fig. 10–12. Two measures of inhibition for seven groups of rats with various intervals between eating and shock (Davitz, Mason, Mowrer, and Viek, 1957, p. 72).

ment which prevented publication of the results for more than a decade. It will be recalled that the interval which is here systematically explored is that between the act of taking and eating food and the occurrence of a subsequent "punishment" in the form of electric shock. Now in order for any study of delayed reinforcement to be valid, it is essential that the delay interval not be "bridged," in any unrecognized or unintended way, so as to make the effect of reinforcement postponment less marked than it would be without such an artifact (on the basis of stimulus trace alone). As we have seen, a possible source of difficulty in the Jenkins experiment (Section VI) is that there may have been some generalization of secondary reinforcement from the stimulus (sound of delivery mechanism) which was immediately followed by food "back" to the stimulus (buzzer) which preceded food by various time intervals (in the different experimental groups). This particular type of difficulty did not arise in the study just reported, but there was another one: the possibility that a small quantity of the food which was presented to the subjects on each daily "trial" *remained in their mouths* during the delay period. If this happened, the food-in-mouth (or mere taste thereof) would be directly associated with shock in *all* groups, and the effort to vary the interval between taking food and the occurrence of shock would be vitiated. Since the food which might remain in the mouth after eating would be dissolved *gradually*, the taste residue would become progressively less and might, therefore, provide a gradient somewhat like the one obtained. In other words, it could be reasoned that the "stimulus trace" from the food and act of eating was in this experiment *chemical* rather than neurological.

We have, even now, no guarantee that the lingering taste of the food did not operate as just suggested. But in an experiment which was conducted for a different purpose (see Section IX) and in which the same source of difficulty could not have existed, Bixenstine (1956) obtained very similar (though less systematic) results: an electric shock administered 20 seconds after eating had a decidedly inhibitory influence, and a shock coming 50 seconds thereafter had a very much smaller but still noticeable effect (see also Bevan & Dukes, 1955). Moreover, the results obtained in the Viek study give gradients sufficiently like those obtained both in researches previously cited and in those to be described in the next section, so that the question of a possible artifact here is not, in any case, a very crucial one (cf. Kamin, 1959).

VIII. Delayed Reinforcement Type-I, Extrinsic Stimuli

Thus far we have reviewed three types of delayed reinforcement experiments. We have discussed experiments in which there was a variable interval between either a response or an environmental stimulus and a reward; and we have just considered an experiment in which there was a variable interval between a response and an ensuing punishment. The remaining question is: What is the effect of varying the interval between an *environmental stimulus* and "punishment," i.e., primary incremental reinforcement? Two rather different experiments will be described, one in some detail, the other more briefly.

The first of these studies, on the effect of varying the interval between an external stimulus and incremental reinforcement ("punishment"), was reported in 1954 by L. J. Kamin. It is entitled, "Traumatic Avoidance Learning: The Effects of CS-US Interval with Trace-Conditioning Procedure." After citing an early attack on this problem by Warner (1932a), Kamin says that the objective of his own study was to explore "the effects of CS-US interval on the acquisition of a shuttle-box avoidance response [see Chapter 2] in dogs" (p. 65).

There were four reinforcement-delay intervals: 5, 10, 20, and 40 seconds, with the interval measured from the onset of a two-second buzzer to the onset of shock which stayed on until the animal "shuttled," i.e., jumped over a low hurdle into the other half of the apparatus (see Fig. 12-19). Thus, the four intervals used, if measured from the *end* of the buzzer to the beginning of the shock, i.e., the true "trace" periods, are in each instance two seconds *less* than the delay values given. The electric shock used with each dog was just below an intensity which would be tetanizing—hence the expression "traumatic" avoidance learning. The interval between trials ranged between two and four minutes, with a mean of three minutes.

Training was continued, within a single session, until each animal had made five successive "avoidance" jumps. The chief testing procedure, involving resistance to extinction, is described thus:

Three minutes after the dog's fifth consecutive avoidance, extinction trials were begun. The CS was still presented at the same intertrial intervals, but the US was never again applied. Ten extinction trials were conducted on the first experimental day. They were followed by a 5 min. "cooling-off" period for the dog. The dog was then returned to its home cage. The second, and all succeeding, experimental days followed the pattern of the first day's extinction trials. The 10 min. observation period was followed by ten CS presentations and by a 5 min. cooling-off period. Thus, each daily extinction session lasted 42 minutes. The extinction trials were continued until the dog had achieved an extinction of five consecutive failures to respond to the CS by jumping. However, if extinction had not occurred within ten days (100 trials), the animal was discontinued (p. 66).

Ten mongrel dogs served as subjects in each of the four experimental groups; and there were two control groups, of five animals each, which were used in order to see to what extent the behavior of the experimental animals might have been a function of the presentation of shock alone, without the occurrence of the warning signal.

As might be expected, it was found "that the number of trials required to reach criterion [of conditioning] increases with the CS-US interval" (p. 67). However, the data which are most clear-cut and interesting for present purposes are those derived during extinction. Figure 10–13 shows the extinction curves for the four experimental groups; and Fig. 10–14 shows the total extinction performance of these four groups as a function of the CS-US interval. The similarity of the latter curve to those previously reproduced in this chapter is striking and serves to increase still further one's confidence that, regardless of whether the antecedent event is a response or an environmental stimulus and regardless of whether the ensuing reinforcement is decremental or incremental, the gradient of reinforcement is negatively accelerated and lasts for upwards of 30 to 60 seconds as a limit.

Fig. 10–13. The course of extinction of an avoidance response in four groups of dogs wherein the danger signal had previously been paired with shock at the intervals indicated (Kamin, 1954, p. 67).

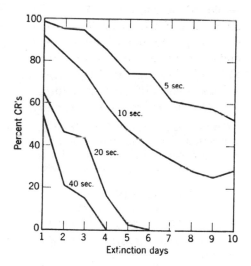

The only other investigation known to the writer in which a systematic attempt was made to study the effect of varying the interval between a danger signal and the painful event thereby signified is one carried out by Davitz & Mason (1957).[5] The details of this experiment will not be given here except to say that, using rats as subjects, these investigators paired a two-second blinking light with a three-second electric shock with various interstimulus intervals (the same as those

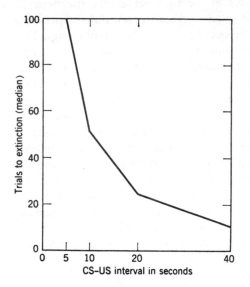

Fig. 10–14. Resistance to extinction ("percent CR's") as a function of training interval between CS and shock (Kamin, 1954, p. 67). Cf. Fig. 10–13.

employed by Mowrer & Viek). The extent to which fear was conditioned to the blinking light was then measured by the capacity of this stimulus to inhibit exploratory locomotion in a test situation. The findings are in essential agreement with those of Kamin, just described, and with those reported by Perin, Perkins, Jenkins, and by Mowrer & Viek, using different procedures.

In conclusion Davitz & Mason say:

On the basis of the evidence from a number of experiments concerning the acquisition of instrumental responses, Spence proposed that all learning under conditions of delayed reward is a function of the effects of immediate secondary reinforcement. The experimental procedure utilized in the present study, however, precluded the possibility of secondary reinforcing cues operating during the delay period. The gradient obtained does not seem to be more parsimoniously accounted for in terms of secondary reinforcement, and casts some doubt upon the adequacy of Spence's hypothesis (p. 73).

[5] For a related approach, with similar results, see Brown (1939) and Mowrer (1940b).

The evidence thus seems to point quite consistently to the conclusion that both decremental and incremental reinforcement, following either an environmental stimulus or a response, can be delayed in mammals for as long as 30 seconds and still result in some degree of conditioning, with the effect becoming progressively greater as the interval between stimulus, or response, and reinforcement is shortened (see also Dmitriev & Kochigina, 1959).

IX. The Problem of Temporal Integration

The biological utility of temporal gradients of reinforcement (made possible by the phenomenon of stimulus trace) is obvious: since a response is more likely to have *produced* (or a stimulus to be a *sign of*) some rewarding or punishing event which occurs immediately thereafter than it is to have produced some temporally remote event of a similar kind, it is clearly an advantage for temporally proximal events to have more of an effect, with respect to learning, than remote ones (see also Mowrer 1960, Chapter 8). It is nevertheless true that the effect of an action performed at one point in time may be considerably delayed; and when this happens unfortunate complications may ensue. It has already been noted, in connection with the discussion of Roberts' experiment on delayed reward, that considerable *mislearning* may result under these circumstances: i.e., since other, irrelevant actions will almost certainly intervene between the truly effective response and the resulting reward, these other actions, coming nearer to the reward in time, will be more strongly reinforced. But, as indicated, there is a self-correcting provision here in that when, as a result of such spurious reinforcement, irrelevant actions are "encouraged," the very fact of their irrelevancy and ineffectiveness means that they will also tend to be extinguished.

There is, however, another type of situation where the complications resulting from delayed reinforcement are not so benign. This is where a given action or response has *two* reinforcing consequences, one a reward and the other a punishment occurring at *different* points in time. Consider this example. Suppose a buzzer sounds, indicating that food is now available to a hungry rat in a little trough; but suppose, also, that there is a "rule" which says that the rat is not to eat the food for three seconds after its appearance and that the punishment for so doing is an electric shock which comes, let us say, 10 seconds after the "taboo" has been violated. As an experiment reported by Mowrer & Ullman (1945) indicates, it is virtually impossible (under the conditions described) for rats to find the *integrative* solution to a problem of this kind, which would be to *wait* briefly after the food has appeared (three seconds or more) and *then* eat the food. What these subjects do instead is to eat the food, immediately upon its appearance, and then get punished later, without ever "seeing the connection."

Or it might be that the situation is reversed: there could easily be a situation in which there was a slight immediate punishment which would prevent the subject from getting to a larger remote reward, just as in the experiment cited a slight immediate gain (immediate vs. slightly delayed eating) wins out over a larger remote punishment (cf. Muenzinger's research on "courage," described in the following chapter).

Thus, through the uneven distribution of reward and punishments in time, the basis is laid for what Shaffer (1936) has called "persistent nonadjustive" behavior. And Hearnshaw (1956), in a presidential address to the British Psychological Society, entitled "Temporal integration and behaviour," has said:

Animals, even the primates, live mainly in the present. They are sense-bound: learned reactions are tied to present stimuli, or subject to but short delay; anticipations are brief. Kohler's (1925) observation is classic: "A great many years spent with chimpanzees leads me to venture the opinion that besides in the lack of speech it is in the extremely narrow limits (in time) that the chief difference is to be found between anthropoids and even the most primitive human beings." In confirmation of this observation we find the temporal maze is a peculiarly difficult task for animals; and that the capacity for delayed response is far less than with quite young children (pp. 17–18).

How, then, do human beings achieve their unique capacity for "time-binding," as Korzybski (1933) has called it? Rather clearly the phenomenon of language (Mowrer, 1960, Chapters 3 and 4) is crucially important here. But certain animal studies give at least intimations of the direction in which the solution to this problem lies.

At the outset of this chapter we reviewed a number of experimental situations in which the temporal gap between an action and a delayed primary reward was subtly spanned by an inadvertant *cue* (secondary reinforcer) of some sort. And in Chapter 5 passing reference was made to a study in which Wolfe (1936) taught chimpanzees to "work" for poker-chip "tokens" which could later be exchanged for food. The latter was thus a *deliberate* attempt to produce the effect which had occurred accidentally in several of the early studies (one of which, incidentally, had been performed by Wolfe himself,

1934) involving delayed primary reinforcement. The trick, in Wolfe's poker-chip study, was to get his animals to subject themselves to a slight immediate inconvenience (light "work" of some sort) as a means of obtaining a promise of rather considerable but belated primary reward (food). Without the "tokens" the animals would never have sensed the relationship; but with the aid of the tokens, which provided immediate *secondary* reinforcement, the animals readily found the "integrative" solution to the problem.

More recently, an experiment along similar lines has been reported by Bixenstine (1956). His objective was to show how rats, in the Mowrer-Ullman type of dilemma, could solve the "temporal integration" problem if aided by a cue, or "token," of some sort. In brief, what this investigator did was this: whenever food was presented and the subject *violated* the rule of waiting, a little light "blinked" briefly and then blinked *again* just before the delayed punishment (shock) occurred. In other words, where Wolfe had provided his subjects with an immediate token, or promise, of reward to come later for present behavior, Bixenstine gave his subjects an immediate token, or "promise," of a *punishment* to come later for present behavior. Again, "integrative learning" resulted:

When Ss are aided by a sign having clear, unambiguous reference to temporally remote, punishing consequences, their integrative capacity is multiplied immeasurably. We may say that the secondary drive properties of the sign (blinking light) at the time of its occurrence during the taboo are the crucial determinants; the point in time where this learned drive is reinforced (i.e., the remoteness of the blinking light and shock combination), though noteworthy, is only of secondary importance (Bixenstine, 1956, p. 165).[a]

Although animals are not wholly lacking in the ability to supply themselves with the tokens, or "symbols," which make integrative problem solving possible, certainly they are severely limited in this connection (see Ferster, 1953; Mowrer, 1960, Chapter 2), whereas man is the symbol user *par excellence*. But while this accomplishment is the touchstone of much of his glory, it can apparently also lead to serious difficulty.

[The study of] temporal integration may not impossibly throw light on some of the primary problems of personality development and breakdown. Bowlby (1951) recently noted that the young child's personality develops hand in hand with a sense of continuity in time. . . . In breakdowns of per-

[a] For yet another use of a cue to span a temporal (and spatial) interval, see Grice & Goldman (1955), Mason (1956), and Dyal (1957); cf. Duryea (1955).

sonality, both mild and severe, temporal disorganization is a common feature. . . . Or consider *les clochoards*, the Parsian down-and-outs recently described by Schneider (1955), whose horizon is the moment, who have no history, nor aspirations, but have surrendered unconditionally to the passage of events. . . . If we are to explain behavior in its most characteristically human forms without having recourse to animism it is to the concept of temporal integration that we must turn (Hearnshaw, 1956, pp. 18–19).[7]

We cannot, of course, at this point pursue these inviting leads without getting very much ahead of our story; but it is useful here to have noted how quickly the study of so simple a matter as gradients of reinforcement, as observed in animals, carries us into problems of human thought, planning, conduct, and adjustment (see also Chapter 8, p. 273). Elsewhere (Mowrer, 1960) we shall return to these matters, but in the meantime it will be our purpose to adhere to a more progressive, systematic, orderly development of a foundation upon which a full human psychology can firmly rest.

X. Temporal Integration and "Superstition"

In the experiments cited in the preceding section (Wolfe's use of poker chips as tokens of ultimate reward and Bixenstine's use of a blinking light as a token of ultimate punishing), the "mediating" stimulus (cf. Mowrer, 1960, Chapter 2) was externally provided for the subject. Although human beings, in language, have a rich reservoir of such mediators, animals are manifestly limited in this connection, although (as we shall presently see) they are not entirely without such resources.

As early as 1948, Skinner published some highly significant observations in a paper entitled " 'Superstition' in the Pigeon." Because it was so compactly written to begin with, this paper is hard to abstract and will instead be quoted at some length.

A pigeon is brought to a stable state of hunger by reducing it to 75 per cent of its weight when well fed. It is put into an experimental cage for a few minutes each day. A food hopper attached to the cage may be swung into place so that the pigeon can eat from it. A solenoid and a timing relay hold the hopper in place for five sec. at each reinforcement.

If a clock is now arranged to present the food hopper at regular intervals *with no reference whatsoever to the bird's behavior*, operant conditioning usually takes place. In six out of eight cases the resulting responses were so clearly defined that two observers could agree perfectly in counting in-

---

[7] For a discussion of similar problems in the context of what he calls "temporal conflicts," see Brown (1957); also Rigby (1954).

stances. One bird was conditioned [spontaneously learned] to turn counter-clockwise about the cage, making two or three turns between reinforcements. Another repeatedly thrust its head into one of the upper corners of the cage. A third developed a "tossing" response. . . .

The conditioning process is usually obvious. The bird happens to be executing some response as the hopper appears; as a result it tends to repeat this response. If the interval before the next presentation is not so great that extinction takes place, a second "contingency" is probable. This strengthens the response still further and subsequent reinforcement becomes more probable. It is true that some responses go unreinforced and some reinforcements appear when the response has not just been made, but the net result is the development of a considerable state of strength (pp. 168–169).

In order the better to grasp what is going on here, it may be helpful to recall Krechevsky's 1932 paper on "hypotheses in rats." In the Skinner situation, it would appear that, to speak loosely, the pigeon "assumes" or "infers" that the appearance of the food must be "contingent" upon *something* which it does and so forms this or that "hypothesis," depending upon adventitious relationships between behavior and reinforcement. Skinner's own account continues:

The experiment might be said to demonstrate a sort of superstition. The bird behaves as if there were a causal relation between its behavior and the presentation of food, although such a relation is lacking. There are many analogies in human behavior. . . . These behaviors have, of course, no real effect upon one's luck or upon a ball half way down an alley, just as in the present case the food would appear as often if the pigeon did nothing—or, more strictly speaking, did something else (p. 171).

So much, then, for Skinner's general remarks. We come now to the more specifically relevant part of his paper, namely his comments and observations concerning the question of delayed reinforcement.

The effect appears to depend upon the rate of reinforcement. In general, we should expect that the shorter the intervening interval, the speedier and more marked the conditioning. One reason is that the pigeon's behavior becomes more diverse as time passes after reinforcement. . . .

Another reason for the greater effectiveness of short intervals is that the longer the interval, the greater the number of intervening responses emitted without reinforcement. The resulting extinction cancels the effect of an occasional reinforcement.

. . . Fifteen seconds is a very effective interval at the drive level indicated above. One min. is much less so. When a response has once been set up, however, the interval can be lengthened. In one case it was extended to two min., and a high rate of responding was maintained with no sign of weakening (p. 169).

As of 1948 Skinner regarded the behavior here described as "superstitious," nonfunctional, which, under the prevailing circumstances, it indeed was. But more recently Ferster (1953) has found that if circumstances are slightly altered, this behavior can become extraordinarily useful. What Ferster did, first of all, was to show that if pigeons were allowed to learn an instrumental "pecking" response with relatively prompt reward, this response extinguished in three out of four birds when the reward was consistently delayed for 60 seconds and that extinction occurred in the remaining bird when the delay was extended to 120 seconds. Then reported Ferster,

> The same Ss that extinguished under 60- and 120-sec. delays were reconditioned on the original variable-interval schedule without delay. Short delays were then introduced and the value of the delays was gradually increased as S's behavior became stable under any particular delay. It was possible in three out of four of the cases to sustain normal rates of response under delays of 60 sec. (p. 224).

Observation of the pigeons indicated that, by virtue of the procedure just described, they had developed "superstitious" responses during the delay interval and that these had become instrumental in bridging the 60-second interval between the originally pecking action and the eventual food reward. Here, Ferster reasoned, the "strength of the pecking response will not be maintained directly by the presentation of food, but depends on the food-reinforced mediating behavior" (p. 224). In other words, once an interval response has been adventitiously reinforced and thus established as "superstitious" behavior, its occurrence apparently links, in some way, the original pecking action with ultimate food reinforcement. Ferster seems to assume that the mechanism is that of "response chaining"; and he regards this interpretation as being supported by the fact that a deliberate attempt on his part to teach pigeons specified (and measurable) responses "which could function in the same way as a 'superstitious' chain conditioned as a consequence of the delayed procedure" (p. 224). But it is also possible that the delay interval was being spanned by the device of secondary reinforcement or, equivalently, second-order conditioning. If, in other words, a given response was "superstitiously" learned as a result of its temporal proximity to the (causally unrelated) appearance of primary reward (food), this would mean (a) that the habit itself (if our general conception of habit formation is valid) consisted of the secondary reinforcement that became conditioned to the back-lash stimulation from the response in question and (b) that this stimulation, if produced in temporal proximity to the truly instrumental response of pecking, can secondarily reinforce that response, i.e., can serve, in Ferster's words, as "the food-reinforced mediating behavior" but does so by means of secondary reinforcement (as previously discussed in this chapter) rather than through the device of stimulus-response chaining.

It would be interesting to see if pigeons would show an increased facility in developing this type of mediating behavior if subjected to a number of *different* situations of the kind described by Ferster. It might be that, with sufficiently extended practice in varied contexts, they would become relatively "expert" in the use of such mediating ("superstitious") responses (cf. Harlow's concept of "learning sets," 1949).

Recently Noble & Alcock (1958) have discussed the difficulty of demonstrating with human subjects the diminishing efficiency of reward as the interval between the "correct," instrumentally effective response and the reward is increased. They say:

There is a common belief that reinforcement and feedback in human learning, just as in rodent learning, must be undelayed and specific if optimal proficiency is to be achieved (p. 407). [But] whether reward or information is withheld seems to be of less consequence than what S does during the time interval between response and after-effect (p. 408).

They then quote Lorge & Thorndike (1935) as follows:

It is almost impossible to prevent human subjects from keeping a connection . . . in mind until the after-effect occurs or from recalling it to mind when the after-effect occurs and then repeating some equivalent of the after-effect. The real relation would then be immediate, regardless of how long an ostensible delay we used (pp. 193–194).

In other words, human beings, with their remarkable skill in symbolic manipulation, can easily keep, or re-establish, the "connection" between two events (action and reward or action and punishment), even though these events are considerably separated in time. For example, if a subject "knows" that a given response is responsible for a given (delayed) effect, he might say to himself, immediately upon completion of the response: "Although there will be a delay now, before I get the reward, I nevertheless *know* I have done the right thing, so all I have to do is wait." Such a sentence could undoubtedly mediate considerable secondary reinforcement. Or it is conceivable (though perhaps less likely) that the subject, instead of anticipating the reward verbally upon completion of the action, will wait and verbally reinstate the action just as or just after the reward occurs.

Being far less versatile in the use of symbols (mediators), the pigeons previously described in this section had to use a relatively crude, but not ineffective, procedure. If they performed some purely arbitrary action repeatedly in the "goal region," i.e., shortly before primary reward occurred, then the response-correlated stimuli took on S^r properties; and if these stimuli are then produced (by the performance of this act) shortly after the occurrence of the relevant, truly instrumental (but temporally remote) action, they served to transmit (by higher-order conditioning) S^r properties to the stimuli produced by the relevant action and thus give it habit strength, so-called. Otherwise, without such a mediating mechanism or activity, behavior from which primary reinforcement is temporally remote will have no chance at all of being learned.

In earlier sections of this chapter, we have reviewed a number of experiments in which the primary gradient of reinforcement was inadvertently bridged by some secondary reinforcer in the experimental situation. In the Skinner-Ferster type of situation, it seems that the subject himself—by means of what Hull has termed a "pure stimulus act" (Mowrer, 1960, Chapter 2)—becomes capable of providing a secondary reinforcer which apparently serves much the same function.

XI. Conclusions and Disclaimers

Our review of the relevant literature shows that one or more investigations have been reported for each of the four types of reinforcement gradient which revised two-factor theory suggests. There are studies on the effect of varying the interval (a) between a response and decremental reinforcement (reward), (b) between an external stimulus (signal) and decremental reinforcement, (c) between a response and incremental reinforcement (punishment), and (d) between an external stimulus and incremental reinforcement (cf. Hilgard, 1956, p. 153). Although the experiments here reported are not beyond possible criticism and alternative interpretation (cf. the Spence-Grice hypothesis), the results converge in suggesting that all gradients of primary reinforcement, both decremental and incremental, cover an interval of something like three-quarters of a minute, at most; and further analysis suggests that this common finding derives from the fact that gradients of reinforcement are based upon the underlying phenomenon of stimulus trace.

As indicated in Chapter 7, there are four kinds of *secondary reinforcement*. None of these seems as yet to have been systematically studied as far as the problem of reinforcement delay is concerned. Presumably all of them operate in a manner roughly equivalent to what has been found to hold for primary reward and punishment. Such studies would of necessity involve the phenomenon of second-order conditioning; and the resulting gradients might, accordingly, be expected to start at a lower level and extend less far than do gradients involving first-order conditioning, i.e., primary reinforcement. Here, it appears, is a relatively little explored area inviting further research.[8] However, the phenomenon of secondary reinforcement has repeatedly entered into our discussions in this chapter in another way: namely, as an "artifact" which, if not carefully controlled, may easily and effectively "bridge" the interval between stimulation and primary reinforcement and vitiate experimental efforts to establish true reinforcement gradients. On the other hand, in circumstances where there is an unavoidable delay of considerable duration between stimulation (or response) and primary reinforcement and where learning is none the less desired, it follows that secondary reinforcement can be very usefully employed (as Wolfe and Bixenstine have shown) as a mediational device (Mowrer, 1960, Chapter 2).

If it be granted, as present evidence seems to warrant, that the gradient of primary reinforcement is, maximally, 30 to 45 seconds in duration and if it be further assumed that this interval is determined by the duration of stimulus traces, then the question arises: Why, in the course of evolution, have living organisms developed nervous systems which mediate traces of this magnitude, rather than markedly shorter or longer ones? Since any answer to this question must be largely speculative, no attempt will be made to deal with it in the present context (but see Mowrer, 1960, Chapter 8). And certain other implications which the facts of delayed reinforcement have for integrative problem solving will also have to be considered at another time (Mowrer, 1960, Chapter 10).

We should, however, note that in discarding the concept of "habit" and positing instead that all learning involves conditioning, revised two-factor theory avoids a common embarrassment. It has long been recognized that the interval between *a stimulus* and a reinforcing state of affairs, if brief, is normally bridged by the phenomenon of stimulus trace. But how, it has been asked, can the interval between *a response* and a reinforcing state of affairs be spanned? It is conceded that a stimulus can and does reverberate for a short time within the nervous system; but no one, apparently, has thought it feasible to posit *response* reverberation, *response* traces. Some writers (notably Thorndike) have seemed to resolve this problem by implying what amounts to

---

[8] Since the above was written, Kamin (1957a, 1957b) has studied the effect of delaying decremental secondary reinforcement type-I. The results are congruent with expectation.

retroactive causation. Others writers (viz., Spence and Grice) have taken a different tack on the problem; but because their analysis is predicated on a continued acceptance of traditional habit theory, it encounters serious difficulties. Because revised two-factor learning theory assumes that responses, in the sense of overt, behavioral acts are never "learned" and that all learning is in the nature of stimulus substitution, the concept of stimulus trace nicely handles all instances of delayed reinforcement.

In certain types of conditioning (see, for example, Hilgard & Marquis, 1940), it has been found that the gradient of reinforcement is extremely short, with conditioning becoming practically non-existent when the CS-UnCS interval is over two or three seconds (cf. McAllister, 1953, Fitzwater & Thrush, 1956). This type of finding might at first seem inconsistent with the evidence cited in this chapter for believing that the gradient of reinforcement typically lasts for something between 30 seconds and a minute. The trouble, it seems, lies in the way in which the conditioning process is conceptualized and experimentally controlled. If one thinks of conditioning as involving mainly, or perhaps exclusively, *emotional* reactions, then there is no difficulty in demonstrating the longer type of gradient; but if one thinks of a "conditioned response" as involving some overt reflex, such as an eye blink or the knee jerk, then one is either dealing with an altogether different type of learning mechanism or with a very inefficient way of demonstrating the more basic phenomenon of emotional conditioning. This is one among many reasons why so little reference is made in this volume to the conditioning of the so-called "short-latency" responses: they are of comparatively little biological importance and do not, apparently, show learning in its most typical and important form.[9]

[9] After class one day, a group of students challenged the above position. *Why,* they wanted to know, are not the short-latency conditioned reflexes just as important and just as "typical" and interesting as the other forms of learning previously stressed. By way of answer the instructor stepped up to one of the students and made a quick, threatening gesture toward his eyes. The student, of course, blinked and was then asked: "Why did you blink your eyes? You *knew* I wasn't going to hit you." A little sheepishly, he said that he did indeed "know" that I was not going to hit him (and, significantly enough, made no effort to avoid a blow by moving his whole body or head), but added that he just "couldn't help" blinking. It occurred "involuntarily." It was then pointed out that this is precisely the reason for regarding the short-latency conditioned reflexes as representing a primitive and nontypical form of learned action. They are strictly "mechanical" and often occur (as in the foregoing instance) uselessly, "stupidly." In a few situations, as with rapidly moving objects approaching the

Nor has any attempt been made to discuss the relationship between the gradient of reinforcement and *amount* of reinforcement; there is a literature on this problem, but to date it has not proved very instructive, since it has been found that this variable is not usually very consequential (but see Chapter 11). Within narrow limits, at any rate, it has been found that a small reward or a small punishment works just as well as "larger" reinforcements; [10] but this fact should not be confused with the effect of *delaying* reinforcement. As the several experiments cited in this chapter consistently show, there is an orderly progression from highly efficient learning at zero or brief delay intervals to no learning at all (without "bridging" stimuli) when the interval is a minute or longer. This gradient, as we have seen, seems to be specifically dependent upon and mediated by the phenomenon of stimulus trace. In some instances, where the action-reinforcement interval exceeds the duration of the stimulus trace, and where this interval is not bridged by external stimuli having secondary reinforcing power, the subject (even though infrahuman) will develop "mediation" responses (Mowrer, 1960, Chapter 2) which serve the same purposes. In situations where these responses occur but do not serve this purpose (or where they are perhaps not understood by the observer), they may be termed "superstitions."

Although the biological utility of learning where there is delayed reinforcement is obvious, certain dilemmas nevertheless arise where *two* reinforcements or "effects" follow a given action and are unevenly distributed in time. Here arises the problem of "temporal integration," which man best solves by means of symbols (Mowrer, 1960); the capacity of lower animals in this connection is severely limited.

---

eyes, it is more important to have a protective response that occurs *quickly* than one under the control of a more discriminating, more "intelligent," but slower-acting ("deliberate") system. The "trouble" with the short-latency reflexes is just this; that in achieving *speed* of occurrence, they *sacrifice integration with the rest of the organism.* They are little mechanisms which function autonomously, independently of the larger, more highly organized system which we call the organism-as-a-whole (cf. Mowrer, 1960, Chapters 6 and 7).

[10] For a good discussion of some of the complications involved in research on this problem, see Fehrer (1956); also Armus (1959), Karsh (1959), and Moll (1959).

11

Unlearning, Conflict, Frustration, and Courage

In the early chapters of this book, attention was especially directed toward the "negative" aspects of learning, i.e., the learning involved in active and passive *avoidance* behavior. In seeking to gain a better, more systematic understanding of these two phenomena, we found ourselves exploring the problem of secondary reinforcement, which logically divides itself into type-1 and type-2. Then, upon further analysis of type-2 secondary reinforcement, we found we were in a position to formulate a new theory of "positive" learning, i.e., *approach* behavior and *habit*. In the immediately preceding chapters, the emphasis has fallen rather evenly upon both the positive and the negative aspects of learning, as thus conceived. Now the time has come to examine the problem of *unlearning*, that is, the question of how learning, in either "direction," can be undone, counteracted, reversed.

At once a paradox will be encountered: If there are two distinct forms of "reinforcement," involving drive decrement and drive increment respectively, and if these are antithetical in their effects, then what is "positive" or "forward" movement with respect to one of these forms of learning will involve a reversal of the other. Thus, learning which is in one sense negative is in another sense positive (cf. Deese, 1952, Chapter 6; Keller, 1954, pp. 31 ff.). One of the important challenges to revised two-factor theory is to see how well it can handle this complication—and the attendant phenomenon of conflict.

It is obvious that unlearning of both hopes and fears can be produced by counterconditioning; but it is also well established that these reactions recede under the less radical influence of "extinction," i.e., elicitation without confirmation. Discussion of the latter phenomenon leads to the topic of "frustration"; and from consideration thereof it is found that a theory of extinction is today emerging which is consistent with the general view of unlearning adopted in this chapter.

In this context we shall examine a phenomenon which, while equally familiar to common sense, has only recently begun to be an object of laboratory study. This is the phenomenon of "courage." As we shall see, it, too, is easily defined operationally and readily lends itself to objective investigation.

I. The Problem of Unlearning in Light of Revised Two-Factor Theory

As indicated in Chapter 2, the original version of Thorndike's Law of Effect squarely confronted the problem of unlearning and had an explanation: punishment, it held, reverses, obliterates, "stamps out" the neurological residue of past learning. Learning, starting at or near "zero," progresses under the influence of reward; and under the impact of punishment, it simply regresses, back toward its starting point. But this approach had no way of accounting for the *conflict* which punishment manifestly produces; nor did it take cognizance of the fact that "punishment" not only interferes with established behavior ("passive avoidance"; see Chapter 2) but also can set up behavior ("active avoidance"; see Chapter 3) where there was no behavior, no action before. One of the major assets of two-factor learning theory as formerly conceived was that it acknowledged and accommodated both of these phenomena. But if the Law of Effect had too little conflict, this version of two-factor theory had, one may say, *too much*.

The dilemma to which the earlier (second) version of two-factor theory led may be summarized as follows. It accepted the Thorndikian hypothesis that the neurological connection between a drive stimulus and an instrumental response is strengthened by reward, but it rejected the complementary notion that such a connection is weakened by punishment. It proposed instead that punishment causes the stimuli produced by the behavior which punishment follows to become conditioned to fear; and it further posited that behavior instigated by fear and reinforced by fear reduction then competes with and often overrides the original behavior. This way of thinking made a place for the phenomenon of conflict, as the Law of Effect did not; but it provided no suggestion as to how conflict may eventually be *resolved*. One learning mechanism, that of motivation and reward, caused a "habit" to be established; punishment, through conditioning, then caused a new motive, that of fear, to come into existence; and its reduction served to reinforce an *antagonistic* "habit." But such antagonism or conflict, once created, might be expected to hold the subject in a sort of rigor or tetany indefinitely—unless some sort of central short-circuiting or, perhaps, "stamping out" of the kind posited by Thorndike mercifully intervened. The question is now: Does revised two-factor theory offer any simpler or more satisfactory way of dealing with this problem?

The principal difference between the second version and the present revision of two-factor theory is that, in the latter, habit formation is made dependent upon conditioning no less than is habit inhibition. In the earlier version, the learning produced by reward was thought of as involving a strengthening of the stimulus-response sequence which leads to the reward; whereas the effect produced by punishment was conceived, not as simply reversing the effects of prior reward, but as leading to the conditioning of fear to stimuli associated with the occurrence of the stimulus-response sequence which elicited the punishment. The unsatisfactory nature of primitive habit theory, as represented by the Law of Effect, first became evident from the study of punishment and avoidance behavior and led to the earlier two-factor position. Now, for reasons previously reviewed, it seems that conditioning is responsible for the effects of reward no less than for the effects of punishment. Hence, all learning is reduced to sign learning (with "feedback" control of behavior; see Chapter 7). By virtue of this new and more consistent position, the problem of unlearning and of conflict is manifestly changed.

Let us begin by reviewing some well-authenticated facts concerning learning and unlearning when independent, external signs are involved. We know that if such a stimulus, as a result of association with one type of reinforcement, is given a particular meaning, this meaning can be changed either by (a) repeated presentation of the stimulus without such reinforcement or by (b) association with the opposite type of reinforcement. For example, if a given stimulus, through association with the onset of pain, has first acquired the capacity to arouse fear, its "meaning" can be changed, in the direction of neutrality, by the repetitive occurrence of the stimulus *without* the pain; *or* the stimulus can be caused to lose its fear-arousing tendency and take on hope-arousing capacity by its repeated conjunction with a *pleasurable* experience of some sort. The first of these procedures is ordinarily referred to as *extinction* and the other as *counterconditioning*.

We may suppose, then, that the selection or elimination of *behavior* is controlled by these same principles, except that here the conditioning involves stimuli that are response-correlated rather than independent. A response which has previously had little or no "habit strength" may be made more likely to occur in a given situation if followed by reward, since the stimuli associated therewith become conditioned to hope; and once established in this way, the same behavior can be nullified either by elimination of the reward or, more swiftly, by replacing the reward with punishment, so that the stimuli associated therewith arouse fear rather than hope or positive expectation. Here no assumption whatever is made concerning changes in the conductance or resistance of the neural connections between the organism's brain and muscles, i.e., in what may be called the "executive" ("ordering") pathways. The change occurs rather in the nature of the "information" relayed *back* to the brain when a given course of action is started or contemplated (i.e., is symbolically rehearsed; Mowrer, 1960, Chapters 2 and 5). It is assumed that if response-produced stimuli become conditioned to fear, the likelihood of recurrence of that response will be decreased and that if response-produced stimuli become conditioned to hope, the likelihood of recurrence will be increased and that, with nonreinforcement, both types of conditioning will extinguish, toward a null or "indifference" point, with a concomitant lessening in response strength or response inhibition, as the case may be.

Thus, if we assume that "habit" is neither a motive-response nor a cue-response *bond* but a matter of hope being conditioned to stimuli associated with the occurrence of a particular response, it is easy to account for loss of habit strength through either extinction (nonreinforcement) or counterconditioning (opposing reinforcement). If the revised two-factor conception of habit formation is valid and if the meaning of external signs can be modified in the ways indicated, then it follows that, by the same principles, behavior itself can be modified by changing the meaning of behavior-connected stimuli. ·

Here, as elsewhere, we shall find that habit is the same as conditioning—that, in fact, it *is* conditioning: the conditioning of hopes to response-correlated, rather than independent, stimuli.

II. Conditioning and Counterconditioning with External Stimuli

In the preceding discussion it has been taken for granted that the affective responses made to external stimuli can be changed according to definite and orderly principles. Before going further it will be useful to examine some of the relevant laboratory evidence for such an assumption. Oddly enough, one of the earliest and best studies of this kind was published in 1920 by John Watson, the great advocate of Behaviorism, in collaboration with Rosalie Rayner. The introductory paragraph of their report reads as follows:

> In recent literature various speculations have been entered into concerning the possibility of conditioning various types of emotional response, but direct experimental evidence in support of such a view has been lacking. If the theory advanced by Watson and Morgan (1917) to the effect that in infancy the original emotional reaction patterns are few, consisting so far as observed of fear, rage and love, then there must be some simple method by means of which the range of stimuli which can call out these emotions and their compounds is greatly increased. Otherwise, complexity in adult response could not be accounted for. These authors without adequate experimental evidence advanced the view that this range was increased by means of conditioned reflex factors. It was suggested there that the early home life of the child furnishes a laboratory situation for establishing conditioned emotional responses. The present authors have recently put the whole matter to an experiment test (p. 1).

There then follows an account of the now-classical Watson-Rayner experiments with the year-old infant, "Albert B." He was "reared almost from birth in a hospital environment; his mother was a wet nurse in the Harriet Lane Home for Invalid Children." He was described as an unusually healthy and unemotional child. In fact, "his stability was one of the principal reasons for using him as a subject in this test" (p. 1). First of all, Albert was shown an array of more or less "furry" objects: "a white rat, a rabbit, a dog, a monkey, masks with and without hair, cotton wool, burning newspapers, etc. . . . At no time did this infant ever show fear . . ." (p. 2).

The plan was to select the white rat as a "conditioned stimulus" and see if it could be made to elicit signs of fear by associating it with the noise produced by striking a "steel bar a sharp blow." The investigators wished to obtain, if possible, answers to the following four questions:

I. Can we condition fear of an animal, e.g., a white rat, by visually presenting it and simultaneously striking a steel bar?

II. If such a conditioned emotional response be established, will there be a transfer to other animals or other objects?

III. What is the effect of time upon such conditioned emotional responses?

IV. If after a reasonable period such emotional responses have not died out, what laboratory methods can be devised for their removal? (p. 3).

The first two conditioning trials employed in this investigation are then described as follows:

> White rat suddenly taken from the basket and presented to Albert. He began to reach for rat with left hand. Just as his hand touched the animal the bar was struck immediately beyond his head. The infant jumped violently and fell forward, burying his face in the mattress. He did not cry, however.
>
> Just as the right hand touched the rat [on the second trial] the bar was again struck. Again the infant jumped violently, fell forward and began to whimper (p. 4).

One week later there were five more "joint stimulations." On the eighth trial, the rat alone was presented.

> The instant the rat was shown the baby began to cry. Almost instantly he turned sharply to the left, fell over on left side, raised himself on all fours and began to crawl away so rapidly that he was caught with difficulty before reaching the end of the table.
>
> This was as convincing a case of a completely conditioned fear response as could have been theoretically pictured. In all, seven joint stimulations were given to bring about the complete reaction. It is not unlikely had the sound been of greater intensity or of a more complex clang character that the number of joint stimulations might have been materially reduced (p. 5).

Five days later Albert was tested for generalization of fear to other objects. Wooden blocks were accepted and manipulated as usual. But then:

> The rabbit was suddenly placed on the mattress in front of him. The reaction was pronounced. Negative responses began at once. He leaned as far away from the animal as possible, whimpered, then burst into tears (p. 6).

Less marked but definite evidences of fear generalization were likewise observed in the little boy's reactions to a dog, a fur coat, cotton wool, and a Santa Claus mask. He was also "completely negative" when one of the experimenters "put his head down to see if Albert would play with his hair" (p. 7). There is thus clear-cut evidence of transfer of fear to objects somewhat similar to the white rat and of no transfer to more dissimilar objects, e.g., wooden blocks.

The experimenters were also able to show that when Albert was placed in a room other than that in which original conditioning has occurred, the rat and other "furry" objects produced some withdrawal and fear tendencies, but they were less marked than they had been in the other situation. Thus it was demonstrated that not only is there a gradient of fear generalization from the original conditioned stimulus (white rat) to other similar objects but that there is also a gradient of generalization in the fear reactions shown by the subject to these several objects from the original learning situation to a different, neutral situation.

What, then, of the "effect of time upon conditioned emotional responses"? (p. 10). As a result of tests made after a lapse of one month, the investigators say:

> These experiments would seem to show conclusively that directly conditioned emotional responses as well as those conditioned by transfer persist, although with a certain loss in the intensity of the reaction, for a longer period than one month (p. 12).

Because of the unavoidable removal of Albert from the hospital setting, Watson and Rayner were unable to experiment with methods which might have eliminated his fear of the white rat and similar objects. Had he been available for a longer period, they would have attempted "reconditioning" by "feeding the subject candy or other food just as the animal is shown" (p. 12) and by providing other pleasant experiences in this context.

An incidental observation made by these workers which is not without interest and relevance here is that, although not a "thumbsucker" under ordinary circumstances, Albert was very prone to put his thumb in his mouth "as a compensatory device for blocking fear and noxious stimuli."

> During the course of these experiments, especially in the final test, it was noticed that whenever Albert was on the verge of tears or emotionally upset generally he would continually thrust his thumb into his mouth. The moment the hand reached the mouth he became impervious to the stimuli producing fear (p. 13).

This type of observation has been repeated in many other types of situation; and it squares well with our assumption that fear and hope are antithetical and that, depending upon which is the stronger, one will counteract the other. It may be that Freud (1916) is correct in his contention that the mouth is an "instinctively" erogenous zone and that stimulation thereof produces a pleasurable sensation no less reflexly and innately than does stimulation of the sex organs (ct. the discussion of the innate "palatability" of certain tastes, Chapter 6). But it is also conceivable that since oral stimulation regularly precedes hunger (and hunger-fear) reduction, it acquires quite powerful secondary-reinforcement properties and, in this way, becomes capable of neutralizing fear. So far as we know, Albert was not especially, if at all, hungry when the tests were conducted with him, so it may at first not seem reasonable for him to have sought, under these conditions, to re-activate stimulation which had been associated with eating. But there are now a good many laboratory demonstrations of the generalization of secondary reinforcement, i.e., the tendency for living organisms, after certain stimuli have been associated with one type of fear reduction, to attempt to reproduce these same stimuli when experiencing fear of a different type. "Anxious eating" has already been alluded to, and "anxious sucking" would seem to be a closely related phenomenon (see Chapter 5).

In view of the inability of Watson and Rayner to study fear *de*conditioning in Albert, it is fortunate that Mary Cover Jones, a few years later, became interested in this problem and carried out a number of illuminating studies. Instead of setting up specific fears experimentally and then introducing conditions designed to "undo" them, Dr. Jones (1924a) undertook the presumably more difficult task of eliminating fears which children had already acquired in their daily lives. Various methods—disuse, verbal appeal, negative adaptation, repression,[1] distraction, and social imitation—were tested for their effectiveness in this connection; but the approach which worked best was that of "direct conditioning." It was described thus:

> During a period of craving for food, the child is placed in a high chair and given something to eat. The fear-object is brought in, starting a negative response. It is then moved away gradually until it is at a sufficient distance not to interfere with the child's eating. The relative strength of the fear impulse and the hunger impulse may be gauged by the distance to which it is necessary to remove the fear object. While the child is eating, the object is slowly brought nearer to the table, then placed upon the table, and finally as the tolerance increases it is brought close enough to be touched. . . . The effectiveness of this method increases greatly as the hunger grows, at least up to a certain point. The case of Peter [reported in detail elsewhere, Jones, 1924b]

[1] It is not clear exactly what procedure Jones implies by the word "repression," but it at least suggests *punishment* of the fear response. We have some understanding of what to expect when independent or response-correlated stimuli are followed by drive increment; but we do not know, in any systematic way, what happens when fear itself is thus reinforced. The problem manifestly needs further attention (see Section VI).

illustrates our procedure; one of our most serious problem cases, he was treated by the method daily or twice daily for a period of two months. The laboratory notes for the first and the last days of the training period show an improvement which we were able to attribute specifically to the training measures used.

Case 30.—Peter. Age 2 years, 10 months.

March 10, 10:15 a.m. Peter sitting in high chair, eating candy. Experimenter entered room with a rabbit in an open mesh wire cage. The rabbit was placed on the table 4 feet from Peter who immediately began to cry, insisting that the rabbit be taken away. Continued crying until the rabbit was put down 20 feet away. He then started again on the candy, but continued to fuss, "I want you to put Bunny outside." After three minutes he once more burst into tears; the rabbit was removed.

April 29, 9:55 a.m. Peter standing in high chair, looking out of the window. He inquired, "Where is the rabbit?" The rabbit was put down on the chair at Peter's feet. Peter patted him, tried to pick him up, but finding the rabbit too heavy asked the experimenter to help in lifting him to the window sill, where he played with him for several minutes.

This method obviously requires delicate handling. Two response systems are being dealt with: food leading to a positive reaction, and fear-object leading to a negative reaction. The desired conditioning should result in transforming the fear-object into a source of positive response (substitute stimulus). But a careless manipulator could readily produce the reverse result, attaching a fear reaction to the sight of food (pp. 388–389).

By way of summarizing her work, Dr. Jones says, in part:

In our study of methods for removing fear responses, we found unqualified success with only two. By the method of direct conditioning we associated the fear-object with a craving-object, and replaced the fear by a positive response. By the method of social imitation we allowed the subject to share, under controlled conditions, the social activity of a group of children especially chosen with a view to prestige effect . . . (p. 390).

In the more detailed report of Peter's "recovery" already cited (Jones, 1924b), the process of reconditioning is shown quantitatively by means of the graph reproduced in Fig. 11-1. The letters shown along the ordinate of this figure represent a range in toleration of the originally fear-producing object from "A, Rabbit anywhere in the room in a cage causes fear reactions" to "P, Fondles rabbit affectionately" and "Q, Lets rabbit nibble his fingers." The graph therefore shows a progressive and decided change in Peter's attitude toward the rabbit, from strong fear to positive interest and affection.

The work of Watson & Rayner and of Jones thus demonstrates that by association with a noxious experience an originally neutral (or even an emotionally positive) object can become a potent fear-producer and that by association with a pleasurable experience an originally neutral, or even an emotionally negative, object can be made to take on emotionally positive and pleasant connotations. Thus we are in agreement with Thorndike in his contention that learning is "reversible," but we depart from his position in two important ways. We assume (1) that the "locus" of learning is not in the S—R bond but in the R:s—r connections. And we assume (2) that learning may move in either direction on a "scale" extending from +1.0 (strong hope) through 0.0 (indifference, neutrality) to −1.0 (strong fear), rather than merely back and forth on a scale extending from 0.0 (no habit strength, no "bond") to +1.0 (maximal habit strength).

Many of the implications which flow from these distinctions have already been noted; but a new one may be appropriately suggested here. According to Thorndike's scheme (of which Hull's is a variant), the "least" habit strength which a given response can have is zero (0.0). Habit strength cannot, in other words, be less than zero in this system, i.e., it cannot have a *negative* value. But in point of fact, we know that such a state can easily exist: e.g., a dog which has been

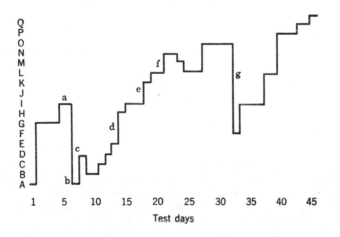

Fig. 11–1. A graph reproduced from Mary Cover Jones (1924b, p. 311) showing the progressive extinction of a fear response in a small boy. The meaning of the capital letters along the ordinate is given in the text. The lower-case letters accompanying the curve itself designate points at which vicissitudes in the daily life of the child or in the experimental situation occurred and facilitated or retarded the extinction and reconditioning process. These are described in some detail in the original report.

severely shocked for raising his right forepaw (or after having it passively lifted) as, let us say, a means of obtaining food, will thereafter not only not make this response—he will *actively resist* ("push against") this response, both when the response is instigated actively (cf. Konorski's experiments, Section X, Chapter 8) and when an attempt is made by the experimenter to "perform" the response for the dog. *Negative* habit strength, or response *resistance*, which we know to be an empirical reality, is readily derivable from revised two-factor theory, but it is not deducible from the Thorndikian theory of learning. In addition, neither can the latter give an explanation of place learning (approach and avoidance), whereas place learning is no less easily accounted for in the present system (Chapter 9) than are response facilitation and active response inhibition.

III. Nonconfirmation versus Counterconditioning: the Fatigue Hypothesis

In the preceding section we have seen some instances of emotional conditioning and counterconditioning to external stimuli. Remaining is the question whether so-called extinction is simply counterconditioning which is carried just to the null point (of no meaning) or involves rather a different process of some sort.

In the second version of two-factor theory, loss of learning through extinction constituted something of an enigma. If it is assumed that "habits," instead of being intrinsically weakened by punishment, are merely blocked by the competing motive of fear, then how is one to interpret the loss of habit strength which occurs with mere extinction, mere nonrewarded repetition? In the introduction of a republished version of an early paper by Mowrer & Jones (Mowrer, 1950a), this problem has been stated—and ostensibly solved—as follows:

> Any careful investigation of the psychology of fear leads to a consideration of the inhibition of behavior that is produced by means of so-called "punishment." Other writers [notably Thorndike] have suggested that this effect comes about by virtue of "punishment" having the capacity to neutralize or reverse the effects of previous experienced "reward." It now seems that inhibition occurs rather as a result of *conflict*, which consists of the incompatibility of the punished response and the response(s) which the punishment itself and the associated fear call forth. (What is said here is intended to apply only to the inhibition of overt *behavior*. How emotional reactions are negatively modified is an independent and, at present, not well understood problem.) [This comment was made in the context of unrevised two-factor learning theory (see Section VI).]

In this paper the same logic is extended to account for the inhibition of habits, not by punishment in the ordinary sense, but by what is often referred to as "extinction." In extinction the only apparent source of conflict is that provided by the *fatigue* resulting from the recurrent, unrewarded perform-ance of a habit. The experiment here reported was designed to test the de-duction that, with other things equal, effortful responses, i.e., responses whose performance generates relatively great fatigue, will extinguish (in-hibit) more quickly than less effortful ones. This inference was confirmed at a high level of confidence (p. 152).

The hypothesis thus put forward might be reformulated, somewhat more colloquially, by saying that both punished and nonrewarded responses are inhibited for basically similar reasons. In the one case it is as if the subject says to himself, "If I perform that response I will get *hurt*." In the other case it is as if the subject says to himself, "If I perform that response I will get *tired*." Both pain and fatigue are forms of discomfort; and it is assumed that they both operate, the one swiftly, the other more gradually, to inhibit any response which produces them.

The experimental findings referred to in the paragraph last quoted are reproduced, in graphic form, in Fig. 11–2. During prior training 30 hungry laboratory rats had learned to press a Skinner bar in order to obtain food, with the bar requiring, at different stages of training, 5, 42.5, and 80 grams of pressure to depress it. The subjects were then

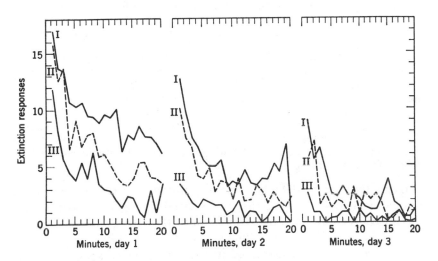

Fig. 11–2. Curves showing the course of extinction of a habit when that habit is easy (I), hard (III), and intermediate (II) with respect to the effort required to execute it (Mowrer and Jones, 1943, p. 374).

randomly divided into three equal groups; and extinction was carried out with the bar so weighted as to require one of the three pressures just listed. As will be seen in Fig. 11–3, there was a decided (and

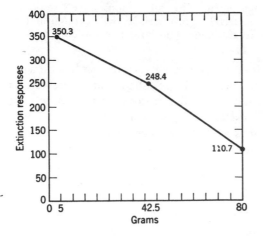

Fig. 11–3. Average number of extinction responses made by three different groups of animals as a function of response effortfulness (Mowrer and Jones, 1943, p. 375).

statistically reliable) relationship between rapidity of extinction and the effort involved in performing the act of bar pressing. In summarizing this part of their investigation Mowrer & Jones say:

> This study takes as its point of departure the hypothesis that the elimination of a response, or habit, through its own nonrewarded repetition involves a conflict in which the fatigue thus generated instigates a response (resting) which is incompatible with and therefore tends to inhibit the original response. Such an hypothesis is confirmed by the finding that the rate at which a nonrewarded response extinguishes is highly correlated with the effortfulness of that response. It is also confirmed by the well-known tendency for an extinguished response to reappear after a lapse of time, since the motive which produces the inhibitory response of resting, namely, fatigue, is thereby eliminated. The fact that the amount of recovery following successive extinctions becomes progressively smaller and may eventually reach zero is due to a change in the "meaning" of both situational and organic cues, which follow familiar learning principles (p. 169).

Using the empirical findings here reported (see also confirmatory studies by Solomon, 1948a, 1948b, and Applezweig, 1951) as the basis for his reasoning, Hull (1943) introduced the terms, "reactive inhibition" (I_R) and "conditioned inhibition" ($_sI_R$), to refer, respectively, to the two phenomena described in the foregoing paragraph. Kimble (1949) has paraphrased Hull's definition of reactive inhibition thus:

Reactive inhibition is essentially a negative drive state closely allied to pain. . . . It is a *response-produced* inhibition which results from or accompanies all effortful behavior whether reinforced or not and dissipates during periods of rest. In this respect I_R resembles fatigue (p. 15).[2]

If nonrewarded repetition of a response is to have anything more than a temporarily depressing influence, it is clear that something must happen comparable to the fear learning involved in the use of punishment. It was therefore assumed, by Mowrer & Jones, that some part of the "reactive inhibition," or fatigue reaction, produced by non-rewarded repetition could become conditioned to stimuli associated with the occurrence of the response in question, so that subsequently the response could be immediately inhibited, instead of having to occur enough times to generate full-fledged fatigue.

This, then, is how the matter of inhibition through extinction was handled in the second version of two-factor learning theory and in Hull's formal theoretical system. However, this can scarcely be the end of the story. In the first place, there is still some question about the empirical validity of the assumption that effortful responses extinguish more rapidly than easy ones. Such an assumption certainly agrees with common observation; and Solomon and Applezweig, as already noted, have reported confirmatory laboratory findings. However Maatsch, Adelman, & Denny (1954), in a paper entitled "Effort and resistance to extinction of the bar-pressing response," report data which they feel go against such an assumption. In their study these writers used an over-all procedure similar to that employed by Mowrer & Jones, but with certain controls which they felt were lacking in the earlier study. Their findings are reproduced in Fig. 11-4, of which the authors say:

The present study indicates that work, within the limits employed, bears no relationship to resistance to extinction, and as a consequence, to the accumulation of I_R. The data obtained by Mowrer and Jones in a comparable situation may be attributed to the differences in habit strength produced by their preliminary training schedule. . . .

The Mowrer and Jones study, far from being convincing evidence of a relationship between work and the accumulation of I_R would seem to support the lack of relationship found in the present study. . . .

[2] Hull frequently referred to the concept of "reactive inhibition" to account for extinction, but almost never used the term "punishment." A rare exception will be found on p. 44 of Hull, Livingston, Rouse, & Barker (1951), where he speaks of "negative reinforcement (punishment) as distinguished from experiment extinction" (Chapter 3, Section III, and Chapter 6, Section VI).

Conflicting results of a similar nature were reported by Montgomery (1951a). . . .

It is concluded, in light of the present study and available literature, that explanations of extinction phenomena based upon the effects of lesser amounts of work, such as might be encountered in Skinner boxes, T mazes, and other common learning situations, are questionable and contingent upon further research in this area (p. 49).

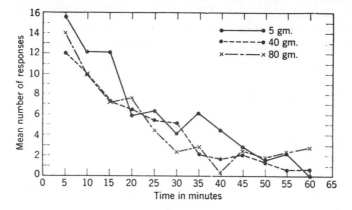

Fig. 11–4. Response extinction as a function of response effort (Maatsch, Adelman, & Denny, 1954, p. 49).

Whether these criticisms of the fatigue theory of extinction will be supported or refuted by further empirical inquiry is an open question (see Aiken, 1957; Lawson & Brownstein, 1957; Stanley & Aamodt, 1954; Capehart, Viney, & Hulicka, 1958; and Chapter 7, Section VI). But there is another issue which has logical precedence over the one raised by Maatsch *et al.* In any case, the fatigue hypothesis is applicable only to the extinction of responses involving the skeletal musculature, i.e., to "habits." The fact is, of course, that purely autonomic responses, such as the galvanic skin reaction (fear) or salivation, also undergo extinction if repeatedly elicited without reinforcement; and there can scarcely be a question here of "fatigue," at least not in any ordinary sense of the term. Only in connection with responses involving skeletal (striated) muscles do we normally speak of fatigue as a consciously experienced countermotivation. Emotional responses, mediated by the autonomic nervous system and involving glands and smooth muscle, can manifestly be conditioned and deconditioned, yet their repeated elicitation does not, so far as we know, generate anything like fatigue. Hence we must have something other than a fatigue theory to account for the extinction of emotional responses. The fatigue theory, as described above, is evidently a form of counterconditioning, rather than extinction in "pure form." The fact seems to be that repeated nonconfirmation of an emotional response (notably hope or fear) also tends to cause that response to disappear. Its disappearance can be hastened by explicit counterconditioning; but, as already noted, mere nonconfirmation seems to be a sufficient condition for the gradual elimination of such responses.[3] The question is: Does such a procedure involve a subtle form of counterconditioning or some different principle or mechanism? This problem will be given special consideration in the next section.

IV. Extinction and the Concept of Frustration

In this volume we have repeatedly seen how unsatisfactory was the treatment of punishment and avoidance learning until the subjective phenomenon of *fear* was acknowledged and systematically related to theory; and we have also followed the growth of interest in so-called secondary reinforcement, which seems to be nothing more nor less than the common experience of *hope*. Contemporary learning theory, with its behavioristic bias, has also been reluctant to acknowledge the reality of *anger*; but that reluctance has been slowly overcome, and this

---

[3] This discussion is given special point by an experiment recently reported by Black (1958), which consisted of teaching dogs an active avoidance response (under threat of electric shock) and then repeatedly presenting the danger signal (without shock) while the subjects were muscularly paralyzed (by curare) but fully conscious and sensate. "Dogs receiving extinction trials while immobilized by d-tubocurarine chloride required fewer trials to reach the extinction criterion and made fewer responses during extinction (when tested after recovering from curarization) than animals which had not received extinction trials under curare" (p. 524). And earlier, Solomon, Kamin, & Wynne (1953) showed that a similar effect can be produced by means of a glass barrier, which prevents dogs from executing a shuttling response and thus forces them to "reality test" (during extinction) and discover that the shock "isn't there" anymore. Hence, on sound experimental grounds (see also Hurwitz, 1955, and Amsel, 1958b), we can say that since the performance of an overt response is not essential for its extinction (see Mowrer, 1960, Chapter 2), it can hardly be argued that the fatigue or effort factor is the *sole* determiner of extinction. However, the fact of emotional extinction in its own right does not exclude the possibility that effort may still operate as suggested by Mowrer & Jones. To coin a phrase, the situation seems somewhat complex: but we may yet find the phenomenon of extinction, in all its guises, can be subsumed under a single master formula (see Section IV).

emotion, like the others cited, is gradually finding its rightful place in the scientific analysis of behavior.[4]

In 1939 Dollard, Doob, Miller, Mowrer, & Sears made the first extended effort to deal with this problem in their book, *Frustration and Aggression*. Despite some useful features, this effort was not very successful. It drew much of its inspiration from psychoanalytic speculations concerning aggression and hostility, as viewed clinically; and it was at the same time dominated, methodologically, by a strong behavioristic slant which required that frustration and aggression be treated in a simple stimulus-response framework, which had little or no place for the intervening variable of anger (cf. Miller & Stevenson, 1936; also Lewin, 1956).

In 1951 Brown & Farber made a more realistic attack upon this problem in an article entitled "Emotions Conceptualized as Intervening Variables—with Suggestions Toward a Theory of Frustration." Heartened by the successful introduction of fear as an intervening variable (and by the emerging recognition of hope), these writers argued, persuasively enough, that the time had come to begin also to consider anger in the context of systematic learning theory. Since Hull's treatment of the latter was the most highly formal and elaborate then available, these writers used it as the matrix for their postulations concerning the role of anger. That system, as we now know, has a number of major (if not fatal) weaknesses: so no attempt will be made here to show the ways in which Brown & Farber related their analysis to it.

One of the many more fortunate features of their paper is that these writers point out the inherent relation between problem solving (trial-and-error learning) and the experience of frustration in the sense of a blocking of on-going behavior. They say:

> This similarity is well exemplified by Dashiell's (1937) use of a schematic diagram of adjustive behavior leading to learning (p. 364) which is identical in its essential relations with his diagram of frustration resulting from a conflict of motives (p. 144). Both schema include factors leading to the blocking of a motivated response, both include barrier-circumventing or "solution" responses and possibilities for readjustment or learning. Melton (1941), following Dashiell, has made a similar analysis of the learning process and has explicitly noted that ". `. . this definition and analysis of learning assumes

---

[4] These three states obviously correspond to what Watson & Morgan (Section II) termed the three "original emotional reaction patterns": fear, love, and rage. But whereas the early Behaviorists saw these solely as "reactions," neobehaviorists go further and recognize their motivational and behavior-determining properties (see Winsor, 1930).

that all instances of learning involve in some degree the frustration of a motivated organism . . ." (p. 669) (Brown & Farber, p. 477).[5]

Now as Brown & Farber point out, many learning theorists have advanced "nonemotional interpretations of frustration" (p. 477); and, in general, the resulting oversimplifications have not been too serious. After all, the white rat has been carefully bred for his *docility;* and, precisely because of their "viciousness," wild rats have been found to be almost worthless as laboratory subjects. But even a highly docilized strain of rats still have some spunk and spirit left in them, as the experiments to be cited presently show. With other species this dimension of behavior has always been apparent.

For instance, Finch (1942) has observed that chimpanzees accustomed to pressing the handle of a spigot to get water will press with much more than usual energy if the water supply is shut off (Brown & Farber, p. 478).

This intensification of on-going behavior (presumably implying increased motivation) is certainly one of the striking behavioral indices of frustration; but in a thoughtful recent paper, Bull & Strongin (1956) point out that frustration may also result in at least a temporary *loss* of interest in the original goal and "fixation on the obstacle."

Thus we are dealing [they say] first and foremost with a special type of conflict between two orienting attitudes which are related but, for various reasons, incompatible—the first one aiming toward a goal, and still operative, though impaired; the second one initiated by the obstacle, and aimed at getting rid of it (p. 531).

These writers further develop their analysis along clinical lines, in a highly interesting and suggestive way; but present purposes will be best served if we return to the Brown-Farber discussion. These writers, having abandoned the strictly S—R (frustration-aggression) approach of Dollard *et al.,* usefully note that, once anger is admitted as a motivational construct, it follows that any of several reactions other than aggression are at least theoretically possible, and they also conjecture that, "Like any unconditioned response, a frustration reaction [anger] might be conditioned to other (perhaps external) 'non-frustration' stimuli" (p. 490). In conclusion Brown & Farber say:

It will be apparent from this treatment of frustration as a determinant of behavior that no attempt has been made to specify precisely which responses will appear in thwarting situations. The present theory does lead to the ex-

[5] The same general point of view was also adumbrated in Shaffer's 1936 book, *The Psychology of Adjustment.*

pectations that the presence of frustration will often result in the intensification of responses, that reactions followed by a reduction in frustration will be reinforced, and that responses associated with frustration in one situation will tend to appear in other thwarting situations. But there is nothing in the theory itself to imply that aggression, for instance, will occur more frequently than withdrawal, or withdrawal more frequently than, say, primitivization [regression] (p. 490).

In an earlier chapter reference has already been made to an attempt by Brown & Farber to test the hypothesis that in a situation originally used by Miller to show, purportedly, the role of escape from a fear-inducing situation as a secondary reinforcer, there might also (or instead) be an element of frustration and that it might thus be *anger* rather than fear which was the relevant secondary motivator and reinforcer. But since this experiment led to negative results, it cannot be regarded as a successful test of the assumption "that reactions followed by a reduction in frustration will be reinforced." However, the assumption "that the presence of frustration will often result in the intensification of responses" has provided the inspiration for a series of quite successful experiments by Amsel and collaborators, the first of which was reported by Amsel & Roussel, in 1952, and summarized as follows:

This experiment was designed to test the assumption that frustration is a motivational state. . . .
Eighteen male albino rats were trained under hunger drive to run down an alley into a goal box, then leave that goal box and run down a second alley into a second goal box distinctively different from the first one. Their time to traverse the alley between Goal box 1 and Goal box 2 was measured during a preliminary period. When this time had reached a stable minimum, their running time and latency in leaving Goal box 1 were measured during test trials. In half of these trials they were frustrated in Goal box 1 [i.e., the expected reward of food was not received]; in the other half they were not. . . .
An implication of the . . . assumption—that strength of performance on frustration test trials should be greater than that during the preliminary trials or that on reward test trials—was strongly supported by the data (p. 368) [see Fig. 11–5].

This finding, that a "frustrated" rat is more motivated than a satisfied one, is congruent with conjectures put forward in Chapter 5. There the assumption is made that a stimulus with secondary reinforcing properties is one which is capable of allaying drive fear, giving "assurances," arousing *hope*. Thus it is almost axiomatic that "frustration," in the objective sense of that term, involves the nonfulfillment, nonconfirmation of an implied "promise" and the emergence, at the very least, of the experience previously termed *disappointment*, which is to say the *loss* of hope and the *return of fear* and the resulting *increase of motivation* found by Amsel & Roussel. This line of reasoning is independently supported by the following observation by Bull & Strongin:

We propose . . . to limit the term frustration to situations where interruption takes on this character of *threat* and automatically produces the mixed type of emergency reaction which is found in all "emotional" response to danger. Thus all frustration would definitely connote the presence of fear, which is not, however, sufficiently overwhelming to cause a complete disappearance of the original goal-oriented tendency (p. 532).

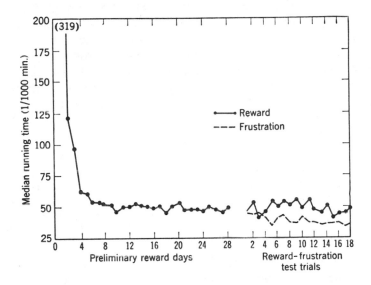

Fig. 11–5. Experimental demonstration of the thesis that frustration may serve to increase the total drive state of an organism (Amsel and Roussel, 1952, p. 367).

It has long been known that fear and anger are physiologically akin —both being characterized by activation of the sympathetic division of the autonomic nervous system (Arnold, 1950; Ax, 1953). And it is conceivable that whether such arousal will be subjectively perceived as anger or as fear *may* depend, in part at least, upon certain perceptual and motor factors, or "sets," on the part of the organism, i.e., upon what may be loosely called the organism's "intentions." Presumably everyone has had the experience of having his "fear turn into anger" or the reverse; and this mutability may be a function of whether *attack* or *retreat* is perceived as the best policy. Could it be that, in at least some situations, William James was right (see p. 48) and that we are afraid because we run (or at least feel that we ought to) and that we are angry because we fight (or feel we ought to)? Here the facts are not at all clear, but this much can apparently be said with some confidence. Just as "appetite" surges up in an organism as it comes close to a goal, anger likewise mounts when a barrier suddenly intervenes. Appetite, as conjectured in Chapter 6, has the effect of providing that last additional bit of motivation sometimes needed to ensure success; whereas anger, it seems, often gives the organism special energy at just those critical points when possible success is about to turn into sure failure (see Haner & Brown, 1955). However, if frustration-induced anger does *not* lead to success, it serves another function which will be explored, more systematically, in the next section.

As will be thus apparent some progress is now being made in articulating the concept of frustration with general behavior theory; and the experimental literature is growing apace. Fortunately this literature has just been reviewed by Amsel (1958a) and need not be reconsidered here.[6] However, it is pertinent to note some of Amsel's opening comments in this connection:

> This paper is based on the proposition that an adequate theory of instrumental behavior must involve three types of goal event: (a) *Rewarding events*—usually the presence of stimuli which evoke a consummatory reaction appropriate to some condition of deprivation; (b) *Punishing events*—noxious stimulation at the termination of a behavior sequence; and (c)*Frustrative events*—the absence of or delay of a rewarding event in a situation where it had been present previously (p. 102).

It is quickly apparent that this writer thinks of each of these events as capable of becoming conditioned to formerly neutral stimuli as, respectively, *hope, fear* and *anger* (although his terminology is slightly different).

---

[6] Special attention should nevertheless be called to the fact that, following the demonstration by Amsel & Roussel that on-going behavior can be intensified by frustration, Bernstein (1957) has shown that frustration can (up to a point at least) increase resistance to extinction, Adelman & Maatsch (1955) report that anger can motivate and reinforce new learning, Wagner (1959) has defended the Amsel hypothesis (with experimental evidence) against a criticism advanced by Seward, Pereboom, Butler, & Jones (1957), and Holder, Marx, Holder, & Collier (1959) have published evidence that anger can be conditioned, much in the manner of fear or hope (see also Zbrozyna, 1958). For a review of earlier attempts to study the relation between frustration, anger, and learning, see Miller (1951b, p. 462; also 1957, p. 1278).

Basically, the position adopted here assumes that all learned, instrumental (goal-oriented) responses depend, to some extent, on classical-conditioned implicit responses. These responses are the learned counterparts of responses elicited by the three types of goal event—rewarding, punishing, and frustrative events—outlined earlier (p. 102).

Revised two-factor theory would differ with this statement only in holding that it is too guarded: if the phrase, "to some extent," were eliminated, the statement would be quite unobjectionable; for it would then assert, simply, that "*all* learned, instrumental (goal-oriented) responses" are, in the final analysis, selected, guided, and controlled by the emotions of hope, fear, and anger as they have been conditioned to response-correlated stimuli, independent stimuli, or both (but cf. Mowrer, 1960, Chapter 5).

Especially interesting and relevant for present purposes is Amsel's development of the notion that "frustrative non-rewarded events determine activating (drive) states, which can be measured as an increase in the vigor of behavior which immediately follows the frustrative events [see Amsel-Roussel experiment], and are also responsible for inhibitory effects, which are at least partly responsible for decreases in strength of the instrumental behavior which is terminated by the frustrative event" (p. 3). *Here* is a theory of extinction with generality and power. The best we have had in the past was the view that extinction occurs because habit strength (hope) is offset (through counterconditioning) by an inhibitory state created by the fatigue or effort generated by the nonrewarded repetition of a response. As Amsel indicates, this may still be a factor in extinction; but it is also very probable that the anger generated by nonreward (disappointment) serves to countercondition hope just as does the fear which is generated by punishment (see also Chapter 12).[7]

[7] Theory in this area is obviously in a state of flux and change. In his 1958b article, Amsel gives some indication of this when he says: "The important change which seems to be going on in our thinking about goal factors is in the conceptualization of the role of nonreinforcement (nonreward). It represents a movement away from Hull's treatment of nonreinforcement (following later Thorndike) as a nonactive factor in behavior (cf. Amsel, 1951, 1958a) and a return to an earlier position, most explicit in Spence's treatment of discrimination learning in the '30ies (Spence, 1936, 1937), in which nonreward is regarded as an active factor determining inhibitory tendencies. In his 1936 paper, after referring to the principle of reinforcement, Spence wrote: 'The second principle to be used is that of inhibition or frustration, which states that when a reaction is not rewarded, i.e., when the final consummatory response is prevented from taking place, the excitatory tendencies . . . are weakened . . . and it is assumed that this weakening is due to an active, negative process' (p. 430)" (pp. 3-4). In this paper Amsel

How much progress has been made during the past 30 years in our understanding of the whole problem of "unlearning" can be nicely illustrated by reference to an article published by Winsor in 1929. At that time, as Winsor pointed out, William James' old Law of Exercise (1890, Vol. I, Chapter 4) was still widely accepted; and he cited a later formulation thereof by Gates (1928) as follows: "Whenever a modifiable connection between a situation and a response is exercised, other things being equal, the strength of that connection is increased" (p. 282). Having become familiar with the phenomenon of experimental extinction (as reported by Pavlov, 1927) and with Dunlap's principle of negative practice (1928), Winsor cogently remarked:

An examination of almost any psychology text which describes the learning process will show that this dual aspect of adaptation has not been taken into consideration. It appears from the texts that the authors conceive of repetitive stimulation as inevitably increasing the probability that the response will continue to be positive. It seems never to have occurred to them that exercise might function in developing a negative response. In fact they try to account for adaptation without this type of response and when they are confronted with the inhibitive behavior assume that it is merely a limitation of the law of exercise (p. 395).

And then, in reference to the results of an experiment which Winsor himself reported, he said:

If we may assume that the increased secretion of the parotid [salivary gland] to the sight of food represents a typical organic habit and that under the conditions of the experiment it was "broken" or eliminated, these data become very significant to students of behavior. They afford a study of the factors which cause a positive or excitatory reaction to be changed into a negative or inhibitory reaction. The factor of exercise is rather clearly shown. If any one aspect of the total situation or organic influence could be singled out as of especial potency in the fixation of inhibition it would be repetition. Other factors remaining constant, this factor of exercise is seen to facilitate

---

does not exclude the factor of fatigue or effort in extinction; but, as already indicated, he is inclined to give greater weight to the *emotional* effects of nonreward. While granting that repeated nonrewarded performance of an act may cause an organism to *get tired* (see Section III), it may, more importantly, also cause the organism to *get mad*. And this *negative* emotion will then countercondition the *positive* emotion (hope) which has previously been conditioned to the sensory feedback from the act in question. Interestingly enough, although Spence has abandoned his originally Hullian position in these matters, he has not followed Amsel in reverting to his earlier views. Say Noble & Alcock (1958): "Spence (1956, p. 151) has forsaken habit-strength interpretations in favor of simple experimental extinction, thereby adopting a Guthrian type of counterconditioning hypothesis" (p. 411). For a recent review of the frustration concept in general—and a bibliography of 257 titles, see Lawson & Marx (1958).

inhibition as well as excitation. An important factor in the breaking of this organic secretory habit, therefore, is use. In order to conserve energy nature is equipped to eliminate false signals as well as to utilize adequate signals. Both processes appear to be subject to the same important basic laws. Whether the reaction develops into a positive or negative habit depends upon the biological significance of the situation. As the significance of the signal to the organism changes, persistence of that signal causes a change in the response (pp. 394–395).

Obviously, as we now know, the sheer occurrence of a response is no guarantee at all that the likelihood of its recurrence will be increased; in fact, as Winsor correctly points out, the repeated performance of a response may lead to its inhibition rather than facilitation. If, however, we somewhat revamp the Law of Exercise, it can be given a new validity. All learning, we now assume, is in the nature of conditioning; and the *sine qua non* for conditioning is the conjoint presentation of a so-called conditioned and unconditioned stimulus. At this level of analysis, so far as we know, the "Law of Exercise," or *repetition*, is unexceptionally true: Every time a CS is followed by the UnCS, the likelihood that the CS will produce the R originally elicited by the UnCS will be increased, provided that we are careful to apply this rule exclusively to *emotional* responses and do not extend it to overt behavior as well (see Section VI). And when a CS is *not* followed by the usual UnCS *or* when it is followed by a different, opposite type of UnCS, the original conditioned reaction is extinguished or (in the case of counterconditioning) replaced by an opposite type of reaction. It is only when we try to apply these principles to behavioral, rather than purely emotional, autonomic reactions that difficulty and confusion arise.

Thus a remarkable evolution of thought may be said to have occurred. For a time it looked as if the Law of Exercise was to be completely eclipsed by the Law of Effect; but as the latter has been probed and reformulated in the course of preceding chapters, we find that it is only a global approximation of facts which are more precisely explained in terms of classical conditioning—and here "exercise," in the sense of stimulus repetition "in contiguity," is of the essence.

V. Maier's Frustration-Fixation Hypothesis

The evidence reviewed in the preceding section adds up to a strong presumption that frustration is often an important factor in the *abolition* of "habits." It was therefore surprising that N. R. F. Maier, in 1949, should advance the notion that frustration, under certain special circumstances at least, results in their *fixation*, rather than elimination. His argument went as follows:

> If [in a Lashley discrimination apparatus, see Chapter 12] the cards are latched in no regular order (i.e., neither a particular card nor a particular position is consistently reward or punished), then there is no response that will permit escape from punishment. In such case the animal normally shows a stage of variability in its choices and soon thereafter it refuses to jump. This resistance to jumping may be overcome by giving the animal an electric shock at the jumping stand, prodding with a stick, or blowing a blast of air on it. Under these conditions the animal can be forced to jump. We speak of this situation as the *insoluble* or *no-solution* problem and regard it as frustrating both because it is a problem that cannot be solved and because pressure is applied to the animal to force a response.
>
> After a short while in the insoluble problem situation and with pressure applied to force behavior, the animal develops a response to the situation that has no adaptive value in the sense that it is adequate to the situation or in the sense that it is superior to any number of other possible responses. Nevertheless, the appearance of the behavior is associated with a decline in resistance to jumping. Thus an animal that is forced to respond in the insoluble problem situation may always choose the card on its right, despite the fact that this choice is punished on half the trials. This type of response is not selected by the method with which reward and punishment are used. At the same time it is not a mere random response but is consistently expressed and so must be considered as a response to the situation (pp. 26–27).

Equally striking, of course, were Thorndike's sudden repudiation of the negative half of his celebrated Law of Effect (see Chapter 2) and Spence's suggestions that there was probably no primary gradient of reinforcement (Chapter 10). While useful in stimulating new research and clarifying theory, neither of these observations has, however, proved basically sound; and it now appears that much the same verdict is in order as regards Maier's novel thesis. Hull once remarked that the "ingenuity" with which psychological experiments are designed is sometimes such that the experimenter himself is misled, no less than his subjects. At the very least, we may say that the Maier procedure involves a great many variables and that the frustration-fixation hypothesis, as advanced by Maier, seems to neglect some of them.

In a review of Maier's book, published in 1950, the present writer suggested that the picture might be clarified by thinking along the following lines. Originally, during the discrimination-training phase of the Maier-type experiment, the rats are motivated by hunger and rewarded, for jumping toward the correct stimulus card, by food. Also, they are punished, by a bump on the nose and a fall into a net below, for jumping toward the incorrect stimulus card. By carefully attending to business, the rats can, of course, bring the incidence of reward up to 100% and reduce the incidence of punishment to 00%. And this is precisely what they tend to do (see the Chapter-12 discussion of discrimination learning). But when the "rules" are changed and the cards are *randomly* locked or loose (instead of the "correct" one always being loose and the "incorrect" one always locked, as during the preceding training), the animals are—understandably enough— "frustrated." Now the best they can probably do is 50% jumps correct (rewarding) and 50% incorrect (punishing); and it is not surprising that they "get mad," refuse to "play," and have to be *forced* to jump under threat of punishment of some kind, from "behind." Neither is it remarkable that, under such coercion, the animals, although continuing to jump, abandon the attempt to "follow" the (now meaningless) positive cue card from one side of the apparatus to the other on successive trials and revert ("regress") to the simpler, easier, and *no less rewarding* practice of always jumping to the *same side*, i.e., developing a "position habit"—or what Maier called a "fixation."

Viewed from the proper perspective, there is nothing in the least paradoxical or exceptional about this finding: the animals have learned a discrimination habit, conditions are changed so that this habit can no longer operate effectively, and the discrimination habit is soon abandoned! Frustration can be said to result in "fixation" only if attention is shifted to a *different* mode of adjustment, which is *simpler* than the discrimination habit and which persists only because of the coercive threat of punishment. Maier has been inclined to refer to such a position habit as "behavior without a goal." Eglash (1951) is probably more nearly correct when he suggests that there is a *change* in goals: from the original interest in obtaining food (which the discrimination habit, if practiced perfectly, provided 100% of the time) to the later interest in avoiding punishment on the jumping stand (which the position habit did 100% of the time—which was just as well as the more complex and, presumably, more difficult "discrimination" habit, which was now no longer functional in the way it originally was, could do).

Maier has held that when an organism's "frustration tolerance" is exceeded, there is a categorical loss of behavioral adaptivity and a resulting "abnormal" stereotyping of action. Our alternative suggestion is that the reversion to a position habit, under the circumstances described, is *realistically justified* and does not at all imply a loss of normal flexibility and intelligence. This view is supported by the fact that some of Maier's animals do *not* "fixate" but continue to experiment with alternative right and left jumping. Moreover, of those animals which do develop the position habit, Eglash (1954) has made the following pertinent observation:

> Whereas fixation suggests rigidity or perseveration, the fixated animal remains as flexible as the normal. This flexibility sometimes [takes] the form of a surprising ingenuity. . . . In addition to displaying a variety of responses, as described by Maier, the fixated animal may drive directly into the net, or leap so lightly that it fails to reach the window. It may assume a passive role: the air blast designed to force the jump blows the animal off the stand (p. 241).
> This adaptability suggests *substitute*, rather than "fixated," behavior (p. 242) [see also Ellen, 1956].

Much has been made of the fact that, once an animal in the Maier-type experiment adopts a position habit (i.e., starts jumping consistently to either the right or the left side of the discrimination apparatus), its resistance to leaving the jumping stand diminishes. And since such a pattern of behavior involves abortive (punishing) jumps on 50% of the trials, it has been argued that the normal responsiveness of the animal to punishment and reward has been lost. It should be remembered, however, that this incidence of failure (and punishment) is *no worse* than would probably be experienced if the animal continued to show some pattern of alternating response; [8] and, besides, the position habit (as already noted) is easier, simpler.

But over and beyond these considerations there are two other interesting possibilities that should be briefly noted. In the review of Maier's book previously cited (Mowrer, 1950c), it was suggested that, once the position habit gets well under way, it may have a tendency to gain momentum through the mechanism involved in the experiment by Whiteis (1955, 1956) which has already been alluded to in Chapter 6 (and will again be considered in Chapter 12). Here fear which is

---

[8] The word "probably" occurs in this sentence for the following reason. It will be recalled that in the frustrating part of Maier's experiment, *one* of the cards is still loose and the other locked on any given trial, just as in the discrimination training, except that now the cards are locked or loose without respect to whether they carry the positive or the negative stimulus cue. Therefore, it would still be conceivable, though most improbable, that an animal, in continuing to jump to both sides of the apparatus, would *just happen* to select the side which, on successive trials, was unlocked. Thus, 100% food reinforcement and no punishment would be experienced. But the odds against such a performance are, of course, astronomically high—as are the odds against a rat's always choosing the locked card. *On the average*, animals would tend to choose a locked card 50% of the time and a loose one equally often, *regardless* of whether they jumped consistently to one side of the apparatus or continued to jump to both sides.

reinforced by punishment at one point in space generalizes "back" to another point in space and produces what, ostensibly, is a sort of behavioral equivalent of perpetual motion. Thus, in the Maier experiment, it is conceivable that the punishment which is intermittently experienced by the rat in performing the position habit would produce fear that would generalize to the jumping standing stand and tend to keep the jumping habit "going" considerably longer than might otherwise occur (cf. Lichtenstein, 1957).

Furthermore, reference has just been made to the fact that, in the "fixated" position habit, punishment is experienced "intermittently"—50% of the time the card is locked and the rat gets a nose bump and a fall, but 50% of the time the card is loose and the rat's jump carries him into a compartment where there is food. And we have already seen (Chapter 4) that intermittent reinforcement, in general, tends to produce greater "resistance to extinction" than does continuous reinforcement, so that it might be that the "fixation" in Maier's experiment arises, in part at least, from this phenomenon (see also Chapter 12).

In any event, it is apparent that Maier's contention that frustration sometimes fixates a habit rather than disrupting it is by no means logically coercive. Instead it seems that we are justified in continuing to assume that the absence of reward, where reward is expected but not reviewed (or is expected in a given amount but less is received, see Tinklepaugh, 1932, and Leary, 1957), generates an affective reaction commonly known as anger. This emotion has now been shown to be capable of intensifying action in progress and, on occasion, to result in aggression toward or attack on a barrier interposed between organism and goal. But when neither intensified effort nor attack succeeds, frustration and the resulting anger have a different effect. They result in a lessening of "habit strength," or hope, by virtue of the fact that anger (like fear in the more drastic punishment situation) produces counterconditioning (Section IV), as a result of which hope is gradually nullified and habit strength destroyed. In the Maier experiment, hope had been conditioned to the positive cue card in the training procedure; but then, in the later part of the experiment, the positive card became no more rewarding than the negative one. In fact, we may say with equal justification that it became *equally punishing*, so that the rat abandoned the earlier habit of "following" the positive cue card and reverted (fatalistically but not unreasonably) to a simple position habit (always right or always left). By the procedure employed in the second part of the Maier experiment, discrimination was indeed rendered insoluble; and the subjects might well be said to have been "frustrated." But also we must note that in the no-solution period what was really happening was that the differential reinforcement for discriminating was totally eliminated (changed from 100/0 to 50/50); and since discrimination was harder work (and now no more rewarding) than was fixation, by the principle of least effort (Sumner & Keller, 1927, Waters, 1937; see also Section III), one would expect exactly the result obtained. In fact, such an outcome would follow from principles discussed much earlier in this book (Chapters 2 and 3) and does not require that the concept of "frustration" be introduced at all.

VI. The Differential Effect of Reward and Punishment on Overt Behavior and on the Emotions

A number of writers in psychology have attempted to handle emotions "just like any other response." The reader may have been surprised to find (in Section II) that Watson, as the chief exponent of Behaviorism, even recognized the existence of emotions. The fact is that, in the sense in which we are using that term, he did not. For Watson, an emotion was merely another example or exhibit of overt behavior; and just as he assumed that other observable reactions could be conditioned, so also could an emotion be. For Watson, emotions, in the sense of a subjective state (or "intervening variable") with motivational properties, simply did not exist (at least not in his formal theoretical system). His position was therefore a thoroughly consistent one but also, for numerous reasons already discussed, thoroughly unsatisfactory.

Hull, Miller, and other "reinforcement theorists" have similarly held that the emotions are subject to the same principles as govern the learning of responses in general. Since they assumed that drive reduction, or reward, was the sole reinforcement mechanism for the development of "habits," they assumed that emotions (to the extent that they acknowledged them) were also "learned" on the basis of reward. This position leads to a number of manifest incongruities, most notable of which is the notion that *fear* is strengthened by *reward* (drive reduction), rather than by punishment (drive induction). As already noted, this is one of the basic issues on which the present approach differs from that of Hull. Here we are assuming that behavioral responses are categorically different from emotional responses: the former are "voluntary" and subject to influence through reward and punishment (and *not* conditionable, strictly speaking), whereas the latter are involuntary and conditionable and not subject to control through reward and punishment, or at least not in the *same way* as are the overt-behavioral responses.[9]

Emotional responses, it is assumed (Sections III and IV), can be counterconditioned; but because they work on an entirely different principle from that involved in behavioral responses, they do not respond to reward and punishment as such. For example, salivation (as an indicator of hope that food will soon be forthcoming) cannot, so far as we know, be strengthened by reward, at least not in the same way that bar pressing, paw lifting, or some other "instrumental" act can be. If we should want to teach a rat to press a bar *harder* and *harder*, as a means of obtaining food, all we would have to do is to withhold reward for relatively weak responses and give it only for increasingly vigorous ones. Under such a regime the incidence of "hard" responses would increase.

Now consider, by contrast, how differently the salivary response behaves. So far as is known to this writer, no attempt has ever been made to perform an experiment in which this response would be treated like an instrumental act, i.e., would be required to occur in specified magnitude before "reward" would be forthcoming. If such an experiment were successful, a Pavlovian dog could be turned into a vertiable "saliva factory," by simply requiring the dog to secrete a little more each time the CS was presented, as the precondition for the presentation of the UnCS (food). If this has ever been done, it is not widely known. And when the Polish neurophysiologist, J. Konorski, was recently in this country, he said he would regard such an experiment as not even worth trying, so certain was he of the outcome: namely, that it would not be successful. Salivation, like conditionable responses in general, is "reinforced" by the *paring* of the CS and UnCS and each omission of the UnCS would presumably *weaken* the salivary reaction to the CS, not strengthen it (but see Perkins, 1955; also Chapter 12). And Konorski went on to say that, quite apart from

[9] In addition to the experimental work previously cited on the emotions of fear, hope, and anger, it should be noted that the reaction of nausea can be conditioned and probably then provides at least a species of the experience commonly termed *disgust*. Loucks (1935) and Konorski (1950) both cite studies in which the sight of a hypodermic needle that had been used to inject morphine into dogs became capable, alone, of producing definite signs of nausea; and persons who have been severely seasick or airsick report that the "mere sight" of a ship or plane can reinstate the experience in attenuated form. Thus far, then, we may say that one "positive" and three "negative" emotions have been identified and operationally defined: hope (or love) on the one hand and fear, anger, and disgust on the other.

the difference in the nervous mechanisms controlling emotional and behavioral responses, there is the fact that the former have no kinesthetic (or related forms of) feedback; in fact, the nervous system which mediates the occurrence of the emotions (i.e., the autonomic) is entirely a motor (efferent) system; and the knowledge of the occurrence of such responses is derived from sense organisms that are connected with the *central* nervous system. Moreover, there are many autonomic responses (e.g., the pupillary response) which can occur, and even be conditioned, without the subject's even "knowing" about it (Gerall, Sampson, & Boslov, 1957).

But perhaps the most striking illustration and indication of the way in which *emotions* and *motions* differ is provided in the realm of fear. A motion, or movement, of some part of the body which is controlled by skeletal (or "striped") muscles can, as everyone knows, be inhibited by punishment; i.e., if the movement occurs and produces certain characteristic response-correlated stimuli, these stimuli, if followed by drive increment, acquire the capacity to arouse fear and thus inhibit, or at least modify, the response on future occasions. But let us consider a fear response which is called out by some objective danger signal: if *this* response were "punished," the effect would be to *augment* the response, not inhibit it, since danger signal followed by drive increment would be the very condition that brought the fear-to-signal response into existence in the first place.

And just as one cannot weaken a fear reaction by "punishing" it, neither can one strengthen it through reward: reward, as we have previously seen, acts to countercondition fear, not reinforce it.

Finally, we need to make explicit one other consideration which is already implied in what has gone before. In this chapter we are exploring the possibility that when hope is not confirmed (as in so-called extinction), the subject not only does not get positively reinforced (by food or the like) but, in addition, experiences the distinctly negative emotion of anger, which tends to countercondition the hope reaction. Now we must ask, what happens when a *fear* is not confirmed? If a stimulus (or stimulus compound) which has previously produced fear is recurrently associated with primary drive reduction rather than with drive induction, the fear is, of course, gradually nullified and ultimately replaced, or counterconditioned, by hope. But what about the situation where, rather than being thus counterconditioned, the fear is simply not confirmed, not reinforced? Here it might seem that the principle of unlearning through counterconditioning meets a limitation. But not so. When a danger signal terminates without the customary reinforcement (noxious stimulation), the organism, as we well know, experiences *relief*, which is a form of secondary decremental reinforcement and ought, therefore, to be capable of counterconditioning fear itself. Thus, just as nonconfirmation of hope produces anger (and/or fear) which counterconditions hope, so also does nonconfirmation of fear produce relief, which likewise can function as a counterconditioner. There is, however, a limiting factor: since frustration (and anger) can presumably occur only so long as there is hope, and since relief can be experienced only so long as there is fear, the counterconditioning, in both instances, will proceed only to the point of neutrality, no reaction, "extinction." Whereas if, in the first case, reduction of a drive other than fear is introduced, the counterconditioning can, obviously, be carried beyond the null point, over to the opposite type of emotional reaction.

Thus we arrive at the conclusion that, in the final analysis, all learning (at least of the emotions; cf. Mowrer, 1960, Chapter 5) involves conditioning principles and that all systematic behavior change is derivable therefrom. So-called instrumental conditioning procedures (Chapter 2) work only with voluntary responses and are derivative phenomena; the basic operation is classical emotional conditioning. And, by the same token, all *un*learning of emotional reactions involves counterconditioning, and not simply the withdrawal or absence of the conditions of reinforcement which have previously prevailed. This view of the matter follows logically from our general systematic position and possesses broad explanatory potency.

VII. Some Experimental Approaches to the Problem

Up to this point our discussion of the way in which emotions and motions are affected by reward and punishment has been largely "theoretical." We now must ask specifically: What is the evidence? The first thing to be noted is that the evidence is, as yet, fragmentary and sparse. Apparently the first, and still one of the few, experimental attacks which have been made on this problem was reported by Gwinn in 1949. This investigator began his study on this premise:

If the response to the punishing stimulus is compatible with the punished act, *punishment will facilitate rather than inhibit an act motivated by fear.* The fear produced by the punishment will strengthen the fear-drive motivating the punished act (p. 260).

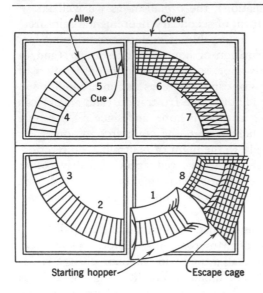

Fig. 11–6. Floor plan of apparatus used by Gwinn (1949, p. 261) in a study of the effects of punishing a fear-motivated escape response in rats.

The apparatus used by Gwinn is shown in Fig. 11–6. In preliminary training, a rat was dropped into this circular maze at section 1, with the entire grill floor electrically charged, except for section 8, which was the floor of the "escape cage." After some initial confusion, the subjects all learned to run quickly from the "starting hopper" to the "escape cage." Then the subjects were put into the starting hopper with no shock on the grill and only fear to motivate them. Again they ran around the alley and into the escape cage. But now a complication was added: shock was reintroduced in sections 6 and 7, so that it acted, in effect, as a "punishment" to the animal for running the maze. The result was that the animals nevertheless continued to run the maze, in fact ran it *more energetically* for a time than did control animals, although eventually they were inhibited and "froze" in front of the entry to section 6. Of this finding, Gwinn said:

The punishment facilitated the punished act, and the facilitation increased with the intensity of the punishment. There was no evidence of inhibition until after many repetitions of the punishment (p. 269).

Thus the results are somewhat ambiguous: they show that although the *first* effect of punishment on a fear-motivated act is to facilitate it, the act is finally inhibited. Although interesting, it is obvious that this experiment does not bear *precisely* upon our problem, which has to do, not with fear-motivated *acts*, but the fear itself. Our assumption would be that what Gwinn did, in substance, was to produce in his subject a *conflict*, between (a) fear of the maze as a whole and the desire to get into the "escape cage" and (b) a more specific fear of entering into sections 6 and 7, which acted as a sort of "bottle-neck" for the escape response. At first the shock experienced in sections 6 and 7 apparently acted, through generalization (Chapter 12), to increase fear of the alley as a whole and to accelerate escape therefrom. But eventually a discrimination set in (as Gwinn himself, p. 268, observes) and the subjects *stopped* running, i.e., fear of *entering* sections 6 and 7 became greater than was the rats' fear of the maze as a whole. In other words, the rats learned that what happened in sections 6 and 7 was *different* from what happened (*now*, as opposed to earlier) in sections 1 to 5. (See also a somewhat similar study by Solomon, Kamin, & Wynne, 1953).

In this experiment, therefore, the subjects were actually not punished for being afraid, but for a particular overt response they made to their fear. Here, as noted, there was the possibility for conflict to develop and eventually to become so great as to inhibit the *original* fear-motivated action. The question, What happens if *fear itself*, rather than a fear-motivated act, is "punished"? thus remained unanswered.

A more direct attack upon this problem has recently been proposed by Perkins & Hertzler (1958). Heart rate, as a direct physiological index of fear, will be used; and, after presentation of a signal, a strong or a weak shock will be presented as a function of whether the heart rate increases or decreases. "Two groups of subjects will be run. For Group A the intensity of the shock will be a positive function of the heart rate just before onset of shock," i.e., the more the heart rate goes up, the stronger will be the shock; and "the shock intensity will be a negative function of heart rate for Group B," i.e., the greater the increase in heart rate, the *less* will be the shock. Here, in Group A, increased heart rate (fear) will be punished, whereas in Group B it will, in effect, be rewarded. To the extent that heart rate is a valid index of fear, revised two-factor theory would predict that "punishment" will *augment* the "response" (heart acceleration) which it follows and that "reward" will have the reverse effect. This, of course, is *not* the way in which other (nonemotional) responses are affected by punishment and reward.

Coppock (1955) has published an article with the intriguing title, "Responses of [Human] Subjects to Their Own Galvanic Skin Responses." Since the GSR is commonly taken as an index of fear (or "anxiety"), it might be expected that the question of what happens to a fear when rewarded or punished was here under investigation; but such was not, or at least not directly, the case. However, the paper contains this interesting sentence:

An unpublished observation made in collaboration with Dr. Robert Glaser in 1949 suggested that the amplitude of GSR's to standard stimulation varies in some subjects with their stated intention or set to "feel fear" or to "feel no fear" (p. 25).

Whether this observation could be confirmed by more systematic experimentation is uncertain; but it is at least suggestive of the phenomenon of "repression." In clinical literature it is not uncommon to read that a given individual "repressed his fear" (of this or that); and the inference might follow that such an inhibition of fear was achieved through a traumatic (punishing) experience of some kind. Despite many conjectures as to how (and if) such repression actually occurs, it is still not well understood; but this passing reference to repr ision provides a natural transition to the next topic.

VIII. The Problem of Conflict Re-analyzed

Reviewing the discussion up to this point, we may say that, within the framework of revised two-factor theory, learning and "unlearning" are conceived as follows. From a point of neutrality, learning can move in either of two directions: stimuli (extrinsic or response-produced) may acquire the capacity to elicit either hope or fear (or certain other "aversive" emotions); and both types of learning can be counteracted by the opposite form of reinforcement or by non-reinforcement (which, in the final analysis, may also involve counter-conditioning; see Section VI). But there is also this difference to be noted: whereas nonreinforcement will ordinarily reverse learning only to the point of neutrality, contradictory reinforcement will, of course, carry learning beyond neutrality, over to the opposite form of conditioning. With these principles one can go a long way toward deriving the known facts of response learning (and unlearning) and place learning (and unlearning) (see Chapter 9).

But what, then, of *conflict?* Is not the very possibility of its occurrence thus excluded, at least in theory, quite as completely as in Thorndike's early formulation of the Law of Effect? The earlier version of two-factor theory was an advance over the Law of Effect in that it took conflict into account and could account for it; but it was weak in that it could not readily explain conflict resolution. Now the revised version of the theory, whatever its other advantages, seems in danger of having no more place in it for conflict than did Thorndike's theory. If, on the basis of past experience, a given situation or response has acquired, let us say, positive significance (hope, promise, secondary reinforcement), and if that situation or response is now as-sociated with negative reinforcement, will not the meaning of the relevant stimuli be modified, automatically and progressively, without conscious conflict or antagonism? If the sign function, or sign-ificance, of a stimulus can be *directly* changed, through either so-called ex-tinction or more explicit counterreinforcement, it is not easy to see how the inner tension and restlessness and the behavior vacillation which characterize conflict could come about. One might expect rather that, with withdrawal or reversal of reinforcement, attitudes, expectations, and action of one type would *quietly* give way to different beliefs and behaviors. This, however, is not what typically occurs. Conflict intervenes as a real and often obvious phenomenon. How can its occurrence be explained, if at all, within the framework of revised two-factor learning theory?

From Chapter 2 a demonstration will be recalled in which a rat, shocked for eating food from the end of a small stick, would alter-nately move toward and then away from the stick (see also Deese, 1952, pp. 121–122). Here, manifestly, was conflict. How to explain it? The stimuli associated with approach to the stick and food have, as a result of their association with electric shock, taken on the capacity to arouse fear. On the other hand, stimuli associated with *retreat* from the stick has never been thus associated and conditioned. Consequently, the animal experiences mounting fear as a result of approaching the stick and relief whenever it reverses its line of pro-gression. Hence, the stimuli associated with the latter behavior take on secondary reinforcement potency and backing-away behavior de-velops as a "habit." But while such behavior reduces the drive of fear, it does not lessen hunger; so when the fear of shock is reduced, the hunger and hunger fear remain and will, sooner or later, instigate the rat once again to move forward.[10]

The key to the conflict observed here is the fact that *different*

---

[10] The author recently observed a similar instance in his own behavior. In his back yard one summer evening he noticed some flowers that needed watering. This stimulus put him in motion toward the watering can. But the can was at some distance and the hydrant still more remote. There was, moreover, the anticipated weight of the water on the return trip. The evening was hot. Move-ment toward the watering can stopped, then a glance at the flowers reinstigated it, etc.

emotions are associated with *different stimuli:* fear with stimuli correlated with the forward motion, relief with stimuli correlated with backward motion. However, there is a further complexity. Moving forward is associated not only with fear of shock but also with hope of food; and moving back is associated not only with relief from shock fear but also with awareness of the persistent hunger. Hence, the very *same* stimuli tend, in both instances, to have contradictory implications; and we may well imagine that their meanings will, as a result, tend to "even out." By this is meant that the opposing meanings, of hope and fear, will undergo a sort of algebraic summation which will eventually bring their net effectiveness somewhere near zero, or neutrality. If the various primary and secondary drives thus involved are well balanced, we might expect, as a final result, that the subject would abandon its oscillatory behavior and *come to rest*. If this equilibrium of forces is disturbed, through mounting hunger or declining fear or both, then the conflict may "break out" again, and no enduring peace will be found until either (a) another way of obtaining food is discovered, (b) the animal discovers that the shock no longer occurs as a result of eating from the stick, or (c) the animal grows weak, loses its hunger, and dies. We, therefore, seem to have here at least a general framework for accommodating many of the major facts of conflict and one which is entirely congruent with the premises of revised two-factor theory.[11]

In an earlier section of this chapter, on extinction and frustration, there is an implied inconsistency which should now be explicitly noted. There it is posited, first, that the anger which results from failure of an expected satisfaction often serves to *intensify* activity in progress and to *increase* (at least temporarily) resistance to extinction; at the same time it is also assumed (by some of the writers cited) that anger is the negative or "aversive" emotion which is generated in so-called extinction situations and which therefore serves to countercondition (or counteract) the hope involved in a given "habitual" mode of response. Grossly, at least, there is a contradiction here: anger is assumed both to reduce and to produce the decline of a habitual response which typically occurs when accustomed reward is withdrawn.

[11] Miller (1944), although operating in a rather different conceptual framework, handles the problem of conflict and conflict resolution in a somewhat similar manner. See also Brown (1957) and Miller (1958). For a discussion of the question of the *permanence* of the inhibitory affect produced by punishment, see Skinner (1938), Estes (1944), Lichtenstein (1950a, 1950b), and Deese (1952, pp. 117 ff.).

It is not yet certain how the resolution of this paradox really goes, but one possibility is this. Bull & Strongin have already noted (Section IV) that frustration and *threat* are intimately related; and it may be that, typically, the *first* reaction to deprivation (loss of accustomed satisfaction) is anger and that when this *energizing* emotion fails of its purpose (*if* it fails), then a *second* emotion supervenes: namely, disappointment, discouragement, despair, depression. Therefore, only in the latter phase of this sequence would we think of counterconditioning (and extinction) as occurring and of the original habit strength (hope) being dissipated (or "worked through," as psychoanalytic writers sometimes say in connection with mourning reactions). At least, such a biphasic interpretation of "extinction" (frustration) would be consistent with the experimental findings of Bernstein, as shown graphically in Fig. 11–7. Here we see that a *brief*

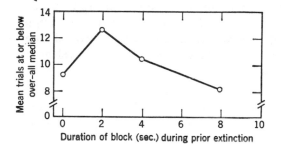

Fig. 11–7. Resistance to extinction of a runway response (in rats) as a function of length of time subjects were held in a special delay (frustration) compartment (Bernstein, 1957, p. 93).

(two-second) detainment of the subject in the course of running a simple maze increases resistance to extinction but that a longer blockage (of eight seconds) *reduces* it, i.e., facilitates the extinction process.

The results of this experiment offer evidence for the occurrence of an increase in response vigor and resistance to extinction with the addition of blocking in avoidance extinction. Both of these findings are consistent with . . . expectations following from a frustration-drive interpretation. A reversal in both response vigor and resistance to extinction occurred when the duration of blocking exceeded a critical point (Bernstein, 1957, p. 93).

However, for reasons which need not be elaborated, the precise meaning of the Bernstein results is not unequivocal; and it may be that they do not necessarily support the particular biphasic theory of frustration here suggested. This theory is nevertheless a plausible possibility—and something to be more specifically explored in the future.

IX. Two Recent Studies Described and Evaluated

In 1939 Razran published a detailed analysis of the then known facts and theories of extinction. In 1956, in a paper entitled "Extinction Re-examined and Re-analyzed: A New Theory," this same writer, on the basis of quite different experimental studies, has arrived at an interpretation of extinction which seems to be pointing in much the same direction as does the present analysis.

Razran begins by noting that, of late, American investigators have been more interested in the study of *instrumental* or *operant behavior* than in what he calls "classical conditioning," by which he means conditioning involving *external*, rather than response-correlated, stimuli. This trend, says Razran, is somewhat unfortunate since, in his opinion, the acquisition and extinction of behavior can be understood in the ultimate sense only in terms of simple, or "classical," conditioning. Razran's argument is built around three main propositions, the second of which "is the most novel and crucial one." It runs as follows:

> The automatic deconditioning in the early stage of extinction is a direct result of the loss of the interceptive and the proprioceptive conditional stimuli (feedback CS's) which in the original conditioning were an integral part of the CR situation and which when the unconditional stimulus is withheld and the evoked reaction is reduced cease to be present (p. 45).

It will not be possible to give a detailed account of what this proposition means to Razran; but it will be sufficiently clear, from the terminology alone, that his thinking is close to that inherent in revised two-factor theory. The general nature of this affinity is made particularly evident in the concluding section of Razran's paper. Entitled "Final Word," it reads thus:

> 1. *The testability (verifiability) of the new theory.* The interoceptive and proprioceptive stimuli held by the theory to be the basis of the deconditioning and counterconditioning in extinction are by no means postulated as any kind of intervening variables. They are observables! As already mentioned, in the last 15 years the Russians have clearly demonstrated both the existence of interoceptive and proprioceptive conditioning (particularly the former) and their interaction with typical exteroceptive conditioning. And while, as far as the writer is aware, no experiment has ever been specifically devoted to a comparison of the CR states of the viscera during alimentary conditioning and during alimentary extinction of conditioning, there is no reason why such an experiment could not be undertaken. Moreover, one could of course compare extinction of, let us say, alimentary conditioning in normal animals and

in animals with de-afferented viscera. The isolation of proprioceptive stimulation presents more of a problem, no doubt, but could also be mastered.

2. *Extinction of operant conditioning.* It has always been the opinion of the writer that a thorough analysis of primary variables in operant conditioning [habit or trial-and-error learning] is difficult, if not impossible, without a prior analysis of such variables in classical conditioning. And it is only such a "prior analysis" which this article offers with respect to extinction of operant conditioning, even though a number of facts presented here have been directly verified, as is known, in operant CR experiments, and the theory, too, is not alien to operant CR thinking. More than that, the writer is by no means ready to accord priority to operant over classical conditioning with respect to theoretical and methodological—and even practical fundamentals of learning. The contrary appears to him to be true, and he indeed deplores the decline of classical CR experimentation in this country. Certainly, such extreme views as expressed recently in this Journal by one author (Smith, 1954) that "conditioning [meaning classical conditioning] is an artifact" are indefensible—and patricidal. They could have been put forward only in total unawareness of the almost 500 well-controlled experiments in classical conditioning for most of which the author's alternate "reinforcement" is a very contorted and unnatural or impossible explanation. True, a large number of these classical CR experiments are, unfortunately, unknown to American readers. Yet they do exist (pp. 49–50).

In the second paragraph quoted, Razran seems to be espousing a position very close to that of revised two-factor theory. "Operant conditioning," i.e., habit formation, is reducible, he conjectures, to "classical conditioning"; and extinction of habits is a matter of "deconditioning and counterconditioning." All learning thus reduces, as in two-factor theory, to sign learning and all extinction to a reversal of the meanings of signs. Here, it seems, is yet *another instance of independent convergence upon a common point of view in these matters from quite dissimilar starting points.*

But we must now turn to what appears to be evidence *against* the general position taken in this chapter. In a recent paper entitled "An Experimental Validation of Conditioned Inhibition," Calvin and co-workers (1956) present experimental data of a quite remarkable kind. They report that if hungry rats are given 30 runs per day in a 10-foot straightaway alley and consistently rewarded with food, they will eventually "extinguish," despite consistent reward and persistent hunger!

In 1954, Gleitman, Nachmias, & Neisser published a paper in which they showed that such an outcome would have to be logically predicted on the basis of certain of Hull's postulates; and since the outcome was so contrary to common sense, they used the prediction as an indication of the unsoundness of the Hullian position. They said:

Necessarily, then, there is no learned act which can be performed for any length of time; its very repetition—regardless of reinforcement—must lead to its eventual elimination. This prediction is at odds with everything we know about the course of learning. The phenomenon of "inhibition of reinforcement" (Hull, 1943) occurs only under quite special conditions, and hardly begins to do justice to this deduction. The learning curve must return to *zero*, regardless of the spacing of trials, and must do so in the *same number of trials* required for experimental extinction after $_sE_R$ has reached asymptote. One does not have to refer to experimental studies to demonstrate the fallacy of this prediction (p. 30).

Yet Calvin *et al.* report dramatic confirmation of this unlikely prediction. They say:

The fact that all of the Ss ceased to run even though reinforced on every trial stands as a striking confirmation of the S—R reinforcement theory of extinction. Certainly the analysis made by Gleitman, Nachmias, and Neisser was a logical one. It was good "common sense." However the beauty of reinforcement theory as elaborated by Spence, Hull, Miller, etc., is its ability to make predictions contrary to common sense. Although the present authors are well aware that current reinforcement theory is far from perfect, it seems to us that as long as it can make predictions of the kind which are validated by the present experiment it will continue to be the dominant theory in the field of learning (p. 4).

The experiment in question has already been described briefly. At this level of exposition the results are striking indeed. There are, however, certain seemingly minor aspects of the experiment which can hardly be without significance. The first is that after the maze runs, the subjects were returned to their living cages and were there given a feeding which supplemented the food obtained as a result of the performance in the maze. In other words, the rats did not "make their living" exclusively by maze running. Indeed, they could get along perfectly well, or even better, *without running the maze at all:* if they loitered or refused to run they were picked up and carried to the home cage, where they received all the food they wanted! So why "run"? Why not simply *wait* instead of *work?*

The nonrunning ("extinction") solution to the problem was, therefore, a perfectly logical one. One may, however, question whether rats would be "intelligent" enough to hit upon it. That they certainly had a "motive" for giving up the work solution and adopting the waiting solution is clear. The authors say:

In closing we would like to mention one more point which seems to support the S—R reinforcement theory of extinction. It took approximately two hours a day to run one spaced S. If the S ran for 85 days it completed 2,550 trials. Each trial meant that the S had run 10 feet making a total of

25,500 feet or a little short of five miles. During this time the E was accompanying the S on his daily trips down the alley. Since the E had to walk both to and from the goal box, he walked approximately 10 miles. Introspective reports indicate that a great deal of conditioned inhibition was accumulating, and in some cases it was touch and go as to who would extinguish first—the S or the E (p. 6).

Many other maze experiments have been carried out with essentially similar procedures, but they usually are limited to one or two hundred trials. Here as many as 2,550 trials, or more, might be involved (before the subjects "extinguished"), so there would be ample opportunity for learning of an unusual and more difficult kind than is ordinarily seen in maze studies. With so much experience, the subjects might well discover that they had a choice between (a) running the maze 30 times and (b) just *waiting* for their meal. Moreover, a rather special feature of the procedure would seem to favor just such learning. The authors say:

If an S failed to enter the goal box [i.e., failed to negotiate the maze] after five minutes it was placed in the goal box. If this occurred on two successive trials the series *was discontinued until the following day* (p. 2; italics added).

In other words, whenever an animal (for whatever reason) delayed in running the maze, it found that it would be *carried* to the goal box —certainly a circumstance conducive to *not running;* and, more than this, if it twice refused to run, it would then be returned to the living cage and given free and full access to food, without "work." If the animal *ran* for the food obtainable at the end of the maze, it had to make 30 such trips before getting anything like a full feeding; whereas, if the animal, on only two trials, simply "sat tight" and waited (for a maximum of 10 minutes), it would get a full feeding "for nothing."

In the Calvin experiment, there were thus two possible solutions to the animals' hunger problem: (1) running the maze repeatedly and (2) simply waiting a maximum of 10 minutes and being returned to the living cage with food present. Viewed in this light, "common sense" would certainly lead us to expect precisely the result obtained. Certainly it is not surprising that the subjects all eventually came to prefer the decidedly *easier* of the two solutions. But we can confidently predict that had the running solution been the *only* one available to the subjects (or if there had been a *long delay* after return to the home cage before feeding occurred), no such "extinction" would have occurred.

Only in a very special sense can the running "habit" here involved be said to have extinguished. It was not that it *lost* habit strength, but rather that another "habit" *got stronger*. The "extinction" of an instrumental response is normally the decrement in such a response which occurs as a result of its repeated performance, *without* the expected reinforcement. Keeping the reinforcement present but providing an *easier* alternative way of obtaining it is pretty clearly a phenomenon of a different order (see Deese's 1952 analysis, pp. 117 ff., of some of Skinner's and Estes' early work on punishment).

We thus end this section with arguments and evidence from Razran's paper actively supporting the general view put forward earlier in this chapter; and the seemingly paradoxical results reported by Calvin *et al.* lose their paradoxical qualities when all the experimental circumstances are taken into account (cf. Dinsmoor, 1956).

X. Kendrick's Repetition of the Calvin Experiment

After this book had gone to press, Kendrick (1958) reported a repetition of the experiment by Calvin *et al.*, with certain modifications, which calls for special consideration. The rational of this replication is given by Kendrick as follows:

The procedure in this [Calvin's] experiment was criticized by Dinsmoor (1956) who pointed out several reasons other than the Gleitman prediction, why the Ss may have stopped running, the most pertinent of which was that Calvin may have inadvertently trained the Ss not to run, because when any S refused to run it was picked up and placed in the goal box with the reward present, thus rewarding the nonrunning behavior.

It was therefore decided to repeat Calvin's experiment in a modified form, with more stringent nonrunning criteria exercised (p. 313).

The apparatus used by Kendrick was a 10-foot straight runway; and, for reasons not explained, the subjects (laboratory rats) were motivated by thirst rather than by hunger (as in the Calvin experiment). Then, after preliminary training, the Ss were treated as follows:

Each S was placed in the starting box facing the door, the door was opened and S ran to the reinforcement dish. Immediately S finished drinking, it was taken out of the goal box and run again. This was repeated for 30 trials for each S. The reinforcement per trial was ¼ cc., so that if S completed the 30 trials it received 7.5 cc. of water. Three hours after the last trial of each S a further drinking period ad libitim of ½ hr. was allowed. The Ss were thus tested under approximately 20 hr. water deprivation.

The criterion for extinction was that on three consecutive days S must refuse to run for water twice consecutively within the first five trials. A refusal was defined as S's failing to stop the running time clock within 5 min. of the door being opened. After the first refusal S was momentarily taken out of the starting box and then put back in again and the door opened. If any S had two consecutive refusals during any part of a day's testing, testing was discontinued for that day, but was not counted as an extinction day. On no occasion was S lifted out of the runway and placed in the goal box for reinforcement if it refused to run (p. 314).

By the criteria here stipulated, after a period of about 33 days (on the average), "all Ss refused to run for their water" (p. 318)! This, surely, is a dramatic result—but what does it mean? Certainly one source of weakness in the Calvin experiment has been eliminated: the rats were *not* carried to the goal box when they refused to go there under their own power. But other ambiguities remain, the principal one of which is that here, again, running the maze was not the *only* way of getting a 24-hour supply of water. It is true that, by running, the rats used in this experiment got it *sooner;* but if they refused to run, they still got all the water they could drink—the only disadvantage being a three-hour wait. Thus the experimental situation was still very unlife-like; for if, in a state of nature, an organism refuses to work for its living, its living will not be brought to it (nor *vice versa*). Hence, it seems forced and misleading to speak of "inhibition of reinforcement" or "conditioned inhibition" in such a situation. If animals had to depend exclusively upon running the maze as a means of getting water, one can be quite certain that they would *not* become "inhibited." In the usual sink-or-swim predicament, organisms *swim.* And if they preferred not to "swim" (run) in the present situation, it must be because the alternative adjustment was in some overall sense preferable.

In the second place, there is the rather singular practice of discontinuing the experiment "for that day" whenever "any S had two consecutive refusals during any part of a day's testing." If these two refusals did not come during the first five trials, they did not contribute to meeting the criterion for "inhibition"; but one cannot escape the feeling that they may have nevertheless *encouraged* "inhibition." Suppose, for all we know, that the rats used in this experiment, in addition to not liking to run the runway, trial after trial, also did not like being picked up and handled by the experimenter. Thus, by not running, the animals could escape from this (presumably disagreeable) situation, with resulting reinforcement of the nonrunning behavior.

The experiment obviously needs to be further replicated, with certain other variations and controls.[12] But if, after all reasonable precautions are taken, the Calvin effect still persists, such a finding would not invalidate the frustration hypothesis; it would simply show that fatigue can also be a factor in bringing about extinction, which the advocates of the frustration hypothesis have not at all disclaimed. For it will be remembered that both the frustration hypothesis and the fatigue hypothesis involve basically the same assumption, namely, that a form of counterreinforcement is involved in extinction; and it presumably does not matter greatly whether this is provided by conditionable anger or by conditionable fatigue—or $_sI_R$, as Hull has conceived it. Both involve the phenomenon of conflict and both achieve their effects, presumably, by counteracting hope. In fact, it could be argued that even the rats in the Calvin-Kendrick type of experiment are "frustrated"—not, to be sure, by failing to find the accustomed quantum of water, but by the factor of effort. But it is perhaps idle to speculate further about this matter until further investigation shows whether the phenomenon is itself valid beyond doubt.

XI. The Psychology of Courage and Perseverance

In a chapter on "experimental neuroses" in his book *Conditioned Reflexes*, Pavlov (1927) describes the following remarkable observation by his student, Dr. Eroféeva (1913):

As was mentioned in the third lecture, a conditioned alimentary reflex can be developed to a most severe electrical stimulus applied to the skin—a stimulus which would normally evoke the inborn defense reaction but to which the animal now responds by an alimentary reaction, turning its head towards the place where the food appears, licking its lips and producing a secretion of typical "alimentary" saliva. In the case which is being described the development of this reflex had been started with the use of a very weak current, which was gradually increased in strength until finally it was extremely powerful. The conditioned alimentary reflex developed in this way remained stable for many months (p. 289).

Here the innate, unconditioned reaction to a noxious stimulus (shock) is overridden or replaced by the conditioned reflex of salivation. In order to achieve this effect, it is necessary, as Frolov (1937),

---

[12] For example, it would be interesting to use a U-maze (with a doorway leading from the goal box back into the starting box), so that the element of handling would be minimized. It is, incidentally, noteworthy that "inhibition of reinforcement" has apparently never been reported in an ordinary bar-pressing situation, where the animal goes from one performance of an act to the next without handling or outside interference of any kind.

in *Pavlov and His School,* points out, for the subject's hunger to be quite intense (often involving loss of "a considerable proportion of its weight"). But the effect is evidently quite striking. Of this experiment Frolov says:

The animal stands quietly on the stand and awaits food. It suffices merely to switch on the electric current and the dog begins to wag its tail and to exhibit a number of obvious "food" reactions, the chief of them being the process of secreting saliva. On gradually increasing the strength of the current, the food reaction does not diminish. Thus, a conditioned food reflex to pain has been established.

In this case, in Yerofeyeva's [Eroféeva's] experiment, we have as it were a *switching over of the nervous energy from the centre of defence movements to the centre of food movements,* the previous reaction becoming inhibited. Those movements of the dog which were previously directed towards completely different requirements, for instance opening the mouth in order to gnaw the [restraining] straps, are now found to be switched over to absolutely different aims and objects, i.e., for better grasping its food, even if the food itself is not yet visible. The entire behaviour of the dog has a completely different appearance from that shown during the elaboration of the reflex. Instead of tenseness of the extremities and vertebral muscles, the dog displays expectation and affability. . . .

The story is told by the scientist G. Bohn, that when Sherrington—who happened to be present at the time of this experiment in Pavlov's laboratory in the Academy of Medicine—saw the changed behaviour of the dog, he exclaimed: "Now I understand the joy with which the Christian martyrs went to the stake!" (pp. 95–97).

Although the chain of inference by which Sherrington arrived at this remark may involve some leaps which we are not prepared to take, we can, however, make good use of both the experiment and Sherrington's comment. The experiment dramatically shows how an external stimulus that is inherently painful can come to release reactions of hope and "joy." Now let us ask what would happen if such a stimulus, instead of being applied by the experimenter, were a "barrier" which an organism had to "cross" en route to some desired goal (cf. Warner, 1928a, 1928b). It is virtually certain that if a rat first ran over a very weakly energized electric grill on its way to food, it would become willing to cross the grill at higher shock intensities, progressively arrived at, which would abruptly stop a naive rat (cf. Brown, 1955). For the experienced rat, the stimuli correlated with running would be conditioned to fear *but also,* and more strongly, to the hope derived from the food reinforcement; whereas a hungry rat, put into the apparatus for the first time with high shock on the grill, would have *only fear* conditioned to running and would be inhibited rather than "courageous." *Courage,* in other words, seems capable of being acquired and to be a function of how the opposing forces in a conflict are balanced. If much fear and little hope are associated with the stimuli which a given action produces, then, with respect to that action, the individual is "timid," "cowardly"; but if there is relatively little fear and much hope, then the action may be boldly executed. The principle is, of course, a familiar one in military training: exposure to slight danger, followed by relief and satisfaction, as a preparation for facing greater danger (cf. Chapter 2, Section II).

To the writer's knowledge only one psychologist has thus far concerned himself with this problem, experimentally, and this research got started by accident. Over a period of several years, K. F. Muenzinger and his students conducted a series of experiments on discrimination learning in which it was found that reward and punishment did not always operate precisely as they might be expected to. Previously it had been taken for granted that one rewarded the "correct" response in a discrimination situation and punished the "incorrect" one. But Muenzinger and co-workers found, for example, that sometimes punishment of the *correct* response markedly facilitated this type of learning. Naturally enough, this finding precipitated a controversy (Wischner, 1947; Mowrer, 1950a, Chapter 12), which we shall not review. Suffice it to say that the paradoxical findings, rather than being a contradiction of our general assumptions about reward and punishment, seem to be traceable to certain unperceived artifacts in the situation. However, these findings served the highly useful purpose of suggesting to Muenzinger a sort of experimental analogue of courage and have prompted him to start thinking about this by no means unimportant problem (cf. Prince, 1956).

The summary of a paper by Muenzinger *et al.* (1952) reads as follows:

The purpose of this study was to find out whether the accelerating effect of electric shock for correct choice (in a non-corrective situation) would manifest itself more readily if the avoidance effect of shock had been overcome previously.

White rats were given 120 trials in a straightaway and received shock in 55 of the trials. They were subsequently trained by the non-corrective method to learn a black-white discrimination. Ss which were shocked for correct turns were only slightly poorer than those shocked for wrong turns. The differences were statistically insignificant.

Among other Ss that had not received any prior experience with shock in the straightaway those trained with shock for correct turns were significantly poorer than those trained with shock for wrong turns.

It is assumed that electric shock in discrimination learning has two functions: (a) producing avoidance behavior, and (b) accelerating learning.

If the tendency to avoid shock is overcome prior to training in the discrimina-
tion box, the accelerating function will manifest itself unequivocally (pp.
118–119; italics added).

And earlier, in the same paper, we read:

It might not be amiss to point out that under the conditions used here the
rats, even though at first disturbed by shock in the straightaway, overcame
their avoidance reaction fairly well and were willing eventually to cross a
grid which must have given them a considerable shock. The gradual increase
in current, no less than the frequent exposure to it (55 times), was probably
an important factor in overcoming undesirable emotional effects, if such
effects existed at the beginning, which is probable (p. 118).

In the paper cited, the word "courage" does not appear; but in a
personal communication Professor Muenzinger has indicated his inclination to think of the behavior in question as at least analogous to
courage. However, as late as 1957 this author (in a paper published
jointly with Baxter) objected to the explicit use of this term, as
follows:

There is a common practice of considering fear as a motivator, which in
our opinion leads to serious descriptive and theoretical difficulties. Elsewhere the senior author (Muenzinger, 1954) has suggested a clear-cut
distinction between the concepts of motivation and emotion through the use
of an all-encompassing frame of reference. If the behavior of the shocked
animals in sets 3 and 4 in avoiding the alley with the signal "shock coming"
is due to fear, which is superficially plausible, what shall we call the behavior
of the animals in sets 1 and 2 which chose quite readily the very alley which
also conveyed the signal "shock coming"? If fear of shock did exist initially
in the [straightaway], it must have changed into something else after 50 runs.
This "something" in human Ss we usually call "courage," but nobody, including ourselves, would want to use such a concept in rats. Would it not be
consistent not to use the complementary concept of fear in rats? We do not
claim that the records of the groups referred to disprove the existence of
fear in rats which have been shocked; we merely suggest that in this case the
use of the concept of fear is superfluous and perhaps misleading (p. 256).

Everyone recognizes the danger of reification in science; but as
far as the concept of fear is concerned, we now seem to be on
eminently safe grounds. As regards "courage," the situation is less
clear. We can, if we wish, define it "operationally," without raising
the issue as to whether it really "exists." But may it not be that courage
is simply the *absence* of fear in situations where it might well be expected to be present? We shall approach this problem again, from a
somewhat different angle, in Chapter 12. In the meantime, it will be
instructive to examine the phenomenon of "perseverance," which is
clearly akin to "courage" (cf. Chapter 12, Section VIII).

Fear of pain is not, of course, the only barrier that obstructs living organisms in their march toward the fulfillment of their needs and wants. *Effort* may likewise cause them to "give up" in circumstances when just a little more persistence would lead to success. Suppose that a hungry rat were put in a Skinner box, with the lever adjusted so that it would deliver a pellet of food only after being pressed 200 times. In the course of its exploration of the new situation, the rat would undoubtedly press the bar a few times; but it would certainly not "stay with" this response long enough to produce any food. Very likely it would starve rather than learn to survive in this way. Or suppose that in such an apparatus, the subject were rewarded with a pellet of food each time it pressed the bar for, let us say, the first 20 times and that then the delivery mechanism were set so that it would produce food only after 200 bar pressings. Here, again, such habit strength as would be built up by the 20 reinforcements would probably be exhausted well before the rat had pushed the bar 200 times. But if the amount of bar pressing required for a pellet of food were *gradually increased*, then one would find, as Skinner himself reports (1938), that a rat could very well "make his living" in this way, hard as it is. The greater resistance to extinction generated by periodic rather than continuous reinforcement will be discussed in another context (Chapter 12); but it will be at once clear from the foregoing that we are here broaching the psychology of "work," "sacrifice," "character."

Also it will be evident that we are here close to a phenomenon which is commonly interpreted as a form of psychopathology, namely so-called *masochism*. Here, ostensibly, the individual is *rewarded*, rather than punished, by pain—a circumstance which, if valid, would constitute no small problem for the homeostatic conception of motivation and behavior. However, such exceptions to homeostasis are probably more apparent than real and arise from a fallacy of observation. As Brown (1955) has pointed out, *all* goal-seeking behavior to some degree involves a detour "through pain"—be it only the factor of effort, apprehension, or the like; and it is only when the "punishment" is relatively great and obvious, with the satisfaction subtle or obscure, that confusion arises. When an individual's goal is known and socially approved, no matter how great the "obstacles," we do not speak of "masochism": instead we speak of determination, persistence, "gumption." Only, it seems, when the goal is covert—as, for example, in the assuagement of guilt—but none the less real and important to the individual himself, and the pain or punishment, *overt*, are we likely to infer, erroneously, that the "pleasure principle" is being violated.

Incidentally, the capacity to experience guilt is undouhtedly a complex phenomenon and one not to be explained in overly simple terms (cf. Mowrer, 1960, Chapter 10); but it is none the less potent (at the human level), and we must not allow our theorizing about behavior to be distorted by neglect or misinterpretation thereof. A spurious (insufficiently analyzed) "example" can always cause much needless difficulty.

12 ═══════════

Generalization, Discrimination, and Skill

In some ways the topics discussed in this chapter are specialized, narrow, technical; but in other ways they are as broad and as significant as the psychology of learning itself. Here we encounter problems which are at once baffling but intriguing. Here, too, we begin to move from the more elementary learning processes to processes that are "higher," more complex. Built, as it is, upon principles delineated in preceding chapters, the present discussion provides, in turn, a basis for the consideration of mediation, language, and other topics which, in the companion volume (Mowrer, 1960), take us from the animal to the more distinctively human level of psychological functioning.

I. Learning and Generalization

In one sense, even the most rudimentary type of learning involves generalization. As an organism discovers, or "learns," that event A (a stimulus or a response) is regularly followed by event B (a reward or a punishment), it may be said to be "generalizing." Even though the learner be a nonverbalizing organism, it is as if its nervous system were saying, "A was followed by B once, A was followed by B twice, A was followed by B three times. . . . A is *always* followed by B!" In this way, by a process of *induction*, the organism generalizes, or "extrapolates," from its past experience to the *future*. On the basis of memory of the past, somewhat paradoxically it *anticipates* what is to come and is thus enabled to behave more adaptively than it could if it did not learn. Thus, ordinary learning may be termed *once-always* "generalization" (but see also Mowrer, 1960, Chapter 8).

There has been some controversy among psychologists about this progressive, step-by-step aspect of learning (Spence, 1940). Doubting that learning is essentially inductive, some writers (e.g., Krechevsky, 1938) have taken the position that it is instead a matter of "insight." Elsewhere (Mowrer, 1960, Chapter 6) we shall examine the latter phenomenon in more detail; but we can anticipate that discussion by suggesting that although insight is real enough, it is not itself a form of learning, properly speaking. Therefore, the fact of insight does not go against the assumption that learning proper is progressive, inductive. Insight, as we shall see, is a *deductive* procedure and thus complements the notion that learning is inductive. There is, it seems, no real contradiction here.

But the once-always type of generalization is not what is usually implied by the term, generalization; it is more commonly used to refer to the fact that if an organism becomes conditioned to respond in a given way, let us say with fear, to a given stimulus or situation, it will also show a tendency to respond *in the same way*, though somewhat less strongly, to *other* stimuli or situations which are "similar to" the stimulus or situation to which the fear was originally conditioned (cf. Chapter 2, Section VI, and Chapter 11, Section II). The biological utility of such a tendency is obvious. If, in a state of nature, a buffalo has a painful, fear-inducing encounter with a wolf, it well behooves the buffalo henceforth to look with apprehension, not only upon this particular wolf, but upon *all* wolves. It may be that *some* wolves are harmless; but there is a kind of over-all biological economy in generalizing in the manner just suggested.

Hence, we may speak of *two kinds* of "generalization": *once-always generalization*, the process involved in ordinary inductive learning; and *one-many generalization*, the tendency of living organisms to react to many similar stimuli or situations as if they were the original stimulus or situation with which a given experience has been associated.

There has been much discussion of the shape of the curve for one-many generalization, or *stimulus generalization*, as it is more often called. If, for example, either human or animal subjects are taught to react in a particular way to Middle-C, i.e., a tone of 265 vibrations per second, they will show a decreasing tendency to make the same response to the tones extending out on each side of, i.e., above and below, Middle-C. Thus, if we represent the original, inductive learning by means of a rising, negatively accelerated "learning curve,' we can think of this learning generalizing off in both directions from the stimulus involved in the original learning. A crude attempt to represent this relationship between "regular learning" and "stimulus generalization" is shown in Fig. 12–1. There may be some errors in the details of this figure, but it is presumed to represent, in a general way, the relationship between the two forms of "generalization" under discussion here.

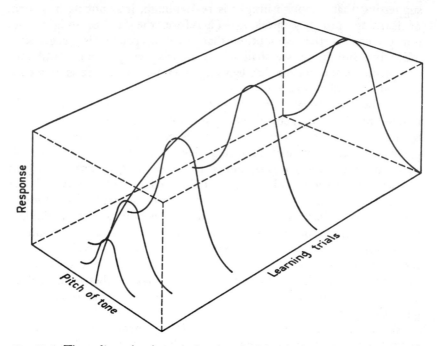

Fig. 12–1. Three-dimensional graph showing the hypothetical relationship between the curve of inductive learning and the generalization gradients radiating off from the curve.

So far as the writer is aware, no empirically derived set of curves such as shown in Fig. 12–1 has ever been published. However, since the original copy for Fig. 12–1 was drawn, Guttman & Kalish (1956) have published the family of curves shown in Fig. 12–2. These show the extent of generalization as a function of response strength at four different stages of response *extinction*. The picture is very similar to that postulated above as representing generalization as a function of the level of response strength during the course of *acquisition*. The general methodology used in obtaining the Guttman-Kalish curves is discussed in the next section.

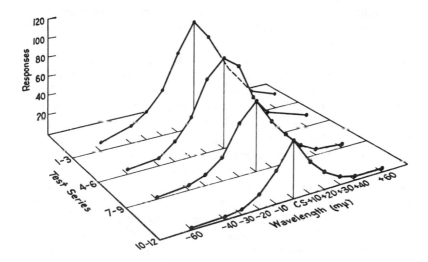

Fig. 12-2. Mean generalization gradients obtained by Guttman & Kalish (1956, p. 85) at four different stages of extinction. Twenty-four pigeons served as subjects in this experiment. These curves, empirically derived, are to be compared with the hypothetical ones shown in Fig. 12-1.

II. Generalization and Discrimination

Is stimulus generalization something that occurs automatically, on the basis of some sort of innate mechanism, or is it, too, subject to modification through experience? This much is well known, that the spread or extent of such generalization can be *narrowed* through learning. If, in the illustration already given, our subjects have been taught to react to Middle-C with fear, we can reduce their tendency to react fearfully to other tones by (a) presenting those tones many times without incremental reinforcement or (b) by having those other tones followed by decremental reinforcement (see Chapter 11). In this way a clear-cut *discrimination* can be established, as a result of which the subject will react with fear only to Middle-C and neutrally or even positively to other nearby tones. Here the shape and magnitude of the double (bidirectional) generalization gradient extending out from the original training tone has been radically restricted as a result of learning, so if the originally more extended gradient is in some sense innately given, it is obviously not irreversibly fixed. Although, as we have seen, it is to the advantage of living organisms to generalize what they have learned in one situation to other similar situations, it is also desirable that, where further experience warrants, they be capable of "correcting" this tendency so that behavior conforms as exactly as possible to existing realities.[1]

Having thus seen the possibility of restricting the range of stimulus generalization by means of discrimination, one wonders if there is any way in which its range might be *extended*. Rather obviously, this could be done, in the illustration given, by also negatively reinforcing tones other than Middle-C. If, in this procedure, the subject first found that Middle-C was dangerous, then that the G above and the F below were dangerous, and that the C above the G and the C below the F were also dangerous, the subject would certainly have a tendency to "infer" that *all tones* are dangerous and probably equally so. Hence, the subject might react to *any tone*, whether above, below, or in between those actually reinforced, quite as vigorously as to the reinforced ones. Here we are dealing with something similar to, if not identical with, what is commonly called *concept formation* (Osgood, 1953; Hilgard, 1956). An auditory stimulus of 10,000 double vibrations per second is certainly very different from one of 60 d.v.s.; but we do apply the term, *tone*, to each of them and to all the intervening frequencies; and if an organism has the "concept" of *tones*, it may be a relatively simple matter to conclude that "tones" *are dangerous* and thus to react with *equal vigor* both to those that have been specifically reinforced and to those that have not been (see concept of *mediation*, as developed in Mowrer, 1960, Chapters 2, 6, and 7). Here we have, in a very real sense, the antithesis of discrimination.

In the interests of brevity, the foregoing discussion has dealt with the matter of generalization and discrimination in rather global terms. Before concluding this section, it will be helpful to review a series of very precise experiments recently reported by Dr. Norman Guttman and colleagues. A good many years ago, B. F. Skinner (1938) suggested a useful method for studying discrimination in animal subjects. If, for example, a pigeon is hungry it will readily learn to peck at a little panel or "key" as a means of obtaining bits of food. Moreover, if a

---

[1] "Allergies" or "sensitivities" may be said to represent failures of "discrimination" at the physiological level. As Selye (1956) has pointed out, the reactions involved, for example, in "hay fever" are highly useful when they occur in response to smoke and certain other gases and irritants; they become pathological only when they "generalize" too broadly and occur in response to biologically harmless substances such as plant pollens.

cue (discriminative stimulus, or S^D) of some sort is introduced, the bird will soon learn to peck at the "key" *only* when the cue is present, not when it is absent (S$^\Delta$); i.e., it learns to respond "on cue." Using this basic procedure, Guttman & Kalish (1956) have been able to derive from the pigeon very pretty generalization gradients for different regions of the color spectrum, as shown in Fig. 12–3. This was done

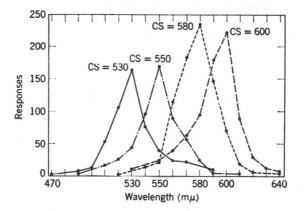

Fig. 12–3. Mean generalization gradients obtained by Guttman & Kalish (1956, p. 83) from four groups of pigeons (six to the group). The gradients for the individual pigeons were very similar.

by teaching the bird to peck when some spectral color, e.g., green (550 mμ), was projected upon the milkglass signal window and not to peck when the window was dark (Fig. 12–4) and then exploring the extent to which lights of *other* hues would be reacted to as if they were the cue for pecking. In a recent popular account of their researches, Guttman & Kalish (1958) say:

We first train the pigeon to peck at light of a certain wavelength, presented in the form of an illuminated disk. The food reward for pecking the disk is given not for each response but on an irregular schedule, controlled by an automatic device which gives food for one response in each minute on the average. The main reason for this system is that we do not want the bird to "expect" a reward for every response, because that would interfere with the later generalization tests. Paradoxically, the irregular reward method produces an extremely eager response by the pigeon. After a few hours of training the bird pecks steadily at the rate of 4,000 to 6,000 times per hour! What is especially important for our purposes, the response persists strongly when we stop giving the reward. The pigeon continues to peck for several hours, at a slowly declining rate. During this period we can carry out extensive generalization tests.

A test consists in presenting the pigeon with monochromatic light at 10 or 12 wavelengths other than the one to which it was trained to respond. The test stimuli are distributed over a considerable range of the color spectrum. If, for instance, the bird was trained to a green at the wavelength of 5,500 Angstrom units, it may be tested on wavelengths ranging from 4,800 Angstroms (blue) to 6,200 Angstroms (orange). These are presented in random order. The whole series of wavelengths is repeated a dozen times, each time in a different order. The bird's response to each disk is measured by its rate of pecking (pp. 78–79).

Fig. 12–4. A portion of the apparatus used by Guttman & Kalish (1958, p. 78) in the study of color generalization in the pigeon. The "cue window," at the right, could be illuminated with any desired color of light or allowed to remain unlighted.

Many earlier attempts have been made to ascertain the exact shape of the curve of sensory generalization, but numerous difficulties have always been encountered which make one somewhat less than confident that the results in any given experiment repr⁻sent the "true" curve. Wickens, Schroder, & Snide (1954) have discussed possible variables that may distort the results obtained in this type of research; and, on the basis of experiments in which special care was taken to avoid artifacts, they conclude "that the gradient of primary stimulus generalization is actually bell-shaped" (p. 56). The results obtained by Guttman & Kalish strongly support this assumption.

In some ways, it is little short of astonishing that the pigeon should "know so much" as it apparently does about the color spectrum. That a bird should differentiate between a pure green and a blue-green on the one side and a yellow-green on the other is perhaps not so surprising; but it does seem remarkable that it should "know" so perfectly that red (640 mμ) is "farther" away from green than is yellow (580 mμ) and that dark blue (420 mμ) is farther away, in the opposite direction, than is light blue (460 mμ).[2] Human beings, in the course of their socialization, nearly always receive at least a limited amount of training which helps them perceive tones with rapid frequencies as "high" and tones with slower frequencies as "low" (see earlier example). But one cannot see anything in the experience of a pigeon that would give it a similar ability to order colors so accurately according to wavelength. The most reasonable inference at present is that this capacity is in some way innately given; yet, if innate, this capacity (as already noted) is subject to modification through training. Pigeons, if given discrimination training, can become capable of differentiating quite sharply between one monochromatic color and another which differs from it in wavelength by only 2 or 3 millimicrons. In other words, the "innate" tendency toward color generalization can be corrected so that the drop in response rate, as one moves from the reinforced stimulus out to unreinforced stimuli, is precipitous rather than gradual.

Furthermore, Honig (1961), working under the direction of Guttman, has shown that, by means of special training, it is also possible to make the "innate" color generalization gradient broader, as well as narrower. As shown by the upper curve in Fig. 12–5, if pigeons receive reinforcement with cues of various hues, they respond about equally well to stimulation from any part of the spectrum. Then, if one hue, let us say pure green (550 mμ), is extinguished, the *extinction* generalizes in the way shown by the lower curve in Fig. 12–5. Thus we see much the same pattern of generalization with both positive and negative reinforcement (Chapter 11), although the two patterns, in absolute terms, are inverted images of each other.

With further training, it would, of course, be possible to modify ("sharpen") the extinction curve, just as it is possible to modify the

---

[2] At the human level, this would be equivalent to one's being able to reproduce the full color spectrum without special knowledge or training.

generalization curve for positive learning. If, for example, after extinction of green, a pigeon repeatedly found that the immediately adjacent color of blue-green was "positive," the curve would rise abruptly from green to blue-green, rather than gradually as shown in Fig. 12–5.

It is obviously possible to use discrimination learning for either of two purposes: (1) to determine the range and acuity of any given receptor system, or (2) to investigate the learning process itself. We are here interested mainly in the latter.

III. Conditioning and Discrimination not Easily Distinguished

Let us suppose that a laboratory rat has been placed in a small compartment, the floor of which is a metal grill through which electric shock can be administered to the rat's feet. Now periodically a buzzer will sound for five seconds, at the end of which time a shock will come on the grill and remain on until the rat, in the course of trial-and-error behavior, leaps into the air. If, when the buzzer is presented, the rat leaps in response to it alone, within the five-second warning period, then the buzzer is terminated and the shock is not presented. In short, the procedure is doubly "instrumental": the leap terminates the danger signal and also prevents the shock from occurring if it occurs to the danger signal alone (see Chapter 2 and 3).

During the course of the first 10 trials, one may get an average of two or three leaps from a group of rats, treated in this manner, to the buzzer alone; but one will note an equal or perhaps even greater number of leaps *in the intertrial interval,* when neither buzzer nor shock is on. How does this happen? After a rat has received the buzzer-shock combination in the experimental situation a time or two, it will be apparent that the rat is afraid of the situation regardless of whether the buzzer is present, or not. In other words, in the beginning the rat becomes quickly conditioned to react with fear to the experimental situation, as such, and does not distinguish sharply between situation-with-buzzer and situation-without-it. However, if the subject is repeatedly put back into the apparatus and given, let us say, 10 trials each day, we observe that the incidence of leaps to situation-with-buzzer increases and the incidence of leaps to situation-without-buzzer *decreases.* This tendency for the "interval" responses to disappear and for the responses to the danger signal to become more reliable is shown in Fig. 12–6. Although the rats become quickly conditioned to fear the situation as a whole, they gradually learn that the situation is really dangerous *only* when the buzzer is present, at other times perfectly safe (cf. Section X). Although a curve such as the ascending one in Fig. 12–6 is often presented as a record of conditioned-response learning, it will thus be apparent that such a curve also importantly involves discrimination learning and does not by any means portray conditioning in pure form. As already indicated, conditioning, in the sense of fear learning, occurs in one or two trials, as can be demonstrated by the fact that a rat, once (or twice) shocked in a given piece of apparatus, will react thereafter very differently if again placed in the apparatus a day, a week, or even many weeks afterwards, without any intervening experience therein. In other words, the rat will "remember" the shock after only one or two encounters with

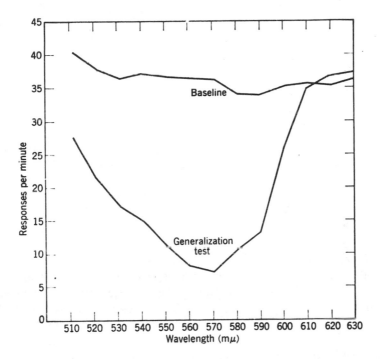

Fig. 12–5. Generalization of extinction (or inhibition) as revealed in a study carried out by Honig (1956, p. 4). Six pigeons served as subjects. Actual extinction took place with a stimulus of 570 mμ. The obtained extinction generalization is shown by the lower line. The level of responding to colors of various hues prior to extinction is shown by the "baseline" at the top of the figure.

it in this situation. Hence, the type of ascending curve shown in Fig. 12–6 gives a very inadequate picture of conditioning in pure form.

Further support for the type of thinking just described is given by the two curves shown in Fig. 12–7. Here the danger signal was a distinct, momentary "tap" caused by the clapper of an electric bell striking the bell just once, the bell immediately thereafter being

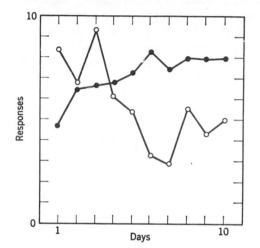

Fig. 12–6. Curves reproduced from Mowrer and Lamoreaux (1951, p. 204), showing the incidence of "avoidance" jumping responses (ascending curve) and the incidence of "interval" jumping responses (descending curve).

"damped." If, within five seconds after the occurrence of this stimulus, the subjects did not leap into the air, they received electric shock, just as did the animals whose performance is shown in Fig. 12–6. But during this five-second danger period the only basis for distinguishing between it and the safe period, between trials, was the *trace* of the tap (Chapter 10). It would, the experimenters reasoned, be more difficult under these conditions for the subjects to distinguish the danger period and the safe period than it would be for subjects in a situation where the danger period was demarcated by a continuous buzzer. The fact that the rats getting the discrete "tap" made more interval responses and fewer avoidance responses seems to indicate clearly that the discrimination had indeed been rendered more difficult for them.

These and other findings that could be cited make it sufficiently evident that the type of criteria commonly used as a measure of conditioning is really heavily contaminated with discrimination learning. Conditioning seems to occur first, and very quickly, to the *total situation;* and only gradually does the subject then differentiate out

of that total stimulus complex the specific stimulus element or combination of elements that is truly significant, specifically meaningful.

A small boy's mother put his new dog out of the house through
the back door. The dog tried immediately to go back into the house
with the woman; and since he was not deterred by the woman's
shouts of "No, no!" the dog was switched a couple of times, until he
was "willing" to remain outside and let the woman enter alone. Later
the boy reported, with some puzzlement, that his dog would not enter
the house with him through the back door. Clearly the dog had been
so conditioned as to fear going into the house through the rear door,
regardless of such seemingly trivial details as to whether he had been
told "No" or "Come on in." Eventually, of course, this kind of discrimination was made; but conditioning, in the gross, over-all sense,
is obviously much more rapid.

In the foregoing we have implied that it is *conditioning* which
occurs when a rat learns to be afraid as a result of having been
shocked in a given piece of apparatus and that it is *discrimination*
that occurs when the rat learns to be afraid in this setting only when a
buzzer is presented. That the distinction even here is not entirely
clear-cut is indicated by the fact that the rat "conditions" so quickly

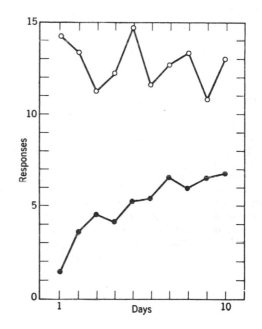

Fig. 12–7. Curves showing the incidence of avoidance responses (below) and the inci-
dence of interval responses
(above) in a situation in which
the danger and safety in the experimental situation are inten-
tionally made more difficult to
discriminate (Mowrer and Lamoreaux, 1951, p. 205).

to the apparatus-as-a-whole only because, from the outset, this situation is already "discriminated" from all other situations in which the rat has ever been. Usually, in discussing discrimination, we speak of a *cue;* and in discussing conditioning, we refer to the conditioned stimulus as a *signal.* Yet these terms are constantly interchanged. For example, Miller (1951b) says: "A learnable drive or reward [i.e., a conditioned fear or hope, in our terms] is one that can be acquired by a previously ineffective *cue* as a result of learning" (p. 436; italics added). And Gentry, a good many years ago (1934), in a study of visual discrimination spoke of a slight change in illumination as a *signal* for the occurrence of an avoidance response. Although, following Gentry, many other investigators have used the so-called conditioned-response method of studying discrimination (cf. also Pavlov, 1927, and his co-workers), the impression seems to persist that there is a *real*, albeit subtle, difference between conditioning and discrimination. Here we can only conjecture that conditioning, as that term is ordinarily used, involves *affective* responses whereas discrimination involves *cognitive* response; but since the latter term will not be given explicit consideration until later (Mowrer, 1960, see especially Chapter 5), this distinction cannot be elaborated here.[3]

IV. Some Interesting Complications

Those writers who, in the past, have wished to stress the discriminative ("cognitive") aspect of learning in contrast to the reinforcement ("conditioning") aspect have sometimes pointed to the fact, long known (Pavlov, 1927), that if a laboratory animal learns to make a particular response, which is then extinguished, relearned, extinguished,

---

[3] For a discussion of the conditioning-discrimination distinction in somewhat different terms, see McGuigan & Crockett (1958). See also Kendler (1959) who, epigrammatically, remarks that "All learning results from learning to discriminate. This is why theories of discrimination are considered as so important" (p. 53). Although the last word has certainly not been said on the relationship between discrimination and conditioning (cf. Section V), the two seem genuinely different or at least not precisely identical. For example, if a rat is put into a particular piece of apparatus and does not react with strong fear, this is not to say that he does not *discriminate* this situation as different, let us say, from his home cage. The discrimination of difference, *perceptual* difference, is easy and immediate; and we may then specifically condition fear to this situation by associating it with electric shock or other traumatic experience. Now we may say, if we like, that the rat has also made an emotional "discrimination" between the two places, but this does not imply that perceptual or "cognitive" discrimination did not previously exist.

etc., successive retrainings and extinctions tend to occur more and more rapidly. Superficially at least, this finding is somewhat difficult for reinforcement theory to explain. However, in 1945, Mowrer & Jones pointed out that both the presence and the absence of a primary reward (such as food) can have *cue* value, quite aside from their reinforcing (or frustrating) functions. And Wickens & Miles (1954), in a paper entitled "Extinction Changes During a Series of Reinforcement-Extinction Sessions," have more recently published particularly good experimental evidence on this score (see Fig. 12–8), which they interpret along much the same lines. They say:

For the animal, there is no difference in the stimulating [experimental] situation on any one day until the completion of the first bar-pressing act. As a consequence of this act and the experimental arrangement, a food pellet is either received or not. Thus, when the bar is confronted on the second trial, traces of reinforcement or nonreinforcement are then present. The experimental procedure is such that on days when traces of reinforcement are present, further responses will be followed by reinforcement, but if these traces are absent, further responding is not reinforced. Hence, to solve the problem, a discrimination on the basis of traces of reinforcement or nonreinforcement must be learned (pp. 316–317).

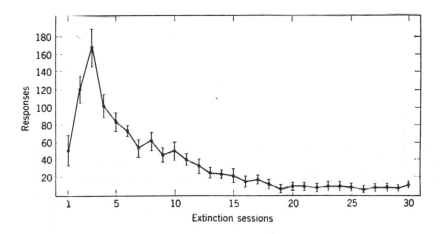

Fig. 12–8. Number of responses made on successive extinctions, with intervening re-acquisition (Wickens and Miles, 1954, p. 316). It is interesting to note that up to the third extinction session, the subjects (rats) had not learned the "meaning" of nonreward following the first response. The marked decrement in number of extinction responses made subsequently indicates that such "meaning" *had* been learned.

In other words, primary reinforcement (food) or nonreinforcement following the first trial of an experimental session has, in addition to its inherent (positive or negative) "motivational" effect (see Chapter 11), also a *cue function*, which indicates whether subsequent responses during that session will or will not be rewarded—and thus worth or not worth the trouble of making (see also Lauer & Carterette, 1957; and Brunswik's 1939 study of repeated reversal of a T-maze habit).

Reinforcement theory has been similarly challenged by the finding, first reported by Harlow (1949) and confirmed by many others, e.g., Meyer (1951), Warren & Baron (1956), Miles & Meyer (1956), that if monkeys (or other laboratory animals) are given a series of discrimination problems they "learn to learn." i.e., become progressively better in their performance even though each discrimination problem or task is distinctive and of equal inherent difficulty. This finding forces a long-overdue recognition of some important facts, but it does not seem to require any new principles of explanation. The present book was first completely written and mimeographed; this version was used for teaching purposes and for obtaining the criticisms of colleagues; and then each of the 12 chapters was revised and new typewritten copy sent to the publishers. The revision of the first two or three chapters required more than two weeks apiece, whereas this chapter was revised in one week. Here each chapter, also, was a "new task," but there was much transfer (generalization) of prior learning, as regards methods of organizing the task, work routines, and many other little "tricks" and conveniences not known at the outset. It seems likely, therefore, that Harlow's monkeys did not so much "learn to learn"; instead, they began to *transfer* the "common elements" from task to task, which is to say, to *generalize* about discrimination-learning tasks (cf. Hebb & Thompson, 1954; Mowrer, 1960, Chapter 10). But Harlow's study is none the less important and useful, for it reminds us of one of the unavoidable hazards of using "naive" animal subjects. Because, in any given learning situation, many *incidental* things have to be learned (or unlearned) in addition to the particular behavior in which the experimenter is specifically interested, our laboratory studies have undoubtedly often made animals appear much "slower" and less intelligent than they actually are. As Harlow's studies dramatically show, when monkeys get their "naïvete" out of the way, they are clever as can be. A large part of man's superiority in "learning" and "problem solving" undoubtedly lies in the fact that to any new situation he brings n-years of "education" *with* him. This problem will be discussed again, in a different context (Mowrer, 1960, Chapter 10).

Finally, attention should be directed to an experiment which has been proposed by Flakus (1958). The conceptual background is formulated thus:

> One theory of avoidance regards the initially neutral stimulus as having acquired the capacity to elicit "fear" or "anxiety." According to Mowrer, for example, fear is a conditioned response, learned according to a stimulus-substitution principle, with the initially neutral stimulus serving as the CS, and some primary noxious stimulus such as shock, as the US. This hypothetical fear response is endowed with drive properties, but more important for the present purposes, the covert stimuli produced by the fear response tend to be regarded as the directing, or cue, stimuli for the observable avoidance response. This is clear from Mowrer's diagrammatic representations of his two-factor theory of avoidance learning, where "conditioning" and "problem solving" are laid "end-to-end." The initially neutral stimulus serves as a cue for the avoidance response only in the sense that it leads to another stimulus, fear, which is capable of evoking this response.
>
> Such a conception, although perhaps tenable for the single-response avoidance situation, seems to slight the possible cue properties of the initially neutral stimulus. If two such stimuli are separately paired with a common noxious stimulus, then presumably they would elicit the same fear response and the same response-produced stimuli. If it can be shown that S is capable of responding differently to the initially neutral stimuli then it seems obvious that they must have a cue function more direct than just eliciting a mediating fear. Perhaps different *patterns of fear* can be established, as Miller once suggested, but this possibility has never been explored (p. 1).

The proposal, quite simply, is to teach laboratory animals to make "two different avoidance responses to two different stimuli," on the assumption that, if this proves possible, there will be "no reason to postulate a hypothetical fear common to the responses" (p. 2.). What this analysis overlooks is the possibility that conditioned fear may still be the motivation common to both responses and that they occur differentially because the two warning signals create, in effect, two different situations, wherein the subjects learn that R_1 will "work" in situation-one and R_2, in situation-two, but not the other way round. Said otherwise: the two stimuli would be alike in their capacity to arouse fear but would differ in their cue properties, as far as overt behavior is concerned. R_1 in the presence of S_1 will be followed by reward but not in the presence of S_2; and similarly, R_2 in the presence of S_2 will be followed by reward but not in the presence of S_1. The proposed experiment does not, it seems, present nearly so sharp a dilemma as at first it might appear to; the reason this is so should become clearer in Section X of this chapter.

V. Conditioning and Discrimination:
The Keller-Schoenfeld-Dinsmoor Hypothesis

Some of the more global reasons for equating the roles of *cues* and *signals* have been delineated in the preceding section. We shall now examine this relationship in a somewhat more specific way. In the same year, Keller & Schoenfeld (1950) and Dinsmoor (1950) put forward the view that in order for a stimulus to act as a secondary reinforcer (type-2), it must also have cue function; and, conversely, it was proposed that any stimulus which acts as a cue, in the sense of "setting the occasion" for a response, will serve also as a secondary reinforcer. Said differently, the proposal was that every such stimulus has *two* functions, depending upon whether it *precedes* or *follows* a particular response. If, for example, a hungry rat is waiting for a stimulus which indicates that bar pressing will be effective as a means of obtaining a pellet of food, that stimulus (S^D) is a *cue* or, more precisely, has cue function with respect to the response which it "releases." On the other hand, if the rat, while waiting for such a cue, discovers that it can *produce* the cue, let us say, by licking the fur on its left flank, then with respect to *this* response the stimulus is a secondary reinforcer. Therefore, reasoned Dinsmoor:

It no longer seems to be necessary to provide separate theoretical accounts of the manner in which a discriminative or [secondary] reinforcing stimulus gains or loses the power to raise the rate of response. The previous distinction between the two types of stimulus appears to be reduced to a distinction between two categories of temporal schedule for the administration of the stimulus. This distinction is relevant chiefly to the determination of the distribution of the stimulus effects among the variety of responses in the organism's repertoire (p. 471).

This position is entirely congruent with the presuppositions of revised two-factor theory. In Chapter 4 we saw that if eating on the part of a hungry rat is contingent upon its getting a particular cue, the rat will quickly learn to press a bar as a means of producing this cue (without further primary reinforcement), thus exhibiting what is ordinarily termed "secondary reinforcement." In Chapter 7 we saw that if eating on the part of a hungry dog is contingent upon the dog's experiencing a particular pattern of kinesthetic and tactile stimulation (produced by the flexing of the right foreleg), then this "cue" will likewise manifest secondary reinforcing properties, as indicated by the dog's developing a paw-flexing "habit." And elsewhere

(Mowrer, 1960, Chapter 3) an important application of this principle in the explanation of language learning will be described.

In 1950 Schoenfeld, Antonitis, and Bersh reported an experiment which seemed particularly convincing in this connection. What these investigators did was this: they presented hungry rats with a distinctive stimulus, not in advance of receiving food (as a sign or cue), but *as* they were chewing and swallowing food already given to them. Here the stimulus was associated with drive reduction and would (according to Hull's postulate) be expected to acquire secondary-reinforcement power; but, coming *after* the food was already obtained, it could have no cue function or properties. It was found that such a stimulus did *not* subsequently reinforce a bar-pressing response, i.e., unlike a stimulus which *precedes* (cues off) the act of eating, this stimulus had no demonstrable secondary reinforcing capacity. And McGuigan & Crockett (1958) have carried out an ingenious experiment on the same problem, which they summarize as follows:

> Two groups of rats were trained such that a stimulus was established as a discriminative stimulus for Group I, but not for Group II. To accomplish this Group I ran [in a straight alley with interchangeable goal boxes] to either a black or a white end box, only one of which contained food. Group II ran to one of two end boxes of the same color, both of which contained food. Performance in a Y maze which had a black and a white end box, neither of which contained food, was used as the test of secondary reinforcement. Two criteria were used: frequency of choice on the first trial and on the first 10 trials. Performance on the first trial was not an effective criterion, but the second criterion indicated that the stimulus that had been associated with reward became a secondary reinforcer for Group I, but not for Group II. It was thus concluded that the prior establishment of a stimulus as a discriminative stimulus is a necessary condition for that stimulus to become a secondary reinforcer (p. 187).

As McGuigan & Crockett point out, this finding goes beyond Hull's postulate that a neutral stimulus needs only to occur ". . . repeatedly and consistently in close conjunction with a reinforcing state of affairs [to] acquire the power of acting as a reinforcing agent" (Hull, 1952, p. 6); and they suggest that "the prior establishment of a stimulus as a discriminative stimulus is sufficiently important to be included as a necessary condition in such general statements as Hull's" (p. 184).

For a time it looked as if there were additional support for the Schoenfeld-Dinsmoor hypothesis in the fact that no one, as yet, had been able to impart clear-cut secondary reinforcing capacity to a stimulus associated with shock termination (see Chapter 6). Here the drive state could be terminated without the subject's doing anything whatever about it, so that there was no basis for regarding the stimulus which signaled shock reduction as a cue; and, as would follow from the theory, such a stimulus seemed incapable of acquiring secondary-reinforcement potential. However, as is well known, one can readily set up a "habit" by means of shock reduction (escape from shock); and, according to our present understanding of what habit is, it consists of secondary reinforcement which has become conditioned to response-correlated stimuli. Thus it would *logically* follow that shock termination can be used to impart reinforcing power to stimulation associated therewith, *without* the latter necessarily having cue properties, in any accepted sense of that term. Furthermore, the researches of Crowder (1958) and Carlton & Marks (1957), which have already been described in Chapter 6, show that stimuli associated with termination of a noxious drive (such as electric shock or coldness) *can* become secondary reinforcers, without also having cue properties. The validity, or at least generality, of the Schoenfeld-Dinsmoor hypothesis is thus considerably impugned.

Moreover, an unpublished study by C. W. Eriksen and D. W. Zimmerman shows a further limitation of this hypothesis. According to this hypothesis, a stimulus which "releases" a response, i.e., has "cue" potential, also has secondary-reinforcement power. The investigators cited put this assumption to the following test. Several rats were trained individually to "shuttle" (see Chapter 2) whenever a tone was sounded. After this behavior was well established, a Skinner bar was made available in the apparatus, depression of which would cause the tone to sound. Thereafter the tone was never presented by the experimenter, but could be produced *ad libitum* by the rat. Although, in the course of its spontaneous activity within the apparatus, each animal eventually touched the bar a time or two, none of them ever "took up" bar pressing. In other words, it was abundantly clear that in *this* situation, the stimulus (tone) which cued off the shuttling response was not something the subjects would readily recreate themselves. Here, manifestly, the "cue" did *not* have the power of secondary reinforcement, in the common sense of the term. Rather, it appeared to be secondarily reinforcing in the *negative* sense, i.e., to act as a secondary punishment rather than as a secondary reward (cf. Chapter 5).

So what, in summation, can be said of the Schoenfeld-Dinsmoor hypothesis? Certainly it is an interesting idea, with some empirical evidence to support it; but, as we have seen, there is also considerable evidence of a contradictory nature. Further inquiry and analysis will be needed to permit us to see the value and limits of this hypothesis in true perspective.

VI. The Consequences of Intermittent Reinforcement Interpreted as Discrimination Failure

In 1939, L. G. Humphreys reported a paradoxical finding. Since "reinforcement" is (by definition) the condition or process that produces learning, a response ought to be learned more rapidly and more firmly if reinforced consistently than if reinforced inconsistently. Yet Humphreys (see also Skinner, 1938) found, as have many later investigators (see review by Jenkins & Stanley, 1950), that a response which is intermittently reinforced has greater resistance to extinction than does a response which, during acquisition, has been reinforced each time it occurs. Since resistance to extinction is a commonly accepted measure of "habit strength," this finding leads to the rather disconcerting inference that a habit is strengthened *more* by a given number of intermittent reinforcements than by the same (or even a greater) number of continuous reinforcements. It is true that if *rate of acquisition* is used as the index of habit strength, this paradox does not arise, since it has been repeatedly shown that intermittent reinforcement produces slower acquisition than does continuous reinforcement (see Jenkins & Stanley, 1950; Grant & Hake, 1951; Grant, Schipper, & Ross, 1952; Reynolds, 1958). The paradox arises only as regards *resistance to extinction*, where it has been found to hold in a wide variety of situations: instrumental animal learning, human verbal learning (Grant, Hake, & Hornseth, 1951), classical conditioning procedures, active avoidance learning (Jones, 1953), and even in situations involving punishment (Deese, 1952, p. 118).

In 1945 Mowrer & Jones reviewed the literature on this phenomenon and found that most speculations concerning its possible explanation were identifiable with either (a) the response-unit hypothesis or (b) the discrimination hypothesis.

(a). *The response-unit hypothesis.* Various studies (Hilgard and Marquis, 1940; Hull, 1943) have shown that the reinforcing effects of reward apply not only to the immediately preceding behavior but also, to a diminishing extent, to the behavior which is temporally more remote from the advent of reward. According to this principle (the "gradient of reinforcement"), we know that under the conditions of the present experiment [involving intermittent reinforcement of bar pressing by rats] it was possible for an animal to be somewhat reinforced for pressing the bar even when this behavior did not immediately produce food. Thus, because an animal was, for example, rewarded only after pressing the bar twice, we should not think of this as press-failure, press-reward, but rather as press-press-reward (p. 184).

When "response" is thus redefined in terms of the whole pattern of behavior which proves effective in producing reward during acquisition, the Humphreys paradox disappears. When "response" is thus redefined, it is found that intermittent reinforcement, far from producing greater "habit strength," actually produces reliably less than does continuous reinforcement (p. 198).

As early as 1938 Skinner had advanced one version of this explanation; and in 1949 Virginia Sheffield (following suggestions derived from Hull) advanced another quite similar one. However, in 1954 Weinstock published an experiment which put this hypothesis under considerable duress. The gist and genious of the Weinstock experiment was that he used *widely spaced* trials (24 hours apart) and still found that intermittent reinforcement led to the Humphreys effect, which it could not readily dc if the response-unit hypothesis were valid. This hypothesis presupposes that when several repetitions of a particular *action* are required to complete an *act*, the reward comes soon enough that the *stimulus trace* from the preceding as well as the last repetition of the action are still present when reinforcement occurs. If successive performances of a given action are widely separated in time, this explanation would not be applicable.

By making certain assumptions about "memory" and "imagery" (see Mowrer, 1960, Chapter 5), it might still be possible to salvage the response-unit hypothesis as an over-all explanation of the Humphreys effect; and even Weinstock does not exclude the possibility that it may *partially* account for the observed results under the ordinary (massed) conditions of intermittent reinforcement. However, the Weinstock findings (which have been subsequently confirmed) strongly suggest that, in any case, some other principle (or principles) is also operative here.

The discrimination hypothesis, as it has been called, holds that intermittent reinforcement leads to greater resistance to extinction than does continuous reinforcement for the reason that in the former circumstances the subject, having experienced runs of nonreinforced trials during acquisition, cannot easily determine when acquisition has ended and "true" extinction has begun, whereas with continuous reinforcement this change is abrupt and clear-cut. In other words, in the extinction that follows continuous reinforcement, the subject quickly "loses hope" and becomes frustrated and discouraged (see Chapter 11); whereas in extinction following discontinuous reinforcement, the subject cannot be sure for a long time that there will be no more reinforcements and so "keeps hoping" and responding. In the one case, the extinction procedure is easily and clearly distinguished from acquisition because the conditions are so obviously different; whereas, in the other case, acquisition and extinction are less markedly different and discrimination is correspondingly more difficult. This hypothesis has received widespread empirical support (Fehrer, 1956; Jones, 1953; Tyler, 1956; Parducci, 1957; Capaldi, 1957; and Lewis & Duncan, 1956, 1957).

While plausible enough from an intuitive, common-sense approach, the discrimination hypothesis has not been very acceptable to the more objectively minded ("noncognitive") learning theorists; so efforts have been made to find alternative interpretations of a less "mentalistic" sort. One of the most noteworthy of these is a study reported by Denny in 1946. This investigator's thinking went as follows. In a so-called intermittent reinforcement procedure, reinforcement is truly intermittent only with respect to *primary* reinforcement. Since, on the so-called nonreinforced trials, the subject enters a compartment or experiences other forms of stimulation which have previously been associated with primary reinforcement, then, here too, *secondary* reinforcement will be experienced. Put loosely, the idea would be that the subject has a sense of having arrived at the "right place," even though on this particular trial there is "nothing there." Hence it might be argued that in so-called intermittent reinforcement, reinforcement is really continuous; and because the total number of trials is likely to be greater here than in a control group receiving continuous primary reinforcement, intermittent primary reinforcement may well result in more *total reinforcement* (primary and secondary combined) than does continuous primary reinforcement alone. If this were the case, a correspondingly greater resistance to extinction would be in no way enigmatic.

The experimental evidence cited by Denny in the 1946 paper supports this hypothesis but is intricate and will not be described here. Instead, let us consider a simpler procedure which was reported by the same investigator in 1948. In an ordinary T-maze, the usual procedure is to have identical goal boxes at the ends of the two "wings" of the maze but with food in only one of these, let us say the one on the right; and on the basis of such differential reinforcement the subject learns to make, consistently, a right turn at the choice point rather than a left turn. But Denny reasoned that this kind of learning could be considerably facilitated if the two goal boxes were themselves clearly differentiated, so that there would be no (or at least less) generalization of secondary reinforcement from the rewarded to the unrewarded goal box. The obtained results supported this inference. Said Denny:

These findings are interpreted as substantiating implications of the principle of secondary reinforcement. It is assumed that in the like end-box group the secondary reinforcement generalized from the correct goal box to the incorrect end box, providing reinforcement for the rat on wrong responses; while in the unlike end-box group stimulus generalization is presumed to be negligible and the animal is consistently reinforced on one side (pp. 248–249).

This finding (which has been confirmed and extended by others, e.g., Ehrenfreund, 1954), that secondary reinforcement can generalize from one goal box to another (similar) one, makes entirely reasonable the assumption that it can also generalize, in the *same* goal box, from one *trial* to another. This, quite simply, was the assumption which underlay Denny's 1946 experiment and the attendant effort to explain, in terms of reinforcement theory, the phenomenon of increased resistance to extinction following intermittent primary reinforcement.

However, even this interpretation, reasonable as it is, has not gone unchallenged. In 1957 Mason reported an experiment which he summarized as follows:

Each of four groups of rats was trained concurrently on both a black-gray and a white-gray discrimination problem [see Fig. 12–9]. When used, the black or white stimulus alley was positive and the gray alley was always negative. Each group learned one of the discriminations under partial (50 per cent) reinforcement of the positive alley, while they learned the other discrimination under complete (100 per cent) reinforcement of the positive alley. Two groups received 300 trials on each discrimination, and the other two groups received 200 trials on the completely reinforced

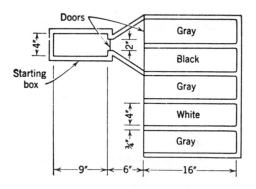

Fig. 12–9. Floor plan of discrimination apparatus used by Mason (1957, p. 265) in testing the Denny hypothesis.

discrimination and 400 trials on the partially reinforced discrimination. Subsequent to this training, the animals were required to choose between the two positive stimuli of the initially learned discrimination (i.e., black and white).

Contrary to the prediction based on the Denny hypothesis concerning the effects of secondary reinforcers in strengthening habits under conditions of partial reinforcement, and in agreement with a prediction derived from the Tolman-Brunswik (1935) theory of expectancies based upon environmental probabilities, 17 of the 20 animals under each condition chose the stimulus alley which had been completely reinforced during the original training. This difference is significant beyond the .01 level of confidence (p. 268).

To this unusually complete yet succinct summary, it need only be added that there were 10 test trials, with both of the positive (black and white) end boxes available; and a choice of one of the boxes on six or more of the 10 trials was regarded as constituting a "preference."

From one point of view, the Mason experiment would seem to be a very fair and straightforward attack on the Denny hypothesis: if intermittent primary reinforcement, as a result of summating with interspersed secondary reinforcement, produces greater *total* reinforcement, then it would indeed appear that Mason's subjects should have preferred the goal box in which intermittent rather than continuous primary reinforcement had been experienced. But there is a subtle complication here: *it is by no means certain that preference and resistance to extinction test the same function.* If, for example, a human being had a choice between two levers, one of which (when operated singly) had previously "paid off" half the time and the other of which had "paid off" on every trial, he would unquestionably choose the latter. But if, with both levers present, he found that the 100%-reinforcement lever was not paying off at all, he might very well conclude that it was out of order (or "empty") and thus stop operating it much sooner than he would stop operating the 50%-reinforcement lever.

At another time (Mowrer, 1960, Chapter 9) we shall discuss the phenomenon of "probabilistic learning" and will then see that it involves a choice between two (or more) response alternatives with different reinforcement ratios, whereas the Humphreys effect, strictly speaking, is limited to *one* response in an extinction situation. Therefore the Mason experiment is something of a combination of the two —and is correspondingly difficult of interpretation. We shall, therefore, in the next section turn to yet another attempt to obtain an experimental decision with respect to this dilemma of intermittent reinforcement.

VII. The Bitterman-Feddersen-Tyler Experiment

In 1953, Bitterman, Feddersen, & Tyler published a paper entitled "Secondary Reinforcement and the Discrimination Hypothesis," which they introduced as follows:

The experiment to be reported is concerned with the relation between the concept of secondary reinforcement and what Mowrer and Jones have called the *discrimination hypothesis*—the assumption that rate of extinction is inversely related to the similarity between conditions of training and extinction. In contemporary learning theory, the effect of change in the afferent consequences of a response upon its resistance to extinction has been considered primarily in terms of the principles of secondary reinforcement—a neutral stimulus acquires reinforcing properties as a function of repeated association with primary reinforcement (Hull, 1943). From this point of view the extinction of a response must inevitably be retarded by stimuli which have been contiguous with reinforcement during training. It is doubtful, however, that the effect of change in the afferent consequences of response can be fully understood in this way. The presence during extinction of stimuli encountered in training may contribute to the similarity of the two series of events and thus, to some extent at least, sustain response independently of previous association with reinforcement. The validity of this conception may be tested under circumstances in which the transition from training to extinction is more readily discriminated in the presence of a secondarily reinforcing stimulus than in its absence (p. 456).

Before examining the results of this experiment, let us review the procedure followed and the logic thereof. The main experiment, employing the animals which the authors refer to as Group II, involved 50% intermittent reinforcement for running a straightaway alley, with a white goal box on reinforced trials and a black one on the nonreinforced trials (or vice versa, as a counterbalance for the possible effects of color *per se*) (cf. Denny, 1948; Saltzman, 1949; also Chapter 4). In order to prevent the subjects from seeing which goal box was present from the start of a run (and thus perhaps just not running on the "negative" trials), the experimenters introduced a gap in the maze, near the end, which the subjects had to leap across. Immediately beyond was a card (with black and white vertical stripes on it) which fell over as an animal jumped against it, thus giving access to the goal box but preventing vision into it. In this way subjects were kept from seeing what the goal box looked like until they were actually in it.

After 10 days of training (10 trials per day) with the procedure just described, the rats were subjected to extinction; but they were now divided into two subgroups, Group II-N, which on all extinction trials found the goal box that had been the nonreinforced one during acquisition, and Group II-S which consistently found the goal box that had been reinforced during acquisition. In other words, if during training the goal box was white on rewarded trials and black on nonrewarded trials, then Group II-N had only the black goal box during extinction and Group II-S had only the white goal box. The results are shown in Fig. 12-10.

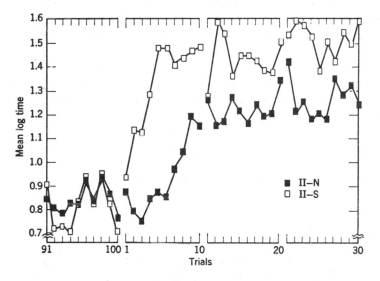

Fig. 12-10. Curves reproduced from Bitterman, Feddersen, & Tyler (1953) showing the greater resistance to extinction (faster running time) of rats (Group II-N)· which encountered only the nonreinforced goal box during extinction as opposed to rats (Group II-S) which encountered the previously reinforced goal box.

As will be seen, the animals which, during extinction, encountered only the previously nonreinforced goal box showed much *greater* (statistically significant) resistance to extinction than did the animals which, during extinction, encountered only the previously reinforced one. Here is dramatic confirmation of the "discrimination hypothesis": the Group II-N animals during extinction encountered conditions (nonreward in black goal box) which had also existed (though not so protractedly) during acquisition and so, not being able to separate acquisition and extinction, kept "hoping" and responding; whereas the

Group II-S animals during extinction encountered conditions (non-reward in *white* goal box) which had *never* existed before, and so immediately reacted to extinction *as extinction*, rather than as continued acquisition.

But this sword cuts both ways: while affording striking confirmation of the discrimination hypothesis, the results of the Bitterman-Feddersen-Tyler study at the same time challenge a hypothesis which is far more basic to our present analysis: the notion that "habit" is the secondary reinforcement which an organism experiences as a result of performing (or "considering"—see Mowrer, 1960, Chapter 7) a given response. Here a response that brought the subject into the white goal box, with its very considerable S^r potency, extinguished *sooner* than did the same response when it brought the subject into the goal box which presumably had *less* S^r capacity. And the authors, taking this observation at its face value, conclude that: "This outcome cannot be understood in terms of the concept of secondary reinforcement" (p. 461; see also the passage already quoted from p. 456). This position, it seems, is based on an incomplete analysis of the results of this investigation. While the results cited do indeed support the discrimination hypothesis, at a gross, molar level of analysis, they do not actually impugn either the secondary-reinforcement conception of habit in general or, for that matter, the particular hypothesis set forth by Denny, as will now be shown.

Thus far only half of the subjects used in the Bitterman-Feddersen-Tyler experiment have been described, i.e., the Group-II (S and N) animals. The Group-I animals (not hitherto mentioned) were also given 50% reinforcement during acquisition; but instead of running into the white box on reinforcement trials and into the black box on nonreinforced trials, they ran into the same (white) box on reinforced and nonreinforced trials alike, as in the usual type of intermittent-reinforcement experiment. Then, for the extinction test, the Group-I animals were divided into two subgroups, one of which (I-S) continued to find the same (white) goal box at the end of the alley, whereas the other (I-N) found a differently colored (black) goal box. The extinction results for the I-S and I-N animals are shown in Fig. 12–11. Taken in conjunction with the results shown in Fig. 12–10, these findings have a number of implications:

1. First we note that the curves in Fig. 12–11 conform quite satisfactorily to the notion that habit is secondary reinforcement. Here we see that those subjects which ran into the same goal box during extinction as the one used during acquisition (I-S) showed visibly

(and reliably) greater resistance to extinction (habit strength) than did those which ran into a goal that had never been associated with food and hunger reduction (I-N). This outcome is strictly in accord with the hypothesis that habit strength is progressively lessened as one eliminates or changes the usual stimulus consequences of a "habitual" (positively reinforced) response.

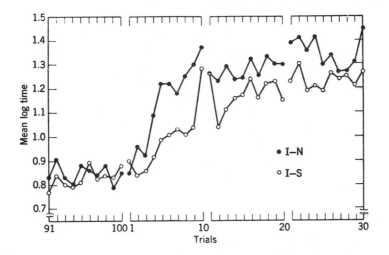

Fig. 12–11. Extinction curves for animals treated the same as those for which results are shown in Fig. 12–10, except that during acquisition they went into one and the same box, rather than into different boxes, on rewarded and nonrewarded trials. During extinction, the Group I-S animals ran into the same box as used during acquisition, whereas the Group I-N animals ran into a different (previously unencountered) box.

2. Then it becomes instructive to put the I-S curve and the II-S curve together on the same graph, as shown in Fig. 12–12. The I-S animals are quite dramatically superior to the II-S animals in terms of resistance to extinction, although both groups found the *same* end box as had been reinforced during acquisition. How, then, explain the difference in outcome? The II-S animals, it will be recalled, had *always* been reinforced (during acquisition) upon entering the (white) goal box, whereas the I-S animals had been reinforced 50% of the time and not reinforced 50% of the time in this box. In other words, as far as the *white box* was concerned, the II-S animals had had what was, in effect, *continuous* reinforcement, whereas the I-S animals had been intermittently reinforced therein. The striking con-

trast between the two curves shown in Fig. 12–12 is therefore the one typically obtained in conventional experiments on intermittent versus continuous reinforcement. The I-S animals had difficulty in discovering where acquisition ended and extinction started, whereas the transition was perfectly obvious for the II-S animals; hence the much more rapid extinction (as the discrimination hypothesis would require) of the latter.

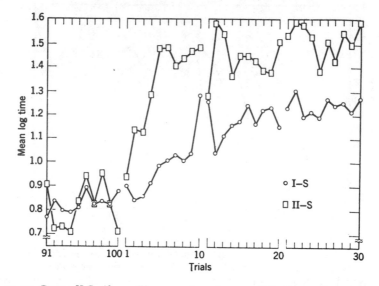

Fig. 12–12. Curve II-S (from Fig. 12–10) and curve I-S (from Fig. 12–11) reproduced on the same coordinates for comparison. The observed difference is in keeping with that usually found following continuous and intermittent reinforcement.

3. It is also instructive to superimpose the I-N and the II-N curves upon the same coordinates (see Fig. 12–13). Here it turns out that 25 of the points in the I-N curve are above the 1.2 latency level, whereas only 15 of the points in the II-N curve are similarly located. This means, simply, that the I-N animals extinguished more easily than did the II-N animals. Here again, during extinction both groups were treated alike objectively, i.e., ran into the same (black) extinction box. But this box had a different *history* ("meaning") for these two groups. The I-N animals had never before encountered it, whereas the II-N animals had encountered this box during acquisition but had never received food in it. However, the fact that it sustained the

running habit during extinction better in Group II-N than it did in Group I-N suggests that the black ("nonreinforcement") box in the II-N group had nevertheless acquired a good deal of secondary reinforcement value. This could not, presumably, have come about through generalization of secondary reinforcement (see Denny and Ehrenfreund), since the two (reinforcement and nonreinforcement) goal boxes used in Group-II training were so manifestly different (white versus black). But there was another mechanism whereby the black goal box could have acquired S^r potency. Since the interval between trials in this experiment was only 20 seconds, an animal might easily run into the black (empty) box and, well before the stimulus trace of this experience had disappeared, it might find itself in the white (baited) box, and since Jenkins (Chapter 10) has shown that a stimulus can acquire secondary reinforcement with temporally delayed primary reinforcement, there would be no reason to deny such a possibility in the present study. However, Elam, Tyler, & Bitterman (1954) have since repeated the Bitterman-Feddersen-Tyler study with distributed practice (a minimum of 15 minutes between trials) and have obtained much the same results, which the authors interpreted as lending further support to the "discrimination hypothesis" and dis-

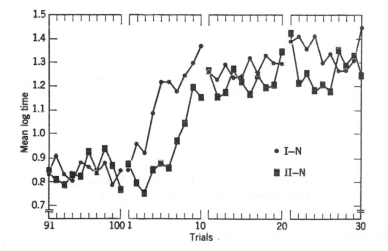

Fig. 12–13. Curve II-N (from Fig. 12–10) and curve I-N (from Fig. 12–11) reproduced on the same coordinates. The superiority of the II-N performance shows that a distinctive end box into which rats run on the nonreward trials in intermittently reinforced acquisition acquires some secondary-reward value.

crediting the whole idea of secondary reinforcement in such a situation. In point of fact, the experiment does force a reconsideration of the *way* in which secondary reinforcement might be operating here; but it does not wholly rule out the influence thereof.

Up to this point we have been proceeding on the assumption that the continued running of the II-N animals was due to the secondary reinforcement provided by the black goal box; but this box was never *directly* associated with food, and the Elam-Tyler-Bitterman study shows that it likewise did not acquire this capacity through delayed presentation of food (on the next trial). Therefore, perhaps the black end box was essentially neutral and the secondary reinforcement which kept the II-N animals responding came from another source. Such a possibility is not far to seek. It will be remembered that the external situation and the subject's response, up to the point of entering the end box, were exactly the same, during training, on both reinforced (white-box) and nonreinforced (black-box) trials. Thus, the pattern of stimulation (visual, tactile, kinesthetic, etc.) which preceded primary reinforcement in the white box during training would be precisely the same as that which preceded entry into the black box during nonreinforced training trials *and* during extinction. Perhaps the secondary reinforcement that kept these animals "going" was not in the end box at all, but in the alley itself!

But why, then, did the II-S animals extinguish more rapidly, since there was the *same* secondary reinforcement in the alley and more still in the (white) goal box? One can conjecture that the experience of not receiving food in the white box was much more frustrating than was the same experience in the black box—the latter, after all, promised nothing and delivered nothing, whereas the white box promised but then did not "keep" its promise—and so led to more rapid counterconditioning and extinction (see Chapter 11, and Mowrer, 1960, Chapter 5, Section III).

VIII. A Noncognitive (Counterconditioning) Version of the Discrimination Hypothesis

Despite ambiguities of the kind discussed in the preceding section, the current literature gives strong support to the view that the greater resistance to extinction of intermittently reinforced habits represents a difficulty of discrimination (Tyler, 1956; Lewis & Duncan, 1956; Capaldi, 1958; Brown & Bass, 1958), in contrast to various other hypotheses which Amsel (1958a) has summarized thus:

Beginning with the "common sense" expectancy interpretation of Humphreys (1939b), there followed the "response-unit" explanation offered originally by Skinner (1938) and tested by Mowrer and Jones (1945); the Hull-Sheffield interpretation (Virginia Sheffield, 1949) in which traces of previous goal events and stimulus generalization decrement are the important factors; the discrimination or sensory integration hypothesis of Bitterman and Tyler and others (Crum, Brown, and Bitterman, 1951; Tyler, 1956; Tyler, Wortz, and Bitterman, 1953); Weinstock's contiguity hypothesis (1954) which suggests that partial reinforcement provides an opportunity for the habituation of competing responses on the nonreward trials during acquisition; some recent Pavlovian interpretations of Razran (1955), the most convincing of which makes partial reinforcement "a case of the efficacy of repeated postextinction reconditionings"; a more recent interpretation of Logan, Beier, and Kincaid (1956) in terms of r_G factors; and a still more recent, contiguity-type interpretation of Hulse and Stanley (1956) which suggests that partial reinforcement training increases resistance to extinction because the partially reinforced subjects have acquired during acquisition something to do in the goal box on nonreward trials (p. 112-113).

The principal objection raised against the discrimination hypothesis is that it is so highly "cognitive" and does not readily lend itself to even a neobehavioristic S—R analysis. For example, Brown & Bass (1958) have characterized this hypothesis as holding that intermittent reinforcement tends "to prolong extinction by making it difficult for S to *see* that extinction conditions are different from those of acquisition" (p. 504). At a common-sense, intuitive level of analysis there is apparently no better description of the facts than this one. But this is not the level at which contemporary learning theory usually operates —and has greatest power. Therefore it is fortunate that Amsel's work on frustration theory (as reviewed in Chapter 11) provides the opportunity for a more "objective" type of analysis.

There is now reason to believe that extinction of a response which has developed on the basis of continuous reinforcement occurs because the emotion of hope which has become conditioned to response-correlated stimuli is counterconditioned by the emotion of disappointment (or anger), which occurs on each extinction trial. Now consider, by contrast, what happens if a habit has developed on the basis of intermittent reinforcement. On nonrewarded trials the subject will, of course, experience disappointment—which will tend to make acquisition somewhat slower, as previously noted in this chapter. But, what is more to the point, each such nonrewarded trial, with its attendant disappointment, is *followed*, sooner or later, by a rewarded trial. Thus, instead of the experience of nonreward (disappointment) becoming a cue for *more* nonreward (as happens in extinction following continuous reinforcement), it becomes a cue *for reward;* and when hope becomes thus conditioned to the experience of nonreward, this experience is decidedly less frustrating, less disappointing, less anger-producing than when there is "no hope."

Another way to put the same notion is to say that intermittent reinforcement of a response does not make the response actually *more resistant* to extinction; instead, intermittent reinforcement *makes extinction less effective*, in the sense that the intermittent reinforcement during acquisition *neutralizes* the normally active agent in extinction, namely frustration (anger, disappointment). As a result, the subject remains hopeful—and "habitful"—longer (sometimes remarkably longer; see Zimmerman, 1957a, 1959) than would otherwise be possible (cf. Kendler & Lachman, 1958, on intermittent reinforcement and resistance to habit *reversal*).

Thus, after a good deal of confusion and "lost motion," we seem to have arrived at a thoroughly satisfactory explanation of the Humphreys paradox. Our error has been in assuming that the greater persistence of a habit following intermittent reinforcement necessarily implied greater "habit strength," instead of realizing that the greater persistence occurs because the normal machinery of extinction has, under these circumstances, been largely put out of operation. Resistance to extinction has been regarded as one of the most reliable means of assaying habit strength. Now we see that, at least under some circumstance, it may be extremely untrustworthy. If, by the means described, the normal effectiveness of nonreward (frustration) is lessened, then, obviously, a habit may show heightened resistance to extinction, not because the habit itself is stronger, but because the forces making for extinction have been *weakened*.

There is only one "catch" in the foregoing argument: How, it may be asked, can nonreward on one trial become the conditioned stimulus for hope if the next (rewarded) trial is delayed beyond the normal span of the gradient of reinforcement (which, as we have seen in Chapter 10, depends upon the phenomenon of stimulus trace)? There is apparently only one satisfactory way of answering this question, and that carries us beyond the scope of the present volume (see Mowrer, 1960, Chapter 5). However, this answer rests upon a well-authenticated set of observations, and we need have no further concern about the problem for the present.

The plausibility and intelligibility of the foregoing argument can perhaps be increased by employing the same assumptions in the context of active punishment, rather than mere nonreward. If, as assumed in Chapter 11, nonreward is functionally equivalent to mild punishment, and if continuous nonreward (as in extinction) is less inhibitory when, during acquisition, nonrewarded trials have been interspersed with rewarded ones, then it would follow that the effect of punishment would be similarly lessened if occasional punishment were experienced during a series of rewarded trials, rather than being applied consistently—and for the first time—from some given point onward. Suppose, for example, that one group of rats were allowed to press a Skinner bar 100 times, receiving a pellet of food each time, and that punishment were then consistently applied on each subsequent trial, in the form of an electrical charge on the bar. There can be little doubt that this would be an effective way of quickly inhibiting the bar-pressing habit. On the other hand, suppose that, during acquisition, the charge were put on the bar only now and then and that the animals, after a punished bar press, would find the bar no longer charged. Here punishment would be followed, not by more punishment, but by no punishment—and continued reward. The result is easily anticipated: when, after 100 trials, the punishment was consistently applied, it would probably be far less inhibiting than in the other group of animals.

We might say that these animals, by the procedure described, had developed "courage" (Chapter 11); or, equally, we might say that they were perverse, rigid, foolhardy. If we, the observers, *wished* to see the subjects over-ride and ignore the shock, we would evaluate their behavior positively—and call it courageous; but if we wished to block the habit and the rats persisted in it, we would then evaluate their behavior negatively. But the *same principles*, it seems, would be involved in both cases.

No one, apparently, has investigated this problem precisely as proposed. Hilgard (1956) reviews the somewhat equivocal studies by Estes (1944) under the following headings: "Punishment Does Not Act as a Negative Reinforcement" (p. 110) and "Intermittent Punishment Is More Effective Than Punishment at Every Occurrence" (p. 111). Perhaps the most relevant finding of the Estes research is that:

If punishment is delivered every time the response is made, the rate of responding is seriously depressed. While it is not depressed as much if punishment is given only occasionally; the effects of punishment persist longer in the latter case" (Hilgard, 1956, p. 110). [See also Akhtar, 1960.]

Tsushima (1959) has pointed out some of the practical implications of intermittent ("inconsistent") punishment as follows:

Since the discovery of the Humphreys effect (Humphreys, 1939b), the psychological meaning of the effect of partial reinforcement has become one of the most interesting topics in the field of learning psychology. This issue becomes quite important when we consider its implications for the relationship between child-rearing practices and personality dynamics and adjustment. Sears and his co-workers (1953), on the basis of their research on the child-rearing antecedents of aggression and dependency in children, drew a theoretical hypothesis that the combination of positive reinforcement and moderate frustration or punishment establishes a drive [habit] of maximum strength. Too much or too little frustration results in a weaker drive. Also Shaffer and Shoben (1956) suggest that frustration generally strengthens a drive.

The present investigation is basically related to the above experiments and ideas, and mainly examines the effects of positive reinforcement with shock punishment in terms of resistance to extinction using albino rats as subjects in an instrumental conditioning situation (p. 1).

In experimentation with rats, Tsushima was able to show that interpolation of occasional punishment during the acquisition of a habit produces greater resistance to extinction (consistent nonreward); but he did not explore the problem of whether greater resistance to *punishment* can be similarly induced. Superficially there is a contradiction between the Estes finding that punishment has a more persistent effect if intermittently applied and Tsushima's finding that intermittent punishment is *less* effective than consistent punishment. This paradox probably hinges upon certain quantitative and other variables which need not be considered here.[4]

[4] The writer has recently had occasion to discuss the Amsel interpretation of the Humphreys effect with Professor Humphreys himself, who raised a very interesting and instructive question. Granted that the Amsel hypothesis is applicable where the habit is a positive, goal-oriented one (and where nonreinforcement might well be expected to generate frustration), could one similarly explain the fact that a *defensive* response, such as the conditioned eyeblink, also shows greater resistance to extinction following intermittent, rather than continuous, reinforcement? Here the omission of reinforcement would be expected to generate *relief* rather than frustration, so that the Amsel hypothesis might not seem to apply. On the grounds that eyelid conditioning is something of an anomaly and probably does not represent conditioning in its most characteristic and significant form, let us shift the example from eyelid conditioning to fear conditioning, as indexed by the psychogalvanic reflex. Here, too, the Humphreys effect is known to hold; and the Amsel hypothesis applies quite nicely, as one may say, in reverse. The Amsel explanation of the extinction of a hunger-motivated habit is that if the habit is executed with the expectation of reward and none is forthcoming, then anger supervenes and counterconditions the hope (type-2 secondary reinforcement) which presumably constitutes the habit's "strength." And as was also pointed out in Chapter 11, if the response which has been acquired and is to be extinguished is fear, then each time the conditioned stimulus is presented and not confirmed, a sense of *relief* is experienced, which counterconditions the fear. Now what presumably happens where a PGR has been

IX. The Discrimination and Counterconditioning Hypothesis Inseparable

Sections VI and VII suggest that, of many possible explanations of the Humphreys paradox which have been advanced, the discrimination hypothesis is in many ways the best. And in Section VIII, it is shown how the discrimination hypothesis can be given a noncognitive reformulation, along the lines recently suggested by Amsel to explain extinction, in general, as counterconditioning. But the essential identity, or at least equivalence, of these two ways of interpreting the Humphreys paradox becomes clearer still if we examine two experiments which have been reported by Tyler, Wortz, & Bitterman (1953) and by Capaldi (1958). These experiments have already been briefly alluded to but deserve special consideration for the reasons just given.

In the first of these experiments, two groups of rats were trained to negotiate a straightaway alley for food under the following conditions. Both groups were reinforced during acquisition 50% of the time, but according to different patterns. In the Group-A animals food was given regularly every-other trial, i.e., alternately; whereas in the Group-R animals food was given also 50% of the time but *randomly*. When tested with no reinforcement whatever, the Group-A animals extinguished decidedly faster than did the Group-R animals.

set up on the basis of intermittent reinforcement is that when, during acquisition training, the danger signal is presented and, on a given trial, is not followed by shock but on the next trial is so followed, nonreinforcement loses its capacity to bring relief, and so is rendered less effective in counterconditioning the fear reaction during extinction proper. That is to say, when nonreinforcement of a danger signal and the resulting relief on certain trials during acquisition training are followed, not by continued nonreinforcement, but again by reinforcement, then the *sign function* of nonreinforcement (see Section IV) is structured in such a way as to reduce the relief-producing value of nonreinforcement, when it becomes continuous in the true extinction period, just as the recurrent withholding of *positive* reinforcement during acquisition training can structure the sign function of such an event so as to reduce its *frustrating* capacity and thus render continuous nonreinforcement less effective during extinction proper. It is presumed that this type of explanation is also applicable, with perhaps minor modifications, to the Humphreys effect as observed in eyelid conditioning and other short-latency skeletal responses. It is, incidentally, also interesting to ask whether the *fatigue* theory of extinction (see Chapter 11) can be similarly used to resolve the Humphreys paradox. The present writer's tentative impression is that it cannot. And if this impression should be sustained by further research and analysis, this would be yet another indication of the greater potency of the frustration theory of extinction, in general.

Now the cognitive version of the discrimination hypothesis would hold that the reason for this outcome is that the Group-R animals never "knew" when reinforcement was going to come during acquisition so could not be sure when true extinction had started, whereas the Group-A animals *did* know when to expect reinforcement and could therefore detect quite precisely the onset of extinction. "But," one might ask, "how can you possibly check such a hypothesis? How can you tell what a rat does or doesn't 'know' or 'expect'?" In answer to this question, Tyler, Wortz, & Bitterman published a graph which is reproduced here as Fig. 12–14. Here the average running times of the Group-A animals on each of the 120 acquisition trials (10 trials per day for 12 days) are clearly plotted, with the open circles representing nonrewarded runs and the closed circles, rewarded runs. During roughly the first half of the acquisition trials, there is no systematic difference in running speeds on the alternately rewarded and nonrewarded trials. But in the second half of the acquisition trials, it is unmistakable that the rats "knew" what they were doing, or at least what was being done *to* them. On the nonrewarded trials they ran regularly and markedly slower than on the rewarded trials, thus indicating that they

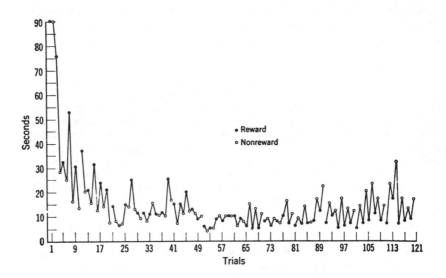

Fig. 12–14. Graph reproduced from Tyler, Wortz, & Bitterman (1953) showing the gradual discovery (by rats) of an alternating pattern of reward and nonreward for runs in a simple alley-type maze. "Knowledge" of this pattern significantly influences the subjects' behavior when reward is withdrawn entirely (see text).

had learned the alternating pattern of reinforcement and nonreinforcement and were decidedly less "hopeful" and less hurried on the non-rewarded trials than they were on the rewarded ones. Hence, one can say with confidence that the Group-A rats would know, quite precisely, when extinction had started, i.e., when conditions had been changed to no reward at all, and would modify their behavior accordingly; whereas the Group-R animals could not make nearly so sharp a discrimination and would be correspondingly slower in modifying their behavior following the withdrawal of reward.

The experiment reported by Capaldi shows the high pertinence of the discrimination hypothesis in an even more dramatic form. Using essentially the same type of apparatus as was employed in the study just described, this investigator ran four groups of hungry rats under the following conditions: Group A-14, 14 acquisition trials with alternate reinforcement and nonreinforcement; Group A-7, seven acquisition trials with alternate reinforcement and nonreinforcement; Group R-14, 14 trials with *random* 50% reinforcement; and Group R-7, seven acquisition trials with random 50% reinforcement. Capaldi gives the rationale of his experiment thus:

The discrimination hypothesis holds that the ease of discrimination between extinction and acquisition trials is a factor in extinction. If increased amounts of training result in greater discriminability between acquisition and extinction trials, then resistance to extinction should decrease with overtraining. Alternating partial reinforcement may fulfill the conditions required by the discrimination hypothesis. Increased amounts of training under an alternate reinforcement schedule may lead to better learning of the pattern of reinforcement itself because of the predictability of the pattern, i.e., reinforcement follows nonreinforcement and vice versa. Better learning of the pattern implies that deviations from the pattern will become more noticeable, and therefore the extinction process should be accelerated. Extinction following random reinforcement should not be especially accelerated by increased amounts of training because of the unpredictability of the pattern and therefore the impossibility of learning the pattern (pp. 367–368).

In other words, using the discrimination hypothesis, Capaldi made the remarkable prediction that if regular 50% alternate reinforcement were used during acquisition, animals which received *more* training would have a better grasp of the reinforcement-nonreinforcement pattern, would therefore discriminate more precisely when extinction (complete nonreinforcement) had set in, and would thus show *less* resistance to extinction. This prediction is strikingly confirmed by the findings shown in Fig. 12–15. Here we see that although the

Group A-14 animals had received twice as many acquisition trials as the Group A-7 animals, they showed decidedly *less* resistance to extinction, i.e., reacted more promptly and more appropriately to the change in reinforcement pattern which marked the onset of extinction. Moreover, the Group R-14 and R-7 animals provided perfect controls for this interpretation; for here we see that when there was nothing that *could* be learned about the pattern of reinforcement-nonreinforcement (because it was random), additional training did *not* result in reduced resistance to extinction.

Here, and in the Tyler-Wortz-Bitterman experiment, is about as conclusive support for the discrimination hypothesis (as over against most other interpretations) as one could ask. However, these findings are equally interpretable in terms of the frustration or counterconditioning hypothesis. In both experiments it is shown that if a rat *expects* reinforcement on a given trial and it is not forthcoming, this failure of reinforcement has a markedly depressing effect upon the rat's

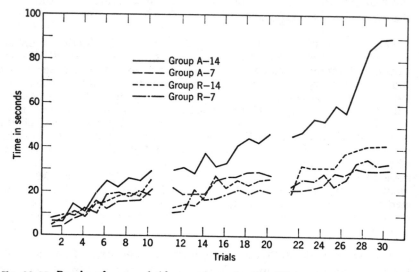

Fig. 12–15. Results of a remarkable experiment by Capaldi (1958) showing that rats which have been given more training in a straightaway alley (Group A-14 as compared with Group A-7) with alternate reward and nonreward display less resistance to extinction (as indicated by slower running). This difference does not appear in comparable groups (R-14 and R-7) which have undergone another pattern of training (random reward and reinforcement). These findings strongly support the discrimination (and frustration) interpretation of the Humphreys effect.

"morale"; whereas, if a rat has no certain knowledge or strong expectation of when reinforcement will or will not occur, failure or withdrawal of reinforcement has a much less decided effect. As already noted, these findings conform exactly to predictions generated by the discrimination hypothesis, but they are equally congruent with the frustration hypothesis. If a rat is *not sure* whether a given trial is the one which is to result in reinforcement, he is not particularly frustrated (surprised, disappointed) if there is no reinforcement; but if, on a particular trial, reinforcement *is* confidently expected and does not materialize, then there will be maximum frustration and correspondingly greater counterconditioning (extinction) of hope and habit strength.

As already indicated, it seems that the discrimination hypothesis and the counterconditioning hypothesis are, in reality, one and the same, the only difference being that the one is formulated in "cognitive" and the other in affective-dynamic terms. In this book we have given major attention to affective rather than cognitive learning; but the experiments just described (along with many other considerations) suggest that every affective event normally has its cognitive counterpart and that a complete psychology of learning must take the latter into account no less than the former. However, the detailed demonstration of this thesis is a task for the book which is to follow and cannot be undertaken in this volume.

X. Temporal Discrimination Exemplified: Avoidance ("Compulsive") Behavior without Objective Warning

If a rat is put into a revolvable cage and shocked every 20 seconds *unless*, during this interval, it revolves the cage (by some minimal amount—say an inch or two), a very interesting type of performance results. Because each "spontaneous" (or interval) response, of walking or running, serves to *avoid* (or at least postpone for 20 seconds) the next "trial," it is clearly to the rat's advantage to make these interval responses; and if they are made with sufficient reliability, the experience of shock can be completely eliminated. Figure 12–16 illustrates the learning that commonly occurs in a situation of this kind. And Sidman (1956), as a result of continuing training of this kind much further, reports that rats and other laboratory animals eventually become highly proficient in such behavior, reaching the point eventually where shock is almost never allowed to occur (cf. Fig. 12–18, p. 480; also see Fig. 12–17, p. 479).

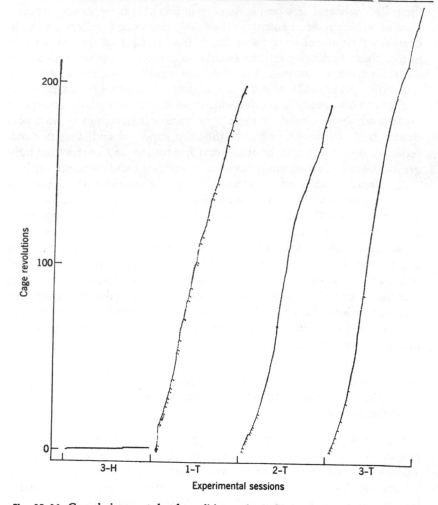

Fig. 12–16. Cumulative records of an albino rat's performance in a revolvable cage when between-trial ("spontaneous") runs postpone the next shock by 20 seconds. An activity baseline, representing the amount of running by the subject during the third of three daily habituation sessions of one hour each, under conditions of no shock, is shown in curve 3-H. Curves 1-T, 2-T, and 3-T represent the amount of running during an hour-long session on each of three successive "training" days. Shocks were applied only when the subject failed, for 20 seconds, to revolve the cage by the prescribed amount (approximately two inches). Shocks are indicated by the lateral spurs on the underside of the curves. (Reproduced from Mowrer & Keehn, 1958, p. 213).

From an intuitive and common-sense point of view, this finding is not very surprising. Yet, in terms of systematic behavior theory, it has occasioned some puzzlement. As we have seen in earlier chapters, avoidance behavior is usually instigated and reinforced, respectively, by the appearance and disappearance of some specific danger signal; whereas, in the situation under discussion, no such signal is immediately apparent and, as a result, some writers have been inclined to see here a possible exception to the principles now generally regarded as governing avoidance learning. However, a little closer scrutiny of this situation indicates that these principles apply here, too, very satisfactorily.

Schaefer (1959) has pointed out that in a situation of the kind described, what first happens is this: the subject learns to discriminate between the state of being *in motion* and the state of being *at rest*. Shock is never experienced by the animal when moving or just after having moved; whereas shock does occur when the animal is at rest. Therefore, the subject will soon begin to feel afraid when at rest and relieved and safe when in motion—and immediately thereafter. Hence, the "danger signal" is the state of rest or inaction; and since the animal can terminate it by moving (and revolving the cage), this behavior will be reinforced by fear reduction quite as much, presumably, as it would be if the danger signal were some external stimulus such as a buzzer or a blinking light, which was turned *off* each time the animal

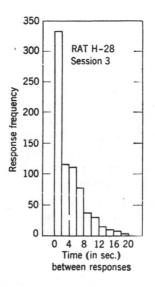

Fig. 12-17. Diagram reproduced from Sidman (1953) showing the distribution of interval responses when such a response will postpone the next "trial" (shock) for 20 seconds if the response occurs within 20 seconds of the preceding response. The distribution of responses shown here is for a rat which has had comparatively little training (cf. Fig. 12-18).

ran. Hence we see how it is that the subject in this experimental setting would be motivated to engage in a very considerable amount of "interval" activity or responding: because this is the way to *eliminate* the "danger signal," i.e., change a dangerous situation into a *safe* one.

However, on both theoretical and empirical grounds, we have reason to believe that a still more refined and efficient discrimination, or "adjustment," can be made here. Strictly speaking, it is not true that action is safe and inaction dangerous. Action is, to be sure, safe enough; but inaction is not necessarily dangerous. It is dangerous *only* when upwards of 20 seconds has elapsed since the preceding response. Therefore, instead of running, stopping, and running again almost immediately (as an inexperienced subject for a time tends to do), an animal can handle this situation—very nicely—by running, stopping, *waiting a time*, and *then*, at the appropriate point, running again (see

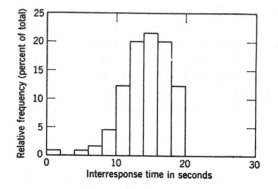

Fig. 12–18. Temporal distribution of "spontaneous" avoidance responses in a well-trained rat (Sidman, 1956, p. 293). The response-shock interval was again 20 seconds.

Fig. 12–18). Here one thinks immediately of the mechanism of *stimulus trace* described in Chapter 10. For the improved type of adjustment just described, all the subject has to do is to learn to discriminate between the *safe* (earlier) and the *really dangerous* (later) parts of the trace; the shocks can thus still be avoided, and without a lot of unnecessary, useless responses in the meantime.

In a well-trained, experienced rat one can see this type of adjustment working very clearly. After having just made a run (or performed whatever other type of response is required in the situation), the animal will appear quite unconcerned and relaxed for a time, grooming itself, rummaging about, or doing whatever else strikes its fancy. But then, as if an inner "timer" of some sort were operating, the rat will presently be "reminded" of the impending danger and will again make the appropriate response. Because the stimulus trace is of limited duration, there is a corresponding limit to the duration of the intertrial interval that can be effectively used here; but within this limit, *temporal discrimination* (or conditioning), though difficult, can nevertheless develop and function quite nicely.

This phenomenon has rather obvious relevance to the psychology of "work" and to certain types of "compulsions" as they appear clinically; and Brady (1958b; also Brady, Porter, Conrad, & Mason, 1958) has shown that monkeys which are subjected to certain schedules of avoidance training of this kind develop lethal stomach ulcers. The article by Mowrer & Keehn (1958) gives a general review of this phenomenon; and Sidman and co-workers are vigorously, and imaginatively, exploring its ramified implications.

XI. Generalization and Apparent Failure of Extinction

The assumption has been made throughout this volume (see especially Chapter 11) that all learning, without occasional reinforcement, undergoes extinction or "oblivesence." Hopes, without fulfillment at least now and then, grow dim; and fears, if not periodically confirmed, subside. Seeming exceptions to this assumption have sometimes been reported. Instances of habits which appear to be "functionally autonomous" (a term popularized by Allport, 1937), upon closer examination, usually turn out to involve subtle sources of secondary reinforcement; and even "memories," in the most subjective sense of the term, fade unless kept alive by occasional recall.

Hilgard & Marquis (1940) have a good review of some of the earlier studies showing unusual persistence of fear reactions; but the problem has been most extensively studied by Solomon and associates, with dogs as subjects. The apparatus used in this line of investigation is shown in Fig. 12–19 and is described by Solomon & Wynne (1953) thus:

> The shuttle box consisted of two compartments separated by a barrier and a guillotine-type gate. The inside dimensions of each compartment were 45 in. long, 24 in. wide, and 40 in. high. The barrier [which the subject had to leap over in order to go from one compartment to the other] was adjustable in height. The gate could be raised by means of a pulley system above the level of the top of the compartments. When the gate was closed it rested on top of the barrier, thus creating a solid wall completely separating the two compartments. . . .
> The barrier was adjusted to approximately the height of the dog's back. Therefore, the dogs could look over the barrier from one compartment to the other when the gate was raised (pp. 2–3).

It should perhaps be added that the "danger signal" employed in the foregoing research involved two distinct stimuli:

The lights above the compartment in which the dog was confined were turned off [by the experimenter] by means of a foot pedal. Simultaneously, the experimenter raised the gate by pulling the counterweight on the pulley system. Therefore, the subject was in relative darkness but was, at the same time, exposed to the presence of the barrier, and immediately beyond it the other compartment was still illuminated. This situation was referred to as the conditioned stimulus pattern (CS), or the "signal" (p. 3).

The authors then summarize the procedure followed and the results obtained in these words:

An experiment in traumatic avoidance learning is reported in which dogs were trained to avoid a just-subtetanizing shock by responding to a signal which preceded the shock by a period of 10 seconds. A shuttle-box jumping response was reinforced as the instrumental avoidance reaction. The dogs received ten trials per day with a 3-min. interval between trials. The results can be stated briefly: (1) During the *escape* phase of learning,

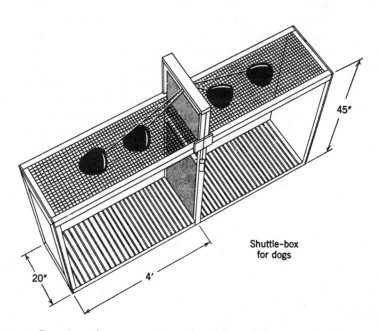

Shuttle-box
for dogs

45"

20"   4'

Fig. 12–19. Drawing of apparatus (reproduced from Solomon and Wynne, 1953) designed and used for avoidance learning in dogs.

when the animals were receiving shocks because they were not "anticipating," the latency of the jumping response decreased rapidly and did
not change significantly after the third trial. (2) The first *avoidance* response, a response to the signal having a latency of less than 10 seconds,
appeared (on the average) on the fifth trial; it was preceded at about
the third trial by the appearance of conditioned emotional reaction to the
signal. (3) The latency of the first avoidance response represented an
abrupt decrease from the escape reaction latencies preceding it. (4) After
the first avoidance trial, the latency of responses continued to decrease in
an orderly manner, while the latencies of the escape reactions did not
change. (5) The latency of avoidance reactions continued to decrease
after the trial on which the last shock was received. (6) The difference
in latency between the last shock trial and the avoidance trial following
it was 9.1 seconds, approximately the magnitude of the CS-US interval.
(7) The sequential patterns of escape and avoidance reactions showed
that some dogs make a complete change from 100% escapes to 100%
avoidances without reversal. (8) Relatively large amounts of shock received
during the first few trials tended to decrease the number of reversals
from avoidance to escape on the trials following the first avoidance response.
(9) Stereotyping of behavior was noted in conjunction with decrease in
emotional reactions. . . .

The results were discussed within the framework of a two-process theory
of learning. Several inadequacies in current learning theories were revealed
in trying to explain our findings (pp. 18–19).

An interesting but not entirely new observation reported here is
that the avoidance performance of the dogs *continued to improve*
after reinforcement, conceived of as shock, ceased to be received.
From one point of view this finding is somewhat paradoxical, but
from another it is entirely reasonable. Fear conditioning apparently
occurred very quickly in this situation and was very durable. Therefore, it is not surprising if the dogs showed improvement in their
behavioral response to the fear after the fear itself ceased to be reinforced. In other words, with the secondary drive of fear well established, the correct response *to the fear* might very well become more
prompt and more precise, under the influence of the secondary reinforcement (decremental type) provided by escape from fear, without
the fear itself receiving any further (incremental) reinforcement. The
same sort of phenomenon and interpretation thereof have been previously suggested by Lichtenstein (1950a).

Also striking is the suddenness with which the shock-avoidance
solution often replaced the shock-escape solution. This is shown in
Fig. 12–20.

But, for present purposes, the most important thing about the behavior modification produced by the type of training described by

Solomon & Wynne is its persistence, often for several hundred trials, without a single readministration of shock (see Solomon, Kamin, & Wynne, 1953). There are several factors that may enter into the explanation of this finding. One is that the shock used was as intense as it could be without locking the dog's muscles so they could not move. One would naturally expect such a shock to be "remembered," with lively apprehension, for a long time. Then, too, it will be noted that spontaneous, interval responses were excluded in the Solomon-

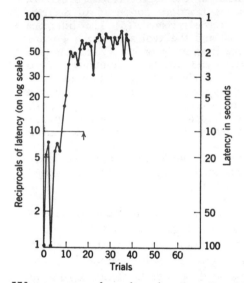

Fig. 12–20. "An individual acquisition curve for a fairly typical subject. Note that the transition from escape responses to avoidance responses is final and complete, with no reversals. Here is an instance of avoidance learning which is not a case of irregular or a periodic reinforcement" (Solomon and Wynne, 1953, p. 6.)

Wynne procedure by the "gate" which was kept closed between trials. Dr. Solomon, in a personal communication, has indicated that he feels this feature of the procedure was quite important in producing the high stability of the avoidance behavior. Perhaps it operated in this way: If, in an avoidance-learning situation, the subject can make the "correct" response between trials, this means that the response may be followed, perhaps quite soon, by a new trial. The new trial involves the occurrence of at least the danger signal (secondary incremental reinforcement), and it may also involve the occurrence of the shock (primary-incremental reinforcement). In either case, we would expect the effect upon the response in question to be a depressing one; so it may be that what the Solomon-Wynne procedure did, actually, was to prevent the "punishment" of the correct response which almost inevitably occurs to some extent (in a fixed-interval schedule of trials) when interval responses are not prevented from occurring. Therefore, since the leaping response, with gate open and light on, was invariably rewarded and never punished, we might expect it to have, perhaps, unusual stability and persistence (cf. Murphy & Miller, 1958).

Just how long dogs trained in the manner indicated would continue to "obey" the "command" to leap over the barrier, given to them by the change in illumination and the opening of the gate, is not known. But it is clear that this type of learning is very resistant to extinction, so much so that Solomon and his co-workers incline to the belief that there is a "partial irreversibility" about such learning. Moreover, Hunt et al. (1941, 1947) have reported long-lasting effects from presumably traumatic starvation in rats, which would also seem to support the notion of "partial irreversibility." There is, however, still some doubt about these findings (cf. Littman, 1956; Levine, 1956; Morgan et al., 1943; Scott, 1955). And in the case of Solomon's findings the possibility is not excluded that fear in the experimental situation is subtly reinforced by contact with the experimenter *outside* that situation. In the barrier-leaping experiment, the experimenter stands nearby; and it is perhaps not unreasonable to assume that the dogs interpret the appearance of the danger signal as a sort of *command from the experimenter*. Outside the experimental situation, the experimenter presumably has considerable contact with the subjects, *in a master-subject relationship;* and *that* relationship is probably reinforced every time the dog questions it! If, therefore, the danger signal in the experimental situation is indeed perceived as a "command" from the experimenter, and if the experimenter gives and, on occasion, reinforces commands outside the experimental situation, it is not unlikely that such reinforcement would carry over (generalize) into the experimental situation and produce there what seems to be virtually permanent "obedience." Might it not be, therefore, that the phenomenal resistance to extinction reported is in reality just an instance of discrimination failure—failure to discriminate, that is, between commands given in the experimental situation which (beyond a given point) are not going to be reinforced and commands given and *reinforced* in all other situations? [5]

[5] The reader may here recall the remarkable resistance to extinction recently reported by Zimmerman (1957a) for rats in a double-intermittent-reinforcement situation, where food rather than shock was the primary reinforcer. Here more than 2,000 performances of a bar-pressing response, established and maintained in rats exclusively upon the basis of secondary reinforcement, are not uncommon. But here, again, the effect (as we have seen in Sections V and VI) is apparently dependent upon a deliberately fostered "failure of discrimination": the failure,

As far as the Solomon findings are concerned, these inferences are entirely speculative. But this line of thought is empirically supported by a striking and now well-authenticated experimental phenomenon. Several years ago J. S. Brown told the present writer of having obtained the following effect. A rat was placed in one end of a runway about six feet long and, through the grill floor, was presently shocked until it ran to the opposite end of the runway and escaped into a small "safety" box. After one or two repetitions of this procedure, the rat would, understandably enough, scamper down the runway and into the safety box, without the shock having to be applied. Such behavior may occur for a good many trials, but eventually it extinguishes. If, however, a section of the grill at the end of the runway, just in front of the safety box, is kept permanently electrified, the running may *never* extinguish (cf. the Gwinn experiment, discussed in Chapter 11; also Hurwitz, 1956a). That is to say, it may never again be necessary to shock the rat in the starting end of the runway as a means of making it run to the safety compartment. This effect was later confirmed in unpublished work by Barbara Lyndon; and Whiteis (1955, 1956) has recently studied it more systematically. Whiteis was able to show, fairly conclusively, that the effect is due to a failure of discrimination. If the whole interior of the runway is homogeneous in appearance, i.e., if the beginning end of the runway looks very much like the opposite end (where shock is experienced), then the fear conditioned to the shock end of the runway readily generalizes to the beginning end; and each time the rat is put into the beginning end, it is so afraid that it is driven out of that end, in the direction of the safety compartment, despite the fact that its route takes it over the energized portion of the floor grill. When a partition, with a small doorway in it, is put in the runway so as to separate the starting segment and the shock segment and when the two compartments thus created are "decorated" differently, the otherwise observed "functional autonomy" breaks down and the rat stops running—provided, of course, that shocks are no longer applied in the starting compartment. In other words, when the two compartments are quite visibly different, the subjects are much more prone to

---

that is, to discriminate between acquisition (occasional primary reward) and extinction (no primary reward). Since this technique of making the boundary between acquisition and extinction vague was not employed in the Solomon-Wynne study, it is conjectured that the persistence of punishment for disobedience ("discipline") *outside* the experimental situation may have "spilled over" and produced unusual resistance to extinction therein.

"reality test," i.e., to wait and see if the shock in the starting compartment is "still there," than when the two areas are visibly just the same; and if, as a result of such testing, rats find that they are now actually safe in the starting compartment, then, sensibly enough, they stop running. It is only when they cannot distinguish between the starting and the shock areas of the runway that they get into and persist in the "vicious circle."

We conjecture, therefore, that the "partial irreversibility" of the fear conditioning reported by Solomon & Wynne was of an analogous character. In the Whiteis experiment, fear in the starting area of the alley proved to be apparently "irreversible" because the animal's fear was getting reinforced in the adjacent area and was generalizing back into the now actually safe area. It seems entirely possible that the discipline which the Solomon-Wynne dogs presumably received everywhere else generalized, in like manner, over into the experimental situation. Eventually, the dogs might learn that the experimenter no longer "meant it" when the command (light change and gate opening) to jump came in the experimental situation; but since this command was initially reinforced so powerfully and since *all other* commands outside the experimental situation were consistently enforced, it would presumably take a very smart (and brave) dog indeed to make such a discrimination. Is it not suggestive that no one has reported similarly persistence "obedience" (resistance to extinction) in the shuttling behavior of rats or other organisms which are ordinarily subjected to obedience (avoidance) training only in the experimental situation? (See also Chapter 6, Section VI.)

Dollard & Miller (1950), in attempting to give a learning-theory account of human neurosis, have made much of the hypothesis (also accepted, though differently expressed, by Freud) that pathological adult fears are simply fears that have been learned by the individual in infancy and persist because the individual fails to realize that "conditions have changed" and that, under the circumstances of adult life, he is now free to do certain things which, in infancy or childhood, were severely tabooed and punished. The evidence reviewed in the preceding pages (see also Mowrer, 1960, Chapter 10) suggests that this is an oversimplification. Conceivably there are some instances where an unnecessary adult fear is kept alive by generalized reinforcement (Solomon example) or by a vicious circle (Whiteis example). However, in human psychopathology the individual's guilt seems real rather than spurious. His fears would therefore reflect a failure far more basic than one of mere discrimination.

XII. Discrimination, Skill, and "Response Generalization"

Throughout this book we have stressed the thesis that a "habit" does not involve *motor learning*, i.e., the strengthening of the neural connection between some stimulus or drive and a particular set of muscles. Instead, "habit" is conceived as a matter of the hopes and fears that have become conditioned to the stimuli that are associated with the occurrence of a given response. And the evidence for such a thesis is already substantial and apparently growing. However, with some justification it can still be asked if there are not at least *some* instances of purely "motor learning," particularly in the domain of the so-called *skills*. It will be pointed out that the violin virtuoso or the Olympic hurdler *must* have his muscles "trained" in special ways. In a sense this is, of course, true. Many skills call for unusual, not to say prodigious, *muscular development;* but fitness and strength of muscle is not what we mean by learning—though "fitness" is admittedly an essential *aspect* of many skills. The learning aspect of the problem has to do with the co-ordination and delicacy of the *control* which the individual has over his musculature.

And how, we must ask, is such control acquired? It is, we conjecture, a matter of *increasingly refined discrimination*. Most musicians and athletes have to study with and be trained by special teachers and coaches; and much of this training consists of intensive instruction in what is *right* and what is *wrong* about their performances. From this kind of tutelage they themselves get a proper *feel* for what is correct, what incorrect. Some of this learning is "motor" in the sense that it involves discrimination between the proprioceptive feedbacks from correct and from incorrect responses; but the process is broader than this. The hurdler can *see*, as well as feel, some of his movements; and, in the case of the violinist, to kinesthesis, sight, and touch is added *sound*. No amount of "purely motor" training will ever make a Kreisler out of a person with "no ear"; and we may conjecture that champion hurdlers need certain other forms of *sensory accuity*, as well as strong legs and lungs.[6]

It will be apparent that this interpretation of skill is not merely consistent with but is virtually demanded by the revised two-factor position. Other writers (e.g., Keller, 1954; Bahrick, Fitts, & Schneider,

---

[6] For a remarkably explicit, earlier statement of this hypothesis, see James (1890, Vol. II, p. 492), where we read: "Professor Beaunis (1889) found that the accuracy with which a certain tenor sang was not lost when his vocal cords were made anaesthetic by cocain. He concludes that the guiding sensations are not

1955; and Gibbs, 1954), on quite independent grounds, have recently advanced a very similar type of interpretation.[7]

Finally there remains to be considered in this section the concept of "response generalization." It is referred to as a concept, rather than as a phenomenon, for the reason that, as we shall attempt to show, it probably reduces to a matter of *stimulus* generalization. Such a conclusion follows from the premise that *psychologically* a response *is* the stimulation which it produces, in the actor and in others. Thus one response is like or unlike another in terms of the stimulation which is contingent upon its occurrences; and we would expect, accordingly, that so-called response generalization would follow the anterior principles governing stimulus generalization.

The term, response generalization, has been applied to the fact that an organism which has been rewarded for making a particular response will tend to reproduce, not only this response, but also responses which are similar but by no means the "same." Sheppard (1958) puts the matter thus:

In addition to stimulus generalization, an analogous phenomenon of response generalization is sometimes supposed to operate so that (a) a stimulus to which one response has been conditioned tends to evoke other responses, and (b) the magnitude of this tendency (for any particular one of these responses) is governed by the dissimilarity between that response and the response originally conditioned. Although this principle of response generalization is also of considerable theoretical importance, even less progress has been made toward the quantitative determination of the shape of the gradient in this case than in the case of stimulus generalization (pp. 242–243).

In a sense, therefore, response generalization is the antithesis of *skill*, which calls for a very precise replication of some standard pattern of action (and return stimulation). It may, in fact, be said to represent the usual, normal tendency of living organisms prior to highly specific training: because the secondary reinforcement that is

---

resident in the laryngeal muscles themselves. They are much more probably in the ear (p. 253)."

[7] If the cogency of our emphasis on the role of discrimination and emotional conditioning in the development of "motor skills" is not fully apparent, it may be helpful to recall how a well-trained musician is affected by hearing a tyro "murder" a familiar selection; or, to take a more general example, how uncomfortable most persons are made by hearing distorted, labored, defective speech. We are *all* highly trained in *this* skill; and when we hear the grossly (or even slightly) inadequate and improper speech of another, we feel some of the discomfort that would occur if the performance were our own. For a review of the theories and practices of speech correctionists in this connection, see Mowrer (1958).

"habit" generalizes from the stimuli produced by the response which has been selectively rewarded to stimuli produced by more or less similar responses, performance has an initially nonprecise, general, even "sloppy" (but not unadaptive) quality. (Only if such generalization occurs will the subject feel rewarded—have a sense of "accomplishment"—on the first several repetitions or *approximations* of the correct response.) With specific nonreinforcement (or punishment) for similar but not (by some criterion) identical responses, these tend to drop out; and performance becomes more precise, artistic, "discriminating." [8]

Here we see, once again, converging evidence of the power of the new two-factor position and the scope and variety of its implications.

XIII. High-Speed Performance and the Problem of Control

However, one technical difficulty, or at least objection, remains. A good many years ago Lashley (1917; see also Lashley, 1951) advanced what may seem to be a rather specific argument against the feedback conception of habit. He pointed out that in rapid typing or performance on a musical instrument, sequences of finger movement may be executed so quickly that there is literally no time for impulses from one movement to get back to the brain before the next movement is initiated. And from this observation he argued that some types of learned, "habitual" action are really patterned sequences involving many predetermined, pre-assembled (Hebb, 1949) individual responses and that such a conception of habit demands the postulation of some sort of purely "central" mechanism, rather than the mixed central-peripheral mechanism involved in the feedback arrangement.

Osgood (1953), in discussing the notion that responses occurring

---

[8] It is not without interest that Sheppard (1958), although operating on the basis of rather different theoretical presuppositions, believes that "considerable evidence can be adduced for the proposition that the gradients of stimulus and response generalization both conform to [the same] exponential decay function" (p. 243). This is another indication that, at bottom, we are here dealing with one and the same phenomenon. It will also be evident that in response generalization, so-called, we are dealing with what has traditionally been termed "transfer of training" or, simply, "transfer." At a recent professional meeting, Bugelski, Goss, Murdock, Perkins, & Wickens (1958) conducted a symposium on "Mediating processes in transfer," which also, in effect, reduced response generalization to stimulus generalization (see also Mowrer, 1960, Chapter 2).

in rapid succession become "chained" together by means of 'cues produced by preceding movements," puts the matter thus:

> This behavioral analysis of the development of instrumental skills, while undoubtedly true in part, is certainly not a sufficient explanation. It relies heavily upon the sensory "feed-back" from responding muscles, and Lashley (1917) long ago pointed out that there simply isn't enough time between the components of a rapidly executed skill for signals to be relayed back and forth over the motor and sensory nerves connecting brain with periphery. He used for illustration a pianist playing a swift cadenza. It seems probable that in the final stages of skill formation cells in the central motor areas become organized in such a way (cf. Hebb, 1949) that the time and ordering of sequential movements is determined at this locus. One of the necessary conditions for the development of such central motor organization is probably a fairly rapid sequence of movements guided by the sensory feed-back mechanism. We need a great deal more information from the neurophysiologists on these points (p. 401).

Actually, Lashley's criticisms were directed against a notion which is somewhat different from that involved in our present conception of habit. Lashley was attacking the then prevalent view that one overt response can become directly "conditioned" to stimulation provided by the immediately preceding overt response and that long series of responses may become "linked together" in this manner, so that, given the occurrence of the first response in the series, the other responses will be automatically "run off," without any sort of central motivation, direction, or control. For reasons previously considered, we do not accept the view that overt actions are directly conditionable and would join Lashley in rejecting the chain-reflex, or "chaining," theory of serial learning. However, as Osgood indicates, in admitting central factors into the picture, we are not at all obliged to exclude the possibility of influential sensory feedback.

Fortunately, Quastler (1955), who is both a neurologist and an engineer, has made a comprehensive analysis of this problem which resolves it in a manner congruent with the assumptions of two-factor theory. In presenting his analysis he says:

> This report contains a series of studies of human performance in information transmission. We have estimated the rates at which information is transmitted by people reading, typing, playing the piano, doing mental arithmetic, or assimilated by glancing at a display of letters, playing cards, scales and dials. In these situations, we have attempted to establish the principal limiting factors. However, our primary interest is not in such things as measuring the number of "bits" per second which a typist can transmit from a script to her keyboard; in fact, we are not primarily

interested in information transmission per second. Rather, our interest
concerns human performance in the general activity of information proc-
essing; this includes, besides transmitting, activities such as perceiving,
filtering, remembering, correlating, learning, selecting a response, etc. (p. 5).

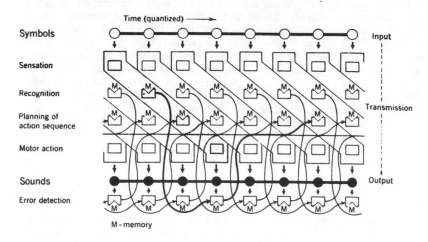

Fig. 12–21. Schematic diagram of component processes of a "simple sequential
task"—music reading—from Quastler (1955, p. 66).

It will not be possible here to go into the details of the Quastler
analysis, but the general tenor of his thinking can be had from the
following excerpt and a diagram taken from the last section of his
report, entitled "Implications of Mechanisms of Information Process-
ing."

[In Fig. 12–21] the sight-reading process, . . . is pictured diagrammatically. The physical events (scripts and sounds) are projected on bands
[which run diagonally, left to right]; the boxes represent mental processes,
or rather, the abstractions here used to describe areas of mental activities;
each box represents a complex system of action. The diagram contains
the *minimum* of components needed to represent the flow of information.
In particular, it applies only to over-learned activities; no allowance is
made for feedback or other checks during any action. It is vastly schematized, assuming the system to be synchronized and leaving out connections between chains which undoubtedly exist. Thus, the diagram is
supposed to represent a simplified version of the activities involved in
sight-reading. We are not proposing to study the organization of these
varied activities; we only conjecture that, seeing that the total task is
learned virtually to perfection, the organization of component activities
ought to be efficient. The whole process involves several diverse acts of

information-processing. What we evaluate is only the over-all result; we have not taken account of the information processes in planning coordinated action nor of that used in the feed-back loop. Accordingly, the statement that a pianist has been shown to transmit about 22 bits/sec does not imply that he processes information at only this rate; it only means that the net result of his activities could be paralleled by an appropriate ideal transducer with a capacity of 22 bit/sec. This observation sheds some light on the main result of this study, the finding that the information measure is relatively invariant over a considerable range of conditions. This phenomenon could be due to some aspect of the elementary processes involved, but it could equally be an expression of the way in which elementary information-handling processes are efficiently organized into a complex system (pp. 66–67).

Clearly, the problem of rapid sequential activity is an intricate one. Lashley's original objections to the chain-reflex interpretation seem well founded, but the same objections do not apply to the revised two-factor conception of habit formation and execution. Many details remain to be worked out as far as this type of interpretation is concerned, as the Quastler analysis indicates; but as far as can be seen at present, there is no known neurological fact or cybernetics principle (see Mowrer, 1960, Chapter 7) which is in opposition to the assumptions demanded by our theoretical position.

No extended analysis of these problems will be undertaken; but it should be pointed out that as *speed* of performance increases, accuracy of *control* tends to decrease. And where responses are being emitted at extremely high rates, "control" in one sense of the term is completely lost in that "mistakes" cannot be corrected before they occur, i.e., cannot be "prevented." In more leisurely performances one has an opportunity to "check" his behavior (both in the sense of inspecting it and, if need be, stopping it) while it is in progress. This advantage is embodied in many aphorisms, such as "Make haste slowly," and "Easy does it." One of the hallmarks of virtuosity and "brilliance" is the very capacity to do things rapidly *and* perfectly. It is not that there *is* no feedback from such behavior but that it arrives too late to be useful as far as the control and *correction* of any given item of behavior is concerned. Hence Lashley and Hebb are probably right in assuming that extremely rapidly sequential performances must presuppose a form of "organization" not required when the pace is more leisurely; [9] yet this fact in no way impugns the notion that

[9] A recently (and still incompletely) reported study by Murdock (see Bugelski *et al.*, 1958) suggests that the speed of sequential actions may depend, after all, upon discrete reaction times. If this should prove to be the case, much of the force of the Lashley-Hebb type of argument would, of course, be lost.

"habits" are, primitively and basically, a matter of the hopes and fears that are conditioned to the sensory (including the imaginal—see Mowrer, 1960, Chapter 5) consequences of their performance.

Sometimes the term "habit" is thought of as applying mainly to well-practiced, semi-automatic, and only partially "conscious" actions, in distinction to behavior that is said to be fully conscious and "voluntary." It must be admitted that some sequences of behavior run off very smoothly, whereas others involve hesitation, choice, and correction. But the difference is apparently one of degree rather than of kind.[10] As indicated in the preceding chapter and elsewhere in this book, the important and basic distinction is rather between *all* such behavior of this kind (involving the skeletal musculature) and the *emotions*, which are truly conditionable and occur outside the sphere of conscious, voluntary control. But, somewhat paradoxically, it is these involuntary reactions and the conscious states they produce which then mediate and motivate the process of choice and volition.

This analysis is carried further in the sequel to this book, *Learning Theory and the Symbolic Processes* (Mowrer, 1960).

[10] Since the above was written, a colleague (who is a bicycling enthusiast) has provided the following report of a remarkable experience: "Recently, as a result of a slight mishap, I found that my bicycle was hard to guide, tending to 'draw' now to the right, now to the left, and so on. Examination by an expert revealed that the front and back wheels were out of alignment (were not 'tracking'); and it was suggested that if I would just keep riding the bike I would probably 'get used to it' and no longer notice the steering difficulty. However, the difficulty continued to be distracting, and I ordered a new fork for the front wheel. But, sure enough, by the time the fork arrived, I was aware of the problem only occasionally; most of the time the bicycle seemed to be quite all right. Then a surprising thing happened: the new fork was installed and for some minutes after I again started riding the bicycle I noticed that my hands—I say, not 'I,' but *my hands*—were alternately turning the handle-bar slightly to the right, slightly to the left, etc. Immediately I realized what had happened: I had learned to *compensate* for the misalignment and therefore became unmindful of it; and, although the misalignment had now been corrected, I was still, automatically and unconsciously, compensating. Of course, this now useless behavior soon disappeared; but, for a time, it provided an unusually clear and striking example of the development of an 'unconscious' skill or habit. As already indicated, I had originally been only too vividly aware of the 'trouble,' but I had no knowledge at all of the solution I had adopted, i.e., what I had learned to *do* about it." It is unclear at present whether this type of observation can or cannot be reconciled with the general point of view expressed in this chapter—and in this book as a whole. Related problems are discussed elsewhere (Mowrer, 1960).

Bibliography and Author Index

The following is a combined bibliography and author index. The numbers appearing in brackets after a bibliographic item indicate the pages on which that item is cited in the text. Nonspecific references to the ideas or work of others are likewise shown in brackets, after all of the specific references have been listed or, if there are no such references, directly after the individual's name.

Aamodt, M. S. (See Stanley & Aamodt, 1954).

Adams, D. K. [278, 324].

Adamson, R. (See Bevan & Adamson, 1959).

Adelman, H. M. (See Maatch, Adelman, & Denny, 1954).

Adelman, H. M. & Maatsch, J. L. (1955) Resistance to extinction as a function of the type of response elicited by frustration. *J. exp. Psychol.*, 50, 61–65 [408].

Aderman, M. (1957) The effect of differential training upon the relative strength of place vs. response habits. Unpublished manuscript [331].

——— (1958) The effect of differential training upon the relative strength of place vs. response habits. *J. comp. physiol. Psychol.*, 51, 372–375 [331].

Adrian, E. D. (1928) *The basis of sensation.* New York: W. W. Norton & Co. [85].

Aiken, E. G. (1957) The effort variable in the acquisition, extinction, and spontaneous recovery of an instrumental response. *J. exp. Psychol.*, 53, 47–51 [402].

——— (See Mowrer & Aiken, 1954).

Akhtar, M. (1959) The effect of intermittent punishment during acquisition of a habit upon subsequent inhibition thereof by means of consistent punishment. (Unpublished research report) [471].

Alcock, W. T. (See Noble & Alcock, 1958).

Allport, F. H. (1924) *Social psychology.* Cambridge, Mass.: The Riverside Press [65].

Allport, G. W. (1937) *Personality: A psychological interpretation.* New York: Henry Holt & Co. [482].

——— (1947) Scientific models and human morals. *Psychol. Rev.,* **54,** 182–192 [12].

Amsel, A. (1950) The combination of a primary appetitional need with primary and secondary emotionally derived needs. *J. exp. Psychol.,* **40,** 1–14 [157].

——— (1951) A three-factor theory of inhibition: an addition to Hull's two-factor theory. Presented at meeting of Southern Society for Philosophy and Psychology (unpublished) [409].

——— (1958a) The role of frustrative nonreward in non-continuous reward situations. *Psychol. Bull.,* **55,** 102–119 [408–409, 468–469, 472].

——— (1958b) The future of Hullian neobehaviorism. (Unpublished paper read at the Washington, 1958, meeting of the American Association for the Advancement of Science.) [403, 409].

Amsel, A. & Maltzman, I. (1950) The effect upon generalized drive strength of emotionality as inferred from the level of consummatory response. *J. exp. Psychol.,* **49,** 563–569 [157].

Amsel, A. & Roussel, J. (1952) Motivational properties of frustration: I. Effect on a running response of the addition of frustration to the motivational complex. *J. exp. Psychol.,* **43,** 363–368 [406–409].

Amsel, R. A. (See Tyler, Weinstock, & Amsel, 1957).

Anderson, E. E. (1941a) The externalization of drive. I. Theoretical considerations. *Psychol. Rev.,* **48,** 204–224 [109, 155–156].

——— (1941b) The externalization of drive. II. The effect of satiation and removal of reward at different stages of the learning process of the rat. *J. genet. Psychol.,* **59,** 359–376 [155].

——— (1941c) The externalization of drive. III. Maze learning by non-rewarded and by satiated rats. *J. genet. Psychol.,* **59,** 397–426 [154–155].

Anderson, N. H. & Grant, D. A. (1957) A test of a statistical learning theory model for two-choice behavior with double stimulus events. *J. exp. Psychol.,* **54,** 305–317 [288].

Andersson, B. & Wyrwicka, W. (1957) The elicitation of a drinking motor conditioned reaction by electrical stimulation of the hypothalamus "drinking area" in the goat. *Acta physiologica Scandiniavca,* **41,** 194–198 [208].

Angell, J. R. (1907) The province of functional psychology. *Psychol. Rev.,* **14,** 61–91 [3–4, 7].

Antonitis, J. J. (See Kish & Antonitis, 1956).

——— (See Schoenfeld, Antonitis & Bersh, 1950).

Applezweig, N. H. (1951) Response potential as a function of effort. *J. comp. physiol. Psychol.,* **44,** 225–235 [400–401].

Arjona, J. H. [24].

Armus, H. L. (1959) Effect of magnitude of reinforcement on acquisition and extinction of a running response. *J. Exp. Psychol.,* **58,** 61–63 [387].

Arnold, M. (1950) An excitatory theory of emotion. In M. L. Reymert (ed.) *Feelings and emotions.* New York: McGraw-Hill Book Co. [407].

Ashby, W. R. (1952) *Design for a brain.* New York: John Wiley & Sons [196].

Atkinson, J. T. (See McClelland, Atkinson, Clark, & Lowell, 1953).

Atkinson, R. C. (See Estes, Burke, Atkinson, & Frankmann, 1957).

Augustine, (399) *Confessions,* quoted from p. 31 of *The age of belief* (1954). Anne Fremantle (ed.). New York: The New American Library [166].

Ax, A. F. (1953) The physiological differentiation between fear and anger in humans. *Psychosomatic Medicine*, 15, 433–442 [407].

Bahrick, H. P., Fitts, P. M., & Schneider, R. (1955) The reproduction of simple movements as a function of proprioceptive feedback. *J. exp. Psychol.*, 49, 437–444 [488].

Bain, A. [258].

Barber, T. X. (1959) Toward a theory of pain: Relief of chronic pain by prefrontol leucotomy, opiates, placebos, and hypnosis. *Psychol. Bull.*, 56, 430–460 [137].

Barker, A. N. (See Hull, Livingston, Rouse, & Barker, 1951).

Barlow, J. A. (1952) Secondary motivation through classical conditioning: One trial nonmotor learning in the white rat. *Amer. Psychol.*, 7, 273 (abstract) [140].

Baron, A. (See Warren & Baron, 1956).

Barrientos, G. (See Wike & Barrientos, 1957).

——— (See Wike & Barrientos, 1958).

Bass, B. (See Brown & Bass, 1958).

Baxter, L. F. (See Muenzinger & Baxter, 1957).

Beck, E. C. & Doty, R. W. (1957) Conditioned flexion reflexes acquired during combined catalepsy and de-efferentation. *J. comp. physiol. Psychol.*, 50, 211–216 [246].

Beck, E. C., Doty, R., & Kooi, K. A. (1958) Electrocortical reactions associated with conditioned flexion reflexes. *EEG Clin. Neurophysiol.*, 10, 279–289 [61].

Beck, R. C. (1957) Secondary reinforcement and shock-motivated discrimination. Unpublished Ph. D. thesis, University of Illinois [140, 144].

Behan, R. A. (See Denny & Behan, 1956).

Beier, E. M. (See Logan, Beier, & Kincaid, 1956).

Bekhterev, V. M. (1913) *La psychologie objective*. Paris: Alcan [6, 42, 44, 68, 90, 93–95].

——— [89].

Belleville, R. E. (See Hill, Belleville, & Wikler, 1954).

Bellows, R. T., & Van Wagenen, W. P. (1938) The relation of polydipsia and polyuria in diabetes insipidus. *J. nerv. & ment. dis.*, 88, 417–473 [71].

Berkun, M. M., Kessen, M. L., & Miller, N. E. (1952) Hunger-reducing effects of food by stomach fistula versus food by mouth measured by a consummatory response. *J. comp. physiol. Psychol.*, 45, 550–554 [195].

Berlyne, D. E. (1950) Novelty and curiosity as determinants of exploratory behavior. *Brit. J. Psychol.*, 41, 68–80 [176].

——— (1960) *Conflict, arousal, and curiosity*. New York: McGraw-Hill [211].

——— (See Gordon & Berlyne, 1954).

Bernstein, B. B. (1957) Extinction as a function of frustration drive and frustration drive stimulus. *J. exp. Psychol.*, 54, 89–95 [408, 425].

Bernstone, A. H. (See Muenzinger, Dove, & Bernstone, 1936).

Bersh, P. J. (1951) The influence of two variables upon the establishment of a secondary reinforcer for operant responses. *J. exp. Psychol.*, 41, 62–73 [145, 369].

——— (See Schoenfeld, Antonitis, & Bersh, 1950).

Bersh, P. J., Notterman, J. M., & Schoenfeld, W. N. (1956) Extinction of a human cardiac-response during avoidance-conditioning. *Amer. j. psychol.*, 69, 244–251 [60].

Bevan, W. & Adamson, R. (1959) Internal referents and the concept of reinforcement. (In press.) [262].

Bevan, W. & Dukes, W. F. (1955) Effectiveness of delayed punishment on learning performance when preceded by premonitory cues. *Psychol. Rep.,* **1,** 441–448 [373].

Bexton, W. H., Heron, W., & Scott, T. H. (1954) Effects of decreased variation in the sensory environment. *Canad. J. Psychol.,* **8,** 70–76 [179–180].

Bicknell. E. A. (See Calvin, Bicknell, & Sperling, 1953).

Bijou, S. W. (1958) Operant extinction after fixed-interval schedules with young children. *J. exp. Analyses of Behavior,* **1,** 25–30 [338].

Bindra, D. (1947) Hoarding behavior in rats: Nutritional, and psychological factors. Unpublished Ph.D. thesis, Harvard University [152].

Birch, H. G. & Bitterman, M. E. (1949) Reinforcement and learning: The process of sensory integration. *Psychol. Rev.,* **56,** 292–308 [219, 279–282].

——— (1951) Sensory integration and cognitive theory. *Psychol. Rev.,* **58,** 355–361 [277, 283].

Bitterman, M. E. (1957) Book review of *Behavior theory and conditioning* by K. W. Spence. *Amer. J. Psychol.,* **70,** 141–145 [46, 264–266].

——— (See Birch & Bitterman, 1949).

——— (See Birch & Bitterman, 1951).

——— (See Crum, Brown, & Bitterman, 1951).

——— (See Elam, Tyler, & Bitterman, 1954).

——— (See Tyler, Wortz, & Bitterman, 1953).

Bitterman, M. E., Fedderson, W. E., & Tyler, D. W. (1953) Secondary reinforcement and the discrimination hypothesis. *Amer. j. psychol.,* **66,** 456–464 [462–464].

Bitterman, M. E., Reed, P. C., & Krauskopf, J. (1952) The effect of the duration of the unconditioned stimulus upon conditioning and extinction. *Amer. J. Psychol.,* **65,** 256–262 [88].

Bixenstine, V. E. (1956) Secondary drive as a neutralizer of time in integrative problem solving. *J. comp. physiol. Psychol.,* **49,** 161–166 [373, 379, 380, 385].

Black, A. H. (1958) The extinction of avoidance responses under curare. *J. comp. physiol. psychol.,* **51,** 519–525 [403].

Black, J. W. (1951) The effect of delayed side-tone upon vocal rate and intensity. *J. Speech & Hearing Disorders,* **16,** 56–60 [247].

Bohn G. (See Frolov, 1937) [433].

Bolden, L. (See Calvin, Clifford, Bolden, & Harvey, 1956).

Bolles, R. C. (1958) The usefulness of the drive concept. In *Nebraska symposium on motivation* (M. R. Jones, Ed.). Lincoln: University of Nebraska Press [262, 272].

Borasio, G. (1952) An experimental investigation of backward, forward, and strictly simultaneous conditioning of fear. Unpublished master's thesis, Kent State University [348].

Boren, J. J. (See Brady, Boren, Conrad, & Sidman, 1957).

——— (See Sidman, Brady, Boren, & Conrad, 1955).

——— (See Sidman & Boren, 1957a).

——— (See Sidman & Boren, 1957b).

Boring, E. G. (1929) *A history of experimental psychology.* New York: The Century Co. [258, 365].

——— (1946) Mind and mechanism. *Amer. J. Psychol.,* **59,** 173–192 [79].

——— (1950) The influence of evolutionary theory upon American psychological thought. Chapter 7 in *Evolutionary thought in America* (Stow Persons, ed.). New Haven: Yale University Press [4].

Boslov, G. L. (See Gerall, Sampson, & Boslov, 1957).

Bousefield, W. A. (1955) Lope de Vega on early conditioning. *Amer. psychol.*, **10**, 828 [24].

Bowlby, J. (1951) Maternal love and mental health. W. H. O. Report [379].

Brady, J. V. (See Sidman, Brady, Boren, & Conrad, 1955).

—— (1958a) Temporal and emotional factors related to electrical self-stimulation of the limbic system. In *Reticular formation of the brain*. Boston: Little, Brown, & Co. [207].

—— (1958b) Ulcers in "executive" monkeys. *Sci. Amer.*, **199**, 95–100 [481].

Brady, J. V., Boren, J. J., Conrad, D., & Sidman, M. (1957) The effect of food and water deprivation upon Intracranial Self-Stimulation. *J. comp. physiol. Psychol.*, **50**, 134–137 [207].

Brady, J. V. & Hunt. H. F. (1955) An experimental approach to the analysis of emotional behavior. *J. Psychol.*, **40**, 313–324 [56–57].

Brady, J. V., Porter, R. W., Conrad, D. G. & Mason, J. W. (1958) Avoidance behavior and the development of gastroduodenal ulcers. *J. exp. Analyses of Behavior*, **1**, 69–72 [481].

Brandauer, C. M. (1953) A confirmation of Webb's data concerning the action of irrelevant drives. *J. exp. Psychol.*, **45**, 150–152 [157].

Braun, H. W., Wedekind, C. E., & Smudski, J. F. (1957) The effect of an irrelevant drive on maze learning in the rat. *J. exp. Psychol.*, **54**, 148–152 [158].

Brody, A. L. (1957) Statistical learning theory applied to an instrumental avoidance situation. *J. exp. Psychol.*, **54**, 240–245 [288].

Brogden, W. J. (1939a) Sensory pre-conditioning. *J. exp. Psychol.*, **25**, 323–332 [281].

—— (1939b) Elaboration of higher-order conditioned responses with food the constant incentive. *Amer. j. physiol.*, **126**, 444–445 [120].

—— (1942) Non-alimentary components in the food-reinforcement of conditioned forelimb-flexion in food-satiated dogs. *J. exp. Psychol.*, **30**, 326–335 [151].

Brogden, W. J., Lipman, E. A., & Culler, E. (1938) The role of incentive in conditioning and extinction. *Amer. J. Psychol.*, **51**, 109–117 [43–55, 57–59, 122].

Bronfenbrenner, U. (1951) Toward an integrated theory of personality. In *Perception, An approach to personality* (Blake and Ramsey, Eds.). New York: The Ronald Press Co. [313–314].

Brown, C. R. (See Dember, 1954) [338–339].

Brown, G. W. (See Cohen, Brown, & Brown, 1957).

Brown, J. S. (1939) A rate on a temporal gradient of reinforcement. *J. exp. Psychol.*, **25**, 221–227 [376].

—— (1942) The generalization of approach responses as a function of stimulus intensity and strength of motivation. *J. comp. Psychol.*, **33**, 209–226 [344].

—— (1953) Problems presented by the concept of acquired drives. In *Current theory and research on motivation: A symposium*. Lincoln: University of Nebraska Press, 1–21 [171, 173, 181, 197].

—— (1955) Pleasure-seeking behavior and the drive-reduction hypothesis. *Psychol. Rev.*, **62**, 169–179 [135, 162, 190, 196, 202, 433, 436].

—— (1957) *Principles of intrapersonal conflict. Conflict Resolution*, **1**, 135–154 [380, 424].

—— [344, 386].

Brown, J. S. & Bass, B. (1958) The acquisition and extinction of an instrumental response under constant and variable stimulus conditions. *J. comp. physiol. Psychol.*, 51, 499–504 [468–469].

Brown, J. S. & Farber, I. E. (1951) Emotions conceptualized as intervening variables—with suggestions toward a theory of frustration. *Psychol. Bull.*, 48, 465–495 [404–406].

Brown, J. S. & Jacobs, A. (1949) The role of fear in the motivation and acquisition of responses. *J. exp. Psychol.*, 39, 747–759 [79, 95–97, 271–272].

Brown, M. L. (See Cohen, Brown, & Brown, 1957).

Brown, P. A. (See Haner & Brown, 1955).

Brown, U. (See Simons, Wickens, Brown, & Pennock, 1951).

Brown, W. L. (See Crum, Brown, & Bitterman, 1951).

Brown, W. O. (See Muenzinger, Brown, Crow, & Powloski, 1952).

Brownstein, A. (See Goodson & Brownstein, 1955).

Brownstein, A. J. (See Lawson & Brownstein, 1957).

Bruce, R. H. (1932) The effect of removal of reward on the maze performance of rats. III. *Univ. Calif. Publ. Psychol.*, 6, 75–82 [141].

Bruch, H. (1943) Psychiatric aspects of obesity in children. *Amer. J. Psychiat.*, 99, 752–757 [162].

Brunswik, E. (1939) Probability as a determiner of rat behavior. *J. exp. Psychol.*, 25, 175–197 [452].

——— (See Tolman & Brunswik, 1935).

Buchanan, G. (See Smith & Buchanan, 1954).

Bugelski, R. (1938) Extinction with and without sub-goal reinforcement. *J. comp. Psychol.*, 26, 121–133 [100, 108, 226, 228–229, 235].

——— (1956) *The psychology of learning.* New York: Henry Holt & Co. [235–236, 331].

Bugelski, B. R., Goss, A. E., Murdock, B. B., Perkins, C. C., & Wickens, D. D. (1958) Symposium: Mediating processes in transfer. *Amer. Psychologist*, 13, 391 [490, 493].

Bull, N. & Strongin, E. (1956) The complex of frustration: A new interpretation. *J. nerv. & ment. dis.*, 123, 531–535 [405, 407, 425].

Burke, C. J. (See Estes, Burke, Atkinson, & Frankmann, 1957).

Burstein, B. (See Delgado & Burstein, 1956).

Butler, B. (See Seward, Pereboom, Butler, & Jones, 1957).

Butler, R. A. (1953) Discrimination learning by rhesus monkeys to visual-exploration motivation. *J. comp. physiol. Psychol.*, 46, 95–98 [175, 177, 339].

Calvin, A. A., Clifford, T., Clifford, B., Bolden, L., & Harvey, J. (1956) An experimental validation of conditioned inhibition. *Psychol. Rep.*, 2, 51–56 [427–428, 430].

Calvin, J. S., Bicknell, E. A., & Sperling, D. S. (1953) Establishment of a conditioned drive based on the hunger drive. *J. comp. physiol. Psychol.*, 46, 173–175 [145–148].

Campbell, B. A. (See Sheffield & Campbell, 1954).

——— (See Sheffield, Roby, & Campbell, 1954).

Campbell, B. A. & Sheffield, F. D. (1953) Relation of random activity to food deprivation. *J. comp. physiol. Psychol.*, 46, 320–322 [197–198, 273].

Campbell, D. T. (1954) Operational delineation of "what is learned" via the transposition experiment. *Psychol. Rev.*, 61, 167–174 [331].

—— (1956) Perception as substitute trial and error. *Psychol. Rev.*, **63**, 330–342 [17].

Capaldi, E. J. (1957) The effect of different amounts of alternating partial reinforcement on resistance to extinction. *Amer. J. Psychol.*, **70**, 451–452 [459].

—— (1958) The effect of different amounts of training on the resistance to extinction of different patterns of partially reinforced responses. *J. comp. physiol. Psychol.*, **51**, 367–371 [468, 473, 475–476].

Capehart, J., Viney, W., & Hulicka, I. M. (1958) The effect of effort upon extinction. *J. comp. physiol. Psychol.*, **51**, 505–507 [402].

Carlton, P. L. & Marks, R. A. (1957) Heat as a reinforcement for operant behavior. Report No. 299, Psychology Department, US Army Medical Research Laboratory, Fort Knox, Kentucky [144, 456].

Carmichael, L. (1946) The onset and early development of behavior. In *Manual of child psychology* (L. Carmichael, ed.). New York: John Wiley & Sons [221].

Carterette, T. S. (See Lauer & Carterette, 1957).

Casey, A. (See Wike & Casey, 1954).

Carr, H. A. (1938) The law of effect: A round table discussion: I, *Psychol. Rev.*, **45**, 191–199 [257].

Cattell, J. McK. (1904) The conceptions and methods of psychology. *Pop. Sci. Monthly*, **66**, 176–186 [5].

Cattell, R. B. (1950) *Personality: A systematic, theoretical, and factual study.* New York: McGraw-Hill Book Co. [79].

Chambers, R. M. (See Coppock & Chambers, 1951).

—— (See Coppock & Chambers, 1954).

Chapman, W. P., Rose, A. S., & Solomon, H. C. (1948) *The frontal lobes*, p. 754. A.R.N.M.D. XXVII, Baltimore [136].

Chase, R. A. (1959) A comparison of the effects of delayed auditory feedback on speech and key tapping. *Science* (in press) [248].

—— (See Sutton, Chase, & First, 1959).

Childe, V. G. (1951) *Social evolution.* New York: H. Schuman [9].

—— (1955) *Man makes himself.* (Rev.) New York: New American Library [10].

Clark, R. A. (See McClelland, Atkinson, Clark, & Lowell, 1953).

Clayton, F. L. (1952) Secondary reinforcement as a function of reinforcement scheduling. *Psychol. Rep.*, **2**, 377–380 [114].

Clifford, B. (See Calvin, Clifford, Clifford, Bolden, & Harvey, 1956).

Clifford, T. (See Calvin, Clifford, Clifford, Bolden, & Harvey, 1956).

Cohen, B. D., Brown, G. W., & Brown, M. L. (1957) Avoidance learning motivated by hypothalamic stimulation. *J. exp. Psychol.*, **53**, 228–233 [209].

Cohn, S. H. & Cohn, S. M. (1953) The role of cybernetics in psychology. *Scientific Monthly*, **76**, 85–89 [245].

Cohn, S. M. (See Cohn & Cohn, 1953).

Cole, Marie-Louise W. (See Hunt, Cole, & Reis, 1958).

Collier, G. (See Holder, Marz, Holder, & Collier, 1959).

Conant, J. B. (1947) *On Understanding Science.* New Haven: Yale University Press [211].

Conger, J. J. (1951) The effects of alcohol on conflict behavior in the albino rat. *Quart. J. Stud. Alcohol.*, **12**, 1–29 [97].

Conrad, D. G. (See Brady, Boren, Conrad, & Sidman, 1957).

—— (See Brady, Porter, Conrad, & Mason, 1958).

────── (See Sidman, Brady, Boren, & Conrad, 1955).

Coppock, H. W. (1950) An investigation of secondary reinforcing effect of a visual stimulus as a function of its temporal relation to shock termination. Ph.D. thesis, University of Indiana [140].

────── (1955) Responses of subjects to their own galvanic skin responses. *J. abnorm. soc. Psychol.*, **50**, 25–28 [421].

Coppock, H. W. & Chambers, R. M. (1951) Prior, immediate, and delayed reward in conditioning the galvanic skin response. Paper read at the Midwestern Psychological Association, Chicago [88].

────── (1954) Reinforcement of position preference by automatic intravenous injections of glucose. *J. comp. physiol. Psychol.*, **47**, 355–357 [195].

Cowgill, D. O. (1948) Variant meanings of the terms conditioning and conditioned response. *J. soc. Psychol.*, **28**, 247–255 [65].

Cowles, J. T. (1937) Food-tokens as incentives for learning by chimpanzees. *Comp. Psychol. Monogr.*, **14**, 1–96 [100, 108].

Craig, W. (1918) Appetites and aversions as constituents of instincts. *Biol. Bull.*, **34**, 91–107 [314–316].

Crespi, L. P. (1942) Quantitative variation of incentive and performance in the white rat. *Amer. J. Psychol.*, **55**, 467–517 [262].

────── (1944) Amount of reinforcement and level of performance. *Psychol. Rev.*, **51**, 341–357 [262–263].

Crisler, G. (1930) Salivation is unnecessary for the establishment of the salivary conditional reflex induced by morphine. *Amer. J. Physiol.*, **94**, 553–556 [246].

Crockett, F. (See McGuigan & Crockett, 1958).

Crosskey, M. A. (See Elithorn, Piercy, & Crosskey, 1955).

Crow, W. J. (See Muenzinger, Brown, Crow, & Powloski, 1952).

Crowder, W. F. (1958) Secondary reinforcement and shock termination. Ph.D. thesis, University of Illinois [144, 456].

Crum, J., Brown, W. L., & Bitterman, M. E. (1951) The effect of partial and delayed reinforcement on resistance to extinction. *Amer. J. Psychol.*, **64**, 228–237 [234, 469].

Culler, E. (See Brogden, Lipman, & Culler, 1938).

────── (See Eccher & Culler, 1941).

────── (See Finch & Culler, 1934).

Cutts, J. (See Hurwitz & Cutts, 1957).

Danziger, K. (1951) The operation of an acquired drive in satiated rats. *Quart. J. exp. Psychol.*, **3**, 119–132 [155–156].

Darwin, C. (1859) *Origin of the species* [2–3, 6, 17].

Dashiell, J. F. (1937) *Fundamentals of psychology.* Boston: Houghton Mifflin Co. [404].

Davis, J. (1958) The reinforcing effect of weak light onset as a function of food deprivation. *J. comp. physiol. Psychol.*, **51**, 496–498 [183].

Davis, J. D. (See Grice & Davis, 1957).

Davis, R. C. (1958) The domain of homeostasis. *Psychol. Rev.*, **65**, 8–13 [210].

Davitz, J. R. (1955) Reinforcement of fear at the beginning and end of shock. *J. comp. physiol. Psychol.*, **48**, 152–155 [85–87].

Davitz, J. R., Mason, D. J., Mowrer, O. H., & Viek, P. (1957) Conditioning of fear: A function of the delay of reinforcement. *Amer. J. Psychol.*, **70**, 69–74 [371–372, 376].

Deese, J. (1952) *The psychology of learning.* New York: McGraw-Hill Book Co. [348, 388, 423–424, 430, 457].

Delafresnaye, J. F. (1954) *Brain mechanisms and consciousness.* (ed.) Springfield, Ill.: C. C. Thomas [186].

Delgado, J. M. R. & Burstein, B. (1956) Attraction and avoidance evoked by septal and rhinencephalic stimulation in the monkey. *Fed. Proc.,* 15, 143 [209].

Dember, W. N. (1954) Seminar report. Department of Psychology, University of Michigan [338, 341].

—— (See Walker, Dember, Earl, & Karoly, 1955).

Dember, W. N., Earl, R. W., & Paradise, N. (1956) Between and within-stimulus alternation; the response to differential stimulus complexity. Unpublished paper, University of Michigan [339].

Dempsey, E. W. (1951) Homeostasis. In *Handbook of experimental psychology* S. S. Stevens ed.). New York: John Wiley & Sons [210].

Denny, M. R. (1946) The role of secondary reinforcement in a partial reinforcement learning situation. *J. exp. Psychol.,* 36, 373–389 [459, 467].

—— (1948) The effect of using differential end boxes in a simple T-maze learning situation. *J. exp. Psychol.,* 38, 245–249 [102, 459–460, 462, 467].

—— (See Maatch, Adelman, & Denny, 1954).

Denny, M. R., & Behan, R. A. (1956) Conditioned hunger drive or conditioned approach? *Psychol. Rep.,* 2, 194 [156].

Deutsch, M. (1954) Field theory in social psychology. In *Handbook of social psychology* (Gardner Lindzey, ed.). Reading, Mass.: Addison-Wesley Pub. Co. [308, 311–312].

Dewey, J. (1896) The reflex arc concept in psychology. *Psychol. Rev.,* 3, 357–370 [4, 9, 259].

—— [173].

Diggs, B. J. (1957) Ethics and experimental theories of motivation and learning. *Ethics,* 67, 100–118 [8–9].

Dinsmoor, J. A. (1950) A quantitative comparison of the discriminative and reinforcing functions of a stimulus. *J. exp. Psychol.,* 41, 458–472 [454].

—— (1954) Punishment: I. The avoidance hypothesis. *Psychol. Rev.,* 61, 34–46 [33, 46, 48–50, 52].

—— (1956) Absurdum revisited; A comment. *Psychol. Rep.,* 2, 255–256 [430].

Dmitriev, A. S., & Kochigina, A. M. (1959) The importance of time as stimulus of conditioned reflex activity. *Psychol. Bull.,* 56, 106–132 [377].

Doane, B. K. (See Heron, Doane, & Scott, 1956).

Dodson, J. D. (See Yerkes & Dodson, 1908).

Dollard, J. (See Miller & Dollard, 1941).

Dollard, J., Doob, L. W., Miller, N. E., Mowrer, O. H., & Sears, E. E. (1939) *Frustration and aggression.* New Haven: Yale University Press [404].

Dollard, J., & Miller, N. E. (1950) *Personality and psychotherapy.* New York: McGraw-Hill Book Co. [137, 487].

Doob, L. W. (See Dollard, Doob, Miller, Mowrer, & Sears, 1939).

Doss, R. (See Reese, Doss, & Gantt, 1953).

Doty, R. W. (See Beck & Doty, 1957).

—— (See Beck, Doty, & Kooi, 1958).

—— (See Nielson, Doty, & Rutledge, 1958).

—— (See Rutledge & Doty, 1957).

Dove, C. C. (See Muenzinger, Dove, & Bernstone, 1936).

Duffy, M. (See Smith & Duffy, 1957).

Dukes, W. F. (See Bevan & Dukes, 1955).

Duncan, C. P. (See Lewis & Duncan, 1956).

——— (See Lewis & Duncan, 1957).

Dunlap, K. (1928) A revision of the fundamental law of habit. *Science,* **67**, 360 [410].

Duryea, R. A. (1955) Stimulus-response asynchronysm and delay of reinforcement in selective learning, *Amer. J. Psychol.,* **68**, 343–357 [379].

Dyal, J. A. (1957) The role of the anticipatory goal response in delay-of-reward and irrelevant-incentive learning. Ph.D. Thesis, University of Illinois [270, 379].

Dykman, R. A. & Gantt, W. H. (1954) Blood pressure conditioned to pain. *Federation Proceed.,* **13**, 127– [60].

Dykman, R. A., Gantt, W. H., & Whitehorn, J. C. (1956) Conditioning as emotional sensitization and differention. *Psychol. Monogr.,* **70**, No. 422 [60, 77].

Earl, R. W. (See Dember, Earl, & Paradise, 1956).

——— (See Walker, Dember, Earl, & Karoly, 1955).

Eccher, W., & Culler, E. (1941) Reciprocal facilitation of the conditioned and conditioning mechanisms. *J. comp. Psychol.,* **31**, 223–231 [119–122].

Eglash, A. (1951) Perception, association, and reasoning in animal fixations. *Psychol. Rev.,* **58**, 424–434 [413].

——— (1954) Fixation and inhibition. *J. abnorm. soc. Psychol.,* **49**, 241–245 [414].

Ehrenfreund, D. (1954) Generalization of secondary reinforcement in discrimination learning *J. comp. physiol. Psychol.,* **47**, 311–314 [460].

Elam, C. B., Tyler, D. W., & Bitterman, M. E. (1954) A further study of secondary reinforcement and the discrimination hypothesis. *J. comp. physiol. Psychol.,* **47**, 381–384 [467].

Elithorn, A., Piercy, M. F. & Crosskey, M. A. (1955) Prefrontal leucotomy and the anticipation of pain. *J. Neurol. Neurosurg. Psychiat.,* **18**, 34–43 [136].

Ellen, P. (1956) The compulsive nature of abnormal fixations. *J. comp. physiol. Psychol.,* **49**, 309–317 [414].

Ellis, N. R. (1957) The immediate effects of emotionality upon behavior strength. *J. exp. Psychol.,* **54**, 339–344 [158].

English, H. B. (1954) *The historical roots of learning theory.* Garden City, N. Y.: Doubleday & Co. [1].

Eriksen, C. W., & Zimmerman, D. W. Unpublished research [177, 456].

Eroféeva, M. N. (1913) [Contribution to the physiology of conditioned reflexes to injurious stimuli.] *Proc. Russian Med. Soc. in Petrograd.,* **80**, (see Pavlov, 1927) [432–433].

Estes, W. K. (1944) An experimental study of punishment. *Psychol. Monogr.,* **57**, 40 pp. [424, 471].

——— (1949) Generalization of secondary reinforcement from the primary drive. *J. comp. physiol. Psychol.,* **42**, 286–295 [156–157].

——— (1950) Toward a statistical theory of learning. *Psychol. Rev.,* **57**, 94–107 [283, 287, 288, 290].

——— (1954) Kurt Lewin. Section 4 in *Modern learning theory* by Estes. Koch, MacCorquodale, Meehl, Mueller, Schoenfeld, & Verplanck. New York: Appleton-Century-Crofts [310]

——— [283, 290].

Estes, W. K., Burke, C. J., Atkinson, R. C., & Frankmann, J. P. (1957) Probabilistic discrimination learning. *J. exp. Psychol.*, **54**, 233–239 [288].

Estes, W. K. & Skinner, B. F. (1941) Some quantitative properties of anxiety. *J. exp. Psychol.*, **29**, 390–400 [56].

Fairbanks, G. (1954) Systematic research in experimental phonetics: 1. A theory of the speech mechanism as a servosystem. *J. of Speech & Hearing Disorders*, **19**, 133–139 [247–248].

—— (1955) Selective vocal effects of delayed auditory feedback. *J. of Speech & Hearing Disorders*, **20**, 333–346 [247].

—— Personal communication [248].

Fairbanks, G. & Jaeger, R. (1951) A device for continuously variable time delay of headset monitoring during magnetic recording of speech. *J. Speech & Hearing Disorders*, **16**, 162–164 [247].

Farber, I. E. (1948) Response fixation under anxiety and non-anxiety conditions. *J. exp. Psychol.*, **38**, 111–131 [60, 95].

—— (1954) Anxiety as a drive state. *Nebraska symposium on motivation* (M. R. Jones, ed.). Lincoln: University of Nebraska Press [137, 173].

—— (See Brown & Farber, 1951).

—— (See Spence & Farber, 1953).

Farber, I. E. & Spence, K. W. (1953) Complex learning and conditioning as a function of anxiety. *J. exp. Psychol.*, **45**, 120–425 [157].

Fedderson, W. E. (See Bitterman, Fedderson, & Tyler, 1953).

Fehrer, E. (1956) Effects of amount of reinforcement and of pre- and post-reinforcement delays on learning and extinction. *J. exp. Psychol.*, **52**, 167–176 [387, 459].

Feokritova, J. P. (1912) [Time as a conditioned stimulus to salivary secretion.] Thesis, Petrograd (see Pavlov, 1927) [368].

Ferster, C. B. (1953) Sustained behavior under delayed reinforcement. *J. exp. Psychol.*, **45**, 218–224 [379, 382].

—— (1957) Withdrawal of positive reinforcement as punishment. *Science*, **126**, 509 [165].

—— (1958) Control of behavior in chimpanzees and pigeons by time out from positive reinforcement. *Psychol. Monogr.*, **461**, 38 [165].

Ferster, C. B. & Skinner, B. F. (1958) *Schedules of reinforcement*. New York: Appleton-Century-Crofts [290]

Finch, G. (1942) Chimpanzee frustration responses. *Psychosomatic Medicine*, **4**, 233–251 [405].

Finch, G., & Culler, E. (1934) Higher order conditioning with constant motivation. *Amer. J. Psychol.*, **46**, 596–602 [119–120].

First, D. (See Sutton, Chase, & First, 1959).

Fitts, P. M. (See Bahrick, Fitts, & Schneider, 1955).

Fitzwater, M. E. & Reisman, M. N. (1952) Comparisons of forward, simultaneous, backward and pseudo-conditioning. *J. exp. Psychol.*, **44**, 211–214 [348].

Fitzwater, M. E. & Thrush, R. S. (1956) Acquisition of a conditioned response as a function of forward temporal contiguity. *J. exp. Psychol.*, **51**, 59–61 [386].

Flakus, W. J. (1958) The acquisition and extinction of two different avoidance responses to two different stimuli. Unpublished research proposal [453].

Fletcher, F. M. (See Muenzinger & Fletcher, 1936).

Fonberg, E. (1958) The manifestation of the defensive reactions in neurotic states. *Acta biologiae experimentalis*, **18**, 89–116 [60].

Foursikov, D. S. (1922) [Effect of external inhibition upon the development of differentiation and of a conditioned inhibitor.] *Russian J. Physiol.*, **4** (see Pavlov, 1927) [119].

Frankman, J. P. (See Estes, Burke, Atkinson, & Frankmann, 1957).

Freeman, G. L. (1940) The relationship between performance and bodily activity level. *J. exp. Psychol.*, **26**, 602–608 [163].

Freud, S. (1916) *Three contributions to the theory of sex.* New York: Nervous & Mental Disease Pub. Co. [394].

———— (1935) *A general introduction to psychoanalysis.* New York: Liveright Publishing Co. [314].

———— (1936) *The problem of anxiety.* New York: W. W. Norton & Co. [95, 260, 291, 301, 314].

———— [260, 291, 301, 314].

Frovlov, Y. P. (1937) *Pavlov and his school.* London: Kegan Paul, Trench, Tribner & Co. Ltd. [98, 119, 432–433].

Galanter, E. H. (1955) Place and response learning: Learning to alternate. *J. comp. physiol. Psychol.*, **48**, 17–18 [331].

Galton, B. B. (See Montgomery & Galton, 1956).

Gans, S. (See Waddell, Gans, Kampner, & Williams, 1955).

Gantt, W. H. (1942) The origin and development of nervous disturbances experimentally produced. *Amer. J. Psychiat.*, **98**, 475–481 [60].

———— (See Dykman, Gantt, & Whitehorn, 1956).

———— (See Light & Gantt, 1936).

———— (See Reese, Doss, & Gantt, 1953).

———— (1949) Psychosexuality in animals. In *Psychosexual development in health and disease* (P. H. Hoch & J. Zubin, eds.). New York: Grune & Stratton [77, 202].

Gates, A. J. (1928) *Elementary psychology.* New York: The Macmillan Co. [410].

Geldard, F. (1953) *The human sense.* New York: Wiley & Sons [299].

Gentry, E. (1934) Cues of signals. *J. comp. Psychol.*, **18**, 227–258 [450].

Gerall, A. A., Sampson, P. B., & Boslov, G. L. (1957) Classical conditioning of human pupillary dilation. *J. exp. Psychol.*, **54**, 467–474 [418].

Gibbs, C. G. (1954) The continuous regulation of skilled response by kinaesthetic feedback. *Brit. J. Psychol.*, **45**, 24–39 [489]

Gibson, J. J., & Mowrer, O. H. (1938) Determinants of the perceived vertical and horizontal. *Psychol. Rev.*, **45**, 300–321 [334].

Ginsburg, N. Personal communication [216].

Girdner, J. B. (1953) Ph.D. Thesis, Duke University Library [184].

Glanzer, M. (1953) Stimulation satiation: An explanation of spontaneous alternation and related phenomena. *Psychol. Rev.*, **60**, 257–268 [338].

Gleitman, H. (1955) Place learning without prior performance. *J. comp. physiol. Psychol.*, **48**, 77–79 [140].

Gleitman, H., Nachmias, J., & Neisser, U. (1954) The S—R reinforcement theory of extinction. *Psychol. Rev.*, **61**, 23–33 [427–428, 430].

Godell, H. (See Wolff & Godell, 1943).

Goldman, H. M. (See Grice & Goldman, 1955).

Goodson, F. & Brownstein, A. (1955) Secondary reinforcing and motivating properties of stimuli contiguous with shock onset and termination. *J. comp. physiol. Psychol.*, **48**, 381–386 [140].

Gordon, W. M. & Berlyne, D. E. (1954) Drive-level and flexibility in paired-associate nonsense-syllable learning. *Quart. J. exp. Psychol.*, **6**, 181–185 [172].

Goss, A. E. (See Bugelski, Goss, Murdock, Perkins, & Wickens, 1958).

Grant, D. A. (See Anderson & Grant, 1957).

Grant, D. A. & Hake, H. W. (1951) Dark adaptation and the Humphreys random reinforcement phenomenon in human eyelid conditioning. *J. exp. Psychol.*, **42**, 417–423 [457].

Grant, D. A., Hake, H. W., & Hornseth, J. P. (1951) Acquisition and extinction of a verbal conditioned response with differing percentages of reinforcement. *J. exp. Psychol.*, **42**, 1–5 [457].

Grant, D. A., Schipper, L. M., & Ross, B. M. (1952) Effects of inter-trial interval during acquisition on extinction of the conditioned eyelid response following partial reinforcement. *J. exp. Psychol.*, **44**, 203–210 [457].

Greenberg, I. (See Seeman & Greenberg, 1952).

Greene, J. A. (1939) Clinical study of the etiology of obesity. *Annals of Int. Med.*, **12** [162].

Grice, G. R. (1948a) An experimental test of the expectancy theory of learning. *J. comp. physiol. Psychol.*, **41**, 137–143 [331, 386].

—— (1948b) The relation of secondary reinforcement to delayed reward in visual discrimination learning. *J. exp. Psychol.*, **38**, 1–16 [280, 358–360].

Grice, G. R. & Davis, J. D. (1957) Effect of irrelevant thirst motivation on a response learned with food reward. *J. exp. Psychol.*, **53**, 347–352 [157–158].

Grice, G. R. & Goldman, H. M. (1955) Generalized extinction and secondary reinforcement in visual discrimination learning with delayed reward. *J. exp. Psychol.*, **50**, 197–200 [379].

Grindley, G. C. (1929) Experiments on the influence of the amount of reward on learning in young chickens. *Brit. J. Psychol.*, **20**, 173–180 [100].

Gulde, C. J. (1941) The effects of delayed reward on the learning of a white-black discrimination by the albino rat. Unpublished Master's thesis. University of Iowa [357–358, 360].

Guthrie, E. R. (1935) *The psychology of learning.* New York: Harper & Brothers [193, 278].

—— (1942) Conditioning: A theory of learning in terms of stimulus, response, and association. In *41st Yearbook, National Society for the Study of Education.* Part II [283].

—— (1946a) Recency or effect—a reply to Captain O'Connor. *Harv. Educ. Rev.*, **16**, 286–289 [284, 286].

—— (1946b) Psychological facts and psychological theory. *Psychol. Bull.*, **43**, 1–20 [287].

—— (1952) *The psychology of learning.* (Rev. ed.) New York: Harper & Brothers [285, 322–323].

—— Personal communication [383–386].

—— [54, 250, 268, 290, 332].

Guthrie, E. R. & Horton, G. P. (1946) *Cats in a puzzle box.* New York: Rinehart & Co., [336].

Guttman, N. & Kalish, H. I. (1956) Discriminability and stimulus generalization. *J. exp. Psychol.*, **51**, 79–88 [440, 442–443, 445].

———— (1958) Experiments in discrimination. *Sci. Amer.*, **198**, 77–82 [443–444].

Gwinn, G. T. (1949) The effects of punishment on acts motivated by fear. *J. exp. Psychol.*, **39**, 260–269 [419–421, 486].

Haas, E. L. (See Warden & Haas, 1927).

Hake, H. W. (See Grant & Hake, 1951).

———— (See Grant, Hake, & Hornseth, 1951).

Hall, J. F. (1951) Studies in secondary reinforcement: I. Secondary reinforcement as a function of the frequency of primary reinforcement. *J. comp. physiol. Psychol.*, **44**, 246–251 [145].

Hamilton, E. L. (1929) The effect of delayed incentive on the hunger drive in the white rat. *Genet. Psychol. Monogr.*, **5**, 131–208 [352–353].

Haner, C. F. & Brown, P. A. (1955) Clarification of the instigation to action concept in the frustration-aggression hypothesis. *J. abnorm. soc. Psychol.*, **51**, 204–206 [408].

Harker, G. S. (1950) An experimental investigation of the effect of changes in the delay of an instrumental response. Unpublished Ph.D. Thesis, University of Iowa [262].

Harlow, H. F. (1949) The formation of learning sets. *Psychol. Rev.*, **56**, 51–65.

———— (1950) Learning and satiation of response in intrinsically motivated complex puzzle performance by monkeys. *J. comp. physiol. Psychol.*, **43**, 289–294 [11, 175, 383, 452].

———— (1954) Motivational forces underlying learning. *Learning theory, personality theory and clinical research—The Kentucky Symposium.* New York: John Wiley & Sons [170–172, 174, 177–182, 185].

Hart, G. (See Miller & Hart, 1948).

Hartley, D. [259, 265].

Harvey, J. (See Calvin, Clifford, Clifford, Bolden, & Harvey, 1956).

Hearnshaw, L. S. (1956) Temporal integration and behaviour. *Bull. Brit. Psychol. Soc.*, No. 30, 1–20 [166, 378, 380].

Heath, R. G. (1955). Correlation between levels of psychological awareness and physiological activity in the central nervous system. *Psychosomatic med.*, **17**, 383–395 [210].

Hebb, D. O. (1946) On the nature of fear. *Psychol. Rev.*, **53**, 259–276 [175].

———— (1949) *The organization of behavior.* New York: John Wiley & Sons [271, 490–491, 493].

———— (1958) The motivating effects of exteroceptive stimulation. *Amer. psychol.*, **13**, 109–113 [237].

Hebb, D. O. & Thompson, W. R. (1954) The social significance of animal studies. In *Handbook of social psychology* (Gardner Linzey, ed.). Reading, Mass.: Addison-Wesley Pub. Co. [176, 185, 452].

Heider, F. (1953) Psychology of interpersonal relations. (Tentative title.) Unpublished manuscript [312].

Henderson, P. K. (1953) Ph.D. Thesis, Missouri University Library [184].

Henderson, R. L. (See Harx, Henderson, & Roberts, 1955).

Hendrix, Gertrude. Personal communication [176].

Henle, M. (1956) On activity in the goal region. *Psychol. Rev.*, **63**, 299–302 [129].

Heron, W. (1957) The pathology of boredom. *Sci. Amer.*, **196**, 52–56 [237].

———— (See Bexton, Heron, & Scott, 1954).

—— (See Thompson & Heron, 1954).

Heron, W., Doane, B. K., & Scott, T. H. (1956) Visual disturbances after prolonged perceptual isolation. *Canad. J. Psychol.*, **10**, 13–18 [179, 237].

Herrnstein, R. J. (See Morse & Herrnstein, 1956).

Hertzler, E. C. (See Perkins & Hertzler, 1958).

Hilgard, E. R. (1956) *Theories of learning.* New York: Appleton-Century-Crofts [103–104, 264–266, 283–285, 287, 291, 314, 330, 384, 442, 471].

Hilgard, E. R. & Marquis, P. G. (1940) *Conditioning and learning.* New York: Appleton-Century [43–44, 49, 55, 346, 348, 386, 457, 482].

Hill, H. E., Belleville, R. E., & Wikler, A. (1954) Anxiety reduction as a measure of the analgesic effectiveness of drugs. *Science*, **120**, 153 [137].

Holder, E. (See Holder, Marz, Holder, & Collier, 1959).

Holder, W., Marz, H. H., Holder, E., & Collier, G. (1959) Response strength as a function of delay of reward. *J. exp. Psychol.*, (in press) [408].

Hollingworth, H. L. (1928a) *Psychology, its facts and principles.* New York: A. Appleton [285]

—— (1928b) The general laws of redintegration. *J. gen. Psychol.*, **1**, 79–90 [285].

Holt, E. B. (1931) *Animal drive and the learning process.* Vol. I. New York: Henry Holt & Co. [179, 315, 320].

Honig, W. K. (1961) Generalization of extinction on the spectral continuum *Psychol. Record*, **11**, 267–278 [445, 447].

Hornseth, J. P. (See Grant, Hake, & Hornseth, 1951).

Horton, G. P. (See Guthrie & Horton, 1946).

Horton, S. W. (See Mowrer, 1950a) [52].

Hulicka, I. M. (See Capehart, Viney, & Hulicka, 1958).

Hull, C. L. (1929) A functional interpretation of the conditioned reflex. *Psychol. Rev.*, **36**, 498–511 [55, 348].

—— (1930) Simple trial and error learning: A study in psychological theory. *Psychol. Rev.*, **37**, 241–256 [105, 384].

—— (1931) Goal attraction and directing ideas conceived as habit phenomena. *Psychol. Rev.*, **38**, 487–506 [105, 270].

—— (1932) The goal gradient hypothesis and maze learning. *Psychol. Rev.*, **39**, 25–43 [226, 348].

—— (1934) The concept of the habit-family hierarchy and maze learning. *Psychol. Rev.*, **41**, 33–152 [226].

—— (1935) Special review: Thorndike's fundamentals of learning. *Psychol. Bull.*, **32**, 807–823 [66].

—— (1937) Mind, mechanism, and adaptive behavior. *Psychol. Rev.*, **44**, 1–32 [226].

—— (1938) The goal gradient hypothesis applied to some "field-force" problems in the behavior of young children. *Psychol. Rev.*, **45**, 271–299 [344].

—— (1943) *Principles of behavior.* New York: Appelton-Century-Crofts [66, 68–71, 93, 99–102, 104–105, 112, 125, 127, 138, 142–143, 145, 157–158, 181, 183–184, 193, 218 219, 262, 278, 305, 337–338, 342–344, 346, 357, 365–367, 400–401, 404, 427–428, 455, 457–458, 462].

—— (1951) *Essentials of behavior.* New Haven: Yale University Press [100, 104, 112].

—— (1952) *A behavior system.* New Haven: Yale University Press [103, 138, 323, 344, 360, 363–364].

——— [7, 22, 75, 89–90, 95, 101, 123, 260–261, 263, 268, 288–289, 301, 306–307, 313, 323, 329, 397, 409, 412, 416].

Hull, C. L., Livingston, J. R., Rouse, R. O., & Barker, A. N. (1951) True, sham, and esophageal feeding as reinforcements. *J. comp. physiol. Psychol.*, **44**, 236–245 [71, 194, 401].

Hulse, S. H., Jr. & Stanley, W. C. (1956) Extinction by omission of food as related to partial and secondary reinforcement. *J. exp. Psychol.*, **52**, 221–227 [469].

Hume, D. [61].

Humphreys, L. G. (1939a) The effect of random alternation of reinforcement on the acquisition and extinction of conditioned eyelid reactions. *J. exp. Psychol.*, **25**, 141–158 [457, 473].

——— (1939b) Acquisition and extinction of verbal expectations in a situation analogous to conditioning. *J. exp. Psychol.*, **25**, 294–301 [469, 471].

Hunt, H. F. (See Brady & Hunt, 1955).

Hunt, J. McV. (1941) The effects of infant feeding-frustration upon adult hoarding behavior in the albino rat. *J. abnorm. soc. Psychol.*, **36**, 338–359 [485]

——— (1959) Experience and motivation: Some reinterpretations. (Unpublished manuscript) [303–304].

Hunt, J. McV., Cole, Marie-Louise W., and Reis, Eva E. S. (1958) Situational cues distinguishing anger, fear, and sorrow. *Amer. J. Psychol.*, **71**, 136–151 [166–168].

Hunt, J. McV., Schlosberg, N., Solomon, R. L., & Stellar, E. (1947) Studies of the effects of infantile experience on adult behavior in rats. I. Effects of infantile feeding frustration on adult hoarding. *J. comp. physiol. Psychol.*, **40**, 291–304 [485].

Hunt, W. A. (1941) Recent developments in the field of emotion. *Psychol. Bull.*, **38**, 249–276 [166].

Hunter, W. S. (1935) Conditioning and extinction in the rat. *Brit. J. Psychol.*, **26** (II), 135–148 [42].

Hurwitz, H. M. B. (1955) Response elimination without performance. *Quart. J. exp. Psychol.*, **7**, 1–7 [403].

Hurwitz, H. M. B. (1956a) Vicious circle behaviour under two shock intensities. Mimeographed paper. Birkbeck College, London [486].

——— (1956b) Conditioned responses in rats reinforced by light. *Brit. J. anim. Behav.*, **4**, 31–33 [184].

Hurwitz, H. B. & Cutts, J. (1957) Discrimination and operant extinction. *Brit. J. Psychol.*, **48**, 90–92 [234].

Huxley, A. (1958) Tyranny over the mind. *Newsdays*, May 31. Garden City, N. Y. [277].

Jacobs, A. (See Brown & Jacobs, 1949).

Jaeger, R. (See Fairbanks & Jaeger, 1951).

James, W. (1890) *Principles of psychology.* (Two volumes.) New York: Henry Holt & Co. [5, 48, 133, 258–259, 408, 488].

Jenkins, W. O. (1950) A temporal gradient of derived reinforcement. *Amer. J. Psychol.*, **63**, 237–243 [223, 368–370, 372, 373, 376, 467].

Jenkins, W. O. & Stanley, J. C. (1950) Partial reinforcement: A review and critique. *Psychol. Bull.*, **47**, 193–234 [457].

Jennings, H. S. (1906) *Behavior of the lower organisms.* New York: Columbia University Press [16, 316].

Johnson, O. (See Morgan, Stellar, & Johnson, 1943).

Jones, E. (1953) *The life and work of Sigmund Freud, Vol. I.* New York: Basic Books [260, 457].

Jones, H. M. (See Mowrer & Jones, 1943).

—— (See Mowrer & Jones, 1945).

Jones, M. B. (1953) An experimental study of extinction. *Psychol. Monogr.,* **67,** 1–17 [459].

Jones, Mary C. (1924a) The elimination of children's fears. *J. exp. Psychol.,* **7,** 382–390 [395–396].

—— (1924b) A laboratory study of fear: the case of Peter. *J. genet. Psychol.,* **31,** 308–315 [395–397].

Jones, R. B. (See Seward, Pereboom, Butler, & Jones, 1957).

Jourard, S. M. (1958) *Personal adjustment: an approach through the study of healthy personality.* New York: The Macmillan Co. [8, 129].

Kalish, D. (See Tolman, Richie, & Kalish, 1946).

Kalish, H. I. (See Guttman & Kalish, 1956).

—— (See Guttman & Kalish, 1958).

Kamin, L. J. (1954) Traumatic avoidance learning: The effects of CS-US interval with a trace-conditioning procedure. *J. comp. physiol. Psychol.,* **47,** 65–72 [374–376].

—— (1956) The effects of termination of the CS and avoidance of the US on avoidance learning. *J. comp. physiol. Psychol.,* **49,** 420–423 [51–53, 55].

—— (1957a) The effects of termination of the CS and avoidance of the US on avoidance learning: An extension. *Canad. J. Psychol.,* **11,** 48–56 [53, 385].

—— (1957b) The gradient of delay of secondary reward in avoidance learning tested on avoidance trials only. *J. comp. physiol. Psychol.,* **50,** 457–460 [385].

—— (1959). The delay-of-punishment gradient. *J. comp. physiol. Psychol.,* **52,** 434–436 [373].

—— (See Solomon, Kamin, & Wynne, 1953).

Kampner, P. (See Waddell, Gans, Kampner, & Williams, 1955).

Kaplon, M. D. (See Wolfe & Kaplon, 1941).

Kappauf, W. E. Personal communication [164].

Karoly, A. J. (See Walker, Dember, Earl, & Karoly, 1955).

Karsh, Eileen B. (1959) The effect of intensity of punishment and number of rewarded and punished trials on running speed in a conflict situation. Yale Ph.D. dissertation: New Haven, Conn. [387].

Keehn, J. D. (1959) On the non-classical nature of avoidance behavior. *Amer. J. Psychol.,* **72,** 243–247 [74].

—— (See Mowrer & Keehn, 1958).

Kelleher, R. T. (1957a) Conditioned reinforcement in chimpanzees. *J. comp. physiol. Psychol.,* **50,** 571–575 [114].

—— (1957b) A multiple schedule of conditioned reinforcement with chimpanzees. *Psychol. Rep.,* **3,** 485–491 [114].

Keller, A. G. (See Sumner & Keller, 1927).

Keller, F. S. (1942) Light aversion in the white rat. *Psychol. Rec.,* **4,** 235–250 [185].

—— (1954) Learning (Reinforcement theory). In *Doubleday papers in psychology.* Garden City, N. Y.: Doubleday & Co. [388, 488].

Keller, F. S. & Schoenfeld, W. N. (1950) *Principles of psychology.* New York: Appleton-Century-Crofts [165, 286, 291, 454].

Kellogg. W. N. (See Spooner & Kellogg, 1947).

Kelly, G. A. (1956) *The psychology of personal constructs.* Vol. I. *A theory of personality.* Vol. II. *Clinical diagnosis and therapy.* New York: W. W. Norton & Co. [287].

Kelvin, Lord [1].

Kendler, H. H. (1959) Learning. In *Annual review of psychology.* Stanford, Calif.: Annual Reviews, Inc. [250–252, 290].

Kendler, H. H. & Lachman, R. (1958) Habit reversal as a function of schedule of reinforcement and drive strength. *J. exp. Psychol.,* 55, 584–591 [470].

Kendrick, D. C. (1958) Inhibition with reinforcement (conditioned inhibition). *J. exp. Psychol.,* 56, 313–318 [430].

Kessen, M. L. (See Berkun, Kessen, & Miller, 1952).

Kimble, G. A. (1949) An experimental test of a two-factor theory of inhibition. *J. exp. Psychol.,* 39, 15–23 [400].

Kincaid, W. D. (See Logan, Beier, & Kincaid, 1956).

Kish, G. B. (1955) Learning when the onset of illumination is used as reinforcing stimulus. *J. comp. physiol. Psychol.,* 48, 261–265 [182–183, 185].

Kish, G. B. & Antonitis, J. J. (1956) Unconditioned operant behavior in two homozygous strains of mice. *J. genet. Psychol.* 88, 121–129 [182].

Kochigina, A. M. (See Dmitriev & Kochigina, 1959).

Köhler, W. (1925) *The mentality of apes.* London [175, 378].

Kohn, M. (1951) Satiation' of hunger from stomach versus mouth feeding. *J. comp. physiol. Psychol.,* 44, 412–422 [195].

—— (See Murray, Wells, Kohn, & Miller, 1953).

Konorski, J. (1948) *Conditioned reflexes and neuron organization.* (Trans. by Stephen Garry.) Cambridge, England: Cambridge University Press [292, 346].

—— (1950) Mechanisms of learning. In *Psychological mechanisms in animal behavior.* New York: Academic Press [292, 345, 417].

—— (1958) Trends in the development of physiology of the brain, *J. ment. sci.*,* 104, 1100–1110 [221–222].

—— (See Miller & Konorski, 1928).

—— [60, 208, 296, 398, 417].

Konorski, J. & Miller, S. (1937) On two types of conditioned reflex. *J. genet. Psychol.,* 16, 264–272 [65].

Kooi, K. A. (See Beck, Doty, & Kooi, 1958).

Korzybski, A. (1933) *Science and sanity.* Lancaster, Penn.: International Non-Aristotelian Library Pub. Co. [378].

Krauskopf, J. (See Bitterman, Reed, & Krauskopf, 1952).

Krech, D. (1949) Notes toward a psychological theory. *J. Personality,* 18, 66–87 [v].

Krechevsky, I. (1932) "Hypotheses" in rats. *Psychol. Rev.,* 39, 516–532 [309, 381].

—— (1937a) Brain mechanisms and variability: II. Variability where no learning is involved. *J. comp. Psychol.,* 23, 139–163 [339].

—— (1937b) Brain mechanisms and variability: III. Limitations of the effect of cortical injury upon variability. *J. comp. Psychol.,* 23, 351–364 [339].

—— (1938) A study of the continuity of the problem-solving process. *Psychol. Rev.,* 45, 107–133 [439].

Kroeber, A. L. (1952) *The nature of culture.* Chicago: University of Chicago Press [9].

* *Journal of mental science.*

Lachman, R. (See Kendler & Lachman, 1958).

Ladd, G. T. (1902) *Outlines of descriptive psychology.* New York: Charles Scribner's Sons [1].

Lamoreaux, R. R. (See Mowrer & Lamoreaux, 1942).

—— (See Mowrer & Lamoreaux, 1946).

—— (See Mowrer & Lamoreaux, 1951).

Lashley, K. S. (1917) The accuracy of movement in the absence of excitation from the moving organ. *Amer. J. Physiol.*, 43, 169–194 [490–491, 493].

—— (1934) Nervous mechanisms in learning. In C. Murchison, ed. *A handbook of general experimental psychology* [298].

—— (1950) In search of the engram. In *Physiological mechanisms in animal behaviour.* New York: Academic Press [56, 274, 278, 365].

—— (1951) The problem of serial order in behavior in *Cerebral mechanisms in behavior. The Hixon Symposium* (L. Jeffress, ed.). New York: John Wiley & Sons [490].

—— (See Spence, 1951a) [278].

Lashley, K. S. & McCarthy, D. A. (1926) The survival of the maze habit after cerebellar injuries. *J. comp. physiol. Psychol.*, 6, 423–433 [246].

Lauer, D. W. & Carterette, T. S. (1957) Changes in response measures over repeated acquisitions and extinction of a running habit. *J. comp. physiol. Psychol.*, 50, 334–338 [452].

Lawson, R. & Brownstein, A. J. (1957) The effect of effort and training-test simularity on resistance to extinction. *Amer. J. Psychol.*, 70, 123–127 [234, 402].

Lawson, R., & Marx, M. H. (1958) Frustration: theory and experiment. *Genet. Psychol. Monogr.*, 57, 393–464 [410].

Leary, R. W. (1957) The effect of amount of reward on serial discrimination learning of rhesus monkeys. MPA program, Chicago [415].

Lee, B. S. (1950) Effects of delayed speech feedback. *J. acoust. Soc. Amer.*, 22, 824–826 [247].

Lee, W. A. (1951) Approach and avoidance to a cue paired with the beginning and end of pain. Unpublished manuscript, Wesleyan University [140–142].

Leuba, C. (1955) Toward some integration of learning theories: The concept of optimal stimulation. *Psychol. Rep.*, 1, 27–33 [185].

Levin, H. (See Sears, Maccoby, & Levin, 1957).

Levine, S. (1956) Unpublished research [485].

Lewin, D. J. (1956) Acquisition, extinction, and spontaneous recovery as a function of percentage of reinforcement and intertrial intervals. *J. exp. Psychol.*, 51, 45–53 [404].

Lewin, K. (1935) *Dynamic theory of personality.* New York: McGraw-Hill Book Co. [313, 343].

—— (1942) Field theory of learning. Yearb. Nat. Soc. Stud. Educ., 41, (II), 215–242 [311, 313].

—— (1943) Defining the "field at a given time." *Psychol. Rev.*, 50, 292–310 [342].

—— (1951) Field theory and learning. In *Field theory in social science* (Dorwin Cartwright, ed.). New York: Harper & Brothers [313].

—— [278, 306, 308, 323–324, 343].

Lewis, D. J. & Duncan, C. P. (1956) Effect of different percentages of money reward on extinction of a lever-pulling response. *J. exp. Psychol.*, 52, 23–27 [459, 468].

Lewis, D. J., & Duncan, C. P. (1957) Expectation and resistance to extinction of a lever-pulling response as functions of percentage of reinforcement and amount of reward. *J. exp. Psychol.*, **54**, 115–121 [459].

Lichtenstein, P. E. (1950a) Studies of anxiety: I. The production of feeding inhibition in dogs. *J. comp. physiol. Psychol.*, **43**, 16–29 [97, 424, 483].

―――― (1950b) Studies of anxiety: II. The effects of lobotomy on a feeding inhibition in dogs. *J. comp. physiol. Psychol.*, **43**, 419–427 [424].

―――― (1957) On the dilemma of fear as a motivating force. *Psychol. Rep.*, **3**, 213–216 [415].

Liddell, H. S. (1944) Conditioned reflex method and experimental neurosis. In *Personality and the behavior disorders* (J. McV. Hunt, ed.). New York: The Ronald Press Co. [44].

―――― (1950) The role of vigilance in the development of animal neurosis. In *Anxiety* (P. H. Hoch & J. Zubin, eds.). New York: Grune & Stratton [368].

Liddell, H. S., James, W. T., & Anderson, O. D. (1934) The comparative physiology of the conditioned motor reflex. *Comp. Psychol. Monogr.*, **11**, 1–89 [60].

Light, J. S. & Gantt, W. H. (1936) Essential part of reflex arc for establishment of conditioned reflex. Formation of conditioned reflex after exclusion of motor peripheral end. *J. comp. Psychol.*, **21**, 19–36 [246–247].

Lilly, J. C. (1958) In: *Henry Ford Hospital Internation Symposium* on the reticular formation of the brain. Boston: Little [207].

―――― (1956) Mental effects of reduction of ordinary levels of physical stimuli. *Psychiat. Res. Reports*, **5**, 1–9 [179, 237].

Lipman, E. A. (See Brogden, Lipman, & Culler, 1938).

Lipps, T. [6].

Littman, R. A. (1956) Infantile experience and adult behavior in the white rat. *J. gen. Psychol.*, **88**, 11–24 [485].

Littman, R. & Wade, E. A. (1955) A negative test of the drive-reduction hypothesis. *Quart. J. exp. Psychol.*, **7**, 56–66 [140–142].

Livingston, J. R. (See Hull, Livingston, Rouse, & Barker, 1951).

Loeb, J. [315].

Logan, F. A., Beier, E. M., & Kincaid, W. D. (1956) Extinction following partial reinforcement and varied reinforcement. *J. exp. Psychol.*, **52**, 65–70 [469].

Lope de Vega [24–25].

Lorente de No, R. (1933) Vestibulo-ocular reflex arc. *Arch. neurol. Psychiat.*, **30**, 245–291 [365–366].

Lorge, I., & Thorndike, E. L. (1935) The influence of delay in the after-effect of a connection. *J. exp. Psychol.*, **18**, 186–194 [353].

Loucks, R. B. (1935) The experimental delimitation of structures essential for learning: The attempt to condition striped muscle responses with faradization of the sigmoid gyrus. *J. Psychol.*, **1**, 5–44 [237–241, 244, 293, 417].

Lowell, E. L. (See McClelland, Atkinson, Clark, & Lowell, 1953).

Lowrey, E. D. (1958) Characteristics of food-carry behavior in the rat. *J. comp. physiol. Psychol.*, **51**, 565–569 [153].

Lyndon, Barbara [486].

McAllister, W. R. (1953) Eyelid conditioning as a function of the CS-US interval. *J. exp. Psychol.*, **45**, 417–428 [386].

McCarthy, D. A. (See Lashley & McCarthy, 1926).

McClelland, D. C. (1955) The psychology of mental content reconsidered. *Psychol. Rev.*, **62**, 297-303 [10-11].

—— (1957) Freud and Hull: Pioneers in scientific psychology. *Amer. Scientist*, **45**, 101-113 [260, 296].

McClelland, D. C., Atkinson, J. T., Clark, R. A., & Lowell, E. L. (1953) *The achievement motive.* New York: Appleton-Century-Crofts, Inc. [113, 141, 271-273, 275-276, 296, 333, 336].

MacCorquodale, K. & Meehl, P. E. (1953) Preliminary suggestions as to a formalization of expectancy theory. *Psychol. Rev.*, **60**, 55-63 [288].

McCurdy, H. G. (See Zener & McCurdy, 1939).

MacDonnell, M. F. (See Siegel & MacDonnell, 1954).

McDougall, W. (1905) *Physiological psychology.* London: Dent [6].

—— (1923) *Outline of psychology.* New York: Charles Scribner's Sons [175].

—— (1919) *An introduction to social psychology,* London: [166].

—— (1938) *The energies of men.* New York: Oxford University Press [79].

McGeoch, J. A. (1942) *The psychology of human learning.* New York: Longmans, Green, & Co. [257].

McGill, T. E. (See Robinson & McGill, 1958).

McGuigan, F. J. (1956) The logical status of Hull's principle of secondary reinforcement. *Psychol. Rev.*, **63**, 303-308 [129].

McGuigan, F. J. & Crockett, F. (1958) Evidence that the secondary reinforcing stimulus must be discriminated. *J. exp. Psychol.*, **55**, 184-187 [455].

Maatsch, J. L. (See Adelman & Maatsch, 1955).

Maatch, J. L., Adelman, H. M., & Denny, M. R. (1954) Effort and resistance to extinction of the bar-pressing response. *J. comp. physiol. Psychol.*, **47**, 47-49 [401, 402].

Maccoby, E. E. (See Sears, Maccoby, & Levin, 1957).

Maier, N. R. F. (1949) *Frustration, the study of behavior without a goal* New York: McGraw-Hill [411, 413-415].

Maier, N. R. F. & Schneirla, T. C. (1942) Mechanisms in conditioning. *Psychol. Rev.*, **49**, 117-134 [280].

Malmo, R. B. (1958) Measurement of drive: An unsolved problem in psychology. in *Nebraska symposium on motivation* (M. R. Jones, ed.). Lincoln: University of Nebraska Press [163, 197, 272].

—— (1959) Activation: A neurophysiological dimension. *Psychol. Rev.*, **66**, 367-386 [211].

Maltzman, I. (See Amsel & Maltzman, 1950).

Mandler, J. M. (1958) Effect of early food deprivation on adult behavior in the rat. *J. comp. physiol. Psychol.*, **51**, 513-517 [130].

Marks, R. A. (See Carlton & Marks, 1957).

Marquis, P. G. (See Hilgard & Marquis, 1940).

Marx, M. H. (1950) A stimulus-response analysis of the hoarding habit in the rat. *Psychol. Rev.*, **57**, 80-91 [151].

Marx, M. H., Henderson, R. L., & Roberts, C. L. (1955) Positive reinforcement of the bar-pressing response by a light stimulus following dark operant pretests with no after affect. *J. comp. physiol. Psychol.*, **48**, 73-76 [184].

Marz, H. H. (See Holder, Marz, Holder, & Collier, 1959).

Mason, D. J. (1956) The relation of quantity, quality, and probability of reward to reaction potential and secondary reinforcement. Ph.D. Thesis, University of Illinois [270, 379].

—— (1957) The relation of secondary reinforcement to partial reinforcement. *J. comp. physiol. Psychol.*, 50, 264–268 [248, 460–461].

—— (See Davitz, Mason, Mowrer, & Viek, 1957).

—— Personal communication [248].

Mason, J. W. (See Brady, Porter, Conrad, & Mason, 1958).

May, M. A. (1948) Experimentally acquired drives. *J. exp. Psychol.*, 38, 66–77 [95].

May, R. (1950) Historical roots of modern anxiety theories. In *Anxiety* (P. H. Hoch & J. Zubin, eds.). New York: Grune & Stratton [169].

Meehl, P. E. (1950) On the circularity of the law of effect. *Psychol. Bull.*, 47, 52–75 [267].

—— (See MacCorquodale & Meehl, 1953).

Melching, W. H. (1954) The acquired reward value of an intermittently presented neutral stimulus. *J. comp. physiol. Psychol.*, 47, 370–374 [234–235].

Melton, A. W. (1941) Learning. In *Encyclopedia of educational research* (W. S. Monroe, ed.). New York: The Macmillan Co. [404].

Melzack, R. (1952) Irrational fears in the dog. *Canad. J. Psychol.*, 141–147 [175].

—— (1954) The genesis of emotional behavior: An experimental study of the dog. *J. comp. physiol. Psychol.*, 47, 166–168 [176].

Meyer, D. R. (1951) Intraproblem-interproblem relationships in learning by monkeys. *J. comp. physiol. Psychol.*, 44, 162–167 [452].

—— (See Miles & Meyer, 1956).

Meyer, M. F. (1911) *The fundamental laws of human behavior;* lectures on the foundations of any mental or social science. Boston: R. G. Badger [6].

—— (1922) *The psychology of the other-one.* Columbia: Missouri Book Co. [308].

—— (1933) That whale among the fishes—the theory of emotions. *Psychol. Rev.*, 40, 292–300 [308].

—— Personal communication [6].

Meynert, T. (1874) *Zur Mechanik des Gehirnbans.* Vienna [5].

Miles, R. C. (1956) The relative effectiveness of secondary reinforcers throughout deprivation and habit strength parameters. *J. comp. physiol. Psychol.*, 49, 126–130 [228–230, 232].

—— (1958a) The effect of an irrelevant motive on learning. *J. comp. physiol. Psychol.*, 51, 258–261 [162].

—— (1958b) Learning in kittens with manipulatory, exploratory, and food incentives. *J. comp. physiol. Psychol.*, 51, 39–41 [180].

—— (See Wickens & Miles, 1954).

Miles, R. C. & Meyer, D. R. (1956) Learning sets in mormosets. *J. comp. physiol. Psychol.*, 49, 219–222 [452].

Miles, R. C. & Wickens, D. D. (1953) Effect of secondary reinforcer on the primary hunger drive. *J. comp. physiol. Psychol.*, 46, 77–79 [99, 170].

Miles, W. R. (See Miller & Miles, 1935).

Miller, N. E. (1944) Experimental studies of conflict. Chapter 14 in *Personality and the behavior disorders* (J. McV. Hunt, ed.). Vol. I. New York: The Ronald Press Co. [344, 416, 424, 428, 453].

—— (1948a) Studies of fear as an acquirable drive: I. Fear as motivation and fear-reduction as reinforcement in the learning of new responses. *J. exp. Psychol.*, **38**, 89–101 [34, 79, 95–97, 127–129, 145, 406].

―― (1948b) Theory and experiment relating psychoanalytic displacement to stimulus-response generalization. *J. abnorm. soc. Psychol.*, **43**, 155–178 [127].

―― (1951a) Comments on multi-process conceptions of learning. *Psychol. Rev.*, **58**, 375–381 [81, 87–88].

―― (1951b) Learnable drives and rewards. Chapter 13 in *Handbook of experimental psychology* (S. S. Stevens, ed.). New York: John Wiley & Sons [56, 100, 135, 138, 141, 151, 173, 176, 202, 272, 408, 450].

―― (1954) Drive, drive-reduction, and reward. Fourteenth International Congress of Psychology, Montreal [179–180, 195].

―― (1957) Experiments on motivation: Studies combining psychological, physiological, and pharmacological techniques. *Science*, **126**, 1271–1278 [208–209, 250, 408].

―― (1958) Central stimulation and other new approaches to motivation and reward. *Amer. J. Psychol.*, **13**, 100–107 [284, 424].

―― (1959a) Liberalization of basic S—R concepts: Extensions to conflict behavior, motivation, and social learning. In *Psychology: A study of a science* (S. Koch, ed.). New York: McGraw-Hill Co. [150, 199–200, 252, 273–274, 328].

―― (1959b) Learning and performance motivated by direct stimulation of the brain. In *Electrical stimulation of the brain: subcortical integrative systems*. D. E. Sheer (Ed.) Austin: University of Texas Press [206–207, 209].

―― [416, 428, 453].

―― (See Berkun, Kessen, & Miller, 1952).

―― (See Dollard, Doob, Miller, Mowrer, & Sears, 1939).

―― (See Dollard & Miller, 1950).

―― (See Murray, Wells, Kohn, & Miller, 1953).

―― (See Myers and Miller, 1954).

Miller, N. E. & Dollard, J. (1941) *Social learning and imitation*. New Haven: Yale University Press [10, 16, 17, 85, 95, 101, 181, 193].

Miller, N. E., & Hart, G. (1948) Motivation and reward in learning. Psychological Film Register, Pennsylvania State University, State College, Penn. [95].

Miller, N. E. & Miles, W. R. (1935) Effect of caffeine on the running speed of hungry, satiated, and frustrated rats. *J. comp. Psychol.*, **20**, 397–412 [350].

Miller, N. E., Sampliner, R. I., & Woodrow, P. (1957) Thirst-reducing effects of water by stomach fistula vs. water by mouth measured by both a consummatory and an instrumental response. *J. comp. physiol. Psychol.*, **50**, 1–5 [195].

Miller, N. E. & Stevenson, S. S. (1936) Agitated behavior of rats during experimental extinction and a curve of spontaneous recovery. *J. comp. Psychol.*, **21**, 205–231 [404].

Miller, S. (See Konorski & Miller, 1937).

Miller, S. & Konorski, J. (1928) Sur une forme particuliere des reflexes conditionels. *C. R. Soc. Bio. Paris*, **99**, 1155–1157 [240, 292].

Milner, P. (See Olds & Milner, 1954).

Miron, M. S. Personal communication [129–130].

Moll, R. P. (1959) The effect of drive level on acquisition of the consummatory response. *J. comp. physiol. Psychol.*, **52**, 116–119 [387].

Molotkov, A. (1910) [The formation of motor association-reflexes to visual stimuli.] Thesis, St. Petersburg (see Razran, 1956) [44].

Monkman, J. A. (See Montgomery & Monkman, 1955).

Monroe, R. L. (1956) The role of drives in human growth. *Merrill-Palmer Quart.*, **3**, 24–35 [273].

Montague, E. K. (1953) The role of anxiety in serial rote learning. *J. exp. Psychol.*, **45**, 91–96 [157, 172].

Montgomery, K. C. (1951a) An experimental investigation of reactive inhibition and conditioned inhibition. *J. exp. Psychol.*, **41**, 39–51 [338, 402].

—— (1951b) The relation between exploratory behavior and spontaneous alternation in the white rat. *J. comp. physiol. Psychol.*, **44**, 582–589 [175, 185].

—— (1953) The effect of hunger and thirst drives upon exploratory behavior. *J. comp. physiol. Psychol.*, **46**, 315–319 [175].

—— (1954) The role of the exploratory drive in learning. *J. comp. physiol. Psychol.*, **47**, 60–64 [338, 340].

—— (1955) The relation between fear induced by novel stimulation and exploratory behavior. *J. comp. physiol. Psychol.*, **48**, 254–260 [175].

Montgomery, K. C. & Galton, B. B. (1956) A test of the drive-reduction explanation of learned fear. Reported in Solomon, R. L., & Brush, E. S. Experimentally derived conceptions of anxiety and aversion. In *Nebraska symposium on motivation* (M. R. Jones, ed.). Lincoln: University of Nebraska Press [140].

Montgomery, K. C. & Monkman, J. A. (1955) The relation between fear and exploratory behavior. *J. comp. physiol. Psychol.*, **48**, 132–136 [176].

Morey, R. (1933) Ph.D. Thesis, Princeton University [162].

Morgan, C. T. (1947) The hoarding instinct. *Psychol. Rev.*, **54**, 335–341 [151–152].

Morgan, C. T. & Stellar, E. (1950) *Physiological psychology.* (Second ed.) New York: McGraw-Hill Book Co. [247].

Morgan, C. T., Stellar, E., & Johnson, O. (1943) Food-deprivation and hoarding in rats. *J. comp. Psychol.*, **35**, 275–295 [485].

Morgan, J. J. B. (See Watson & Morgan, 1917).

Morris, C. [12].

Morse, W. H. & Herrnstein, R. J. (1956) The maintenance of avoidance behavior using the removal of a conditioned positive reinforcer as the aversive stimulus. *Amer. Psychol.*, **11**, 430 [164].

—— Personal communication [165].

Mowrer, O. H. (1938) Preparatory set (expectancy)—A determinant in motivation and learning. *Psychol. Rev.*, **45**, 61–91 [26, 344].

—— (1939) A stimulus-response analysis of anxiety and its role as a reinforcing agent. *Psychol. Rev.*, **46**, 553–565 [93, 95, 127].

—— (1940a) Anxiety-reduction and learning. *J. exp. Psychol.*, **27**, 497–516 [95].

—— (1940b) Preparatory set (expectancy)—Some methods of measurement. *Psychol. Monogr.*, **52**, No. 2, 43 [376].

—— (1947) On the dual nature of learning: A reinterpretation of "conditioning" and "problem solving." *Harv. Educ. Rev.*, **17**, 102–148 [19, 76, 78].

—— (1950a) *Learning theory and personality dynamics.* New York: The Ronald Press Co. [34, 52, 60, 68, 87, 171, 177, 337, 398, 434].

—— (1950b) Comment on Estes' study: "Generalization of secondary reinforcement from the primary drive." *J. comp. physiol. Psychol.*, **43**, 148–151 [137, 157].

—— (1950c) Review of N. R. F. Maier, *Frustration*—The study of behavior without a goal. *Science, III*, 434 [412, 414].

—— (1952) Learning theory. *J. educ. Research*, **46**, 475–495 [79].

—— (1953a) Is "habit strength" merely "secondary reinforcement." Unpublished paper [89, 223].

—— (1953b) Motivation and neurosis. In *Current theory and research in motivation*—A symposium. Lincoln: University of Nebraska Press [79, 223, 225, 248].

—— (1954) Ego psychology, cybernetics, and learning theory. In *Learning theory, personality theory and clinical research: The Kentucky Symposium*. New York: John Wiley & Sons [202].

—— (1956) Two-factor learning theory reconsidered, with special reference to secondary reinforcement and the concept of habit. *Psychol. Rev.*, **63**, 114–128 [19, 89, 223, 234].

—— (1958) Hearing and speaking. An analysis of language learning. *J. of Speech & Hearing Disorders*, **23**, 143–152 [489].

—— (1959) The dean of American Psychology takes a stand: review of R. S. Woodworth's *Dynamics of behavior contemporary psychology*, **4**, 129–133 [301].

—— (1960) *Learning theory and the symbolic processes*. New York: John Wiley & Sons [1, 11–13, 19–21, 26, 31, 39, 49, 61, 90, 109, 163, 174, 184, 201, 210, 215, 217, 220–221, 228, 237–238, 258–261, 267, 277, 279, 282, 286, 290, 299, 301, 303, 305, 308–309, 313, 316, 323, 327–329, 331, 334–335, 341–342, 349, 360, 362, 377–380, 384–385, 387, 391, 403, 409, 419, 438–439, 442, 452–453, 458, 464, 468, 470, 487, 493–494].

—— [266, 453].

—— (See Davitz, Mason, Mowrer, & Viek, 1957).

—— (See Dollard, Doob, Miller, Mowrer, & Sears, 1939).

—— (See Gibson & Mowrer, 1938).

—— (See Whiting & Mowrer, 1943).

Mowrer, O. H. & Aiken, E. G. (1954) Contiguity vs. drive-reduction in conditioned fear: temporal variations in conditioned and unconditioned stimulus. *Amer. J. Psychol.*, **67**, 26–38 [81, 87–88, 140, 348].

Mowrer, O. H. & Jones, H. M. (1943) Extinction and behavior variability as functions of effortfulness of task. *J. exp. Psychol.*, **33**, 369–386 [336, 398–401, 403].

—— (1945) Habit strength as a function of the pattern of reinforcement. *J. exp. Psychol.*, **35**, 293–311 [12, 451, 457, 462, 469].

Mowrer, O. H. & Keehn, J. D. (1958) How are inter-trial "avoidance" responses reinforced? *Psychol. Rev.*, **65**, 209–221 [236, 291, 294, 478, 481].

Mowrer, O. H. & Lamoreaux, R. R. (1942) Avoidance conditioning and signal duration—a study of secondary motivation and reward. *Psychol. Monogr.*, **54**, No. 5, 1–34 [51, 55].

—— (1946) Fear as an intervening variable in avoidance conditioning. *J. comp. Psychol.*, **39**, 29–50 [73, 95, 119].

—— (1951) Conditioning and conditionality (discrimination). *Psychol. Rev.*, **58**, 196–212 [37, 238, 448–449].

Mowrer, O. H. & Solomon, L. N. (1954) Contiguity vs. drive-reduction in conditioned fear: the proximity and abruptness of drive-reduction. *Amer. J. Psychol.*, **67**, 15–25 [83, 88].

Mowrer, O. H. & Ullman, A. D. (1945) Time as a determinant of integrative learning. *Psychol. Rev.*, **52**, 61–90 [370, 377, 378].

Mowrer, O. H. & Viek, P. (1948) An experimental analogue of fear from a sense of helplessness. *J. abnorm. soc. Psychol.*, **83**, 193–200 [71, 134, 376].

Muenzinger, K. F. (1954) The need for a frame of reference in the study of behavior. *J. gen. Psychol.*, **50**, 217–236 [378, 435].

—— Personal communication [378, 435].

Muenzinger, K. F. & Baxter, L. F. (1957) The effects of training to approach vs. to escape from electric shock upon subsequent discrimination learning. *J. comp. physiol. Psychol.*, **50**, 252–257 [435].

Muenzinger, K. F., Brown, W. O., Crow, W. J., & Powloski, R. F. (1952) Motivation in learning: XI. An analysis of electric shock for correct responses into its avoidance and accelerating components. *J. exp. Psychol.*, **43**, 115–119 [378, 434–435]

Muenzinger, K. F., Dove, C. C., & Bernstone, A. H. (1936) Serial learning: II. The bi-directional goal gradient in the endless maze. *J. genet. Psychol.*, **50**, 229–241 [348].

Muenzinger, K. F. & Fletcher, F. M. (1936) Motivation in learning. VI. Escape from electric shock compared with hunger-food-tension in the visual discrimination habit. *J. comp. Psychol.*, **22**, 79–91 [179].

Munn, N. L. (1950) *Handbook of psychological research on the rat.* Cambridge, Mass.: The Riverside Press [197].

Murdock, B. B. (See Bugelski, *et al.*, 1958) [493].

—— (See Bugelski, Goss, Murdock, Perkins, & Wickens, 1958).

Murphy, J. V., & Miller, R. E. (1958) The effect of intertrial responding on conditioning and extinction of avoidance behavior. *J. comp. physiol. Psychol.*, **56**, 256–261 [485].

Murray, E. J., Wells, H., Kohn., M., & Miller, N. E. (1953) Sodium sucaryl: A substance which tastes sweet to human subjects but is avoided by rats. *J. comp. physiol. Psychol.*, **46**, 134–137 [190].

Murray, H. A. (1938) *Explorations in personality.* New York: Oxford University Press [173, 343].

Myers, J. A. (1949) An experimental study of the reinforcing value of food for non-hungry rats. M. A. thesis, University of Iowa Library [151].

Myers, A. K. & Miller, N. E. (1954) Failure to find a learned drive based on hunger; evidence for learning motivated by exploration. *J. comp. physiol. Psychol.*, **47**, 428–436 [150, 179, 181, 340].

Nachmias, J. (See Gleitman, Nachmias, & Neisser, 1954).

Neff, W. D. (1953) Physiological psychology. In *Annual Review of Psychology*, **4**, 255–272 [195].

Nefzger, W. D. (1957) The properties of stimuli associated with shock reduction. *J. exp. Psychol.*, **53**, 184–188 [140].

Neisser, U. (See Gleitman, Nachmias, & Neisser, 1954).

Nelson, Amelia K. (See Pratt, Nelson, & Sun, 1930).

Nezdanova, Z. A. (1940) Trans. Pavlov Physiol. Lab., **9**, 355 [346].

Nielson, H. C., Doty, R. W., & Rutledge, L. T. (1958) Motivation and perceptual aspects of subcortical stimulation in cats. *Amer. J. Physiol.*, **194**, 427–432 [207, 244].

Noble, C. E., & Alcock, W. T. (1958) Human delayed-reward learning with different lengths of task. *J. exp. Psychol.*, **56**, 407–412 [383, 410].

Notterman, J. M. (See Bersh, Notterman, & Schoenfeld, 1956).

Nowlis, V. (See Sears, Whiting, Nowlis, & Sears, 1953).

O'Connor, V. J. (1946) Recency or effect?—A critical analysis of Guthrie's theory of learning. *Harv. Educ. Rev.*, **16**, 194–206 [284, 286, 363].

O'Kelly, L. I. (1954) The effect of preloads of water and sodium chloride on voluntary water intake of thirsty rats. *J. comp. physiol. Psychol.*, **47**, 7–13 [195].

—— Personal communication [233].

Olds, J. (1953) The influence of practice on the strength of secondary approach drives. *J. exp. Psychol.*, **46**, 232–236 [129].

—— (1956a) *The growth and structure of motives*. Glencoe, Ill.: The Free Press [191].

—— (1956b) Pleasure centers in the brain. *Sci. Amer.*, **195**, 105–116 [207, 209].

—— (1956c) A preliminary mapping of electrical reinforcing effects in the rat brain. *J. comp. physiol. Psychol.*, **49**, 281–285 [207].

—— (1958) Effects of hunger and male sex hormone on self-stimulation of the brain. *J. comp. physiol. Psychol.*, **51**, 320–324 [207].

Olds, J. & Milner, P. (1954) Positive reinforcement produced by electrical stimulation of septal area and other regions of rat brain. *J. comp. physiol. Psychol.*, **47**, 419–427 [206–209].

Osgood, C. E. (1953) *Method and theory in experimental psychology*. New York: Oxford University Press [138, 281, 442, 490–491].

Overton, R. K. (1958) *Thought and action*. New York: Random House [365].

Paradise, N. (See Dember, Earl, & Paradise, 1956).

Parducci, A. (1957) Alternative measures for the discrimination of shift in reinforcement-ratio. *Amer. J. Psychol.*, **70**, 194–202 [459].

Pavlov, I. P. (1927) *Conditioned reflexes*. (G. V. Anrep, Trans.). London: Oxford University Press [5, 7, 14, 68, 98, 100, 119, 125, 127, 163, 194, 222, 254, 257–258, 262, 293, 305, 346–348, 365–366, 368, 410, 432, 450].

—— (1932) The reply of a physiologist to psychologists. *Psychol. Rev.*, **39**, 91–127 [63, 74–75].

—— [15–19, 21–22, 25, 31, 39–43, 47, 58, 63–66, 68, 76, 89–90, 92–95, 99–101, 123–124, 214, 278, 291, 307, 313, 323–324, 433].

Pennock, L. (See Simons, Wickens, Brown, & Pennock, 1951).

Pereboom, A. C. (See Seward, Pereboom, Butler, & Jones, 1957).

Perin, C. T. (1943a) A quantitative investigation of the delay of reinforcement gradient, *J. exp. Psychol.*, **32**, 37–51 [262].

—— (1943b) The effect of delayed reinforcement upon the differentiation of bar responses in white rats. *J. exp. Psychol.*, **32**, 95–109 [262, 356, 357, 360, 369, 372, 376].

Perkins, C. C. (1947) The relation of secondary rewards to gradients of reinforcement. *J. exp. Psychol.*, **37**, 377–392 [262, 356, 357, 360, 369, 372, 376].

—— (1955) The stimulus conditions which follow learned responses. *Psychol. Rev.*, **62**, 341–348 [348, 417].

—— (See Bugelski, Goss, Murdock, Perkins, & Wickens, 1958).

Perkins, C. C. & Hertzler, E. C. (1958) An experimental study of the role of reward in conditioned change in heart rate. Mimeographed paper [421].

Petropavlovsky, V. P. (1934) [The methodology of conditioning motor reflexes.] *Fiziol.* zb. SSSR, **17**, 217–225 (see Razran, 1956) [44].

Pfaffman, C. (1951) Taste and smell. In *Handbook of experimental psychology* (S. S. Stevens, ed.), 1143–1171. New York: John Wiley & Sons [190].

Piercy, M. F. (See Elithorn, Piercy, & Crosskey, 1955).

Plato [275].

Porter, R. W. (See Brady, Porter, Conrad, & Mason, 1958).

Postman, L. (1947) The history and present status of the law of effect. *Psychol. Bull.*, **44**, 489–563 [22].

Powloski, R. F. (See Muenzinger, Brown, Crow, & Powloski, 1952).

Pratt, C. (See Schlosberg & Pratt, 1956).

Pratt, K. C., Nelson, Amalie K., Sun, K. H. (1930). *The behavior of the newborn infant.* Columbia: Ohio State University Press [190].

Prince, A. I., Jr. (1956) Effect of punishment on visual discrimination learning. *J. exp. Psychol.*, **52**, 381–385 [434].

Protopopov, W. (1909) [Motor association-reflexes to sound.] Thesis, St. Petersburg (see Razran, 1956) [44].

Quastler, H. *et al.*, (1955) Human performance in information transmission. Part II. Sequential Tasks. Report R-62, Control Systems Laboratory, University of Illinois, Urbana [491–492].

Rand, A. L. (1941) Results of the Archbold Expeditions. No. 34. *Bull. Amer. Mus. Nat. Hist.*, **78**, 213–242 [175].

Rayner, R. (See Watson & Rayner, 1920).

Razran, G. (1939) The nature of the extinctive process. *Psychol. Rev.*, **46**, 264–297 [426, 430].

——— (1955a) A note on second-order conditioning—and secondary reinforcement. *Psychol. Rev.*, **5**, 327–332 [113].

——— (1955b) Partial reinforcement of salivary CR's in adult human subjects: preliminary study. *Psychol. Rep.*, **1**, 409–416 [469].

——— (1956a) Backward conditioning. *Psychol. Bull.*, **53**, 55–69 [349].

——— (1956b) Extinction re-examined and re-analyzed: A new theory. *Psychol. Rev.*, **63**, 39–52 [426].

——— (1956c) On avoidance learning before the familiar American studies: "Avoidant vs. unavoidant conditioning and partial reinforcement in Russian laboratories." *Amer. J. Psychol.*, **69**, 127–129 [44–45].

——— (1957) Soviet psychology since 1950. Invited address, Annual Meeting of Eastern Psychological Association. Mimeographed [15].

Reed, P. C. (See Bitterman, Reed, & Krauskopf, 1952).

Reese, W. G., Doss, R., & Gantt, W. H. (1953) Autonomic responses in differential diagnosis of organic and psychogenic psychoses. *Arch. neurol. psychiat.*, **70**, 779–793 [60].

Reis, Eva E. S. (See Hunt, Cole, & Reis, 1958).

Reisman, M. N. (See Fitzwater & Riesman, 1952).

Restle, F. (1957) Discrimination of cues in mazes: A resolution of the "Place-vs.-Response" question. *Psychol. Rev.*, **64**, 217–228 [331].

Reykowski, J. [57].

Reynolds, W. F. (1958) Acquisition and extinction of the conditioned eyelid response following partial and continuous reinforcement. *J. exp. Psychol.*, **55**, 335–341 [457].

Rhoades, J. M., & Wyers, E. J. (1956) Effect of blindness on saccharine intake and manipulatory activity in rats (Abstract.) *Amer. J. Psychol.*, 11, 445 [181].

Richie, B. F. (See Tolman, Richie, & Kalish, 1946).

Riesen, A. H. (1940) Delayed reward in discrimination learning by chimpanzees. *Comp. Psychol. Monogr.*, 15, 1–53 [357–358, 360].

Rigby, W. K. (1954) Approach and avoidance gradients and conflict behavior in a predominantly temporal situation. *J. comp. physiol. Psychol.*, 47, 83–89 [380].

Ritchie, B. F. (1954) A logical and experimental analysis of the laws of motivation. In *Nebraska symposium on motivation* (M. R. Jones, ed.). Lincoln: University of Nebraska Press [248].

Roberts, C. L. (See Marx, Henderson, & Roberts, 1955).

Roberts, W. H. (1930) The effect of delayed feeding on white rats in a problem cage. *Pedagogical seminar and J. genet. Psychol.*, 37, 35–58 [354–356, 367, 377].

Robertson, E. G. (1954) *Brain*, 77, 232– [207].

Robinson, J. S., & McGill, T. E. (1958) Comparison of place and response learning in a simultaneous-successive discrimination-learning situation. *J. comp. physiol. Psychol.*, 51, 627–630 [331].

Roby, T. B. (See Sheffield & Roby, 1950).

——— (See Sheffield, Roby, & Campbell, 1954).

Roe, Anne & Simpson, G. G. (1958) *Behavior and evolution*. New Haven: Yale Press. [4].

Rogers, C. R. (1956) Intellectualized psychotherapy. On G. Kelly's *Psychology of personal constructs*. In *Contemporary Psychol.*, 1, 357–358 [287].

Roosevelt, F. D. [133].

Rose, A. S. (See Chapman, Rose, & Solomon, 1948).

Rosenbleuth, A. (1934) Central excitation and inhibition in reflex changes of heart rate. *Amer. J. Physiol.*, 107, 293–304 [366].

Ross, B. M. (See Grant, Schipper, & Ross, 1952).

Roth, L. (1954) *I'll cry tomorrow*. New York: Popular Library [270].

Rouse, R. O. (See Hull, Livingston, Rouse, & Barker, 1951).

Roussell, J. (See Amsel & Roussell, 1952).

Rutledge, L. T. (See Nielson, Doty, & Rutledge, 1958).

Rutledge, L. T., & Doty, R. W. (1957) Differential action of chlorpromazine on reflexes conditioned to central and peripheral stimulation. *Amer. J. Physiol.*, 191, 189–192 [97].

Saltzman, I. J. (1949) Maze learning in the absence of primary reinforcement: A study of secondary reinforcement. *J. comp. physiol. Psychol.*, 42, 161–173 [109–114, 214, 353, 462].

Sampliner, R. I. (See Miller, Sampliner, & Woodrow, 1957).

Sampson, P. B. (See Gerall, Sampson, & Boslov, 1957).

Samuels, I. (1959) Reticular mechanisms and behavior. *Psychol. Bull.*, 1–25 [210].

Schaefer, V. H. (1959) Differences between strains of rats in avoidance conditioning without an explicit warning stimulus. *J. comp. physiol. Psychol.*, 52, 120–122 [479].

Scharlock, D. P. (1955) The role of extra-maze cues in place and response learning. *J. exp. Psychol.*, 50, 249–254 [331].

Schipper, L. M. (See Grant, Schipper, & Ross, 1952).

Schlosberg, H. (1934) Conditioned responses in the white rat. *J. genet. Psychol.*, 45, 303–335 [42, 44–45].

—— (1936) Conditioned responses in the white rat: II. Conditioned responses based upon shock to the foreleg. *J. genet. Psychol.*, **49**, 107–138 [55].

—— (1937) The relationship between success and the laws of conditioning. *Psychol. Rev.*, **44**, 379–394 [55, 65, 266].

—— (See Woodworth & Schlosberg, 1954).

Schlosberg, H. & Pratt, C. (1956) The secondary reward value of inaccessible food for hungry and satiated rats. *J. comp. physiol. Psychol.*, **49**, 149–152 [141].

Schlosberg, N. (See Hunt, Schlosberg, Solomon, & Stellar, 1947).

Schneider, P. (1955) The minimum man. *Listener*, **54**, 1, 397 [380].

Schneider, R. (See Bahrick, Fitts, & Schneider, 1955).

Schneirla, T. C. (See Maier & Schneirla, 1942).

Schoenfeld, W. N. (1950) An experimental approach to anxiety, escape, and avoidance behavior. In *Anxiety* (P. H. Hoch & J. Zubin, eds.). New York: Grune & Stratton [52, 291–292].

—— (See Bersh, Notterman, & Schoenfeld, 1956).

—— (See Keller & Schoenfeld, 1950).

Schoenfeld, W. N., Antonitis, J. J., & Bersh, P. J. (1950) A preliminary study of training conditions necessary for secondary reinforcement. *J. exp. Psychol.*, **40**, 40–45 [234, 455].

Schroeder, H. M. (See Wickens, Schroeder, & Snide, 1954).

Science Illustrated (1946) Eating your heart out? Vol. 1, No. 7, Oct., 1946 [162].

Scott, J. H. (1955) Some effects at maturity of gentling, ignoring, or shocking rats during infancy. *J. abnorm. soc. Psychol.*, **51**, 412–414 [485].

Scott, T. H. (See Bexton, Heron, & Scott, 1954).

—— (See Heron, Doane, & Scott, 1956).

Sears, E. E. (See Dollard, Doob, Miller, Mowrer, & Sears, 1939).

Sears, P. S. (See Sears, Whiting, Nowlis, & Sears, 1953).

Sears, R. R. (1951) A theoretical framework for personality and social behavior. *Amer. Psychol.*, **6**, 476–483 [10].

Sears, R. R., Maccoby, E. E., & Levin, H. (1957) *Patterns of child rearing*. Evanston, Ill.: Row, Peterson & Co., [10, 340].

Sears, R. R., Whiting, J. W. M., Nowlis, V., & Sears, P. S. (1953) Some child rearing antecedents of aggression and dependency in young children. *Genet. Psychol. Monogr.*, **47**, 135–243 [472].

Seeman, W. & Greenberg, I. (1952) Secondary reinforcement and acquired drives: A note. Unpublished paper [101, 142].

Selye, H. (1956) *The stress of life.* New York: McGraw-Hill [442].

Seward, J. P. (1950) Secondary reinforcement as tertiary motivation. A revision of Hull's revision. *Psychol. Rev.*, **57**, 362–374 [201, 225, 267–268].

—— (1951) Experimental evidence for the motivating function of reward. *Psychol. Bull.*, **48**, 130–149 [271, 275].

—— (1956a) Reinforcement and expectancy: Two theories in search of a controversy. *Psychol. Rev.*, **63**, 105–113 [269, 278].

—— (1956b) Drive, incentive and motivation. *Psychol. Rev.*, **63**, 195–203 [200, 269, 289].

Seward, J. P., Pereboom, A. C., Butler, B., & Jones, R. B. (1957) The role of prefeeding in an apparently frustration effect. *J. exp. Psychol.*, **54**, 445–450 [408].

Shaffer, L. F. (1936) *Psychology of adjustment.* Boston: Houghton Mifflin Co. [378, 405].

Shaffer, L. F. & Shoben, E. G. (1956) *The psychology of adjustment*. Boston: Houghton Mifflin Co. [472].

Shand, A. F. (1914) *Foundations of character*. London: Macmillan & Company [165].

Sheffield, F. D. (1948) Avoidance training and the contiguity principle. *J. comp. physiol. Psychol.*, **41**, 165–177 [54–55].

—— (See Campbell & Sheffield, 1953).

Sheffield, F. D. & Campbell, B. A. (1954) The role of experience in the "spontaneous" activity of hungry rats. *J. comp. physiol. Psychol.*, **47**, 97–100 [198–200, 273].

Sheffield, F. D. & Roby, T. B. (1950) Reward value of a non-nutritive sweet taste. *J. comp. physiol. Psychol.*, **43**, 471–481 [192–194].

Sheffield, F. D., Roby, T. B., & Campbell, B. A. (1954) Drive reduction versus consummatory behavior as determinants of reinforcement. *J. comp. physiol. Psychol.*, **47**, 349–354 [193].

Sheffield, Virginia F. (1949) Extinction as a function of partial reinforcement and distribution of practice. *J. exp. Psychol.*, **39**, 511–525 [458, 469].

Sheppard, R. N. (1958) Stimulus and response generalization: deduction of the generalization gradient from a trace model. *Psychol. Rev.*, **65**, 242–256 [489–490].

Sherman, M. (1927) The differentiation of emotional response in infants. I. Judgments of emotional responses from motion picture views and from actual observation. *J. comp. Psychol.*, **7**, 265–284 [166].

Sherrington, C. S. (1906) Integrative action of the nervous system. New Haven: Yale University Press [65, 221–222].

—— (See Pavlov, 1927) [433].

Shnirman, A. L. (1925) New data in the reflexology and physiology of the nervous system, *Symposium of the Society of Experimental Biology*, No. 1, p. 218 [346].

Shoben, E. G. (See Shaffer & Shoben, 1956).

Sidman, M. (1953) Two temporal parameters of the maintenance of avoidance behavior by the white rat. *J. comp. physiol. Psychol.*, **46**, 253–261 [294, 479].

—— (1956) Drug-behavior interaction. *Annals of the New York Academy of Sciences*, **65**, 282–302 [477, 480].

—— (See Brady, Boren, Conrad, & Sidman, 1957).

Sidman, M. & Boren, J. (1957a) A comparison of two types of warning stimulus in an avoidance situation. *J. comp. physiol. Psychol.*, **50**, 282–287 [50].

—— (1957b) The relative aversiveness of warning signal and shock in an avoidance situation. *J. abnorm. soc. Psychol.*, **55**, 339–344 [177].

Sidman, M., Brady, J. V., Boren, J. J., & Conrad, D. G. (1955) Reward schedules and behavior maintained by intracranial self-stimulation. *Science*, **122**, 830–831 [210].

Siegel, P. S. & MacDonnell, M. F. (1954) A repetition of the Calvin-Bicknell-Sperling study of conditioned drive. *J. comp. physiol. Psychol.*, **47**, 250–253 [147].

Simmons, R. (1924) The relative effectiveness of certain incentives in animal learning. *Comp. Psychol. Monogr.*, **2**, No. 7, 1–79 [352–353].

Simons, C. W., Wickens, D. D., Brown, U., & Pennock, L. (1951) Effective of the secondary reinforcing agents on the primary thirst drive. *J. comp. physiol. Psychol.*, **44**, 67–70 [99, 171].

Simpson, G. G. (See Roe & Simpson, 1958).

Skinner, B. F. (1932) On the rate of formation of a conditioned reflex. *J. genet. Psychol.*, **7**, 274–286 [226].

———— (1935) Two types of conditioned reflex and a pseudo type. *J. genet. Psychol.*, **12**, 66–77 [65].

———— (1938) *The behavior of organisms.* New York: Appleton-Century-Crofts [100, 108–109, 117, 122–123, 193, 223, 235, 272, 355, 424, 436, 442, 457–458, 469].

———— (1948) "Superstition" in the pigeon. *J. exp. Psychol.*, **38**, 168–172 [59, 380–381].

———— (1950) Are theories of learning necessary? *Psychol. Rev.*, **57**, 193–216 [289].

———— (1953a) *Science and human behavior.* New York: The Macmillan Co. [8, 48–50, 52, 165].

———— (1953b) Some contributions of an experimental analysis of behavior to psychology as a whole. *Amer. Psychol.*, **8**, 69–78 [219, 224, 290–291].

———— (1958) Reinforcement today. *Amer. Psychol.*, **13**, 94–99 [273].

———— [58, 283, 287, 290].

———— (See Estes & Skinner, 1941).

———— (See Ferster & Skinner, 1958).

———— (1959) John Broadus Watson, Behaviorist. *Science*, **129**, 197–198 [6].

Smith, K. (1954) Conditioning as an artifact. *Psychol. Rev.*, **61**, 217–225 [427].

Smith, M., & Duffy, M. (1957) Evidence for a dual reinforcing effect of sugar. *J. comp. physiol.*, **50**, 242–247 [189, 191].

Smith, M. P. & Buchanan, G. (1954) Acquisition of secondary reward by cues associated with shock reduction. *J. exp. Psychol.*, **48**, 123–126 [140].

Smudski, J. F. (See Braun, Wedekind, & Smudski, 1957).

Snide, J. D. (See Wickens, Schroeder, & Snide, 1954).

Solomon, H. C. (See Chapman, Rose, & Solomon, 1948).

Solomon, L. N. (See Mowrer & Solomon, 1954).

Solomon, L. N. & Swanson, A. M. (1955) Establishment of a secondary drive based on thirst. Unpublished manuscript [147, 151].

Solomon, R. L. (1948a) The influence of work on behavior. *Psychol. Bull.*, **45**, 1–40 [400–401, 485].

———— (1948b) Effort and extinction rate: A confirmation. *J. comp. physiol. Psychol.*, **41**, 93–101 [400].

———— (See Hunt, Schlosberg, Solomon, & Stellar, 1947).

———— (See Wynne & Solomon, 1955).

Solomon, R. L., Kamin, L. J., & Wynne, L. C. (1953) Traumatic avoidance learning: The outcomes of several extinction procedures with dogs. *J. abnorm. soc. Psychol.*, **48**, 291–302 [403, 421, 484].

Solomon, R. L., & Wynne, Lyman C. (1950) Avoidance conditioning in normal dogs and in dogs deprived of normal autonomic functioning. (Abstract). *Amer. J. Psychol.*, **5**, 264 [240].

Solomon, R. L. & Wynne, L. C. (1953) Traumatic avoidance learning: Acquisition in normal dogs. *Psychol. Monogr.*, **67**, 1–19 [60, 481–482, 484, 486–487].

———— (1954) Traumatic avoidance learning: The principle of anxiety conservation and partial irreversibility. *Psychol. Rev.*, **61**, 353–385 [97, 60, 240].

Spence, K. W. (1936) The nature of discrimination learning in animal. *Psychol. Rev.*, **43**, 427–449 [409].

———— (1937) Analysis of the formation of visual discrimination habits in the chimpanzee. *J. comp. Psychol.*, **23**, 77–100 [409].

———— (1940) Continuous versus non-continuous interpretations of discrimination learning. *Psychol. Rev.*, **47**, 271–288 [439].

———— (1947) The role of secondary reinforcement in delayed reward learning. *Psychol. Rev.*, **54**, 1–8 [234, 249, 356, 358–361, 363, 376, 386, 412, 428].

———— (1950) Cognitive versus stimulus-response theories of learning. *Psychol. Rev.*, **57**, 159–172 [218].

———— (1951a) Theoretical interpretations of learning. In *Comparative psychology* (C. P. Stone, ed.), 3rd ed. New York: Prentice-Hall [69, 105, 219, 261, 278, 309, 323].

———— (1951b) Theoretical interpretations of learning. In *Handbook of experimental psychology* (S. S. Stevens, ed.). New York: John Wiley & Sons [265, 283, 285, 288].

———— (1954) Current interpretations of learning data and some recent developments in stimulus-response theory. *Learning theory, personality theory, and clinical research. The Kentucky Symposium.* New York: John Wiley & Sons [157].

———— (1956) *Behavior theory and conditioning.* New Haven: Yale University Press [89, 103, 105, 113, 200, 250, 263–264, 266, 410].

———— (1958) A theory of emotionally based drive (D) and its relation to performance in simple learning situations. *Amer. Psychol.*, **13**, 131–141 [157].

———— [249, 428].

———— (See Farber & Spence, 1953).

———— (See Taylor & Spence, 1952).

Spence, K. W. & Farber, I. (1953) Conditioning and extinction as a function of anxiety. *J. exp. Psychol.*, **45**, 116–119 [172].

Spencer, H. [3].

Sperling, D. S. (See Calvin, Bicknell, & Sperling, 1953).

Sperry, R. W. (1951) Mechanisms of neural maturation. In *Handbook of experimental psychology* (S. S. Stevens, ed.), pp. 236–280. New York: John Wiley & Sons [220–221].

Spooner, A. & Kellogg, W. N. (1947) The background conditioning curve. *Amer. J. Psychol.*, **60**, 321–334 [348, 349].

Spragg, S. D. S. (1940) Morphine addiction in chimpanzees. *Comp. Psychol. Monogr.*, **15**, No. 7 [135].

Stagner, R. (1951) Homeostasis as a unifying concept in personality theory. *Psychol. Rev.*, **58**, 5–17 [210].

Stanley, J. C. (See Jenkins & Stanley, 1950).

Stanley, W. C. & Aamodt, M. S. (1954) Force of responding during extinction as a function of force required during conditioning. *J. comp. physiol. Psychol.*, **47**, 462–464 [234, 402].

Stanley, W. C. (See Hulse & Stanley, 1956).

Starytzin, S. E. (1926) [The method of forming motor association-reflexes in dogs through stimulation of the pads of their paws.] *Sbornik Posviashebonny Bekhterevu*, 133–143 (see Razran, 1956) [44].

Stellar, E. (1951) The effects of experimental alterations on metabolism on the hoarding behavior of the rat. *J. comp. physiol. Psychol.*, **44**, 290–300 [152–153].

———— (See Hunt, Schlosberg, Solomon, & Stellar, 1947).

———— (See Morgan & Stellar, 1950).

———— (See Morgan, Stellar, & Johnson, 1943).

Stepien, L. (See Stepien & Stepien, 1958).

Stepien, I., & Stepien, L. (1958) The effects of ablations of the sensori-motor cortex of instrumental (type II) conditioned reflexes. I. The lesions of sensory cortex in dogs. Bulletin de l'academie polanaise des sciences, **6**, 309–312 [296, 298].

Stern, W. (1938) *General psychology from the personalistic standpoint.* New York: The Macmillan Company [166].

Stevenson, S. S. (See Miller & Stevenson, 1936).

Stone, G. R. (1950) The effect of negative incentives in serial learning: II. Incentive intensity and response variability. *J. gen. Psychol.,* **42**, 179–224 [46, 48].

Strongin, E. (See Bull & Strongin, 1956).

Sullivan, J. J. (1950) Some factors affecting the conditioning of the galvanic skin response. Unpublished Ph.D. dissertation, State University of Iowa [88].

Sullivan, J. W. N. (1949) *Limitations of science.* New York: Mentor Books, New American Library, Viking Press [1].

Sumner, W. G., & Keller, A. G. (1927) *The science of society.* (Three volumes.) New Haven: Yale University Press [416].

Sun, K. H. (See Pratt, Nelson, & Sun, 1930).

Sutton, S. Chase, R. A., & First, D. (1959) Bibliography: delayed speech feedback. *J. speech & hearing research,* **2**, 193–200 [247].

Swanson, A. M. (1955) Secondary mechanisms in the control of behavior: Response selection in the absence of primary drive and primary reward. Unpublished Doctor's dissertation, University of Illinois [148–149].

—— (See Solomon & Swanson, 1955).

Switzer, S. C. A. (1930) Backward conditioning of the lid reflex. *J. exp. Psychol.,* **13**, 76–97 [346].

Taylor, Janet A. (1951) The relationship of anxiety to the conditioned eyelid response. *J. exp. Psychol.,* **41**, 81–92 [157].

Taylor, Janet A. & Spence, K. W. (1952) The relationship of anxiety level to performance in serial learning. *J. exp. Psychol.,* **44**, 61–64 [172].

Thompson, W. R. (See Hebb & Thompson, 1954).

Thompson, W. R. & Heron, W. (1954) The effect of early restriction on activity in dogs. *J. comp. physiol. Psychol.,* **47**, 77–82 [175].

Thorndike, E. L. (1898) Animal intelligence. An experimental study of the associative processes in animals. *Psychol. Monogr.* **2**, No. 4 (Whole No. 8) [5, 7, 16, 349–350].

—— (1911) *Animal intelligence.* New York: The Macmillan Co. [367].

—— (1913) *Educational psychology, Vol. II. The Psychology of Learning.* New York: Teachers College, Columbia University [23, 217, 254–255, 257–258, 285, 319, 349, 353–354, 361].

—— (1931) *Human learning.* New York: Century Co. [22, 64, 193, 217–218].

—— (1932a) Rewards and punishment in animal learning. *Comp. Psychol. Monogr.,* **8**, 1–65 [22].

—— (1932b) *The fundamentals of learning.* New York: Teachers College, Columbia University [22, 64, 66, 225, 285].

—— (1933) An experimental study of rewards. *Teach. Coll. Contr. Educ.* No. 580, **72**, 174 [348].

―――― (1935) *The psychology of wants, interests, and attitudes*. New York: Appleton-Century [278].

―――― [15, 17–19, 21, 25, 28, 39, 41, 47, 63, 65, 75–76, 89–90, 92–95, 123–124, 260, 275, 291, 305, 307, 313, 323–324, 329, 385, 390, 397–398, 409, 412].

―――― (See Lorge & Thorndike, 1935).

Thrush, R. S. (See Fitzwater & Thrush, 1956).

Tinbergen, N. (1950) The hierarchical organization of nervous mechanisms underlying instinctive behaviour. In *Physiological mechanisms in animal behaviour*. Symposia of the (British) Society for Experimental Biology. New York: Academic Press [216].

―――― (1953) *Social behavior in animals*. New York: John Wiley & Sons [216].

Tinklepaugh, O. L. (1932) Multiple delayed reaction with chimpanzees and monkeys. *J. comp. Psychol.*, 13, 207–243 [415].

Titchener, E. B. [10–11, 187].

Tolman, E. C. (1922) A new formula for behaviorism. In *Collected papers in psychology* (1951). Berkeley: University of California Press [278, 303, 306, 320–325].

―――― (1933) Sign-gestalt or conditioned reflex? *Psychol. Rev.*, 40, 246–255 [322, 328, 335].

―――― (1934) Theories of learning. In *Comparative psychology* (F. A. Moss, ed.), pp. 367–408. New York: Prentice-Hall [324, 326–329].

―――― (1945) A stimulus-expectancy need-cathexsis psychology. Republished in *Collected papers in psychology* (1951). Berkeley: University of California Press [193, 321].

―――― (1948) Cognitive maps in rats and men. *Psychol. Rev.*, 53, 189–208 [330].

―――― (1955) Principles of performance. *Psychol. Rev.*, 62, 315–326 [323].

―――― [278. 303, 306, 320–324].

Tolman, E. C., & Brunswik, E. (1935) The organism and the causal texture of the environment. *Psychol. Rev.*, 42, 43–77 [461].

Tolman, E. C., Richie, B. F., & Kalish, D. (1946) Studies in spatial learning. II. Place learning versus response learning. *J. exp. Psychol.*, 36, 221–229 [330–331, 334].

Traum, Alice. (See Mowrer, 1950a) [52].

Troland, L. T. (1928) *The fundamentals of human motivation*. New York: D. Van Nostrand Co. [316, 318–320].

Tsushima, T. (1959) The effects of combination of positive and negative reinforcement—an experimental analogue of child-rearing practice. M. A. Thesis, University of Illinois. Urbana [471–472].

Tuttle, H. S. (1946) Two kinds of learning. *J. Psychol.*, 22, 267–277 [65].

Tyler, D. W. (1956) Extinction following partial reinforcement with control of stimulus-generalization and secondary reinforcement. *Amer. J. Psychol.*, 69, 359–368, [459, 468–469].

―――― (See Bitterman, Fedderson, & Tyler, 1953).

―――― (See Elam, Tyler, & Bitterman, 1954).

Tyler, D. W., Weinstock, S., & Amsel, A. (1957) Theoretical interpretations of runway studies of partial reinforcement. Symposium presented at Midwest Psychol. Association, Chicago, May, 1957 [234].

Tyler, D. W., Wortz, E. C., & Bitterman, M. E. (1953) The effect of random and alternating partial reinforcement on resistance to extinction in the rat. *Amer. J. Psychol.*, **66**, 57–65 [469, 473–474, 476].

Ullman, A. D. (1951) The experimental production and analysis of a "compulsive eating symptom" in rats. *J. comp. physiol. Psychol.*, **44**, 575–581 [158–159, 161–162].

—— (See Mowrer & Ullman, 1945).

Underwood, H. Personal communication [332].

Valentine, C. W. (1930) The innate bases of fear. *J. genet. Psychol.*, **37**, 394–419 [176].

Van Wagenen, W. P. (See Bellows & Van Wagenen, 1938).

Verplanck, W. S. (1954) E. R. Guthrie's Theory of Learning. In *Modern learning theories*, (Estes *et al.*). New York: Appleton-Century-Crofts [290].

Viek, P. (See Davitz, Mason, Mowrer, & Viek, 1957).

—— (See Mowrer & Vick, 1948).

Viney, W. (See Capehart, Viney, & Hulicka, 1958).

Voeks, V. W. (1948) Postremity, recency, and frequency as bases for prediction in the maze situation. *J. exp. Psychol.*, **38**, 495–510 [283–284].

—— (1950) Formalization and clarification of a theory of learning. *J. Psychol.*, **30**, 341–362 [285].

von Linne, K. [2].

Waddell, D., Gans, S., Kampner, P., & Williams, A. (1955) A comparison of place and response learning in very young rats. *J. comp. physiol. Psychol.*, **48**, 376–377 [331].

Wade, E. A. (See Littman & Wade, 1955).

Wagner, A. R. (1959) The role of reinforcement and nonreinforcement in an "apparent frustration effect." *J. exp. Psychol.*, **57**, 130–136 [408].

Walk, R. D. (1958) Personal communication [139].

—— (1959) Fear and Courage: A psychological study. Cornell University (mimeographed) [139].

Walker, E. L. (1957) Learning. In *Annual review of psychology* (Farnsworth, P. R., ed.). Palo Alto, Calif.: Annual Reviews [v].

Walker, E. L., Dember, W. N., Earl, R. W., & Karoly, A. J. (1955) Choice alternation: I. Stimulus vs. place vs. response. *J. comp. physiol. Psychol.*, **48**, 17–18 [182].

Warden, C. J. & Haas, E. L. (1927) The effect of short intervals of delay in feeding upon speed of maze learning. *J. comp. Psychol.*, **7**, 107–116 [351–353].

Warner, L. H. (1928a) A study of thirst behavior in the white rat by means of the obstruction method. *J. genet. Psychol.*, **35**, 178–192 [433].

—— (1928b) A study of hunger behavior in the white rat by means of the obstruction method. *J. comp. Psychol.*, **8**, 273–299 [433].

—— (1932a) The association span of the white rat. *J. genet. Psychol.*, **41**, 57–90 [325, 374].

—— (1932b) An experimental search for the "conditioned response." *J. genet. Psychol.*, **41**, 91–115 [325].

Warren, J. M. & Baron, A. (1956) The formation of learning sets by cats. *J. comp. physiol. Psychol.*, **49**, 227–231 [452].

Waters, R. H. (1937) The principle of least effort in learning. *J. gen. Psychol.*, **16**, 3–20 [416].

Watson, J. B. (1907) Kinesthetic and organic sensations: their role in the re-

actions of the white rat to the maze. *Psychol. Monogr.*, **8**, No. 33, 1–100 [285].
—— (1914) *Behavior: An introduction to comparative psychology.* New York: Henry Holt & Co. [4, 6].
—— (1916a) The effect of delayed feeding upon habit formation. (Abstract) *Psychol. Bull.*, **13**, 77 [350–351, 353].
—— (1916b) The place of the conditioned reflex in psychology. *Psychol. Rev.*, **23**, 89–116 [4].
—— (1917) The effect of delayed feeding upon learning. *Psychobiology*, **1**, 51–60 [187, 350, 416].
—— (1926) Experimental studies on the growth of the emotions. In *Psychologies of 1925.* Worcester, Mass.: Clark University Press [93].
—— [187, 416].
Watson, J. B. & Morgan, J. J. B. (1917) Emotional reactions and psychological experimentation. *Amer. J. Psychol.*, **28**, 163–174 [392, 404].
Watson, J. B. & Rayner, R. (1920) Conditioned emotional reactions. *J. exp. Psychol.*, **3**, 1–14 [392, 394–396].
Webb, W. B. (1949) The motivational aspect of an irrelevant drive in the behavior of the white rat. *J. exp. Psychol.*, **39**, 1–4 [157–158].
Wedekind, C. E. (See Braun, Wedekind, & Smudski, 1957).
Wegner, N. (See Zeaman & Wegner, 1954).
Wegner, N. & Zeaman, D. (1958) Strength of cardiac conditioned responses with varying unconditioned stimulus durations. *Psychol. Rev.*, **65**, 238–241 [88].
Weinstock, S. (1954) Resistance to extinction of a running response following partial reinforcement under widely spaced trials. *J. comp. physiol. Psychol.*, **47**, 318–322 [458, 469].
Weinstock, S. (See Tyler, Weinstock, & Amsel, 1957).
Welker, W. I. (1956) Effects of age and experience on play and exploration of young chimpanzees. *J. comp. physiol. Psychol.*, **49**, 223–226 [176].
Wells, H. (See Murray, Wells, Kohn, & Miller, 1953).
Wenzel, B. M. (1958) Relative resistance to reserpine of responses based on positive, as compared to negative, reinforcement. Paper delivered at meeting of American Psychological Association, Washington, D. C., Sept. 2, 1958 [97].
Wever, E. G. (1930) The upper limit of hearing in the cat. *J. comp. Psychol.*, **10**, 221–234 [325].
Wheeler, W. M. (1928) *The social insects: their origin and evolution.* New York: Harcourt, Brace & Co. [315].
White, L. A. (1949) *The science of culture.* New York: Farrar, Straus, & Co. [9].
White, R. K. (1936) The completion hypothesis and reinforcement. *Psychol. Rev.*, **43**, 396–404 [226].
—— (1943) The case for the Tolman-Lewin interpretation of learning. *Psychol. Rev.*, **50**, 157–186 [323].
White, R. T. (1953) Analysis of the function of a secondary reinforcing stimulus in a serial learning situation. Ph.D. dissertation, The University of Buffalo [235].
Whitehorn, J. C. (See Dykman, Gantt, & Whitehorn, 1956).
Whiteis, U. E. (1955) A study of the effects of punishment on avoidance behavior. Unpublished Ed. D. thesis, Harvard University [177, 414, 486–487].
—— (1956) Punishment's influence on fear and avoidance. *Harv. Educ. Rev.*, **26**, 360–373 [177, 414, 486].

Whiting, J. W. M. Personal communication. (See Farber, 1954) [137].

——— (See Sears, Whiting, Nowlis, & Sears, 1953).

Whiting, J. W. M. & Mowrer, O. H. (1943) Habit progression and regression —a laboratory study of some factors relevant to human socialization. *J. comp. Psychol.*, **36**, 229–253 [175, 337].

Wickens, C. (See Wickens & Wickens, 1942).

Wickens, D. D. (1938) The transference of conditioned excitation and conditioned inhibition from one muscle group to the antagonistic muscle group. *J. exp. Psychol.*, **22**, 101–123 [15, 334].

——— (See Bugelski, Goss, Murdock, Perkins, & Wickens, 1958).

——— (See Miles & Wickens, 1953).

——— (See Simons, Wickens, Brown, & Pennock, 1951).

Wickens, D. D. & Miles, R. C. (1954) Extinction changes during a series of reinforcement-extinction sessions. *J. comp. physiol. Psychol.*, **47**, 315–317 [451].

Wickens, D. D., Schroeder, H. M., & Snide, J. D. (1954) Primary stimulus generalization of the GSR under two conditions. *J. exp. Psychol.*, **47**, 52–56 [444].

Wickens, D. D. & Wickens, C. (1942) Some factors related to pseudo-conditioning. *J. exp. Psychol.*, **31**, 518–526 [348].

Wiener, N. (1948) *Cybernetics*. New York: John Wiley & Sons [1].

Wiertheimer, M. [288].

Wike, E. L., & Barrientos, G. (1957) Selective learning as a function of differential consummatory activity. *Psychol. Rep.*, **3**, 255–258 [250].

——— (1958) Secondary reinforcement and multiple drive reduction. *J. comp. physiol. Psychol.*, **51**, 640–643 [141].

Wike, E. L. & Casey, A. (1954) The secondary reward value of food for satiated animals. *J. comp. physiol. Psychol.*, **47**, 441–443 [153].

Wikler, A. (See Hill, Belleville, & Wikler, 1954).

Williams, A. (See Waddell, Gans, Kampner, & Williams, 1955).

Williams, K. A. (1924) The reward value of a conditioned stimulus. *Univ. Calif. Publ. Psychol.*, **4**, 31–55 [109].

Winsor, A. L. (1929) Inhibition and learning. *Psychol. Rev.*, **36**, 389–401 [410, 411].

——— (1930) Observations on the nature and mechanism of secretory inhibition. *Psychol. Rev.*, **37**, 399–411 [404].

Wischner, G. J. (1947) The effect of punishment on discrimination learning in a non-correction situation. *J. exp. Psychol.*, **37**, 271-284 [434].

Wolfe, J. B. (1934) The effect of delayed reward upon learning in the white rat. *J. comp. Psychol.*, **17**, 1–21 [379–380, 385].

——— (1936) Effectiveness of token rewards for chimpanzees. *Comp. Psychol. Monogr.*, **12**, No. 60, 1–72 [109, 141, 378].

Wolfe, J. B. & Kaplon, M. D. (1941) Effect of amount of reward and consummative activity on learning in chickens. *J. comp. Psychol.*, **31**, 353–361 [193].

Wolff, H. G. & Godell, H. (1943) The relation of attitude and suggestion to the perception of and reaction to pain. *Res. Publ. Ass. nerv. ment. Dis.*, **23**, 434-448 [135].

Wolpe, J. (1950) Need reduction, drive reduction, and reinforcement: A neurophysiological view. *Psychol. Rev.*, **57**, 19–25 [218, 267].

——— (1952) The neurophysiology of learning and delayed reward. *Psychol. Rev.*, **59**, 192–199 [60, 218–219, 267].

Woodbury, C. B. (1942) A note on "passive" conditioning. *J. gen. Psychol.*, **27,** 359–361 [240, 241].

Woodrow, P. (See Miller, Sampliner, & Woodrow, 1957).

Woodworth, R. S. (1918) *Dynamic psychology.* New York: Columbia University Press [18, 64–65, 301].

—— (1921) *Psychology.* New York: Henry Holt & Co. [79, 176].

—— (1938) *Experimental psychology.* New York: Henry Holt & Co. [277, 300, 343].

—— (1947) Reinforcement of perception. *Amer. J. Psychol.*, **60,** 119–124 [278–279, 282, 300].

—— (1958) *Dynamic psychology.* New York: Henry Holt & Co. [6, 69, 300–304].

Woodworth, R. S. & Schlosberg, H. (1954) *Experimental psychology.* New York: Henry Holt & Co. [26, 53].

Wortz, E. C. (See Tyler, Wortz, & Bitterman, 1953).

Wyckoff, L. B. (1959) Toward a quantitative theory of secondary reinforcement. *Psychol. Rev.*, **66,** 68–78 [234].

Wyers, E. J. (See Rhoades & Wyers, 1956).

Wynne, L. C. (See Solomon, Kamin, & Wynne, 1953).

—— (See Solomon & Wynne, 1950).

—— (See Solomon & Wynne, 1953).

—— (See Solomon & Wynne, 1954).

Wynne, L. C. & Solomon, R. L. (1955) Traumatic avoidance learning: acquisition and extinction in dogs deprived of normal peripheral autonomic function. *Genet. psychol. monogr.*, **52,** 241–284 [60].

Wyrwicka, W. (See Andersson & Wyrwicka, 1957).

Yerkes, R. M. & Dodson, J. D. (1908) The relation of strength of stimulus to rapidity of habit formation. *J. comp. Neurol. Psychol.*, **18,** 459 [171].

Young, P. T. (1948) Studies of food preference, appetite, and dietary habit. VIII. Food-seeking drives, palatability and the law of effect. *J. comp. physiol. Psychol.*, **41,** 269–300 [192].

—— (1949a) Emotion as disorganized response—a reply to Professor Leeper. *Psychol. Rev.*, **56,** 184–191 [172].

—— (1949b) Food-seeking drive, affective process, and learning. *Psychol. Rev.*, **56,** 98–121 [187, 271, 275–276].

—— (1955) The role of hedonic processes in motivation. In *Nebraska symposium on motivation.* Lincoln: University of Nebraska Press [187–188].

—— (1959) The role of affective processes in learning and motivation. *Psychol. Rev.*, **66,** 104–125 [192].

Youtz, R. E. P. (1938) Reinforcement, extinction, and spontaneous recovery in a non-Pavlovian reaction. *J. exp. Psychol.*, **22,** 305–318 [328].

Zbrozyna, A. W. (1957) The conditioned cessation of eating. *Bulletin de l'Academie Polanaise des Sciences*, **5,** 261–265 [165].

—— (1958) Withdrawal versus withholding of positive reinforcement. *Science*, **127,** 1456–1458 [165].

Zeaman, D. (1949) Response latency as a function of the amount of reinforcement. *J. exp. Psychol.*, **39,** 466–484 [262]

—— (See Wegner & Zeaman, 1958).

Zeaman, D. & Wegner, N. (1954) The role of drive reduction in the classical conditioning of an autonomically mediated response. *J. exp. Psychol.,* **48,** 349–354 [88].

Zener, K. (See Spence, 1951a) [278].

Zener, K. & McCurdy, H. G. (1939) Analysis of motivational factors in conditioned behavior: I. The differential effect of changes in hunger upon conditioned, unconditioned, and spontaneous salivary secretation. *J. Psychol.,* **8,** 321–350 [142].

Ziegler, H. P. (1957) Electrical stimulation of the brain and the psychophysiology of learning and motivation. *Psychol. Bull.,* **54,** 363–382 [209].

Zimmerman, D. W. (1957a) Analysis of a method for producing stable secondary reinforcement. (Unpublished research memorandum.) [113–118, 144, 171, 214, 470, 485].

——— (1957b) Durable secondary reinforcement. *Psychol. Rev.,* **64,** 373–383 [115–118].

——— (1958) A method of obtaining longer-lasting secondary reinforcement. Ph.D. Theses, University of Illinois [118].

——— (1959) Sustained performance in rats based on secondary reinforcement. *J. comp. physiol. Psychol.* (in press) [118, 470].

——— Personal communication [248–249].

Subject Index

Because this book does not contain a special summary chapter, attention is called to summarizing statements which appear from time to time as the development of argument seems to call for them. Page references to these statements will be found listed under "Summaries" and occasionally under the topic which is specifically involved.